Fourth Edition

Teaching Special Students in the Mainstream

Rena B. Lewis
San Diego State University

Donald H. Doorlag
San Diego State University

Merrill, an imprint of Prentice Hall
Englewood Cliffs, New Jersey   Columbus, Ohio

Library of Congress Cataloging-in-Publication Data
Lewis, Rena B.
    Teaching special students in the mainstream / Rena B.
Lewis, Donald H. Doorlag.—4th ed.
        p.   cm.
    Includes bibliographical references and index.
    ISBN 0-02-370502-7
    1. Special education. 2. Mainstreaming in education. 3.
Teaching. I. Doorlag, Donald H.
    LC3965.L46   1995
    371.9—dc20   94-3463
                                                      CIP

Cover photo: © Gabe Palmer/The Stock Market
Editor: Ann Castel Davis
Developmental Editor: Carol S. Sykes
Production Editor: Linda Hillis Bayma
Photo Editor: Anne Vega
Text Designer: Anne Flanagan
Cover Designer: Anne Flanagan
Production Buyer: Deidra M. Schwartz
Electronic Text Management: Marilyn Wilson Phelps,
 · Matthew Williams, Jane Lopez, Karen L. Bretz

This book was set in Transitional 511 by Prentice Hall and
was printed and bound by Quebecor Printing–Hawkins.
The cover was printed by Phoenix Color Corp.

 © 1995 by Prentice-Hall, Inc.
A Simon & Schuster Company
Englewood Cliffs, New Jersey 07632

Earlier editions © 1991 by Macmillan Publishing Company and © 1987, 1983 by Merrill Publishing Company.

Photo credits: Scott Cunningham/Merrill and Prentice
Hall, pp. 3, 65, 74, 91, 123, 159, 259, 297, 333, 359, 383,
385, 415, 417, 424, 445, 471, 497, 533; Kevin Fitzsi-
mons/Merrill and Prentice Hall, pp. 7, 241; Mary
Hagler/Merrill and Prentice Hall, p. 519; Larry
Hamill/Merrill and Prentice Hall, pp. 11, 17, 31, 37, 41,
93, 104, 106, 144, 201, 266, 349; T. Hubbard/Merrill and
Prentice Hall, p. 392; Tom Hutchinson/Merrill and Prentice Hall, p. 131; David Napravnik/Merrill and Prentice
Hall, pp. 71, 214; Barbara Schwartz/Merrill and Prentice
Hall, pp. 371, 503; Anne Vega/Merrill and Prentice Hall,
p. 516; Tom Watson/Merrill and Prentice Hall, pp. 29,
161, 180, 219, 447, 453, 489; Todd Yarrington/Merrill and
Prentice Hall, pp. 67, 153, 165, 189, 193, 261, 342, 377,
434, 459, 473, 485.

Printed in the United States of America

10 9 8 7 6 5 4 3 2

ISBN: 0-02-370502-7

Prentice-Hall International (UK) Limited, *London*
Prentice-Hall of Australia Pty. Limited, *Sydney*
Prentice-Hall of Canada, Inc., *Toronto*
Prentice-Hall Hispanoamericana, S. A., *Mexico*
Prentice-Hall of India Private Limited, *New Delhi*
Prentice-Hall of Japan, Inc., *Tokyo*
Simon & Schuster Asia Pte. Ltd., *Singapore*
Editora Prentice-Hall do Brasil, Ltda., *Rio de Janeiro*

*To the regular class students
who are special to us:*

*Dylan Lewis
Kristi Doorlag
Scott Doorlag*

Preface

This book is about two things: special students and teaching. It is designed to prepare the professional educator to effectively teach the range of students found in the typical elementary or secondary classroom. It provides information about four groups of students with special needs: students with disabilities, gifted and talented learners, individuals from culturally and linguistically diverse backgrounds, and students at risk for school failure. In addition, it presents practical strategies for adapting standard instruction to meet the learning needs of all members of the mainstreamed classroom.

The Fourth Edition

The fourth edition has been thoroughly updated with the addition of several new topics and expanded coverage of others. Included are discussions of important areas such as these:

- The Individuals with Disabilities Education Act (IDEA) and the Americans with Disabilities Act (ADA)
- The full inclusion movement and other current issues and trends

- Prereferral intervention strategies
- The team approach to collaboration and consultation
- The inclusion of students with severe disabilities in neighborhood schools and general education classes
- Instructional adaptations for students with attention deficit disorder (ADD) and attention deficit hyperactivity disorder (ADHD)
- Intervention strategies for students with traumatic brain injury
- Considerations for mainstreaming students with autism
- Augmentative communication strategies, including facilitated communication

The fourth edition reflects current research in the fields of special and general education (more than 200 new references have been added), and there is information on the newest technologies available for use in mainstreamed classrooms. Several of the "Spotlight on Technology" sections now feature software recommended for students with special needs, and a new appendix has been added on sources of software and assistive devices.

Organization and Content

In organizing this book, we have attempted to maintain a noncategorical approach to instruction while acknowledging the differential impact of student characteristics on school performance. To accomplish this, the first eight chapters of the book (and the last) address the needs of all special students and their teachers. The chapters dealing with instructional methods (chapters 9 to 17), in contrast, are tied to specific populations of students and the types of school problems they most often encounter. However, the instructional strategies discussed in these chapters are relevant for any student with the same difficulties. For example, because students with learning disabilities are characterized by the problems they experience mastering basic skills, the chapter entitled "Teaching Students with Learning Disabilities" includes techniques for teaching reading, written language, and math skills. These techniques can and should be used with other students facing similar skill acquisition problems.

The 18 chapters of this book are divided into five major segments. The first part, "Introduction to Mainstreaming," identifies the purposes of mainstreaming, provides a rationale for a team approach to the solution of educational problems, and describes the major instructional needs of mainstreamed special students.

The second part, "Skills for the Mainstreaming Teacher," addresses the needs of the educator. Strategies are provided for achieving four basic instructional goals: adapting instruction, managing classroom behavior, promoting social acceptance, and coordinating the classroom learning environment. Also, there is information on the effective use of computers and other technologies in the mainstreamed classroom.

In the third part, "Methods for Mainstreaming Students with Disabilities," teaching strategies are suggested for a variety of different types of special students. These include students with learning disabilities, mild mental retardation, behavioral disorders, communication disorders, physical and health impairments, and vision and hearing impairments.

This part also discusses interventions for individuals with four other types of disabilities: students with attention deficit disorders (ADD) and attention deficit hyperactivity disorders (ADHD) (chapter 9), severe disabilities (chapter 10), autism (chapter 12), and traumatic brain injury (chapter 13).

The fourth part, "Methods for Mainstreaming Students with Other Special Needs," recommends instructional techniques for three other groups of students with special needs: gifted and talented individuals, students from culturally and linguistically diverse backgrounds, and students at risk for school failure.

The final part, "The Future of Mainstreaming," examines past mistakes, current practices, and some of the promising approaches that will give new directions to the mainstreaming of special students in school and society.

Special Features

Throughout this book are several types of special features. The "Tips for the Teacher" sections answer some of the questions teachers most often ask about mainstreaming. "For Your Information" boxes highlight important facts, and those entitled "Exceptional Literature" recommend fiction, biography, and professional works related to different kinds of special needs. Information about the use of new technologies in mainstreamed classrooms appears in the "Spotlight on Technology" sections. Each chapter ends with "Things to Remember," a brief summary of the major points of the chapter. Also included at the end of each chapter are suggested activities, which extend the information presented in the chapter by providing opportunities for school observations, interviews with practicing professionals, perusal of the special and general education literature, and so on.

At the end of the text, an appendix provides contact information for publishers of instructional software and manufacturers of assistive devices. Special terms are highlighted in the text in bold print as they appear; each is defined in the glossary.

Information for Instructors

Although the chapters in this book are designed to be read in the order in which they appear, some instructors find other sequences more beneficial to their students. For example, some instructors prefer to proceed from Part I of the book directly to Parts III and IV, leaving the chapters on skills for teachers until after students have gained information on the special needs of various populations.

The fourth edition has an enhanced instructor support package, including an instructor's manual, test bank, and a video package. The instructor's manual is organized by chapter and contains objectives, terminology, a detailed outline, and a set of questions appropriate for class discussion, essay assignments, and essay exams. The test bank, also organized by chapter, includes more than 1,000 objective test questions (multiple-choice, true-false, and completion). The test bank is available in print format and on disk for IBM and Macintosh computers. The video package demonstrates mainstreaming in a variety of classroom settings using current teaching techniques.

Acknowledgments

Our greatest debt is owed to our students and the special and general educators and educators-in-training who asked the difficult questions that prompted the writing of this book. We also wish to thank the colleagues who served as reviewers for this edition: Mary Banbury, University of New Orleans; Robert J. Evans, Marshall University; Nancy Halmhuber, Eastern Michigan University; and Quisar Sultana, Eastern Kentucky University. Thanks also to Kris English for her contributions in the area of mainstreaming strategies for students with hearing impairments, and to Tamarah Ashton-Coombs for her assistance in the preparation of the instructor's manual and test bank that accompany this book. In addition, sincere thanks go to our editors at Merrill: Ann Castel Davis, Carol Sykes, and Linda Bayma.

Last, but never least, we say thanks once more to our partners, Jim and Deanne, for continuing their support and understanding through yet another edition.

Rena B. Lewis
Donald H. Doorlag

Contents

■
■ ■
■ ■
PART V

*The Future of
Mainstreaming*   *531*

I

Introduction to Mainstreaming

1 Mainstreaming for Success

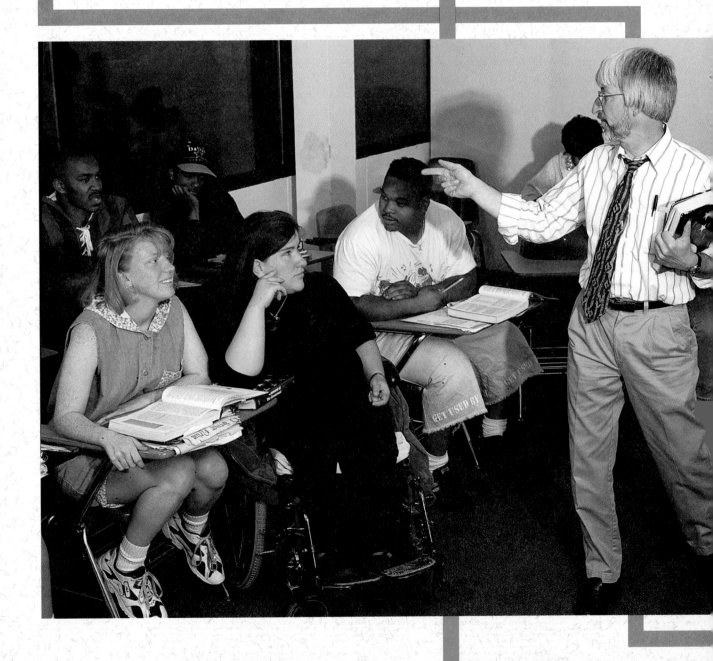

Behind each classroom door lies a world of diversity. In a typical class of students, there is a wide range of abilities. Some students learn easily; others require much assistance. Some are well behaved; others, mischievous. Some are friendly; others, ill at ease with their peers. In addition, students perform differently at various times and under different circumstances. The class leader may be overcome with shyness when asked to speak at a school assembly. The student who excels in science may write and spell poorly. Addition and subtraction problems may be easy for a student, but multiplication may be extremely difficult. Such variations contribute to the wonder of individuality.

When special students are members of a class, the range of diversity increases. Students with disabilities, gifted and talented students, and students from culturally and linguistically diverse backgrounds are indistinguishable from their peers in most ways. However, their learning needs may be more serious or more compelling. Such students are individuals with different personalities, preferences, skills, and needs. Like all students, they present a challenge to the teacher.

This book is for teachers who wish to learn more about special students. It is also about good teaching. All students, particularly those with special learning needs, deserve special care and special teaching. This book provides teachers with the skills needed to deal with the complex and often perplexing diversity that lies behind the classroom door.

■ MAINSTREAMING

Mainstreaming* refers to the inclusion of special students in the general educational process. Students are considered mainstreamed if they spend any part of the school day with regular class peers. In a typical mainstreaming program, special students in regular classrooms participate in instructional and social activities side by side with their classmates. Often they receive additional instruction

_____

* Words appearing in **boldface** in the text are defined in the Glossary.

and support from a special educator such as a resource teacher. That instruction may take place within the general education classroom or outside of it in a setting such as a resource room.

Special students are those with special learning needs. Because of these needs, they require instructional adaptations in order to learn successfully. This book considers four types of students special: pupils with disabilities, gifted and talented individuals, students from culturally and linguistically diverse backgrounds, and students at risk for school failure. Because of physical, cognitive, or emotional disabilities, some children and adolescents receive special education services in addition to (or, in some cases, in place of) the general educational program. Other special students may not be offered special programs in their schools, but their special learning needs soon become apparent to the teacher of the regular classroom.

Integration of special students into the mainstream of education differs according to the needs of the individual. The amount of time in which special students participate in regular class activities varies from student to student. For some the mainstream is their full-time permanent placement; for others mainstreaming occurs only for a portion of the school day. There is also variation in the type of activities in which mainstreamed students take part. Some interact with regular class peers primarily on a social basis; others are included for both social activities and classroom instruction. In the area of instruction, many participate in most of the regular class curriculum, whereas others are mainstreamed only for selected subjects.

Mainstreaming is an educational program that varies with the needs and abilities of the student. It is characterized by the meaningful interaction of special and typical students in social activities and/or classroom instruction. Mainstreaming has been defined in many ways; for a sample of several different viewpoints, see Figure 1–1.

In the definition of Kaufman, Gottlieb, Agard, and Kukic (1975), mainstreaming is described as temporal, instructional, and social integration. Not only are special students placed in an educational environment with typical peers for some specified amount of

FIGURE 1–1
Mainstreaming Is . . .

Mainstreaming is usually defined in relationship to students with disabilities. As you read the quotations below, think about the process of mainstreaming as it relates to all types of special students: youngsters with disabilities, gifted and talented individuals, students from culturally and linguistically diverse groups, and those at risk for school failure. For special students, mainstreaming is . . .

- the social and instructional integration of handicapped students in a regular education class for at least a portion of the school day (Schulz & Turnbull, 1983, p. 49)

- maximum integration in the regular class combined with concrete assistance for the regular class teacher (Gearheart, Weishahn, & Gearheart, 1988, p. 5)

- providing special education and related services to exceptional children while they attend regular classes and schools (Reynolds & Birch, 1988, p. 1)

- the integration of children with learning, behavioral, and/or physical problems into regular education settings and programs unless their problems are so severe that they cannot be accommodated in regular programs (Cartwright, Cartwright, & Ward, 1989, p. 10)

- a belief which involves an educational placement procedure and process for exceptional children, based on the conviction that each such child should be educated in the least restrictive environment in which his educational and related needs can be satisfactorily provided for (The Council for Exceptional Children, 1976, p. 43)

- the temporal, instructional, and social integration of eligible exceptional children with normal peers based on an ongoing, individually determined, educational planning programming process, and requires clarification of responsibility among regular and special education administrative, instructional, and supportive personnel (Kaufman, Gottlieb, Agard, & Kukic, 1975, p. 5)

time (temporal integration), they participate meaningfully in the academic activities of the general education class (instructional integration) and are accepted as members of that class by their teacher and classmates (social integration). Integration to this extent is a real possibility for many special students, particularly those with mild learning and behavior problems. However, severe disabilities may prevent some special students from full participation in all instructional aspects of the regular class.

Inclusion is a newer term that is sometimes used to describe the mainstreaming process. Initiated by professionals interested in severe disabilities (Stain-

back & Stainback, 1985; Thousand & Villa, 1990), the full inclusion movement calls for reform of practices that exclude and segregate individuals with disabilities. Advocates of full inclusion maintain that the general education classroom is the most appropriate full-time placement for all students with disabilities, not only those with mild learning and behavior problems but also those with more severe disabilities. In this model, students do not leave the mainstream to receive special services; instead, support is provided within the regular classroom setting. However, many special education professionals disagree with the assumption that full-time mainstreaming is the only appropriate placement for students with disabilities. They argue that other options, such as resource rooms, should be available so that educational programs can be tailored to the specific needs of individual students. This is the position of the Council for Exceptional Children (CEC), the major professional organization in special education. According to the *CEC Policy on Inclusive Schools and Community Settings* (1993),

> CEC believes that a continuum of services must be available for all children, youth, and young adults. CEC also believes that the concept of inclusion is a meaningful goal to be pursued in our schools and communities. In addition, CEC believes children, youth, and young adults with disabilities should be served *whenever possible* in general education classrooms in inclusive neighborhood schools and community settings [italics added].

As discussed later in this chapter, this position is consistent with current federal laws and their requirements for placement of students with disabilities in the "Least Restrictive Environment."

Including students with special needs in general education programs is not a new idea. In the early days of education in the United States, classrooms served a wide variety of individuals, including some students with disabilities. The one-room schoolhouse with its range of ages and skills is an example. Kirk and Gallagher (1979) describe a mainstreaming program that began in 1913 for students with vision losses. Students spent part of their day in the regular classroom and part in a special "sight saving class."

Today, most special students begin school in the mainstream and receive the majority of their education there. Many never leave the regular classroom. Some, if learning problems become apparent, are identified as disabled and receive special education services. Of these, few are served in special classes and special schools. Those who do attend separate programs often join their regular class peers for social activities and for instruction in nonacademic subjects such as art, music, and physical education. However, most students with disabilities are educated in regular classes with part-time special services provided if necessary. In the school year 1990–91, for example,

the regular classroom was the primary educational placement for 68% of this nation's children and youth with disabilities (U.S. Department of Education, 1993). Consider the stories of Donna and Josh that follow. Donna and Josh are students with disabilities who participate fully in general education while receiving special assistance in problem areas. They are examples of successfully mainstreamed students.

■ Donna

Donna is 8 years old and likes to swim, roller-skate, and eat hot dogs. She and her two best friends, Katie and Sue, walk to school together each morning. They are all in Ms. Cole's second grade class. Donna likes school this year, but last year was very different. Donna is a special student; she has learning problems. In first grade Donna had great difficulty with reading. This year she works with the resource teacher for a half hour each day, and she's beginning to make progress in reading. In her second grade class she does well in math and handwriting, and she can keep up with her classmates in spelling. Donna is successfully mainstreamed.

■ Josh

Josh is a high school student who is planning to attend college when he graduates. He wants to study chemistry or physics. This year he's taking English, American history, biology, and geometry. Josh is a special student; he has a physical disability and travels by wheelchair. Josh rides a special bus to school and attends an adaptive physical education class. Josh writes and types slowly, so he sometimes needs extra time to complete tests and assignments. His grades in all his classes are excellent, and he has many friends. Josh is successfully mainstreamed.

Later in the chapter we will take a look at portions of the Individualized Education Programs for Donna and Josh.

■ STUDENTS WITH SPECIAL NEEDS

Most discussions of mainstreaming concentrate on only one type of special student: children and adolescents with disabilities. Students who have a disability that negatively affects their school performance are served by special education, and federal laws uphold their right to a free, appropriate, public education. In this textbook, however, we have expanded the concept of special students to include three other groups with learning needs significant enough to warrant special consideration. These are gifted and talented students (often served by special education but not protected by the laws for learners with disabilities); students from culturally and linguistically diverse backgrounds; and students at risk for school failure. The special needs of these students, like those of many students with disabilities, can often be accommodated within the regular classroom.

Special students are a heterogeneous group. They may learn quickly and easily or with great difficulty. Their school behavior may be beyond reproach or frequently inappropriate. Some have sensory or physical disabilities. Others stand out because of their speech, language, or culture. Despite their special needs, such students can and do learn. However, more than most students, they require good teaching to succeed in the mainstream.

Students with disabilities may have special learning needs because of a cognitive, physical, sensory, language, or emotional disability. According to

Public Law 101-476, the Individuals with Disabilities Education Act of 1990, students with disabilities include those with

> mental retardation, hearing impairments including deafness, speech or language impairments, visual impairments including blindness, serious emotional disturbance, orthopedic impairments, autism, traumatic brain injury, other health impairments, or specific learning disabilities.

Another disability, attention deficit disorder (ADD), is covered under other federal legislation.

Some of the terms that describe disabilities in federal laws are replaced or changed in common usage. For example, most special educators prefer *behavioral disorders* to *serious emotional disturbance*. Also, *orthopedic impairments* are often called *physical disabilities*, and the term *ADD* may be changed to *ADD/ADHD* to include students with attention deficit hyperactivity disorder.

Students with learning disabilities have adequate general intelligence and are able to succeed in many school tasks. However, because of specific disabilities in areas such as attention, perception, and memory, they experience difficulty in school. They may encounter learning problems in one or more, although usually not all, academic subjects. In contrast, students with mental retardation generally are delayed in most, if not all, academic subject areas. They are characterized by a slower rate of learning and difficulty with reasoning tasks.

Students with behavioral disorders may have adequate academic achievement despite poor classroom behavior, or their behavior problems may interfere with learning. Such students may be disruptive or withdrawn, they may experience difficulty controlling their own behavior, or they may lack the skills necessary for building and maintaining interpersonal relationships with peers and adults.

Communication problems are primary in students with speech and language disorders. A student's speech may be difficult for others to understand, or language development may be delayed. Students with autism experience difficulty in socialization as well as in communication. With vision and hearing disorders, the disability is sensory. Individuals with vision disorders may be blind or partially sighted; those with hearing disorders may be deaf or hard of hearing. In either case, learning takes place through the senses still available to the student.

Students with physical disabilities and health disorders may participate fully in regular class activities. However, those with limited physical mobility, such as those who travel by wheelchair, may take a less active role. Some with chronic health problems may have special needs because of prolonged school absences. In general, students with physical and health needs can learn successfully in the mainstream. For many of these special students, their physical problems have little effect on their ability to learn.

Two other groups of individuals with disabilities are often members of mainstream classes: students with traumatic brain injury (TBI) and those with attention deficit disorder (ADD) or attention deficit hyperactivity disorder (ADHD). Most students with TBI are members of regular classes when the accident or other trauma that causes the injury to the brain occurs, and most return to that setting after hospitalization and rehabilitation. Students with ADD/ADHD typically remain in the general education setting while receiving assistance for problems in attention, impulsivity, and hyperactivity.

Like learners with disabilities, **gifted and talented students** are exceptional. Although they usually do not encounter school failure, their special abilities require special teaching. Gifted students are unusually bright; they may learn quickly and excel in all areas. They may be far ahead of their peers in the mainstreamed classroom and thus require special attention and instruction. Some gifted students are creative; others may have special abilities in specific areas such as art, music, drama, and leadership. Opportunities for expression of creativity and talents can be provided within the mainstreamed classroom.

Students from culturally and linguistically diverse backgrounds present a different type of challenge. Although many students from diverse groups do not need special assistance to succeed in the mainstream, some do. The customs, traditions, and values of their culture may set them apart from their peers and hinder their acceptance. Some students may be fluent speakers of English, others may be bilingual in English and another language, and still others may be just beginning to acquire English language skills. If communication is difficult, learning problems may result.

Also posing a challenge to the teacher are **students at risk for school failure.** Although these students are not considered disabled under the law, their current performance and future welfare are threatened by a host of complex societal problems: poverty, homelessness, child abuse, and drug and alcohol abuse. They are the potential school dropouts, potential or actual delinquents, runaways, teenage parents, and suicide risks. Like other special students, students at risk have very real educational needs that must be addressed if the likelihood for school failure is to be reduced.

Special students come to the attention of their teachers when they require instructional assistance in order to succeed in school. Their needs, however, are similar to those of their peers, although probably more serious and long-standing. Every class, no matter how homogeneous, has its bright and not-so-bright students, its troublemaker or behavior problem, and its student with a transitory physical disability in the form of a broken arm or leg. Special students only enhance the range of skills and abilities within the regular classroom. To learn more about special students, see "For Your Information" on page 9. Boxes such as these, placed throughout the book, present facts of interest to teachers.

ORIGINS OF MAINSTREAMING

Most special students today are educated in mainstreamed classrooms. If identified as disabled, gifted, or in need of English language instruction, they may also receive part-time services from a trained specialist such as a special education teacher. In some cases, that professional provides support to students (or to the teacher) within the regular classroom; in others, students leave the classroom for brief periods to receive instruction in a resource room or other setting. In either case, special students remain with their peers for all regular class activities in which they can successfully participate.

Not all special students spend the majority of the school day in the regular classroom. Special classes (and, in some locations, special schools) are available for students with severe disabilities whose instructional needs are different from and more intense than those of their age peers. Although educated in separate programs, these students enter the mainstream for nonacademic and social activities whenever feasible. Also, they may increase their level of participation in the general education program as they acquire new skills and/or as professionals become more proficient at providing them the support they need to succeed in the regular classroom. The door to the mainstreamed classroom remains open to all students with special needs.

This has not always been so. Mainstreaming, as it is known today, has had a long developmental period. In the early days of education in the United States, special students were placed in regular classes because this placement was the only one available. Special services were virtually nonexistent. Students with special needs did not receive assistance from trained specialists; teachers were left to cope with special students as best they could. Students considered difficult to teach, such as those with severe disabilities, were often excluded from public education.

With the growth of special education and other such services, changes occurred. Children and adolescents with severe disabilities, who had been denied an education, were provided with special schools. Regular class students with learning and behavior problems were removed from the mainstream of education and placed in separate special classes. Because those students were having difficulty meeting the demands of the regular class, intensive full-time special education services were seen as the remedy. It was thought that the needs of students with disabilities could best be served by specially trained teachers in special situations, far from the mainstream.

Although the idea of providing special services to students with special needs was a worthwhile notion, serious problems grew out of the special class movement. It was soon discovered that full-time special education was not the answer for most students with disabilities. Many special students did not require full-day services. Many were able to participate in at least some of the activities of the regular class; all could benefit from contact with their peers. But students in special classes were removed from the mainstream of education; special classes were often located in obscure places in the school building. Special class students were also segregated from their peers and often excluded from typical school activities such as assemblies. In addition, the labeling process set special students further apart from their peers. In order for students to qualify for special services, it was necessary to determine the existence of a disability. Students were tested and, often on the basis of inadequate assessments, were labeled brain injured, mentally retarded, or emotionally disturbed. Labels such as these did not provide useful educational information for the classroom teacher or the special educator; worse, they attached stigma to special students.

Another major problem was the inappropriate placement of students in special classes. Students who spoke little or no English were tested in English and labeled retarded. Students from diverse cultures were compared with middle-class, Anglo American peers and were found different, therefore inferior. Such students were placed in special classes side by side with students with disabilities. And once removed from the mainstream, a student had little chance to return. Special class placement was virtually permanent.

These practices were soon recognized as problems. Parent groups, such as the Association for Retarded Citizens and the Learning Disabilities Association of America (formerly the Association for Children with Learning Disabilities), became active in support of appropriate services for all special students. Leaders in special education began to speak out against special class abuses; the article "Special Education for the Mildly Retarded—Is Much of It Justifiable?" by Lloyd Dunn (1968) is an example. Researchers like Jane Mercer (1973) accumulated evidence that students from diverse groups were vastly overrepresented in special classes. *The Six Hour Retarded Child*, by the President's Committee on Mental Retardation (1969), found that many students were disabled only in the school situation. Court cases were filed. The *Diana* suit (1970, 1973) attacked testing abuses with students who did not speak English; the *Larry P.* case (1972, 1979, 1984) pointed up abuses with students from diverse cultures.

As more and more information became available, the prevailing educational philosophy began to shift. With the report of the Project on Classification of Exceptional Children by Hobbs (1975, 1976), the disadvantages of labeling became apparent. Normalization, or the belief that individuals with disabilities have the right to as normal an existence as possible, became an accepted goal of special services (Nirje, 1969; Wolfensberger, 1972). The pendulum swung away from segregation of special students in separate special schools and classes and toward inclusion in the mainstream of education. This viewpoint was endorsed not only by parents and professional educators but also by state and federal laws such as Public Law 94-142, the Education for All Handicapped Children Act of 1975.

As "For Your Information" on page 12 explains, PL 94-142 expanded the idea of normalization and applied it to school programs by requiring that students with disabilities be educated in the least restrictive environment—that is, alongside their peers without disabilities—whenever feasible. Some professionals call this practice mainstreaming; others use the term *integration* to underscore the need to move away from separate, segregated programs. More recently, advocates for students with severe disabilities have recommended the full inclusion of all students, whatever their special needs, in general education programs (Stainback & Stainback, 1990a). The term *inclu-*

sion serves as a reminder that some models of service delivery are characterized by their "exclusion" of students perceived to be difficult to teach.

MAINSTREAMING TODAY

Today, mainstreaming is a reality. However, there are several important differences between current mainstreaming practices and those of several decades ago. First, today the regular classroom is not the only service available to students with special needs, although it is viewed as the most appropriate option for many. Second, rather than being allowed to flounder and fail in the mainstream, students with disabilities are provided with aid and assistance including, when necessary, individualized instruction from a specialist.

Third, general education teachers also receive assistance from specialists. Professionals such as resource teachers or special education consultants may aid in planning educational programs for mainstreamed students, provide suggestions for modification of regular class activities, and supply special materials and equipment. The general educator, as part of the mainstreaming team, contributes by sharing information and ideas with parents and specialists.

According to federal law, alternative placements must be available for students with disabilities whose educational needs cannot be met in mainstreamed classes. However, such students are encouraged to interact with regular class peers in any way feasible. For example, in many districts students once placed in special schools are now members of special classes located within regular schools. This greatly enhances their opportunities to interact with age peers. In addition, special classes are not viewed as permanent placements; students may reenter the mainstream at some time in the future if they are able to benefit from the general educational program.

Although school districts typically offer a range of special education services for students with disabilities, services for other types of special students are less common. If available, programs for students who are gifted, talented, bilingual, or at risk for school failure are similar to those offered by special education. That is, students are mainstreamed in regular classes for a portion of their school day and receive individualized services from specialists as necessary. Most programs also provide assistance and support to the regular classroom teacher.

BENEFITS OF MAINSTREAMING

The benefits of mainstreaming are many. Special students remain with their peers; they are not segregated from the normal activities of the school. Labeling is deemphasized. Students leave the classroom for special help, not to see the teacher of students with mental retardation or emotional disturbance. Resource room services have aided in decreasing the stigma attached to special education because resource teachers often serve students with many different types of special needs. In addition, research indicates that students with disabilities can achieve academic success in mainstreamed class-

Landmark Legislation for Persons with Disabilities

*T*wo federal laws passed in the 1970s have had dramatic impact on the lives of individuals with disabilities in the United States. Two newer laws, passed in the 1990s, follow the same tradition as earlier legislation and extend the rights guaranteed to persons with disabilities.

Legislation Related to Education

Public Law 94-142, the Education for All Handicapped Children Act of 1975, had as its major provision the guarantee of appropriate educational services to all school-aged students with disabilities. Although the act itself did not include the term *mainstreaming,* it is sometimes called the mainstreaming law because it requires that students with disabilities be educated with regular class peers to the maximum extent appropriate. Listed here are the major provisions of PL 94-142:

- All students with disabilities are guaranteed a free, appropriate public education.
- An Individualized Education Program (IEP) must be developed for each student with disabilities.
- Parents have the right to participate in planning their child's educational program.
- Students with disabilities are to be educated in the least restrictive environment, that is, with students not identified as disabled, whenever possible.
- Tests and other assessment procedures used with students with disabilities must not discriminate on the basis of race, culture, or disability.
- Due process procedures must be in place to protect the rights of students with disabilities and their parents.
- The federal government provides some funding to states to help offset the costs involved in educating students with disabilities.

Public Law 101-476, the Individuals with Disabilities Education Act of 1990, the current update to PL 94-142, introduced several modifications. Known as IDEA, this law:

rooms. Success is most likely when general education instruction is individualized and when support is available not only to students with special needs but also to their teachers (Leinhardt & Pallay, 1982; Madden & Slavin, 1983).

Current practices safeguard against the inappropriate placement of students in special education programs. Every effort is made to keep special students in mainstreamed situations, and those students in separate special programs are encouraged to participate in as many of the school's regular activities as feasible. For example, they should attend school assemblies, use the playground with other classes, and eat at the regular lunch time.

Regular class students benefit from association with their special peers. The inclusion of individuals with

- changed the language of the law so that the term *handicap* is replaced with *disability;*
- added autism and traumatic brain injury to the list of disabilities covered under the law and called for study of the condition of attention deficit disorder;
- required that IEPs address needed transition services for students ages 16 and older (and younger students, as appropriate);
- defined as support services "assistive technology device" and "assistive technology service"; and
- provided funding for the recruitment of persons from diverse groups into careers in special education.

Civil Rights Legislation

Section 504 of the Vocational Rehabilitation Act of 1973 applies to people of all ages. Known as the civil rights act for persons with disabilities, it provides that:

> no otherwise qualified handicapped individual in the United States . . . shall, solely by reason of his handicap, be excluded from the participation in, be denied the benefits of, or be subjected to discrimination under any program or activity receiving federal financial assistance.

Section 504 forbids discrimination in employment, in admissions to institutions of higher education, and in the provision of health, welfare, and other social services (Berdine & Blackhurst, 1985). Also, it entitles school-aged children with disabilities to a free, appropriate public education.

Public Law 101-336, the Americans with Disabilities Act of 1990, or ADA, is a comprehensive law designed to "provide a clear and comprehensive national mandate for the elimination of discrimination against individuals with disabilities." To this end, ADA prohibits discrimination in employment, public accommodations (e.g., restaurants, hotels, theaters, and medical offices), services provided by state or local governments, public transportation, and telecommunications.

disabilities in school activities is a realistic introduction to U.S. society. As "For Your Information" on the next page shows, regular class students learn about those different from themselves and have the opportunity to learn that the differences are unimportant.

Teachers and specialists also gain when special students are mainstreamed. Special educators are able to serve more students. Special classes usually contain only 10 to 15 individuals, whereas resource programs may serve as many as 25 to 30 students. Also, specialists are able to concentrate on the special learning needs of the student and are not forced to duplicate the efforts of the regular classroom. General educators benefit, too, in the support they receive from the mainstreaming team. Specialists provide special students with individualized help and are available to

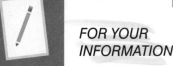

Students' Perceptions of Mainstreaming

Until quite recently, Jessica Rose attended a special school for students with multiple disabilities. Last fall, however, Jessica became a fifth grader; with support from a special education teacher, Jessica was included as a member of a grade 5 general education classroom located in a regular neighborhood school. Jessica's parents, Peggy and Tim, describe Jessica as a beautiful 9-year-old who is nonverbal, nonambulatory, and unable to feed, dress, or care for herself. Her fifth grade classmates have a somewhat different perspective. Read a sample of their responses (presented here in their original form) when they were asked at the end of the year to describe what it was like to have Jessica in their class:

- I feel that Jessica has changed my life. How I feel and see handicapped people has really canged. My friends used to make fun of handicaped children. When I saw Jessica I was scared and I didn't know what of. I used to think about handicaped people being really weak and if I would touch her I would hurt her but now I think diffrently.
- Whenever I'm around Jessica I feel very special. I feel lucky to be able to interact with her. When I look at Jesse and then look at myself I look back at how I used to be. I never used to look at a disabled person without staring at them. I've learned alot from Jesse. She taught me how to accept peopl's differences. Jessica is very special to me. She's a pleasure to be around.
- I feel like she is just a normal person. I though that I would not ever have a eperence with a handycaped but I do now. I feel lucky to have this experience. I use to feel unconferble but now I do not. I like her in our room now.

assist the teacher in meeting the needs of students mainstreamed in the regular classroom.

Of course, difficulties may occur in the mainstreaming process. General education teachers who have little experience with special students may be reluctant to participate. Students, both typical and special, and their parents may be apprehensive. These problems are exacerbated when financial and personnel resources are reduced; there may be fewer services for special students and less assistance to teachers of mainstreamed classrooms. Such difficulties are minimized when general education teachers are skilled in dealing with special students.

One purpose of this book is to help teachers develop the necessary skills. See "Tips for the Teacher" to learn about meeting the needs of special students as well as those of the other pupils in the classroom.

SPECIAL EDUCATION AND MAINSTREAMING

Special education is specially designed instruction to meet the individual needs of special students. According to Kirk and Gallagher (1979), special education is "those additional services, over and above the regular school program, that are provided for

- I think it is great that Jessica is in our room. Jessica is very fun. She laughs and smiles a lot. Sometimes she crys but that is OK. I have learned that Handicapped people are just like the others. I used to say "ooh" look at that person but now I don't I have a big heart for handicapped because they are interesting they can do things that other people can't do. I think Jessica has changed because she is with lots of other kids.
- I like Jessica a lot and I enjoy it a lot when I hear her giggle. I feel just because she is in a wheelchair that doesn't mean she is bad. I have learned a lot about Jessica. Jessica will allways be my friend.
- I really like having Jessica in my class. Before she came I always had thought people in wheelchairs were real weak. I was wrong. Jessica is really quite strong. I never really thought that she could have feelings because she was handicapped. She can have feelings too. She can paint with guided help. I never thought she could paint. Having Jessi in my class has taught me stuff others might never know.
- I think that I used to be scared of handy caped people but now that Jessica came in I am not scared anymore. Because I think we should be treated equally. Because we are all the same.
- I really like Jessica in my class. Befor I met her I never really cared about handycapt people. Jessie is really nice and I like her alot. Jessica is almost like a sister to me. I like to spend my recess playing with her. I thought a handycapt kid would never be part of my life but now one and alot more are.

exceptional children to assist in the development of their potentialities and/or the amelioration of their disabilities" (p. 22). Heward and Orlansky (1992) define special education in another way:

> Special education is individually planned, systematically implemented, and carefully evaluated instruction to help exceptional learners achieve the greatest possible personal self-sufficiency and success in present and future environments. (p. 23)

Special educators serve students identified as having disabilities: students with learning disabilities, behavioral disorders and emotional distur-

bances, mental retardation, speech and language disorders, autism, physical and health disorders, traumatic brain injury, and vision and hearing disorders. Many states also provide special education services to gifted and talented students. Students from culturally and linguistically diverse backgrounds, unless they are also disabled or gifted, are not eligible for special education; instead, they may receive services from specialists in bilingual education or from teachers of English for speakers of other languages.

Special education services are available to both special students and their teachers. These services

TIPS FOR THE TEACHER

Teaching Special Students and All the Others

A s the teacher of a regular classroom, you are the person who is responsible for the education of your students. Each of the children or adolescents in your charge has specific learning needs; each is an individual. When special students are members of your class, you may feel overwhelmed. Don't! Special students have specific learning needs, just like the other students in your class. They are individuals, just like their peers. Their differentness comes from the severity of their needs. They require more help in some areas than typical students do. In these areas they receive special education. In your classroom they participate in general education. Some adaptations of instructional procedures or the classroom environment may be necessary, but many "regular" students also need such changes.

Shortly after the passage of PL 94-142, Mills (1979) made several suggestions for teachers of mainstreamed classrooms. These suggestions are still good ones, and, although they deal specifically with students with disabilities, many can be applied to the other types of special students who are mainstreamed.

- Develop the necessary skills.
- Think positively.
- Know your own strengths and weaknesses.
- Insist on in-service.
- Seek assistance.
- Utilize parents.
- Prepare your class.
- Smile.

This last suggestion deserves more explanation. Mills elaborates:

> These are kids, too. They need the same love and warmth as do all children and may need a little assurance of the mainstream's desire to have them there. The other children won't accept the child with problems if the teacher isn't ready to do so. Be a leader in your own class; set the stage for a positive learning environment for all children. (p. 16)

range from special consultation provided to the teacher of a student with disabilities, to special instruction delivered to a special student a few minutes per day by a special education resource teacher within the regular classroom or in the resource room, to full-day special classes for students with severe and comprehensive disabilities.

Several other **related services** may be provided to special students if necessary. These include psycho-logical services for assessment and counseling, transportation, speech and language services, special physical education, rehabilitation counseling, and physical and occupational therapy. Auxiliary services such as these are available to help special students derive the maximum benefit from special education.

Many different professionals may provide service to the same student with disabilities. For example, Donna, the 8-year-old student introduced earlier in this chapter, receives instruction from her second grade teacher, Ms. Cole, and from the resource teacher. Josh, the high school student, attends four different subject matter classes, sees the adapted physical education teacher, and receives special transportation services. In addition, the resource teacher coordinates his program and provides assistance to his general education teachers as necessary.

For mainstreamed students such as Donna and Josh, the team that provides advice regarding their educational program can be viewed as the mainstreaming team. It is made up of the student's classroom teacher (or teachers), any specialists who work with the student, the parents of the student, and, when appropriate, the special student. Each of these individuals has an important role in planning and executing the mainstreaming experience. The team approach is critical in fostering communication, cooperation, and collaboration among those interested in the education of the special student.

One of the functions of the team is to plan the student's educational program. As soon as a student is found to be eligible for special educational services, the team meets to make several important instructional decisions. After the student's present level of performance in important educational areas is identified, the team plans the student's program for the next year, and annual goals and short-term objectives are established. The next decision concerns placement. The extent to which the student is able to participate in the general education classroom is determined, and special education and related services are provided to meet the remaining educational needs. In this way the student's needs determine the amount and kind of special services to be provided. Placement outside the regular class occurs only when absolutely necessary.

The educational plan devised by the mainstreaming team is called the **Individualized Education Program,** or IEP. It is a written plan agreed upon by a team that includes the student's parents and often the student. An IEP is prepared for each student who receives special education services. The IEP is available to all team members and must be reviewed at least once a year, and more often if necessary.

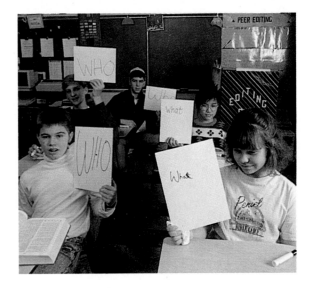

A sample IEP form is shown in Figure 1–2. On this form, the team records information about the student's present performance and lists annual goals and short-term objectives. Special education services are described, and the extent to which the student will participate in the general education program is noted. At the bottom of the form is a space for parents to indicate their approval of the educational program and placement.

Portions of the IEPs for Donna and Josh appear in Figure 1–3. Included for each student are present levels of educational performance, annual goals, and the persons responsible for achieving those goals. After that come descriptions of the educational services to be provided. Note that both special education services and the amount of regular class participation are specified.

Placement in the mainstream is considered optimal for students with disabilities if they are capable of coping with regular class demands. As Figure 1–4 illustrates, a range of special services is available, and many of these include at least part-time placement in the regular classroom. For example, a special educator may collaborate with the classroom teacher to identify appropriate instructional adaptations for one or more mainstreamed students or

FIGURE 1–2
IEP Form

JACKSON COUNTY PUBLIC SCHOOLS
INDIVIDUALIZED EDUCATIONAL PROGRAM

Student_____ Birth Date_____ School _____
This IEP effective from_____ until_____ To be reviewed _____
                  (date)   (date)   (date)

Members of IEP Committee	Current Program Placement
Name Position _____ _____ _____ _____ _____ _____ Dates of IEP meetings _____	☐ Self-contained, full-time ☐ Self-contained, part-time ☐ Resource room ☐ Regular class with supportive services ☐ Other (specify) _____

Extent to which student will participate in regular education program (include percentage of time to be spent in regular classroom):

Related Services to be Provided

	Beginning date	Ending date	Person/ agency responsible
☐ Speech therapy	_____	_____	_____
☐ Occupational therapy	_____	_____	_____
☐ Physical therapy	_____	_____	_____
☐ Counseling	_____	_____	_____
☐ Other (specify)	_____	_____	_____

PRESENT LEVEL OF PERFORMANCE	ANNUAL GOALS	EVALUATION CRITERIA

SHORT-TERM OBJECTIVES	DATES		TEACHING STRATEGIES
	Begun	Completed	

☐ I participated in the development of my child's IEP, and I approve of the plan.
☐ I did not participate in the development of my child's IEP, but I approve of the plan.
☐ I do not approve of my child's IEP, and request that the plan be reviewed.

Signature of Parent or Guardian _____ Date _____

Note. Reprinted with permission of Merrill, an imprint of Macmillan Publishing Company, from *Exceptional Children* (p. 371) by W. L. Heward and M. D. Orlansky, Copyright © 1980 Merrill Publishing Company, Columbus, Ohio.

FIGURE 1–3
Portions of the IEPs for Donna and Josh

Donna

Current Grade: 2

Present Levels of Educational Performance

■ Donna is in good health with normal vision, hearing, and motor abilities. She is well adjusted and gets along well with her peers.

■ Donna's listening and speaking skills are age-appropriate. She performs at grade level in math and handwriting.

■ Donna is able to say the alphabet and identify all letters. She knows most of the consonant sounds and the short sound of *a*. Her sight vocabulary is approximately 70 words. Donna reads on the primer level.

■ Donna is able to spell most of the words in the first grade spelling text (although she cannot read them all). She receives passing grades in spelling in her second grade classroom.

Annual Goals

1. By the end of the school year, Donna will read at a beginning second grade level with 90% accuracy in word recognition and comprehension.
   Person responsible: Resource teacher

2. By the end of the school year, Donna will increase her sight vocabulary to 150 words.
   Person responsible: Resource teacher

3. By the end of the school year, Donna will know the short and long sounds of the vowels.
   Person responsible: Resource teacher

4. By the end of the school year, Donna will read and spell at least 70% of the second grade spelling words.
   Person responsible: Second grade teacher

5. By the end of the school year, Donna will successfully complete second grade requirements in math, handwriting, science, social studies, art, music, and physical education.
   Person responsible: Second grade teacher

Amount of Participation in Regular Class

■ Donna will participate in the second grade class for all subjects except reading.

Special Education and Related Services

■ Donna will receive special instruction in reading (Annual Goals 1, 2, and 3) from the resource teacher for 30 minutes daily.

assist in the regular classroom by teaching lessons to a small group that includes a student with special needs. The array of special education service options is sometimes viewed as a continuum. The continuum extends from placement in the general education classroom with no special services or supports to options that serve small numbers of students with very severe needs, such as a hospital school for young children with cancer.

In selecting placements for special students, it is necessary to follow the principle of **Least Restric-** **tive Environment,** or LRE. The LRE for a student with disabilities is believed to be the appropriate placement closest to the mainstream of education. For students unable to function successfully in a regular class, placement in a special class within a public school is less restrictive (i.e., closer to the mainstream) than placement in a separate school or residential facility. This concept does not imply that students should be placed in less intensive settings simply to bring them closer to the mainstream. Their placement must be feasible; they must have a

FIGURE 1–3
continued

Josh

Current Grade: 10

Present Levels of Educational Performance

- Josh is unable to move his legs and has difficulty with fine-motor tasks involving eye-hand coordination. He is able to travel independently by wheelchair.

- Josh's general health is good. His hearing and vision are within normal limits. He is well adjusted and friendly and appears to get along well with his peers.

- No academic problems are apparent. Josh received As and Bs in Grade 9 classes and scored well above average in group academic achievement tests.

- Josh communicates better orally than in writing because of motor difficulties. His handwriting and typing are slow and require much effort.

Annual Goals

1. By June, Josh will successfully complete all 10th grade requirements, including physical education.

   Persons responsible: General education teachers, resource teacher, adapted physical education teacher

2. By June, Josh will improve in handwriting and other types of fine-motor tasks.

   Persons responsible: General education teachers, resource teacher, adapted physical education teacher

Amount of Participation in Regular Classes

- Josh will participate in regular 10th grade classes four out of five periods per day.

Special Education and Related Services

- Josh will receive special transportation services between his home and the school.

- Josh will attend an adapted physical education class one period per day.

- The resource teacher will provide consultation as needed to Josh's regular class teachers.

good chance of successful performance. The goal is the least restrictive *and* most appropriate placement possible. For most students with disabilities, this means the regular classroom with special services for the student and teacher.

CURRENT ISSUES AND TRENDS

In the past decade, several important factors have begun to influence general education, special education, and their collaboration in the mainstreaming of special students. The educational reform movement is one major trend. The 1980s produced a series of commission reports and recommendations aimed at improving the quality of U.S. schools. Best known among these is *A Nation at Risk: The Imperative for Educational Reform* by the National Commission on Excellence in Education (1983); it begins with these words:

Our Nation is at risk. . . . [T]he educational foundations of our society are presently being eroded by a rising

FIGURE 1–4
Placement in the Least Restrictive Environment

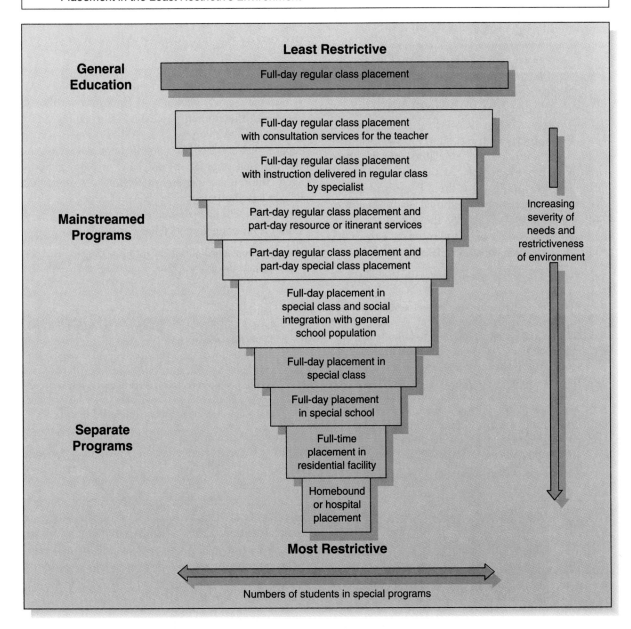

General Education

Least Restrictive

Full-day regular class placement

Full-day regular class placement
with consultation services for the teacher

Full-day regular class placement
with instruction delivered in regular class
by specialist

Mainstreamed Programs

Part-day regular class placement and
part-day resource or itinerant services

Part-day regular class placement and
part-day special class placement

Full-day placement in
special class and social
integration with general
school population

Full-day placement in
special class

Full-day placement
in special school

Separate Programs

Full-time
placement in
residential facility

Homebound
or hospital
placement

Most Restrictive

Increasing severity of needs and restrictiveness of environment

Numbers of students in special programs

tide of mediocrity that threatens our very future as a Nation and a people. (p. 5)

This report and others calling for educational reform led to the excellence in education movement. Among the results of this movement were an increased emphasis on content area subjects (as opposed to basic skills), longer school days and years, higher expectations and grading standards, and more stringent discipline requirements.

The next wave of reforms led to the school restructuring movement and efforts to increase the decision-making powers of educators through site-based management models. At the same time, the nation's governors led by then-President Bush agreed on six national educational goals (*America 2000*, 1990). Modified slightly, these goals became the framework for President Clinton's Goals 2000 education legislation enacted in 1994:

- By the year 2000, all children in America will start school ready to learn.
- By the year 2000, the high school graduation rate will increase to at least 90 percent.
- By the year 2000, American students will leave grades 4, 8, and 12 having demonstrated competency over challenging subject matter including English, mathematics, science, foreign languages, arts, history, and geography, and every school in America will ensure that all students learn to use their minds well, so they may be prepared for responsible citizenship, further learning, and productive employment in our modern economy.
- By the year 2000, United States students will be first in the world in mathematics and science achievement.
- By the year 2000, every adult American will be literate and will possess the knowledge and skills necessary to compete in a global economy and exercise the rights and responsibilities of citizenship.
- By the year 2000, every school in America will be free of drugs and violence and offer a disciplined environment conducive to learning.

Goals 2000 calls for a number of reforms such as drug-free schools and improved high school graduation rates. Math and science achievement is stressed, but attention is also given to universal literacy and readiness for school. In addition, the term *all students* is defined as including not only typical students and those who are academically talented but also students with disabilities, those from diverse cultural and ethnic groups, those with limited proficiency in English, and those who are disadvantaged.

Another major trend is the changing nature of the school-aged population in the United States. As reform movements lead to more rigorous educational standards, the student population is becoming more diverse and in many ways less able. Reeves (1988) reports that children are now the poorest segment of the national population; one of every four school-aged children is a member of a family whose income falls below the poverty line. Several general population trends will have dramatic effects on the needs of students entering general education classrooms:

- As the general population ages, the proportion of the young who are members of minority groups—particularly blacks and Hispanics—will expand dramatically.
- As the gap between rich and poor grows wider, a larger and larger percentage of children will fall below the poverty line.
- As shifts in the traditional patterns of marriage and child-rearing continue, fewer children will have the emotional and educational advantages of a two-parent family, parents who are themselves educated, and close supervision after school. (Reeves, 1988, p. 17)

In addition, according to the Individuals with Disabilities Education Act (1990), the fastest-growing segment of the U.S. population is persons with limited proficiency in English language skills.

Changes such as these will increase the number of students at risk for school failure. This suggests that educational reform efforts that divert funds away from remedial programs may be moving in the wrong direction. There is a need for more support for low-performing students and their teachers, not less (McLoughlin & Lewis, 1994).

Within special education, there has been much debate about an idea called the regular (or general) education initiative (Davis, 1989). Contrary to its name, this movement did not originate in general education. However, it concerns general education because its basic premise is that students with disabilities should be educated in the mainstream. Although this does not sound like a new idea, the proponents of the regular education initiative (REI) suggest that pull-out programs such as special education resource room services contribute to fragmented service delivery and that many students with mild disabilities could and should receive all of their education in general education settings (Reynolds, Wang, & Walberg, 1987; Wang & Birch, 1984; Wang & Walberg, 1988; Will, 1986b). According to Lewis (1989), in REI

> the placement-of-choice would be the regular classroom, albeit an *enhanced* regular classroom in which powerful instructional technologies such as cooperative learning and peer tutoring are routinely employed to increase the probability of academic and social success of low-achieving students. (p. 49)

Critics of REI point to the need for a continuum of services for students with disabilities, point out methodological weaknesses in the research used to support REI, and call for continued study of intervention techniques (e.g., cooperative learning, teacher consultation, peer tutoring) that could increase the likelihood of student success in the mainstream (Fuchs & Fuchs, 1988; Hallahan, Keller, McKinney, Lloyd, & Bryan, 1988; Kauffman, Gerber, & Semmel, 1988; Lloyd, Crowley, Kohler, & Strain, 1988).

While REI focuses on students with mild disabilities, a similar movement calls for increased integration of students with severe disabilities. Leaders such as Stainback and Stainback (1985, 1990b, 1992) and Thousand and Villa (1990) advocate the full-time inclusion of all students, including those with severe disabilities, in regular classrooms in neighborhood schools. Others disagree. Groups such as the Council for Exceptional Children (1993), the Division for Learning Disabilities (1993), the National Joint Committee on Learning Disabilities (1993), and the Learning Disabilities Association of America (1993) maintain that one educational option is not sufficient. Instead, a variety of special education programs should be available to serve the diverse needs of students with disabilities.

Another trend in special education is increased interest in preschool and postsecondary age groups.

Public Law 99-457 focuses attention on young children with disabilities and their families. As part of this federal law, states may offer programs for infants and toddlers with disabilities; with very young children, an Individualized Family Services Plan (IFSP) guides the delivery of services instead of an IEP. Federal special education laws also address the needs of adolescents and young adults with disabilities. For example, the Individuals with Disabilities Education Act of 1990 requires a transition plan for all high school students with disabilities in order to ensure coordination between school programs and postschool options such as vocational training, postsecondary education, employment, and adult services.

At present, the effects of educational reform movements and the changes in student demographics are just beginning to become apparent in general education. Special education is directing some of its efforts to the early childhood years in an attempt to reverse or at least slow the effects of disabilities on young children's readiness for school. There is also debate about the relationship of special and general education and the most effective ways of promoting the social and instructional integration of students with disabilities. As this debate continues, it will become increasingly important for general and special educators to collaborate in the search for solutions to the educational problems facing all types of special students, not only those with identified disabilities.

GENERAL EDUCATION TEACHERS AND SPECIAL STUDENTS

The teacher of a mainstreamed classroom makes several contributions to the success of special students. The teacher is often the first professional to identify the special needs of students and to initiate the referral process. The classroom teacher is also a source of valuable information about current school performance when students are assessed for possible special education services. As part of the mainstreaming team, the teacher participates in planning the student's educational program and in developing the IEP.

The teacher's most important role is implementation of the special student's general education pro-

People First Language

Language is a powerful tool. When talking or writing about people with disabilities, professionals should make every effort to use language that reflects positive attitudes, not negative stereotypes. One important consideration is putting the person first, not the disability. Consider these examples from the California Governor's Committee for Employment of Disabled Persons (1990):

> DON'T SAY . . . "Mr. Lee is a *crippled teacher* and *confined to a wheelchair.* All of his students are *normal."*
> BUT INSTEAD SAY . . . "Mr. Lee is a *teacher with a disability.* He is a *wheelchair-user.* All of his students are *nondisabled.*

The Research and Training Center on Independent Living (1990) provides several suggestions in its pamphlet *Guidelines for Reporting and Writing about People with Disabilities* (1990):

- Do not use generic labels for disability groups, such as "the retarded," "the deaf." Emphasize people not labels. Say *people with mental retardation* or *people who are deaf.*
- Put people first, not their disability. Say *woman with arthritis, children who are deaf, people with disabilities.* This puts the focus on the individual, not the particular functional limitation. . . .
- Emphasize abilities not limitations. Consider: *uses a wheelchair/braces, walks with crutches,* rather than confined to a wheelchair, wheelchair-bound, or is crippled. Similarly, do not use emotional descriptors such as unfortunate, pitiful, and so forth.

For more information about "people first language" or to obtain a copy of the *Guidelines,* contact the Media Project, Research and Training Center on Independent Living, Bureau of Child Research, University of Kansas, Lawrence, KS 66045.

gram. This process sometimes requires adaptation of classroom procedures, methods, and/or materials to guarantee success for the student with special needs. Regular class activities should be coordinated with the special services received by the student. And communication between parents and professionals is crucial.

In addition, the regular classroom teacher may help to evaluate the student's progress not only in the general education program but also in the areas served by specialists. Evaluation is a critical step in the educational process because it helps determine program modifications. Figure 1–5 presents the educational process, including the final step of evaluation. This diagram also provides a summary of the mainstreaming teacher's roles.

Even though these roles are not new ones for the teacher, special students may require special teaching skills. The first part of this book provides basic information about mainstreaming. Chapter 1 has presented the concept and some of the benefits of mainstreaming, has introduced special students and special education, and has briefly described the roles of the mainstreaming teacher. Chapter 2 will acquaint the teacher with all the members of the mainstreaming team. In chapter 3 the special needs of special students will be explored.

In Part II, teachers will learn about special teaching tools needed for mainstreaming. Each of the chapters in that section deals with an important skill area: adapting instruction, managing behavior, promoting social acceptance, coordinating the classroom learning environment, and integrating computers and other technologies into classroom learning activities. In the third and fourth parts of this book, these skills are applied to each type of special learner.

Before turning to chapter 2 to meet the mainstreaming team, check your understanding of this chapter by consulting the section entitled "Things to Remember."

ACTIVITIES

Here are several activities that will help increase your understanding of the concepts presented in this chapter. Some are designed to acquaint you with the literature on mainstreaming. Others are explorations of current programs and practices in your local schools and community. You will find activities such as these at the end of each chapter.

1. Arrange a visit to an elementary, middle, or high school. Talk with the principal or one of the staff members about the special services at the school. What types of programs are available? Is there a

---

FIGURE 1–5
The Special Education Process

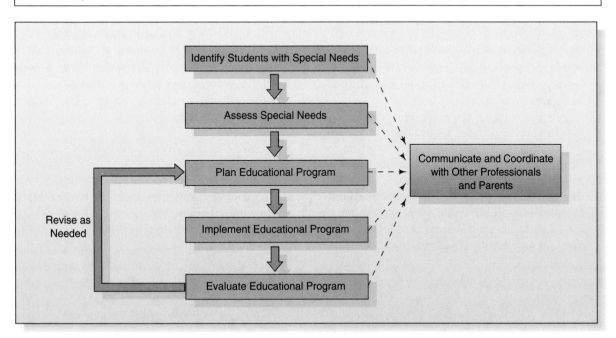

Identify Students with Special Needs

Assess Special Needs

Plan Educational Program

Implement Educational Program

Evaluate Educational Program

Revise as Needed

Communicate and Coordinate with Other Professionals and Parents resource teacher who provides part-time special services to students with disabilities? If possible, visit a regular class in which special students are mainstreamed. Observe the students carefully. Can you tell which are identified as special?

2. Interview several general education teachers about their perceptions of mainstreaming. Have they taught mainstreamed special students in their classrooms? If so, what special learning needs did these students have? What do the teachers believe are the advantages and disadvantages of mainstreaming?

3. Select one or two of the major educational journals in your field. Look for articles that present useful suggestions for adapting instruction for mainstreamed students. You may also wish to look at some of the journals in special education. Two that feature practical articles about educating students with disabilities are *Intervention in School and Clinic* and *Teaching Exceptional Children.* Despite its title, *Teaching Exceptional Children* includes suggestions for both elementary and secondary teachers.

4. Read the article by Madeleine C. Will (1986b), "Educating Children with Learning Problems: A Shared Responsibility." To whom is Will referring when she says "children with learning problems"? What reforms does Will recommend?

5. The major professional organization in special education is the Council for Exceptional Children, or CEC. Many communities have local CEC chapters, and student chapters are often found at colleges and universities. The national CEC office is located at 1920 Association Drive, Reston, VA 22091. Get in touch with your local or state CEC, or write to the national headquarters to learn more about this organization. Is it concerned with all types of special students? Are its members only special education teachers? How does it attempt to improve educational services for students with disabilities?

2 *The Mainstreaming Team*

The team approach is not new in education. Most professionals are aware of individuals who work together as a team to accomplish some common goal. Teams can be established at different levels within the educational system for a variety of purposes, such as selection of instructional materials, development of curriculum, and evaluation of educational programs. These school teams work to plan, evaluate, or improve various aspects of the educational system.

In special education, the team approach has traditionally been used to decide whether students should receive special services. Groups of specialists, often called placement or child study teams, have met to determine whether students were eligible for special education services and, if so, to select the special educational placement of most benefit to the student.

Today, not only special educators but also general education teachers and parents assist in making important decisions about the education of special students. Moreover, the purpose of the team approach to mainstreaming goes beyond that of placement. Team members collaborate to plan and evaluate the mainstreaming experience for students with special needs, and the educators on the team work to implement the plan in the classroom.

It is important to remember that not all students with educational problems need special education services. Often problems can be resolved by modifying the student's current instructional program in the regular classroom. The team approach can help here, too, when professionals work together to adapt instructional strategies to meet the student's educational needs within the general education classroom.

MAINSTREAMING TEAMS

Mainstreaming teams are established within a school to initiate, facilitate, supervise, and evaluate the mainstreaming program for students with special needs. Teams are found at all levels of education, from infant programs through high school. Mainstreaming teams serve one or more of the following purposes: (a) assist teachers in meeting the educational needs of students within the regular classroom;

(b) determine whether students are eligible for services such as special education; and (c) plan, monitor, and evaluate the provision of special services. In this book, we call any team that performs one or more of these functions a mainstreaming team.

Although the team approach is required by federal special education legislation, there is much variation from district to district and from state to state in the names given to different teams and the responsibilities that these teams assume. As described in the "For Your Information" section on the Individuals with Disabilities Education Act, two types of teams are mandatory: the multidisciplinary team and the IEP team. The multidisciplinary team is responsible for determining whether a student is eligible for special education services; it is sometimes called the *special services committee, special education committee,* or *placement committee.* Once a student is found eligible, the IEP team is charged with planning and monitoring that student's Individualized Education Program. The IEP team may be called the *IEP committee* or the *educational planning team.* In some districts, one team assumes both the duties of the multidisciplinary team and those of the IEP team.

The third type of mainstreaming team is designed to assist teachers to solve problems in the general education classroom, before referrals are made to special education or other types of special services. This team may be called the *student study team,* the *prereferral committee,* or the *teacher assistance team.* Although not required by federal laws, such teams are mandatory in some states and districts.

This book advocates that general and special educators work together as a team when making educational decisions about all students with special needs, particularly those who are served in the mainstream. To this end, we call the teams that promote the successful integration of special students in regular classes mainstreaming teams. These teams should be concerned with not only students identified as having disabilities but also students being considered for special education and similar services. For students with disabilities, state and federal laws and regulations describe the purpose, responsibilities, and membership of the teams that make educational decisions. For other special students such as gifted and talented individuals, students from culturally and linguistically diverse backgrounds, and students at risk for school failure, there may be no laws or regulations that require the team approach. However, this book will stress the importance of mainstreaming teams in helping all special students succeed in the general education program.

Mainstreaming teams are composed of individuals directly involved with the education of the mainstreamed special student. Included are general and special educators, some of whom may provide direct service to the student. Other professionals such as school psychologists, speech-language pathologists, and school nurses are involved as necessary. School administrators serve as resources to the team, and the parents of the student are an important addition. Although typically not professional educators, parents are able to provide information about the student and thus play a significant role in the educational decision-making process. If appropriate, the special student should be encouraged to participate.

Mainstreaming teams are multipurpose in nature. Major duties are the planning, implementation, and evaluation of educational programs for mainstreamed students with special needs. A team considers students experiencing difficulty in school and determines, first, whether the general education program can be modified to meet student needs. If this cannot be accomplished, students are assessed to decide whether they are eligible for special education or another type of special service. A team then works to plan a specific educational program for each student. Several team members may be responsible for implementation of that program. For example, the special education resource teacher may assist the general education teacher in adapting instruction for the student in the regular classroom. Or the special teacher may provide the student with part-time instruction in mathematics while the regular classroom teacher takes responsibility for all other subject matter areas. At regular intervals (at least yearly), a team evaluates the student's progress and makes any needed programmatic changes.

Mainstreaming teams provide a vehicle for general and special educators to effectively carry out their shared responsibility for the education of students with special needs. They provide the opportunity for parents and professionals, sharing a common concern for the education of special students, to work together to share information and expertise.

Important Provisions of PL 101-476, the Individuals with Disabilities Education Act (IDEA)

*P*ublic Law 101-476, the Individuals with Disabilities Education Act (IDEA), is the 1990 amendment of Public Law 94-142, the Education for All Handicapped Children Act of 1975. These federal laws provide guidelines for many of the activities and procedures that take place in special education, including requirements for two types of teams: the multidisciplinary team and the IEP team. Check the explanations of the following terms to further your understanding of federal special education laws:

- *Multidisciplinary team*. This group of professionals with appropriate training and experience evaluates students referred for consideration for special education services. Although the composition of this team varies according to the needs of each particular student, it must include a teacher or other specialist with knowledge in the area of the suspected disability. The multidisciplinary team considers referral information, assesses the student, and then determines whether the student is eligible for special education services. The team can recommend an educational placement, but final placement decisions are made by the IEP team.

- *IEP team*. This group develops, reviews, and revises the IEP. Individualized Education Programs are written for all students with disabilities who receive special education services and must be reviewed, and revised as necessary, at least annually. The IEP committee may include the following members: (a) a representative of the school, other than the student's teacher, who is qualified to provide or supervise the provision of special education; (b) the student's teacher(s) (general and/or special education); (c) one or both of the student's parents; (d) the student, when appropriate; (e) other individuals requested by the school or parents; and (f) if the student has recently been evaluated, an individual who is able to interpret the results of that evaluation.

- *Due process hearing*. If the school or the parents of a student with disabilities are not satisfied that the student is receiving an appropriate educational program, an impartial due process hearing can be requested. Hearings attempt to resolve disagreements regarding issues such as identification, evaluation, and educational programs and placements. When a hearing is requested, the student remains in the current placement until the disagreement is resolved.

- *Related services*. These are services offered to students with disabilities to supplement special education programs. They include transportation and other developmental, corrective, and supportive services such as speech pathology and audiology, psychological services, counseling, physical and occupational therapy, recreation, and diagnostic medical services. Rehabilitation counseling and social work services were added as related services by IDEA.

■ *Child find*. Active programs are maintained by state and local education agencies to identify unserved students in need of special education.

■ *Nondiscriminatory assessment*. Assessment is nondiscriminatory when it does not penalize students for their native language, race, culture, or disability.

■ *Confidentiality*. The provisions of IDEA guarantee "confidentiality in the disclosure of information that may unnecessarily identify a student as having a disability" (Strickland & Turnbull, 1990, p. 261). Parents of students with disabilities must be informed of the confidentiality requirements for personally identifiable information (e.g., name, address) and must give consent before this information can be released to anyone outside the school district. The district must maintain confidential records of each student, and these records must be accessible to parents. Legally responsible parents and guardians "have the right to fully review any educational records maintained on their child by the school before an IEP meeting or due process hearing, within 45 days of any request to do so" (Strickland & Turnbull, 1990, p. 25). In addition, they can request (a) explanation or interpretation of information, (b) amendments to records, (c) deletions of information in the records, and (d) a due process hearing to resolve disagreements regarding proposed modifications in the records.

■ *Parent surrogate*. If a parent of a student with disabilities is not available to work with the school, a surrogate parent can be appointed. The surrogate parent approves the student's placement, works on the IEP committee, and serves as an advocate for the student.

■ *Transition services*. Under IDEA, these services must be provided according to the individual needs of each student with disabilities. A statement of the needed transition services must be included on each IEP no later than age 16 (or when it is determined appropriate for a younger student) and annually thereafter. Transition services are defined as "a coordinated set of activities for a student, designed within an outcome-oriented process, which promotes movement from school to post-school activities, including post-secondary education, vocational training, integrated employment, continuing and adult education, adult services, independent living, or community participation" [PL 101-476, Sec. 602(a) (19)].

FIGURE 2–1
The Team Approach to Mainstreaming

Marvin and Jake

Marvin and Jake are 15-year-old freshmen at Jefferson High. They have always been somewhat less-than-average students with minor problems in school, but they have never been considered for special education services. This year Mr. Morse, the boys' English teacher, has decided to ask that their cases be reviewed. In English class Marvin is disruptive and uncooperative; he fails to complete most of his writing assignments. Those that are finished are usually late and of poor quality (Marvin's average grade on writing assignments is 38%). In addition, when bothered by Marvin's outbursts, the other students in the class retaliate by commenting on his poor progress, which leads to arguments in class and in the hall after class. Jake also is doing poorly on his assignments, often turning them in late (Jake's average grade on assignments is 59%). He is late to class several times a week and appears to be confused about assignments; he seldom asks questions and never participates in class discussions.

The student study team at Jefferson High reviewed Mr. Morse's request for assistance and decided that they would like additional information about both students. Mr. Morse was asked to collect data on their academic performance and classroom behavior. He carefully recorded their daily grades and collected samples of their work. He also collected information on the frequency of Marvin's classroom disturbances and arguments

and the occurrence of Jake's tardiness and classroom participation. The special education resource teacher observed both of the students during their English classes and carefully reviewed samples of their work.

After the team's review of this information, it was decided that it was most appropriate for Mr. Morse to attempt to meet Jake's educational needs without referral to special education. The team suggested that Mr. Morse establish a reinforcement system to encourage Jake's arriving in class on time, writing down directions for his English assignments and their due dates, completing the assignments, and participating in class. Mr. Morse was to continue to collect data on Jake's performance. The remedial English resource teacher was contacted for information about appropriate instructional materials for a student such as Jake. In addition, the special education resource teacher offered to provide periodic consultation services to Mr. Morse.

The review of Marvin's case led to the determination that a formal referral should be submitted and a full-scale review conducted. An assessment plan was developed, the parents' approval obtained, and the assessments carried out. Mr. Morse collected additional data on Marvin's in-class performance. The school psychologist and the special education resource teacher assessed Marvin's overall academic performance and his general ability. The school counselor visited Marvin's parents to discuss home performance.

In effective teams, there is open communication and cooperation among members. Communication is the sharing of information that will assist in providing a more appropriate education for students. Formal meetings establish a working relationship among team members that can then be continued and solidified in informal contacts. For example, team members may compare notes about a student's progress by chatting in the teacher's lounge, by tele-phone, or in a home visit with the family. The team works together, with each team member contributing a different viewpoint. Parents, teachers, and other professionals collaborate to provide the best education possible for the special student. See Figure 2–1 for a glimpse of mainstreaming teams in action.

Three features set mainstreaming teams apart from other types of educational teams. First, these

The counselor also contacted Marvin's math, science, and history teachers to determine how he was doing in those classes.

A multidisciplinary team—composed of the vice principal, the counselor, Mr. Morse, the special education resource teacher, the school psychologist, Marvin, and Marvin's mother—then met to review the assessment data. Results indicated that Marvin has good general ability and is able to read at grade level. His grades in subjects other than English are passing but low. Marvin's writing skills are very poor, particularly in the areas of spelling, grammar, punctuation, and capitalization. In addition, he lacks the social skills necessary for establishing interpersonal relationships; he experiences particular difficulty relating to peers. From these results the team concluded that Marvin was qualified for special education services.

The next step was developing an IEP for Marvin. According to the plan agreed on by the IEP team, Marvin will continue to attend his regular academic classes, including English. He will also see the resource teacher one period per day for special instruction in written expression. In addition, the resource teacher will meet at least once a week with Mr. Morse to assist in adapting Marvin's writing assignments. The school counselor will work with Marvin to develop the skills Marvin needs to get along with other students. The counselor, resource teacher, and Mr. Morse will meet with Marvin to establish a contract system to reward successful completion of classroom assignments and appropriate classroom behavior.

The IEP is to be evaluated in 6 months. In the interim the school counselor will monitor Marvin's progress in all of his ninth grade classes. Marvin and his mother agree with the IEP goals and the special services to be provided. Optimistic about Marvin's future, they believe that with help Marvin will succeed in the mainstream.

The three teams involved in developing and implementing Marvin's educational program at Jefferson High were all mainstreaming teams. The teams shared members, and the primary goal of each was to improve the educational program provided for Marvin by matching his specific needs with an appropriate educational program directed at improving his ability to function in the mainstream. The student study team examined his current performance and considered whether modifications could be made in Marvin's current regular classroom program. The multidisciplinary team considered his eligibility for special education after it had been determined that his needs could not be fully met in his current program. The IEP team (which at Jefferson High has the same membership as the multidisciplinary team) identified appropriate educational goals for Marvin, decided who was going to provide the services needed to meet those goals, and then decided what modifications were to be made in his current placement.

teams consider each student individually. When recommendations are made, they are specific in nature and have direct application to the student's educational program. This practice is different from the operation of many educational teams that consider the needs of groups of students. For example, teams may make general recommendations about all the third grade classes in the district or all the basic freshman English classes at a certain high school.

The mainstreaming team, however, focuses its attention on one student at a time.

Second, mainstreaming teams are composed of both general and special educators and other professionals as needed. Team composition is truly multidisciplinary. In the past, each of these disciplines often worked separately to provide instructional services, and there was a minimum of communication with others. This approach frequently led to poor coordination of educational programs for students with special needs, with overlap in some areas of the curriculum and neglect of others. Frequently the instructional strategies used from setting to setting were inconsistent. The team approach can reduce or eliminate this problem by setting up a coordinated educational plan that clearly specifies the responsibilities of each team member.

Third, mainstreaming team membership varies according to the special needs of the student under consideration. Although the resource teacher (or the special education consultant) and the building principal or an appropriate designee may serve on the teams for most special students, the parents and general education teachers who participate will change as each new student is considered. Other professionals may become a part of the team as students with different needs are studied. For example, the school nurse may be a necessary team member for a student with a physical disability but not for a student with learning disabilities.

In addition, one mainstreaming team, the IEP team, must include not only professionals but also the parents of the student with special needs and, if appropriate, the student as well. This is a radical departure from past practices. The parents and student now have the right to be active members of the educational planning team and to provide input regarding instructional needs, goals, and programs. They have access to the information concerning the student and participate in making important decisions about educational placement and programming.

▇ ROLES OF TEAM MEMBERS

Mainstreaming teams are made up of a variety of different members. Both special education and general education are represented. Teachers and administrators are included as well as specialists such as psychologists, physical therapists, and counselors. In addition, parents and special students themselves may participate in team deliberations. Each of these individuals plays an important role on mainstreaming teams.

Building Principals

School principals or vice principals serve as key members of mainstreaming teams. As administrators they are responsible for the general education programs and often the special education programs housed within their buildings. In large elementary or secondary schools, the vice principal with supervisory responsibilities for the special education program may represent the principal on mainstreaming teams.

The principal often schedules and chairs the team's formal meetings. Although usually not directly responsible for implementing any portion of the student's IEP, administrators do influence the operation and effectiveness of the mainstreaming effort. They are the educational leaders of the school and, as such, are aware of the school's program and personnel resources. Their activities and the attitudes they convey can help establish the necessary school climate for developing educational programs that serve a wide variety of learners and for building successful mainstreaming programs.

Special Education Administrators

Special education directors are responsible for supervising the provision of appropriate educational programs for all the students with disabilities within a district. Their primary activities include the direction of intensive special education programs (such as special schools) as well as the provision of support services to special classes, resource programs, and consultants to general education teachers within regular school buildings. Frequently they are responsible for developing in-service training programs to help regular class teachers work more effectively with students with disabilities.

On mainstreaming teams, special education administrators assist in the review of assessment information and help the team examine appropriate special education placement options. In some districts, these professionals serve on the team only when students likely to require placement in separate special classes or schools are considered.

General Education Teachers

The involvement of general education teachers is critical because they have firsthand experience with students with special needs in their classrooms. They share ideas with parents and other professionals, and they assist in devising strategies for successful mainstreaming programs. If these teachers do not participate on the team, the effectiveness of the mainstreaming effort is compromised.

At the secondary level, students with special needs often are served by a number of general education teachers, and the school counselor may be designated as the teachers' representative on mainstreaming teams. The counselor collects information from each teacher about a student's classroom performance and reports to the team. The counselor is then responsible for conveying team decisions and recommendations to each of the student's teachers. Of course, it is possible (and often desirable) for sec-

ondary teachers to serve as members of the team, as in the example of Mr. Morse, Marvin's and Jake's ninth grade English teacher (Figure 2–1).

General education teachers who have worked with students being considered for special education services can provide the team with much information. They are aware of special strengths students may have, students' past responses to various instructional programs and procedures, and specific areas in which students may require the most assistance. The presence of these teachers on the team can assure that all important classroom information is considered. In addition, their experience with individual students may temper the interpretation of assessment results or the types of recommendations made by the team.

General education teachers responsible for implementing a portion of the IEP should be involved in the team's discussion of assessment results and any other relevant information gathered by professionals or provided by parents. Teachers can describe their classroom programs and their perceptions of a student's ability to participate in regular class activities. They can also benefit from the team's discussion of ways to adapt the general education program. As soon as the IEP or the modified classroom program is initiated, the classroom teacher can inform the team of the student's progress in the mainstream class. This input helps the team evaluate the current program in order to make any necessary changes.

Special Educators

In addition to general education teachers, **special teachers** also provide instructional services to students with disabilities. The special educators most likely to serve on the mainstreaming team are those assigned to a classroom or office within the student's regular school. The special educator may be a teacher-consultant who provides assistance to general education teachers with special students in their classes. Or the special educator may be a resource room teacher who provides direct service to special students as well as consultation to their teachers. The special class teacher also may participate as a member of the team; this teacher serves students who require more intensive special education but who may be mainstreamed for selected activities.

Itinerant special education teachers who work with mainstreamed students with disabilities also serve on the team as necessary. **Itinerant teachers**, who travel from school to school, may be specialists in the education of students with speech and language impairments, visual impairments, hearing impairments, physical or health impairments, or other special needs. One of the most common itinerant specialists is the **speech-language pathologist**, who serves students with communication disorders. These and other specialists serve on the team when a student likely to receive their specific services is being considered.

Special educators fulfill a variety of roles on the team. Often they are responsible for organizing the mainstreaming team, conducting the meetings, and monitoring the services provided to students with disabilities. They may observe a student in the regular class and conduct much of the educational assessment. Special education teachers explain the differ-

ent types of available special services and describe in detail the support services for general education teachers. Also, these professionals help interpret assessment results and assist the team in formulating the educational plan. In the implementation of the IEP, they provide direct services to special students and consultant services to regular classroom teachers.

The special teacher most likely to provide instruction to a specific student should serve on the mainstreaming team when that student's educational program is being planned. This involvement provides the special educator with the opportunity to meet the student and his or her parents and teacher(s). The special educator thus becomes familiar with the student's current performance and specific educational needs, as well as with the views of the student's regular classroom teacher(s), the student's parents, and other professionals concerned with the student's education.

Parents and Students

At first, parents may be reluctant to participate in the activities of mainstreaming teams, particularly if past contacts with the school have been primarily negative. They may also be apprehensive about becoming a member of a team composed mainly of professionals. Team members may need to give them a great deal of reassurance regarding the importance of their involvement.

Programs are more effective for students when parents are active participants. Parents can provide the team with information about the special student's performance outside the school setting. They are also able to assist in establishing appropriate educational goals. In addition, parents contribute to the team effort by specifying which aspects of the educational program can be supported or supplemented within the home. The parents' awareness of the specific program designed for their child and the resultant coordination between home and school can make an important difference for many students. Moreover, the team's concern for the needs of their child may win parental support for the mainstreaming effort.

The team should make every effort to include the special student's parents as fully participating team members. If possible, conflicts between parents and professionals should be resolved at the team level. However, if parents do not agree with the recommendations made by the team, they may request a hearing to appeal the team's decisions. The school district also has the right to appeal if it believes that the parents are not acting in the student's best interests.

Special students participate in the activities of the team when it is appropriate. As a general rule, students who have reached junior high and high school age are the most likely to be included. Students attending team meetings should be encouraged to discuss their reactions and perceptions regarding possible educational goals and placements.

School Psychologists

School psychologists assist in gathering assessment information about special students. In addition to administering tests and other assessments, psychologists may observe the student in the regular classroom, interview the parents, or consult with other professionals who have information about the student's recent performance. Their participation on the team also involves explanation or interpretation of assessment results.

School psychologists generally have training in counseling and classroom management. However, their responsibilities in assessing students, writing reports, and serving on several mainstreaming teams throughout the district often consume most of their time. Because they are usually required to serve more than one school, they may not be available for consultation with a teacher who has an immediate concern.

School Social Workers

School social workers assist in collecting information from parents, coordinating the efforts of the team with community agencies, and observing the student's interactions in settings outside the classroom. They are able to provide consultative services to parents, teachers, and students themselves.

School Counselors

Although counselors are most likely to be found at the secondary level, in some districts they are available for students of all ages. Counselors serve in a number of roles on mainstreaming teams and provide direct services to students with special needs. They assist in gathering information from teachers, school records, parents, and community agencies (particularly when school social workers are not available). Special students may receive counseling or educational guidance from these professionals. Counselors at the secondary level often coordinate the educational programs for special students and assume responsibility for communicating information about each student's progress to the student's teachers, parents, and the student.

School Nurses

The school nurse may collect appropriate medical information regarding special students; for example, nurses can screen students for possible vision or hearing problems. As team members, nurses assist in interpreting a student's medical records and reports and in explaining the educational implications of medical information. They may provide services to students with physical disabilities, those with chronic illnesses, or others needing continual medical attention. In addition, they assist parents in obtaining medical services for their children.

Other Team Members

Other persons serve on mainstreaming teams when their special expertise is needed. For instance, for students with physical disabilities, professionals such as **physical therapists**, **occupational therapists**, and **adapted physical education teachers** are important team members. When young students with disabilities are entering school, it is important to obtain information from the early childhood specialist who is familiar with their progress in infant or preschool programs and can facilitate the transition into the school program. For secondary students, **vocational rehabilitation counselors** may be an important addition. **Audiologists** contribute to the team's understanding of hearing losses, and medical personnel may assist when students with health impairments are considered. Another possible addition is the instructional aide who has worked closely with the special student.

Although these individuals may serve on mainstreaming teams, the effective team involves only those members who are necessary for careful and complete consideration of the student's special needs. Large teams of more than five to seven members become unwieldy, and productivity declines. At the minimum, however, every team should include the student's parents and his or her general and special education teachers.

IDENTIFICATION AND PREREFERRAL INTERVENTIONS

A primary function of mainstreaming teams is identification of students with special needs. Students with special educational needs are located and adjustments made in the general education program to respond to their needs. If classroom modifications do not improve student performance, the student is formally referred for special education services and assessed; the team then determines whether the student is eligible for special education services. Although this may not appear to be a complex task, a number of important factors must be taken into account.

Identification

Federal and state laws and regulations specify procedures for educational agencies to follow in the identification process. Team members must fully understand these legal requirements. (Usually the administrators or special educators on the team take primary responsibility for keeping abreast of rules and regulations.) For example, it is the responsibility of each school district to locate all students with disabilities in need of special education and then to provide appropriate services. Each state also has specific regulations regarding district responsibilities in this and other areas, such as notification of parents, due process procedures, and confidentiality of student records.

Many classroom teachers may be unaware of the types of special education services offered within their districts (or even within their school buildings). Also, they may not know the specific criteria or standards that are used to determine whether students are eligible for special education services. Mainstreaming teams should make sure that this information is available to all educators and other interested parties, such as parents and appropriate community agencies.

Anyone within the school community can refer students for consideration for possible special education services. Most **referrals** originate with regular classroom teachers, but many come from parents, counselors, social welfare agencies, and physicians. Mainstreaming teams should set up clear referral procedures; the steps in the process should then be communicated to all teachers and staff within the building as well as to parents and others who may initiate referrals. However, it is important to consider other possible options within the general education program before beginning referral procedures. Research indicates that, once students are referred, they are likely to be assessed (92%) and ultimately placed in special education (73%) (Algozzine, Christenson, & Ysseldyke, 1982).

Prereferral Interventions

Classroom teachers refer students for special education and other types of support services for many reasons. In one recent study, the most common reasons were general academic problems, difficulty in reading, and behavioral problems such as inattentiveness (Lloyd, Kauffman, Landrum, & Roe, 1991). However, before a referral is made, several strategies are available that the teacher can use to try to solve the instructional problem. Because of *when* they occur, these strategies are often called **prereferral interventions**.

Interventions undertaken during the prereferral stage often eliminate the need to refer students for special education or other special services. For example, a change in instructional strategies or an adaptation of the classroom learning environment may lead to improved student performance. Although not mandated by federal special education laws, prereferral interventions are required or recommended by more than half the states (Carter & Sugai, 1989). In many states, school personnel must document that all possible general education interventions have been attempted before a student can be formally referred for special education services.

Data Collection.   When students experience difficulty with some aspect of the general education program, one of the first steps teachers should take is collection of data to describe the instructional problem. This information allows the teacher to verify the existence of the problem, describe its characteristics, and determine its severity. For example, if a teacher is concerned about a student's off-task behavior during the time set aside for journal writing, the teacher could conduct an observation to determine how often the student is off-task. If results indicate that the student is writing in his or her journal only about half the time and talking with peers the other half, the teacher would likely conclude that the problem is severe enough to warrant some type of intervention.

Collaboration with Parents and Colleagues.
Once the instructional problem is described, it is often useful to confer with other professionals who

are familiar with the student in question. The student's former teachers may be able to describe interventions that they have found effective for similar problems; current teachers can share their experiences with the student and their observations of his or her ability to cope with classroom demands. Parents, too, can provide information about the student. In some cases, simply making parents aware of the problem is an effective intervention. For example, if the problem concerns homework, parents may decide to increase their supervision of the student's study sessions or make a valued activity (such as watching television) contingent upon the completion of all assignments.

In some districts, special educators such as resource teachers or teacher-consultants work with general educators to help them modify classroom programs to meet the needs of students not yet referred for special education services (Idol, 1993; Sugai & Tindal, 1993). In many schools, teachers can also seek assistance from teams of colleagues. These teams are known by several different names: *teacher assistance teams, student study teams, prereferral assistance teams,* and so on. They are typically composed of several general educators representing

TIPS FOR THE TEACHER

Working with Other Professionals During Prereferral

Special education consultants and teacher assistance teams provide prereferral services to general educators in order to resolve educational problems within the regular classroom. To make the best use of these services, consider the following suggestions:

1. The job of the consultant or team is to assist you in developing a plan for working with the "target" student. The consultant or team is not there to dictate what should be done for the student or to "take over" the student's educational program.
2. The student continues to be your responsibility and you are in charge of his or her educational program.
3. Establish an agreement as to your role and that of the team or consultant. It may not be necessary to have this agreement in writing, but it is important that everyone be aware of each other's expectations.
4. It is important that you and the consultant or team work together collaboratively. While your training and experience may be different from that of special education professionals, you are responsible for the quality of the program in your classroom, you are aware of the needs of your students, and you can describe their history while they have been in your classroom. The team or consultant is there to assist you.
5. Try to keep the focus of the discussions on the problems the "target" student has experienced. Be as specific as you can in your statements, and don't digress regarding other problems.
6. Provide specific information on the behaviors of the student and on the interventions you have tried. Data on the number of times a behavior occurs or how long it persists, the performance of the student in problem academic or social areas, or the success of an intervention can assist the team or consultant in providing feedback to you. You may be asked some questions regarding this information to clarify the team's understanding of the problem.

different grade levels or subject areas; other members may include an administrator such as the principal, a specialist such as a special educator, and parents. Their major role is to collaborate with teachers in solving instructional problems. The research on teacher assistance teams (Chalfant & Pysh, 1989) and consultation services (Doorlag, 1989a; Graden, Casey, & Christenson, 1985; Idol, 1993) indicates that these approaches are quite successful in solving

problems at the classroom level, thereby reducing the number of referrals to special education.

Idol and West (1991) emphasize the collaborative nature of the team approach. The teacher seeking assistance becomes a member of the team and participates fully in the problem-solving process. This process involves six steps:

- Step 1: Entry/Goal Setting
- Step 2: Problem Identification

7. The team or consultant may suggest that additional data be collected on the problem behavior. Attempt to facilitate the collection of these data, but if you are not comfortable with the type of data to be collected, how the data should be collected, or how much of your time will be required, share these concerns and resolve the specifics of the data collection process. Some teams or consultants can assist with the initial collection of data on students.

8. The team or consultant should help you develop more than one possible intervention for the problem behavior. Don't expect the "one magic solution." Do expect to be actively involved in providing suggestions and developing possible interventions.

9. Implement the interventions in the way they were developed by you and the team or consultant. If you are not comfortable with the intervention or are unsure of the specifics, ask for clarification or assistance. The consultant or a team member may be able to demonstrate the intervention or inform you of other teachers using similar techniques that you could observe.

10. Be sure that a plan is devised to evaluate the effectiveness of the intervention(s). This plan should specify the type of data needed to evaluate the intervention. It should also include the length of time the intervention should be attempted and the alternative interventions that should be attempted if the initial one fails. Set a date for you and the team or consultant to review the progress of the intervention and to consider next steps. If it later becomes necessary to refer the student for special education services, be sure to share the information you have collected on the student and the interventions attempted.

11. Consider your work with the team or consultant as an opportunity to gain new skills in working with special students. Once these skills are mastered, they will help you work with other students with similar problems.

12. Provide feedback to the team or consultant. This feedback will help improve the prereferral services provided to you and other teachers.

- Step 3: Intervention Recommendations
- Step 4: Implementation of Recommendations
- Step 5: Evaluation of the Action Plan and the Team Process
- Step 6: Follow-Up/Redesign (pp. 77–78)

For example, in step 3, the entire team (including the student's classroom teacher) brainstorms possible solutions to the instructional problem, evaluates the advantages and disadvantages of each solution, and then selects the most appropriate one. Consult the "Tips for the Teacher" section to learn more about working with teacher assistance teams and special education consultants.

Team deliberations are most fruitful when the teacher is able to clearly describe the student's problem and any attempts to remedy it. The student intervention checklist shown in Figure 2–2 is one method for recording this type of information. The

FIGURE 2–2
Student Intervention Checklist

Name _____ Age _____ Date _____

Teacher _____ Grade _____

1. **Area(s) of Concern**

_____ academic   _____ language   _____ gross motor   _____ hearing

_____ behavior   _____ speech   _____ fine motor

_____ emotional   _____ physical   _____ vision

2. What kinds of strategies have been employed to resolve this problem?

   A. **Records Review and Conference**

   _____ student conference(s)   ___ review of educational records

   _____ parent conference(s)   ___ vision   ___ medical   ___ hearing

   B. **Environmental Modifications**

   _____ class seating arrangement   _____ group change   ___ other

   _____ individual seating   _____ teacher change

   _____ schedule modification   _____ teacher position in class

   C. **Instructional**

   _____ modifications in methods used with group or class

   _____ modifications in learning aids used with group or class

   _____ individual methods with regular materials

   _____ individual learning aids with regular materials

   _____ individual methods and materials different from group or class

   D. **Management**

   _____ modification in classroom management system

   _____ use of systematic group management techniques

   _____ use of individual behavior management techniques

3. What methods are currently employed to address the concern? _____

_____

_____

_____

4. Where does this student stand in relationship to others in class, group or grade regarding systemwide tests, class average behavior, completion of work, etc.?

Student Behavior	Class or Group or Grade Behavior

5. Is the concern generally associated with a particular time, subject, or person?

6. In what areas, under what conditions, does this student do best?

7. Assistance requested (observation, materials, ideas, etc.):

_____

_____

_____

_____

Assistance provided:

Dates	Nature of Assistance	Individuals Responsible	Outcome

Permission granted by the publisher for noncommercial reproduction.

Note. Reprinted with the permission of Macmillan College Publishing Company from *Developing and Implementing Individualized Education Programs,* 3/e by Bonnie Baran Strickland and Ann P. Turnbull. Copyright © 1990 by Macmillan College Publishing Company, Inc.

teacher begins by noting the area or areas of concern (e.g., academic achievement, classroom behavior) and the steps already taken to solve the problem (e.g., student or parent conference). He or she then describes the student's present performance and current classroom procedures. At the end of the checklist, the teacher identifies the type of assistance he or she is seeking, and there is space for the team to record the results of its deliberations and the outcomes of any interventions.

Classroom Modifications. A number of prereferral intervention strategies involve changes in the instructional program of the regular classroom. To improve student performance, modifications can be made in any aspect of the program: the classroom curriculum, how instruction is delivered, the types of learning activities in which students participate, how students are graded, the physical arrangement of the classroom, and strategies for managing student behavior.

Curricular adaptations are changes in the body of knowledge and skills taught to students. One option is to retain the standard grade-level curriculum but teach only a portion of it—those areas determined to be the most important. Another option is the substitution of an alternative curriculum. In the regular classroom, this usually involves teaching the prerequisite skills that students lack and/or the use of curricular materials from a lower grade level. For example, a fifth grade teacher might use fourth grade reading materials for some students in the class.

Instructional adaptations are the most common type of classroom modification. These changes may involve any part of the teaching-learning process: the teacher's instructional methods and strategies, learning activities and instructional materials, performance requirements for students, testing and grading procedures, and grouping arrangements. Examples are as follows:

- Providing additional instruction in areas where students experience difficulty
- Structuring practice activities so that students have ample time to master one set of skills before moving on to the next

- Modifying task requirements so that students can listen rather than read or give answers orally rather than write
- Giving students extra time to complete exams and assignments
- Allowing students to use aids such as calculators and dictionaries
- Reducing the number of problems students are required to solve or the number of paragraphs they must write
- Grouping students with similar needs for instruction and changing the composition of the groups, as needed

Management adaptations are changes in the classroom behavior management system. The teacher may need to provide additional instruction to all students on the rules for classroom conduct. Or he or she may need to modify the standard classroom management system if several students begin to display inappropriate behaviors. In some cases, it may be necessary to begin a systematic behavior change program for one or more students with more severe behavioral problems. For example, the teacher and student might negotiate a behavioral contract in which the student agrees to reduce his or her inappropriate behavior, and in exchange the teacher promises to provide a suitable reward.

Environmental adaptations are changes in the physical environment of the classroom. For example, a teacher may modify the arrangement of student desks and the location of learning materials in order to make classroom activities accessible to a student who uses a wheelchair. Students with vision and hearing disorders may be seated near the front of the room, if that is where instruction typically occurs. Students who act out and those who have difficulty focusing their attention may also be seated near the teacher. The classroom itself may be arranged so that there are areas for several different types of activities including large- and small-group instruction, independent study, work at the computer, and so on.

According to recent research, general education teachers use several different techniques to modify instruction for students with special needs. However, although teachers consider many kinds of classroom modifications valuable, they are less positive about their feasibility (Johnson & Pugach, 1990; Ysseldyke, Thurlow, Wotruba, & Nania, 1990). In general, teachers are most likely to introduce interventions that they themselves can accomplish quickly and easily within their own classrooms (Ellett, 1993; Johnson & Pugach, 1990). Some of the most common strategies are modifying assignments so they are shorter or less difficult, allowing students to respond orally on tests, and offering preferential seating (Bacon & Schulz, 1991; Munson, 1986).

General Education and Community Resources.

In addition to making modifications in their own classrooms, teachers can draw upon the resources of the general education program to assist students with school problems. Although there will be differences among schools in the types of resources available, all teachers have access to some level of support within their school, district, and community.

The use of students as instructional assistants is one example. Students act as tutors to other students, which thereby increases the amount of individualized instruction that takes place within the classroom. Peer tutoring programs are inexpensive in terms of both time and money, and research supports their effectiveness for increasing the skill levels of students with school achievement problems (Lloyd, Crowley, Kohler, & Strain, 1988). Parents, other family members, and community volunteers can also act as assistants within the classroom.

The general education program may offer a number of resources: schoolwide peer tutoring and/or peer counseling programs, academic assistance in the computer lab, Chapter 1 programs for low-income students, reading and math labs or tutorial services, programs for students learning English, bilingual education, enrichment opportunities for students with special gifts and talents, and so on. The community may offer additional resources such as after school programs with homework assistance, big brother and big sister programs, sports activities and clubs, or a homework hotline with telephone tutors. School and community resources such as

these are one set of options that teachers should consider when they select prereferral interventions for students with special needs.

◼ REFERRAL AND ASSESSMENT

In some cases, prereferral interventions do not solve the problems that students are experiencing in the regular classroom. When this happens, the next step is referral. A multidisciplinary team considers the referral information, including the data collected during the prereferral stage, and determines whether there is sufficient evidence of a problem to warrant continued investigation. If there is, the team proceeds to the next step in the provision of special services, assessment.

Referral

When students are formally referred to the multidisciplinary team, specific time lines and notification procedures are followed, assuring that each student is reviewed in a timely manner as required by state and federal laws. Good educational practice dictates that any identified need be considered promptly, without relegating the student to a waiting list (as often occurred in the past). Delays deny the student access to appropriate services and also frustrate the individual making the referral.

Many different individuals can refer students for consideration for special education. The general education teacher, however, is the primary referral source because classroom teachers observe students daily in the school setting, constantly monitoring their physical status, academic performance, classroom behavior, and social interactions. Classroom teachers are able to compare the performance of one student with that of current classmates as well as students from previous school years.

Classroom teachers differ in the number and type of referrals they make to special education. Some teachers refer a high percentage of their students; others refer none. This discrepancy may occur for a number of reasons. Teachers may not have a clear understanding of how serious a student's problems should be before special education services are considered. Some teachers may not be aware of the special programs or consultation services that are available; others may already be capable of adapting their classroom program to meet the needs of a wide range of students. Still others may be unfamiliar with the appropriate referral procedures, or they may feel that referrals reflect negatively on their ability as a teacher and classroom manager. Most classroom teachers fall somewhere between the two extremes. Generally, the more teachers know about dealing with students with unique needs—and about the types of special services available, the criteria for special education, and the referral procedures—the more accurate and appropriate their referrals.

The exact procedure for making referrals varies greatly from school to school and from district to district. It can involve completing a short form with a minimal amount of information, an elaborate checklist, or a report requiring detailed data on the student's current and past performance. As part of the referral process in many districts, teachers must document the steps they have taken to meet the student's educational needs within the regular classroom. Figure 2–3 provides an example of a prereferral intervention checklist that a teacher might be asked to complete.

Students are referred for special education if they have special needs that interfere with their school performance *and* if these needs cannot be adequately met within the general educational program. Blankenship and Lilly (1981) provide the following guidelines:

> As a basic principle teachers should refer students when two conditions exist: (1) the student is experiencing significant difficulty in the classroom, and (2) the teacher is unsuccessful in solving the problem as it exists. Many students experience difficulty in learning and not all should be referred for special education. Individual teachers have strengths in dealing with certain types of learning and behavior problems, and are confident that they can handle these problems as they occur. *If the teacher is handling a problem successfully, the student should not be referred.* (p. 36)

Although special students may exhibit a variety of problems, their needs generally cluster into one or more of the following areas:

- *Physical needs*—difficulty with one or more of the senses, with mobility or motor coordination, or with physical activities requiring strength and stamina.
- *Academic needs*—poor performance in relation to peers in one or more areas of the curriculum. These needs may be evident in the communication skills of listening and speaking, academic areas such as reading and mathematics, and/or content areas such as science and history.
- *Classroom behavior needs*—difficulty in controlling inappropriate behaviors that interfere with other students, the instruction of the classroom, or the student's own study activities. Either acting-out or withdrawn behaviors may be considered inappropriate.
- *Social needs*—poor ability to establish and maintain interpersonal relationships, either with peers or with adults.

Information on special needs such as these is reported in a referral form such as that illustrated in Figure 2–4. This sample form asks for specific information about the student's current performance and his or her reactions to any instructional adjustments made by the teacher. Members of mainstreaming teams work hard to make careful placement decisions and provide educators and parents with specific programmatic recommendations. To accomplish these tasks, specific, accurate, and objective data are needed. It is difficult for teams to provide assistance when given only general information, such as "the student is slow," "acts out in class," "never talks," or "works below grade level."

Specific statements that describe the current status of the student are much more helpful. Examples of pertinent types of information to include on referral forms are

- correct and error rates on academic assignments and the level of academic performance as compared with that of other students in the classroom,

FIGURE 2–3
Prereferral Intervention Checklist

Appropriate activities on this checklist must be completed before referring a student for assessment for special education services. Place the date that activities were completed in the space next to the activity. This form must accompany the referral form.

1. _____ Reviewed student educational records to determine longevity of concern and previous interventions.

2. _____ Established that student has passed vision and hearing screening or referred student for vision and hearing screening.

3. _____ Met with student to discuss concerns and possible solutions.

4. _____ Met with parents to discuss concerns and possible solutions.

5. _____ Collected and analyzed recent examples of student's classwork.

6. _____ Collected specific information from records and performance regarding student's academic skills.

7. _____ Collected specific information from the record and class regarding student's behavior.

8. _____ Brainstormed with co-teachers to obtain strategies that have worked in other similar cases.

9. _____ Identified in writing the student's specific educational problem.

10. _____ Consulted with counselor regarding student's behavior.

11. _____ Consulted with resource teachers in school to discuss concerns and obtain strategies.

12. _____ Obtained observation by another teacher or school resource to obtain information regarding concern.

13. _____ Developed and implemented instructional strategies with assistance of other educators.

14. _____ Developed and implemented a behavior management plan with other educators.

15. _____ Obtained or developed instructional learning aids to address this student's problem.

16. _____ List any other modifications, interventions, or strategies you have attempted to maintain this student in the classroom.

_____

_____

_____

_____

Teacher Signature _____ Date _____

Permission granted by the publisher for noncommercial reproduction.

Note. Reprinted with the permission of Macmillan College Publishing Company from *Developing and Implementing Individualized Education Programs*, 3/e by Bonnie Baran Strickland and Ann P. Turnbull. Copyright © 1990 by Macmillan College Publishing Company, Inc.

FIGURE 2–4
Referral for Special Education Services

Directions: Teachers or other individuals referring a student for special education services should complete all sections of this form. The completed form should be sent to the principal's office for processing. Complete and specific information will assist the multidisciplinary team and the IEP committee in determining the student's need for service. Use behavioral descriptions whenever possible.

Teacher _____ Grade/Class _____ Report Date _____

Student _____ Age _____ Birthdate _____

1. What is the student's problem? How does it affect his or her ability to participate in classroom activities?

2. How frequently does the problem occur? (For example, once a week? Six times a week?)

3. What changes have occurred in the behavior during this school year?

4. What changes in classroom activities, assignments, procedures, and so on, have you made to try to solve the problem? What are the results of these changes?

5. What are the student's major strengths and talents?

6. What special interests, hobbies, or skills does the student have?

- the frequency with which inappropriate behaviors occur during the class period or school day, or
- the number of assignments completed by the student and an analysis of the student's errors.

Specific information on the success or failure of changes in classroom instruction or management is also extremely helpful. The more objective and complete the data provided in the referral, the more accurately the team will be able to determine what additional assessment information is needed, what types of special education services should be considered, and which educational recommendations are appropriate.

Assessment

When the mainstreaming team has determined that a referred student may be in need of special education services because adaptations of the general education program have not resolved the student's problems, the team designs a complete assessment plan and presents it to the student's parents for their approval. The assessment plan indicates which tests and other evaluation procedures will be used in the assessment of the student. The assessments used with special students must meet several criteria. They must be administered in the student's native language (when feasible) or other mode of communication (e.g., sign language). They must be validated for the purpose for which they are used, and they must be administered by trained personnel in conformance with the instructions provided by the producers of the assessment instruments. No single instrument can serve as the sole criterion for determining an appropriate educational placement for a student. Tests and other evaluations should assess specific areas of educational need for each student; typical concerns are academic performance, classroom behavior, and social skills. The student should be assessed in all areas that are related to the suspected disability. In addition, the general education teacher can assist by providing curriculum-based assessment information relating to the student's past performance in the classroom setting.

The assessment information, collected from various sources by the team and presented in a written report, indicates the student's present levels of performance. This information is used to determine whether the student is eligible for special education services; if so, it serves as the basis for designing an educational plan and determining the appropriate educational placement for the student.

Under federal laws, eligibility for special education services is determined by two criteria: it must be established that the student has a disability, *and* there must be evidence that the disability in some way adversely affects the student's educational performance. Satisfying one criterion but not the other is not sufficient. For example, many students with school problems do not meet eligibility requirements because they are not disabled. Similarly, a student with a mild disability (e.g., a mild vision loss or physical disability) would not qualify for special education services if he or she were not experiencing educational difficulties.

THE INDIVIDUALIZED EDUCATION PROGRAM

Once it has been determined that a student is eligible for special education, the next step is design of the Individualized Education Program or IEP. This written plan must be developed prior to the start of special education services. The IEP, which must be reviewed and modified at least annually, should include

1. a statement of the student's present levels of educational performance;
2. a list of annual goals that the student is expected to achieve;
3. a set of short-term instructional objectives, written in measurable terms, for each annual goal;
4. the specific special educational services needed by the student;
5. a description of the extent to which the student will participate in the general education program;
6. dates for the initiation and termination of special education services;

7. a statement describing and justifying the educational placement;
8. objective criteria, evaluation procedures, and schedules for determining progress toward instructional objectives;
9. identification of the individuals responsible for implementing the IEP and evaluating the student's progress;
10. a list of the team members who developed the IEP; and
11. a signature indicating parental approval of the IEP.

With older students, the IEP must also contain a description of needed transition services.

A review of the student's present levels of performance may indicate a variety of educational needs. It may not be appropriate, or possible, to deal with each of these areas in the IEP. Possible annual goals should be determined by the team and then ranked in priority order. When the goals have been selected, specific instructional objectives are prepared. Objectives should be stated in observable terms for each of the IEP goals; the criteria for successful performance of each objective are then specified.

The sample IEP presented in Figure 2–5 outlines the student's present levels of performance and provides goals and objectives in the curriculum area of math. Although the format used to present information may vary from district to district, the essential components should be present in all IEPs written for special students.

The mainstreaming team is responsible for assuring that the student's educational program is implemented as specified in the IEP. Instructional recommendations and service provisions called for in the IEP are to be followed unless the plan is modified by the team and the changes are approved by the student's parents.

An annual evaluation of the IEP is required, but it may be necessary to determine the appropriateness of the IEP well before it is a year old. The mainstreaming team should be open to reconsidering the special educational needs of a student if one of the team members believes that the IEP is in need of revision. Data should be systematically collected and presented to the team for their review prior to the actual team meeting. Any changes made in the IEP must be approved by the student's parents prior to implementation.

The annual evaluation of the student's progress can be conducted in the same manner as that used for the initial assessment of the student. However, this is neither practical nor necessary with the majority of special students. The annual evaluation is much more specific; it is concerned with the student's progress toward the goals and objectives stated in the IEP. Much of the evaluation information required will have been collected on an ongoing basis during the school year by the general and special educators providing service to the student. The continuous collection of data allows the teacher to make immediate modifications in the student's instructional program. Also, continuous data are more sensitive to the small incremental changes in performance often observed with special students.

Information should also be collected on a regular basis from the parents of students with special needs. It is important to continue their involvement with the team and elicit their perceptions of their child's progress in school and at home. When data are collected from parents, it is appropriate to share information with them about the school performance of the student.

The IEP is a formal instructional plan designed for and based upon the specific individual educational needs of each student with disabilities. It should clearly communicate to all team members the exact nature of the student's educational program. The IEP coordinates the efforts of the team by specifying what the team is attempting to accomplish, who is responsible for implementing each component of the plan, and which evaluation procedures will be used to determine the student's progress. Development of the IEP requires the team to carefully review each student's needs. The time spent in this analysis helps to improve the quality of the mainstreaming experience for each special student.

IEP Responsibilities of General Educators

General education teachers have many questions about IEPs and their responsibilities in the IEP process. Some of the most commonly asked questions (and their answers) appear here.

Does the classroom teacher participate in the development and review of IEPs? General education teachers usually serve on the IEP committee when students they have referred enter special education. When students with disabilities are mainstreamed and receive both general and special education services, the teacher in the regular classroom may aid in the development of the IEP. At the elementary level, most teachers choose to participate. At the secondary level, however, a staff member such as the school counselor is often selected to serve as the classroom teachers' representative on the IEP committee.

Is the IEP a contract? Are teachers legally responsible for meeting each of the goals on the IEP? The IEP is a contract because schools and agencies are legally responsible for providing the services indicated on the IEP. However, teachers are not held legally accountable for accomplishing IEP goals and objectives. Nevertheless, teachers do have the responsibility for making good-faith efforts to assist the students in accomplishing the goals and objectives stated in the IEP (Strickland & Turnbull, 1990).

Do IEPs cover both special education and general education programs? The IEP must state the extent to which the student will participate in the general education program. Goals and objectives are written for only those portions of the school day in which students require specialized services. If major adaptations are made in regular classroom procedures, then those will be reflected in IEP goals and objectives. However, for most mainstreamed students, regular class goals are not needed.

Who is responsible for implementing the IEP? The IEP states who is responsible for implementing the special education programs to meet each of the annual goals. In most cases this will be the special educator. However, if the IEP contains regular class or even home goals, then the general education teacher or the parent may be named as one of the persons responsible.

Who may see the IEP? Copies of the IEP are available to the student's parents and each of the persons responsible for implementing the IEP. Many districts do not distribute copies of the IEP to all mainstreaming teachers because of the cost of copying and because IEPs are considered confidential documents that must be stored securely. To see the IEPs of mainstreamed students, teachers should contact the special educator or their school principal.

NAME   Molly Davis   SEX   Female   GRADE   6th   DATE OF BIRTH   4/5/82   C.A.   12

ADDRESS   1700 Green Street   TELEPHONE NUMBER   345-8970

PARENT(S), GUARDIAN(S), SURROGATE   Tom and Louise Davis

Date of the IEP meeting(s)   Initial meeting 9/9/94 Final meeting 9/10/94

	TEAM MEMBER	POSITION	SIGNATURE
Chairperson	Kate Turner	Director, Special Education	
	Dennis Fredericks	6th grade teacher	
	Mary Beth Godwin	Resource Room Teacher	
	Ann Ross	Reading Teacher	
	Tom Davis	Father	
	Louise Davis	Mother	

Present placement of child   Regular class + Resource Room

Recommendation for placement   Regular class + Resource Room

Percentage of time in the regular education program   66%

Justification for placement: Molly should be in the resource room for at least one hour of instruction in reading and language arts. She should receive additional 45 minutes of instruction in math in the resource room. All additional services should be carried out in the regular classroom including special instruction in spelling.   Date of program entry 9-15-94   Anticipated duration of special education or related services   9-94 to 6-95   Summary of special education and related services needed: Resource room—special education services. Materials—no special materials except a programmed math book for practice in the regular class. Related services—none.

Area of Instruction   <u>Math</u>

Summary of current functioning level: <u>Facts</u> On timed probes, Molly could quickly compute addition facts to 5 and subtraction facts with minuends to 5. However, she was very slow and inaccurate on more difficult facts. She has no knowledge of x facts. <u>Operations</u>: On both the KEYMATH test and informal tests, Molly could perform + and − operations involving no regrouping. <u>Money</u>: Can name and tell value of coins. <u>Time</u>: Can tell time to hour and half hours. <u>Fractions</u>: no skills.

Long-Term Goals	Short-term objectives Major milestones (★See attached sequences)	Services needed to meet goals/ objectives	Annual Review
Will solve addition and subtraction facts.	When given a sheet of + facts with sums to 10, will write answer with 40 per minute and no more than one error. When given a sheet of + facts with sums to 18, Molly will write answers with 40 per minute and no more than one error. When given a sheet of subtraction facts with minuends to 10, Molly will write answers with 40 per minute and no more than one error. When given a sheet of subtraction facts with minuends to 18, Molly will write answers with 40 per minute and no more than 1 error.	Resource Room— Mary Beth Godwin	
Will solve addition computations involving 3 digit plus 3 digit with regrouping.	When given 20 problems, 2 dig. + 1 dig. with regrouping, Molly will write answers with 95% accuracy. When given 20 problems, 2 dig. + 2 dig. with regrouping, Molly will write answers with 95% accuracy. When given 20 problems, 3 dig. + 3 dig. with regrouping, Molly will write answers with 95% accuracy. (More complete sequence attached.)	Resource Room— Mary Beth Godwin Additional practice using Sullivan Programmed Math Books in Regular Class—Dennis Fredericks	

Procedures for evaluating progress toward long-term goals:

Facts: Daily timings will be taken on facts with daily performance graphed. A posttest will be given on all addition and subtraction facts.

Addition Operations: Daily probes will be taken on addition computations.

Note.   Adapted with permission of Merrill, an imprint of Macmillan Publishing Company, from *Teaching the Mildly Handicapped in the Regular Classroom* (2nd ed., pp. 28–29) by J. Affleck, S. Lowenbraun, and A. Archer, Copyright © 1980 Merrill Publishing Company, Columbus, Ohio.

SPECIAL EDUCATION PROGRAM OPTIONS

Special education programs vary in the opportunities for mainstreaming afforded to students with special needs. Some of the programs permit special students to spend their entire school day in the regular classroom (least restrictive), whereas other programs exclude the students from any interaction with their regular class peers (most restrictive). The remainder of the programs fall between these two extremes. Each type of program is designed to serve students with disabilities with a specific type or intensity of educational need.

The mainstreaming team is responsible for assuring that each student receives educational services in the most appropriate setting that is also the Least Restrictive Environment (LRE). The regular classroom is not the LRE for all students. For some special students, the special class or the special school is the LRE. The majority of special students, however, can benefit from spending at least part of their school day in the regular classroom.

When the mainstreaming team considers the appropriate placement for each special student, it generally has a number of special education program or placement options available at the school or within the district. Options may vary from district to district, but those noted in chapter 1 (Figure 1–4) are typical for students in the K–12 school levels. They range in intensity from residential schools to full-time participation in the regular class. Other types of programs, such as home-based programs in which special educators work directly with parents, are available for infants or preschool students; programs such as community-based vocational programs may be offered for older students with severe disabilities.

As Figure 2–6 illustrates, three major categories of placement options are available for students with disabilities. In the first, regular class programs, students are members of general education classes and the general education teacher takes primary responsibility for their instruction. These programs serve the greatest number of students with disabilities. In the second option, special class programs, students are members of special education classes, and the special education teacher takes primary responsibility for their educational program. The third option, more restrictive programs, serves the smallest number of students with disabilities. It is designed for the students with the most severe, comprehensive, and specialized needs.

Regular Class Options

Regular Class.   The regular classroom is the least restrictive of all the educational placement options. Students not currently identified as special students spend their entire school day in the regular classroom; neither the students nor their teachers receive any direct special education services. The majority of special students begin their educational careers in this setting. For most students identified as having disabilities, the goal is to provide appropriate educational programs to assist in developing the skills necessary for returning to the regular classroom. For some special students with more severe disabilities, this goal may not be realistic.

Indirect services that do not relate to any particular student with special needs may be provided to general education teachers and their classes. For example, in-service training opportunities may be offered to teachers by the special education staff in areas such as special education legislation, referral procedures, or techniques for working with students with learning or behavioral problems. Students enrolled in regular classes may participate in special assemblies that explain various types of disabilities and encourage the acceptance of all individuals, regardless of their unique needs. Special education teachers may visit elementary or secondary classes to discuss alternative communication systems, such as Braille, sign language, or electronic communication devices. Students in the regular class may be trained by special educators to serve as classroom assistants or cross-age tutors in special education classrooms.

Students placed in the regular class may have received special education services at one time but are now able to function appropriately in the regular classroom with no special services. For instance, a

FIGURE 2–6
Program Options

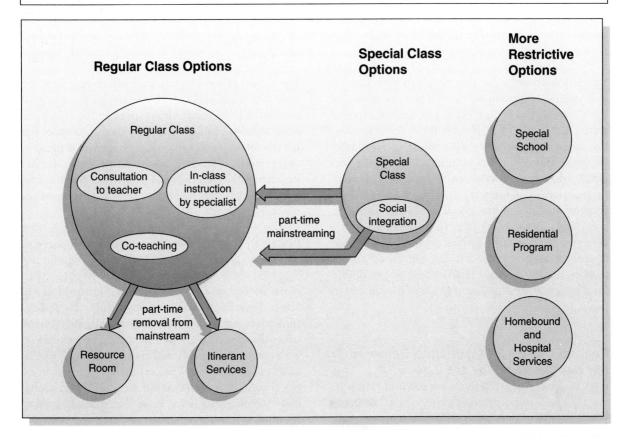

student with a hearing impairment may have received special education services in the past but is now fitted with an appropriate hearing aid, has been trained to use and care for it properly, and is able to supplement the information received via the hearing aid with speechreading skills. A student with a visual impairment may now have appropriate glasses, magnification devices, or other devices or skills that permit independent functioning in the regular classroom. Students who have been identified as special at one time do not necessarily require special services throughout their educational careers. Many acquire the skills needed to function in the mainstream without special support.

Regular Class with Consultation to the Teacher.

In this placement option, the special student spends the entire school day in the regular classroom and receives no direct special education services. Instead, the general education teacher receives services; a special educator provides consultation on the needs of special education students mainstreamed in the teacher's classroom.

Consultation services can take a number of forms. A specialist, such as a special education consultant or a school psychologist, may assist the teacher in designing and implementing a behavior management program for a student with classroom behavior problems. An itinerant teacher of students with visual impairments may furnish the teacher with large print or Braille editions of class textbooks and provide information on how these materials can best be used. The special education resource teacher may help the teacher modify the regular reading or math program for a student with learning disabilities in the class.

Specialists who provide consultation services typically have extensive experience in both general and special education settings. They are aware of the needs of general education teachers and special students. Their goal is to assist the teacher in gaining access to appropriate materials and developing the skills and confidence required to meet the students' educational needs, not to evaluate classroom instruction or management. General education teachers should feel free to call on special education consultants for aid in adapting instruction, managing behavior problems, and promoting social acceptance of special students. Whereas the general education teacher has the primary instructional responsibility for the special student, the consultant is available to facilitate successful mainstreaming.

Regular Class with Instruction Delivered in the Regular Class by the Specialist.

This type of service is a relatively recent innovation in most schools and districts. In this option, students with disabilities receive special education services within the general education classroom. Instead of leaving their classroom to visit a specialist, students remain where they are. The specialist comes to the student's class and delivers services there.

The special education services are provided in the general education classroom by a special educator working alone or with a trained assistant. These staff members "can support integrated special students in many ways, including (a) making adaptations when needed; (b) assisting the classroom teacher in working with a student; (c) coaching nondisabled peers; (d) providing direct instruction; and (e) facilitating positive interactions among students" (Hamre-Nietupski, McDonald, & Nietupski, 1992, p. 8).

The amount of support provided by specialists to students who are integrated full-time in general education classrooms depends on the needs of each indi-

vidual student. For students with mild learning problems, the specialist may visit the classroom for a brief period each day to deliver specialized instruction to target students and perhaps some of their peers with similar needs. For students with more severe disabilities, it may be necessary to provide support throughout the entire school day. In many cases, the amount and nature of services required will change over the course of the school year. For example, the specialist may be able to reduce time spent in the classroom once a cadre of peer tutors or other volunteers has been trained to assist the special student. Or the general education teacher may feel that he or she has developed the skills necessary to work with the special students, which thereby reduces the need for specialist support.

The advantages of this program option have been described by educators concerned with a range of special students, from those with milder disabilities (e.g., Wiedmeyer & Lehman, 1991) to those with more severe disabilities (Hamre-Nietupski et al., 1992). Benefits include the opportunity for special students to have continuous interactions with general education peers, reduction of the stigma associated with having a disability and receiving special education services, increased opportunities for exposure to the general education curriculum, and greater probability that the skills being learned are useful for other "normalized" settings. These educators also note that the success of this type of program is dependent on continuous cooperative planning between general and special educators to assure that the educational needs of all students in the classroom are met.

Regular Class with Co-teaching.

A variation of the specialist teaching in a regular class is the co-teaching model. In this option, a general educator and a special educator co-teach a class composed of students with and without disabilities. For example, if the class includes 30 students, 20 may be typical students and 10 students with identified disabilities. The teachers share responsibility for all the students in the class, with the special educator providing specialized interventions for students with special needs, as required.

Regular Class and Resource Room or Itinerant Services. In this service option, special education services are generally provided to special students in a setting outside the regular classroom. However, the students continue to spend the majority of their school day in the general education class.

The **resource room** is usually located within the student's regular neighborhood school. At a regularly scheduled time each day (or several times a week), students leave their general education classroom to participate in special instruction in the resource room. Resource programs, common in both elementary and secondary schools, may serve several types of special students (e.g., those with learning disabilities, physical disabilities, mild mental retardation), or they may limit service to only students with one particular disability.

A trend exists for resource room programs to include different types of special students. In these cross-categorical or multicategorical resource rooms, there is no longer a reliance on the idea that the special student's disability determines the educational needs of that student. One resource teacher may provide educational programs for several groups of students, including those identified as having physical disabilities, learning disabilities, behavioral disorders, and mild mental retardation. This capability exists because the educational needs of these students are often quite similar despite their different disabilities.

Consultation services, such as those described earlier, are often provided for the general education teachers of the special students enrolled in a resource room program. These services can assist the teacher and facilitate the coordination of regular class and resource instructional activities.

The services provided by itinerant special education teachers, who travel from school to school, are managed in somewhat the same way as those of resource programs. Students with special needs may spend the majority of their day in the general education classroom, but they leave the classroom daily (or several times a week) to receive the services of itinerant teachers, such as speech and language clinicians. Whereas resource room teachers generally serve only special students who spend the majority of their day in the regular class, itinerant teachers may also serve students enrolled in a special class.

Resource and itinerant teachers serve the majority of the special students receiving special education services today. They supplement and support the general educational program by providing assistance to special students and their regular classroom teachers. Although special students usually leave their mainstreamed classrooms to receive special education services, special educators (or their instructional aides) occasionally teach small instructional groups within the regular class. As noted in the previous section, in this service arrangement, the special student receives all instruction, both regular and special, within the general education classroom.

Special Class Options

Special Class and Regular Class. **Special classes** are located within regular elementary or secondary schools. Students receiving service in this placement option spend the majority of their school day in the special class and some time each day in the regular classroom. Participation in the regular class can vary from approximately half a day to only a few minutes. This is the most restrictive of the educational environments in which the student still spends time in the mainstream.

Special students placed in this program option need intensive special education services. The student's regular class involvement is planned in curriculum areas in which success is fairly certain. Regular class participation for such students is limited to the period of time in which they can function successfully without becoming frustrated or creating a disruption.

Special classes can be operated for students in any of the categories of special education (e.g., students identified as having mental retardation, physical disabilities, or behavioral disorders). General education teachers working with students in this option generally have consultation services available to assist them in designing and implementing appropriate instructional programs.

Full-Time Special Class and Social Integration.
An increasing number of students with severe disabilities are being integrated into regular school campuses at all levels of education. This trend is the result of a recognition of the need to integrate these individuals with their normal age peers whenever possible. While many of these students may never attend regular academic classes, it is possible for them to participate in social integration activities at the school such as lunch periods, assemblies, or recreational activities. Such activities offer students with severe disabilities the opportunity to interact with other students and gain the skills needed to function independently. At some schools programs may involve reverse mainstreaming in which general education students participate in activities in the special class. These programs are particularly appropriate for preschool and early elementary students.

Full-Time Special Class.
Students placed in this program option are no longer in the mainstream, for they spend their entire school day in the special class. Special class programs are generally available at both elementary and secondary levels for students with different types of disabilities. Special classes may have different focuses, but the main goal of all such classes is to provide an intensive program to develop skills that will prepare students for adulthood and, if possible, return to the mainstream.

Special classes for students with physical, language, vision, and hearing disorders may be concentrated at the lower elementary level. These students are readily identified at an early age, and providing intensive instruction in preschool or as soon as the students enter the elementary grades can enable them to enter the mainstream at an earlier age. Special classes for these students at the secondary level are somewhat less common; by this time students have either acquired the necessary skills to function in the mainstream, or they have been placed in special school programs.

Special classes for students with behavioral disorders, mental retardation, and learning disabilities are most typically found at the upper elementary, junior high, and high school levels. As these students progress through school, the discrepancy between their performance and that of their peers becomes apparent, particularly if they do not receive appropriate educational services. The special class provides intensive services to students with serious educational needs that cannot be successfully met in the regular classroom.

At one time, special classes served as the primary special education program option between the regular class and the special school options. Their use has diminished as other less restrictive programs, such as the resource room and teacher consultants, have become popular.

More Restrictive Options

Special School.
Special schools are generally the most restrictive placement option regularly offered by the public school system. Placement in this option is generally based on the premise that students placed in such a program cannot presently benefit from inclusion in the mainstream. This program typically serves students with more severe disabilities (e.g., those with multiple disabilities, severe behavioral disorders, severe mental retardation). In the past, one justification for the concentration of students in one special school was the centralization of specialized services. It was thought that when psychologists, social workers, and physical and occupational therapists were housed in one building, they would be available to assist special education teachers in meeting the educational needs of the students. However, concerns over the segregation of these students from their age peers have led to the mandated closing of many special schools and the distribution of the students onto integrated regular school campuses (Pumpian, 1988; Sailor, Gee, & Karasoff, 1993).

Residential Program.
Residential programs primarily serve two groups of special students. The first includes those who need intensive services that cannot be provided in less restrictive special education settings within the regular school program. Students in this group may be those with severe behavioral disorders, severe or profound mental

retardation, and severe multiple disabilities. These students may require specialized educational services and medical care that cannot be provided either in public schools or by their parents at home. In the residential setting, the 24-hour program permits the coordination of medical, psychological, educational, and other services.

The other students served in residential facilities are those who reside in a sparsely populated area that cannot practically offer a special program to serve their educational needs. When schools are so far from home that students cannot travel to school on a daily basis, the placement becomes residential. Placements of this type are becoming much less frequent as communities continue to expand the special education services offered locally.

As school districts have assumed more responsibility for offering appropriate educational programs to all students with disabilities, a change has occurred in the role of the residential school. For example, a few years ago a residential school may have served all the students with visual impairments in a state. Today, the majority of these students attend local school programs. Fewer students live at a residential facility, and those who do have severe or multiple disabilities.

The residential setting is the most restrictive special education setting because the students do not have regular contact with typical peers. In many cases they are also restricted from normal community and home contacts. However, for some students with very special needs, this is the least restrictive placement in which they can function successfully.

Homebound and Hospital Services.

A relatively small number of students are provided their education at home or in a hospital setting. This arrangement is generally not permanent, but it may occur for various periods of time each year depending on the needs of the particular students. These students may have physical disabilities, health impairments, or emotional or behavioral disorders that interfere with their attendance in classes at school. Typically a teacher visits the student several times a week to provide instruction and furnish the educational materials needed by the student. If the

students have been mainstreamed or are capable of completing regular class assignments, the general education teacher may be asked to assist in providing assignments and materials to the teacher of homebound or hospitalized students.

Programs for Infants and Preschoolers with Disabilities

Public Law 99-457, the Education of the Handicapped Act Amendments of 1986, includes provisions designed to assure that infants and toddlers (birth through age 2) and preschoolers (ages 2 through 5) are provided with appropriate special education services. These services typically involve a multidisciplinary, interagency program that coordinates a wide variety of services for young children with or at risk for disabilities and their families. Each state is expected to design a program in which various education and human service agencies collaborate to provide services such as medical and educational assessment, speech and language intervention, physical therapy, and parent counseling and training. The early intervention services are identified and implemented according to an Individualized Family Services Plan (IFSP) that is developed by a multidisciplinary team that includes the child's parents. Key elements of these programs are (a) the early identification and resolution of problems that may contribute to developmental delays in order to maximize the child's potential for independent living in society and (b) the coordination of these efforts with the programs for school-age students to improve the transition of the young children from early childhood to school programs.

Many program options are available to students with special needs. Districts provide a continuum of services ranging from the regular classroom to more intense separate programs. Most special students, however, are able to succeed in the mainstream if provided with appropriate support services.

In chapter 3, we will look more closely at special students, their learning needs, and the challenges they provide to the mainstreaming teacher.

THINGS TO REMEMBER

- The goal of the various types of mainstreaming teams is to assure that special students are provided an appropriate education based on their individual abilities and needs.
- Mainstreaming teams are composed of school administrators, general and special education teachers, parents, special students themselves (when appropriate), and other professionals whose expertise relates to the needs of the student.
- Mainstreaming teams identify and assess students with disabilities, develop the IEP, determine an appropriate placement, and periodically evaluate student progress. Teams also assist the general education teacher in meeting the educational needs of other special students who may be experiencing difficulty within the regular classroom.

- Placement of the special student must be in the LRE for that student.
- Individualized Education Programs include information about the student's current performance, the goals and objectives of the educational program, necessary special services and placement, the amount of participation in the regular classroom, and procedures for evaluating student progress.
- The IEP, including the student's placement, must be evaluated at least annually. No placement should be considered permanent.
- The special student's disability does not indicate the appropriate program or placement. Each student's placement must be based on his or her special needs in the areas of academics, classroom behavior, and social performance.
- Consultation is generally available to regular class teachers working with mainstreamed

students. Teachers should request this service if it is needed.
- Special education consultants and teacher assistance teams can help teachers develop the skills needed to provide interventions for students with problems; if the prereferral interventions are successful, these students may not require special education.
- Prereferral interventions include the collection of data to describe the learning problem, collaboration with colleagues and parents, classroom modifications, and use of available general education and community resources. The most common types of classroom modifications are curricular, instructional, management, and environmental adaptations.
- General and special educators share responsibility for the education of special students in the mainstream.

ACTIVITIES

1. Visit a local elementary or secondary school that provides services for special students. What are the school's mainstreaming teams called? Who serves on the teams? How often do they meet? Do they consider only students with disabilities? Gather information that will help you explain the operation of these teams to another educator. If possible, obtain permission to observe a team meeting.

2. Interview two individuals from a local school who serve on the same mainstreaming team. Select persons who represent different roles—for example, a parent and a special educator, a general education teacher and a psychologist, or a speech-language clinician and a counselor. Compare their opinions of the operation and effectiveness of the team. You may want to ask questions such as these: What is the purpose of the team? Are all team members encouraged to participate in delib-

erations? Are assessment results explained so that all members can understand them? Are the IEPs that are developed appropriate to the needs of special students? Is each student's progress reviewed periodically? Summarize your findings, noting whether there is agreement between the perceptions of the two team members.

3. Read two journal articles on the team approach or on consultation as it relates to the education of special students. *Exceptional Children* and *Remedial and Special Education* are journals that often address these topics. Write a brief summary and evaluation of each article you read.

4. Contact a local school district to find out what types of special education programs are offered. Are resource rooms, special classes, and all the programs described in this chapter available? How have program options changed in the past 5 years? Compare your findings with those of someone who has investigated another district. Explain why programs may vary from district to district.

5. Several organizations are designed to serve parents of special students. Two of the most promi-

nent are the Learning Disabilities Association of America (LDA), whose national headquarters is at 4156 Library Road, Pittsburgh, PA 15234, and the National Association for Retarded Citizens (NARC), located at 2709 Avenue E East, Arlington, TX 76011. Are there local chapters of these organizations in your community? Contact a local or national office of LDA or NARC to learn the purpose of these groups. Do they provide information about special students? Serve as advocates for parents? Work for better special education legislation? What should classroom teachers know about these organizations?

6. There have been several studies of general educators' views on classroom modifications for students with special needs. Examples are the articles by Ellett (1993), Johnson and Pugach (1990), and Ysseldyke et al. (1990). Read one of these articles to find out the types of modifications that teachers feel are most valuable. Are the most valuable interventions the ones that teachers consider most feasible?

3 Special Students, Special Needs

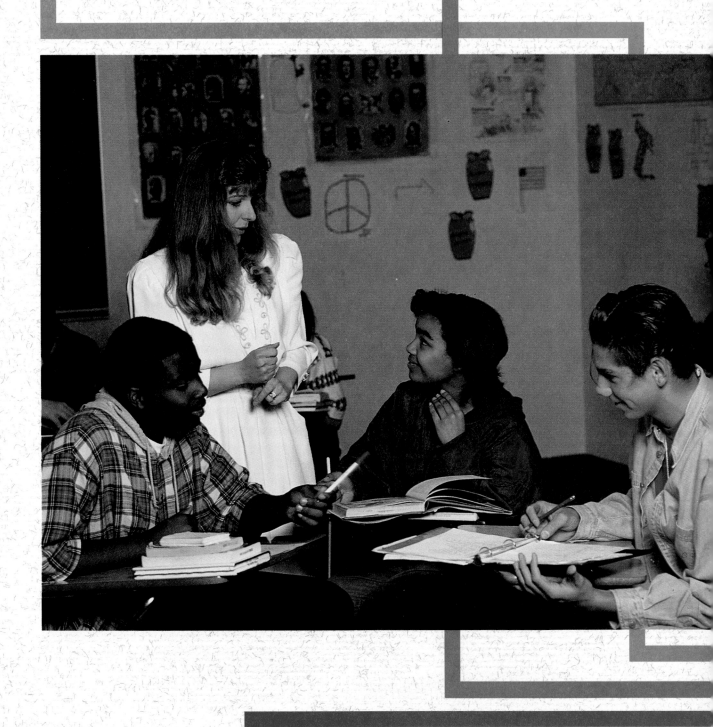

■ *Jody's vision is limited; her textbooks, work-sheets, and other reading materials are in large print.*

■ *Luis has diabetes; he takes medication and must carefully monitor his diet and physical activity.*

■ *George has poor reading skills; he uses taped textbooks for reading assignments, and he is learning to "take notes" in class with a tape recorder.*

■ *Tom is impulsive and often leaves his seat, speaks out in class, and interrupts the work of other students; he and his teacher have set up a program to help Tom control these behaviors.*

■ *Annette is very bright and academically far ahead of her peers; she works on special assignments in subjects that interest and challenge her.*

Special students such as these can succeed in the regular classroom with the assistance of the mainstreaming team. Because their educational needs are not radically different from those of their peers, they can participate in many aspects of the general education program without special educational interventions. In areas where adaptations of the regular program are necessary, support services are available to the student and to the classroom teacher. Special materials and equipment are provided, such as the large-print books needed by students with vision disorders and the tape recorders and taped texts needed by students with reading problems. The school nurse assists students with physical and health needs. The resource teacher works with the classroom teacher to set up behavior change programs for disruptive students and enrichment activities for advanced students. In this way the members of the mainstreaming team collaborate to meet the needs of special students within the regular classroom.

■ SPECIAL STUDENTS

Special students include those with disabilities, gifted and talented students, individuals from cultur-ally and linguistically diverse backgrounds, and students at risk for school failure. Although not all are mainstreamed full-time for instruction, most special students have relatively mild learning problems and are thus able to succeed in the regular classroom.

Students with special needs make up a sizable portion of the school community. In a collection of 100 students, there may be 9 or 10 with disabilities and 3 to 5 who are gifted; depending on the community, any number of students may be from diverse groups. Learning disabilities, mild retardation, behavioral disorders, and speech and language disorders are the most common disabilities; physical, health, vision, and hearing disorders are relatively rare. Mild disabilities are much more frequent than severe disabilities. It is likely that at least 75% of the special education population has mild learning needs that can be met, at least in part, in the regular classroom.

Students with Learning Disabilities

Teachers often use the word *puzzling* to describe students with **learning disabilities**. These students are average, even bright, learners who encounter difficulties in specific school subjects. Because they seem capable and do learn some things quickly and easily, their failure to learn in other areas is perplexing.

Students with learning disabilities have adequate intelligence. Their learning problem is not due to hearing or vision impairments, physical or health disorders, or emotional disturbance. The reason for their poor school performance is much more subtle and elusive: they have difficulty processing information. **Information processing** (sometimes called *psychological processing*) refers to the way in which persons receive, store, and express information. Students with learning disabilities may have difficulty receiving information because of attention or perception problems, their memory may be poor, or they may have difficulty communicating information to others because of expressive language problems. Students with learning disabilities may use poor strategies for learning (Alley & Deshler, 1979; Lewis, 1983); for example, such students may be passive learners who fail to become actively involved in the

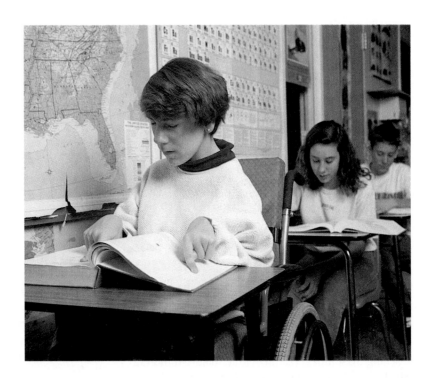

learning task (Torgesen, 1977). When given a list of spelling words to learn or a textbook chapter to read, such students may simply stare at the page, or read and reread it, without actively studying its content.

Despite adequate general ability, students with learning disabilities experience school learning problems. They appear able to achieve, but their performance in school falls short of expectations. Even more perplexing than this discrepancy between expected and actual achievement is the variability of performance that characterizes individuals with learning disabilities. They are successful in some areas while having great difficulty in others. In addition, their performance may vary from day to day; teachers often comment that students with learning disabilities appear to know something one day but forget it the next.

Many different labels have been used to describe students with learning disabilities. Although the emphasis today is on educational terminology, it is still possible to encounter medical terms. For example, students with learning disabilities may be called *brain injured, brain damaged, neurologically*

impaired, minimally brain dysfunctioned, or *perceptually handicapped;* these labels refer to the theory that learning disabilities are due to some type of damage to the central nervous system. There are also medical terms for common academic problems: *dyslexia* (difficulty in reading), *dyscalculia* (difficulty in math), and *dysgraphia* (difficulty in writing). More recent additions to the medical terminology associated with learning disabilities (and with behavioral disorders) are *attention deficit disorder* (ADD) and *attention deficit hyperactivity disorder* (ADHD).

There has been much debate over what constitutes a learning disability and how the condition should be defined. One widely accepted definition, which has been incorporated into several state and federal special education laws, is that of the National Advisory Committee on Handicapped Children (1968):

A disorder in one or more of the basic psychological processes involved in understanding or in using language, spoken or written, which may manifest itself in an imperfect ability to listen, think, speak, read, write, spell, or to do mathematical calculations. . . . The term does not include children who have learning problems which are primarily the result of visual, hearing, or motor handicaps, of mental retardation, or of environmental, cultural, or economic disadvantage.

This definition, like most definitions of learning disabilities, excludes other disabilities and points to information-processing deficits as the reason for poor school performance. In the regular classroom, students with learning disabilities may have special needs in the areas of academic, behavioral, social, and physical performance.

Academic Needs. Students with learning disabilities typically experience difficulty in one or more of the basic school subjects. Young children may enter school with poor listening or speaking skills. In the early grades, acquisition of language arts skills such as reading and spelling may prove difficult. For most elementary-aged students with learning disabilities, reading is the major stumbling block in academic achievement. However, some fare well in this area yet have specific disabilities in other subjects such as math or handwriting.

The basic skill problems of students with learning disabilities persist into junior high and high school (and beyond). These students may fail to acquire reading, writing, and perhaps math skills at a level equal to that of their peers. Although able to cope with the content of secondary-level courses, many students with learning disabilities achieve poorly because of their inability to read texts and complete written assignments. Those with poor listening skills find lecture presentations a serious problem.

Behavioral Needs. Some students with learning disabilities, particularly in the elementary grades, are characterized by a high activity level. Such students may be constantly in motion and, as a result, may have difficulty paying attention to school tasks. Others, not overactive, may be impulsive and distractible; they, too, may have difficulty focusing their attention on appropriate aspects of the learning environment.

Older students with learning disabilities often have behavioral needs in the areas of classroom conduct and study skills. They may be unable to work independently (at least in part because of poor academic skills). Their attention span may continue to be a problem, and their organizational skills may be poor. In addition, there is some evidence of a link between juvenile delinquency and learning disabilities in adolescents (Keilitz, Zaremba, & Broder, 1979).

Social Needs. The social arena is another area in which students with learning disabilities may perform poorly. Research (e.g., Bryan, Pearl, Donahue, Bryan, & Pflaum, 1983) indicates that some children and adolescents with learning disabilities have social perception deficits. That is, they may lack the skills needed for understanding and communicating appropriate social messages. Social communication requires not only speech but also more subtle cues such as facial expression, vocal inflection, and body language; it becomes particularly important when students enter the peer-conscious world of the adolescent.

Physical Needs. Students with learning disabilities do not have obvious physical needs; in appearance they are indistinguishable from their regular class peers. However, some students with learning disabilities have motor coordination problems. They may appear clumsy and may perform gross-motor skills, such as running and jumping, poorly. Fine-motor skills such as cutting, manipulating small objects, and mastering the use of pencils and pens may also be troublesome areas. In school, motor problems such as these become evident in physical education and art activities and in academic tasks requiring handwriting.

Special Services. For students with disabilities severe and comprehensive enough to warrant placement in separate programs, many districts offer special classes. However, the majority of students with learning disabilities remain in the mainstream throughout their educational careers and receive special services on a part-time basis from professionals such as resource teachers. Because students with learning disabilities have average ability and are able to perform as well as regular class students in some areas, they are excellent candidates for mainstreaming.

Students with Behavioral Disorders

Behavioral disorders are a more obvious disability than learning disabilities. Students with behavioral disorders are often described by teachers as behavior problems or troublemakers. They may be rowdy, unruly, disruptive, and even aggressive. Some, whose behavior does not call attention to itself as readily, may appear withdrawn or depressed. All are characterized by inappropriate school behavior. Although most students with behavioral disorders have adequate intelligence as well as acceptable hearing, vision, and physical abilities, they often show poor achievement in academic skills. Some students, however, achieve satisfactorily despite inappropriate classroom behavior.

The term *behavioral disorders* includes a wide range of disabilities. The most severe are seen in students with serious emotional disturbance, such as individuals with psychotic behavior and childhood schizophrenia; such students generally require intensive special education services and are not included in regular class instructional programs. However, most students with behavioral disorders have relatively mild problems that can be dealt with successfully in the mainstream. In fact, the special needs of many of these students are virtually identical to those of the problem student found in every classroom.

Even though apparently obvious, the disability of behavioral disorders is difficult to describe and define. It is necessary to decide which behaviors are appropriate and which are not. The problem is further complicated by the fact that all students behave inappropriately at one time or another in their school careers. Kauffman (1977) sidesteps some of these problems by defining students with behavioral disorders as

those who chronically and markedly respond to their environment in socially unacceptable and/or person-

ally unsatisfying ways but who can be taught more socially acceptable and personally gratifying behavior. (p. 23)

This definition contains several important points. First, behavioral disorders are chronic and severe. The student's behavior must be inappropriate over time, not a one-time occurrence. The student's behavior problem must also be serious; it must in some way impair the student's ability to function in the school environment. Second, behaviors are judged to be inappropriate by either social or personal standards. This allows not only teachers and parents but also students themselves to determine problem behaviors. It also provides for inclusion of behaviors such as withdrawal that may be socially acceptable but are detrimental to the student. Third, Kauffman's definition recognizes that behavior is learned and that students with behavioral disorders are able to acquire more acceptable responses to their environment. This point is crucial for teachers who seek to change the behavior of their students.

The definition proposed by Bower (1969) is widely accepted by educators and is included in many special education laws. It describes students with behavioral disorders as those who show at least one of the following characteristics "to a marked extent" and "over a period of time":

1. An inability to learn which cannot be explained by intellectual, sensory, or health factors. . . .
2. An inability to build or maintain satisfactory interpersonal relationships with peers and teachers. . . .
3. Inappropriate types of behaviors or feelings under normal conditions. . . .
4. A general, pervasive mood of unhappiness or depression. . . .
5. A tendency to develop physical symptoms, pains, or fears associated with personal or school problems. (pp. 22–23)

A student need not exhibit all five of these characteristics to be identified as having a behavioral disorder; only one is necessary, although students may meet several of the criteria. This definition stresses the educational aspects of behavioral disorders by focusing on learning problems, student-teacher relationships, and school phobia problems.

Like the definition of learning disabilities proposed by the National Advisory Committee on Handicapped Children, the Bower definition contains an exclusion clause: The learning problems of students with behavioral disorders must not be due to retardation, vision or hearing disorders, or health impairments.

As Heward and Orlansky (1992) remark, definitions of behavioral disorders "agree that a child's behavior, to be considered disordered, must differ markedly (extremely) and chronically (over time) from current social or cultural norms" (p. 190). In the regular classroom, this means that students with behavioral disorders may have special needs in the areas of social and academic, as well as behavioral, performance.

Behavioral Needs. Children and adolescents with behavioral disorders are a heterogeneous group who exhibit a wide range of inappropriate classroom behaviors. These students may be disobedient, aggressive or overly shy and retiring. One way to conceptualize this array of possible problem behaviors has been suggested by Quay (1979), who describes four typical patterns or dimensions of disordered behavior: conduct disorder, socialized aggression, immaturity, and anxiety-withdrawal.

Students with conduct disorders are aggressive, defiant, uncooperative, disobedient, and disruptive. Their behavior is judged socially unacceptable by teachers and others in authority. Students falling under the socialized aggression dimension also are perceived as behaving inappropriately. They are socialized in that they belong to gangs, but they participate in delinquent activities such as truancy and theft. Less obvious dimensions are immaturity and anxiety-withdrawal. Immature students appear delayed in development; they may be passive, have a short attention span, appear preoccupied, and daydream. Students characterized by anxiety and withdrawal appear fearful, timid, depressed, and lacking in self-confidence.

Students with behavioral disorders may have difficulty following classroom rules and meeting teachers' expectations for appropriate school conduct.

Although aggressive students are the ones most easily and quickly identified by teachers, withdrawn and immature students also require special help. In junior high and high school, the truancy problems of predelinquent and delinquent students complicate their difficulties in meeting school demands.

Social Needs. Students with behavioral disorders often have trouble establishing interpersonal relationships. Their inappropriate behaviors may make them unattractive to peers and to teachers. They may lack the social skills necessary to make and keep friends. In addition, the self-concept of students with behavioral disorders is often low, especially in individuals who are anxious and withdrawn. And the problem perpetuates itself. Students with poor social skills remain friendless, and their self-esteem suffers; students with low self-esteem are unwilling to risk interpersonal relationships.

Academic Needs. Students with behavioral disorders, like those with learning disabilities, often experience difficulty with basic school skills. Most studies of the academic achievement of students with behavioral disorders find poor performance in reading, math, and other subjects such as spelling and language (e.g., Rubin & Balow, 1978). Some evidence suggests that math achievement problems may be more serious than reading problems (Bower, 1969). The precise relationship between academic underachievement and inappropriate classroom behavior, however, is difficult to assess. Students may act out or withdraw as a reaction to school failure, or problem behaviors may interfere with successful school learning. In either case, most students with behavioral disorders require instruction in both behavioral and academic skills.

Special Services. Some students with behavioral disorders require intensive special education services in special classes, special schools, and even residential facilities. Most, however, are able to participate in at least some aspects of regular classroom instruction. Some may spend part of their day in a special class and part in the mainstream. Others take part more fully in regular class activities and receive only part-time special services. The mainstream is generally the most appropriate placement for students with mild behavioral disorders, provided, of course, that necessary support services are available to students and teachers.

Students with Mild Mental Retardation

Students with mental retardation have comprehensive learning problems. Because of below-average intellectual ability, they may learn slowly and may appear delayed in most areas of school performance when compared with their age peers. Tasks requiring reasoning and abstract thinking may be particularly difficult for them.

Mental retardation is one of the oldest areas of study within the field of special education, and there is general agreement regarding the definition of this disability. According to the American Association on Mental Retardation (1992),

> *Mental retardation* refers to substantial limitations in present functioning. It is characterized by significantly subaverage intellectual functioning, existing concurrently with related limitations in two or more of the following applicable adaptive skill areas: communication, self-care, home living, social skills, community use, self-direction, health and safety, functional academics, leisure, and work. Mental retardation manifests before age 18. (p. 1)

Less-than-average intelligence is central to the concept of mental retardation. Individuals considered retarded are those whose general aptitude for learning is impaired. Intellectual functioning is assessed by intelligence or IQ tests; these measures contain several types of verbal and nonverbal reasoning and problem-solving tasks. General ability level is established by comparing the performance of one student with that of others of the same age. Individuals who fall within the lowest 2% to 3% are considered retarded; that is, their intellectual performance is significantly subaverage in comparison to that of their peers. However, as Heward and Orlansky (1992) point out, measurement of intelli-

gence is not an exact science, and it is possible for IQ scores to change significantly over time.

In addition to poor intellectual performance, students must show impaired **adaptive behavior** in order to be considered mentally retarded. Adaptive behavior, sometimes referred to as social competence, is "the effectiveness or degree with which individuals meet the standards of personal independence and social responsibility expected for their age and cultural group" (Grossman, 1983, p. 1). It is the way in which students meet the expectations of the total social environment, not merely those of the school. Expectations for adaptive behavior vary with the age of the student. Parents expect preschool youngsters to learn to walk, talk, and interact with family members; teachers expect school-aged children to learn to read, write, do math, and interact with peers; society expects adults to be gainfully employed and get along in the community. Expectations also vary across cultures. For example, while American teachers expect their students to ask questions and participate in discussions, Asian parents expect their children to be quiet and obedient and listen to adults without asking questions or challenging their authority (Cheng, 1987).

Thus, students with mental retardation are characterized by both below-average intellectual ability and deficits in adaptive behavior. A low IQ score alone is not sufficient to determine retardation; the student's learning problem must be substantiated in the home, neighborhood, and community. The problem must also become apparent during the developmental period (i.e., before age 18). Older persons whose intellectual abilities are impaired by an injury, accident, or illness are not considered mentally retarded.

Within the group of students considered mentally retarded are several levels of abilities. Students with mild retardation, as the term is used in this book, are those who are able to learn basic academic skills. The special needs of students with severe retardation are more serious and comprehensive. Students with severe disabilities may be educated in a full-day special class; such classes are typically located on regular school campuses to facilitate social interactions between students with severe disabilities and typical students. In some cases, however, students with severe disabilities are fully included in general education classes with support from special education personnel. Severe disabilities are discussed more fully in a later section of this chapter.

Many students with mild retardation are mainstreamed because they are often able to participate in the instructional activities of the regular classroom. The special needs of this group, which makes up approximately 80% of the population identified as retarded, are in the areas of academic, behavioral, social, and physical performance.

Academic Needs. Students with mild retardation generally master academic skills at a slower rate than regular class students of the same age. Because they enter school somewhat behind their peers, they may not be ready to begin formal academic instruction immediately. Individuals with mild retardation are able to acquire basic school skills, but their achievement is below grade-level expectations. Nonetheless, most individuals with mild retardation acquire upper-elementary-level reading and math skills by the completion of their school career (Kirk & Gallagher, 1979).

Some aspects of school learning are especially troublesome for students with mild retardation. They may have difficulty focusing attention, remembering, and transferring information and skills learned in one setting to another situation. Tasks involving abstract reasoning, problem solving, and creativity pose special problems. For example, students with mild retardation perform less well on arithmetic reasoning tasks than on straightforward computational problems.

In the elementary years, the discrepancy between the age of students with mild retardation and their achievement level is not great. In adolescence, the gap widens. At the secondary level, such students often receive intensive career education programs that stress vocational training. Despite their evident learning needs, students with mild intellectual disabilities may be identified as retarded only during their school years. Outside the school environment, with its academic demands, individuals with mild retardation do not have obvious needs.

Behavioral Needs. As a group, students with mild retardation display more problem behaviors than their regular class peers, perhaps because of the slower rate of learning of students with mild retardation. Their repertoire of classroom behavioral skills may be appropriate for their developmental level but not for their age group. Another possible factor is the low frustration tolerance of many students with mild retardation. Repeated failure in school and social situations contributes to this decreased capacity for handling frustration.

Social Needs. Students with mild retardation may not be socially accepted by their age peers. Lacking social skills, they may be rejected or ignored. This difficulty in establishing interpersonal relationships may be due to the apparent immaturity of students with mild retardation. Their social skills are not well developed in comparison with those of their age peers, and their problem behaviors may make them unattractive. Also, the play and leisure interests of students with mild retardation may be inappropriate for their age.

Physical Needs. Not all individuals with mild retardation have special physical needs; indeed, some excel in the physical area. However, as a group, these students are somewhat deficient in motor skills. When compared with their age peers, they perform less well in tasks requiring agility, coordination, strength, and dexterity (Bruininks, 1977). In addition, youngsters with mild retardation show vision problems and hearing losses more frequently than do typical students.

Special Services. Students with mild retardation are educated in a range of settings. Many, however, are mainstreamed for at least part of the school day. Students with mild retardation may be placed in a special class and may then attend regular programs for nonacademic activities. Others are mainstreamed for the majority of the day while receiving part-time special education services. As with all special students, decisions regarding the amount of regular class participation for pupils with mild retardation must be made on an individual basis.

Students with Other Disabilities

Many mainstreamed classrooms include students with disabilities other than learning disabilities, behavioral disorders, and mild mental retardation. Among these are speech and language disorders, physical and health disorders (including traumatic brain injury), and vision and hearing impairments. Students with attention deficit disorder or attention deficit hyperactivity disorder are also frequently served in general education settings. Students with autism and those with other types of severe disabilities are mainstreamed in some districts; in others, they receive more comprehensive special education services.

Communication Disorders. Among the most common of all disabilities are **speech and language impairments.** According to Van Riper (1978), speech is considered abnormal "when it deviates so far from the speech of other people that it calls attention to itself, interferes with communication, or causes the speaker or his listeners to be distressed" (p. 43). Articulation disorders, or difficulty with the production of sounds, are the most typical speech problem, especially in young children. Other possible trouble areas include voice problems and disorders of fluency, such as stuttering.

Speech is the production of sounds for the communication of oral language. Oral language includes not only the expression of messages by speaking but also the reception of messages by listening. Students with language impairments may experience difficulty in either or both areas. Some students show an overall delay in language development. Others have particular difficulty with a specific component, such as grammatical structure (syntax) or the meaningful aspects of language (semantics).

In the regular classroom, students with speech and language disorders have special academic and social needs. In addition to receiving special help from speech-language pathologists, they may require instruction in listening skills, vocabulary, grammar, and oral expression. In the social area, students with communication problems may find interpersonal encounters stressful. Such students may need assistance in order to become a part of the social group of the regular classroom.

Physical and Health Impairments. This group of students is relatively small (less than 1% of the school-aged population) but extremely diverse. **Physical and health impairments** encompass a multitude of different conditions and disabilities that range from mild to severe and from invisible to obvious. According to Sirvis (1982), this group includes individuals with *functional limitations* "related to physical skills such as hand use, trunk control, mobility" (p. 384) and individuals with *medical conditions* that affect strength and stamina.

Students with physical disabilities include those with missing limbs, spinal cord injuries causing paralysis, and conditions such as muscular dystrophy. Two of the most common physical problems are cerebral palsy and epilepsy. Cerebral palsy is a motor impairment caused by damage to the brain; it results in difficulty with coordination. Epilepsy is a convulsive disorder; students with epilepsy may have seizures during which they lose consciousness and motor control. Examples of health problems that may affect school performance are diabetes, cardiac conditions, asthma, hemophilia, and cancer.

In the regular classroom, students with physical and health disorders may encounter few difficulties; if special needs do arise, they are likely to be in the areas of physical, academic, and social performance. Special services may be provided by adapted physical education teachers or other motor specialists; school nurses help with students needing special diets, medication, or activity restrictions. For students with physical mobility problems (such as individuals who walk with crutches or those who travel in wheelchairs), it may be necessary to modify the physical environment of the school to allow access. Instructional materials are adapted for students whose physical problems make writing difficult. Although students with physical and health impairments are not poor achievers as a group, those with chronic medical conditions may miss much school

and may fall behind their peers as a result. Social acceptance is another possible problem area, particularly for students with conspicuous disabilities.

Traumatic brain injury was recognized as a separate disability by PL 101-476, the Individuals with Disabilities Education Act. The National Head Injury Foundation Task Force defines traumatic brain injury as

> an insult to the brain, not of a degenerative or congenital nature, but caused by an external physical force that may produce a diminished or altered state of consciousness which results in impairment of cognitive abilities. (as cited in Tucker & Colson, 1992, p. 198)

The most common causes of head injuries in school-aged individuals are motor vehicle accidents, falls, sports injuries, and, in some parts of the country, assaults (Mira & Tyler, 1991). Students with traumatic brain injury often have physical, academic, and social-behavioral needs. Such students receive educational services in hospital settings, at home, and in a variety of school placements, including mainstreamed classrooms.

Sensory Disorders. Another small group of students with disabilities includes those with **vision impairments** and **hearing impairments.** Many school-aged individuals are able to see and hear normally despite vision and hearing problems; their difficulties either have responded to medical treatment or are corrected by eyeglasses or hearing aids. Such students are not considered disabled. Only those whose senses remain impaired after treatment and correction are identified as having a vision or hearing impairment.

Students with vision impairments may be **blind** or may have **low vision.** Individuals who are blind receive so little information through the eyes that they must learn through their other senses; for example, they use the sense of touch to read braille. Students with low vision, although visually impaired, are able to use their residual vision to learn. In the regular class, students with vision problems may have physical, academic, and social needs. They may require assistance in learning to move about the school and classroom environments; itinerant or resource teachers assist by teaching students basic orientation and mobility skills. These specialists also locate and provide any special materials and equipment needed for academic instruction; some examples are large-print books, braille materials, raised or embossed maps, tape recorders and taped textbooks, magnification devices, and computers with "talking" word processing programs. In the social area, students with vision impairments may need encouragement to interact with sighted peers.

Students with hearing disorders may be **deaf** or **hard of hearing**. Individuals who are hard-of-hearing hear well enough to understand speech, usually with the assistance of a hearing aid. Students who are deaf, however, receive so little information through the ears that the sense of hearing is not useful for speech comprehension. In the regular classroom, students with hearing impairments may have special physical, academic, and social needs. Difficulty in speech and language development is one of the major educational problems associated with hearing loss. Students with hearing impairments may require classroom adaptations in order to use the skills taught by special educators. For example, sitting near the front of the classroom helps in hearing or speechreading the verbal instructions of the teacher.

Some students with hearing impairments communicate with speech; others use a manual communication system such as sign language. Interpreters may accompany some students who are deaf to the regular classroom, particularly at the secondary level; interpreters are hearing individuals who translate the spoken word into manual signs and vice versa. Students with hearing losses may be academically delayed in subjects related to language, such as reading, spelling, and written expression; they may receive special instruction from a resource or itinerant teacher in these areas. Speech and language problems may also inhibit the social interaction of students with hearing losses. If they communicate via speech, articulation problems may make them difficult to understand; those who use manual communication may be isolated from peers unless they, too, have acquired basic signing skills.

Attention Deficit Disorder and Attention Deficit Hyperactivity Disorder.
According to the American Psychiatric Association (1987), attention deficit hyperactivity disorders are characterized by "developmentally inappropriate degrees of inattention, impulsiveness, and hyperactivity" (p. 50). In contrast, hyperactivity is not considered a component of attention deficit disorder. ADD and ADHD appear to be quite common; a 1991 policy memorandum of the U.S. Department of Education estimates that 3% to 5% of the school-aged population has significant educational problems related to ADD or ADHD. Students with ADD or ADHD may experience difficulty in academic achievement in addition to their behavioral problems.

Many students with ADD or ADHD are served in general education programs. Although these disorders are not included as disabilities under current federal special education laws, some students may meet eligibility qualifications for other disabilities such as learning disabilities, serious emotional disturbance, or other health impairments. In addition, the U.S. Department of Education (1991) has ruled that students with ADD or ADHD are eligible for services under Section 504 of the Rehabilitation Act of 1973. Under this law, students with ADD or ADHD may receive special education services, related services, and/or adjustments in the general education program.

Autism. Kauffman (1993) calls autism a "pervasive developmental disorder" because it affects all areas of functioning and it is identified before a child reaches 3 years of age. Individuals with autism have difficulty engaging in interactions with other people; experience marked delays in language development; may use echolalic speech (i.e., instead of responding to a question, the person with autism echoes or repeats the question); and engage in behaviors such as tantrums, self-stimulatory repetitive activities, and self-mutiliatory acts (Kauffman, 1993; Lovaas & Newsom, 1976).

Experts often disagree about autism. Some maintain it is a severe behavioral disorder; others suggest it is a severe disorder of language or a type of health impairment (Heward & Orlansky, 1992). Because of this controversy, autism was designated as a separate disability under the Individuals with Disabilities Education Act of 1990. Clearly, students with autism have special needs in all areas: behavioral, social, academic, and physical performance. These students are often served in special schools or classes. In recent years, some students with autism have been mainstreamed in general education classes as part of the full inclusion movement. When that occurs, special education personnel must provide comprehensive support services in the regular classroom to assist the general education teacher and increase the probability that the student with autism will benefit from the mainstreaming experience.

Severe Disabilities. Students with severe disabilities have the most serious and comprehensive needs of all the individuals served by special education. Such students have severe mental retardation and/or show significant developmental delays; their cognitive disabilities are often accompanied by physical, health, communication, and sensory impairments. The U.S. Department of Education describes students with severe disabilities as

. . . those who because of the intensity of their physical, mental, or emotional problems, or a combination of such problems, need educational, social, psychological, and medical services beyond those which are traditionally offered by regular and special education programs, in order to maximize their potential for useful and meaningful participation in society and for self-fulfillment. (*Federal Register,* 1988, p. 118, as cited in Heward & Orlansky, 1992)

In the past, students with severe disabilities were served in special schools and residential programs. Today, however, these students typically attend special classes in regular schools. Like students with autism, students with severe disabilities are fully included in general education classes in some districts.

In working with special educators and others who serve students with disabilities, one of the first things that most general educators notice is terminology. Because special education is a technical field, many terms are used to describe disabilities. Abbreviations, designed as shortcuts in communication, are also used abundantly. However, statements like "Joel has a BD and an LD, and his IEP says the RR is the LRE for him" certainly do not further communication. Translations of some of the common abbreviations used in special education are listed in "For Your Information" on pages 78 and 79.

Other Special Students

Mainstreamed classrooms typically contain, in addition to regular class students, not only students with disabilities but also individuals with special gifts and talents. In many towns and cities, students from culturally and linguistically diverse backgrounds may also be class members. In addition, classrooms often include students at risk for school failure. Members of these three groups of students may have special learning needs.

Gifted and Talented Students. These students, who are estimated to make up 3% to 5% of the school-aged population, may be exceptionally bright (i.e., gifted), have special talents in areas such as art or music, or be both gifted and talented. One definition of this group is found in federal law.

> The term *gifted and talented children* means children and, whenever applicable, youth who are identified at the preschool, elementary, or secondary level as possessing demonstrated or potential abilities that give evidence of high performance capabilities in areas such as intellectual, creative, specific academic, or leadership ability, or in the performing and visual arts. . . . (Section 902, PL 95-561, Gifted and Talented Children's Act of 1978)

Gifted students are characterized by above-average performance on measures of intellectual performance; they may excel academically in all subjects or be particularly advanced in one. Some have creative ability that allows them to produce unusual or novel solutions to problems. Talented students may excel in leadership, drama, art, music, dance, or other areas.

Many states provide special educational opportunities for this diverse group of students. Some gifted individuals are allowed to enter school early and accelerate quickly through the curriculum, perhaps skipping one or several grades. Others attend special schools or classes. Most common, however, is regular class placement with part-time special services either in a resource setting or through special enrichment activities such as seminars or after-school programs.

In the regular classroom, gifted and talented students may have special academic and social needs. Those who are advanced academically benefit from special learning projects and assignments to help them continue their development. Some, however, although bright, may achieve poorly in relation to their potential; for example, they may be unmotivated, lack prerequisite skills, become bored with what they perceive as elementary-level instruction, or fail to achieve because a disability interferes with their performance. Students who are creative and talented may be academically advanced or typical of individuals their age; whatever their academic ability, they require guidance to develop their talents. Some gifted and talented students have excellent social skills; others, especially those with extraordinary abilities, may need assistance in relating to

their age peers. It is also possible for special populations to overlap. A student who is both culturally diverse and disabled may also be identified as gifted, and some gifted youngsters may be at risk for school failure.

Students from Culturally and Linguistically Diverse Backgrounds. Culturally diverse individuals are those reared in a culture that is at variance with that found in the school or different from the dominant culture in the United States. These students face at least two sets of expectations—those of the home and those of the school—and many times these expectations are discrepant. Included within this group are linguistically diverse students; these youngsters may speak languages other than English or be bilingual in English and the language of the home. Some students from culturally and linguistically diverse backgrounds have special learning needs; others do not.

Students who speak little or no English are likely to be members of minority cultures. They are at an extreme disadvantage in school if both their language and experiential background sets them apart from their peers. Many schools offer such students bilingual education, in which they develop English language skills while learning more about their own culture and the dominant culture of the United States. Minority students include Native Americans and Alaskan natives, Asians and Pacific Islanders, African Americans, and Hispanics. African Americans and Hispanics are the two most prevalent minority groups in the United States today. Within the Hispanic group are individuals of Mexican, Cuban, Puerto Rican, or other Spanish culture or origin. Some minority students are bilingual, some may be considered culturally diverse, but many are English-speaking members of the dominant American culture.

Culturally diverse students are those whose background and experiences differ from those of their peers. Cultural differences must be defined in terms of local norms. For instance, a Christian student may be perceived as culturally different in a predominantly Jewish community; a student who

Making Sense of Special Education Abbreviations

Special educators are sometimes accused of speaking in jargon and "alphabet soup." Here are some of the abbreviations commonly used in discussions of students with disabilities. If you hear one that is not on this list and you fail to understand its meaning, stop the speaker and ask for an explanation. Remember that communication can occur only if the listener is able to comprehend the speaker's message.

ADA   The Americans with Disabilities Act of 1990

ADD   Attention deficit disorder

ADHD   Attention deficit hyperactivity disorder

BD   Behavioral disorder; often used synonymously with emotional disturbance (ED)

COHI   Crippled and other health impairment; an older term sometimes applied to physical and health disorders (Note: The term *crippled* is considered pejorative.)

ED   Emotional disturbance

EMR   Educable mental retardation; an older term that refers to mild mental retardation (MMR)

FAPE   Free and appropriate public education; refers to the basic guarantee of federal laws such PL 94-142, the Education for All Handicapped Children Act, and IDEA

HH   Hard of hearing

speaks with a Boston accent may appear out of place among residents of the Deep South.

Students with ethnic, linguistic, and cultural backgrounds different from those of their peers add diversity and variety to the general education classroom. However, they may have special academic and social needs. Those still developing skills in understanding and speaking English may experience difficulty with academic instruction. Others may fail to meet teacher expectations because of different entry-level skills or different cultural values and motivational systems. Social acceptance may be withheld by peers unaccustomed to cultural variations.

Students at Risk for School Failure. Students can be at risk for many reasons. They may live in an impoverished family with inadequate housing, poor nutrition, and little or no medical care; with their basic needs in jeopardy, such students often have few resources left to devote to school learning. Others may be slow learners who, although they do not have disabilities, learn at a pace that falls somewhat below grade level expectations. Some students are unmotivated to achieve in school, and as a result their academic performance is less than satisfactory. Older students with a history of poor school achievement may become truant or contemplate leaving school. According to the National Coalition of Advocates for Students (1985), one of every four students who enters the ninth grade drops out before graduating from high school.

Every classroom contains students at risk for school failure, although it is difficult to determine

HI	Hearing impairment
IDEA	The Individual with Disabilities Education Act of 1990
IEP	Individualized Education Program
LD	Learning disability; also called specific learning disability (SLD) and language and learning disability (LLD)
LRE	Least Restrictive Environment
MMR	Mild mental retardation
MR	Mental retardation
OHI	Other health impairment; refers to health disorders
OI	Orthopedic impairment; refers to physical disabilities involving the skeletal system
PH	Physical handicap
PL	Public Law, as in PL 94-142
POHI	Physical and other health impairment
RR	Resource room
SC	Special class, also called special day class (SDC)
SED	Serious emotional disturbance; used in federal law to refer to emotional disturbance (ED)/behavioral disorders (BD)
SH	Severely handicapped; often used to describe individuals with severe retardation and/or multiple serious disabilities
TBI	Traumatic brain injury
TMR	Trainable mental retardation; an older term that refers to moderate and severe retardation
VI	Vision impairment

precisely how many general education students fit within this category. Many types of students can be considered at risk. Among these are potential school dropouts, students with suicidal behaviors, those who use or abuse alcohol or other drugs, teenage mothers, victims of child abuse or neglect, those with eating disorders, and delinquents.

At-risk students often have needs in the area of academic performance; they may fail to achieve, show little interest in instructional activities, or achieve at levels far below their potential. Some students may also show special needs in the area of behavior; they may exhibit inappropriate behavior in the classroom or begin to develop very serious problems such as drug and alcohol abuse, gang activity, and delinquency. Social acceptance may be a problem particularly for students who fail to meet the school's expectations for achievement and the peer group's expectations for behavior.

SPECIAL NEEDS

It is common practice to divide special students into separate groups or categories such as students with learning disabilities, those with mental retardation, and so on. In the classroom, however, the special needs of these students are often so similar that distinctions among categories become blurred. It also becomes difficult to differentiate between students with identified disabilities and some of their regular class peers with similar learning problems.

Academic needs are common. The acquisition, mastery, and application of school skills proves difficult for many special students and for many of their

Special Needs

- A student may have a disability without being handicapped. A disability is some sort of impairment. It becomes a handicap only when it interferes with performance in some important area.
- Male students with special needs are more common than female students. No one knows exactly why this is so. It may be that males are more susceptible to the inheritance of learning problems and disabilities. Or it may be related to the cultural expectations for students of different sexes.
- There is no relationship between physical disabilities and intelligence. People with severe physical problems may be bright, and individuals with mental retardation may have no physical disabilities.
- Most special students are not identified as disabled until they encounter difficulty in school. Children identified in the preschool years have serious or obvious disabilities or conditions that place them at risk for developmental delays.
- Given the right circumstances, any student could be considered culturally different. For example, a student who moves from Texas to New England will encounter new speech patterns, foods, social customs, and even sports activities.

classmates. Children are expected to enter school with listening, speaking, and other readiness skills. In the primary years (grades 1, 2, and 3), the basic skills of reading, writing, and mathematics are taught; at the intermediate level (grades 4, 5, and 6), students learn to use these skills to acquire information in content areas such as science and social studies. In junior high and high school, the focus of the curriculum shifts to these content areas; mastery of basic skills is assumed. For many students, this assumption is unwarranted; they are not able to read, write, and calculate at the level expected in the secondary grades. Those who have acquired rudimentary basic skills may fail to acquire content area knowledge and concepts. Still others may require alternatives to the general education curriculum; their major educational need may be career education with an emphasis on vocational training.

Classroom behavior needs frequently occur among special students and their general education peers. Elementary school students are expected to obey their teacher and others in authority, adhere to the rules of classroom conduct, and get along with their peers both during instruction and in less structured situations such as lunch and recess. These expectations are also true for secondary students. In addition, however, it is assumed that they have developed the study skills and work habits necessary for independent learning. Many students require assistance in meeting these expectations for classroom behavior.

Students may also have special *physical needs*. Children are expected to enter school with intact vision, hearing, and physical abilities. Those with sensory losses cannot participate in many classroom activities designed for sighted and hearing students. Many students, including those with physical and health disorders, cannot walk, run, or play games and sports as well as their regular class peers. They have special needs in the area of physical development.

Special students and others often have *social needs*. Young children are expected to know how to make friends with their classmates. Instruction is often presented in group situations that require students to interact with both their teacher and peers. Many school activities are at least partly social in nature; personal interactions take place during lunch, recess, assemblies, and field trips and in clubs, organizations, and sports teams. Social skills become increasingly important as individuals approach adulthood; secondary students are expected to build and maintain friendships and begin establishing interpersonal relationships as preparation for courtship and marriage. Because they may appear to be different in some ways, special students may have difficulty gaining acceptance from their regular class peers. Students with poor social skills (whether they are identified as special or not) need instruction and training in this area.

Most students require assistance in one or more of these areas at some time during their school careers. Special students are no exception. However, with special students it is possible to predict some of the areas in which they are likely to encounter difficulty. As shown in Table 3–1, it is probable that all will have special academic and social needs. Some may also have needs in the areas of classroom behavior and physical development. This diagram depicts only the typical needs of groups of students; it is certainly possible for students with speech and language disorders to display problem behaviors or for students with physical disabilities to require no special academic assistance.

There are many similarities among special students and between special students and their regular class peers. This is particularly true in relation to students with mild disabilities: learning disabilities, behavioral disorders, and mild retardation. These

TABLE 3–1
Typical Needs of Special Students

| Special Students | Special Needs | | | |
	Academic	Classroom Behavior	Physical	Social
Learning disabilities	X	X	X	X
Behavioral disorders	X	X		X
Mental retardation	X	X	X	X
Speech/language	X			X
Physical/health	X		X	X
Vision/hearing	X		X	X
ADD/ADHD	X	X		X
Autism	X	X	X	X
Severe disabilities	X	X	X	X
Gifted/talented	X			X
Students from diverse groups	X			X
Students at risk	X	X	X	X

students make up perhaps 5% to 7% of the school population. They are physically indistinguishable from their regular class peers and are usually not identified as special until they experience failure in school. They begin school in regular classes and receive the majority of their education in mainstreamed situations. According to Hallahan and Kauffman (1976), students with mild disabilities cannot be differentiated by the causes of their learning problems, the methods found effective in their instruction, or their behavioral characteristics. All have academic, behavioral, and social needs that may require adaptations in general education classrooms.

When adaptations are made for special students, general education teachers often wonder how to explain these changes to the rest of the class. Students may wonder why others are receiving special treatment. Ideas for handling this situation are listed in "Tips for the Teacher."

■ CAUSES OF LEARNING PROBLEMS

For most special students, the cause or **etiology** of their learning problem is unknown. Although a host of causative agents have been identified, it is often impossible to state with certainty which was responsible for the disability of a particular student.

Causes can be classified according to when they occurred in the life of the individual: prenatal (before birth), perinatal (during the birth process), or postnatal (after birth). An example of a prenatal cause is rubella or German measles. If contracted by a woman during the first three months of her pregnancy, rubella can lead to hearing, vision, physical, and cognitive disabilities in the fetus as it develops. Oxygen deprivation during the birth process is a perinatal cause, whereas a head injury sustained in an auto accident at 3 years of age is a postnatal cause.

Another view of etiology is the dichotomy of hereditary and environmental factors. Some types of deafness are inherited, and there is some indication that reading problems tend to run in families. Environmental causes of learning problems include poor nutrition, lack of sensory stimulation, and inadequate instruction.

The causes of learning problems are of interest for two reasons: treatment and prevention. Medical research has developed treatments for some known etiologies and preventive techniques for others. For example, the Salk vaccine has virtually eliminated the crippling disease of polio in the United States, and progress is being made in use of gene therapy for conditions such as muscular dystrophy. In education, the emphasis is on environmental causes of learning problems. Research indicates that early education of children with special needs may lessen or prevent later learning problems (Casto & Mastropieri, 1986; White, Bush, & Casto, 1986). Education itself is one of the environmental influences on students, one that can precipitate learning problems. Poor or inappropriate instruction has been cited as a major factor in the development of school problems. Reynolds and Birch (1982) contend that "most pupil behaviors called learning disabilities and behavior disorders are best acknowledged as the consequences of failure to provide enough high quality individualized instruction" (p. 237).

■ ASSESSMENT OF SPECIAL LEARNING NEEDS

Assessment is the process of gathering information about students to make important educational decisions (McLoughlin & Lewis, 1994). In special education and other supplementary school services, it is necessary to determine whether students meet certain legal requirements before services can begin. In special education, for example, students are considered eligible for services only if they are disabled and if their disability has a negative effect on school performance. That is, students must experience difficulty in school, and that difficulty must be attributable to a disability.

Classroom Assessment

General educators play many roles in the assessment process. As discussed in chapter 2, it is typically the classroom teacher who refers students for special education and other types of assessment. In addition, teachers collect all sorts of information

Explaining Classroom Modifications to Peers

*I*t is sometimes necessary to make changes in classroom activities so that students with special needs can succeed. For example, students with academic needs may be given special assignments or may be required to complete only part of the work assigned to the rest of the class. Those with behavioral needs may earn special rewards for good behavior. The rest of the class may become curious about why these students rate special treatment from the teacher. Teachers can prevent problems from occurring by following these suggestions:

■ Don't call undue attention to students with special needs. Treat them as you would any other student in your class.
■ When special assignments are necessary, give them privately. Then, when the class is working on individual assignments, the student with special needs will not be conspicuous.
■ Group students with similar learning needs together. If a student with a disability requires extra instruction in reading, set up a small group that includes peers with similar needs. If students with special needs have difficulty following class rules, consider beginning a behavior program for the entire class.
■ When class members have questions, answer them promptly and honestly. Acknowledge that you are individualizing assignments and activities so that everyone in the class can learn successfully. A matter-of-fact response will usually satisfy curiosity and allay any feelings of resentment.

about their students. Some of the assessment strategies that classroom teachers use most often are

■ observation of students as they engage in academic activities and social interactions;
■ analysis of students' errors and correct responses on work samples such as homework assignments, tests, essays, and math papers;
■ administration of quizzes and exams to assess student progress toward instructional goals; and
■ interviews with students to learn more about their attitudes, viewpoints, and the strategies they use to interact with classroom tasks.

These techniques are all considered **informal assessment** strategies. Unlike the formal, norm-referenced tests often used in special education, their purpose is not to compare one student's performance to that of others of the same age or grade. Instead, they are curriculum-based because they focus on students' mastery of the instructional goals addressed in the regular classroom.

Informal techniques fit well with the current move toward alternative assessment in general education. This approach is also known as authentic assessment, outcome-based assessment, and performance assessment (Worthen, 1993). Its proponents call for less reliance on traditional achievement tests, particularly those made up of multiple-choice questions, and more emphasis on authentic tasks that require students to demonstrate problem-solving abilities rather than rote memory skills.

At present, **portfolio assessment** is the most popular tool for alternative assessment (McLoughlin & Lewis, 1994). Portfolios are simply collections of student work gathered over time; however, students are responsible for selecting their best work for inclusion in the portfolio and for evaluating their own progress (Grady, 1992). Teachers evaluate the contents of a portfolio with the same informal techniques used to analyze other types of student work samples.

One major reason for the collection of data is to evaluate the effectiveness of instruction. When done systematically, this is called **clinical teaching** (McLoughlin & Lewis, 1994). First, the teacher gathers data about student performance on the task in question. Then, an intervention is introduced and data collection continues. Any of the informal assessment strategies described earlier can be used in clinical teaching: observation, analysis of student work samples, quizzes, and so on. The intervention is considered successful if results indicate that student performance has improved.

Curriculum-based measurement (CBM) is an informal assessment strategy used in special education to monitor student progress (Deno, 1985, 1987; Shinn & Hubbard, 1993). It is easy to use and sensitive to small changes in students' skill levels, which makes it a useful measurement technique for clinical teaching. In CBM, the teacher collects very brief samples of important student behaviors. For example, to assess oral reading skills, students read aloud for 1 minute while the teacher (or an assistant) records the number of words read correctly. This "probe" is administered frequently (e.g., two or three times each week), and results are graphed to provide a visual record of the student's progress. In clinical teaching, this graph is inspected to determine whether desired changes occurred when the new intervention was introduced.

Assessment for Program Eligibility

When students are referred for special education assessment, a multidisciplinary team is formed to plan the process of gathering information about the need for extraordinary services. **Norm-referenced tests** are typically used for this type of assessment. These tests provide information about a student's status in relation to other students of the same age or grade; this type of comparison is needed to determine whether a student's problem is severe enough to warrant special educational intervention.

The tests are administered by trained specialists to one student at a time. Group administration procedures are not used because they can depress the performance of students with special learning needs. Group tests require students to read, write, and attend to test tasks for a relatively long period of time. On individually administered tests, a student's knowledge of science can be separated from his or her reading skills because the tester reads the questions to the student; also, if the student's attention wavers, the professional can help the student refocus on the task at hand.

No matter what disability is suspected, the team will collect information on three major areas of functioning:

1. *Intellectual performance.* Tests of intellectual performance, sometimes called intelligence or IQ (intelligence quotient) tests, are used to assess the student's skills in reasoning and problem-solving tasks. These measures do not determine innate potential; instead, they assess a student's aptitude for academic tasks (McLoughlin & Lewis, 1994).
2. *Academic achievement.* At the beginning of assessment, tests that include several academic subjects (e.g., reading, spelling, composition, mathematics, content area knowledge) are administered to identify broad areas of need. Then, more specific measures (e.g., a test of reading skills) are used to pinpoint areas of difficulty.
3. *Area of disability.* In special education assessment, it is necessary to establish the existence of a disability. For instance, in mental retardation, the team will study intellectual performance and adaptive behavior. In learning disabilities, the focus is information processing, and in behavioral disorders, severe and long-standing conduct disorders. Federal laws provide regulations for determining eligibility, and states and school districts supplement these with additional guidelines.

Figure 3–1 lists and describes some of the individually administered norm-referenced tests used most often in special education assessment. Included

FIGURE 3–1

Measures Used in Special Education

Measures of Intellectual Performance

Wechsler Intelligence Scale for Children-Third Edition—Contains 13 tests that assess verbal and nonverbal reasoning in students ages 6 to 16; results include global IQ scores (Verbal, Performance, and Full Scale IQ) as well as scores for four cognitive factors: Verbal Comprehension, Perceptual Organization, Freedom from Distractibility, and Processing Speed. Called the *WISC-III*, this is the most commonly used measure of intellectual performance in schools.

Woodcock-Johnson Psycho-Educational Battery-Revised, Tests of Cognitive Ability—Estimates overall intellectual performance and provides measures of seven cognitive factors: Long-Term Retrieval, Short-Term Memory, Processing Speed, Auditory Processing, Visual Processing, Comprehension-Knowledge, and Fluid Processing; designed for ages 2 to 90+.

Stanford-Binet Intelligence Scale: Fourth Edition—Assesses four areas of intellectual performance in persons from age 2 to adulthood: Verbal Reasoning, Abstract/Visual Reasoning, Quantitative Reasoning, and Short-Term Memory. This test is the current version of the original IQ test devised in the early 1900s by Binet and Simon.

Measures of Overall Academic Achievement

Peabody Individual Achievement Test-Revised—Includes tests of General Information, Reading Recognition, Reading Comprehension, Mathematics, Spelling, and Written Expression for students in grades K through 12.

Wechsler Individual Achievement Test—A newer measure with 8 subtests that assess reading, mathematics, and written language as well as listening and speaking skills; designed for grades K through 12.

Woodcock-Johnson Psycho-Educational Battery-Revised, Tests of Achievement—Contains 14 tests to assess Reading, Mathematics, Written Language, and Knowledge (science, social studies, and humanities) for ages 2 to adulthood.

Wide Range Achievement Test 3—More limited in scope, the *WRAT3* assesses spelling, arithmetic, and reading recognition skills in students ages 5 through adulthood.

Measures of Specific Academic Skills

Woodcock Reading Mastery Tests-Revised—Used to identify strengths and weaknesses in Word Identification, Word Attack, Word Comprehension, Passage Comprehension, and reading readiness skills in K–12 and college students.

KeyMath Revised—Offers 13 subtests to assess mathematics skills in Basic Concepts, Operations, and Applications; normed for grades K through 9.

Test of Written Spelling-2—A dictation spelling test of Predictable and Unpredictable Words for ages 6 to 18.

Test of Written Language-2—Identifies strengths and weaknesses in areas of written language such as vocabulary, spelling, and style in students ages 7 to 18; one part of the *TOWL-2* requires students to write a story describing a picture.

are measures of intellectual performance as well as academic achievement tests.

Although classroom teachers do not administer tests such as these, test results are often discussed in the deliberations of the mainstreaming team. To help teachers become better acquainted with the tests and other data collection procedures used in special education, common assessment tools and techniques are discussed throughout this book. However, this book places most emphasis on the types of assessment tools that teachers find useful in the classroom. These are typically informal assessments—measures and strategies devised by teachers to answer specific questions about the academic, social, physical, and behavioral needs of their students. The measures also tend to be curriculum-based rather than norm-referenced; that is, their purpose is to compare a student's performance to the demands of the local curriculum and the expectations in a particular classroom.

■■■ SKILLS FOR THE MAINSTREAMING TEACHER

General education teachers play an important role in the prevention and treatment of school learning problems. With appropriate instruction, students with disabilities and others with special learning needs can succeed in the mainstream. The next chapters of this book focus on the major skills needed by teachers to adapt instruction, manage behavior, promote social acceptance, and coordinate the learning environment in the mainstreamed classroom. These skills are simply good teaching procedures; they can be used with any student, special or not. Good teaching skills focus on the needs of the student (rather than any particular disability), and they are based on the following four assumptions about special students and the teaching-learning process.

All students can learn. Despite any special needs they may have, all individuals are able to acquire new skills and absorb new information and attitudes. Students learn at different rates, and the same person may learn some things more quickly than other things. Although much is known about different types of special students and their disabilities, it is impossible to accurately predict the specific areas in which they will experience difficulty. However, we do know that they *can* and, with proper instruction, *will* learn.

Learning is determined by changes in behavior. Learning is a process of change. Students acquire new skills, become more proficient in previously learned skills, and learn to perform in certain ways. Teachers evaluate students' progress by their behavior; that is, they observe students' overt responses and infer that learning has occurred. Students demonstrate that they have learned academic, classroom conduct, and social skills in many ways; they may display new behaviors, a greater number of appropriate behaviors, or fewer inappropriate behaviors. Teachers monitor the learning process by noting what students say in class discussions, what they write on assignments and exams, and how they act in the many situations of the school day.

Teaching involves manipulation of the environment. If learning is the change of student behaviors, then teaching is the arrangement of the learning environment to maximize the chance that desired behaviors will occur. In instruction, teachers have control over two important factors: the **antecedents** and **consequences** of student behaviors. An antecedent is anything that precedes or comes before a behavior; typical teaching activities such as lectures, small-group discussions, text readings, and written assignments are all instructional antecedents that can be manipulated to enhance learning. Consequences, or events that follow behaviors, include grades, teacher praise or scolding, and rewards (remember gold stars?) and punishments; these, too, are powerful tools that can be used to facilitate learning. Just as students learn at different rates, they also respond differently to instructional antecedents and consequences. Although there is no one sure-fire teaching method, material, or reward system, empirical evidence suggests that

- Both special students and their regular class peers may have special learning needs. Special needs occur in the areas of academic, classroom behavioral, physical, and social performance.
- Special students, as a group, typically experience difficulty in academic and social areas;

some students also have special behavioral and physical needs.
- Information about special needs is more useful to the teacher than knowledge of the student's categorical label.
- Causes of learning problems are important if they help in treatment or prevention.
- Teachers use informal assessment tools to gather information for instructional decisions.

- Appropriate instruction can prevent some learning problems and help to overcome others.
- Teachers manipulate the learning environment to produce changes in the behavior of students.
- Data-based instruction is efficient and effective in teaching special students the behaviors needed to succeed in the mainstream.

some instructional procedures are more effective than others. For example, direct instruction methods that focus on skill development have been found useful for teaching basic academic skills (Stevens & Rosenshine, 1981).

Data collection increases teaching efficiency. Because there are almost unlimited options to choose from in setting up an instructional system of antecedents and consequences, it is important to approach the task systematically. After the desired student behavior is stated as precisely as possible, the most simple and straightforward strategy for teaching that behavior is tried. The teacher collects information about the behavior before instruction and also during the instructional intervention. If the behavior changes in the desired way, the intervention is considered successful; if it does not, the teacher proceeds to a more complex or intensive instructional strategy. In this way, instructional decisions are made on the basis of data rather than on guesses or hunches; teaching becomes more efficient, with the end result that students learn more. This data-based approach to instruction is particularly beneficial for special students and others who encounter difficulty in learning.

Turn to the next chapter to see how these assumptions about the teaching-learning process can be applied to the adaptation of instruction for mainstreamed special students.

ACTIVITIES

1. Disabilities are not the same as handicaps. However, some disabilities interfere with the performance of tasks required by certain professions. For example, consider blindness for a painter or deafness for a musician. Are there any disabilities that would be handicaps for a teacher? If so, what are they? What disabilities would a teacher be able to overcome? Be prepared to discuss your answers to these questions.

2. Interview two or more general educators about the students they teach. Are students with disabilities included in their classrooms? If so, what types of special needs do these students have? Are there others in the classroom with similar needs? What kinds of classroom modifications have the teachers made to accommodate the special needs of these students?

3. Many special education journals concentrate on one disability. For instance, the Council for

Exceptional Children publishes *Behavioral Disorders, Education and Training in Mental Retardation,* and *Learning Disabilities Research and Practice.* Select one or two of these journals, and look at several recent issues. Did you find any articles on the inclusion of students with special needs in regular classes?

4. Talk with an adult who has a disability. Ask about the ways in which the disability affects daily life. If the person had the disability as a child, ask about school experiences. Were special education services available? Was the person mainstreamed?

5. A person's culture affects many perceptions. Talk with someone from a culture different from yours, and compare your experiences. You might discuss foods, dress, manners, or traditional celebrations or holidays. Also, compare the ways in which different cultures view the birth of a child with a disability. Are persons with disabilities treated differently by different cultures?

II

Skills for the Mainstreaming Teacher

4 Adapting Instruction

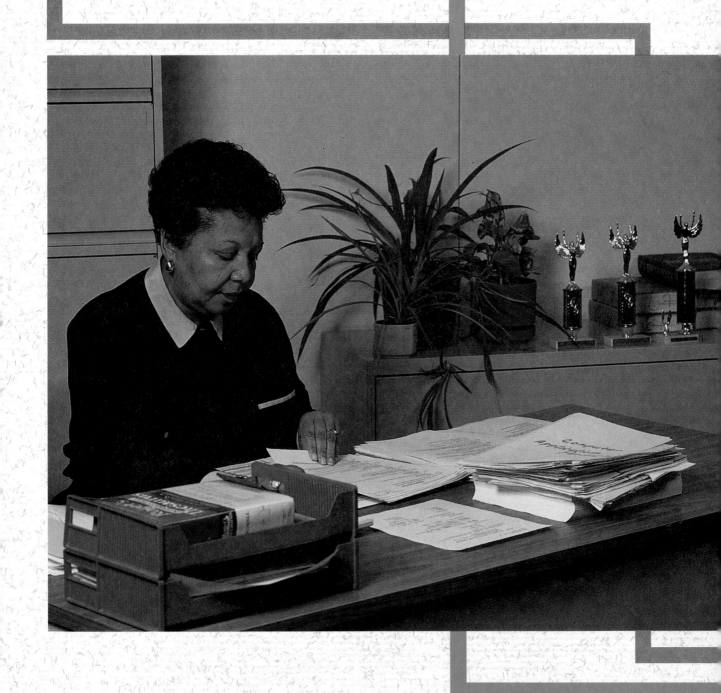

■ *Eleanor, a fourth grader, reads at the beginning third grade level.*

■ *Patrick can solve math computation problems with ease, but he has trouble with word problems.*

■ *Erin's handwriting is barely legible, and the assignments he turns in are wrinkled, messy, and full of crossed-out words.*

■ *Although Patty seems to understand the information presented in chemistry class, she has failed every quiz this semester.*

■ *Ian's essays contain excellent ideas, but his spelling, grammar, and punctuation are atrocious.*

■ *Billy is habitually late to class, and he often forgets to do his homework.*

■ *Dan's vocational skills are good, but he'll have difficulty completing job applications.*

Students such as these have special needs in the area of academic performance. For them to succeed in the regular classroom, it may be necessary to adapt instructional procedures. In order to do this, general education teachers should be familiar with the typical **academic problems** of mainstreamed students and their peers, methods for gathering data about academic performance, and strategies for adapting **instruction** to meet special needs.

ACADEMIC PROBLEMS IN THE CLASSROOM

Students can experience difficulty with academic instruction at any age and in any subject. Such students come to the attention of their teacher when their classroom performance does not meet teacher expectations. Elementary teachers often describe students with academic problems as "achieving below grade level" in one or more subjects. Secondary teachers, on the other hand, take note of students who receive poor or failing grades in specific courses, such as English 9, biology, American history, or woodshop.

School learning involves the acquisition of both information and skills. Students are expected to absorb vast amounts of information in academic subjects and to develop and sharpen their thinking and learning skills. Problems can occur in any one of the three stages of learning: acquisition, maintenance, and generalization. **Acquisition** is initial learning, **maintenance** is the recall of previously learned material, and **generalization** is the application or transfer of learned material to similar situations and problems. Students may require more time to learn new information and skills, have difficulty sustaining performance over time, or fail to apply old learning to new situations.

Teachers evaluate student responses to determine whether learning is occurring as expected. Students respond in the classroom in a number of ways: oral answers to teacher questions, participation in class discussions, in-class assignments and homework, and quizzes and examinations. Academic problems are suspected if one (or more) of the following response patterns is evident:

■ *High number of incorrect responses.* The majority of the student's responses are incorrect, or the student's accuracy rate falls below the criterion set by the teacher. For example, George solves only 6 out of 10 subtraction problems correctly; the teacher's criterion is 90% accuracy.
■ *Low number of responses.* The student fails to respond to a significant number of questions, problems, or activities. For example, Henry answers only 7 of the 15 questions at the end of the chapter.
■ *Inconsistent responses.* The student's responses to the same question, problem, or activity vary in correctness from time to time. For example, Thelma writes all 20 spelling words correctly on the Wednesday practice quiz but scores only 40% on the test on Friday.

Of course, if many students show response patterns such as these, the first step would be to evaluate classroom instructional procedures.

Inappropriate response patterns can be seen in any school subject. One typical trouble spot is **basic skills;** listening, speaking, reading, writing, and mathematics often are difficult for students to acquire, maintain, and generalize. The written language skills of reading and writing are built on the oral language skills of listening and speaking. Students may have trouble with the reception of information (listening and reading), the expression of information (speaking and writing), or all aspects of the communication process. The development of basic skills is a high-priority instructional goal in the elementary grades. Special students may experience difficulty with the rote aspects of these skills (e.g., word recognition, handwriting, spelling, mathematics facts and computation) or with the more conceptual aspects (e.g., reading comprehension, written expression, mathematical problem solving).

At the secondary level, instruction centers on **content area subjects** rather than basic skills. The academic curriculum is organized according to bodies of knowledge: English (including both composition and literature) and other languages; science (biology, chemistry, physics); higher math (algebra, geometry, trigonometry); the social sciences (history, social studies, geography); and other areas such as art, music, and physical education. However, academic problems in basic skills may persist; students may not have acquired (or maintained) adequate reading, writing, and mathematics skills, or they may be unable to apply these skills to the acquisition of new information. Students may also have difficulty learning the skills, information, concepts, and principles of particular content areas. Poor organizational and study skills may also interfere with student performance.

Career education is another aspect of school learning in which academic problems can arise. According to Brolin (1983), career education "is not simply preparation for a job. It is also preparation for other productive work roles that comprise one's total career functioning" (p. vii). One aspect of career education is specific vocational training experience at the secondary level. Career education also includes the application of basic skills and content area information to the solution of daily life prob-

lems, such as reading menus, making change, and selecting appropriate items to purchase. Students may have difficulty in the acquisition of specific vocational skills, such as typing, mechanical drawing, or welding. They may also have difficulty in the generalization of basic work habits, such as punctuality and task completion, and the application of school learning to job and community situations. Easing the transition from school to the world of work is one of the major concerns in career education today.

Because academic instruction is one of the major goals of U.S. education, academic problems are a concern to classroom teachers at all levels. However, as Montgomery (1978) points out, not all variations in student performance are learning problems.

> Johnny reads with his book turned sideways, or kneels instead of sitting on his chair, or wears his jacket in class. Do we "fix" him or let him be? Before we can answer that question realistically we must ask, "Is it a problem for Johnny—or for us?" Does it hamper Johnny's learning, or do we see it as a problem because of our own preoccupation with things being normal, with Johnny acting like everyone else? (p. 112)

■ PRINCIPLES OF INSTRUCTION

Despite their special learning needs, mainstreamed students have the necessary skills to participate in many regular classroom activities. They may take part in all instructional aspects of the general education program, or they may be mainstreamed only for selected subjects. The decision is made on the basis of three factors: the student's skills in the subject area, the amount of instructional support required to ensure the student's active participation, and the usefulness or functionality of the academic subject for the student. When students are mainstreamed only for those subjects that are useful to them and in which successful performance is probable, the general education curriculum is appropriate; that is, *what* is taught need not be modified by the mainstreaming teacher. However, it is often necessary to alter instructional procedures, that is, *how* skills and information are taught to special students.

Much is known today about what teachers can do to have positive effects on student performance. This knowledge comes from a large body of research on teaching behaviors, sometimes known as the teacher effectiveness literature (Brophy & Good, 1986; Medley, 1982; Rieth & Evertson, 1988; Rosenshine & Stevens, 1986; Weil & Murphy, 1982). The major factors found to have a positive influence on student achievement are listed here (Weil & Murphy, 1982):

■ Teachers maintain an *academic focus* in selecting classroom activities and directing classroom work.

■ Teachers maintain *direction and control* in the management of the classroom learning environment.

■ Teachers hold *high expectations* for the academic progress of their students.

■ *Students are accountable* for the satisfactory completion of classroom work.

■ Students work together, showing *cooperation* rather than competition.

■ The affective climate of the classroom learning environment is *not negative*.

Among the most critical concerns in fostering student achievement are the quantity and pace of instruction (Brophy & Good, 1986). Both concerns are related to an opportunity to learn. Learning increases when more time is devoted to academic pursuits and when students are actually engaged in learning during that time. Learning also increases when students move through the curriculum at a brisk pace, provided that students maintain a high rate of successful performance.

Both quantity and pace of instruction can be enhanced by active teaching. According to Brophy and Good (1986), in active teaching "the teacher carries the content to the students personally rather than depending on the curriculum materials to do so" (p. 361). The teacher directs the learning experience, and students "spend most of their time being taught or supervised by their teachers rather than working on their own (or not working at all)" (p. 361). Active teaching has also been called **direct teaching** (or *direct instruction*). In direct teaching, the teacher demonstrates appropriate strategies for the performance of the learning task, allows maximum opportunity for students to respond, and provides systematic and frequent feedback on their task performance (Lewis, 1983).

Lloyd and Carnine (1981) call this *structured instruction*, or the "carefully organized manipulation of environmental events designed to bring about prespecified changes in learners' performance in skill areas of functional importance" (p. viii). It is **individualized instruction**, designed to meet the needs of each student. This does not mean that instruction must be individual, delivered by one teacher to one student. Stevens and Rosenshine (1981) view instruction as individualized when a high proportion of student responses are correct. Good instruction can occur in large groups, small groups, or one-to-one; the criterion is student success.

As shown in Figure 4–1, instruction takes place in a series of steps involving both teacher and student(s) and progressing from the active direction of the teacher (teaching) to the active involvement of the student(s) (learning). There are five steps: curricular choice, presentation, practice, mastery, and application.

1. *Selection of the learning task.* To make this curricular decision, the teacher considers the scope

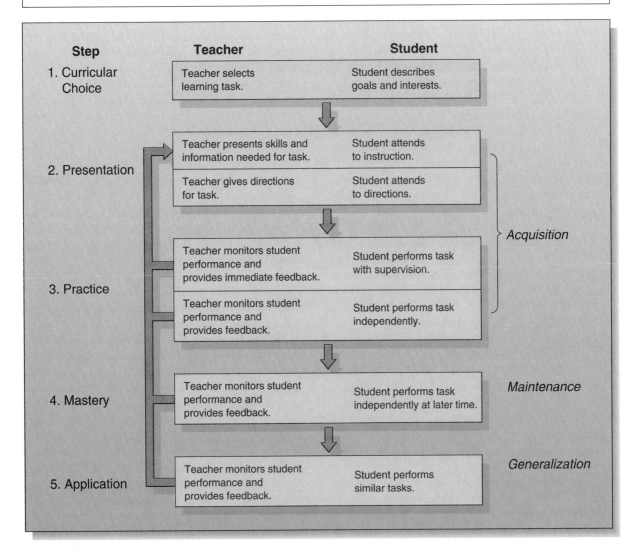

and sequence of the general education curriculum, the skills and information already acquired by the student, and the student's current interests and learning needs. The learning task represents the goal of instruction, and successful performance of this task is the desired student behavior.

2. *Presentation to the student of the material necessary for task performance.* The teacher uses procedures such as lectures, in-class activities, and reading assignments to provide the student with the skills and information required for the task. The teacher may model or demonstrate the skill or explain new information by presenting rules, principles, and examples. Then the teacher gives directions for the performance of the task. The student's role at this stage is to give adequate

attention to instruction and feedback to the teacher if instruction is unclear.

3. *Practice of the learning task.* The student first performs the task under the close supervision of the teacher (guided practice); gradually the teacher's guidance is withdrawn, and the student performs independently (independent practice). The teacher's role is to monitor student performance and provide feedback to the student regarding the adequacy of task performance. In guided practice, feedback is immediate, whereas in independent practice it is delayed. If a high proportion of student responses is incorrect, the teacher returns to the presentation step. Presentation and practice lead to acquisition of skills and information.

4. *Mastery of the learning task.* At some later time, the student performs the task independently, and the teacher monitors student responses. If performance is not adequate, it may be necessary to return to the practice steps or even to the presentation steps. Mastery is determined by maintenance of previously acquired learning.

5. *Application of previous learning.* The student performs tasks similar to the original learning task. If the teacher notes poor performance at this step, it may be necessary to reteach the original task through presentation and practice or to devise a new instructional sequence in which generalization of skills or information is taught directly. Application generalizes previous learning.

The teacher directs instruction by selecting the desired student behavior, arranging instructional antecedents, and providing consequences such as feedback regarding performance accuracy. Even though the teacher is the instructional manager, student factors that influence learning must also be considered. Several of these are described in Table 4–1. In addition, the principles of teaching discussed in the following sections should guide the instructional process.

Before proceeding, it is important to differentiate between direct instruction and an alternative approach, **discovery learning.** In discovery learning, information and skills are not taught directly.

Instead, the teacher arranges the learning environment and students explore that environment as they attempt to discover the facts, concepts, principles, and skills that make up the school curriculum. For example, many proponents of the whole language approach to reading and writing instruction recommend discovery learning (Gersten & Dimino, 1993; Keefe & Keefe, 1993; Mather, 1992). Students are expected to become proficient readers and writers by "exposure to and participation in many experiences involving written language" (Richeck in Lerner, Cousin, & Richeck, 1992, p. 227), not through direct teaching.

Unfortunately, some students do not succeed in programs in which discovery learning is the norm (Gersten & Dimino, 1993). Students with mild disabilities and others at risk for academic learning problems are more likely to succeed when instruction is presented using the principles of direct teaching (Vergason & Anderegg, 1991). As Morsink and Lenk (1992) point out, effective instruction of students with special needs can take place in any setting, general education or special, if teachers "(a) engage in teacher-directed instruction, (b) provide students with opportunities for active academic responding, (c) use high rates of contingent reinforcement, and (d) adapt teaching strategies to accommodate individual differences" (p. 36).

Select Appropriate Learning Tasks

Selection of the learning task is a critical instructional decision. No matter how excellent the teaching procedures, instruction will not be effective if the task selected is inappropriate for the learner. Task selection is even more critical for students with special needs because they may learn new information and skills more slowly than their peers. The teacher should select the most important portions of the general education curriculum as target behaviors. In making these decisions, priority should be given to skills and information that are useful both now and in the future. Special educators often use the term *functional* to refer to such learning tasks, whereas general educators talk about *authentic* tasks.

TABLE 4–1
Facilitating Learning

Factor	Principle
Meaningfulness	A student is more likely to be motivated to learn things that are meaningful to him or her.
Prerequisites	A student is more likely to learn something new if he or she has all the prerequisites.
Modeling	A student is more likely to acquire a new behavior if he or she is presented with a model performance to watch and imitate.
Open communication	A student is more likely to learn if the medium used in the learning situation is structured so that the teacher's messages are open to the learner's inspection.
Novelty	A student is more likely to learn if his or her attention is attracted by relatively novel presentations.
Active appropriate practice	A student is more likely to learn if he or she takes an active part in practice geared to reach an instructional objective.
Distributing practice	A student is more likely to learn if practice is done in short periods over time.
Fading	A student is more likely to learn if instructional prompts are withdrawn gradually.
Pleasant conditions and consequences	A student is more likely to learn if the instructional conditions are pleasant.

Note. From "General Principles of Learning and Motivation" by N. A. Carlson, 1980, *Teaching Exceptional Children, 12,* pp. 60–62. Copyright 1980 by The Council for Exceptional Children. Adapted by permission.

In addition, tasks should be described as precisely as possible. Some, such as Mager (1984), advocate the use of instructional objectives, which are statements of the desired student behavior in specific, observable terms. They spell out the conditions under which the behavior should occur and the criterion for successful performance of the behavior. Objectives help clarify the goals of instruction. Unlike broad goals such as "Students will become better readers," instructional objectives are stated with precision: "When presented with a 100-word passage from a book or story written at the grade 3 level, students will read the passage aloud with no more than 5 word recognition errors."

After the desired student behavior is identified, the teacher chooses instructional activities to present the skills and information required for task performance. Most teachers use commercial programs and supplement them with teacher-made materials and activities. The teacher must be sure that ready-made programs present all necessary skills and information and do not include extraneous or irrelevant material. The teacher must also consider current performance level when placing a student in a program sequence. For example, grade 9 texts may not be appropriate for ninth graders who read at the seventh grade level. Students should be placed in educational programs at a level at which they can succeed, that is, their instructional level.

Break the Learning Task into Teachable Subcomponents

Tasks often require several skills or many different kinds of information for successful performance. Sometimes, particularly with commercial education programs, **task analysis**—the breaking down of tasks into smaller subtasks—is necessary. When the components of the task are identified, they can be presented to students in a systematic fashion. First, the prerequisites for learning the task should be considered. For example, students who have not learned to solve multiplication problems will encounter difficulty in calculating the area of a room. If necessary prerequisite skills are not present, instruction should begin with them. Next, the

learning task is divided into subtasks. The subtasks may be a series of sequential steps or a collection of important subskills. An example of a task that can be broken into steps is addition of three-digit numbers; first the numbers in the ones column are added, then the numbers in the tens column, and finally the numbers in the hundreds column. Other tasks made up of a sequence of subtasks are building a model and locating a reference in the library. Writing a friendly letter is a task that can be divided into component subskills: handwriting (or keyboarding), spelling, capitalization, punctuation, and paragraph writing. Other such tasks are telling time, making change, and reading with comprehension.

The identification of subtasks and subskills allows the teacher to make decisions about the order in which skills and information will be presented. With tasks that are sequential in nature, subtasks are generally taught in the order in which they occur. With tasks made up of several components, the easier subskills are presented first. For example, in cursive writing instruction, simpler letters, such as lowercase *a* and *o*, are taught before more difficult letters, such as uppercase *F* and *G*.

Use Systematic Instructional Procedures

Effective instruction follows the demonstration-prompt-practice model. After the teacher presents a demonstration or explanation of the skills and information necessary for performance of the learning task, the student attempts to perform the task with prompts or assistance from the teacher. The student then **practices** the task independently. In other words, presentation is followed by guided practice, then independent practice.

In **demonstration,** the teacher may model the performance of new skills. If factual information is being presented, the teacher may simply tell students the new material. For example, in mathematics instruction, teachers can model appropriate performance by stating a fact or a rule, performing a task as students watch and listen, or asking one student a question while others observe (Lloyd & Keller, 1989). When information is conceptual, principles and examples are used to aid in explanation

A n objective, according to *Webster's New Collegiate Dictionary,* is "something
   toward which effort is directed; an aim, goal, or end of action." In education,
objectives clearly state the aim of instruction. Their purpose is to direct the
teacher in the selection of instructional activities.

Writing clear and useful instructional objectives is not an easy task. One common mistake is confusing objectives with goals. Goal statements are less specific
than objectives; they generally describe only the behavior of interest and the
direction in which the behavior should change.

Goal: By the end of the school year, Jaime will increase his sight word vocabulary.
Goal: Next semester Susie will be absent from school fewer days.

Instructional objectives, in contrast, are much more detailed. They include specific information about the exact behavior in question, the conditions under which
the behavior should occur, and the criterion for successful performance of the
behavior (Mager, 1984).

Objective: When given a simple job application form,
                    (*conditions*)

              Jack will write his complete name and address
                    (*behavior*)

              in legible handwriting with no errors in spelling.
                    (*mastery criterion*)

One of the most important (and most difficult) steps in writing objectives is
stating student behaviors in observable and measurable terms. The statement
"Louise will write her name" is observable, but "Henry will know the meaning of all
new vocabulary words" is not. Look at the lists of words below. The "observables"
are action verbs; you can easily see whether someone is writing or walking. The
"nonobservables" cannot be seen; it is not possible to see whether someone is
understanding, knowing, or appreciating.

Observables	*Nonobservables*
Write a letter	Understand subtraction
Point to the answer	Know state geography
Say the alphabet	Appreciate sculpture
Read aloud from the text	Realize the importance of budgeting
Raise hand to volunteer	Differentiate hand tools
Look at the teacher	Attend to class lectures
Name the U.S. presidents	Perceive the main idea
Draw a triangle	Draw conclusions

(Kameenui & Simmons, 1990). In one method (Close, Irvin, Taylor, & Agosta, 1981), the teacher presents new concepts directly, then cites relevant examples; guided practice is provided when students answer direct questions, and then the teacher repeats and summarizes the original presentation.

In the prompt or **guided practice** stage, students are given opportunities to perform the task under the supervision of the teacher. This should occur before independent practice to ensure that students do not practice incorrect responses. In guided practice, the teacher gives immediate feedback to students regarding the accuracy of their responses; correct responses are confirmed, and incorrect responses are corrected. This step can be done individually, with small groups, or with the entire class. For example, the teacher can present new material to the class and then conduct a short question-and-answer session with all students. Stevens and Rosenshine (1981) recommend this technique and advocate the use of factual questions and whole-group unison responses.

In **independent practice,** the teacher continues to provide students with feedback or knowledge of results. Because this form of practice usually takes place in individual work sessions in class or as homework assignments, the time delay between student performance and feedback from the teacher is greater.

Direct teaching is another important feature of effective instruction. Skills are taught directly, and teaching activities are designed to be as close to the instructional goal as possible. For example, if the goal is for students to read words aloud, the teacher does not include activities such as matching words with pictures, looking up words in the dictionary, or writing sentences using the words. Instead, the teacher models, and students practice, reading words aloud.

Two other major considerations are maximizing the number of student responses and monitoring the accuracy of student performance. First, because students learn by responding, it is important to maximize the number of response opportunities available to each student. The goal is as many student responses as possible within given time limits. Second, because

students learn by receiving information about the quality of their responses, it is important to monitor student performance by the frequent collection of data. Teachers (and students themselves) should collect information about the number and accuracy of student responses; this should occur frequently, even daily, but at the minimum once a week. This information provides feedback to both students and teachers. If the total number of student responses or the proportion of correct responses becomes low, the teacher can modify the instructional procedures.

Effective instructional strategies can be incorporated into any type of teaching situation for any age learner. Rosenshine and Stevens (1986) suggest that there are six fundamental steps that teachers should follow in the instructional sequence:

1. Review, check previous day's work (and reteach, if necessary)
2. Present new content/skills
3. Guide student practice (and check for understanding)
4. Feedback and correctives (and reteach, if necessary)
5. Independent student practice
6. Weekly and monthly reviews (p. 379)

This sequence is based on the demonstration-prompt-practice model; it is easily adapted to any subject matter area and is equally appropriate for elementary and secondary students. For more information about the specific procedures for each step, consult Figure 4–2.

Archer and Gleason (1989a) suggest that lessons based on the demonstration-prompt-practice model be divided into three important components:

1. *Opening of the lesson.* The teacher gains the attention of the students and reviews any skills or knowledge areas critical to the content of the lesson. Then, he or she states the goal of the lesson and tells why the skill to be learned is important and when and where it will be used.
2. *Body of the lesson.* The teacher models the new skill and provides two types of guided practice: prompt and check. First, the teacher uses prompting to assist students in performing the new skill. Second, the teacher checks the students' progress by having them perform the new skill without assistance. According to Archer and Gleason

Direct Teaching

*I*f you wish to teach spelling skills, here is one direct instruction method you can use. Be sure to select words that the students know the meaning of and can read. Then teach spelling.

Teacher:	Let's spell the word *avalanche.* Watch me.
	(Teacher writes a word on board and says letter names.)
	A-v-a-l-a-n-c-h-e, avalanche. Everyone say that with me.
Teacher and students:	*A-v-a-l-a-n-c-h-e, avalanche.*
Teacher:	Right. *Avalanche* is spelled *a-v-a-l-a-n-c-h-e.* Now, everyone, write *avalanche* on your paper.
Students:	(Students write word.)
Teacher:	Did you write *a-v-a-l-a-n-c-h-e, avalanche?* Good! Everyone say it with me.
Teacher and students:	*A-v-a-l-a-n-c-h-e, avalanche.*
Teacher:	*Avalanche* is spelled *a-v-a-l-a-n-c-h-e.* Now, turn your paper over and write *avalanche.*
Students:	(Students write word.)
Teacher:	Did you write *a-v-a-l-a-n-c-h-e, avalanche?* Good spelling.

This presentation requires only 2 or 3 minutes. In this short time the teacher has modeled the spelling of the word for the class once by writing it and five times orally. Students have spelled the word twice orally, have written it twice, and have been provided with immediate feedback each time. In just a few minutes each student in the class can be provided with several response opportunities.

(1989a), with simpler skills, "MODEL, PROMPT and CHECK can occur in quick succession (e.g., *'This word is* against. *Say the word with me. What word?')*" (p. 5).

3. *Close of the lesson.* The teacher ends the lesson by reviewing the critical information presented and providing a preview of the next lesson. Then students are assigned work for independent practice.

Consider Both Speed and Accuracy

In selecting and describing learning tasks, teachers should determine whether the instructional goal is rapid or accurate performance. This decision influences both presentation and practice.

For most learning tasks, particularly those that involve skills, both speed and accuracy are desired. The teacher demonstrates rapid, accurate performance; students practice for accuracy first and then speed. It is imperative in skill acquisition to provide practice that ensures that students acquire both accuracy and speed. If skills such as reading and writing are performed slowly, their usefulness decreases.

In skill acquisition, initial practice activities emphasize accuracy. Research suggests that students should achieve a 70% to 90% success rate during guided practice and at least a 90% success rate during independent practice (Englert, 1984; Rieth & Evertson, 1988; Rosenshine & Stevens, 1986). How-

FIGURE 4–2
Steps in Instruction

1. **Daily Review and Checking Homework**

   Checking homework (routines for students to check each other's papers)

   Reteaching when necessary

   Reviewing relevant past learning (may include questioning)

   Review prerequisite skills (if applicable)

2. **Presentation**

   Provide short statement of objectives

   Provide overview and structuring

   Proceed in small steps but at a rapid pace

   Intersperse questions within the demonstration to check for understanding

   Highlight main points

   Provide sufficient illustrations and concrete examples

   Provide demonstrations and models

   When necessary, give detailed and redundant instructions and examples

3. **Guided Practice**

   Initial student practice takes place with teacher guidance

   High frequency of questions and overt student practice (from teacher and/or materials)

   Questions are directly relevant to the new content or skill

   Teacher checks for understanding (CFU) by evaluating student responses

   During CFU teacher gives additional explanation, process feedback, or repeats explanation—where necessary

   All students have a chance to respond and receive feedback; teacher insures that all students participate

   Prompts are provided during guided practice (where appropriate)

   Initial student practice is *sufficient* so that students can work independently

   Guided practice continues until students are firm

   Guided practice is continued (usually) until a success rate of 80% is achieved

4. **Correctives and Feedback**

   Quick, firm, and correct responses can be followed by another question or a short acknowledgment of correctness (i.e., "That's right")

---

ever, instruction should not stop with achievement of accuracy; further guided practice stressing speed should be given. This approach helps develop automatic responses that are both quick and accurate and also helps prevent students from acquiring slow response habits.

Maximize Engaged Time

Engaged time refers to the minutes and hours during which students are actively involved and partici-

pating in instruction. During that time they are "on task," whether that means listening to the teacher, watching a science experiment, answering the teacher's questions, reading, or writing. As engaged time increases, learning increases.

Students are engaged in learning for only certain portions of the school day because many noninstructional activities intrude. Even during time allocated for instruction, student attention may be directed elsewhere (Bulgren & Carta, 1992). In one study (Karweit & Slavin, 1981), actual instruction in elementary mathematics classes accounted for only

Hesitant correct answers might be followed by process feedback (i.e., "Yes, Linda, that's right because . . .")

Student errors indicate a need for more practice

Monitor students for systematic errors

Try to obtain a substantive response to each question

Corrections can include sustaining feedback (i.e., simplifying the question, giving clues), explaining or reviewing steps, giving process feedback, or reteaching the last steps

Try to elicit an improved response when the first one is incorrect

Guided practice and corrections continue until the teacher feels that the group can meet the objectives of the lesson

Praise should be used in moderation, and specific praise is more effective than general praise

5. **Independent Practice (Seatwork)**

Sufficient practice

Practice is directly relevant to skills/content taught

Practice to overlearning

Practice until responses are firm, quick, and automatic

Ninety-five percent correct rate during independent practice

Students alerted that seatwork will be checked

Students held accountable for seatwork

Actively supervise students, when possible

6. **Weekly and Monthly Reviews**

Systematic review of previously learned material

Include review in homework

Frequent tests

Reteaching of material missed in tests

Note: With older, more mature learners, or learners with more knowledge of the subject, the following adjustments can be made: (1) the size of the step in presentation can be larger (more material is presented at one time), (2) there is less time spent on teacher-guided practice and (3) the amount of overt practice can be decreased, replacing it with covert rehearsal, restating and reviewing.

Note. From B. Rosenshine and R. Stevens, "Teaching Functions." Reprinted with permission of Macmillan Publishing Company from *Handbook of Research on Teaching*, Third Edn., Merlin C. Wittrock, Editor, pp. 376-391. Copyright © 1986 by the American Educational Research Association.

81% of the scheduled instructional time, and students were found to be engaged during only 68% of the time scheduled for instruction. Student inattention accounted for the greatest loss of learning time.

Similar results are reported by other researchers. In a study of regular classrooms, although 78% of class time was allocated to instruction, mainstreamed special students were actively engaged only 63% of that time (Rich & Ross, 1989). Christenson and Ysseldyke (1986) compared regular classes and resource rooms and found that, regardless of the setting, students with learning disabilities and their peers spent less than 30 minutes of a 95-minute instructional period actively responding to academic tasks.

Student engagement can be increased in several ways. First, teachers should make full use of scheduled instructional time. Other activities such as clerical and housekeeping chores should not be done during the time allotted to teaching and learning. Make every minute count!

Second, teachers should emphasize instruction rather than independent practice. Research indicates that students show much higher engagement

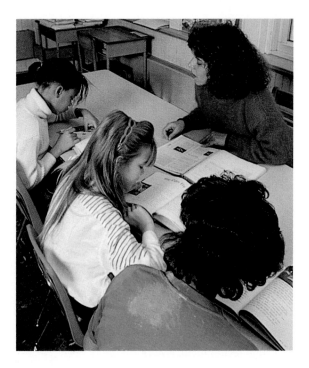

all of the students in the group respond in unison to questions posed by the teacher. Heward, Courson, and Narayan (1989) recommend including several brief (5- to 10-minute) choral response sessions throughout the school day for different academic subjects. The questions asked should require short answers (no more than three words), and only one correct response should be possible. Another technique is group writing. The teacher asks a question or poses a problem (e.g., "What does the word *democracy* mean?"), and each student writes his or her response. Class members then discuss their answers and make corrections, as needed.

Englert (1984) presents several suggestions of ways to increase the amount of class time allocated to learning and methods for promoting student engagement during allocated learning time. The teacher checklist in Figure 4–3 summarizes these suggestions. For instance, teachers should spend at least 80% of class time in instructional activities and interact with 70% or more of their students each hour.

Give Clear Task Directions

For students to succeed, the directions for the learning task must be clearly stated and understandable. Before giving directions, the teacher should be sure that students are paying attention. Directions can be presented orally, in written form, or both. If directions are complicated and contain a number of steps, they should be broken down into subsets. For example, teachers who say, "Get out your math book and a sheet of paper, turn to page 46, do the even-numbered problems in Section A, the odd-numbered problems in Section C, and the first three story problems at the top of page 47" will likely find that their directions are not followed.

Directions can be simplified by presenting only one portion at a time and by writing each portion on the chalkboard as well as stating it orally. When using written directions, the teacher must be sure that students are able to read and understand the words and comprehend the meaning of the sentences. Also, directions should be presented immediately preceding the learning task (Rosenkoetter & Fowler, 1986). Students beginning an assignment at

rates in teacher-led activities than in seatwork tasks (Rieth & Evertson, 1988).

Third, instruction should be designed to engage student attention. Materials and activities should be selected so that they are attractive, interesting to students, and at an appropriate level of difficulty. The length of the lesson should be neither too short nor too long; if the lesson is too long, student interest and attention may decline. The pace of instruction should be brisk. While not rushing students, the teacher should ensure that instruction proceeds at an energetic tempo with few pauses, hesitations, interruptions, or opportunities for boredom.

Fourth, engagement increases when students are required to respond. Students should be provided with as many response opportunities as possible; students actively involved in asking and answering lesson-related questions are engaged in learning. Maximum response opportunities that result in high proportions of correct responses are basic to successful instruction.

Group responding is one way to increase the number of active student responses. In **choral responding,**

FIGURE 4–3
Are You Making Optimal Use of Class Time?

Respond to each item in terms of the extent to which it describes yourself: (1) not at all descriptive, (2) descriptive to a small extent, (3) descriptive to a moderate extent, (4) descriptive to a large extent, (5) descriptive to an extremely large extent.

Competencies

Allocated Time

		Performance Evaluation
1.1	Maximizes time in instruction by continually scheduling students in direct instruction (e.g., interacts with 70% or more of the students per hour).	1 2 3 4 5
1.2	Minimizes time in non-instructional activities (e.g., spends 80% or more of class time in instructional activities).	1 2 3 4 5
1.3	Keeps transition time between lessons short (e.g., no more than 3 minutes between change of students and activity; no more than 30 seconds when a change of activity only).	1 2 3 4 5
1.4	Established procedures for lessons that signal a clear beginning and end.	1 2 3 4 5
1.5	Gains all students' attention at the beginning of the lesson and maintains student attention during lesson at 90% level.	1 2 3 4 5
1.6	Prepares students for transitions in advance by stating behavioral expectations and informing students that lesson is drawing to a close.	1 2 3 4 5

Engaged Time

2.1	Maintains students' attention during seatwork at 80% levels or higher.	1 2 3 4 5
2.2	Monitors seatwork students continuously through eye scanning.	1 2 3 4 5
2.3	Circulates among seatwork students between lessons to assist students and to monitor progress.	1 2 3 4 5
2.4	Maintains seatwork accuracy at 90% level or higher.	1 2 3 4 5
2.5	Tells rationale for seatwork and communicates the importance of the assignment.	1 2 3 4 5
2.6	Provides active forms of seatwork practice clearly related to academic goals.	1 2 3 4 5
2.7	Sets seatwork and assignment standards (neatness, accuracy, due dates).	1 2 3 4 5
2.8	Uses tutoring (e.g., peer, volunteers, aides) and other specialized instructional technology to increase opportunity for active academic responding during seatwork.	1 2 3 4 5
2.9	Establishes procedures for early finishers, students who are stalled, and those seeking help.	1 2 3 4 5
2.10	Schedules time to review seatwork.	1 2 3 4 5
2.11	Requires that students correct work and make up missed or unfinished work.	1 2 3 4 5
2.12	Gives informative feedback to students in making written or verbal corrections.	1 2 3 4 5

Note. From "Measuring Teacher Effectiveness from the Teacher's Point of View" by C. S. Englert, 1984, *Focus on Exceptional Children, 17*(2), p. 9. Copyright 1984 by Love. Reprinted by permission.

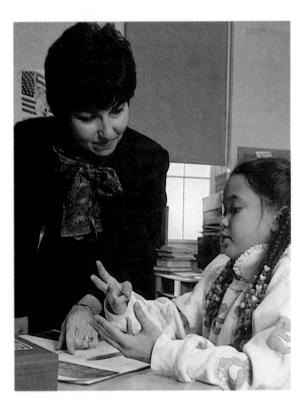

loss of teacher attention and praise or other unpleasant consequences. Because behaviors followed by pleasant consequences are more likely to occur again, teachers should make a systematic effort to reward successful task performance.

One powerful consequence is feedback to the student or **knowledge of results.** The student responds, and the teacher comments about the accuracy of the response; correct answers are confirmed, and incorrect answers are corrected. Students provided with information about the acceptability of their responses tend to modify their performances to increase the number of correct responses. Eventually they begin monitoring their own performances rather than relying on teacher feedback. Suggested ways of providing feedback are listed in "Tips for the Teacher" on page 108.

In addition to knowledge of results, other types of consequences can be used. Teachers can reward successful task performance with attention, praise, and compliments; with letter or number grades; with recognition of the student's accomplishment before peers or parents; and with awards, privileges, and special activities.

Consequences, like instructional antecedents, are powerful tools for promoting successful classroom performance, and their use will be described in more depth in the next chapter. However, consequences must be used systematically. They should follow behaviors as closely in time as possible, especially when students are in the acquisition stage of learning. Consequences should also be used consistently. Behaviors confirmed as correct and rewarded on one day should receive the same consequences on the next day.

10 A.M. are not likely to recall or follow the directions given by the teacher at 9:30 A.M.

Teachers can determine whether directions are clear by attending to feedback from students. Puzzled expressions and failure to follow the directions are immediate cues that directions are unclear. If students are asked to repeat the directions to the teacher, misunderstandings become apparent. Clear directions are an important part of effective instruction, and clarity is one of the teacher characteristics most valued by students. Figure 4–4 presents a checklist for students to use in assessing their teachers' clarity.

Provide Consequences for Successful Task Performance

In most classrooms, a variety of consequences are available for the teacher's use. Successful task performance may be followed by teacher attention, praise, special privileges, or awards. Unsuccessful performance, on the other hand, may result in the

Check for Maintenance and Generalization

The majority of the time spent in instruction is devoted to acquisition of skills and information. However, if students are to use what they have learned in later school and life situations, maintenance and generalization are also important. It cannot be assumed that tasks performed successfully today will also be performed successfully next week,

FIGURE 4–4
The Clear Teacher Checklist

As your teacher I hope I am clear. In order to improve my ability to be clear I need your help. Below are 28 statements that describe what clear teachers do. Read each statement and place a check mark in the column that tells how often I perform the behavior that is described. In that way I'll know what I do well and what I need to improve.

(Put a check ✓ in one box after each statement.)

As our teacher, you:

	All of the time	Most of the time	Some of the time	Never	Doesn't apply to our class
1. Explain things simply.					
2. Give explanations we understand.					
3. Teach at a pace that is not too fast and not too slow.					
4. Stay with a topic until we understand.					
5. Try to find out when we don't understand and then you repeat things.					
6. Teach things step-by-step.					
7. Describe the work to be done and how to do it.					
8. Ask if we know what to do and how to do it.					
9. Repeat things when we don't understand.					
10. Explain something and then work an example.					
11. Explain something and then stop so we can ask questions.					
12. Prepare us for what we will be doing next.					
13. Give specific details when teaching.					
14. Repeat things that are hard to understand.					
15. Work examples and explain them.					
16. Give us a chance to think about what's being taught.					
17. Explain something and then stop so we can think about it.					
18. Show us how to do the work.					
19. Explain the assignment and the materials we need to do it.					
20. Stress difficult points.					
21. Show examples of how to do classwork and homework.					
22. Give us enough time for practice.					
23. Answer our questions.					
24. Ask questions to find out if we understand.					
25. Go over difficult homework problems.					
26. Show us how to remember things.					
27. Explain how to do assignments by using examples.					
28. Show us the difference between things.					

"The Clear Teacher Checklist" is based substantially on research findings contained in the article by Kennedy et al. in *Journal of Educational Research,* Sept./Oct. 1978.

Note. From *Practical Application of Research,* 1981, 3(3), p. 4. Copyright 1981 by Phi Delta Kappa's Center on Evaluation, Development, and Research, Bloomington, IN. Reprinted by permission.

Providing Students with Feedback

- When students respond correctly, tell them! A simple "Yes," "Right," "Good," or "Correct" lets a learner know that the answer was on target.
- If a student's response is correct but hesitant, the teacher should provide process feedback. The response is confirmed and the teacher explains why it was correct. For example, the teacher might say, "Yes, John, that's correct. The first word in every sentence begins with a capital."
- If students give incorrect responses, again they should be told. The teacher can say "No" or "Not quite." If the teacher believes a student answered incorrectly because he or she did not understand the question or was not paying attention, the question should be repeated.
- The next step is the use of a correction procedure. After making the student aware that the response was incorrect, the teacher should help the student produce the correct answer. The teacher can model the correct response.

Teacher:	Spell *this.*
Student:	*T-h-e-s.*
Teacher:	No, *this* is spelled *t-h-i-s.* Spell *this.*
Student:	*T-h-i-s.*
Teacher:	Right!

With some learning tasks a prompt can be given.

Teacher:	Read this word: *shut.*
Student:	*Cut.*
Teacher:	Not quite. The first sound is *sh.* Read it again.
Student:	*Shut.*
Teacher:	Good reading.

Or the task can be made easier.

Teacher:	Who was the first president of the United States?
Student:	Lincoln.
Teacher:	No. Was it George Washington or Thomas Jefferson?
Student:	Washington.
Teacher:	Correct.

Knowledge of results is a powerful tool for helping students learn. However, when students make errors, feedback alone is not sufficient. To help students learn the correct response, correction procedures must also be used.

next month, or next semester. Acquisition does not guarantee maintenance. Skills and information, particularly those that are verbal in nature, are forgotten if not practiced. To enhance maintenance, task performance should be monitored over time, and practice should be provided when necessary.

Generalization cannot be assumed, either. Students may perform quite well on one task but be unable to transfer their learning to a similar task. For example, words spelled correctly on a spelling test may be misspelled in a book report or essay. Generalization is crucial because there is insufficient time to teach all the possible situations in which particular skills and information may be needed. Teachers can promote transfer by evaluating its occurrence; if necessary, the teacher can demonstrate how skills and information are used in many different situations and then provide students with practice in generalization.

If Change Is Needed, Try the Least Intrusive Intervention First

Data on student performance may indicate the need for a change in instructional procedures. Student responses may be infrequent, inconsistent, or less accurate than desired. To increase the likelihood of successful performance, the learning task is made easier—by changing teaching procedures, modifying materials and activities, or altering task requirements. Several ways of accomplishing this are described later in this chapter.

However, unsuccessful performance should not result in the immediate substitution of an alternate task. First, the original task should be modified in an attempt to increase response accuracy. The simplest, least dramatic changes should be tried first; for instance, task failure may be due to insufficient practice or poor understanding of the directions. Intense interventions such as radically different instructional procedures, new materials and activities, or abandonment of the original task should be used only when all other options have been exhausted.

The principles of instruction presented here apply to learners of all ages and all ability levels.

The instructional technique used to help you learn these principles has been direct presentation with occasional examples. Another appropriate technique is the use of nonexemplars, or examples of noninstances. In teaching colors, we show students several examples of red and then introduce the concept of nonred by showing blue, yellow, green, and pink objects. See Figure 4–5 for nonexemplars of effective instructional strategies.

It is possible for teachers to use effective instructional techniques but to apply these techniques unequally with different groups of students. Research indicates that teachers treat high achievers and low achievers quite differently. For example, in one study (Alves & Gottlieb, 1986), teachers in mainstreamed classrooms interacted less frequently with students with disabilities than with their classmates without disabilities. Students with disabilities also were asked fewer questions by their teachers and received less feedback on their performance. For instruction to be truly effective, it must address the needs of all students within the classroom.

■ METHODS FOR GATHERING DATA

Information about student performance helps the teacher make instructional decisions. For example, data are gathered to determine the student's current level of academic performance before instruction begins. Such information aids in planning the educational program and placing the student in the correct portion of the instructional sequence. During instruction, data are used to evaluate student progress and to explore reasons for poor performance; this information helps to determine whether instructional adaptations should be made.

Although many types of assessment techniques are available, in most cases informal assessment rather than formal testing is the method of choice for gathering information about a student's classroom performance. One approach to informal assessment is **curriculum-based assessment** (CBA), which Gickling and Thompson (1985) define as "a procedure for determining the instructional needs

FIGURE 4–5
Common Mistakes in Instruction

Inappropriate Instructional Strategy	Example
Instructional content is presented sporadically, rather than sequentially and systematically over time.	The teacher presents an exercise demonstrating syllabication of words. He provides a verbal description of the process and written exercises which he scores. The next day a different concept is taught. Observation shows that syllabication activities are taught again 2 weeks later; the same procedure is used.
Well-written instructional activities are followed by nonspecific evaluation.	Although the teacher develops written lesson plans complete with behavioral objectives and teaching procedures, the evaluation component generally consists of such global statements as "It seems to go pretty well" or "I should make the material more relevant."
Conditions for independent seatwork are not stated clearly.	The teacher initiates and leads a group. Five minutes later Ruthie approaches the teacher and asks for help with her seatwork. The teacher excuses herself to help Ruthie. An observer notes that reading is resumed but is interrupted five more times in the 15-minute reading session.
Reading activities are geared to frustration rather than to comprehension level.	The teacher asks Dotty to read a three-paragraph (64-word) selection during an individual instruction session in a resource room. An observer's record shows that the teacher supplied (read) 22 words that Dotty failed to read.
Children's error rates are consistently high.	Tommy hands in a math exercise, and the teacher says, "OK." Observation reveals that he made 7 errors in the set of 15 problems. A question elicits this response: "Oh, he knows that; it's just sloppy work." No data are available to confirm or deny the statement.
Additional learning trials are presented after criterion has been met.	Mark, a 10-year-old member of a class for educable mentally retarded children, proudly reads his primer to an observer. A question reveals that he has been reading it without error for the last 2 weeks.

Note. From "A Teacher's Guide to Instructional Programming" by J. W. Tawney, C. G. Kruse, P. T. Cegelka, and D. L. Kelly, 1977, *Teaching Exceptional Children, 10,* pp. 2–6. Copyright 1977 by The Council for Exceptional Children. Adapted by permission.

of students based on the student's ongoing performance in existing course content" (p. 206). That is, the curriculum of the student's classroom is used as the yardstick by which to measure educational progress. Results of such assessments have immediate instructional applications. Skills that the student has not yet mastered become the next goals in the instructional sequence. The sections that follow provide principles for gathering useful information about student performance.

Determine the Student's Current Levels of Performance

Before beginning instruction, teachers are interested in finding out what skills have already been acquired by the student. The group achievement tests given routinely to students in many school districts are one source of this information. Measures such as the *Comprehensive Tests of Basic Skills*, the *Metropolitan Achievement Tests*, and the *Stanford Achievement Tests* provide information about the level of performance in basic skills such as reading and mathematics. For example, results may indicate that a sixth grade student is performing at a fifth grade level in reading comprehension, a sixth grade level in mathematics, and a fourth grade level in written language.

Stone, Cundick, and Swanson (1988) suggest that results of group achievement tests can be used to identify students who may need interventions such as special education. They recommend using the 5th percentile as a cutoff point. Percentile rank scores indicate the percentage of a test's norm group that a particular student's performance equals or exceeds. Thus, a student scoring at the 5th percentile would show achievement equal to or better than 5% of norm group peers (and worse than 95% of that group).

Reynolds, Zetlin, and Wang (1993) recommend a somewhat different procedure, "20/20 Analysis." Results of group achievement tests are studied to identify two groups of students who benefit from adaptations of the general education program: (a) students with learning problems, defined as students who fall in the lowest 20% (i.e., below the 20th percentile), and (b) high achievers, defined as students who fall in the highest 20% (above the 80th percentile).

Because student achievement levels change over time, only recent achievement test results are of interest. However, even recent test data should be considered with caution because test tasks may differ from classroom learning tasks. Also, some students do not perform to the best of their ability on tests administered in group settings. In general, standardized measures such as group achievement tests are not the best source of information about current levels of performance; instead, more informal measures such as placement tests, inventories, and criterion-referenced tests should be used.

Measures of current student performance are provided in many commercial educational programs and textbook series. These placement tests assess the student's skill levels and provide information about where in the educational program the student should begin. If these measures are not available, the teacher can devise informal assessments such as inventories and criterion-referenced tests.

Inventories are measures that sample a variety of different skills and information within a subject matter area. They are designed to estimate the approximate level of student functioning. For instance, an informal math inventory would not assess all aspects of a mathematics curriculum. However, it might include a range of problems sampling knowledge of basic number facts, skills in basic operations (addition, subtraction, multiplication, and division), and ability to solve problems requiring regrouping. Student performance on this inventory would give the teacher some information about which skills have been acquired and which have not. An informal handwriting inventory appears in Figure 4–6; this measure provides general information about current levels of performance in the skill area of handwriting.

For more specific data, more precise measures are necessary. **Criterion-referenced tests** assess whether students have mastered the educational goals stated in instructional objectives. The teacher selects an objective, sets up the necessary conditions, and sees whether students are able to perform well enough to meet the criterion for acceptable performance. For

FIGURE 4–6
Handwriting Inventory

Print your name on the line below.

Fill in the missing letters.

a cd fg ij l no qr tu w y

Print the uppercase (capital) letter that goes with each of the lowercase (small) letters below.

a A

b ___   f ___   d ___

g ___   r ___

Copy this sentence in your best printing.

Foxes and rabbits are quick, but turtles are slow.

Write your name in cursive on the line below.

Finish writing the cursive alphabet.

a b c

Write the following words in cursive.

dog ___   like ___   and ___   the ___

Write this sentence in your best cursive handwriting.

At the zoo you can see lions and tigers, elephants, bears, and monkeys.

FIGURE 4–7
Observations of Academic Performance

Student: Juan

Subject: Science 9

Task: Homework Assignments

Day	Number of Questions	Number of Responses	Number of Correct Responses	Percentage of Correct Responses
Monday	7	7	3	43%
Tuesday	9	9	4	44%
Wednesday	6	6	3	50%
Thursday	10	10	5	50%
Friday	8	8	3	38%

example, to determine mastery of the objective "Students will write the names of at least 45 of the states with no errors in spelling," the teacher simply directs students to write the name of each of the states. Responses are acceptable if they are state names and if they are spelled correctly. Students with fewer than 45 correct responses have not yet met the objective and should receive further instruction.

Evaluate Progress

Information about student performance during instruction provides the teacher with feedback about the effectiveness of teaching procedures. Before instruction begins, it is important to pretest students to establish a performance baseline. This initial performance then becomes the reference point for evaluating progress in the instructional program.

Systematic observation is a useful technique for monitoring pupil progress. As chapter 5 will explain, observation is a flexible technique that can be used with a variety of student behaviors. In academic instruction, observation generally focuses on the number of responses made by the student and the proportion (or percentage) of correct responses. Figure 4–7 presents an example in which the teacher observed Juan's performance on science assignments for a 1-week period. Although Juan answered all the questions, the proportion of correct responses never rose above 50%. Thus, the teacher will modify instruction in an attempt to increase response accuracy.

As discussed in chapter 3, curriculum-based measurement is an effective strategy for monitoring student progress (Deno, 1985, 1987; Fuchs, 1986, 1987; Howell, Fox, & Morehead, 1993). Deno and Fuchs (1987) describe the procedures needed to establish a system of curriculum-based measurement in the classroom. The teacher decides what to measure and how to measure it, then formulates a specific instructional goal and objective. In the example provided by Deno and Fuchs (1987), the goal is

In 19 weeks, when presented with stories for 1 minute from Level 2-SRA series, Michael will read aloud 80 words with no more than 6 errors. (p. 13)

The accompanying objective is to increase the number of words Michael reads correctly by an average of 2.6 words per week.

The teacher assesses this student's progress by having him read randomly selected passages from his reading text for 1-minute periods. These data are collected frequently, at least twice a week. The student's performance is graphed (see Figure 4–8), and his progress is compared with the aimline, a diagonal line extending from his baseline performance to the instructional goal.

Analyze Reasons for Task Failure

When task performance is unsatisfactory, the student's responses can be analyzed to help locate problem areas. Called **error analysis,** this technique involves scoring each response as correct or incor-

---

FIGURE 4–8
Curriculum-Based Measurement

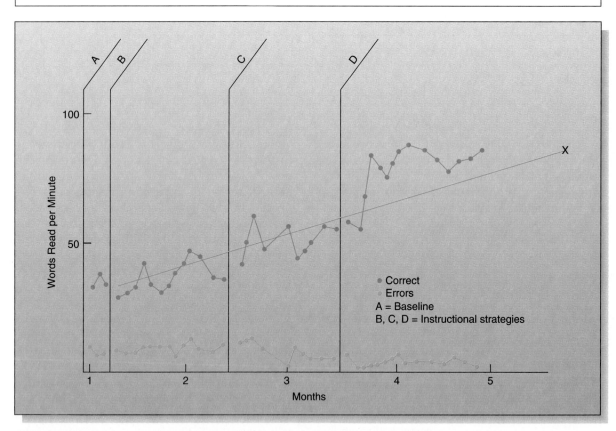

Note. From "Developing Curriculum-Based Measurement Systems for Data-Based Special Education Problem Solving" by S. L. Deno and L. S. Fuchs, 1987, *Focus on Exceptional Children, 19*(8), p. 15. Copyright 1987 by Love. Reprinted by permission.

---

rect and then looking for error patterns. For example, a student may solve only 8 of 22 addition problems correctly; by systematically analyzing the student's responses, the teacher may find that all errors involved problems requiring regrouping and that the student was using an inappropriate strategy, such as failing to carry:

$$
\begin{array}{r}
42 \\
+\ 39 \\
\hline
711
\end{array}
$$

Use the essay in Figure 4–9, which was written by a ninth grade student, to practice your error analysis skills. The punctuation errors have been analyzed for you; consider the capitalization mistakes and then the misspellings. Do you see any patterns in the errors?

If student performance is poor (few responses are made, or most of the responses are incorrect), analyzing the task rather than the specific student errors may be helpful. With task analysis, the task is broken down into component parts, and then students are asked to perform each of the parts. In this way, the subtasks that are causing the most difficulty can be identified, and instruction can begin with those areas.

FIGURE 4–9
Writing Sample for Error Analysis

Essay
last year I was in the musical "Annie get your gun" that gat me started in the preforming arts. I have tryed out for the teater to be in "annie get your gun, kismit, and music man but I didn't make it today I am trying out for a choir at the high shcool I tryed out for the wizerd of oz

Error Analysis

Punctuation

Number of periods needed in the essay _____5_____

Number of correct responses made by the student _____1_____

Percentage of correct responses made by the student _____20%_____

Capitalization

Number of capital letters needed in the essay _____

Number of correct responses made by the student _____

Percentage of correct responses made by the student _____

Spelling

Number of words written by the student _____

Number of correct responses made by the student _____

Percentage of correct responses made by the student _____

STRATEGIES FOR ADAPTING INSTRUCTION

When students have difficulty acquiring skills and information, the teacher adapts instruction to better meet the students' needs. Teachers can modify instructional materials and activities, change teaching procedures, or alter the requirements of the learning task. Several of the specific strategies for instructional adaptations appear in Figure 4–10. These should be used in an attempt to improve student performance before more involved modifications are made. Note that the strategies are arranged in numerical order from 1 to 10. Number 1 should be tried before number 2, number 2 before number 3, and so on. Of course, before these methods are used, teachers should be sure that the learning task is at an appropriate level of difficulty for the student.

Modify Materials and Activities

The first type of adaptation to try is modification of instructional materials and activities. The learning task remains the same; what is changed is the way in which the necessary skills and information are presented to the student. Three possible strategies are the clarification of task directions, addition of prompts to the learning task, and correction of specific student errors (items 1, 2, and 3 in Figure 4–10).

Clarify Task Directions.   Students may perform tasks poorly if the directions for the task are unclear. Several changes can make directions more understandable:

- Give directions both orally and in writing.
- Restate oral directions in simpler language.
- Give only one or two oral directions at a time.

FIGURE 4–10
Adapting Instruction

IF students experience difficulty in task performance,
TRY these adaptations of . . .
Materials and activities:
  1. Clarify task directions
  2. Add prompts to the learning task
  3. Teach to specific student errors
Teaching procedures:
  4. Give additional presentation of skills and information
  5. Provide additional guided practice
  6. Make consequences for successful performance more attractive
  7. Slow the pace of instruction
Task requirements:
  8. Change the criteria for successful performance
  9. Change task characteristics
 10. Break each task into smaller subtasks
BEFORE selecting an alternate task.
IF NECESSARY, substitute a similar but easier task or a prerequisite task.

- Be sure students are able to see directions written on the chalkboard.
- Keep written directions on the student's reading level.
- Explain any new or unfamiliar terms.

After giving directions, the teacher should demonstrate task performance and then answer any questions students may have.

Add Prompts.   *Prompts* or *cues* are any features added to learning tasks that assist students in task performance. Prompts can be verbal, visual, or physical and can either call attention to the cues already available in the learning task or introduce an artificial cue system.

Prompts are often used to make critical features of the learning task more noticeable. For example, if students confuse addition and subtraction symbols, teachers might circle the symbols, make them larger, write them in red, or remind students to "check each problem to see whether you add or subtract." If students read aloud without attending to punctuation, punctuation marks can be underlined, highlighted, or color-coded to make them stand out.

Artificial prompts can also be added to learning tasks. In handwriting instruction, for instance, guidelines are provided to assist beginning writers. Another example is the use of underlining; teachers who underline important words and phrases on the board are providing prompts. Teachers can also give verbal prompts or reminders; for example, before students begin to write a paragraph, the teacher might say, "Remember to begin each sentence with a capital letter."

Any learning task can be made easier by the use of prompts. However, as students learn, it is important to withdraw the prompts from the task, fading them gradually (as shown in Figure 4–11) to maintain successful student performance.

Teach to Specific Student Errors.   If students make consistent errors that affect overall task performance, the teacher should focus on the correction of those errors. This approach is effective if a few types of errors account for the majority of incorrect responses. For example, if a student writes the cursive alphabet correctly with the exception of the letters *m* and *n*, these letters should be singled out and taught directly. Or if oral reading is characterized by frequent repetitions ("I want . . . I want to go to the . . . I want to go to the store . . . I want to go to the store to buy . . ."), the teacher should attempt to correct this error. However, if task failure is due to several types of errors (or too few responses), it is probably necessary to modify the procedures used in teaching.

Change Teaching Procedures

If modification of instructional activities and materials does not result in successful performance, the next step is to adapt the teaching procedures. Strategies include additional presentation, additional practice, changing the consequences, and slowing the pace of instruction (items 4, 5, 6, and 7 in Figure 4–10).

Give Additional Presentation of Skills and Information.   An additional presentation of the skills and information necessary for task performance may be appropriate. With this strategy, the teacher demonstrates skills and explains information. A repetition of the original presentation may produce the desired results. However, the teacher must usually provide a more complete (or simpler) explanation, additional examples, or several instances in which the skill is modeled.

Provide Additional Guided Practice.   Poor task performance may be improved by additional guided practice. The teacher can increase the amount of practice by requiring more student responses, lengthening practice sessions (although not to the point of student fatigue), or scheduling extra sessions throughout the school day. To make practice more effective, teachers can increase both the amount and the quality of their feedback to students. To increase the amount, feedback can be given after every response rather than after every

FIGURE 4–11
Fading Prompts from the Learning Task

Faded visual prompts in the instruction of one-digit–plus–two-digit addition with carrying

Faded visual prompts used in the instruction of one-digit into two-digit division

Faded visual prompts used in the instruction of one-digit–times–two-digit multiplication

Faded visual prompts used in the instruction of two-digit multiplication

Note. Reprinted with permission of Merrill, an imprint of Macmillan Publishing Company, from *Teaching the Mildly Handicapped in the Regular Classroom* (2nd ed., p. 107) by J. Affleck, S. Lowenbraun, and A. Archer. Copyright © 1980 Merrill Publishing Company, Columbus, Ohio.

third or fifth answer. To increase the quality of feedback, the teacher can describe important features of the student's behavior in addition to telling the student whether the task was performed correctly. The statement "That's right. You remembered to put a period at the end of the sentence" tells the student that the response was accurate and points out the specific behavior for which praise is given.

Make Consequences for Successful Performance More Attractive.

This strategy involves changing the consequences of the behavior rather than its antecedents. Consequences for successful performance include knowledge of results and rewards supplied by the teacher. To increase the effect of knowledge of results, teachers can improve the quality of feedback, as previously described. In addition, students become more aware of their performance if they are involved in data collection procedures. They can place an *X* or a check mark beside each correct response on their assigned papers and then plot their performance on a graph.

The reward system in use in the classroom may also need to be altered. Students may require incentives to begin or complete a task. And teachers may need to reward approximations toward successful task performance (e.g., 60% accuracy, then 70%, etc., until the criterion is achieved). The nature of the rewards used by the teacher may also require modification; things perceived by teachers as rewards may be less attractive to students.

Slow the Pace of Instruction.

If changes in antecedents and consequences do not produce acceptable performance, slowing the pace of instruction may be necessary. The learning task and the time allotted for instruction remain the same, but less material is presented and practiced. For example, the teacher may demonstrate telling time to the hour and to the half hour in two separate sessions rather than one. If this strategy is unsuccessful, the teacher should consider altering the requirements of the learning task.

Alter Task Requirements

The learning task itself can be modified to enhance student success. Possible strategies are changing task criteria, changing task characteristics, and breaking the task into smaller subtasks (items 8, 9, and 10 in Figure 4–10).

Change the Criteria for Successful Performance.

The criteria for successful performance generally address three aspects of the task: quantity, speed, and accuracy. The requirements for each can be reduced. The number of questions, problems, or activities to be performed can be lessened. The time limits imposed can be increased so that speed demands are relaxed. Or a lower accuracy rate can be accepted. However, the teacher should maintain reasonable accuracy requirements to ensure that the student is learning the task.

Change Task Characteristics.

Task characteristics include the conditions under which the task is performed and the nature of the behavior itself. If the task requires students to perform from memory without aids and assistance, the teacher might allow the use of aids. For example, students may be able to solve multiplication problems if they can use an aid such as a multiplication table or a pocket calculator. Presentation and response modes can also be changed. A task's presentation mode is the way it presents information; for example, many classroom tasks require reading skills. Instead of reading, students might listen to lectures and tapes or watch television, films, and filmstrips. Response modes can also be modified. Instead of writing, students might type, answer orally, tape-record their responses, or dictate them to a peer.

Break Tasks into Smaller Subtasks.

If alteration of task characteristics and criteria does not produce success, the task is probably too complex and should be broken into smaller subtasks. For example, if writing (or dictating or tape-recording)

- Students may experience difficulty in the acquisition, maintenance, and generalization of basic skills, content area information, and career education material.
- Academic problems are indicated by a high number of incorrect responses, a low number of responses, or an inconsistent response pattern.
- Instruction is individualized when a high proportion of student responses is correct.
- In systematic instruction the learning task is selected, material necessary for task performance is presented, and practice is provided; skills are taught directly and the demonstration-prompt-practice technique is used.
- Increasing student engagement by increasing response rate accelerates learning.
- Student performance data provide information about current levels of functioning, rate of progress, and reasons for task failure.
- When student performance is unsatisfactory, teachers introduce the least intrusive instructional modification first.
- Materials and activities are modified by clarifying task directions, adding prompts, and correcting specific student errors.
- Teaching procedures are changed by providing additional presentations and practice, making consequences more attractive, and slowing the pace of instruction.
- Task requirements are altered by changing the criteria for successful performance, changing task characteristics, and breaking the task into smaller subtasks.
- Substitution of an alternate learning task, the most drastic instructional change, is used only as a last resort.

an essay is overwhelming to a student, the teacher can set up a series of smaller tasks: selection of a topic, writing the title, formulation of the topic sentence for the first paragraph, and so on. This strategy is the last in a series of instructional modifications; the next step is to substitute an alternate task.

Select an Alternate Task

When student performance remains poor despite instructional adaptations, the teacher should consider replacing the learning task with an alternate task. Two choices are possible: a similar but easier task or a prerequisite task.

Substitute a Similar but Easier Task. The teacher can select an alternate task similar in nature to the original task but easier for students to perform. For example, if students are unable to cope with the history textbook (even in taped form), the teacher can substitute another text that covers the same material but in less depth and at a lower reading level. This allows students to proceed at their own levels and rates while remaining in the same general subject area as their peers.

Substitute a Prerequisite Task. The most drastic intervention available to the general education teacher is replacement of the original learning task with a prerequisite task. For example, if students with poor basic skills are unable to solve algebraic equations (even with the aid of a calculator), the teacher may substitute instruction in math facts and the operations of addition, subtraction, multiplication, and division. This strategy should be the last employed in the regular classroom because it involves the most radical change from typical classroom procedures. Students whose needs cannot be met with this strategy are candidates for special education services.

The next chapter discusses typical behavior problems and presents strategies for managing the classroom behavior of regular class students, including those with special needs.

1. Read the article entitled "Variables Related to the Effective Instruction of Difficult-to-Teach Children" by H. Rieth and C. Evertson (1988). This article summarizes recent research on effective instruction. What are its major conclusions?
2. Arrange to observe in a special or general education classroom. Explain to the teacher that you are interested in seeing how much of the school day is actually spent in instruction. Observe and keep a log of the teacher's activities for an hour or so. How much time is spent in large-group instruction? Small-group instruction? Supervision of students' independent work? Noninstructional duties?
3. Task analysis is used to break tasks into teachable subcomponents. Select one of the tasks that follow, and list all of the steps necessary to complete the task. Check your analysis by trying to do the task using only the steps you have listed.

   - Brushing your teeth
   - Looking up a number in the phone book
   - Frying an egg
   - Making a bed
   - Writing a check

4. Ways of adapting instruction include changing the characteristics of the task and the performance criteria. Try your hand at modifying this objective:

   When given a page of 25 math problems, the student will write the correct answers to at least 20 problems within 5 minutes.

   Describe how you would alter the task for each of the modifications listed here; the first one is done for you.

Modification	*Altered Task*
reduce quantity	give student only 20 problems
reduce speed	
reduce accuracy	
change conditions	
change presentation mode	
change response mode	

5. Explain why substitution of an alternate learning task should be the last type of instructional modification attempted.

5 Managing Classroom Behavior

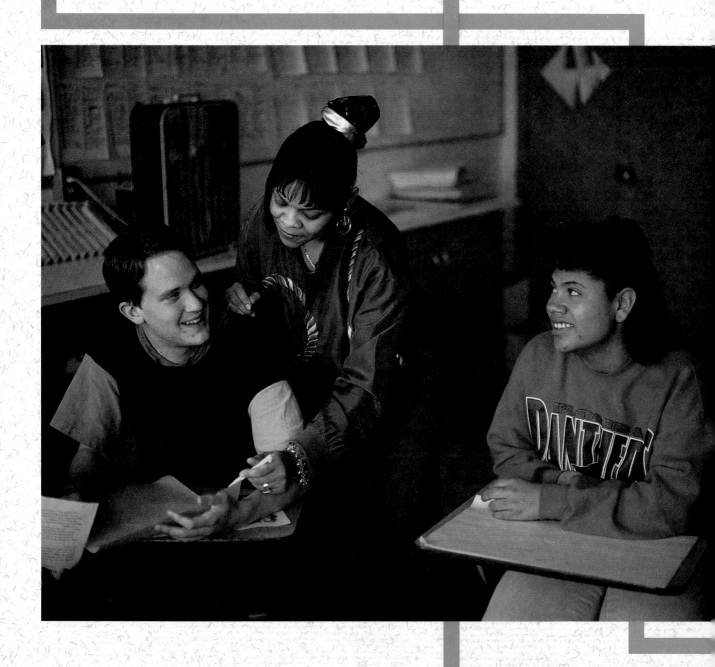

■ *Henry is late for class at least 2 days each week.*

■ *Maxine hasn't completed an assignment this semester.*

■ *Several times each day, John interrupts the teacher's lecture by talking and making noises.*

■ *Pablo argues and fights with other students in the classroom.*

■ *During independent study time, Lisa looks around the room and watches other students or writes notes to her friends.*

■ *Sue doesn't ask questions in class; in fact, the only talking she does is at lunch with her two close friends.*

■ *Willie is seldom in his seat; he seems to be constantly "on the move," and he holds the record for the longest round-trip to the pencil sharpener.*

■ Classroom behavior problems such as these are not rare occurrences. They are a sampling of the problem behaviors that teachers face daily in a mainstream classroom.

BEHAVIOR PROBLEMS IN THE CLASSROOM

Behavior problems are exhibited by regular class students and special students of all ages and at every grade level. Some students call attention to themselves only in the classroom; others also experience difficulty on the playground, in the school cafeteria, on the way to and from school, at home, and in the neighborhood.

The behavior problems of students frequently contribute to their placement in special education programs. When students with special needs return to the mainstream, teachers in general education are often concerned that their problem behaviors will interfere with the operation of the classroom. In addition, such behaviors may hinder the special stu-

dents' academic achievement and may have a negative effect on their acceptance by others.

Two major types of behavior problems are of concern to the teacher: inappropriate classroom behavior and poor study skills. Behaviors that interfere with classroom instruction, impede social interaction with teacher and peers, or endanger others are considered **classroom conduct problems**. Examples of inappropriate classroom behaviors are talking out, fighting, arguing, being out of one's seat, swearing, and avoiding interactions with others. Immature and withdrawn behaviors also fall under this category. Behaviors that interfere with the special student's academic performance and/or the teacher's ability to assess academic progress are considered **study skill problems**. Typical study skill problems are failure to complete assignments, poor attention during lectures or class discussion, failure to follow directions, and poor management of study time.

Problem behaviors are exhibited in one of three ways: low rate of appropriate behaviors, high rate of inappropriate behaviors, or absence of the appropriate behavior from the student's repertoire. Different management strategies are linked to each type of problem behavior.

■ *Low rate of appropriate behaviors.* Students exhibit appropriate behaviors but not as frequently as expected or required. For example, a student may be able to complete homework assignments but chooses to do so only 10% to 20% of the time. Also, students may behave appropriately in one setting but not in another. For instance, a student with disabilities may work well in the resource room but may find it difficult to work in a small-group setting in the general education classroom. To alleviate these problems, the teacher sets up a systematic program to increase the occurrence of appropriate behaviors or to help students generalize behaviors from one situation to another.

■ *High rate of inappropriate behaviors.* Inappropriate behaviors that are troublesome to teachers occur frequently or for long periods of time. Examples include students who are out of their seats 30 to 40 times per day, those who talk during 50% to 60% of the class lecture, and those

Behavior Problems

FOR YOUR INFORMATION

■ According to a recent nationwide study, in six of the past seven years, the general public believed that the second most important problem in public schools (after the use of drugs) was lack of discipline. Lack of discipline was considered the most important school problem in 16 of the 17 years prior to 1986 (Elam, Rose, & Gallup, 1993).

■ The National Education Association (NEA) surveyed teachers and found that 54% believe that "student behavior interferes with teaching" ("NEA Survey," 1980, p. 49).

■ One major study reported that 60% of elementary school children are identified by at least one of their teachers as having a behavior problem (Rubin & Balow, 1978).

■ In effective classrooms, the teacher's classroom management program maximizes the time students spend on learning tasks, and student achievement increases (Smith, Finn, & Dowdy, 1993).

■ Students with poor social behaviors do not achieve as well academically as peers with appropriate social skills. Improving performance in personal interactions and task-related social skills increases both academic performance and social acceptance (Cartledge & Milburn, 1986; Gresham, 1984; Zirpoli & Melloy, 1993).

■ The behaviors that are appropriate in the classroom are determined by the teacher, the policies of the school, and the beliefs of the community. An inappropriate behavior for one teacher may be totally acceptable to another.

who use profanity 5 to 10 times in one class period. To overcome these high rates of inappropriate behavior, teachers attempt to decrease the frequency or duration of the undesired behavior by increasing appropriate behaviors that are incompatible. For instance, to decrease running in the classroom, the teacher can work to increase the frequency of walking.

■ *Absence of the appropriate behavior from the student's repertoire.* Students may not yet have learned the appropriate behavior for social interaction or classroom functioning. The age or grade level of a student is not an accurate predictor of behavioral competence; it is necessary to consider each student individually. For instance, sixth graders may not know how to start a con-

versation or how to organize their time to ensure completion of assignments. To remedy this, the effective teacher directly teaches the new behavior (conversation skills or time management), provides instruction on when and how the behavior is to take place, and carefully builds practice and review opportunities into the instructional sequence (Emmer, 1981; Olson & Platt, 1992).

Behavior problems do not occur in isolation. The way in which the classroom learning environment is arranged and the actions of others can promote, initiate, or reinforce inappropriate behaviors. If classroom behavior problems are to be understood and managed, not only the behavior of the target student but also that of the teacher and peers must be examined. For example, a sarcastic comment from a teacher can initiate a verbal retort from the student. Classmates who laugh at clowning or wisecracks assure that similar behaviors will recur.

Students show inappropriate behavior when they have not learned correct responses or have found that acting inappropriately is more rewarding than acting appropriately. Such behavior problems do respond to instruction. According to one point of view within the education community, behavior problems belong to the teacher, not the student. This viewpoint holds that it is not the students who fail; instead, educators have failed to develop acceptable student behaviors. Opinions on, and results of, research into student behavior in the schools are presented in "For Your Information" on page 125. Figures 5–1 and 5–2 provide checklists of both teacher and student behaviors to consider as possible factors contributing to student misbehavior in the classroom.

▨▨▨ PRINCIPLES OF MANAGING BEHAVIOR

Students who exhibit inappropriate behaviors require a classroom management system that is systematic, consistent, and concerned with both the prevention and cure of problem behaviors. This system should provide for group management yet be flexible enough to allow individualization for the problems of one specific student.

Behavior management follows many of the same principles used in adapting academic instruction. Teachers state precise goals, break behaviors into teachable subcomponents, institute systematic management procedures, and collect data to monitor student progress. Whereas instruction (as discussed in chapter 4) deals primarily with academic skills, behavior management is concerned with classroom conduct and study skills; in both, the teacher arranges the classroom environment to produce changes in student behavior. The following paragraphs present principles to follow in setting up a systematic behavior management program.

Remember That Behavior Is Learned

Problem behaviors are learned behaviors that have developed from the student's experiences and reinforcement history. Sometimes called **operant behaviors**, they are under the voluntary control of the individual. Because behavior is learned, students can acquire new ways of acting; present behaviors can be replaced or supplemented. The learning of new behaviors occurs at different rates for different students, and instructional procedures affect individuals differently. This individuality is particularly important with students with special needs, who may require extra time or additional practice. They are certainly capable of acquiring new behaviors but may need a more systematic management program than their regular class peers.

Consider Both the Antecedents and the Consequences of Behavior

As suggested earlier, behaviors do not happen in isolation. The occurrence of a behavior is affected by the events that precede it and the consequences that follow it. Antecedents and consequences are both important in the management of behavior. New skills can be taught, or current behaviors can be modified, by either altering antecedent events or conditions and/or by manipulating consequences. As a general rule, if antecedents are contributing to the behavior, teachers should first alter the antecedent conditions and then consider changing the consequences. For example, if students fail to follow directions, the first step may be to alter the directions. A change from "Get back to your seat!" to "Would you please return to your seat?" may produce the desired behavior.

It is also possible to modify both antecedents and consequences at the same time. According to Walker (1979),

> Simultaneous manipulation of antecedents and consequences is probably the most effective method for changing behavior. An example of the manipulation of both antecedents and consequences would be in the case where a teacher carefully defines classroom rules

FIGURE 5–1

Possible Contributions to Misbehavior: A Checklist of Teacher Behavior

■ *Am I consistent in responding to children's behavior?* If your response to children's conduct—good or bad — is unpredictable, children will have difficulty learning how they are to behave. Your students should know what the consequences of appropriate behavior and misbehavior will be. Give clear directions; hold firm to your expectations; and be consistent in following through with rewards and punishment.

■ *Am I rewarding the right behavior?* Children who present difficult management problems often are ignored when they are behaving appropriately. Often, about the only time they receive attention is when they are criticized or reprimanded for misbehavior. Sometimes teachers make the mistake of praising them (for something else) or making physical contact with them (in attempts to offer loving correction) when they misbehave. Make sure that children are receiving your attention primarily when they are behaving appropriately. You must make certain that desirable conduct receives a hefty amount of recognition and the misbehavior does not.

■ *Are my expectations and demands appropriate for children's abilities?* When expectations are too high, children feel too much pressure and experience too much failure. When expectations are too low, children become bored and may feel resentful. Make certain that your expectations fit each child's ability level so that the child is challenged while his or her progress is obvious.

■ *Am I tolerant enough of children's individuality?* Children have as much right as adults to express their individuality. Many children rebel against teachers who demand strict uniformity and regimentation or are unwilling to encourage appropriate individuality. Make certain that your rules and expectations allow sufficient room for harmless preferences and idiosyncrasies.

■ *Am I providing instruction that is useful to children?* People do not learn quickly or happily when they see no point in what they are doing. First, you must make sure that you have chosen the most important things to teach. When children do not see the importance of what you are teaching, you must point out to them the value of what they are learning. If they still do not understand, you must find a way to make the material interesting or worth their while—perhaps by offering meaningful rewards or privileges for learning.

■ *Are children seeing desirable models?* Children are great imitators of their teachers and their high-status peers. Make certain that if children are imitating you, they are behaving appropriately. Monitor your own behavior, and change it if necessary. Call attention to the desirable conduct of children's peers. Point out the kind of behavior you want to see.

■ *Am I generally irritable and overreliant on punishment as a control technique?* Teachers set a tone in their classrooms by their general attitudes toward persons and events. A teacher who is easily upset, frequently short-tempered, quick to punish minor misbehavior, and hesitant in expressing approval is virtually certain to foster irritability and defiance in students. General irritability and a focus on punishment suggest depression; and a teacher's depression may contribute to children's depressive behavior.

■ *Am I willing to try a different tack on the problem or to seek the help of colleagues or consultants?* A teacher who resists the suggestions of others, who insists on "going it alone," or who discards any different approach as useless or doomed to failure is not likely to be successful for long. Teaching today presents complex behavior management problems for which even the most competent teacher needs consultation. An attitude of openness and a willingness to look outside oneself are essential to success.

Note. From "Classroom Management: Teacher-Child-Peer Relationships" by J. M. Kauffman, P. L. Pullen, and E. Akers, 1986, *Focus on Exceptional Children, 19*(1), p. 3. Copyright 1986 by Love. Reprinted by permission.

FIGURE 5–2
Possible Contributions to Misbehavior: A Checklist of Student Behavior

Is the child overdependent on you? Children who cannot work independently are a constant source of interruption of the teacher's work and their peers' concentration. Their frequent demands for help, or their refusal to work without the teacher's constant oversight, are wearing on the teacher and may trigger rivalry from peers.

Does the child have difficulty concentrating and paying attention? Learning requires focused attention. A child's lack of attention to task requires additional teacher effort, provides an inappropriate model for peers, raises the probability of disruptive behavior, and lowers the probability of academic success.

Does the child become easily upset under pressure to achieve? The world contains many sources of pressure for productive activity and achievement. Therefore, a classroom without any pressure whatsoever for achievement is an unrealistic and debilitating environment. Children's resistance to expectations for performance is a source of frustration for the teacher and for peers who are striving to achieve.

Is the child's work sloppy? Reflective, careful work is needed in the workplace, and it should be expected in the classroom. Teachers are justified in requiring reasonably neat, thoughtful responses. Teaching is difficult and progress is slow when the child has not learned good work habits and impulse control.

Does the child tease, annoy, or interfere with the work of other students? Annoyance or hassle by neighbors or coworkers is a common and sometimes serious source of stress for adults and children. A child who interferes with the lives of others becomes a source of bad feelings and a sinkhole for the energies of teachers and peers.

Is the child negative toward schoolwork, self, teachers, or peers? Faultfinding, whining, and criticism—whether directed toward others or oneself—induce negative responses in others. These characteristics often are indicative of depression, and they tend to make others feel depressed.

Does the child have poor personal hygiene or habits of self-care? People, young or old, who are dirty or smelly are less likely to be approached socially or to be befriended by others than are those who maintain good hygiene and self-care. Teachers will have difficulty being positive toward children whose odor or appearance is offensive.

Is the child usually withdrawn or reticent? A withdrawn or reticent child is easily overlooked by teachers and peers. A child with those characteristics is unlikely to be drawn into positive, reciprocal social exchanges without special intervention.

Does the child engage in self-stimulation or self-injury? Excessive or socially inappropriate self-stimulation is incompatible with learning and social acceptance. Self-stimulation and self-injury usually are off-putting to others and inhibit normal psychological and physical development.

Is the child aggressive toward teachers or peers? Aggression in the form of verbal threats, intimidation, extortion, or physical attack heightens anxiety and stress in all parties involved. An aggressive child can be expected to induce hostility and counter-aggression in others.

Note. From "Classroom Management: Teacher-Child-Peer Relationships" by J. M. Kauffman, P. L. Pullen, and E. Akers, 1986, *Focus on Exceptional Children, 19*(1), p. 5. Copyright 1986 by Love. Reprinted by permission.

and then allows children to accumulate minutes of free time for following them. (p. 46)

Reduce Behavior Management Problems with Careful Organization of the Classroom

The physical organization of the classroom, the procedures established for movement within the classroom, and the quality of the instructional program all play important roles in determining the frequency of behavior problems. Careful arrangement of such things as physical space, student seating, storage of instructional materials, and student traffic patterns can greatly reduce the potential for disruptions of instructional activities and the occurrence of behavioral problems. Appropriate instructional programs and streamlined classroom procedures are also likely to reduce behavior problems. Chapters 4 and 7 provide specific suggestions for adapting instruction and coordinating the classroom learning environment.

Increase the Occurrence of Behaviors by Reinforcement

Behaviors followed by reinforcers are more likely to occur again. A student who receives praise from the teacher for raising her hand to speak in class is more likely to raise her hand the next time she wishes to contribute something. This is an example of **positive reinforcement**; the behavior is followed by the presentation of a pleasant (or positive) event that makes the behavior more likely to recur. This is a constructive procedure that helps students feel better about themselves. Examples of positive reinforcers are praise, special privileges, positive notes to students and parents, early dismissal for lunch, and special awards. Positive reinforcement is a powerful tool for managing and changing behavior.

Although less favored, negative reinforcers also increase the probability that behaviors will recur. In **negative reinforcement**, the behavior is followed by the removal of an aversive (unpleasant or punishing) event or condition. A student who completes his homework to stop the nagging of his teacher and parents is being negatively reinforced; that is, the desired behavior, finishing the assignment, is followed by the removal of the aversive event, nagging, and is thus more apt to recur in the future. The student who stops talking to classmates and begins working to stop the frown of the teacher is also being negatively reinforced. Negative reinforcement should not be confused with punishment; negative reinforcers increase the occurrence of a behavior by removing something that is aversive. However, because it is a negative approach, negative reinforcement may produce avoidance, escape, or aggressive behaviors on the part of the student (Zirpoli & Melloy, 1993).

Reinforcement is most effective when the reinforcer is clearly associated with the specific behavior and is presented closely following that behavior. The effect of reinforcing a student with immediate praise for entering class on time is much greater than complimenting the student at the end of the day. Reinforcement should be immediate, systematic, realistic, and meaningful to students in order to be effective. Table 5–1 gives examples of reinforcement procedures that influence the strength of a behavior.

Decrease the Occurrence of Behaviors by Removing Reinforcers or Introducing Aversive Events

The strength of a behavior decreases when it is followed by an aversive event or when it stops being followed by a reinforcer. The student who no longer receives laughs and snickers from peers for muttering profanities will generally decrease this activity. Tardiness will decrease if students lose privileges (such as time in the game center) for each minute they are late; the same is true for students who lose the use of the family car for coming home after curfew.

Extinction is the removal of reinforcers that have previously followed the behavior. If the objective is to decrease an inappropriate behavior that has been reinforced in the past, the reinforcer is withheld. For example, the teacher may wish to decrease the number of times Mike talks out in class. If the teacher has been reinforcing Mike's out-of-turn

TABLE 5–1
Procedures to Change Behaviors

Learning Concepts	Educational Procedures	Effects on Behavior	Examples of Positive or Aversive Events Presented or Removed
Positive reinforcement	Behavior is followed by positive event	Increase in strength of behavior	Smile, approval, affection, task completion, money, special privileges, recognition, passing grade
Negative reinforcement	Behavior is followed by removal of aversive event	Increase in strength of behavior	Frown, criticism, poor grade, threat of restriction of use of car, rejection, nonattention
Extinction (of behavior previously strengthened by positive reinforcement)	Behavior is not followed by positive event associated with previous occurrence	Decrease in strength of behavior	Smile, approval, affection, peer attention, bonus, special privilege
Extinction (of behavior previously strengthened by negative reinforcement)	Behavior is not followed by removal of aversive event associated with previous occurrence	Decrease in strength of behavior	Criticism, rejection, threat of loss of privileges, poor grade
Punishment: Presentation of aversive events	Behavior is followed by aversive event	Decrease in strength of behavior which results in the aversive event	Criticism, poor grade, rejection by peers, threat of dismissal from club
Punishment: Removal of positive events through time-out or response cost	Behavior is followed by temporary or permanent loss of positive events	Decrease in strength of behavior which results in loss of positive events	Smile, approval, affection, money, privilege, group membership

Note. From *Learning and Behavior Characteristics of Exceptional Children and Youth: A Humanistic Behavioral Approach* (p. 210) by William I. Gardner, 1977, Boston: Allyn and Bacon. Copyright 1977 by Allyn and Bacon. Reprinted by permission.

responses by attending to them, this positive reinforcer must be withdrawn; the teacher should ignore Mike's comments until he raises his hand. Although extinction procedures will reduce and eliminate a behavior, their use may be somewhat frustrating. A teacher may be unable to identify or control all the classroom reinforcers. In addition, the effect of extinction procedures is not always immediate; there may even be a temporary increase in the student's undesirable behavior before it decreases. For example, the frequency of Ann's tantrums might increase until she realizes the teacher's attention can be gained only by exhibiting appropriate behaviors.

Some inappropriate behaviors should be ignored from the outset (e.g., occasional call-outs, brief whisperings). Behaviors falling into this category are (a) those of short duration that are not likely to spread or persist, (b) minor deviations from classroom rules, and (c) behaviors where a reaction from the teacher would interrupt a lesson or draw undue attention to the behavior. Procedures that decrease behaviors more rapidly (such as punishment or overcorrection) should be considered if the behavior to be reduced is harmful to others (such as fighting) or if it causes a major disruption of the classroom (such as yelling or stealing).

The presentation of an aversive event following a behavior is called **punishment**. Examples of punishers are verbal reprimands, criticism, and low grades. Two of the milder punishment procedures often used in the general education classroom are response cost and time-out. In **response cost**, an inappropriate behavior is followed by the loss or withdrawal of earned reinforcers or privileges. In **time-out**, the student is removed from an event that is reinforcing, or reinforcement is withdrawn for a specified period of time. Time-out may involve **contingent observation** (viewing from the "sidelines"), exclusion time-out (excluding students from observing or participating in activities without leaving the room by, for example, turning their chair toward the wall or placing it behind a screen), or temporary removal from the room. Time-out is effective only if it is carefully planned and systematically implemented and if its effects are carefully evaluated and documented (Cuenin & Harris, 1986).

Punishment is a negative procedure that can rapidly decrease a behavior. However, it should be used only if more positive approaches are not appropriate or feasible. Before punishment is used with special students, teachers should carefully check district and state policies and regulations regarding its use in a school setting as there is an increasing concern about the potential misuse of many negative procedures. In addition, the permission of their parents should always be obtained because punishment can harm students' self-concept and can produce avoidance, escape, or aggressive behaviors.

Punishment is most effective if it is combined with positive reinforcement. This combination will bring about more rapid and effective changes than the use of either procedure alone (Walker, 1979). For example, a student who runs in the classroom will learn appropriate behavior more quickly if he or she receives both positive reinforcers (such as praise and extra recess time) for walking and also punishers (such as loss of earned free time or verbal reprimands) for running.

Identify Consequences That Are Meaningful to Students

To have the desired effect on behavior, consequences must be meaningful to the student. This is true for both positive and negative consequences. A consequence that is positive for one person may be negative for another. For example, going to the library is positive for the book lover but not necessarily so for the sports addict; watching a football game may be a negative activity for those who like to play tennis or visit museums. In addition, the effect of a specific consequence on an individual can change under different conditions. Earning a dessert for completing classwork is reinforcing to a student under most conditions; however, an offer of a banana split for doing the dishes would not be appealing even to the most avid dessert lover who had just eaten a huge meal.

Educators often assume that students are motivated by grades; however, for many special students, grades are aversive. They have received poor grades that resulted in ridicule from their peers and negative feedback from their parents and teachers. For them grades are no longer positive consequences, and other reinforcers must be found.

It is possible to misinterpret the potential effects of a consequence. A teacher may use verbal reprimands as an aversive consequence for inappropriate behavior. However, the teacher's attention may be a positive reinforcer for the student, regardless of the nature of the attention. On the other hand, verbal praise from a teacher may have the effect of a punisher; for instance, to adolescents, praise from a teacher may be distasteful if given in front of their peers.

Consequences must have meaning to their recipients. For instance, most teachers would soon tire of receiving grades instead of paychecks for their work. Pay is not bribery; it is the presentation of a meaningful reinforcer for hard work. Because the paycheck is negotiable, teachers can choose which secondary reinforcers they wish to purchase.

Beware of Noneducational Interventions

Periodically, methods that claim to bring about dramatic changes in the behavior of students appear in the field of education. Many of these are noneducational treatments and interventions. For example, special diets, medication, and therapies (e.g., relaxation therapy) may claim to solve academic and social problems. Teachers should exercise extreme caution in considering such approaches. Most are medical-type interventions; many have little empirical evidence to support their usefulness (Silver, 1987). Information about the use of drugs to manage hyperactivity and other behavior problems is presented in "Tips for the Teacher."

If questions arise, the teacher can consult the school nurse, counselor, special educator, or principal. Noneducational procedures should not be used with special students unless the use of a particular

The Use of Drugs in Managing Hyperactivity

*A*uthors such as Axelrod and Bailey (1979), Kauffman (1993), and Walker (1979) have discussed the concerns frequently raised about the effectiveness of drugs in managing hyperactivity and other inappropriate student behaviors. These experts have noted the need for continuing research in this area and indicate that teachers should approach the medical management of behavioral problems with due caution. Axelrod and Bailey (1979) suggest the following guidelines for the use of drug treatment in school settings:

1. Physical examinations should be prerequisites to commencing and continuing drug treatment. This is necessary not only to monitor possible physiological problems, but also to determine whether physical anomalies might be causing problem behaviors.
2. Drugs should be considered only when there is a demonstration of inordinately inappropriate behavior. . . . The mere claim from a parent or teacher that a child's behavior warrants drug treatment is insufficient.
3. Before drug treatment is implemented, behavior modification procedures or other remedial techniques should be attempted.
4. Children who receive drugs should be exposed to two different dosage levels, a baseline phase, and a placebo condition. Whenever possible, drug and placebo conditions should be conducted in a double blind manner.
5. A continual, preferably daily, record of a child's behavior should be maintained. This should be done not only when attempting to determine a child's appropriate drug treatment, but throughout treatment.
6. The effects on at least one behavior that should increase and one behavior that should decrease should be monitored.
7. Minimal goals for each behavior of interest should be specified in advance. Only when drug treatment meets the prespecified goals should the treatment be continued.
8. During the course of drug treatment, the child should periodically be drug free. If the child's behavior again becomes disorderly, it may be concluded that the drugs were responsible for the previously noted improvement. If the child's behavior remains appropriate, it may be possible to permanently discontinue drug use.
9. Drug treatment should not be considered a permanent solution to a youngster's problems. When drug therapy is considered necessary, it might be combined with more standard educational procedures. As the package of techniques improves a student's behavior, it may be possible to wean the student from drug treatment. (pp. 547–548)

procedure for a particular student has received the full endorsement of the mainstreaming team and the parents have given their informed consent.

METHODS FOR GATHERING DATA

Gathering data on the classroom behavior and study skills of students is an essential component of a behavior management program. General education teachers can collect information through informal techniques such as direct observation of behavior and behavior inventories. Teachers use such data to determine students' current levels of performance, identify antecedents and consequences that may influence behavior, determine the effectiveness of the intervention program, and communicate progress to students and parents. Knowledge of progress can be a strong reinforcer for students.

Direct Observation of Behavior

The most useful method for gathering information on classroom behavior and study skills is the direct observation of student behavior. Observations are usually conducted in the classroom setting by the teacher, an aide, or a trained volunteer; in some cases, students can be trained to collect information on other students or on their own performances.

Although teachers observe students every day, such observations are usually not systematic or precise; general impressions do not provide enough information for planning intervention programs. Instead, direct observations should be carefully planned and should follow the steps outlined in the following paragraphs.

Specify the Behavior to Be Observed. The first task is to specify the behavior of interest to the teacher. This behavior must be described as specifically as possible. If it is stated clearly, two or more observers will be able to agree on whether the student has produced the behavior. Imprecise descriptions of behaviors make them difficult to observe

and measure. The statements "Jack is hyperactive," "Mark is nasty," "Judy is restless," and "Sam has poor study habits" lack specificity and leave much to the interpretation of the observer. Descriptions such as "Louis hits other students," "Wen-Chi leaves her seat frequently," "Candy talks out without raising her hand," and "Jose doesn't turn in his homework assignments" are more precise.

At times, teachers may wish to collect data on the overall performance of a student in order to identify specific problem behaviors. Sulzer-Azaroff and Mayer (1977) suggest narrative recording or sequence analysis for this purpose. In **narrative recording**, the observer describes all the behaviors displayed by the student during the observation period; this record is then analyzed to determine whether there is any pattern in the student's behaviors. **Sequence analysis** is more systematic; the observer describes each behavior and attempts to identify its antecedent and consequence. Table 5–2 presents a portion of a sequence analysis of John's behavior during instruction. Examination of the events that precede and follow a behavior yields much more information than is obtained in a simple observation.

However, narrative recording and sequence analysis may not be practical ways for the general education teacher to collect data. The teacher may be unable to undertake a detailed observation such as this while managing all of the activities of a regular classroom. One solution is to have someone other than the classroom teacher conduct the observation; this person could be an instructional aide, an adult volunteer, a special education teacher or consultant, or even a peer tutor. Another technique is to develop a simpler observation system. In any event, when the task is to identify problem behaviors, it is important to consider not only the behavior itself but also the effect of antecedents and consequences on it.

Select a Measurement System. As soon as a behavior has been identified and specifically described, the system to observe and measure the behavior can be selected. There are several different types of behaviors, and their nature influences the

TABLE 5–2
Example of a Sequence Analysis

Time	Antecedent	Behavior	Consequence
9:05	Teacher asks the class a question.	John raises hand.	Teacher calls on Bill.
9:07	Teacher asks question.	John yells answer.	Teacher reprimands John.
9:11	Teacher asks question and reminds students to raise hands.	John raises hand.	Teacher calls on John and compliments him for raising his hand.

kind of measurement system chosen. One type is that of permanent products such as completed assignments, worksheets, and essays, which are available for review at a later time. Other behaviors are more transitory; they must be observed at the time of the occurrence. Examples include fighting, verbal outbursts, stealing, and being out of one's seat. These behaviors may be discrete (i.e., like writing and talking, they have a definite beginning and ending), or they may be continuous (e.g., studying). Some transitory behaviors can be converted into permanent products if they are audio- or videotaped for later study.

Several methods of recording data are possible during an observation:

1. *Permanent product or work sample analysis.* A sample of the student's work is evaluated, and information such as the number of problems correct is recorded.
2. *Event recording.* The number of times a behavior occurs within a time interval is noted; for example, the teacher counts the number of times a student leaves her seat during one class period.
3. *Duration recording.* The length of time a behavior occurs is recorded; for example, the teacher times how long a student takes to complete an assignment.

4. *Interval recording.* The occurrence or nonoccurrence of a behavior is noted within a specific time interval; for example, the teacher might observe that Bill was reading his science book during only two of the five 3-minute observation periods.

Which method to use depends on the type of behavior and the kind of data that will be most useful to the teacher. Also, the system must be easily implemented by the observer. Table 5–3 describes several kinds of information that result from the different recording systems: percentage, frequency, duration, and interval data.

Permanent product and **event recording** produce frequency data that can be converted into percentage data. Percentages and frequencies are appropriate measures for academic, classroom, and study skills behaviors. A teacher might be interested in the percentage of words read correctly or the percentage of time students spent on a task. Frequency data indicate the number of occurrences of a behavior. In order to compare frequencies, the teacher should be sure that observation periods are equal in length and that the student has the same opportunity to produce the behavior during each observation period. For example, results would be misleading if a student's questioning behavior during the teacher's lecture were compared with that student's

TABLE 5–3
Measures of Behavior

Measure	Derived From	Example	Application
Percent	Number of units correct out of number of total units recorded	8 math problems correct out of 10 total math problems: $\frac{8}{10} \times 100 = 80\%$ accuracy	When a measure of accuracy is of concern without regard for time or proficiency
Frequency	$\dfrac{\text{Count of behavior}}{\text{Observation time}}$	12 handraises in a 6-minute observation period: $\frac{12}{6} = 2$ handraises per minute	When it is desired to know how often a distinct behavior occurs within a period of time
Duration	Direct measures of length of time	A child tantrums for 15 minutes	When the total length of time a continuous behavior occurs is desired
Intervals	Number of fixed time units in which behavior occurred or didn't occur	Children are observed for 30 seconds, then the observer records whether or not behavior occurred during the interval. Observers then repeat the process. Usually data is expressed in terms of percentage of intervals during which behavior occurred. $\frac{5 \text{ intervals}}{10 \text{ intervals total}} \times 100 = 50\%$ of intervals	When total duration is not possible and an estimation of the occurrence of continuous behavior is desired

Note. From "An Applied Behavioral Analysis Research Primer for Behavioral Change Personnel" by M. A. Koorland and D. L. Westling, 1981, *Behavioral Disorders, 6,* p. 166. Copyright 1981 by the Council for Children with Behavioral Disorders, The Council for Exceptional Children. Reprinted by permission.

questioning behavior during a discussion period. Frequency data gathered during unequal observation periods can be more easily compared if they are transformed into rate information, which is simply the number of times a behavior occurs within a certain period (e.g., 8 times per minute; 17 times per hour). Examples of rate data are the number of math problems completed correctly per minute or the number of tantrums per day. Rate and percentage data are easy to compare. For instance, it is possible to compare the percentage of correct responses or the rate of reading words from one day to the next even if the student does not read the same number of words per day.

Duration recording is useful if the length of time the student engages in a behavior is of interest. For example, teachers might note the amount of time students require to line up for lunch or the time a student takes to begin work after the teacher gives directions. Duration can be reported in actual time units (e.g., Katie cried for 14 minutes; Elijah now starts his work within 15 seconds after the teacher gives his group the assignment) or as a percentage (e.g., Ralph was out of his seat 10% of the school day).

Interval recording is particularly useful for the teacher of a regular class because it does not require that students be observed continuously. McLoughlin and Lewis (1994) describe several of the different interval recording systems:

> With these techniques, the observer determines whether a behavior occurs during a specified time period. The class day, period, or activity is broken down into short intervals of a few minutes or even a few seconds, and a record of the presence or absence of the target behavior is kept for each interval. These techniques can also be used with discrete behaviors if a complete record of every occurrence is not necessary.
>
> Several variations of interval recording and time sampling are available.
>
> ■ *Whole-interval recording.* The student is observed for the entire interval, and the observer notes if the target behavior occurs continuously throughout the interval. Observation intervals are very brief, usually only a few seconds.
> ■ *Partial-interval time recording.* The student is observed for the entire interval, but the observer notes only if the behavior occurred at least once during the interval. Again, time intervals are very brief.
> ■ *Momentary time sampling.* The student is observed only at the end of each interval; at that time, the observer checks to see if the behavior is occurring. Intervals are usually longer—3, 5, or even 15 minutes—making this a more convenient method for classroom teachers. However, it is less accurate than [whole- or partial-] interval recording techniques because much of the student's behavior goes unobserved. (p. 99)

Figure 5–3 provides an example of the use of momentary time sampling with an entire class. In this example, the teacher was interested in determining what percentage of the class was on-task during reading instruction. The same type of observation system could also be used with individual students or small groups.

Decide Who Will Observe and How Often Observations Will Occur.

Observers must be able to record data accurately and consistently. If the teacher is the only adult in the classroom, the kind and frequency of observations that are possible may be limited. However, the teacher can record data while conducting instruction or while assisting students; devices such as clipboards, data sheets, stopwatches, and counters are helpful. Some behaviors can be self-recorded if students are monitored by the teacher and reinforced for accurate recording. For more information about conducting observations in the regular classroom, see "Tips for the Teacher" on page 139.

The frequency of observations depends on several factors, including the availability of the student, the type of behavior being observed, the observation system, and the availability of the observer. Data collection should occur frequently, but observations usually require only a short period each day. The observation must be long enough to obtain an accurate picture of the student's behavior. The time of day or the length of the observation should be adjusted if the teacher believes that this sample of behavior is not typical.

Collect and Graph Baseline Data.

Baseline data are collected under the natural conditions of the classroom before any intervention is begun. Baseline data are generally gathered for at least 5 days to ensure that the extremes of the behavior have been established. These data, recorded on a graph, are used to determine the rate or magnitude of the problem, to suggest possible interventions, and later to set the standard for evaluating the effectiveness of instruction. Baseline data may indicate that the behavior believed inappropriate is not as frequent or

---

FIGURE 5–3
Observation Using Momentary Time Sampling

Student(s) observed:	Entire class
Behavior observed:	Number of students on-task, working on independent assignment or actively participating in assigned group activity
Measurement system:	Momentary time sampling (observer determines the number of students on-task at the end of each interval)
Length of interval:	5 minutes
Time of measurement:	Reading instruction time (9:00–9:52 A.M.)
Data recorded:	Number of students on-task/Number of students in class (percentage can be calculated for each observation or for the entire period)
Results:	Over the entire time scheduled for reading instruction, 62% of the students in the class were on-task. However, the percentage of students on-task decreased as the class progressed.

Observation Time	Data	Observation Time	Data
9:05	24/30 = 80%	9:30	18/30 = 60%
9:10	27/30 = 90%	9:35	15/30 = 50%
9:15	24/30 = 80%	9:40	12/30 = 40%
9:20	21/30 = 70%	9:45	15/30 = 50%
9:25	21/30 = 70%	9:50	9/30 = 30%

Class totals: 186/300 = 62%

---

intense as hypothesized; if so, a behavior change program is not necessary. When the teacher is sure that the desired behavior is not part of the student's repertoire or when a behavior is injurious to the student or others, baseline data need not be collected.

Graphing data permits the teacher and student to easily see the behavior and its rate of occurrence. Graphs can present baseline data, progress during intervention, and later the maintenance of behavior after intervention has been discontinued. Graphs are an excellent way to communicate progress to parents and other educators. Figure 5–4 presents an example of a graph that could be used in the classroom.

Collect Data During Interventions. Data collected during the intervention phase help the teacher determine whether the intervention is having the desired effect on behavior. The teacher can then decide whether the intervention program should continue as originally developed or be modified to improve its effectiveness.

Intervention data should be gathered for a minimum of 5 days. Longer data collection periods permit a more careful evaluation of the program's effectiveness. Figure 5–4 shows information collected by the teacher about Elsie's completion of assignments. During the intervention phase, Elsie was rewarded

Techniques for Conducting Observations in the Regular Classroom

O ne typical concern of teachers in regular classrooms is that they do not have time to set up and run behavior management programs. They are busy teaching 30 or more students and cannot drop everything to systematically observe the behavior of a specific pupil. However, several techniques allow the teacher to conduct observations while carrying on regular instructional activities. It is not necessary to stop teaching to observe; in fact, it is almost impossible to teach without observing! Try the following suggestions for integrating observations into your classroom procedures:

1. Carry a small card such as an index card; on it list the names of one or two target students and the problem behaviors you wish to observe (e.g., hitting, being out-of-seat, talking to others). Place a tally mark on the card (and possibly the time the behavior occurred) each time the behavior occurs. Start this system with one or two students and gradually expand it as your skills improve.
2. Require students to record on their in-class work their starting and finishing time. This approach permits the calculation of rate as well as frequency and accuracy data. Students can also note the times they leave and return to their desks; then the total amount of time in-seat each day or each period can be calculated.
3. Carry a stopwatch to measure the duration of behaviors. For example, start the watch each time Maynard leaves his seat, and stop it when he returns. Continue this (without resetting the watch) and time each occurrence of the behavior. At the end of the observation period, note the total amount of time recorded.
4. To count behaviors without interfering with the operation of the class, use wrist counters (golf counters), supermarket counters, paper clips moved from one pocket to another, navy beans in a cup, and other inexpensive devices.
5. Have a seating chart in front of you as you talk to the class. Place a tally mark by a student's name for each target behavior, such as asking a question, talking out, or answering a question correctly.
6. Recruit volunteers to observe in the classroom. Older students, parents, senior citizens, college students, or other students in the class can be excellent observers. If the teacher has developed a method to record the data and clearly stated the behavior to be observed, a nonprofessional should be able to conduct the observation.

FIGURE 5–4
Graphing Baseline and Intervention Data

Behavior observed: Assignments completed by Elsie

Intervention: 3 minutes in the game center for each
                  assignment completed

Student: Elsie

Percentage of
Assignments
Completed

Baseline   Intervention

Day

with 3 minutes in the game center for each assign-ment she finished on time; this was the only way Elsie could earn time in the game center, an activity she enjoyed very much. After 1 week, Elsie's teacher decided that the intervention was working and that it should be continued.

Informal Assessment

Informal behavioral assessment is another method of gathering data about student performance. Teacher-made or commercially prepared behavior rating scales and inventories designed to provide informa-tion about the student's present level of functioning are used to identify potential target behaviors that may need modification. They are most useful as screening devices, suggesting areas for further assess-ment by direct observation of behavior.

Informal measures should reflect the behavioral expectations of the teacher. Rating scales and inven-tories, like task analyses, generally break broad cate-gories of behavior into smaller subcomponents. In constructing or selecting an inventory, the teacher

should be sure that all important aspects of class-room behavior are included. Figure 5–5 shows a portion of the personal-social behavior section of the *Pupil Rating Scale Revised* (Myklebust, 1981), with which the teacher (or other educators or the par-ents) can rate each student on behaviors such as cooperation, attention, and organization. Because measures such as these rely somewhat upon the interpretation of their users, results may be less objective and less precise than those obtained with direct observation of behavior.

STRATEGIES FOR MANAGING AND IMPROVING BEHAVIOR

Teachers can use several strategies in the manage-ment of classroom behavior and the development of study skills. Most effective are intervention pro-grams based on student performance data; these programs help students learn new behaviors, increase or maintain appropriate behaviors, and decrease inappropriate behaviors. Because class-room and study skills are learned behaviors, many of

FIGURE 5–5
Behavior Inventory

Cooperation	Rating
Continually disrupts classroom; unable to inhibit responses	1
Frequently demands attention; often speaks out of turn	2
Waits his/her turn; average for age and grade	3
Above average; cooperates well	4
Excellent ability; cooperates well without adult encouragement	5

Attention	
Never attentive; very distractible	1
Rarely listens; attention frequently wanders	2
Attention adequate for age and grade	3
Above average in attention; almost always attends	4
Always attends to important aspects; long attention span	5

Organization	
Highly disorganized; very slovenly	1
Often disorganized in manner of working; inexact, careless	2
Maintains average organization of work; careful	3
Above-average organization; organizes and completes work	4
Highly organized; completes assignments in meticulous manner	5

Completion of Assignments	
Never finishes even with guidance	1
Seldom finishes even with guidance	2
Average performance; follows through on assignments	3
Above-average performance; completes assignments without urging	4
Always completes assignments without supervision	5

Tactfulness	
Always rude	1
Usually disregards feelings of others	2
Average tact; behavior occasionally inappropriate socially	3
Above average in tactfulness; behavior rarely inappropriate socially	4
Always tactful; behavior never socially inappropriate	5

Note. From *The Pupil Rating Scale Revised* by H. R. Myklebust, 1981, New York: Grune & Stratton. Copyright 1981 by Grune & Stratton. Reprinted by permission.

the principles of instruction presented in chapter 4 remain applicable.

The goal in behavior management is to establish a learning environment in which students are accepted as individuals but in which there are definite guidelines for acceptable classroom conduct. This goal is communicated most effectively to students by posi-

tive behavior change approaches. Students understand the need for guidelines and accept them if they are applied fairly, equally, and consistently. However, questions may arise when behavior change programs are used with some students but not with others. See "Tips for the Teacher" on the following page for ideas on how to handle this situation.

Explaining Special Behavior Programs to Regular Class Peers

*D*ifferential treatment of students is often a concern to teachers. However, no teacher is able to treat all students exactly alike, and students themselves realize that some may require a different type of instruction or additional attention from the teacher. In an individualized classroom, special interventions designed to improve the behavior of one or two target students should draw little attention. Try the following suggestions when implementing behavior change programs in the classroom:

1. If questions do arise, explain that each student has different needs, and some may need special help, special reinforcers, or other program modifications to enable them to learn appropriate social and academic skills.
2. Do not expect to place every student on a different special program. Instead, design programs for the entire class. For example, class members might earn points for assignments completed, books read, and so on. This type of system can be easily adjusted so that one or two students can earn additional reinforcers for accomplishment of special target behaviors.
3. An intervention program should interfere as little as possible with the operation of the class. Teachers can provide students with reinforcers without interrupting classroom activities and without calling attention to the student in question. However, it is essential that the student being reinforced knows it! The teacher can make a mark on the chalkboard, give the student a silent signal, write on a card at the student's desk, or place poker chips or other tokens in a jar.
4. Include other students in the program. Rewarding nearby classmates when the target student is successful often contributes to the effectiveness of the program and the classmates' attitudes toward the special student.
5. Teachers using programs that base decisions on data and careful manipulation of antecedents and consequences find that the benefits of the approach far outweigh its disadvantages.

Managing and improving classroom behavior is a systematic process of identifying expected student behaviors, analyzing student performance to see whether it meets expectations, and implementing interventions when necessary. Figure 5–6 presents the step-by-step process followed by the teacher to plan, develop, implement, evaluate, and revise interventions.

The need for intervention can be reduced through preventive planning. Expectations for behavior should be communicated to students; students who meet expectations should receive positive reinforcement. If intervention is needed, the least intrusive approach should be attempted first; often a change in seating, a careful explanation of class rules, a demonstration of the expected behavior, or a mild reprimand in private can eliminate the problem. Intensive behavior change programs should be used only when less dramatic methods have proven to be unsuccessful.

FIGURE 5–6
Systematic Behavior Management Model

1. State the behavioral expectations for all students.
2. Determine whether students meeting expectations are receiving reinforcement to encourage maintenance of these behaviors.
3. Determine whether some students do not meet expectations. If so, do they know and understand the expectations? Do they have the prerequisite skills for the behaviors?
4. For students with inappropriate behaviors, identify target behaviors to be achieved.
5. Select an observation system, and collect baseline data on each behavior.
6. Analyze data to determine the need for an intervention program.
7. If data indicate the need for an intervention, determine whether the target behavior needs to be learned, increased, or decreased.
8. Select (or design) the intervention that uses the most positive approach.
9. Implement the intervention.
10. Collect data on student performance.
11. Analyze the data to determine the need to continue, modify, or terminate the intervention. Take required action.
12. When the behavior is at the desired level and is no longer dependent on the intervention, continue to collect maintenance data and return to step 4.

Establish Behavioral Expectations and Communicate Them to Students

Students are often unaware of the behavioral expectations for a specific classroom situation. Although more able students are capable of interpreting expectations from environmental cues (e.g., teacher signals, behavior of other students), students with behavior problems often do not interpret these cues. They need specific direction and instruction to know how they are expected to act. Effective classroom managers have been found to be particularly skilled in establishing classroom rules and procedures that communicate behavioral expectations to students (Doyle, 1986). Research results suggest that effective teachers take the following measures:

1. *Establish classroom rules and procedures at the start of the year.* Effective managers do not wait until problems occur; they anticipate potential problems prior to the beginning of school.

2. *Introduce rules and procedures on the first day of the class.* When rules and procedures are communicated to students immediately (from the beginning of the first day of school), they need not guess what the expectations are. Information overload is avoided by introducing the most essential rules and procedures first and presenting others as they are needed. The rules are posted or given to students as a handout, and new students are immediately oriented to the classroom expectations when they arrive in class.

3. *Explain rules and procedures clearly and teach them deliberately to students as part of a system for classroom operation.* A rationale is provided and instruction continues until the students have the rules and procedures mastered.

4. *Make rules and procedures concrete, functional, and explicit so that they contribute to the accomplishment of work and the order of the classroom.* The statements should be few, clear,

and plainly stated. They should indicate the desired behavior (e.g., "Work quietly at your desk," "Respect other people's property") rather than all the undesired behaviors (e.g., "Don't talk when you are working at your desk," "Don't write on the desks").

5. *Associate rules and procedures with clear signals that indicate when students are to carry out or stop specific behaviors or activities.* For instance, the teacher may use a specific phrase (e.g., "Please close your books and straighten your materials") to indicate that it is time to stop the current activity and quietly prepare to move to the next class or activity. In addition, the teacher may need to remind students about acceptable conduct prior to activities that are likely to elicit inappropriate behaviors (e.g., "You may sharpen your pencil but remember not to talk to others").

6. *Demonstrate or model rules and procedures and then allow students to rehearse them.* The teacher demonstrates both the correct and incorrect forms of the behavior (e.g., sitting at a desk, getting to the pencil sharpener). The demonstration enables the students to discriminate the dimensions of the behavior. Students are then given an opportunity to practice the required behavior. Mastering rules and procedures is similar to learning academics; it requires teacher instruction and feedback combined with student practice.

7. *Design rules and procedures to anticipate possible classroom interruptions or problems and to manage these situations.* For example, students may be expected to continue working when classroom visitors enter the room or to stop all activities immediately and line up quickly and quietly when there is a fire drill. Although these events may occur infrequently, expectations should be established and practiced.

8. *Monitor closely how well students follow rules and procedures.* Appropriate behavior is reinforced, and inappropriate behavior is stopped promptly. The teacher must be able to enforce the rules and procedures that are specified; failure to do so diminishes or eliminates their effectiveness. Rules should be modified or eliminated if they prove to be ineffective, unenforceable, or no longer needed. Specific teacher practices for monitoring and enforcing rules and classroom behaviors are presented throughout this chapter.

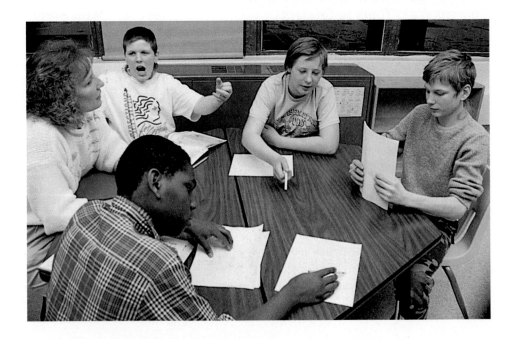

Prevent Inappropriate Conduct by Monitoring Behavior and Providing Feedback

To prevent behavior problems from occurring, teachers must be constantly aware of the behavior of their students and provide them with feedback regarding their performance. This process is as important in developing and maintaining appropriate classroom conduct and study skills as it is in providing academic instruction.

Two important skills related to preventing behavior problems have been identified by the research on effective teaching. These are (a) the ability to simultaneously monitor one or more groups while directing the activities of another and (b) the ability to direct the activities of those students who are not involved in the lesson being conducted by the teacher (Englert, 1984). The first skill requires that teachers position themselves to permit a continual visual scanning of the entire class so that they can observe and make eye contact with students not involved in the lesson. The second skill involves more than observation; it requires that the teacher respond to the observed behavior with verbal or nonverbal signals (e.g., frown, finger point, head nod) that will redirect the student to the assigned task. Effective managers do this without interrupting the lesson they are conducting.

The combination of providing positive attention for appropriate behavior and ignoring inappropriate behavior is frequently advocated for decreasing behavior problems. However, it is more effective to use positive attention for appropriate behavior together with the careful use of **negative attention** (i.e., a verbal or nonverbal response indicating disapproval) for inappropriate behavior (Jones & Eimers, 1975; Jones & Miller, 1974). This combination can be implemented without interfering with the activities of the classroom if teachers follow certain guidelines:

1. *Identify potentially disruptive behaviors at an early stage.* The teacher anticipates the need to act by observing student actions that are likely to lead to inappropriate behaviors.
2. *Develop a repertoire of quick, low-intensity gestures and verbalizations that signify that a student is not following the accepted guidelines.* For example, the teacher may say "John" (student's name) or "That's all" to get the student's attention and identify the current activity as inappropriate.
3. *Establish physical proximity to the disruptive student and orient yourself toward the student.* This strategy may involve the teacher's moving closer to the student and facing him or her to signal that the teacher is aware of, and does not approve of, the student's behavior. At the same time, the teacher maintains direction of an instructional group. Teacher movement around the room and a tight horseshoe arrangement of desks facilitates the use of this procedure.
4. *Promptly respond to inappropriate student behavior.* The teacher uses negative attention to interrupt the student's disruptiveness before it can produce approval or attention from peers.
5. *With negative attention, use a facial expression and tone of voice that is consistent with disapproval.* It is important to communicate to the offending student that the teacher is registering disapproval.
6. *After negative attention, provide immediate reinforcement and attention when the student displays the appropriate behavior.* This identifies the accepted behavior and reaffirms that appropriate behaviors are reinforced and inappropriate behaviors are punished.
7. *If necessary, use prompting to elicit the desired behavior, and then reinforce the student immediately.* Effective teachers actually require misbehaving students to practice the appropriate behavior until they have exhibited it at the established criterion level; these teachers often drill students until they perform the behavior automatically.

Reinforce Appropriate Behavior

It would be wonderful if all students behaved appropriately in school because their teachers expected them to or because it was intrinsically rewarding. However, this expectation is simply not realistic for many students. Teachers need to help students learn that accomplishments themselves can be rewarding. To do this, a powerful tool—reinforcement—is available.

When appropriate behaviors occur, they should be rewarded. To be effective, the reinforcer should follow the desired behavior. Rewards should not be provided when students promise to exhibit the behavior at some time in the future. Only performance is rewarded. *If* the student behaves appropriately, *then* the reward will occur. Appropriate behaviors should also be reinforced immediately. Reinforcers are most effective when delivered immediately after the occurrence of the behavior. For example, if the target behavior is completion of assignments, the student should be reinforced when handing in his or her paper. The reinforcer would lose its effect if it were delivered several hours later, after the teacher had corrected the paper.

When students are learning new behaviors, each occurrence should be reinforced. Continuous reinforcement rewards an appropriate behavior every time it happens. This is the most effective schedule for establishing a new behavior or for increasing the occurrence of an infrequent behavior. As soon as the behavior has become established, the reinforcers can be delivered according to one of the intermittent schedules described in Table 5–4; intermittent reinforcement requires less attention than the continuous schedule. If reduction in reinforcement is gradual, the student will eventually maintain the desired behavior with little reinforcement. Schedules of reinforcement should move from continuous to fixed interval/ratio and then to variable interval/ratio. With variable schedules, students are less able to predict when reinforcement will occur because reinforcers are given after an average period of time (interval) or after an average number of responses (ratio). For example, a variable ratio of 1:10 may deliver the reinforcer after 8 responses, then 7, then 13, as long as the *average* is 1 reinforcer for every 10 responses.

Provide Reinforcers That Are Valued by Students

Reinforcers of little value to students soon lose their effect. The simplest method of finding out what students perceive as rewarding is to ask them. Figure 5–7 is an example of an inventory that can be used to discover students' reinforcement preferences.

Another method of gaining this information is to observe how students use their free time.

It is also important to use a variety of reinforcers. Of the many types available, those that have strong effects on behavior are preferred. Following are several types of reinforcers found to be useful in the classroom:

1. *Social reinforcement.* Social attention or interaction with teachers and peers is a strong reinforcer for most students. It is easy to deliver and is naturally available in the school environment. It can be provided immediately after the occurrence of the desired behavior, and the effects can be generalized to other settings. When social reinforcement is provided, the teacher should tell the student the reason for the reward. The teacher can say (or write on the student's paper), "Good reading," "Nice job on the assignment," "I like the way you lined up for recess," or "Your handwriting is very easy to read." The teacher can also try smiles and, for younger students, hugs; these and other forms of positive attention are easy to give, free, and the supply is unlimited.

2. *Activity reinforcers.* Activities are also strong reinforcers. Any activity that the student enjoys can serve as a reward for the performance of a less desired task. This approach is known as the **Premack Principle**. If Joe finishes his math, then he can feed the gerbil; or if the class works quietly all morning, then they will see a movie after lunch. Other examples of activity reinforcers are spending time in the listening center, watching television, reading comics or magazines, helping the teacher, and watching filmstrips. These reinforcers are readily available in the school and involve minimal cost.

3. *Tangible reinforcers.* Objects such as certificates, notes to parents, toys, and school supplies can also serve as reinforcers for students. However, tangible reinforcers should be used only after social and activity reinforcers have proved too weak to support the occurrence of the behavior. When tangible reinforcers are delivered, they should always be accompanied by a social reinforcer; over time, the tangible reinforcer can be gradually faded so

TABLE 5–4
Intermittent Schedules of Reinforcement

Name of Schedule	Definition of Schedule	Effects on Behavior	
		Schedule in Effect	Schedule Terminated (Extinction)
Fixed Ratio (FR)	Reinforcer is given after each X responses.	High response rate.	Irregular burst of responding. More responses than in continuous reinforcement, less than in variable ratio.
Fixed Interval (FI)	Reinforcer is given for first response to occur after each X minutes.	Stops working after reinforcement. Works hard just prior to time for next reinforcement.	Slow gradual decrease in responding.
Variable Ratio (VR)	Reinforcer is given after X responses on the average.	Very high response rates. The higher the ratio the higher the rate.	Very resistant to extinction. Maximum number of responses before extinction.
Variable Interval (VI)	Reinforcer is given for first response after each X minutes, on the average.	Steady rate of responding.	Very resistant to extinction. Maximum time to extinction.

Note.   From *The Acting-Out Child: Coping with Classroom Disruption* (p. 103) by Hill M. Walker, 1979, Boston: Allyn and Bacon. Copyright 1979 by Allyn and Bacon. Reprinted by permission.

that it is replaced by just the use of the social reward. Disadvantages of tangible reinforcers include their cost (in terms of money or time to prepare) and a possible loss of effectiveness if they are provided too frequently. In addition, many parents and educators disagree with their use. Because they are not universally available, their effects may not generalize to other school settings.

4. *Edible reinforcers.*   The use of edibles should be considered only if social, activity, and tangible reinforcers have been found ineffective. Edibles have disadvantages similar to those of tangible reinforcers. If edibles are used, their presentation should always be paired with the delivery of a social reinforcer.

5. *Negative reinforcers.*   Unlike other forms of reinforcement, negative reinforcers are removed when the desired behavior occurs. For example, the teacher can eliminate 2 math problems for each 10 that are completed correctly. Or the teacher's

FIGURE 5–7
Reinforcement Inventory

1. If you could do anything you wanted to do this afternoon, how would you spend your time? _____

   _____

2. Name your three favorite television shows: _____

   _____

   _____

3. What is your favorite thing to do in each of these seasons:

   summer _____ fall _____

   winter _____ spring _____

4. If someone gave you $5 today, how would you spend it? _____

5. What is the best movie you ever saw? _____

6. Who is the adult you like the best? _____

7. Name your three favorite foods: _____

   _____

   _____

8. If you could play a quiet game with anybody in this school, who would you play with?_____

   _____

9. What are your three wishes? _____

   _____

   _____

10. What do you like to read about?_____

    Finish these sentences:

11. When I'm alone, I like to _____

12. It makes me really happy when my teacher _____

    _____

13. When I grow up, I_____

14. The most fun at home is when_____

15. If I could take home something from school, I would take home _____

    _____

16. If I were the teacher in this room, I would _____

    _____

Note. Reprinted with permission of Merrill, an imprint of Macmillan Publishing Company, from *The Resource Room* (p. 62) by M. F. Hawisher and M. L. Calhoun. Copyright 1978 Merrill Publishing Company, Columbus, Ohio.

frown can disappear when students begin working. Like the more positive reinforcers, these have a place in the classroom. When negative reinforcers produce the desired behavior, the student should be rewarded. For example, when the student begins to work, the teacher can stop frowning *and* praise the student for working.

The variety of reinforcers available in the classroom is limited only by the teacher's imagination. Additional examples are listed in "Tips for the Teacher" on page 150. Remember, though, that social, activity, tangible, and edible reinforcers are rewards only if they are valued by the student.

Use Token Economies to Deliver Reinforcers

In a **token economy**, students are presented with tokens rather than reinforcers after the occurrence of a desired behavior. Such a system can be used with one student, small groups, or the entire class. Students collect the tokens—such as poker chips, gold stars, or points—and later trade them for backup reinforcers listed on a **reinforcement menu**. Tokens should be delivered as soon as the desired behavior has occurred and should always be paired with a social reinforcer. In setting up a token economy, the teacher should

- specify and define the behaviors that earn tokens;
- use tokens that are appropriate for the students;
- develop and post a menu that includes a variety of reinforcers and a wide range of costs—students should be able to "cash in" for either high- or low-cost reinforcers;
- allow students to help in developing the menu;
- revise the menu regularly to ensure variety;
- use a record system that is clear and cannot be sabotaged by students (who might add points or take the tokens of others);
- give students frequent opportunities to cash in (daily or at least several times per week);
- set up a cash-in system that takes a minimal amount of time and does not disrupt the operation of the class;

- provide clear rules to staff for distribution of tokens; and
- gradually reduce the value of the tokens to increase reliance on more natural reinforcers.

Token systems have been shown to be effective with regular class students and students with special needs (Smith et al., 1993), and they are easily understood by teachers and students. The menu allows students to select their own rewards. Also, token systems accommodate students who have difficulty waiting for their reinforcers; they can cash in when they want to. When the token economy is first set up, students tend to cash in frequently; however, as they grow accustomed to this system, they are able to wait for longer periods. Figure 5–8 presents a reinforcement menu that can be used in a token economy.

With Older Students, Use Contingency Contracts

Contingency contracts are written agreements between the student and teacher that indicate what the student must do to earn a specific reward. These agreements, like most contracts, are negotiated; both parties must accept the terms. Because they involve negotiation and require students to assume responsibility for fulfilling their part of the bargain, contracts are probably best for older students.

Homme, Csanyi, Gonzales, and Rechs (cited in Blankenship & Lilly, 1981) provide the following rules for developing contracts in the classroom:

1. The contract payoff (reward) should be immediate.
2. Initial contracts should call for and reward small approximations.
3. Reward frequently with small amounts.
4. The contract should call for and reward accomplishment rather than obedience.
5. Reward the behavior after it occurs.
6. The contract must be fair.
7. The terms of the contract must be clear.
8. The contract must be honest.
9. The contract must be positive.
10. Contracting as a method must be used systematically. (p. 235)

Classroom Reinforcers

*H*ere are several examples of different types of reinforcers appropriate for use in school settings. Social and activity reinforcers have special appeal since they are usually available at no cost to the teacher.

	Social	Activity	Tangible	Edible
Elementary-aged students	Hug Positive comments: "Good job," "I like the way you raised your hand," "You really pay attention" Pat on the back	Helping teacher Popcorn party Being team leader Reading with a friend Time in the computer center Choosing game for P.E. Extra minutes of recess X minutes of free time Cleaning the chalkboard Eating lunch with teacher	Toys Crayons Pencils Erasers Paper Art materials Books Stars Good note to parents	Cereal Fruit Cake Nuts Popcorn Ice cream Sandwich Milk
Adolescents	Signal or gesture of approval Handshake Positive comment on appearance Positive comments: "Great job," "Best work I've seen," "Great to see you working so well"	Field trip Free time Early lunch Choosing class activity Listening to record for X minutes Attending a concert	Pens Paper Rental of tapes/CDs School supplies Sports equipment Magazines Posters Positive note home	Teacher buys lunch. Popcorn Chips Juice Candy Fruit Soft drinks

FIGURE 5–8
Reinforcement Menu

Reinforcers	Points
Apple	10
Cookie	10
Pencil	10
Popcorn	10
Small candies	15
Lanyard materials	25/yd.
Large candies	45
Gum	45
Viewing educational videotape (10 minutes)	50
Viewing entertainment videotape (10 minutes)	100
Pen	100
Grab bag	100
Cassette tape recorder (rental)	100
Tokens for video games	150
Hamburger at fast-food restaurant	500
Free time	500
Time with the computer	500
Shampoo and set	500
Time for game with a friend	700
Lunch with the teacher	750
Blank cassette tapes	1,000
Music tapes	1,500
CDs	2,500
Price as marked:	
Paperbacks of your choice	____
Magazines (Motorcycle, Car, Autocross, etc.)	____
Movie tickets/passes	____
Models	____
Records	____
Field trip	____

A sample contract form, providing space for recording the agreement that has been negotiated between the student and the teacher, is shown in Figure 5–9. A good contract identifies the responsibilities of both parties and the consequences if the terms are not fulfilled.

Teach Behaviors by Shaping

Shaping involves the reinforcement of successive approximations or small progressive steps toward the desired behavior. The technique of shaping is used to teach new behaviors or increase the occurrence of behaviors exhibited infrequently. For example, shaping can be used with a student who completes only one or two assignments per week, when the desired behavior is eight assignments per day. First, a target of one completed assignment per day is established. This is reinforced until the student regularly finishes the daily work. Then the target is raised to two, then three assignments, and so on, as the student progresses toward the ultimate goal of eight assignments

> **FIGURE 5–9**
> Contingency Contract

Official Contract

Effective Dates: From _____ to _____

This contract involves an agreement between _____ and
(Teacher/Parent)

_____. This agreement will be reviewed on the following
(Student)

date(s) _____ and can be renegotiated at any time by

agreement of both parties.

When _____ (Student) does the following: _____

_____

_____

then _____(Teacher/Parent) will: _____

_____

_____

According to this agreement the teacher/parent will provide the agreed-upon
reinforcers to the student only if he or she fulfills his or her part of the contract. If
the student does not fulfill his or her part of the agreement, the reinforcers will be
withheld.

Teacher/Parent Signature _____ Date_____

Student Signature _____ Date_____

---

per day. For the student who completes no assignments, the beginning target might be a few problems or items of each assignment; this goal would be gradually increased toward the classroom goal of eight completed assignments per day.

Use Modeling to Improve Student Behavior

Modeling involves the reinforcement of another individual, the model, for exhibiting the desired behavior in the presence of the target student. The target student is then reinforced when he or she imitates the modeled behavior. For example, the model seated near the target student might be reinforced for studying; the teacher clearly identifies the reason for the reinforcement by saying, "I like the way you are working quietly in your seat." When this behavior is imitated by the target student, he or she is also rewarded.

Consider Involving Peers in Behavioral Programs

Involving class members in implementing programs designed to improve student behavior can be effective. Students can often provide strong reinforcers for the behavior of their peers, and in many cases they are able to monitor and respond to behaviors that the teacher might miss. The use of peers can involve either individual or group programs.

Group contingencies involve establishing a criterion level for the entire group, and the distribution of reinforcement to individual class members is based on the performance of the entire group. For example, a teacher concerned with the high number of talk-outs (average of 45 per day) could establish a system in which the entire class earns 5 minutes of extra recess if there were no more than 20 talk-outs the previous day. As the students improve, the teacher can gradually reduce the number of talk-outs accepted (e.g., they might be reduced by 1 each week).

Team-based contingencies involve grouping students into teams that compete against each other. As with group contingencies, individual students can help or hurt their team. A teacher wishing to increase the amount of homework completed might establish a prize based on the percentage of assignments completed for the week. The prize (i.e., consequence) could be awarded in one of several different ways: (a) only the team with the highest percentage wins, (b) each team wins that reaches a percentage higher than

a preset criterion (e.g., 95%), or (c) the prize earned by each team is based on the percentage of assignments completed by that team (e.g., a team completing 50% of the assignments earns 30 minutes in the computer area, whereas the team that completes 100% earns 1 hour). Greater changes are usually achieved by dividing groups into teams than by concentrating on whole groups.

Another way of involving peers is to have group members share in the consequences earned by a particular student. A rather withdrawn student in a regular class might earn points for each social interaction with a peer. Peers might seek to increase their interactions with that student if the entire class receives an extra minute of recess for every 10 points earned by the student. Similarly, a student who is easily distracted might experience fewer interruptions from classmates if they are all earning reinforcers for increases in the student's on-task behavior.

Peers can be trained to reinforce students such as the withdrawn or distractible students described above. They might provide the reinforcement for such students, especially if they earn reinforcers for the other student's performance. They might also be used to record the other student's performance (e.g., actual interactions or the amount of on-task behavior); these data may be more accurate than teacher-collected data.

Although such programs can be effective, teachers must consider several factors before involving peers in interventions. First, all the students involved must be able to perform the desired behavior. Otherwise, students may be subjected to potential physical or verbal abuse. Second, individual students should not be able to subvert the efforts of the group. Third, students should not be able to do the work required of others in order to improve the performance of their group. The interactions resulting from these programs can be very reinforcing to the students involved, and they often lead to improved transfer of behaviors and to positive interactions outside the typical classroom setting. As with other interventions, careful planning increases the likelihood of success.

Involve Students in Managing Their Own Behavior

Students can be directly involved in managing their own behavior by (a) participating in setting goals, (b) self-monitoring, or (c) assisting in the intervention itself by evaluating their own performance and rewarding themselves for appropriate behavior. If they learn techniques that help improve their behavior in one setting, they can often transfer those skills to other settings.

Teachers can identify several areas in which students need to improve their behavior. The students themselves, especially those at the secondary level, can help to set goals for improvement in these areas, or they can choose other areas of need. Assisting in identifying goals increases students' active involvement in improving their own behavior.

Self-monitoring can take a number of forms. Students may simply be required to judge whether they are "working" at the end of each 5- to 10-minute segment of the class period or at the time a teacher-set buzzer rings. They might also record and graph their daily spelling performance, the number of times they leave their desk, or the length of time they are away from their desk each day. In addition, the number of talk-outs or the number of social interactions they ini-

tiate can be recorded by the students. Self-monitoring needs to be supervised by the teacher, with reinforcement provided for accuracy; reinstruction should be provided if the data are not consistent with those collected by the teacher. Self-monitoring decreases the demands on the teacher for collecting data, and it also makes students acutely aware of their own behavior.

A variety of interventions can be self-administered by students. They can learn to evaluate and self-reinforce their own performance in class. For example, they might give themselves points or check marks for improving their spelling performance or for reducing the amount of time they are out of their seats during a day. Self-punishment might involve deducting points for talking out in class or failing to complete a homework assignment. Other approaches might involve teaching students a strategy to use in resolving various kinds of problems they encounter. Students might be taught to ask specific questions or to make specific self-statements (i.e., **self-instruction**) to help themselves develop problem-solving skills (e.g., "What am I supposed to do? What is my plan? How do I do it?"). A combination of these various approaches (e.g., self-instruction followed by self-reinforcement) can actively involve students in improving their own behavior. It also increases the chance of the intervention's success and the generalization of newly learned skills to other situations.

Involve Parents in Behavior Management Programs

Parents are often willing and helpful participants in behavior management programs. They can provide continuation of the intervention program at home; for instance, parents can reinforce students for time spent doing homework. They can also assist by providing reinforcers for the school behavior of their children. For example, if students earn a certain number of points in school, parents can provide a special activity, such as a camping trip, or a gift, such as a baseball glove or doll.

Positive notes to parents from teachers can be reinforcing both for students and for parents. Many parents of special students have received few good reports from school. A note from a teacher praising

FIGURE 5–10
Are You Managing the Classroom Effectively?

Respond to each item in terms of the extent to which it describes yourself: (1) not at all descriptive, (2) descriptive to a small extent, (3) descriptive to a moderate extent, (4) descriptive to a large extent, (5) descriptive to an extremely large extent.

Competencies

Classroom Set-up and Organization

1.1	Arranges physical space and instructional materials to minimize disruptive movement around classroom and to facilitate easy access to high-use materials.	1 2 3 4 5
1.2	Establishes and implements minimally disruptive traffic patterns and procedures.	1 2 3 4 5
1.3	Establishes and implements procedures for nonacademic class business (e.g., tardiness, material use, movement in and out of room, distributing materials, talk among students, bathroom breaks).	1 2 3 4 5
1.4	Establishes and implements procedures for academic business (e.g., seatwork procedures, obtaining help, volunteer behavior during small group, learning centers, set-up and take-down of lessons).	1 2 3 4 5

Teaching Rules and Procedures

2.1	Communicates clearly what behavior will be tolerated and what will not.	1 2 3 4 5
2.2	Gives behavior reminders and statements of desired behavior in advance of activity.	1 2 3 4 5
2.3	Clearly introduces rules, procedures, and consequences at beginning of school year and whenever needed.	1 2 3 4 5
2.4	States rules, posts rules, and provides discussion of rules at the time of their introduction.	1 2 3 4 5
2.5	Presents examples and non-examples of rules and procedures.	1 2 3 4 5
2.6	Requires student rehearsal of rules and procedures.	1 2 3 4 5
2.7	Monitors rule compliance and provides specific behavioral feedback.	1 2 3 4 5
2.8	Consequates rule noncompliance by stopping inappropriate behavior immediately and requiring students to practice the procedure until it is performed automatically.	1 2 3 4 5

Maintaining Rules and Procedures

3.1	Positions self in the room to provide high degree of visibility (e.g., can make eye contact with all students).	1 2 3 4 5
3.2	Scans constantly and makes eye contact with all students on an equal basis.	1 2 3 4 5
3.3	Detects disruptive behavior early and cites rule or procedure in responding to disruptive behavior.	1 2 3 4 5
3.4	Reinforces appropriate performance through specific praise statements (e.g., states specific behaviors).	1 2 3 4 5
3.5	Administers praise contingently.	1 2 3 4 5
3.6	Includes students in the management of their own behavior.	1 2 3 4 5
3.7	Uses nonverbal signals to direct students when teaching other groups of students.	1 2 3 4 5

Note. From "Measuring Teacher Effectiveness from the Teacher's Point of View" by C. S. Englert, 1984, *Focus on Exceptional Children, 17*(2), p. 5. Copyright 1984 by Love. Reprinted by permission.

THINGS TO REMEMBER

- To function successfully in the general education classroom, students may need to increase some behaviors, decrease others, and learn new ways of acting.
- Classroom behavior problems interfere with instruction and social interactions; study skills problems affect a student's academic performance.
- Intervention may be necessary if there is a low rate of appropriate behavior, a high rate of inappropriate behavior, or an absence of the appropriate behavior from the student's repertoire.
- Behavior is learned and can be taught; it is increased by reinforcement and decreased by the removal of reinforcers or the introduction of aversive events.
- Behaviors do not occur in isolation; their antecedents and consequences must be considered.
- Direct observation of student behavior provides the most useful data for classroom teachers.
- Class rules and procedures make students aware of the expectations for behavior.
- Methods of using reinforcers to change behavior include token economies, contingency contracts, and group contingencies.
- Preventing behavior problems involves careful monitoring of students, reinforcement of appropriate behaviors, and use of negative teacher attention for potentially disruptive behavior.
- Students can participate in self-management of behavior by setting goals, monitoring their own performance, or implementing interventions such as self-reinforcement or self-instruction.
- Effective reinforcers are those valued by the students.

the accomplishments of a student can increase the level of praise that the student receives at home.

Before involving parents in intervention programs, teachers should be sure that the parents are willing and able to implement procedures consistently. If home and school programs are not well coordinated, the effectiveness of both may decrease. Consistency can be improved by providing some parent training or with frequent communication between parents and teachers. Englert (1984) provides several suggestions for improving classroom behavior management techniques. The checklist in Figure 5–10 summarizes these suggestions.

Techniques for promoting the social acceptance of special students in the mainstreamed classroom are discussed in the next chapter. Thank you for reading to the end of this chapter. When you complete your review of "Things to Remember" and the activities listed below, you may want to reward yourself with a short break or a beverage.

ACTIVITIES

1. Collect observation data on an individual (friend, student, teacher) during five separate observation periods. Be sure you have identified a specific behavior to observe (such as being on-task). Record and graph the data using a format similar to the one presented in this chapter. When you are finished, show your graph to another individual; can that person interpret your data? Can you speculate about what antecedents and consequences contribute to the occurrence of the behavior? Describe an intervention you might use if you wished to change the behavior.
2. Interview both a special educator and a general education teacher. Obtain information about the approaches they advocate for managing students in the regular classroom. What do they consider to be problem behaviors? According to the teachers, are special techniques needed for special students, or are the behavior problems of all stu-

dents managed in generally the same way? Ask the teachers to describe how they use student performance data in behavior change programs. Do they collect data before beginning a program? During the program? How do they decide when a program is working? When it needs to be changed?

3. Develop a set of rules for a classroom you have recently observed. Describe the class and establish five to eight rules using the guidelines stated in the chapter. Explain specifically how you would implement these rules at the beginning of a school year. Identify potential problems you might experience in implementing your rules, and describe how you would deal with these problems.

4. Read and summarize two articles that discuss token economies, contracting, or one of the other techniques described in this chapter. Journals such as *Psychology in the Schools, Journal of Applied Behavior Analysis, Education and Treat-ment of Children,* and *Behavior Modification* often feature articles on these topics.

5. Consider different viewpoints on classroom discipline. Contact local school districts to learn about their policies. Also, get in touch with a national teachers' organization, such as the American Federation of Teachers or the National Education Association. Compare the policies of local districts with those of the professional organization you contact. What changes would you make in these policies? Why would you make these changes?

6. Develop a reinforcement menu for a school-aged student. Begin by interviewing the student using the inventory presented in Figure 5–7. You may want to add questions and observe the student in different situations. Then develop a menu that includes at least 10 items, ranging in cost (points) from cheap to expensive. Describe how a general education teacher could use this menu when implementing a behavior change program.

6 Promoting Social Acceptance

Juan has been mainstreamed for a month and still eats lunch alone.

Jackie, who travels by wheelchair, is the only girl in her fifth grade class who hasn't been invited to a birthday party yet this year.

June dislikes talking in class because the other students make fun of her speech.

Even though Matt's classroom behavior has improved, his teacher is reluctant to have him join the class for assemblies and field trips.

Maria's American history teacher wants her to read the text like everyone else rather than listen to special tapes.

The school janitor is irritated because Hank's crutches leave marks on the floors of the classroom, halls, and bathroom.

Mike attends a class for students with severe disabilities that was moved to the regular school campus last month. Although members of his class work in the lunchroom, attend assemblies, and use the playing fields and the gym for physical education, students in the general education program avoid social or verbal interactions with Mike and his classmates.

Several of the parents of Tim's classmates are concerned about his mild seizures; they wonder whether Tim's condition is contagious.

Special students participating in educational programs in the mainstream often suffer rejection during their school years. They have often been rejected by their regular class peers, their teachers, or the parents of their classmates. This lack of acceptance has a negative effect on not only their self-concept but also their school performance (Heron & Harris, 1993; Schumaker & Hazel, 1984). To be effective, a mainstreaming program must make provisions for improving the social skills of special students and enhancing their social integration. This requirement holds true both for special students who enter the regular class from a special program and for those who have never left the mainstream setting.

SOCIAL PROBLEMS IN THE CLASSROOM

Many special students encounter difficulty in social interactions with general education peers and teachers. One source of this difficulty can be the behavior of the special student. At least equally important are the attitudes and feelings of the general population. Many people have little accurate information about special students, and this lack of knowledge can create fear and prejudice.

Special students may fail to conform to the expectations of school and society. They may not look or act the same as other students. For teachers and peers unfamiliar with special students, these differences can create apprehension, distrust, and even hostility. The abilities, talents, and needs of the special student are frequently overlooked.

Some special students can be easily identified; their appearance or their actions are visibly different. One example is the student who travels by wheelchair. Others have no observable signs but stand out when their performance falls below expectations. For instance, students with learning disabilities are indistinguishable from their peers until they are asked to read or write or do math.

Throughout their school careers, special students encounter failure. When placed in the regular classroom, they may be apprehensive about attempting activities. This fear of failure and feeling of incompetence may cause them to withdraw. This withdrawal can contribute to their rejection and make it difficult for even the most effective and creative teacher to provide an appropriate learning situation (Gresham, 1984; Meisgeier, 1981).

Special students can be as delayed in their social development as they are in other areas (Odom, McConnell, & Chandler, 1994). Thus, poor social skills can be another factor in their rejection

(Hollinger, 1987). Many special students are not as capable as regular class peers of initiating and sustaining appropriate social relationships. For example, the research of Bryan and Pflaum (1978) found students with learning disabilities lacking in the language skills necessary for effective social communication. Special students may fail to develop appropriate social skills because they have fewer friends and are rated significantly lower in sociometric status than their peers (Asher & Taylor, 1981; Drabman & Patterson, 1981; McIntosh, Vaughn, & Zaragoza, 1991; Ray, 1985). Or it may be that special students have difficulty using social cues; some misperceive their social standing and feel that they are better accepted by peers than they actually are (Heron & Harris, 1993). According to Bryan and Bryan (1977), students with learning disabilities exhibit more aggressive or negative behaviors, are less accurate in interpreting nonverbal communications, and "emit a lot [of] nasty statements to their peers" (p. 142). Drabman and Patterson (1981) describe excep-

tional students as "opposing peers, displaying disruptive behavior and exhibiting withdrawal behavior" (p. 48). It is difficult to determine the cause of the problem: Friendless students have little opportunity to develop social skills, and those with poor skills are unlikely to form friendships.

At the secondary level, these problems may increase. In adolescence, social interaction with peers becomes extremely important. For special students who have spent the majority of their educational careers segregated from age peers, the transition to the mainstream environment can be hazardous. Special students not only may lack a common experiential background with regular class students but also may be delayed in the acquisition of important social skills. These obstacles, combined with the barriers to acceptance in the general education class, magnify the difficulty of promoting the social acceptance of special secondary students.

Research indicates that regular class students and teachers do not consistently accept the special

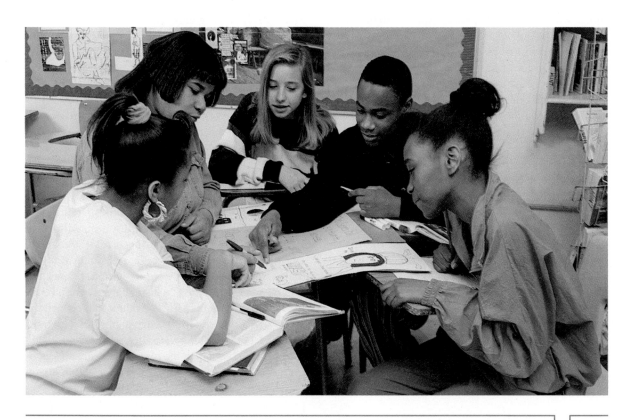

student (e.g., Drabman & Patterson, 1981; Gans, 1985; Garrett & Crump, 1980; Gottlieb & Leyser, 1981; Sabornie & Kauffman, 1985). Teachers and peers are more likely to ignore social interactions initiated by special students. And teachers are more critical of their behavior, provide fewer praise statements, and consider them less desirable as students (Heron & Harris, 1993); this is especially apparent if the students are boys (e.g., Schlosser & Algozzine, 1980; Slate & Saudargas, 1986; Stitt et al., 1988).

One factor that influences teacher attitudes is labeling. When students are identified by a negatively perceived label (e.g., learning disabilities, mental retardation), teachers are less able to objectively observe, rate, and plan appropriate interventions for their behavior (Campbell, Dodson, & Bost, 1985). Although the effects of labeling on social acceptance have not been consistently supported by research (Gottlieb & Leyser, 1981), evidence is adequate to caution against reliance on labels for educational information. For instance, Gillung and Rucker (1977) found that teachers expected less from students who were labeled than from unlabeled students with identical behaviors. Alves and Gottlieb (1986) reported that teachers involved students with disabilities in fewer academic exchanges; these students were asked fewer questions and were given less feedback than their peers without disabilities. In a study conducted by Reschly and Lamprecht (1979), students' labels lowered the initial expectations of teachers; however, as teachers spent more time with special students and observed their behavior, expectations became more realistic. Thus, labels can be misleading and can have a negative effect, at least on the initial acceptance of special students by their teachers.

Another factor that can contribute to the rejection of special students by general education teachers and administrators is a lack of special training and experience (Heron & Harris, 1993; Martin, 1974). Some teachers are afraid that they do not have the skills necessary for teaching special students. Others may feel that working with these students is not as gratifying as working with typical individuals. Teachers with negative attitudes toward special students can convey these feelings to all the individuals in the class and thereby further reduce the chance for successful mainstreaming (e.g., Garrett & Crump, 1980; Heron & Harris, 1993).

A portion of the problem related to the attitudes toward students with special needs can be attributed to former special education practices. For some time, special classes were virtually the only special education service available for students with disabilities. Special educators advocated that these students be removed from the mainstream and entrusted to the care of a specialist in a separate class setting. As a result, general education teachers were not encouraged to attempt to meet the needs of special students within the mainstream setting. At present, however, a variety of part-time special education services are available for both the special students and their general education teachers. In addition, mainstreaming and inclusion are now common practices, and training programs for general education teachers currently require some level of preparation in dealing with the needs of students with disabilities. One important aspect of effective special education programs is ensuring that the collaboration and consulting role of the special educator helps regular class teachers realize that special students can successfully participate in general education settings for a portion of the school day that is appropriate for each student.

The parents of special students can also contribute to the social problems of their children. Parents can be overly protective and restrict a student's involvement in normal social activities, which thereby reduces the opportunities for acquiring friends and fosters a limited experience base. Parents reluctant to allow their child to experience failure can actually be increasing the probability that failure will occur in future social interactions. In addition, the parents of general education students can also influence the acceptance of special students. Some may resist inclusion in the general education program if they believe that it will reduce the quality of their children's education. Other parents may discourage their children from interacting with the special students in the class. These negative attitudes are often based on limited information about, and limited experience with, special students.

*H*ave you ever wondered about how to interact with a person with disabilities? Here are several suggestions:

- Converse with an individual with disabilities in spirit, content, and approach as you would with anyone else.
- When you think someone with a disability may need assistance, ask, "Do you need help? How should I help you?"
- Do not shout at blind persons. They have lost their *vision* not their hearing.
- Do not "talk over" or provide the words for someone who stutters or speaks with difficulty. Be patient and listen, and let the person speak for himself.
- *Always FACE* a person with a hearing impairment. Be sure the person can see your lips; speak clearly without exaggerating lip movements.
- Speak directly to a person with disabilities. Do not direct your conversation to an attendant, assistant, or nearby companion as if she did not exist.
- Do not call special attention to a person with disabilities. Approach her as another person who happens to have a disability—*not* as a disability that belongs to a person.

Note. From "Some Social Tips for Non-Disabled Folks," *Report from Closer Look*, Spring 1981, p. 5. Adapted by permission.

PRINCIPLES FOR ENHANCING SOCIAL ACCEPTANCE

When rejected by general education teachers and peers, special students may perform more poorly, both socially and academically. The self-concept of rejected students can be improved. In addition, because they are not encouraged to participate in classroom activities, rejected students may fall further behind in all skill areas. Simply including special students in regular classes does not guarantee their social acceptance or their acquisition of improved social skills. In most cases, the general education teacher must participate in developing and implementing a systematic program designed to improve the students' social skills and to increase their social integration. Effective mainstreaming and inclusion programs require that educators pay

attention to the social needs as well as to the academic, behavioral, and physical needs of their students (Gresham, 1984; York, Vandercook, MacDonald, Heise-Neff, & Caughey, 1992). The principles described in the following paragraphs assist in planning and implementing a successful program for social acceptance.

Change Attitudes with Information

Attitudes are extremely important. The attitudes of the teacher have a significant effect on the attitudes of the students within the class; negative feelings toward special students can be communicated by the teacher (Cartledge, Frew, & Zaharias, 1985; Garrett & Crump, 1980; Simpson, 1980). Teachers should realize that their words and actions provide a model for students; they should attempt to convey a positive attitude that encourages acceptance of the special student. Attitudes are affected by information. When students and adults increase their knowledge about special students, their attitudes improve (Donaldson & Martinson, 1977; Handlers & Austin, 1980; Simpson, 1980). Information dispels misconceptions and clarifies misunderstandings; prejudice and fear decrease. Teachers and regular class peers become more accepting as they learn more about the abilities and problems of special students (Fiedler & Simpson, 1987; Simpson, 1980).

Knowledge about special students can be gained in many ways. Students and teachers can read or view films, videotapes, and television programs about special students. Also, simulations of disabilities can be used to increase understanding. Visits to special education settings can be arranged, or special students and adults can be interviewed or invited to the general education classroom. Even higher levels of exposure can be gained if teachers volunteer to accept special students in their classes or regular class students are encouraged to work as peer tutors with special students. As more is learned about special individuals, they appear less different, more familiar, and more acceptable.

Recognize the Similarities Between Special and Regular Class Students

Teachers and students may form opinions about the abilities of a special student solely on the basis of physical appearance, labels, or occasional behaviors. Assumptions made by teachers are extremely important because they may influence instructional expectations for the student. A student's looks or assigned label is an insufficient database for programming decisions or for predicting the characteristics of his or her personality. Although it is easy to jump to conclusions, more information is necessary before educational plans and predictions can be made. What is needed is specific assessment information about the student's skills and abilities and an opportunity to observe the student in the classroom. Knowledge that a student has a vision impairment,

for example, raises the anxiety level of the teacher. More pertinent is information that, although the student reads braille materials, she is able to participate in class discussions, benefit from lectures, and interact socially with her classmates. When the team determines that students are able to benefit from placement in the general education classroom, those students do not need to be protected by the teacher. They should be included in as many activities as feasible and treated like any other student in the mainstreamed classroom—that is, as individuals.

Teachers often talk about the behaviors and characteristics of the special students in their classrooms. However, in most cases the academic problems and inappropriate behaviors of special students are also evident in many of their "normal" peers. If teachers were to list the typical behaviors, traits, and concerns of regular class students, they would find that these are also typical of special students. Special students are children and adolescents with identified needs; despite these needs, however, they remain individuals. As Turnbull and Schulz (1979) state, "A difference is only a difference when it makes a difference. . . . [C]hildren [with disabilities] have far more similarities than differences with the [children without disabilities]" (p. 48).

Prepare Students in the Regular Class for Mainstreaming

Regular class students are often isolated from any contact with special students. Consequently, general education students may never have met a person with a disability unless a special individual is among their family, friends, or neighbors. This limited knowledge and experience can lead to the development of prejudice and nonaccepting attitudes and a natural discrimination against individuals who are different. Evidence suggests that "discriminatory responses may exist as relatively normal patterns of behavior" (Simpson, 1980, p. 2).

The attitudes of students in the regular class can be improved and their acceptance of special students in the mainstream increased (Donaldson, 1980; Fox, 1989; Guralnick, 1981; Johnson & Johnson, 1984;

York et al., 1992). Before special students are placed in the regular class, activities should be conducted to provide information and skills to regular class students. For example, students can learn about disabilities and gain skills in assisting special students in the classroom. Such experiences also benefit special students who never leave the regular classroom. This training can be provided by general educators or general and special educators working together.

Prepare Special Students for Inclusion in the Mainstream

One of the reasons for rejection of special students is their frequent lack of social skills. In most cases, students with disabilities should be provided with specific training in the social skills needed to function successfully in school and the community (Brady & McEvoy, 1989; Cartledge, Frew, & Zaharias, 1985; Gresham, 1984; Hollinger, 1987; Schumaker & Hazel, 1984). Special students are able to acquire appropriate social behaviors; however, this is not likely to occur if students are only provided with opportunities to interact with peers and adults. Specific instruction, including modeling and practice, is usually necessary and can be provided in either the special or the general education classroom. In fact, the most successful social skills interventions are those that are structured for individuals or small groups and designed to be conducted over long-term periods (McIntosh et al., 1991).

Prepare Parents for Mainstreaming

Parents of both regular class and special students can make important contributions to the social acceptance program. The attitudes they convey to their children influence their children's attitudes, the teacher's efforts, and the school program. Parents often have concerns about special students being involved in the general education program because they are uncertain about the effects on their children. Informing parents about the needs of special students, the purpose of the program, and the impact on their children will help gain their support. It is important that parents realize that after students leave school, they will all be intermingling in the community. The school program helps prepare them for this involvement.

METHODS FOR GATHERING DATA

Data collection is just as important in promoting social acceptance as it is in instruction and modification of classroom behavior. Assessment information can determine the current attitudes and social behaviors of students and teachers. If the effectiveness of a social acceptance program is to be evaluated, data should be collected both before and after the program is implemented. In addition, continuous monitoring of progress is necessary so that program modifications can be made.

Information about social skills and acceptance can be gathered from many sources: regular class and special students, general and special education teachers, other professionals, and parents. Various methods are used in assessment. **Sociometric measures** provide information about how special students are perceived by general education peers. Teacher opinions can be obtained in interviews or teacher ratings or rankings of class members. Self-concept measures, such as those in Figure 6–1, are used to see how special students feel about themselves. In addition, the observational techniques described in chapter 5 assist in finding out about the types of social behaviors exhibited by special students and their social interactions with teachers and peers. McLoughlin and Lewis (1994) describe a variety of assessment devices useful in a social acceptance program. These include measures of self-concept, attitudes toward school, interactions with teachers, and peer relationships.

One of the most popular methods for gathering data about acceptance and rejection of special students is the sociometric measure. Sociometric devices, which measure the attitudes of group members toward one another, are often recommended for finding out how well special students are accepted by peers (Polloway & Patton, 1993). Results can serve as an overall index of the social skill development of special students (Cartledge & Milburn, 1986; Luftig, 1989). These devices are relatively simple, quick to administer, and easy to interpret, but it is important to note that while they provide an overall measure of the acceptance of students, they do not identify specific behaviors or skills that require intervention.

As shown in Table 6–1, several different types of sociometric measures are used. Students can be

---

FIGURE 6–1
Assessing Self-Concept

Adjective Check List

Directions: Put an *X* by each word that describes you.

_____ 1. smart	_____ 7. quarrelsome	_____ 13. bothersome
_____ 2. funny	_____ 8. fidgety	_____ 14. cranky
_____ 3. tired	_____ 9. energetic	_____ 15. eager
_____ 4. happy	_____ 10. friendly	_____ 16. honest
_____ 5. blue	_____ 11. shy	_____ 17. lazy
_____ 6. busy	_____ 12. sad	_____ 18. selfish

Behavioral Check List

Directions: Put an *X* by each description that fits you.

_____ 1. makes friends easily	_____ 6. seems to lack confidence
_____ 2. not as smart as most kids	_____ 7. is a good leader
_____ 3. likes to be alone	_____ 8. enjoys school
_____ 4. is fun to be with	_____ 9. feelings are easily hurt
_____ 5. laughs a lot	_____ 10. daydreams a lot

Note. Reprinted with permission of Merrill, an imprint of Macmillan Publishing Company, from *Teacher Diagnosis of Educational Difficulties* (2nd ed.) by R. M. Smith, Copyright © 1982 Merrill Publishing Company, Columbus, Ohio.

TABLE 6-1
Sociometric Methods

Method	Description	Example	Scoring	Comments
Nomination	Requires students to name classmates who fit a particular sociometric criterion. Can be based upon positive or negative criteria.	Name three classmates whom you would like to have sitting near you (positive). Name three classmates whom you do not like to have sitting near you (negative).	A student's score is the total number of nominations received from classmates. (Tally those with positive and negative criteria separately.)	Scores are generally stable over time. Not as stable for very young children. Ratings are obtained on only those students nominated.

Rating scale	All students in the class are listed, and a rating scale (e.g., 1 = low and 5 = high) is provided. Each student in the class is rated.	Circle the number which best indicates your opinion. I would like to study with . . .
		
		       Not A
		      at all lot
		Joe 1 2 3 4 5
		Mary 1 2 3 4 5
			Each student's score is an average of their ratings from all students.	All students are rated by all other students in the class. Has high test-retest reliability.

Paired-comparison	The most preferred classmate is chosen from all possible pairings of students in the class.	Circle the classmate in each pair with whom you would most like to study. 1. John or Martha 2. John or Sam . . . 40. Martha or Sue	A student's score is the number of times he or she was chosen by other students in all the possible pairings.	All students are rated by all other students. Has high test-retest reliability. Administration and scoring take more time than other methods.

Note. From "Social Outcomes of Mainstreaming: Sociometric Assessment and Beyond" by S. R. Asher and A. R. Taylor, 1981, *Exceptional Education Quarterly, 1*(4), pp. 13–30. Copyright 1981 by PRO-ED, Inc. Adapted by permission.

asked to nominate favorite peers, rate their class-mates, or choose between pairs of students. The nomination method tends to be a measure of friend-ship, whereas rating scales tend to assess the student's level of acceptance. General acceptance of special students by their peers is probably a more appropriate instructional goal than an increase in the students' number of friendships. This point should be considered when selecting a sociometric device (Asher & Taylor, 1981).

Before using sociometric methods to gather data about social acceptance, teachers should consider district and school policies. These methods involve the collection of confidential information, and some schools allow their use only with parental permission. Results should be treated with caution; when students are asked to rate other students, they should be encouraged to keep the nature of their responses confidential. Also, it is important that teachers not share overall ratings with students, particularly those who may already have a poor self-concept (McLoughlin & Lewis, 1994). Sociometric devices also tend to lose their sensitivity to changes in the behavior of children over 10 years old. Finally, they provide little diagnostic information regarding which social skills should be taught, and, if used too frequently, they may actually contribute to the rejection of some students (Schumaker & Hazel, 1984).

Direct observation techniques are helpful in assessing and monitoring the specific social skills exhibited by special students (e.g., Prasad, 1994) and the behaviors of teachers and peers toward special individuals. Direct observation can take place in analogue settings (i.e., simulated situations, such as role playing or a contrived play setting) or a natural environment. Frequent data collection is important to ensure that the initial assessment is valid and to evaluate interventions to provide a measure of the timeliness of program modifications. Data can be recorded on a graph to allow analysis of behavioral changes over time. Examples of appropriate targets for direct observation include the frequency of positive statements made by the teacher to the special student or the number of social interactions between the special student and a regular class peer.

Rating scales and checklists are also useful in collecting information about a student's performance. Typically, these measures list specific behaviors that are likely to occur in a particular setting. The teacher completes the checklist or rating scale following an observation of the student. For example, a student may be observed participating in an instructional group and then rated on a number of classroom behaviors (e.g., "The student attends to the teacher's instructions? The student raises his or her hand before responding? The student maintains eye contact when talking with the teacher?"). The teacher can simply check the items that describe the student's behavior or rate the quality of the behaviors observed (i.e., from Inappropriate to Appropriate on a 5-point scale).

Behavioral rating scales may also offer a broader set of items that provide more general descriptions of behaviors (e.g., "The student participates appropriately in an instructional group"). A person who knows the student well (a teacher, parent, peer, or even the student in question) reads each description and then rates the student on a numerical scale (e.g., from 1 to 7). Checklists and rating scales permit the collection of consistent information from several different observers to assess the skill level of the student, identify problem behaviors, or assess the student's progress.

Parents can aid in gathering data by reporting on the special student's social interactions in the home, neighborhood, and community. They can also keep a record of the type of comments the student makes about school or self. This information can reflect changes in the student's self-concept or attitudes toward school.

Figure 6–2 presents a checklist for evaluating the social environment of the classroom. It can be used to assess not only teacher behavior but also peer behavior and the curriculum. Use this measure to find out about the social climate of your classroom.

FIGURE 6–2
Social Environment Checklist

Teacher's Behavior

Direct Influence

- Can the teacher specifically state both appropriate and inappropriate student classroom behaviors he/she would like to increase or decrease?

- Does the teacher frequently follow appropriate behavior with encouragement and praise?

- Does the teacher refrain from punishing and criticizing students and rather consistently withdraw his/her attention following inappropriate behaviors?

- Does the teacher objectively record (tally, tape-record, use counter) and evaluate the frequency and consequences of his/her behaviors to document the effects they have on student behavior?

- Does the teacher clearly specify the classroom guidelines, responsibilities, and limitations for students?

Indirect Influence

- Has the teacher continued to grow by adapting teaching plans to meet the needs of each group of students?

- Is the teacher aware of any personal, social, racial, or mental prejudices and does she/he attempt to overcome these through objective teaching and evaluation methods?

- Has the teacher devised a method of getting the students' perceptions and feedback on the teacher and the class (questionnaire, suggestion box)?

- Does the teacher encourage and reinforce self-expression and participation from all the members of the class?

Peer Behavior

- Can the teacher identify the classroom leaders, followers, and isolates?

- Can the teacher identify the peer-group norm base and stereotypes that are held by the class?

- Can the teacher identify and redirect inappropriate peer attention (laughing at a class clown, picking on a . . . child [with a disability]) to promote more constructive activities?

- Does the teacher attend to the problems of the quiet, withdrawn children as much as to the acting-out problem children?

FIGURE 6–2
continued

- Does the teacher use concrete activities and arrangements to maximize the social acceptance and participation of all the children?

- Do the classroom physical arrangements (seating plan) and group activities consider both the elimination of behavior problems and enhancement of social relationships?

Curriculum

- Does the curriculum encourage high levels of student independence and initiative?

- Does the curriculum present a balanced emphasis on students' personal social development and academic skill development?

- Does the curriculum provide challenging new ideas that require students to develop skills in analytic and evaluative thinking?

- Is the curriculum enhanced with a motivational system that guarantees that each child will have a successful learning experience?

- Does the curriculum require participation and interaction from the teacher and students?

- Does the curriculum encourage interaction and cooperation among the students?

- Is the subject content relevant to the interests and backgrounds of the students?

- Is an effort made to meaningfully relate the concepts covered in class to every-day experiences?

- Does the curriculum provide ample opportunity for student enrichment by fre-quently introducing new and different ideas and problems?

- Is motivation enhanced through liberal use of teacher praise and encouragement?

- Are students with special skills allowed or encouraged to share their expertise with their classmates?

- Is an attempt made to incorporate student ideas and suggestions into the instructional program?

Note. Reprinted with permission of Merrill, an imprint of Macmillan Publishing Company, from *Evaluating Educational Environments* (pp. 120–125) by R. M. Smith, J. T. Neisworth, and J. G. Greer, Copyright © 1978 Merrill Publishing Company, Columbus, Ohio.

STRATEGIES FOR PROMOTING ACCEPTANCE OF SPECIAL STUDENTS

Teachers can use several methods to increase the likelihood that special students will be socially accepted. These methods are directed toward general education students and teachers, parents, and special students themselves. Whereas general educators are typically responsible for implementing these strategies, special educators are available to provide necessary assistance.

Inform Regular Class Students About Disabilities

Increasing their knowledge about individuals with disabilities improves the attitudes of general education students and teachers (e.g., Donaldson, 1980; Fiedler & Simpson, 1987; Handlers & Austin, 1980; Schultz & Torrie, 1984). Students should be informed about disabilities, preferably before special students enter the regular classroom. Instruction can take many forms. Teachers can present information directly to younger students; more advanced classes can conduct some of their own research. Some teachers may develop texts and workbooks to use with their students (Schultz & Torrie, 1984); others may use commercially developed materials such as the *Kids on the Block Series* (Aiello & Shulman, 1989), books that present stories about special students. Special educators such as the resource teacher can direct general education teachers and students to other sources of information about disabilities. For example, many books, films, instructional materials, and even television programs discuss various types of disabilities. See "Tips for the Teacher" for some suggestions.

The goal of instruction is to increase awareness of both the abilities and the problems of special students. The teacher can introduce the concept of individual differences and point out that each person is unique, with a distinct array of strengths and weaknesses. At the same time, the similarities between regular class and special students should be emphasized (Schulz & Turnbull, 1983). Typical disabilities should be identified and discussed; students should learn why some individuals require special assistance. It is also possible to describe typical special education services and compare these with the general education program. The lives of famous people with disabilities, such as Helen Keller and Franklin D. Roosevelt, can be studied. Class discussions provide the opportunity for students to exchange information, experiences, and feelings about people with disabilities. Teachers should direct these discussions and clarify or correct any misperceptions or misinformation.

Provide Regular Class Students with Experiences with Special People

Attitudes of regular class students are also affected by meeting and interacting with individuals with disabilities. One way to provide this experience is to invite special adults to the classroom; students can listen to the viewpoint of the person with disabilities and then ask questions. Another method is to visit special education programs such as the resource room or special class located within the school. Older students can also be given assignments to interview an adult with disabilities. The teacher should guide all of these experiences by ensuring that students prepare appropriate questions prior to visits, interviews, and discussions.

Simulation is another way of experiencing disabilities. Simulations assist regular class students in understanding the problems experienced by special individuals and thereby improve the regular class students' level of acceptance (Aiello, 1979; Handlers & Austin, 1980; Israelson, 1980). Some possible simulation activities are traveling around the school in a wheelchair, wearing a blindfold during lunch or art, using earplugs to limit hearing, and attempting to communicate without speaking. For younger children, puppets with various disabilities provide a type of simulation; students can talk with the puppets or become the puppeteers (Binkard, 1985). All simulations should be carried out in a businesslike manner. Following the activities, students should write or talk about their experiences to ensure that they have no misconceptions.

Mainstreaming Materials for General Education Students

*M*any instructional materials are available to help acquaint regular class students with the needs of their peers with disabilities. Several films, filmstrips, and audiotapes are described by Pasanella and Volkmor (1981):

- *"Hello Everybody . . ."* is a series of six filmstrips with audio cassettes (10 minutes each) portraying elementary through secondary students with various disabilities in a mainstream setting. Appropriate for use with students third grade through high school. Available from SFA, James Stanfield Film Associates, P.O. Box 1983, Santa Monica, CA 90406. Titles include
  Hearing and Speech Impairment (Danny)
  Visual Impairment (Toni)
  Orthopedic Impairments (Jed)
  Developmental Disabilities (Sheila)
  Learning Disabilities (Matt)
  Behavior Disorders (Laura, John, Ken)
- *"People You'd Like to Know"* is a series of 10 color films (10 minutes each) portraying students 11–14 years of age with various disabilities in a mainstream setting. Appropriate for use with students third grade through high school. Available from Encyclopedia Britannica Educational Corporation, 425 North Michigan Avenue, Chicago, IL 60611. Selected titles include
  Mary (Hearing and Speech Impairment)
  Harold (Visual Impairment)
  John (Cystic Fibrosis)
  Paige (Down Syndrome)
  Mark (Learning Disability)
- *"Like You, Like Me"* is a series of 10 animated films portraying students with various disabilities in a mainstream setting, both in and out of school. Appropriate for use with students from preschool through primary. Available from Encyclopedia Britannica Educational Corporation, 425 North Michigan Avenue, Chicago, IL 60611. Selected titles include
  Let's Talk It Over (Epilepsy)
  Let Me Try (Mental Retardation)
  Let's Be Friends (Emotional Disturbance)
  Doing Things Together (Prosthetic-Hand)
  Everyone Needs Some Help (Hearing/Speech Impairment)
  See What I Feel (Visual Impairment)

Schulz and Turnbull (1983) have also prepared a list of materials for use in mainstreaming programs. These include resource materials for the teacher, mainstreaming materials for nondisabled students, and children's books about disabilities. Following are their suggestions:

- *Mainstreaming: What Every Child Needs to Know about Disabilities.* Units of instruction designed for grades one through four are provided in the areas of blindness, deafness, physical disabilities, and mental retardation. Instructional activities include using classroom discussions; simulations; exposure to aids and appliances; guest speakers; and books, movies, slides, and videotapes. Excellent resource lists are also included. The Exceptional Parent Press (Room 700, Statler Office Building, Boston, MA 02116).

- *Kids Come in Special Flavors: Classroom Experience Collection.* This collection of social integration materials includes a teacher's guidebook of detailed activities and resource lists, storybooks, cassette tapes for acquainting students with hearing impairments, paper and pencil tasks for simulating problems of the students with mental retardation and learning disabilities, and equipment related to the special needs of students with visual and orthopedic impairments. It is aimed at the elementary level. Kids Come in Special Flavors (Box 562, Forest Station, Dayton, OH 45405).

- *Everybody Counts! A Workshop Manual to Increase Awareness of Handicapped People.* A collection of simulation activities covering the full range of disabilities is included in this guidebook. Detailed instructions and graphic illustrations enable the reader to implement the activities with success. The activities are geared to the secondary level. The Council for Exceptional Children (1920 Association Drive, Reston, VA 22091).

- *Put On a Handicap.* A teacher's manual and a record provide a range of instructional activities including simulations, discussions, and examining prosthetic aids and appliances. The record contains songs that are educational and fun. Kimbo Educational Materials (Box 477, Long Branch, NJ 07740).

- *I Am, I Can, I Will.* This series featuring Mr. Rogers includes fifteen titles aimed at helping children with disabilities understand their feelings. The titles are available in several media formats including films, videotapes, audio cassettes, and books. Teacher guides are also available with suggestions for follow-up activities to encourage the expression of feelings. Hubbard Scientific (P.O. Box 104, Northbrook, IL 60062).

- *The Kids on the Block.* Six handcrafted and engaging puppets representing a range of disabilities are available in this program. A teacher's guide is also available that includes ten scripts, numerous ideas for follow-up activities, and an extensive bibliography of children's literature related to disabilities. The Kids on the Block (c/o Barbara Aiello, Suite 1040, Washington Building, Washington, DC 20005).

- *Special People Behind the Eight-Ball.* This book is a compilation of an extensive annotated bibliography of literature categorized according to disabilities. Books appropriate for both elementary and secondary levels are included. The Exceptional Parent Bookstore (296 Boylston Street, Boston, MA 02116).

- *Different From You and Like You Too.* This filmstrip explores the concept of individual differences and encourages children to ask questions of their peers with disabilities. It is suitable for an elementary audience. Lawren Productions, Inc. (P.O. Box 666, Mendocino, CA 95460).

Literature can also be used to provide experience with special people. A wealth of fiction, biography, and autobiography is available about individuals with special needs; much is appropriate for students to read or to listen to. Part III of this book focuses on specific disabilities, and the "Exceptional Literature" boxes suggest books to read about special people.

Structure Interactions Between Regular Class and Special Students

Classroom and other interactions between regular class and special students have a greater chance for success if teachers provide guidelines. If the general education student's initial contact with a peer with disabilities is purposeful and occurs in a well-structured situation, positive attitudes are more likely to develop. Four techniques for structuring interactions are cooperative learning experiences, group rewards, special friendship programs, and peer or cross-age tutoring programs.

In **cooperative learning**, regular class and special students work together as a team to complete activities or assignments. These teams, which operate in mainstream settings, are small groups of students with a range of abilities (i.e., low-, moderate-, and high-achieving individuals). According to the research reviewed by Gottlieb and Leyser (1981) and Johnson and Johnson (1980), cooperative learning is superior to both competitive learning and individualistic learning. In competitive situations, students attempt to outdo each other; in individualistic situations, the achievement of each student is unrelated to that of any other student. Cooperative learning increases the special student's opportunity to experience success (Slavin, 1990; Snell & Brown, 1993), it provides practice in school skills (Foyle & Lyman, 1990), and the social interactions involved promote the development of the special student's social skills (Andersen, Nelson, Fox, & Gruber, 1988; Johnson & Johnson, 1989) and their acceptance by regular class peers (Slavin, 1987; Slavin, Madden, & Leavey, 1984).

The teacher plays an important role in establishing and guiding the cooperative learning approach. Gottlieb and Leyser (1981) outline the following steps:

a. teacher specifies the instructional objectives;
b. selects the group size most appropriate for the lesson;
c. assigns students to groups and assures that the small groups are heterogeneous with students [with and without disabilities] in the same group;
d. specifies a structured role within the cooperative groups for the . . . students [with disabilities];
e. makes the requirements for the . . . child [with disabilities] reasonable;
f. provides appropriate materials to the groups;
g. explains the task and the cooperative goal structure;
h. trains . . . [all students] in helping, tutoring, teaching, and sharing skills; and
i. observes interactions. (p. 67)

It is important to consider that learners with disabilities may require some additional special preparation or support to allow them to participate effectively in cooperative learning activities (Johnson & Johnson, 1989). The special student may require preparatory coaching or instruction in the social or academic skills required to participate in a group. Other students may need instruction on how to best teach or encourage their group member with disabilities. Descriptions of various methods of using cooperative learning in the classroom, plus highlights of research findings, are provided in Figure 6–3.

A second method of structuring interactions is the use of group rewards (discussed in chapter 5). The teacher sets up a system in which students can earn classroom reinforcers when (a) regular class students interact positively with special students, (b) a special student performs a desired behavior, (c) class members reinforce a student with behavior problems for an appropriate behavior, or (d) class members ignore a student's inappropriate behaviors. Class members pool their earnings, and the entire class is rewarded. These approaches lead to an increase in the number of positive interactions with special students and thereby help to improve the attitudes of regular class students (Heron & Harris, 1993; Salend, 1987).

A third technique is to encourage the development of friendships through communication, social interactions, and recreational activities involving regular class and special students. As friends, students are encouraged to provide support and assistance to others. For example, this support may involve assisting students with physical or visual disabilities in their travels around school or providing a student with severe disabilities the opportunity to learn and practice age-appropriate skills while participating in games or verbal interactions with others (Falvey, Grenot-Scheyer, & Bishop, 1989).

Programs designed to promote friendships vary greatly in their structure. Teachers may reinforce natural interactions, provide students with information or skills related to their interactions, or establish more structured programs that actually provide training for regular class students in how to assist and develop interactions with special students (Campbell, 1989; Perske & Perske, 1988). These programs may build peer support by (a) fostering proximity of students with disabilities with their regular class peers, (b) encouraging the development of support and friendship, (c) teaching support and friendship skills, (d) fostering respect for individual differences, and (e) providing a positive model for appropriate interactions (Stainback, Stainback, & Wilkinson, 1992). The implementation of programs that encourage friendships becomes especially important as more students with disabilities spend increasing amounts of time in general education programs.

The use of students as tutors is a fourth approach. General education students can help special students as peer tutors (working with age- or classmates) or cross-age tutors (working with younger tutees). Regular class students gain in experience and information by working with students with special needs, and special students benefit from the instruction and the model provided by the regular class tutor. Tutoring programs have demonstrated their effectiveness in many situations (Heron & Harris, 1993; Jenkins & Jenkins, 1985; Krouse, Gerber, & Kauffman, 1981; Maheady, Sacca, & Harper, 1988; Strain, 1981a, 1981b). Students have been found to be effective teachers with withdrawn individuals, acting-out students, and those with academic needs. Tutors should receive specific training prior to their service, be provided with structured and carefully prescribed lessons, meet frequently with their tutee, and be continually monitored with

needed reinforcement and reinstruction provided by the teacher. In addition, peer tutors should be warned that they may be rejected at first but that this response will most likely diminish as instruction proceeds (Doorlag, 1989a; Gable, Strain, & Hendrickson, 1979).

Special students can also serve as peer or cross-age tutors. These experiences can provide the special student with new status, increased acceptance by other students in the school, opportunities to develop social skills, and practice and improved performance in academic skill areas (Cochran, Feng, Cartledge, & Hamilton, 1993). For instance, a special student may help a classmate practice spelling words, or a sixth grade special student may enjoy practicing third grade math if this occurs during the tutoring of a third grade student. Special students serving as tutors should be provided the same type of training and assistance suggested for other tutors. These students often benefit more than their tutees from this educational experience (Osguthorpe & Scruggs, 1986). See "Tips for the Teacher" on page 178 for more ideas about how teachers can help general education students accept their special peers.

Increase the Social Skills of Special Students

For many special students, the development of appropriate social skills improves their chances of gaining social acceptance and succeeding in the mainstream (Heron & Harris, 1993; Nelson, 1988; Zaragoza, Vaughn, & McIntosh, 1991). Drabman and Patterson (1981) say that "it is important that integrated exceptional children display as many positive characteristics as they can to facilitate acceptance by nonexceptional peers" (p. 54). Social skills are best developed through direct instructional procedures, following the same principles as academic instruction and provided as a regularly planned component of the instructional day (Sugai & Tindal, 1993). Initially, the teacher describes why the skill is needed, how the skill is performed, when it is to be used, and what its specific components are. Appropriate social behaviors are modeled for the special student by the teacher and peers or by videotapes

FIGURE 6–3
Cooperative Learning Approaches

Cooperative learning methods are aimed at reducing student isolation and perceived hostile climates that exist in highly competitive classrooms, and at increasing students' ability to interact and work with other students toward common goals. The most widely used cooperative learning methods include

- **Student Teams-Achievement Divisions** (STAD)—Students assemble in teams of four or five members mixed according to achievement level, gender, and ethnicity to master the material covered in a lesson just presented by the teacher. Subsequently, they individually take a quiz on that material. The team's overall score is determined by the extent to which each student *improved* over his or her past performance. The team demonstrating the greatest improvement is recognized in a weekly class newsletter.

- **Teams-Games-Tournament** (TGT)—The procedure in TGT is the same as that used in STAD, but instead of taking quizzes, the students play academic games in tournaments with other members in the class whose past performance was similar to their own. The team score is also based on individual improvement. The balance of the groups involved in the tournament are maintained by weekly adjustment of group members based on their performance.

- **Team Assisted Individualization** (TAI)—Teams of elementary or middle school math students are established and evaluated in the same manner as in STAD and TGT. This procedure uses placement tests to determine each student's individualized level and they proceed at their own rate. Teammates check each other's instructional work and help each other with problems. Student performance is based on individual tests and team rewards are based on the number and accuracy of units completed each week. TAI is based on a specific set of materials and its individualized features make it very appropriate for heterogeneous groups.

- **Cooperative Integrated Reading and Composition** (CIRC)—A comprehensive program for teaching reading and writing that involves pairs of students from different reading groups using basal readers and working on decoding, vocabulary, writing, spelling, and comprehension activities. Teacher instruction is provided to a team while others are working on individual activities and is usually followed by team practice, preassessments for the team, and tests. Tests are not taken until the team members determine their teammate is ready.

- **Jigsaw**—Students meet in five- or six-member teams. The teacher gives each student an item of information which the student must "teach" to the team.

Students are then individually tested for their mastery of the material. **Jigsaw II** is the same, except that students obtain their information from textbooks, narrative material, short stories, or biographies. The class is then quizzed for individual and team scores.

- **Learning Together**—After the teacher has presented a lesson, students work together in small groups on a single worksheet. The team as a whole receives praise and recognition for mastering the worksheet.

- **Group-Investigation**—This is a more complex method, requiring students to accept greater responsibility for deciding what they will learn, how they will organize themselves to master the material, and how they will communicate what they have learned to their classmates.

These methods share four positive characteristics. (1) The cooperation required among students prevents one student from doing most of the work for the others. (2) In spite of the cooperative nature of the groups, each student must learn the material in order to improve his or her own score and the team score. (3) Even low achievers who may not contribute greatly can receive recognition since scores are based on individual improvement, however small, over past performance. (4) Students are motivated to cooperate since they receive not just a grade on a piece of paper, but public recognition from the teacher and the class.

Cooperative learning methods have positive effects in several areas. They contribute significantly to student achievement—to an equal extent in both elementary and secondary schools; in urban, suburban, and rural schools; and in diverse subject matter areas.

Schools with racially or ethnically mixed populations do not necessarily have better intergroup relations based solely on student proximity. However, when dissimilar students work together in small groups toward a common goal and are allowed to contribute equally, they will learn to like and respect one another.

Cooperative learning methods also increase acceptance and understanding among students with disabilities and their nondisabled classmates. They also have a positive effect on student self-esteem.

Students who participate in cooperative learning like school more than their peers who are not allowed to work together; they are better able to interact appropriately with others and to understand another person's point of view.

Note. From Slavin, R. E. (1981). "Synthesis of Research on Cooperative Learning," *Educational Leadership, 38,* p. 659. Reprinted with permission of the Association for Supervision and Curriculum Development. Copyright 1981 by ASCD. All rights reserved. Adaptations based on *Cooperative Learning: Theory, Research, and Practice* by R. E. Slavin, 1990, Englewood Cliffs, NJ: Prentice-Hall. Copyright 1990 by Prentice-Hall, Inc. Adapted by permission.

Enhancing Social Acceptance

- Be open and honest with your students. Don't avoid answering questions.
- Discuss disabilities with your class.
- Invite guest speakers—parents of children with disabilities or adults with disabilities.
- Read books to your class about people with disabilities.
- Hold class discussions. Allow students to ask questions and explore feelings.
- Emphasize how much alike we are, rather than how different we are.
- Take the mystery away from adaptive aids such as wheelchairs, braces, and hearing aids by exposing children to them and providing explanations of how they work.
- Try simulation exercises such as a blind walk or a soundless movie.
- Encourage a buddy system.
- Arrange for students without disabilities to work with special students as helpers or tutors.
- Look for ways to capitalize on the strengths of the student with disabilities and provide status and recognition through athletics, drama, the school newspaper, chorus, or as peer tutors.
- Locate and view media—filmstrips and films—on individuals with disabilities.

Note. Reprinted with the permission of Macmillan Publishing Company from *Teaching Handicapped Students in the Mainstream,* 2/e by A. L. Pasanella and C. B. Volkmor. Copyright ©1981 by the University of Southern California and by Macmillan College Publishing Company, Inc.

and films. The student is then questioned about the skill and the steps involved in it and is provided with the opportunity to practice the new behaviors. It is important that the teacher make use of prompts, praise, and corrective feedback during each of the steps of instruction. Providing multiple examples of how the skill is used and opportunities to practice in other settings improves the chance that the skills learned in the classroom will generalize to other settings (Cartledge & Milburn, 1986; Doorlag, 1989b; Rinn & Markle, 1979; Schumaker & Hazel, 1984; Winget & Kirk, 1991).

Instructional materials are available to assist in the teaching of social skills. Examples of programs designed for elementary grade students are listed here:

- *Skillstreaming the Elementary School Child* by McGinnis and Goldstein (1984)
- *DUSO—Revised: Developing Understanding of Self and Others* by Dinkmeyer and Dinkmeyer (1982)
- *ACCEPTS* (A Curriculum for Children's Effective Peer and Teacher Skills) *Social Skills Curriculum* by Walker and others (1983)
- *Getting Along with Others: Teaching Social Effectiveness to Children* by Jackson, Jackson, and Monroe (1983)
- *Social Skills in the Classroom* by Stephens (1978)

Meisgeier (1981) describes a program for mainstreamed students in the secondary grades. Designed for adolescents, *The Social/Behavioral Curriculum* covers four major areas: responsibility, communication, assertiveness, and problem solving. Other programs designed for older students—*Skillstreaming the Adolescent* (Goldstein, Sprafkin, Gershaw, & Klein, 1980) and *The ACCESS* (Adolescent Curriculum for Communication and Effective Social Skills) *Program* (Walker, Todis, Holmes, & Horton, 1988)—provide teachers with guidelines and activities for teaching social skills at the junior and senior high levels.

Programs such as these typically cover several social skill areas. They often include checklists or rating scales designed to assess student behavior and identify appropriate areas in which to begin social skills instruction. For example, the *ACCEPTS* program offers a placement test that is designed to assess the five areas covered in the program: classroom skills (e.g., attending to teachers, following rules), basic interaction skills (e.g., maintaining eye contact, speaking in a moderate tone), getting along skills (e.g., sharing, assisting others), making friends skills (e.g., being clean and neat, complimenting others), and coping skills (e.g., appropriately expressing anger, ignoring teasing). This program includes specific lesson plans and scripts for the teacher to follow for each of the skill areas taught. Optional videotapes provide both positive and negative examples of the student behavior taught in each lesson, or the teacher can reenact these scenes from the description provided. The advantages of programs such as *ACCEPTS* and *ACCESS* are that their structured lessons permit them to be implemented readily by the teacher with a minimal amount of preparation because the lessons have been designed and field-tested by individuals with experience in teaching social skills. Others, such as the *Skillstreaming* programs, are more flexible; they provide less structured guidelines for lessons, behavioral steps for each skill, a general lesson format, and suggested learning and homework activities.

Another approach to the development of social skills is the use of **cognitive behavior modification**, or cognitive training approaches. These methods focus on improving behavior by changing the thinking strategies of the student in order to develop skills that can be used in a variety of settings with a minimum of external support. Students are involved as active participants in the program—they are aware of the behaviors targeted for change, receive training in how the change program will operate, and are actively involved in the intervention (Henker, Whalen, & Hinshaw, 1980). Cognitive training programs teach students strategies such as how to (a) use a sequence of steps to deal with a problem (self-instruction), (b) consider several solutions to a situation (problem-solving), (c) collect and record data on their performance and evaluate the consequences of each alternative used (self-monitoring/self-evaluation), or (d) reinforce themselves for acceptable performance (self-reinforcement). It is important that the students are provided adequate instruction and practice in the use of cognitive training approaches; implementation of this type of program requires that teachers reward students for accurate evaluation of their own behaviors (Zirpoli & Melloy, 1993).

Cognitive training is an efficient approach because it allows teachers to train students to become responsible for portions of their instructional program; the teacher then assumes a monitoring role. A typical cognitive training program to teach social problem solving includes

- problem definition (specifically define the problem),
- goal statement (identify what you want to accomplish),
- delay response (determine ways to stop and think before you act),
- determine alternatives (identify as many solutions to the problem as possible),
- consider consequences (evaluate the different consequences that may follow each alternative solution),
- decision making/implementation (implement the alternative selected as most appropriate),
- review results (provide a self-evaluation and correct errors in strategies used in order to improve results in future), and
- provide reinforcement (provide yourself a "pat on the back" for improving).

Introduce Students to the Mainstream According to Their Individual Needs

For some students with disabilities who are not currently in mainstream settings, adjustment to mainstreaming can be made easier for the special student (and for the teacher and students in the general education class) if inclusion is carefully planned and occurs gradually. For instance, the first step can be an informal meeting between the special student and the general education teacher. Then the student can visit the classroom when regular class students are not present. The next approximation can be participation in a nonacademic activity, such as music or art. These first steps are important because they allow the student to become acquainted with the new teacher, students, and classroom before academic demands are made. They also help the teacher learn about the new student and begin to plan effective instructional and social acceptance programs. It is important to note that not all students with disabilities require a gradual introduction into the general education program; this must be determined on an individual basis as part of the planning for the implementation of the student's IEP.

Upgrade the Teacher's Information and Skills

At present, about 80% of the states require teachers to learn about mainstreaming special students before they receive a teaching certificate or credential (Allinder & Peterson, 1992). However, some teachers have limited knowledge and experience with students with disabilities. Their teacher preparation program may have provided only a minimal amount of training in working with these students, and they may not have had the opportunity to learn about special students through in-service training.

Because of the strong relationship between attitudes and information, teachers should be sure they have adequate knowledge about special students and the appropriateness of different educational interventions (Gable, Laycock, Maroney, & Smith, 1991). The strategies recommended for informing general education students about disabilities (e.g., visitations, simulations, readings, films, discussions) are also appropriate for teachers. Educators can direct their own study or request assistance in getting this information and training from resources available in their district or region.

While teachers often have support available from special educators, it is "essential that the regular class teacher assume primary 'ownership' and accept responsibility for the education of a student with disabilities, just as he/she does for all students on the class list" (Putnam, 1992, p. 132). In order to carry out this responsibility effectively, teachers should strive to upgrade their own skill levels. For example, research indicates that teachers make more negative comments to special students, ask them fewer questions, and provide them with less feedback. This affects the attitudes of students in the regular class as well as the self-concept and achievement of the special student. Because it is important to provide positive support for the appropriate behaviors of special students, teachers should assess their own behavior. They can count the different types of statements they make (e.g., positive, negative, instructional) and determine which are made most frequently to special students. Teachers can collect these data by self-recording while the class is in progress or by using observers or tape recorders.

Communicate with and Involve Parents

Parents should be informed of the purpose of programs implementing mainstreaming or inclusion and the effects these programs will have on their child's education. Parents of special students may be concerned that their child will be rejected by students and teachers in the general education class. They also may regret the loss of the special attention and services provided in the special education program. In addition, they may fear that their child will experience failure in the mainstream. On the other hand, parents of typical students in the regular class often believe that mainstreamed special students require a great deal of the teacher's attention and that the amount of instruction their children receive will be reduced. They may also be concerned that a special student's behavior will have a negative effect on the behavior of their children.

Many of the apprehensions of parents can be eliminated if they are provided with accurate information concerning the mainstreaming program. For example, the PTA can feature programs on the needs of special learners, pamphlets explaining mainstreaming can be sent to all parents, and the acceptance of special students can be a topic of discussion at parent-teacher conferences. Parents of special students will receive specific information at the meeting of the IEP team. Regular class students can assist by communicating accurate information about special students to their parents.

Teachers should communicate regularly with parents to ensure that they remain informed about the mainstreaming program. Parents of special students often hear from the school only when their children behave inappropriately; they receive limited information about accomplishments and successes. In addition, special students may convey distorted reports of classroom occurrences to their parents; for example, they may say that "all" the students in the regular class pick on them. Parents of general education students also need direct communication from the teacher; they may have misconceptions about mainstreaming because their children talk about only the negative acts of the special students. Parents of all students should be informed that they are important to their children's program and should be encouraged to visit the classroom if they have questions (Heron & Harris, 1993).

According to Kroth (1981), parents should be recognized as their children's major teachers and professionals as consultants to parents. The Mirror Model of Parental Involvement advocated by Kroth (see Figure 6–4) suggests that, even though professionals may provide parents of special students with information and skills, those parents also are able to aid professionals and other parents. With appropriate assistance, parents can improve their skills in working with their children, help professionals assist the students at school, and aid students and other parents in understanding and working with their special children (Binkard, 1985).

Edgar and Davidson (1979) recommend that communication with parents include information about specific events and activities. Professional terms such as *mainstreaming* and *Least Restrictive Environment* should be avoided; educators should

FIGURE 6–4
Mirror Model of Parental Involvement

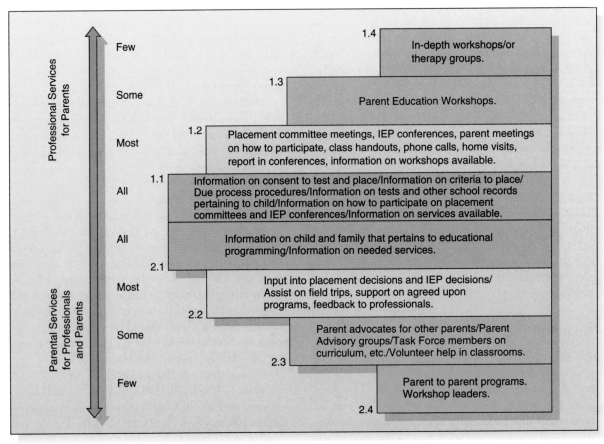

Note. Reprinted with permission of Merrill, an imprint of Macmillan Publishing Company, from "Involvement with Parents of Behaviorally Disordered Adolescents" by R. Kroth. In *Educating Adolescents with Behavior Disorders* (p. 129) by G. Brown, R. L. McDowell, and J. Smith (Eds.). Copyright © 1981 Merrill Publishing Company, Columbus, Ohio.

use words everyone understands. Communication should occur on a regular basis so that parents keep in touch with the program, are informed of current events, and begin to accept and support mainstreaming. Figure 6–5 presents the opinions of the parent of a special student about issues that teachers should consider when working with parents. Although the original statement was directed to special education teachers (Roland, 1989), it contains information that all individuals working with the parents of special students should contemplate.

FIGURE 6–5
A Parent of a Special Student Speaks to Educators

The following recommendations to teachers about working with parents of special students were written by Peggy Roland, who is "the mother of a 12-year-old daughter with education difficulties" (Roland, 1989, p. 3). While the statement was originally directed to special education teachers, it contains concerns and advice that should be considered by others working with special students and their parents.

I'd like to express a few thoughts on behalf of the parents of your students.

Please be frank and *honest* with us. We need the information you have to share and we respect your professional advice and expertise. It may be painful for us to listen to what you have to say but inside we feel relief just hearing something. Our path has been, and always will be, long, but knowing you are there helps.

Please respect us, our children, our families, but above all, the feelings and thoughts that we have shared with you. You may believe we are unrealistic, opinionated, or guilty of ignoring the obvious, but it is probably the best we can manage at the moment. Tomorrow, perhaps even an hour from now, we may express very different feelings.

"They laugh so as not to cry." Such true words! Tears come easily and frequently and they are as much a surprise to us as they are to you. Don't be embarrassed or feel guilty when we cry. Take it as a sign of our humanness and feelings of safety that we react so when we're with you. Many people in the outside world understand neither our laughter nor our tears.

The same is true when we lash out or act defensive. Anger comes with the pain. That anger has no focal point so you may bear its brunt very undeservedly. For that we apologize. Do try to understand that it is usually not directed at you personally but rather at a situation which makes us feel very helpless and, often, very alone. Lashing out may be our overreaction to knowing we can't change the way things are.

Your work and continuing efforts on behalf of our disabled children mean more to us than we can ever explain. Without you, our children would not have achieved the sense of self-worth, the academic and physical success, the societal acceptance they have achieved. Without you, our families would be in more upheaval and distress. Please try to understand that our lives may be just a little different from the average; we have learned to take life one day, sometimes one hour at a time and to be aware and appreciative of the smallest steps while still maintaining our sense of humor and balance.

We are part of this vast thing called life and you are a most important and integral part of our lives. Thank you for being there and helping us establish and maintain a quality of life appropriate for *all* the members of our family.

We look forward to another year of working together!

Note. From "A Parent Speaks to Special Educators" by P. Roland, August 1989, *Exceptional Times*, p. 3.

Teachers and parents must be committed to carrying out the least restrictive alternative concept for handicapped children. If handicapped individuals are ever to be fully accepted in our society, this integration should occur as early and widely as possible. Educators should be willing to put forth their best efforts to make a regular class experience rewarding and enriching for handicapped students. Special class teachers can do much to make these mainstreaming successes happen.

The key to a successful mainstreaming experience is preparation. The checklist below can serve as a guide for the special class teacher in preparing not only the handicapped students, but also the other people who must support the mainstreaming effort. Before placing each handicapped student in a mainstreamed setting, the teacher should examine and work on each element of the checklist, until most, if not all, of the "yes" boxes can be checked.

1. Handicapped student:

Yes No

☐ ☐ Is familiar with rules and routine of the regular classroom?

☐ ☐ Follows verbal and written directions used in the regular classroom?

☐ ☐ Remains on-task for adequate time periods?

☐ ☐ Has expressed a desire to participate in the regular class setting?

☐ ☐ Reacts appropriately to teasing, questions, criticism, etc.?

☐ ☐ Student's IEP objectives match instructional objectives in regular class?

2. Regular class teacher:

Yes No

☐ ☐ Has been given rationale for mainstreaming activities and asked to cooperate?

☐ ☐ Has information about handicapped student's needs, present skills, and current learning objectives?

☐ ☐ Has been provided with special materials and/or support services as needed?

☐ ☐ Has prepared class for mainstreaming?

☐ ☐ Has acquired special helping skills if necessary?

☐ ☐ Will be monitored regularly to identify any problems that arise?

3. Nonhandicapped peers:

Yes No

☐ ☐ Have been informed about handicapped student's participation and about handicapping condition (if appropriate) with the opportunity to ask questions?

☐ ☐ Have been asked for their cooperation and friendship toward handicapped student?

☐ ☐ Have learned helping skills and praising behaviors?

4. Handicapped student's parents:

Yes No

☐ ☐ Have received verbal or written information about mainstreaming situation?

☐ ☐ Have been asked to praise and encourage child's progress in regular and special class?

5. Nonhandicapped students' parents:

Yes No

☐ ☐ Have been informed about mainstreaming activities at PTA meeting, conferences, or through other vehicle, and asked for their cooperation?

6. School administrator:

Yes No

☐ ☐ Has been informed about specifics of mainstreaming activities?

☐ ☐ Has indicated specific steps she or he will take to encourage and support these activities?

Note. From "Helping Teachers Integrate Handicapped Students into the Regular Classroom" by J. C. Dardig, 1981, *Educational Horizons, 59,* pp. 124–130. Copyright 1981 by *Educational Horizons.* Adapted by permission.

THINGS TO REMEMBER

- Mainstreaming programs should emphasize the social acceptance of special students because rejection can damage both self-concept and academic performance.
- Special students may be rejected if they do not look or act like their peers; another contributing factor is that some special students have poor social skills.
- Attitudes are very important; the attitudes of teachers influence the attitudes of their students.
- Attitudes are affected by information; the more teachers and peers know about special students, the more likely they are to accept them.
- Regular class students, special students, and parents should be prepared for mainstreaming.
- Sociometric measures are often used to find out how special students are perceived by their peers.
- Behavioral rating scales and checklists are used to help assess a student's social skill performance, identify problem areas that may require instruction, or assess the student's progress.
- Instruction about disabilities, experiences with special people, and structured interactions with special students can be provided to help general education students (and teachers) gain information.
- Special students can learn appropriate social skills; however, it is usually necessary to provide instruction in this area.
- Parental support for the mainstreaming program can be increased by explaining the purpose of the program, letting parents know how it will affect their children, encouraging parents to participate, and keeping parents informed through frequent communication.

In this chapter, several techniques for promoting the social acceptance of special students in the regular classroom have been described. Consult the checklist in Figure 6–6 to review factors important in preparing to serve special students. Next, you will learn about coordination skills for management of the total learning environment. Before proceeding, however, check "Things to Remember" to review ways to enhance social acceptance.

ACTIVITIES

1. Visit a general education classroom that includes mainstreamed students. Select one special student and one regular class peer to observe. Watch each of these students for approximately 30 minutes, and collect information about the number of times each of the following interactions occurs: the student talks to other students, the student talks to the teacher, other students talk to the student, the teacher talks to the student. Compare your results for the two students. Do you find any differences? Does one seem to be better accepted by peers and teacher than the other?

2. Interview a special student who spends part of the school day in a mainstreamed setting. How does the student feel about the mainstreaming experience? Does he or she feel comfortable in the regular class setting? How positive does the student perceive the attitudes of the teacher and regular class peers to be? Does he or she feel accepted or rejected? Summarize your findings, and use them to prepare a list of questions you might use to interview another mainstreamed student.

3. Select two articles that discuss social acceptance of special students. Journals such as *The Exceptional Parent, Journal of Special Education*, and *Teaching Exceptional Children* would be good places to look. Read the articles to find sugges-

tions for promoting the social acceptance of students within the general education classroom.

4. Talk with special and general education teachers from two different schools about ways to improve the social acceptance of mainstreamed students. What suggestions can they offer? What have they tried in the past that has worked? Ask about activities for teachers, students, parents, and staff members such as secretaries, custodians, and bus drivers.

5. Design a classroom activity that you could use to help regular class students be more accepting of special students. First, decide on a specific goal, and then describe the methods you would use to reach this goal. Include ideas about how you would go about implementing this program in your classroom and how you would evaluate its effectiveness.

6. Locate one of the social skills training programs mentioned in the chapter (e.g., *ACCEPTS, Skillstreaming the Adolescent),* and use the program to teach a lesson on a specific skill to one or more of your friends, colleagues, or students. Write a short report on your experience, and describe specifically how you would use the lesson (or its techniques) with a special student mainstreamed in a general education classroom setting.

7 Coordinating the Classroom Learning Environment

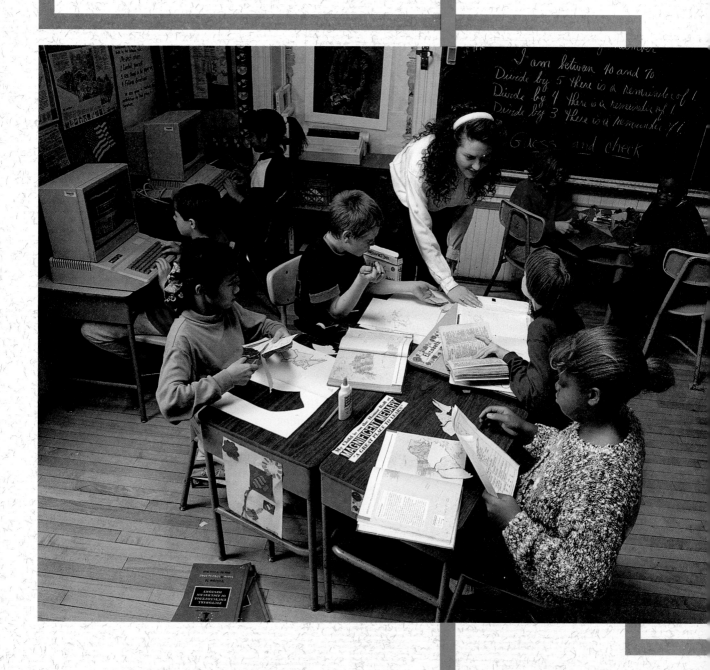

In the mainstreamed classroom, teachers adapt instruction, manage behavior, and promote the social acceptance of students with special needs. In addition, the teacher is responsible for the arrangement, management, and coordination of the total learning environment.

COORDINATION SKILLS FOR THE TEACHER

As managers, teachers structure the physical environment in which learning takes place and within these physical surroundings set up the instructional environment. To do this, teachers coordinate many different resources: time, people (including both students and instructional personnel), and educational materials and equipment. Management skills aid in the successful coordination of the mainstreamed classroom.

According to Stephens (1980), classroom management is "what teachers do to help make student life in the classroom pleasant, meaningful, safe, and orderly." Stephens outlines six classroom management elements that teachers should consider:

- *Demographics*, the group's composition
- *Physical environment*, the use of the room and its furnishings
- *Time*, the amount of time available in the class and the teacher's and students' use of it
- *Student encouragement*, ways that students are reinforced for performance
- *Provisions for interacting*, among the students and with teachers
- *Differentiating instruction*, the extent to which and how the instruction is individualized (p. 4)

The management skills of the teacher have been found to be related to the amount of student learning; good managers are more able to adapt instruction to student needs, particularly in heterogeneous classes (Evertson, Sanford, & Emmer, 1981). This chapter describes several of the factors to consider in managing the total learning environment. Included are principles for arranging the physical environment, organizing the instructional environment, using educational technologies, and coordinating time and other resources.

The teacher can structure the learning situation in many different ways. He or she receives a room, students, curriculum guidelines, and some standard instructional materials (such as grade level textbooks); all other factors are under the teacher's control. Because there is a great deal of freedom in the selection of options, teachers should be aware of the reasons underlying their choices.

Figure 7–1 is a learning style questionnaire based on the work of several persons (Dunn & Dunn, 1978, 1979; Gartner & Riessman, 1977; Lewis, 1980; Pasanella & Volkmor, 1981; Renzulli & Smith, 1978; Schubert, Glick, & Bauer, 1979). Read this survey and determine which conditions *you* favor for learning. Consider your tolerance for environmental variations (noise, distractions, physical surroundings), your personal work habits (time of day, attention span, closure, rate), and your favorite learning methods (other learners, structure, presentation and response modes, activities, reinforcement). Then compare your preferred learning style with your present teaching style.

Many teachers, in arranging the physical and instructional environments, select options that reflect their own preferences as learners. Depending on the needs of the students in the classroom, this approach may or may not be successful. Teachers should be familiar with many different ways to structure the learning environment so that management decisions can take into account not only the preferences of the teacher but also those of the students.

ARRANGING THE PHYSICAL ENVIRONMENT

The **physical environment** is made up of the classroom and its furnishings. The nature of the physical environment and its arrangement have an effect on the behavior of both teachers and students (Smith, Neisworth, & Greer, 1978). For example, environmental constraints make it difficult to teach running skills in a closet, demonstrate cooking and food preparation techniques in a gymnasium, or supervise small-group discussions in a large auditorium with fixed seats. Environment exerts the greatest influence on the nonacademic performance of students.

FIGURE 7–1
What Is Your Learning Style?

When do you work best? What type of learning environment do you prefer? Is the learning environment that *you* prefer the one you provide for students? If so, please reconsider. Your goal as a teacher is to meet the needs of the students!

Factor	Preference
Noise	Do you work best in absolute silence? in a quiet room? with music playing? with television on? with others talking?
Distractions	Are you able to work with many visual distractions (e.g., interesting pictures, bulletin boards, objects)? Can you work near a window? with people moving about? Do you work best with your desk or table clear?
Physical surroundings	Do you work best sitting upright in a straight-backed chair? an easy chair? on the floor? Do you prefer a desk or table for writing? Can you work anywhere at all? Do you work best if it is warm? cool? Are the best conditions those where you can eat? drink? move about at will?
Time of day	Is early morning the best time for you to learn? midmorning? midday? afternoon? evening? late at night? When are you most alert?
Attention span	Are you able to concentrate only a few minutes? a half hour? for long periods of time? until the work is done? How often do you need to take a break? Are you able to get back to work immediately after a break?
Closure	Do you want to finish a task once you've started it, or can you stop working at any point in the task? Do you like to take breaks in the middle of tasks? have work interrupted before it's completed? have to stop before you have finished?
Rate	Are you a fast or slow worker? Do you spend the most time planning? doing the task? checking your work?
Other learners	Do you like to work alone or with others? with peers or adults? If you work one-to-one, should the other person be the teacher? another student? Do you enjoy working in small groups? teams? committees? large groups?
Structure	Are you most comfortable when all task requirements are clearly spelled out for you? when you can make some choices? when you have complete freedom?
Presentation mode	In learning about something new, would you rather read about it? hear someone talk about it? see it in pictures? watch a film or videotape? listen to an audiotape? watch someone demonstrate it? try it yourself? try explaining it to someone else?
Activities	Which of the following instructional activities help you learn: lecture? discussion? projects? drill? peer teaching? independent study? games? programmed instruction? simulation? role playing?
Response mode	Do you like to show what you've learned by writing reports? taking exams? telling others? demonstrating how to do it? expressing it artistically?
Reinforcement	Do you need incentives to do a good job? peer approval? praise and recognition from the teacher? tangible rewards? grades? pay? satisfaction that you did your best?

Reviews of research (Doyle, 1986; Weinstein, 1979) conclude that classroom characteristics affect attitudes and social behavior but have little impact (with the exception of seating arrangements) on student achievement. In the following paragraphs are several principles to consider in arranging the physical environment of your classroom. Keep in mind that some aspects of the physical environment, such as classroom seating arrangements, are easy to modify; others, such as the size of the classroom and the colors of its walls, are less amenable to change.

Ensure a Safe and Barrier-Free Environment

A primary concern with any environment is the safety of its inhabitants. In mainstreamed classrooms, students with physical and sensory disabilities require special precautions. For example, books, other objects, and clutter on the classroom floor are hazards for students with balance problems or poor eyesight. Students with limited mobility may need help to move out of the school quickly during fire drills; students who are deaf may need visual cues in order to react in emergency situations.

Another major consideration is **access** to the school and classroom. Many of the newer school buildings are designed to be barrier-free; that is, **architectural barriers** are avoided, to allow individuals with disabilities entry to and use of the facility. Buildings have elevators and ramps, stairs have handrails for persons with crutches or canes, doorways are wide enough to allow wheelchairs to pass through, and bathroom facilities are specially designed. Drinking fountains, lockers, vending machines, trash cans, towel dispensers, and telephones are installed so that they can be easily reached by a person in a wheelchair. In older schools that do not have these features, it may be necessary to make modifications to allow access to students with disabilities.

The environment of the classroom should also be barrier-free. The room should be arranged to allow easy travel between desks and tables. Instructional materials should be placed within reach, and storage space should be provided for special equipment such as magnification devices, crutches, and adapted keyboards for computers. In addition, bookshelves, chalkboards, and bulletin boards should be conveniently located and low enough to permit their use by students in wheelchairs.

Make the Working Conditions Pleasant

A pleasant physical environment is one that is both comfortable and attractive. The comfort of students and teachers depends on factors such as temperature, ventilation, lighting, and noise level. Classroom temperature should be moderate; hot or cold environments may hinder performance. Ventilation should be adequate so that the room is not stuffy. All work areas should be well lighted and free from glare; some students with vision disorders may require special lighting. Windows permit natural illumination but may offer distractions to students; these distractions can be avoided by building windows above eye level or by temporarily drawing the drapes. Noise can also distract students from their work or interfere with their ability to hear others speak. D'Alonzo, D'Alonzo, and Mauser (1979) recommend the use of soundproofed walls, carpeting, acoustical ceiling tiles, and drapes to decrease unwanted environmental sounds.

The attractiveness of the learning environment is important. Weinstein (1979) found that attractive classrooms helped improve attendance, participation, and attitudes toward instruction. One aspect of aesthetic appeal is the use of color. Smith, Neisworth, and Greer (1978) caution against dark or bright colors for classroom walls; they say that "wall surfaces should be light in tone and subdued though not drab in hue, so that they can better function as a pleasant background for whatever is placed on them or occurs in front of them" (p. 134). The room decor also affects its attractiveness. Furnishings, bulletin boards, pictures, posters, mobiles, and displays of educational materials and equipment all contribute to visual appeal. These stimuli should be interesting and enjoyable to look at without being sources of distraction.

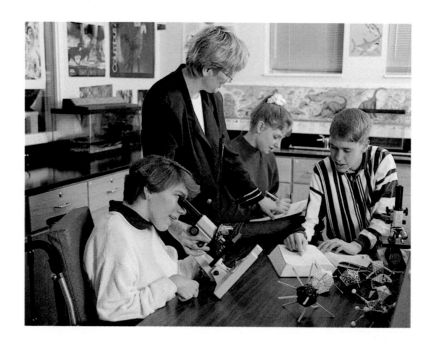

Obtain Appropriate Furniture and Special Equipment

Classroom furniture should be comfortable, attractive, durable, and functional. The primary furnishings of most classrooms (with the exception of specialized classes such as shop and home economics) are chairs and tables or desks. Chairs should be the correct size; students should be able to sit comfortably with their backs supported and their feet on the floor. Tables and desks should be level and should provide adequate writing space and leg room. Special tables and desks may be needed by persons in braces or wheelchairs.

Students with vision, hearing, and physical disabilities often require special classroom equipment. Students may bring with them some types of special equipment: wheelchairs, canes, braces, crutches, hearing aids, and eyeglasses. Other types are furnished by the special education teacher. For example, students with vision disorders may use a braille notetaker or a slate and stylus to write, an abacus or talking calculator for math, and optical aids and magnification devices. Those with hearing losses may need amplification equipment. Students with

physical disabilities may require lapboards for writing, automatic page turners for reading, or special standing tables. Chapters 12 and 13 describe the special equipment needs of students with sensory and physical problems.

Arrange Space Functionally

Classroom space should be divided into performance areas or zones to accommodate routine activities and tasks (Berdine & Cegelka, 1980; Mercer & Mercer, 1993). Stowitschek, Gable, and Hendrickson (1980) suggest that, in planning the room arrangement, teachers consider typical student groupings, storage needs for materials and equipment, and procedures for distribution and collection of materials and student work.

When the room is divided into separate areas, one essential consideration is space for instruction. Usually at least two areas are needed: one for large-group instruction and another for small-group instruction. As shown in Figure 7–2, desks and chairs can be arranged in many different ways for large-group instruction. Typical patterns are straight

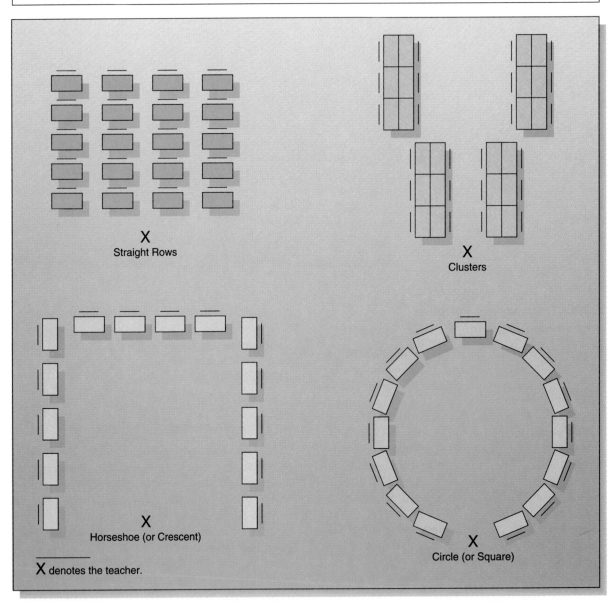

X
Straight Rows

X
Clusters

X
Horseshoe (or Crescent)

X
Circle (or Square)

X denotes the teacher.

rows, clusters of desks, and configurations in the shape of horseshoes, crescents, circles, and squares. Some arrangements for small-group instruction are shown in Figure 7–3. Arrangements can use chairs only, both tables and chairs, or clusters of desks.

In some classrooms, small-group instructional areas are set up for specific subjects or activities. For example, in classrooms that use learning centers or stations, there may be separate areas for math, language arts, and science. These areas can be used by the teacher for direct instruction or by students for independent study or auto-instructional activities. Mercer and Mercer (1993) recommend a separate area for each subject, even at the secondary level; for example, a classroom in which English is taught could be divided into grammar, literature, free reading, and listening areas.

In addition to instructional areas, each student should have an individual work space. Usually the student's desk is the space where he or she works independently and takes part in large-group instruction. Students should have storage space in their desks or, if tables are used instead of desks, in cupboards, cabinets, or bookcases. Care should be taken to ensure that individual work areas are relatively quiet and private. Some students may benefit

from separate work areas. Cubicles, carrels, booths, and partitions can be used to set up private office areas for students who are highly distractible or who have difficulty sustaining attention.

Teachers also need a work and storage area, which is usually the teacher's desk. Some teachers do not use their desks as a work area during school hours; they may move from place to place throughout the classroom or station themselves in one of the small-group instructional areas. The classroom should be arranged so that the teacher can visually monitor students' activities throughout the school day. Stainback, Stainback, and Froyen (1987) say that "the teacher should be able to make a visual sweep of the room and detect when students need assistance and what social interactions are occurring" (p. 12).

Other areas can be incorporated into the classroom if desired. A separate storage location may be needed if materials and equipment are not housed in learning centers. Some teachers set up a specific location at which students pick up their work for the day and return completed assignments. The classroom computer may be placed at the back or side of the room, so that students can interact with instructional programs without disturbing the work of others. Another option is a free time or recreational

FIGURE 7–3
Small-Group Arrangements

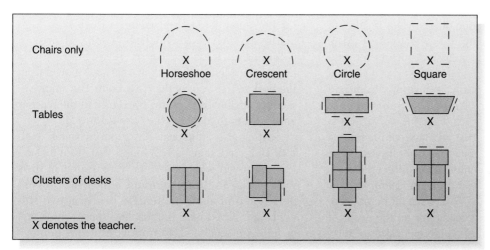

area with games, tapes, books, and other types of reading materials. Time in this area can be used as reinforcement for appropriate behavior, completed work, or accurate performance.

The plan for an elementary grade classroom in Figure 7–4 includes areas for several types of activities. Student desks are clustered for either large- or small-group instruction. There are listening centers and study carrels, a partitioned area for quiet study or games, and a small carpeted area with beanbag chairs. Three tables are available for small-group work, and storage space is ample and conveniently located. There are also many possibilities for flexibility; the placement of desks and tables can be easily changed and the portable chalkboard can serve as a temporary partition.

The relationship among the different areas within the classroom should be carefully planned. According to Doyle (1986), the major concerns are provision of separate areas for different instructional purposes, careful design of classroom traffic patterns, and minimization of density. It is also important to arrange classroom space to encourage smooth and quick transitions between instructional activities (Rieth & Evertson, 1988). Among the factors to consider are these:

1. *Sound.* Separate quiet areas from noisy areas.
2. *Convenience.* Store equipment, supplies, and materials near where they are used; locate instructional groups near the chalkboard.
3. *Movement efficiency.* Make traffic patterns direct; discourage routes that lead to disruptions (e.g., students distracting others when turning in assignments or moving to new activities). Also, make sure that traffic areas are uncluttered and wide enough to accommodate the flow of student traffic, particularly during transitions from one activity to another (Stainback, Stainback, & Froyen, 1987).
4. *Flexibility.* Ensure that all classroom activities can be accomplished; make areas multipurpose or use different arrangements for different tasks. Stainback, Stainback, and Slavin (1989) recommend classrooms with "areas that can be opened, closed, or screened off depending on the needs of students when working on different tasks" (p. 140).

5. *Density.* Arrange student seating so that personal space is preserved; avoid crowding. High density can reduce attentiveness and increase dissatisfaction and aggressiveness (Doyle, 1986; Zentall, 1983).

When arranging classroom space, the teacher should not consider it permanent. New arrangements should be tried as often as necessary to increase the effectiveness of the learning environment. As Polloway and Patton (1993) comment, "every teacher should periodically review why the room is arranged as it is. There is no one best way to arrange a classroom, but some ways are clearly superior to others" (p. 59).

Consider Educational Goals in Making Seating Arrangements

How students are arranged in relationship to each other can affect their academic performance, classroom behavior, and social interactions. Weinstein (1979) concludes from a review of research studies that achievement is related to seat position: in classrooms arranged in rows, students sitting in the front center seats participate more, are more attentive, and spend more time on task. This finding may be due to the availability of more cues from the teacher (e.g., increased eye contact, better reception of nonverbal messages) (Doyle, 1986). It may also be due to self-selection if students choose their own seats or to the tendency of teachers to seat low achievers farther away from the teacher's desk than high achievers (Alves & Gottlieb, 1986). However, according to Heron and Harris (1993), low achievers improve academically as their seats are moved from the back to the front of the classroom. This improvement is attributed to closer proximity to the teacher and the stimuli to which they should attend.

Seating also influences classroom behavior. Axelrod, Hall, and Tams (1972) found that study behaviors improved when students were seated in rows rather than in groups around tables. To prevent behavior problems, inattentive or disruptive students are placed near the teacher; those who argue or fight are separated. Disruptive students improve

FIGURE 7-4
Classroom Plan

Note. Reprinted with permission of Merrill, an imprint of Macmillan Publishing Company, from *Teaching Students with Learning Problems* (3rd ed., p. 85) by C. D. Mercer and A. R. Mercer, Copyright © 1989 Merrill Publishing Company, Columbus, Ohio.

their behavior when grouped with well-behaved students (Stainback, Stainback, & Froyen, 1987). In some cases, teachers may move students to separate areas, away from their peers. Students who act out or display serious inappropriate behaviors may be removed to a time-out area. Those who are highly distractible can be seated in individual study carrels or booths. However, teachers should consider all possible alternatives before physically isolating students from others in the classroom.

Social interaction can be facilitated by seating arrangements. Smith, Neisworth, and Greer (1978) note that interaction increases when students are seated close to each other or opposite one another. Heron and Harris (1993) observe that verbal communication tends to move across tables rather than around them. They recommend seating a low-verbal student across from a high-verbal student to enhance performance. In this arrangement, the low-verbal student is better able to receive the verbal messages and the facial and gestural cues of the peer model.

The physical environment of the mainstreamed classroom can be arranged in many ways to promote successful student performance. The environmental checklist in Figure 7–5 summarizes several important concerns.

▬ ORGANIZING THE INSTRUCTIONAL ENVIRONMENT

The **instructional environment** of the classroom includes the procedures, materials, and equipment used by the teacher to increase student performance. The teacher organizes the curriculum, groups students, and sets up delivery systems for the presentation and practice of skills and information. This structure directly affects nonacademic performance as well as student achievement. Students actively involved in appropriate instruction are less likely to exhibit problem behaviors and more likely to feel good about their competence. Several principles are important to consider in arranging the instructional environment.

Organize Curricular Skills and Information

Although the scope and sequence of the general education curriculum is usually well specified for the teacher, there is opportunity to arrange the skills and information in different ways. The traditional organization follows academic subjects; this is most apparent at the secondary level, where the curriculum is broken down into separate courses. At the elementary level, skills and information can also be divided into different subjects, such as language arts, mathematics, social studies, and science.

An alternate way of organizing the curriculum is the **unit approach,** which cuts across subject matter areas (Polloway & Patton, 1993). Meyen (1981) describes unit teaching as a generic instructional approach that integrates instruction "on academic and social skills, with information structured around a common theme building on the previous experience of students" (p. 3). Topics of interest and importance to students become the vehicle for teaching academic skills. For instance, Meyen (1981) suggests experiential themes, such as transportation, the community, leisure time, and the newspaper. The teacher organizes the unit around a central theme and includes activities in each of the core areas: communication skills, math, social competencies, safety, health, and vocation.

Many teachers use units as a supplement to the regular curriculum. While continuing instruction in specific academic subjects, they also introduce activities related to a special topic or interest area. Examples are space travel, February holidays, contributions of African Americans, and endangered species. This approach is more common at the elementary level but can also be adapted for secondary-aged students.

If units are carefully planned to ensure the inclusion of several important academic skills, they are a valuable addition to the instructional environment. Units include a variety of different activities, and the teacher can tailor instruction to the needs of the individual students within the classroom. In addition, the use of themes that interest and motivate students can increase their willingness to participate in academic activities.

FIGURE 7–5
Physical Environment Checklist

Physiological Effects

Illumination

- Is there adequate light for reading and other demanding visual tasks?
- Is the lighting throughout the classroom varied and home-like?
- Is lighting used to help define the different activity areas of the room?
- Is the lighting warm yet not glaring?

Temperature

- Can adequate air movement be obtained when needed?
- Is there an adequate supply of fresh air?
- Are temperatures controlled within a comfortable range (68–74°)?
- Are children assisted in making necessary clothing adjustments for the room temperature?
- Is humidity adequate year round?

Noise

- Can windows be opened without interference from outside noise?
- Is the noise level of each classroom controlled so that the activities of the other classrooms are not disturbed?
- Is the teacher rarely asked to repeat what he/she has said?

Color

- Are the colors in the classroom pleasantly varied?
- Is color used to define areas of the room and to attract attention to important educational displays?
- Are the colors in the room subdued, mellow, and pleasing?

Materials

- Does the classroom contain furnishings, materials, and displays in addition to typical institutional furnishings?
- Do teachers and students bring in a variety of materials and displays related to current assignments?
- Are learning materials and displays well organized by topics or learning area?
- Have excessive, unorganized materials been removed to eliminate confusion or distraction?

FIGURE 7–5
continued

Spatial Effects

- Are related compatible activities arranged together and unrelated, incompatible activities separated within the classroom?
- Have an appropriate time and place been designated and assigned for all activities?
- Is there a variety of places where different-sized groups can meet and work?
- Are there special places that individual children can go (a) for isolation, (b) for rest and quiet, (c) to let off steam, (d) to reward themselves, (e) for private instruction, (f) to work independently, (g) to be disciplined privately?
- Can children enter, leave, clean up, and dress, etc. without disturbing others?
- Can children space themselves as they need or desire?
- Do the relative amounts of space allocated to various activities reflect their importance in the teaching program?

Physical Effects

- Is the environment kept clean?
- Are the furnishings (desks, displays, etc.) moveable to provide a variety of groupings and areas within the room for different learning tasks?
- Can the teacher control visual distractions between groups of children (by separating groups, raising room dividers, etc.)?
- Are storage facilities accessible to the students for getting out and putting away materials which they are allowed access to?
- Have high physical barriers been eliminated so that the teacher has visual access to the entire room?

Setting Effects

- Can the teacher identify an "overcommitted" setting (one in which most children are observers rather than performers and leaders) and then attempt to create new, smaller work or activity groups?
- Have physical barriers to children with disabilities been removed?
- Does the teacher periodically change the environment to improve the teaching program?
- Does the teacher systematically observe and evaluate the effects of the environment on the social behaviors and learning of the class?

Note.   Reprinted with the permission of Macmillan College Publishing from *Evaluating Educational Environments* by R. M. Smith, J. T. Neisworth, and J. G. Greer. Copyright ©1978 Macmillan College Publishing Company, Inc.

Another method of organizing curriculum is the blending or integration of academic subjects. For example, at the elementary level, the whole language approach integrates the language arts of listening, speaking, reading, and writing (Lapp & Flood, 1992). Skills are taught in the context of authentic communication tasks, not as separate (and isolated) subjects (Westby, 1992). Writing across the curriculum is another example. In this approach, secondary students are expected to practice their writing skills in all subjects, not just in English classes.

Group Students for Instruction

Before presentation of skills and information can begin, the teacher must decide how to group students. Two factors must be determined: group size and group type. The number of students per group can vary from one (in a tutoring situation) to the entire class. Class size is a factor in instruction; it has been noted that student achievement increases as the number of students in the class decreases (Glass & Smith, 1978). However, this does not necessarily mean that classes of 30 or more students should always be broken into several groups for instruction. Using the whole class as a group is an efficient way of presenting new material, if that material is appropriate for all of the students (Brophy & Good, 1986). Also, providing guided practice for the entire class at once is an effective use of time. For instance, if the time allotted for mathematics is 1 hour, the teacher can spend only 2 minutes with each of 30 individual students or can devote the entire period to the class as a whole.

When it is necessary to present different material to different students, small groups are appropriate. According to Brophy and Good (1986), small groups are necessary in beginning reading instruction and in highly heterogeneous classes. Also, smaller groups can lead to greater student participation (Mercer & Mercer, 1993). Small groups generally range in size from three to seven or eight individuals. For some students, individual instruction is needed; this can be presented by the teacher or other instructional personnel, such as peer tutors, aides, and volunteers.

The criterion used to group students together often determines the size of the group. The most typical criterion is homogeneity: students of similar ability, at similar levels, or with similar skills are placed in one group. For example, a placement test might be given to pinpoint each student's current instructional level and the results used to form instructional groups. A **skill-specific group** is made up of students requiring instruction in the same skill area. This type of homogeneous grouping, although temporary because skill needs change, is the most effective means of individualizing instruction.

Heterogeneous groupings can also be used for instruction. Smith, Neisworth, and Greer (1978) point out that in this type of group, lower-functioning students are provided with models; for example, students with articulation problems can benefit from hearing the more appropriate speech of their peers. Also, heterogeneous grouping can be used to promote the development of social skills (Bossert & Barnett, 1981). In groups with a range of skills represented, Affleck, Lowenbraun, and Archer (1980) recommend individualizing by using the same task to develop different skills. For example, having students read a short story can be used for instruction in several types and levels of comprehension skills.

Flexible grouping is the practice of using several kinds of grouping formats at different times; this allows all students to interact with one another (Schubert, Glick, & Bauer, 1979). Although skill-specific grouping remains the most effective for the purpose of instruction, several of the other methods suggested by these authors may be appropriate for nonacademic and social activities. Examples are grouping by common interests, grouping by choice, proximity grouping, alphabetical grouping, and grouping by counting off.

Set Up Systems for Monitoring Practice

Opportunities for practice are provided after new material is presented. During practice, student performance is monitored, either directly by the teacher or through the use of **auto-instructional learning materials.** Stowitschek, Gable, and Hendrickson (1980) define self-instructional materials as those "with which the learner can interact by himself or herself" (p. 191). Students receive feedback from the materials and thus are able to practice independently without the assistance of the teacher. This approach frees the teacher for other activities, such as direct instruction.

Among the different forms of auto-instruction are self-correcting materials, programmed learning, and mediated instruction. **Self-correcting materials** are those that provide the student with the correct answer so that responses can be checked for accuracy. For example, math fact flashcards with the problem on one side and the answer on the other allow immediate feedback. Teachers can also prepare answer keys for independent practice activities and encourage students to check and correct their responses. Mercer and Mercer (1993) point out that this works well with students who have a history of academic failure because they are able to make (and correct) mistakes privately. See "Tips for the Teacher" on pages 204-205 for more information about self-correcting materials.

Programmed instruction is another method that allows students to monitor their own practice. Figure 7–6 describes and illustrates this approach. The learner covers the answers on the right-hand side of the page and attempts to answer the questions; each response can then be checked immediately. Heron and Harris (1993) note that programmed instruction allows learners to progress at their own rate through small, incremental steps that build on previous learning.

Mediated instruction is any procedure that includes the use of media. For example, many computer software programs provide programmed instruction or practice activities with immediate feedback and correction of errors. Another example is the use of audiotapes for auto-instruction. de Grandpre and Messier (1979) suggest that teachers develop self-instructional tapes to aid secondary students in reviewing material before exams. The student listens to a tape-recorded question, stops the tape, writes an answer, and then continues the tape to find out whether the response is correct. The tape directs the student to correct any errors immediately.

A **learning center** is a common way to organize auto-instructional materials for independent classroom practice. According to Berdine and Cegelka (1980), a learning or interest center is "an area especially designed for auto-instructional use by the student" (p. 212). Centers provide independent work for one or several students in one or several skill areas. A typical arrangement is by academic subject; for example, Petreshene (1978) recommends four basic centers for elementary classrooms: writing, computational math, individualized spelling, and discovery (manipulative math or science).

Learning centers should be based on specific instructional objectives, house all necessary media and materials, and provide clear and simple directions for student activities. Pretests allow students to select appropriate activities; several kinds and levels of activities should be included in each center. Another important component is a record-keeping system; for example, checklists can be used to note which activities each student has completed. Student progress is measured by posttests or other evaluation devices.

FIGURE 7–6
Programmed Instruction

Programmed instruction does three things:

First, it breaks learning tasks down into small steps. These small _____ help learners avoid making mistakes. That, then, is the first purpose of programmed instruction—to break material into small steps to help learners avoid making

_____.

    steps

    mistakes

Second, programmed instruction requires that students make active responses while they work. These active _____ are often made by filling in blanks in the programmed material.

    responses

Third, as you respond actively by filling in each _____, you can check immediately to see whether you made a correct response. This immediate knowledge of correct response is the reinforcement built into the program. When you see that you gave the correct response, that knowledge is your

_____.

    blank

    reinforcement

Note. From *Individualizing Instruction* (2nd ed., p. 241) by C. M. Charles, 1980, St. Louis, MO: C. V. Mosby. Copyright 1980 by C. V. Mosby. Reprinted by permission.

Learning centers can be constructed so that practice activities are individualized. Centers promote independence, free the teacher for other duties, and encourage students to work cooperatively. Like other types of auto-instructional systems, they also provide students with immediate feedback on the adequacy of their performance during practice.

Provide Guidelines for Student Behavior

Classroom rules and routines help structure the learning environment. Many students need guidelines for behavior and benefit from consistently enforced rules. As noted in chapter 5, rules for classroom conduct are helpful for students of any age. Madsen, Becker, and Thomas (1968) recommend that classroom rules be short and to the point, few in number, and phrased positively (e.g., "Keep your hands to yourself" rather than "Don't hit others"). Affleck, Lowenbraun, and Archer (1980) add that rules should be simple, clearly stated, and directly enforceable by the teacher. Classroom rules should be explained to students and reviewed frequently.

Structure can also help the academic performance of students. When consistent classroom routines are established, students are aware of what they should do, where they should be, and how they should act. For example, there may be a specific time and place in the classroom for turning in assignments. Some teachers provide each student with a daily assignment card that spells out each of the activities that must be completed. Raison (1979) suggests that secondary teachers establish a routine pattern of assignments (e.g., quiz on Wednesdays, essay due on Fridays) and provide students with a weekly assignment sheet. Eaton and Hansen (1978) advocate the use of student work folders; these can contain the schedule for the day, assignments to be completed, answer keys, and check-off sheets to record finished tasks.

Another way to provide structure is the use of prompts and models. Somewhere in most elementary classrooms is a model of the alphabet for stu-

TIPS FOR THE TEACHER

Self-Correcting Instructional Materials

With instructional materials that are self-correcting, students receive immediate feedback on the accuracy of their response. Some of the most common teaching tools contain self-correcting features. For example, at the end of many textbooks are the answers to all or some of the questions and problems.

Teachers can also design self-correcting materials to meet the needs of specific students. One example of an easy-to-make device that can be used for almost any school subject is suggested by Mercer and Mercer (1993):

> Strips are cut in one side of a manila folder and then the folder is laminated. Worksheets containing problems and answers are inserted into the folder so that only the problem is presented. The student uses a grease pencil or a felt-tip pen to write her responses under each problem. Then the worksheet is pulled upward, and the answers appear in the strip.

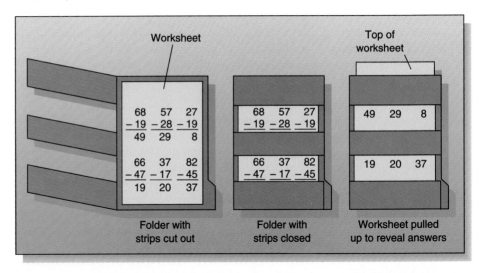

Note. Reprinted with the permission of Macmillan College Publishing Company from *Teaching Students with Learning Problems,* 4/e by Cecil D. Mercer and Ann R. Mercer. Copyright ©1993 Macmillan College Publishing Company, Inc.

dents to consult if they have difficulty forming letters. This technique can be used in most other subjects. For example, procedures for long division, alphabetizing, or constructing a paragraph can be written on the board. These prompts help students to function independently.

Use Systematic Record-Keeping Procedures

A great many sources of data are available to the teacher in the regular classroom, and it is easy to become overwhelmed by masses of information.

Flashcards are another example of a self-correcting material. The question or problem appears on one side of the card and the other side contains the answer. Like the folder device, flashcards are easy to make and can be adapted for many different subjects. Also, students can use flashcards for independent practice or for review sessions with a peer.

Math facts   State capitals

Opposites   Chemical symbols

When students use self-correcting materials for class assignments, teachers often ask how to prevent them from merely copying down the correct answers. Here are three ways to avoid this problem:

- Within each activity or assignment, include a few questions or problems for which the answer is not provided. These items serve as probes to determine whether students can transfer skills to questions for which the answers are not supplied.
- Have students correct each other's work. Students can trade assignments, or one or two individuals can be selected to be graders for the period or the day.
- Distribute answer keys only after students have completed their work; be sure, however, that the feedback occurs as soon after completion of the assignment as possible.

However, by using systematic record-keeping procedures, the teacher can collect sufficient information to make informed instructional decisions.

Teachers generally collect and record two types of data: activities completed (e.g., math workbook, pages 32–34) and actual measures of student performance on tests, quizzes, and other achievement indices (e.g., spelling test, 75%). Keeping detailed records of every activity completed by every student is probably not necessary. However, student performance should be measured in each major subject area at least once per week and more often if students are encountering difficulty.

One way to make data collection simpler is to enlist the aid of students. After correcting their academic work, they can record their scores or the number of correct responses. For example, Figure 7–7 shows George's daily assignment sheet for Monday. After completing an activity, he checks his answers with the key provided, records his score, and then corrects his mistakes. George can also learn to graph his scores so that he and his teacher can easily see his progress from day to day.

Smith, Neisworth, and Greer (1978) recommend that the following information be collected and recorded for each instructional objective: the date instruction began, the date the objective was achieved, and the student's performance level at completion. For groups of students working on the same skill, the teacher can simply record the starting and ending dates of instruction and the individual scores of each student.

Systematic record keeping requires consistency. Teachers should decide what data will be collected, how frequently, and what methods will be used for recording. It is best to begin gradually, perhaps with one or two subjects per week. The record-keeping system should be one with which the teacher is comfortable. Some teachers use grade books or loose-leaf notebooks divided into sections by academic subjects. Others favor a file folder for each instructional group or a 5 × 8 index card for each student. The most important factor is that data are collected regularly, recorded in a systematic fashion, and then utilized to determine whether instructional modifications should be made.

USING EDUCATIONAL TECHNOLOGIES

In a broad sense, the technology of education includes all types of instructional strategies and approaches; thus, systematic instruction and behavior management techniques could be considered educational technologies. More common, however, is the

FIGURE 7–7
Daily Assignment Sheet

Work for ___Monday___

Name ___George___

MATH	Do page 68, numbers 1 through 12.	I did it _____ I scored it _____ I corrected it _____	My score was _____ right.
SPELLING	Do page 42, numbers 4, 6, 8, 9, 10, 11, and 15.	I did it _____ I scored it _____ I corrected it _____	My score was _____ right.
READING	Read pages 6 and 7. Do worksheet 17A.	I did it _____ I scored it _____ I corrected it _____	My score was _____ right.

use of the term **educational technology** to refer to equipment and media with potential for contributing to the instructional process: computers, television and radio, audio- and videotapes, and so on. As Norris commented in 1977, technologies such as these have the capability to "revolutionize the quality, productivity, and availability of education" (p. 451).

In the mainstreamed classroom, both modern and traditional technologies can aid the teacher in providing individualized instruction and enhancing the standard curriculum. Several breakthroughs in the development of **assistive technology** make this particularly true for students with disabilities. For example, assistive technologies allow students who cannot see to hear the words that appear on a computer screen. Other students, unable to type on a computer keyboard, can write by speaking into a microphone. Special educational applications of technology are described throughout the rest of this book in sections entitled "Spotlight on Technology." The "Spotlight" in this chapter focuses on a very common technology, the audiotape recorder, and how this device can be used to enhance instruction for students with special needs and their peers.

Be Aware of Available Technologies

To use technology wisely, teachers must be aware of the resources available in their school and community and must keep informed about new developments. A vast array of technologies is currently available, and many are valuable tools for the presentation and practice of skills and information.

One way of classifying educational technologies is by their communication mode: visual, auditory, or multisensory. Visual media and equipment include photographs and cameras, slides and slide projectors, filmstrips and filmstrip projectors, and transparencies and overhead projectors. Visual technologies are often used with students with hearing losses. For example, with captioned films and television programs, the audio portion of the show is presented on the screen in text; the student reads the print captions, just as an English speaker would read the subtitles in a foreign film.

Records and record players, audiotapes and tape recorders, audio compact discs (CDs) and CD players, and radios are auditory technologies. They can be used by an entire class or selected individuals who listen through headphones. Students with vision losses benefit from auditory devices such as the talking calculator.

Multisensory technologies are common; these include language masters, films, videotapes, television, computers, and interactive videodisc technology. The language master, an adaptation of the tape recorder, uses a card with an audiotape affixed to the bottom. As the card with its printed message moves through the machine, the audiotape plays.

An important trend is the increased use of computers for classroom instruction and other educational purposes. **Computer-assisted instruction,** or the direct delivery of instruction to learners via computers, has proved effective with several types of learners, including students with disabilities. In addition, computers are useful tools for teachers. As Lewis (1993) points out, "technology can increase teachers' professional productivity and reduce the amount of time that must be spent in noninstructional classroom duties" (p. 126). The next chapter in this book focuses on strategies for using computers and other technologies in the mainstreamed classroom.

Match Technologies with Educational Goals

Educational technologies can be used for many types of instructional goals. It is important, however, to analyze the purpose of instruction and ensure that the medium selected is the most appropriate one available. The use of sophisticated technology, when a simple explanation from the teacher would suffice, is not effective management of instructional resources.

Technologies serve five major instructional functions in the classroom. They aid in the presentation of new material, provide practice opportunities, serve as rewards for appropriate behavior, and promote the development of social skills. In addition, assistive technologies allow students with special needs to bypass

Tape Recorders

*A*udiotape recorders and players are one of the most common technologies available today. Tape players, particularly personal stereos, are popular with students of all ages. According to Mercer and Mercer (1993), these devices have several advantages for classroom use. They are inexpensive, easy to operate, small in size, and portable. When used with headphones, they are quiet. Only the student wearing the headphones hears the tape so that others in the classroom are not distracted.

Teachers can use tape recorders as part of instruction in several ways. Mercer and Mercer (1993) provide several suggestions:

1. A tape can be made of reading material (for example, basal reader, stories, and magazines). The student can read along with the tape to practice reading. Thus, the tape can provide feedback, increase speed, and help the student identify and practice difficult words.
2. In a language experience activity, the student can use the recorder to make a tape of a story. Later, the student can write out the story from the tape with a peer, aide, or teacher.
3. Oral directions can be put on tape to accompany seatwork activities. The student who has difficulty with oral directions can play the tape until the directions are understood.
4. Spelling tapes are useful for practice and taking tests. One commonly used format includes (a) the spelling word; (b) the word used in a sentence; and (c) a pause, a beep, and the word spelled correctly. The pause can be eliminated by

disabilities so that they can participate in the same types of classroom learning activities as their peers.

Almost any type of technology can be used to present new information: films, filmstrips, television, video- and audiotapes, overhead transparencies, computer and interactive videodisc programs, and so on. Likewise, several types of media offer opportunities for practice. For example, many computer programs provide students with immediate feedback so that they can monitor their own performance during independent practice.

Technology activities can also serve as rewards. For example, some teachers set up classroom management programs in which students can earn time

to listen to radios or tapes, work with the computer, or watch videos. Production activities can also be reinforcers; students might take photos, make an audio recording of something they have written, or produce a videotape.

In the social area, technology can be used for both instruction and practice. For instance, students might view videotapes of interpersonal interactions that model appropriate skills. Or, the teacher (or a peer assistant) could videotape students as they participate in role plays of typical social situations; the tapes could then be used for discussion and feedback. To promote social acceptance, many teachers take photographs of class members for a bulletin having the student stop the recorder to write the word and then start it to check the spelling.

5. Stories, facts, or a report of an event can be recorded. News programs, commercials, telephone messages, weather reports, and teacher-made content can be used. The student listens and then responds to comprehension questions. For example, a weather report is taped, and the student is required to answer the following questions: High temperature? Low temperature? Any rain? Forecast for tomorrow? What season is it?

6. One-minute samples of instrumental music can be taped for students to use in conducting timings. These tapes usually begin with the word "start" and end with "stop." The teacher may prefer to use only the words and omit the music. In place of a kitchen timer, tapes of different time spans can be used to mark the end of any timed activity.

7. Correction tapes can be used to provide feedback to students who have completed math seatwork.

8. Music can be recorded on tapes for students to listen to when they have completed an assignment. Also, pleasant background music can be played while students are engaged in activities such as cleaning up, settling down after recess, free-choice, seatwork, or art.

9. At the secondary level, class lectures and discussions can be taped. These tapes can be used to help the students review or understand the material.

Note.   Reprinted with the permission of Macmillan College Publishing Company from *Teaching Students with Learning Problems,* 4/e by Cecil D. Mercer and Ann R. Mercer, Copyright ©1993 Macmillan College Publishing Company, Inc.

board or class book. This approach helps acquaint students with one another at the start of the school year and can also be used to teach about individual differences and similarities.

MANAGING TIME AND OTHER RESOURCES

When the physical and instructional environments have been arranged and the teacher begins to implement the classroom educational program, coordination skills become crucial. The teacher, as manager of the total learning environment, supervises the allocation, organization, and use of essential learning resources: time, educational materials and equipment, and instructional personnel. Principles for coordination of these resources appear in the following sections.

Manage Instructional Time Effectively

Time is a valuable and irreplaceable resource; its effective use is essential in the classroom and in other areas of a teacher's busy life. **Time management**, however, is a skill that most teachers and other professionals need to improve. Several of the key points in time management appear in "Tips for the Teacher."

Time Management

1. *Set goals.* What are your long-term goals? What are your goals for the next semester? Consider all aspects of your life: professional, personal, social, family, and community.
2. *Establish priorities.* Which of your goals are most important? Separate your goals into those of high value, moderate value, and low value.
3. *Analyze present time use.* Are you using your time to reach your high-priority goals? Keep a log or diary for a few days and see.
4. *Eliminate time wasters.* Spend your time on priority tasks that lead to high priority goals.
5. *Recognize the difference between "urgent" and "important."* Urgent tasks are those that demand immediate attention; they may or may not be important tasks that lead to your high priority goals.
6. *Don't procrastinate.* Instead, break large tasks into smaller manageable tasks. Begin a smaller task immediately.
7. *Make a daily list of things to do.* Make one list and update it daily; be sure to assign a priority to every item on the list.
8. *Begin with high-priority tasks.* Completion of these tasks will reap the most benefit; low-priority tasks can be postponed.
9. *Ask yourself, Is this the best use of my time right now?*

Note. Suggestions from *Getting Things Done* by E. C. Bliss, 1978, New York: Bantam Books; *Get it All Done and Still Be Human* by T. and R. Fanning, 1979, New York: Ballantine Books; *How to Get Control of Your Time and Your Life* by A. Lakein, 1974, New York: New American Library; *Working Smart* by M. LeBoeuf, 1980, New York: Warner Books; and *How to Put More Time in Your Life* by D. Scott, 1981, New York: New American Library.

In the classroom, teachers manage time by establishing a daily schedule. A schedule divides the day into segments and allots specific amounts of time to different activities. Time should be scheduled so that student engagement in important learning tasks is maximized (Englert, 1984). The highest-priority tasks should be given the most time, and noninstructional activities should be kept to a minimum.

Several suggestions for scheduling, presented by Mercer and Mercer (1993), are appropriate for both the elementary grade teacher, who schedules the entire school day, and the secondary grade teacher, who schedules several different class periods.

Among these suggestions are the following recommendations:

- Schedule for maximum instructional time.
- Proceed from short work assignments to longer ones.
- Alternate highly preferred with less preferred tasks.
- Provide a daily schedule for each student.
- Schedule assignments that can be completed in one school day.
- Provide time cues.
- Plan a variety of activities. (pp. 126–128)

The Premack Principle is also important to consider when designing an instructional schedule.

According to Polloway and Patton (1993), "It is often called 'grandma's law' because it is reminiscent of the traditional dinner table remark, 'If you eat your vegetables, then you can have dessert'" (p. 102). Thus, schedule highly preferred activities after less preferred activities. For example, *if* students finish their assignments, *then* they can select a free time activity.

It is usually best to begin with a structured schedule that includes several short activities. As students progress, the activities can become longer, and more choices can be offered. The schedule should be shared with students and remain consistent from day to day, providing a guideline to help students know what they should be doing at any time during the day. Figure 7–8 shows a schedule for a 55-minute secondary class; times are allocated for a class opening and closing, direct instruction, small-group center activities, and independent seatwork.

Select Learning Materials Wisely

Instructional materials, media, and equipment are other resources that teachers manage. A major consideration is their selection. Few teachers have unlimited funds, and budgets for materials must be used wisely. Smith, Neisworth, and Greer (1978) recommend the evaluation of both the technical and practical aspects of instructional materials. One important technical factor is whether the material has been validated, that is, proven to be effective for its recommended use. Practical considerations include the cost of the material, the number of students with whom it can be used, the strength of its physical construction, and its portability. According to Goodman (1978), characteristics such as difficulty level, presentation sequence, input modes, and modes of response should also be considered. The checklist in Figure 7–9 contains several important factors to take into account when evaluating instructional materials.

Teachers often design their own teaching materials if commercial ones are unavailable or too costly. When time and effort are devoted to the production of new instructional tools, the teacher should be sure to make materials that will last. Cohen and Hart-Hester (1987) say, "Never make a material twice;

FIGURE 7–8
Sample Schedule for a Secondary Class

Time	Amount		Activity
9:00	5 minutes	Opening:	Welcome, collection of assignments, directions for today's activities
9:05	15 minutes	Group A:	Small group instruction with teacher
		Group B:	Independent seatwork
		Group C:	Small group work at center
9:20	15 minutes	Group A:	Independent seatwork
		Group B:	Small group work at center
		Group C:	Small group instruction with teacher
9:35	15 minutes	Group A:	Small group work at center
		Group B:	Small group instruction with teacher
		Group C:	Independent seatwork
9:50	5 minutes	Closing:	Feedback on today's activities, directions for tomorrow's assignments

FIGURE 7–9
Checklist for Evaluating Instructional Materials

Instruction

1. Are instruction procedures for each lesson clearly specified?

2. Does the material provide a maximum amount of direct teacher instruction on the skills/concepts presented?

3. Does the direct teacher instruction provide for active student involvement and responses?

4. Are the direct instructional lessons adaptable to small-group/individual instruction?

5. Is a variety of cueing and prompting techniques used to elicit correct child responses?

6. When using verbal instruction, does the instruction proceed in a clear, logical fashion?

7. Does the teacher use modeling and demonstration when appropriate to the skills being taught?

8. Does the material specify correction and feedback procedures for use during instruction?

Practice

1. Does the material contain appropriate practice activities that contribute to mastery of the skills/concepts?

2. Are the practice activities directly related to the desired outcome behaviors?

3. Does the material provide enough practice for the slow learner?

4. Does the material provide for feedback on responses during practice?

5. Can the learner complete practice activities independently?

6. Does the material reduce the probability of error in independent practice activities?

Sequence of instruction

1. Are the scope and sequence of the material clearly specified?

2. Are facts/concepts/skills ordered in a logical manner from simple to complex?

3. Does the sequence proceed in small steps, easily attainable by the handicapped learner?

Content

1. Does the selection of the concepts and skills adequately represent the content area?

2. Is the content consistent with the stated objectives?

3. Is the information presented in the material accurate?

4. Is the information presented in the material current?

5. Are various points of view concerning treatment of minorities and handicapped people, ideologies, social values, sex roles, socioeconomic class, etc., objectively represented?

6. Are the content and topic of the material relevant to the needs of the handicapped students as well as to the other students in the regular classroom?

Behavioral Objectives

1. Are objectives clearly stated for the material?

2. Are the objectives consistent with the goals for the classroom?

3. Are the objectives stated in behavioral terms including the desired child behavior, the criteria for measurement of the behavior, and the desired standard of performance?

Entry Behaviors

1. Does the material specify the prerequisite student skills needed to work with ease in the material?

2. Are the prerequisite student skills compatible with the objectives of the material?

Initial Assessment/Placement

1. Does the material provide a method to determine initial placement into the material?
2. Does the initial placement tool contain enough items to accurately place the learner into the material?

Ongoing Assessment/Evaluation

1. Does the material provide evaluation procedures for measuring progress and mastery of objectives?
2. Are there sufficient evaluative items to accurately measure learner progress?
3. Are procedures and/or materials for ongoing record keeping provided?

Review/Maintenance

1. Are practice and review of content material provided?
2. Are review and maintenance activities systematically and appropriately spaced?
3. Are adequate review and maintenance activities provided for the slow learner?

Motivation/Interest

1. Are reinforcement procedures built in or suggested for use in the program?
2. Are procedures specified for providing feedback to the student on his/her progress?
3. Has the program been designed to motivate and appeal to students?

Adaptability to Individual Differences

1. Can the pace be adapted to variations in learner rate of mastery?

2. Can the method of response be adapted to the individual needs of the learner?
3. Can the method of instruction be adapted to the individual needs of the learner?
4. Can the child advance to subsequent tasks when he has demonstrated proficiency?
5. Can the learner be placed in the material at his own level?
6. Does the material offer alternative teaching strategies for students who are failing to master an objective?

Physical Characteristics of the Material

1. Is the format uncluttered?
2. Is the format grammatically correct and free of typographical errors?
3. Are photographs and illustrations clear, attractive, and consistent with the content?
4. Are the type size and style appropriate to the students?
5. Are auditory components of adequate clarity and amplification?
6. Are the materials durable?
7. Can the materials be easily stored and organized for classroom use?

Teacher Considerations

1. Is a teacher's manual or set of teacher guidelines provided?
2. Are teacher instructions clear, complete, and unambiguous?
3. Does the material specify the skills and abilities needed by the instructor to work effectively with the material?

Note. Reprinted with permission of Merrill, an imprint of Macmillan Publishing Company, from *Teaching the Mildly Handicapped in the Regular Classroom* (2nd ed., pp. 125–127) by J. Affleck, S. Lowenbraun, and A. Archer. Copyright © 1980 Merrill Publishing Company, Columbus, Ohio.

make it durable from the start" (p. 57). For example, elementary grade teachers can laminate supplementary math problem worksheets; secondary grade teachers may wish to keep a file or notebook of class handouts or directions for homework assignments. In addition, teacher-designed materials should be saved for several years. A worksheet or activity from last year, although not useful this year, may be just the thing that is needed *next* year.

Commercial materials as well as those made by teachers should be stored within the classroom so that they can be easily located and retrieved by students and teachers alike. Mercer and Mercer (1993) recommend the use of a filing system for organization; materials are organized by subject area (e.g., reading) and then by skill (e.g., comprehension). A skill file system designed for student use is described by Stowitschek, Gable, and Hendrickson (1980). Practice materials are sequenced according to skills, and skill tests are included. In addition, the book *Getting Organized* (Winston, 1991), although not written specifically for educators, gives several suggestions that can be used in establishing a management system for classroom materials.

Recruit, Train, and Supervise Instructional Personnel

In many cases, teachers do not have instructional aides, and they may view themselves as the only human instructional resource in their classrooms. However, two excellent sources of assistance are available to every teacher: peer tutors and adult volunteers.

Peer tutors are students who assist by teaching other students. They can come from the same class or can be older, more advanced students (usually called cross-age tutors). Students can learn to perform many instructional duties: they can be scoring monitors and check others' assignments; teach specific skills to individuals in need of extra help; or deliver reinforcers such as points, verbal praise, and feedback (Jenkins & Jenkins, 1985; Stowitschek, Gable, & Hendrickson, 1980). Ehly and Larsen (1980) conclude from a review of research that peer tutoring produces learning gains not only for the learner but also for the tutor. Thus, while tutoring is generally used to provide extra assistance to low-functioning students, such students also can improve their skills by becoming tutors. For instance, a sixth grader with special needs might be assigned as a cross-age tutor in a second grade classroom. This experience could provide motivation and recognition to the older student while benefitting both individuals academically. Krouse, Gerber, and Kauffman (1981) caution that tutoring programs should ensure that the student who is tutored is not stigmatized.

Adult **volunteers** can also provide instructional assistance. Platt and Platt (1980) describe a program that recruited parents and retired persons to help in the schools. Each volunteer was asked to specify areas of interest; choices included working with students on a one-to-one basis, working with small groups, performing clerical duties, and supervising activities outside the classroom.

Training must be provided for instructional personnel, whether they be adults or students. In one program (Heron, Heward, & Cooke, 1980; Parson & Heward, 1979), tutors were taught four skills: preparing learning materials, prompting student responses, praising correct answers, and plotting the results of the tutoring session. Teachers must also supervise and monitor the performance of tutors and volunteers. They can meet with their assistants before instruction or provide written directions. Each assistant should be observed frequently, and further training should be provided as needed. Consult "Tips for the Teacher"

Peer Tutors and Adult Volunteers

*P*eer tutors and adult volunteers are valuable instructional resources. They assist the teacher by taking responsibility for some of the more routine duties in the classroom. One of the first steps in beginning a peer tutoring or adult volunteer program is specification of the duties that these assistants will assume. Remember when choosing tasks that it will be necessary to train tutors and volunteers to perform them.

Student tutors can be trained to

- provide students with feedback about response accuracy,
- correct written assignments,
- deliver reinforcers such as verbal praise and points in a token economy,
- teach specific skills to individuals or small groups of students,
- supervise independent activities such as learning centers, and
- administer simple assessments.

Adult volunteers can be trained to perform any of the duties suggested for student tutors. They can also learn to

- supervise small groups of students in the classroom, at lunch, during assemblies, and so on;
- collect and record data on student performance;
- assist in the preparation of instructional materials;
- perform routine clerical duties; and
- help with classroom housekeeping chores.

When selecting duties for peer tutors, keep in mind that they are students. Choose tasks that relate directly to school learning; save clerical and housekeeping chores for adult volunteers.

Another important consideration is the system that the teacher will use to communicate with tutors and volunteers after these classroom assistants are trained. Hammill and Bartel (1986) suggest using a notebook that contains three different forms:

- *Tutor's Lesson Plan*—a description of the instructional activities, procedures, and amount of time to be spent on each
- *Tutor's Log Sheet*—a reporting form for the tutor to record student performance data and any observations about the tutoring session
- *Teacher's Note*—a page for the teacher to give feedback to the tutor, praise good performance, and suggest ideas for changes

for additional information about peer tutors and adult volunteers.

This chapter has presented several principles for the arrangement, management, and coordination of the classroom learning environment. The next chapter describes techniques for the effective use of one important type of instructional resource: computers and other technologies. Before going on, check "Things to Remember" to review coordination skills.

ACTIVITIES

1. Several educational journals offer suggestions to teachers about coordination of the classroom learning environment. Examples are *Teaching Exceptional Children, Focus on Exceptional Children,* and *Intervention in School and Clinic.* Find an article that interests you and summarize its recommendations.

2. Visit a school, university, shopping mall, or library to check its accessibility. Are there architectural barriers that would deny access to some individuals with disabilities? Watch for curbs, stairs, and steep inclines. If ramps are provided for wheelchairs, try traveling by this route. Is it less direct? Are information signs (e.g., signs on restrooms, elevators, telephones) in raised print and braille?

3. Check the library, educational materials center, and catalogues from school supply houses for self-correcting materials. You might also want to consult the book *Self-Correcting Learning Materials for the Classroom* by Mercer, Mercer, and Bott (1984). Are such materials available for subjects you teach? Are they more or less expensive than other materials? In your opinion, could students use them independently? What types of self-correcting materials could you design and make yourself?

4. Talk with teachers who have used peer tutors or adult volunteers in their classrooms. How were the classroom assistants selected or recruited? Were they provided with a training program? How did the teacher communicate with these helpers? Ask the teachers to discuss the advantages of tutors and volunteers. Are there any disadvantages?

5. One of the most exciting areas in education today is technology. Try to discover some of the latest technological innovations designed for use in education. You might contact a local school district or browse through a recent issue of *Electronic Learning, Technology & Learning,* or *The Computing Teacher.* Consider how the new technologies you identify could be used to improve instruction for students with special needs.

8 Using Computers and Other Technologies in the Classroom

Today, computers are a common feature of schools and classrooms in the United States. In 1981–1982, however, less than 40% of school districts owned computers (Quality Education Data, Inc., 1985). Numbers grew dramatically in the 1980s so that, by 1987, almost every public school in the United States owned at least one computer (Office of Technology Assessment, 1988; Scrogan, 1988). By the early 1990s, more than 2.5 million computers were being used for public school instruction, with a national average of one computer for every 19 students (Market Data Retrieval, as cited in Kinnaman, 1992).

Computer technology has great potential for assisting teachers in the delivery of quality instructional programs, particularly for students with special needs. As Lance observed in 1977, "If a truly appropriate education is to be provided for each child, teachers must be supported by a technology that will permit them to deal with a vast range of individual differences. A teacher cannot wing it with a few textbooks and a ditto machine" (p. 94). That technology is now available: computers, CD-ROM, interactive videodisc, telecommunications, more traditional educational technologies such as audio- and videotape players and recorders, and **assistive devices** such as electronic communication aids and talking calculators designed specifically for persons with disabilities. When used appropriately, these technologies can help teachers individualize instruction in the mainstream classroom.

Computers and other technologies represent only one of the many types of instructional tools available to teachers, however. They are not a panacea for the ills of education. What they do offer is an additional medium for instruction, another way for teachers to attempt to meet student needs.

CLASSROOM USES OF COMPUTERS

According to Taylor (1981), a classroom computer can be a tutor, tool, or tutee. The *tutor* role is the most familiar to teachers; the computer acts as a teaching assistant and delivers instruction to students. This application is called **computer-assisted instruction** (CAI). When the computer is used as a *tool*, it assists the student (or other user) in accomplishing some task. For example, a student writing a term paper might compose the paper at the computer, using a word processing program. The computer acts as a *tutee* when the student becomes the tutor and teaches the computer something, as when a student programs a computer with a computer language such as **Logo**.

Computers serve all three of these purposes in schools today. Students learn new material through CAI and practice what they have learned with computer drills. Computers assist students and teachers in writing and in the management of information; administrators and school clerical staff also take advantage of these computer applications. The computer becomes a tutee for secondary students in programming classes and for younger children creating designs with the Logo language. Figure 8–1 summarizes the research findings regarding computer use with both typical learners and those with special needs.

Computers are versatile tools that can be used for a variety of educational purposes. They offer several potential advantages as a medium for instruction:

- *Computers allow individualization of instruction.* Computers are also called personal computers (PCs) because they are intended for use by one person. They are a technology for individuals. If there were 35 students in a classroom, each sitting at a computer, these students could be learning or practicing skills in 35 different content areas. Or they could all be working on the same content, but each at the skill level appropriate for his or her level of learning. In addition, most computer programs allow learners to proceed at their own pace. Some programs also let teachers (or students) make choices about how instruction will take place. For example, the teacher might be able to choose how many times a question or problem will be repeated before the student is presented with the correct answer.
- *Computers motivate students.* Novelty is an important factor in motivation, and computers are still a new enough instructional medium to

FIGURE 8–1
Research Findings Regarding Computer Use

- When computers are used, students tend to learn the material in less time.

- The use of computers seems to result in increased attention, motivation, and time on task.

- The general effects of computer instruction are similar regardless of the type of software used. This does not imply that the quality of individual software is not a factor, but rather that one category of software has not consistently been found to be superior to others.

- Exceptional as well as nonexceptional learners tend to view the computer in the instructional setting quite positively.

- Drill-and-practice is the most frequent type of program used. This type of program is most useful with lower-ability students but has been found to be effective overall.

- Higher-ability students appear to benefit the most from the use of computers in terms of the amount and diversity of learning attained. This would appear consistent with the learning characteristics of this group.

- Using computers appears to more easily provide education to students who have typically been difficult to reach and teach.

- Computers are helpful in reviewing previously learned material. This may be a very significant factor in mainstreamed settings.

- The most effective use of computers is when they are used to supplement other instruction.

- Use of computers leads to better social interaction when students work jointly than when they work in isolation or when they work in traditional ways with traditional instruction.

- Computers do not stifle creativity nor do they dehumanize education.

- The benefits of computers are not inherent. The environment in which they are used and the way in which they are used are the determining factors.

- Teachers remain excited about the technology but do not spend much time actually using computers in the instructional process. Computers continue to be used in ways that are isolated from the instructional mainstream.

Note. From "Computers and Exceptional Individuals" (p. 12) by A. E. Hannaford, in J. D. Lindsey (Ed.), *Computers and Exceptional Individuals* (2nd ed.), 1993, Austin, TX: PRO-ED. Copyright 1993 by PRO-ED, Inc. Reprinted by permission.

excite students' interest. In addition, many computer programs use a game format so that learning activities seem more like play than work. Some programs also personalize instruction by addressing the student by name. For instance, Olivia might type in her name at the start of the program and then see on the screen, "Olivia, get ready to learn about asteroids!" Another motivating feature, particularly for students with learning needs, is that many programs provide feedback to the learner in a nonjudgmental manner. If the student makes an error, the program simply says, "Not quite, Olivia. Try again."

■ *Computers allow new types of learning and new ways of accomplishing old tasks.* With computers, teachers can provide students with a variety of learning experiences not usually possible in a traditional classroom setting. For example, using computer programs called **simulations**, students might learn to manage a lemonade stand, invest in the stock market, command troops in a Civil War battle, conduct a series of chemistry experiments, or travel to Jupiter. Obviously, these experiences would be difficult or impossible to duplicate in the classroom. Computers also provide new ways of doing old tasks. With **word processing programs**, for example, writing becomes a somewhat different process. As soon as the writer has entered text into the program, that text can be modified and manipulated quickly and easily. The writer can add or delete words or phrases, change the order of sentences or paragraphs, format the text in many different ways, and even add graphics. This flexibility makes writing an easier task for students because errors are less difficult to correct.

■ *Computers help special students bypass or compensate for disabilities.* Computers permit many special students to bypass physical or sensory limitations so that they can take part in regular classroom activities. For example, a student who is paralyzed and able only to nod his head can "type" on a computer by using a special switch mounted on the headrest of his wheelchair. Or a student who is blind can use a computer to translate her braille essay into regular print that her teacher can read. Computers can also help students compensate for

their difficulties in basic academic skills. Students who spell poorly, for example, can write with a word processor, then use a spelling checker program to help locate misspelled words.

There are also potential disadvantages to classroom computer use. Computers are only as good as the computer programs they run, so the selection of instructionally sound software is critical. Not all computer programs are based on sound principles of instruction; and although a wide selection of educational software is now available, it may not be possible to find a program that fits the content, level, and interest needs of a particular student.

In addition, most programs do not provide field test data to support their effectiveness. Although research shows that computers can improve student performance (Stowitschek & Stowitschek, 1984), further study is needed to identify the specific program features most likely to facilitate learning (Hofmeister & Thorkildsen, 1984).

Another potential area of difficulty is access to computer equipment. There may be only a few computers in the school; teachers may need to share a computer across several classrooms or schedule their students in a central computer lab for a limited time each week. In addition, computers become outmoded as new versions are introduced, and software designed to run on newer systems may not work on older ones.

COMPUTERS AND OTHER TECHNOLOGIES

Among the most common technologies currently used in education are computers, CD-ROM players, interactive videodisc players, and devices called modems that allow computers to be used for telecommunications. The sections that follow provide a brief description of each of these technologies.

Computers

Several different types of computers are found in schools today, but the most popular brands are Apple, Macintosh (a type of Apple computer), and

IBM. According to Bruder (1993), a 1992–1993 study of computer use in the United States by Market Data Retrieval found that 74% of all districts use Apple computers for instruction, 58% use the Macintosh, and 48% use IBM.

Despite the variety in computer brands and models, all computer systems share the same basic components. Understanding the purpose of each of these components helps teachers understand how computer systems work; however, it is certainly not necessary to acquire in-depth technical knowledge in order to operate a computer or to use one effectively in the classroom.

■ *Input.* First, there must be some way for the person who uses the computer system (the user) to send information to the computer. The most common input device is the computer **keyboard**. This resembles a typewriter keyboard with a few additional keys; it can be built into the computer or can be a separate (but connected) unit. The **mouse**, another common input device, sits on the desk next to computer. See Figure 8–2 for these and other components of a computer system.

■ *Output.* The computer also must be able to send information to the user. The **monitor**, which looks like a television screen, is used for this purpose. Some computers have color monitors, a nice feature for many educational programs; others have monochrome monitors. Most computers also contain one or more speakers to transmit auditory information to the user.

■ *Central processing unit.* The **central processing unit**, or CPU, is the "brain" of the computer. It directs the flow of information through the computer and controls all operations.

■ *Memory.* **Memory** is where information is stored within the computer. Some of the computer's memory holds information permanently. For example, some computers come with a programming language such as **BASIC** in their permanent memory. The other type of memory is not permanent; information is remembered only until the computer is turned off.

FIGURE 8–2
Components of a Computer System

Note. From *Special Education Technology: Classroom Applications* by R. B. Lewis. Copyright © 1993 by Brooks/Cole Publishing Company, Pacific Grove, CA. Reprinted by permission.

Memory is measured in units such as **bits**, **bytes**, **kilobytes**, and **megabytes**. A byte, which is made up of bits, is "the smallest information unit and represents a letter, number, or symbol" (Taber, 1983). One kilobyte (1 K) is equal to approximately 1,000 bytes and one megabyte (1 MB) to about 1,000,000 bytes. Computers are described by the amount of memory they contain and the more memory available, the better. Thus, a computer with 4 MB of memory is considered more desirable than a computer with 2 MB of memory.

■ *Storage.*   The most usual way of storing information for later use is to record it on a computer **disk**. Disks (sometimes called *floppy disks* or *diskettes*) are used with computers just as film is with cameras or tape with tape recorders. Disks store computer programs or data that the user creates; a wide variety of preprogrammed disks can be purchased commercially. Disks are placed in a device called a **disk drive** so that the information they store can be sent to the computer.

Hard drives are large-capacity storage units that are often built into computers. They are used to store copies of frequently used programs; when a program is on the computer's hard drive, the user does not need to load that program from a floppy disk.

Computer equipment is called **hardware**. Hardware includes the computer itself (which houses the CPU, memory, and perhaps a hard drive) and the keyboard, mouse, monitor, and disk drive. Software refers to the **programs** that are stored on computer disks.

A **peripheral** is any computer device that is peripheral to (i.e., not really necessary for) the operation of the computer. A common peripheral is the computer printer, an output device that transfers information to a printed page. Joysticks, similar to the controls used in video arcade games, are another type of input device. Some peripherals are specially designed to facilitate computer use for persons with disabilities; these are described later in this chapter.

Multimedia

Multimedia is one of the newest trends in educational computing. Multimedia computers and software programs present information to users through a combination of several different media. While traditional programs are typically limited to text and graphics, multimedia software may offer animation, video, audio (e.g., music, sound effects, and voice), and high quality photos and artwork. For example, in addition to reading a text description of elephants and seeing a drawing, the student may be able to look at color photos of different types of elephants, hear a recording of an elephant's call, and watch a video of a mother elephant interacting with her calf.

One drawback of multimedia programs is the amount of storage space they require. For example, many modern educational software programs do not fit on one floppy disk; programs requiring six, seven, or eight disks are quite common. One solution to this problem is the use of high-capacity storage media instead of traditional computer disks.

CD-ROM discs resemble the audio CDs on which music is stored. *CD* stands for compact disc; *ROM* means read-only memory. With computers, CD-ROM discs can only be "read"; the user cannot alter them or "write" new information on them. One CD-ROM disc can store a tremendous amount of information: approximately 250,000 pages of text, 15 hours of recorded audio, or 15,000 color photos (Holzberg, 1991; Oehring, 1992; Salpeter, 1988). For instance, it is possible to purchase one CD-ROM disc that contains the complete works of Shakespeare and another that holds an entire encyclopedia. To use CD-ROMs with a computer, that computer must be equipped with a special CD-ROM drive.

Videodiscs are another high-capacity storage medium. They look like large CDs and, like CD-ROM discs, they are able to store large amounts of information. As their name implies, videodiscs are used most often for videos and high-quality still photos; they also contain two audio tracks. A videodisc can be played from start to finish; for example, videodisc versions of movies are available for home entertainment. In education, however, videodiscs tend to be used interactively rather than linearly. That is, instead of simply playing the videodisc, the teacher or student selects segments of the program with which to interact. For instance, after watching a short video segment introducing the history of Mexico, a student might be asked to select which topic to explore first: pre-Columbian civilizations, the colonial era, or independence.

To play a videodisc, a videodisc player and a monitor or television are necessary. Three methods are used to control the videodisc player: a hand-held controller (similar to a remote control device for a television), a barcode reader (similar to those used in grocery stores to read the barcodes on consumer products), or a computer and specially designed software (Lewis, 1993). When videodiscs are used with a computer, two monitors are required: one for the computer and the other for the videodisc player. See Figure 8–3 for an example of a CD-ROM disc and a videodisc.

Linking Computers: Networks and Telecommunications

Although computers are designed for individual users, they can also be linked together. One way of doing this is by a **network**, often called a *local area network* or LAN. For example, all the computers in a school computer lab can be networked together so that they share a printer. Or, the entire school can be networked so that computers in various classrooms, offices, and the library/media center can share software and communicate with each other. When a school is networked, students may be able to access databases in the library/media center from their classroom computer; in addition, students in different classrooms may be able to work collaboratively on projects such as a school newspaper.

Telecommunications is another method for linking computers. Specifically, it "is the process of transferring information over a distance via a conduit such as telephone lines" (Lewis, 1993, p. 365). Two computers located far from each other can communicate over phone lines if each is equipped with a device called a **modem.** Or, one computer equipped with a modem can use telephone lines to connect to a commercial information service such as America OnLine, Prodigy, or CompuServe. In many states, teachers also have access to the Internet, the international information highway.

With telecommunications, teachers and students in different states, regions, and countries can communicate and exchange electronic mail (E-mail). In addition, users can consult a number of databases and other information sources. For example, SpecialNet, a commercial information service for persons interested in special education, offers electronic mail, conferences, bulletin boards, and databases on technology, law, and other topics.

FIGURE 8–3
CD-ROM Disc and Videodisc

Note.   Photo by Scott Cunningham/Prentice Hall and Merrill.

EDUCATIONAL SOFTWARE

Educational software was once a scarce commodity, but that is certainly not the case today. Now thousands of instructional software programs are available (Sivin & Bialo, 1988). According to the Office of Technology Assessment (1988), more than 10,000 educational programs have been produced by approximately 900 commercial firms. Most current programs are technically excellent, many are educationally sound, and the number and variety of instructional programs continue to increase.

Instructional programs are available for most areas of the school curriculum, including basic skills subjects such as reading, spelling, writing, and mathematics as well as content area subjects such as science, social studies, and history. There is instructional software for preschool children, programs to teach computer literacy and programming skills, and programs that address career education and the development of prevocational and vocational skills.

Software can be classified by curriculum area or by the type of instructional mode used to present the content. The most common types are tutorials, drill-and-practice programs, simulations, problem-solving programs, educational games, teacher utility programs, and software tools such as word processors and data management programs.

Tutorials

Tutorials are designed to present content that is new to the learner. They introduce and explain new skills or information and then supervise the student's first attempts to practice and apply this new material. For example, *Word Attack Plus!* (Davidson & Associates)* offers several activities for learning vocabulary words, beginning with a tutorial that presents each new word and its meaning. Although tutorials assume no prior experience with the content to be presented, the learner may need prerequisite skills or information to take full advantage of instruction.

---

* See the Appendix for contact information for the software publishers and producers of assistive devices mentioned in this book.

For instance, basic math skills would be needed to benefit from a tutorial on adding fractions.

Of course, for any tutorial (or any other type of instructional program), students must have sufficient computer skills to operate the program. And in many cases students must also be able to read and interpret the information that appears on the screen. Typing and spelling skills may also be needed for the learner to respond to questions in the program.

Drill-and-Practice Programs

Drill-and-practice programs, one of the most common types of academic software, provide learners with the opportunity to practice material to which they have already been exposed. Drill programs do not present new material or attempt to teach new skills or explain new concepts. Instead, they review material introduced previously, giving students practice so that performance can improve. Most drill programs provide students with immediate feedback on the accuracy of their responses, and many impose speed demands to encourage students to respond both quickly and accurately.

One variation of drill-and-practice software is arcade-type instructional programs. Their purpose is the same as that of any drill program, but they incorporate the features of arcade games in an attempt to motivate learners. For example, in one early program, the student piloted a helicopter and spelled words by shooting the letters in order. In other programs, the student might work against the clock trying to answer questions or problems correctly in order to prevent a spaceship from crashing or extraterrestrials from launching their missiles. Arcade-type programs often incorporate color, graphics, and sound effects to enhance their appeal to young learners.

Simulations

Often used for enrichment activities in content area subjects, these programs provide students with experience in situations difficult or impossible to duplicate in the classroom. For instance, students might command troops in a Revolutionary War battle, manage a household budget, or travel to Mars.

One of the most popular social studies programs is *The Oregon Trail* (MECC), in which students simulate the pioneers' journey across the United States.

Simulations provide students with information about the situations they will encounter and then ask them to make decisions. The student space travelers, for example, might need to select provisions for their journey and chart the route they will follow. When the simulation begins, events unfold and more choices must be made; in many simulations, there is an element of chance so that students may be unsuccessful despite careful planning and prudent decisions. Simulations, unlike tutorials and drills, are discovery learning activities. Students are expected to learn about the situation or event in which they participate and to draw conclusions about the important variables within that situation by perceiving the consequences of the decisions they make.

Programs to Teach Problem-Solving Skills

Problem-solving programs are not tied to any one curriculum area; instead, their purpose is to set up a learning environment in which students can practice critical thinking and acquire skills in problem analysis and solution. A good example of this type of software is Logo, a programming language designed for children. It is essentially content-free, and, as Seymour Papert (1980) explains in *Mindstorms*, it places the child in control of the computer, rather than letting the computer control the child. Papert suggests that "in teaching the computer how to think, children embark on an exploration about how they themselves think" (p. 19).

Although Logo is perhaps the most comprehensive system for teaching thinking skills, several other programs are available that attempt to achieve the same end. These programs pose a problem and then allow students to gather information about the problem, suggest alternative solutions, and evaluate the effectiveness of each. For example, in *The Factory* (Sunburst Communications), students are provided with a set of machines with which to manufacture a product that matches the model presented by the program. The order in which the machines are used affects the outcome, so students must experiment in order to come up with the right product.

Educational Games

There is a plentiful supply of games software, and some of these programs are of value in the classroom. Games can be used to teach thinking skills, provide practice in the application of academic skills, and serve as a leisure activity rewarding appropriate classroom behavior. Most of the traditional board games, such as Monopoly and Scrabble, are available as computer programs, as are card games and word games such as hangman. Another variety, adventure games, is quite similar to simulations, except that the situations that are portrayed are selected for their entertainment value rather than their educational value. In adventure games, participants often engage in role playing, and decisions made by the player alter the course of the adventure. Arcade-type computer games are perhaps the most popular games outside the classroom; players earn points by skillful maneuvering and careful aim while they do battle with some opponent, make their way through a maze or labyrinth, or play the electronic version of some sport or conventional arcade game.

Software Tools

The most widely used software tool in school settings is the word processing program. Word processors present the user with the computer equivalent of a blank sheet of paper—an empty screen—and then provide a system for entering text onto that screen. Their main value, however, is the ease with which that text can be changed and manipulated. The writer can correct errors quickly and easily, alter the sequence and format of the text, and then store what has been written for later use. In addition, a number of programs can be used in conjunction with word processors, including those that check and correct spelling and grammar and even thesaurus programs that suggest alternative word choices.

There are many popular word processors. Some, designed specifically for younger students, offer fea-

Introducing Students to Database Management Programs

Lesson Title	Lesson 1: Introducing Database Management
Grade Level	4–12
Content Area	Language, Social Studies, Critical Thinking
Goal	Students will understand what a database is and how it works.
Time Required	1–3 hours
Preparation	Materials needed: File box, file folders, labels, computer, database program, blank disk, blackboard, paper and pencil for each student

Conducting the Lesson

1. Ask students if they've ever used a file box, file cabinet, etc., and if they know what it's used for.
2. Open the box and ask how you would find what you're looking for (label on box, folders, etc.).
3. Ask students if they would like to teach the computer to be an electronic file cabinet, and see who can find information best—an electronic file cabinet or a person with a file box.
4. Put a label on the file box: *Mrs. Smith's Class* (use *your* name).

---

tures such as simple operation and large-sized text. Others have the capacity to "talk"; that is, students can hear the text they have written read aloud. A **desktop publishing program** is a special type of word processor that allows writers to add graphics to their text. In education, the best-known desktop publishing programs are *The Children's Writing and Publishing Center* (Learning Company) and its recent update, *The Writing Center.*

Database management programs are a popular type of software tool with teachers, and students use them in some content area subjects. Examples are *AppleWorks* (Claris), *ClarisWorks* (Claris), and *Microsoft Works* (Microsoft); these are integrated programs that contain both a word processor and a database management system (as well as other features such as spreadsheets for manipulating numerical information). Database programs assist in the organization and management of large bodies of information; in effect, they create a computer-based filing system. The user determines the type of information to be stored and the exact data to be included in each record. The major value of such a record-keeping system is that, once the information has been

---

5. Ask the class to brainstorm the kinds of information that might "fit" into the box. List these on the blackboard (for example, names of students, birthdays, hobbies, favorite subjects).
6. Have the class select three. Ask each student to write the three categories on his/her paper and fill in the information (for example, Name, Suzie Smith; Birthday, June 3, 1973; Favorite Color, Red).
7. Load the database program into the computer, insert the file disk, and design a form to collect the data while the students watch.
8. Ask for a volunteer to sit in the computer chair and enter his/her data. (You may need to point to the keys to speed up the process.) If time allows, let 2–3 others also enter data. Finish the class's data entry yourself.
9. Give each student a file folder and a label. Ask them to put their name on it and to put their papers in it. Put the folders in the file box.
10. Ask students if they think the computer remembers what was entered. Flash through the files to make sure.
11. Ask for a volunteer to race the computer to see how many students were born in 1973. Set up the program to sort by year of birth, and give the file box to the volunteer.
12. Read out the data as it is sorted by the computer.
13. Ask the students which was faster, more fun, easier, etc.

Follow-Up

Ask the students for other categories to sort. Ask the students if there is additional information that should go in the file box.

Note.   From *Special Magic: Computers, Classroom Strategies, and Exceptional Students* (p. 69) by M. Male, 1988, Mountain View, CA: Mayfield. Copyright 1988 by Mayfield Publishing. Reprinted by permission.

stored, it can be sorted and retrieved quickly and easily. For example, if a teacher has set up a database on the classroom software collection, he or she can quickly retrieve the names of the programs within that collection that provide drill in spelling or all those programs that cost less than $50. In social studies, students might search a database on the states to identify all the states that entered the union after 1900 or all that are smaller than Virginia (Hunter, 1984). See "Tips for the Teacher" for a sample lesson plan to introduce students to database management programs.

Teacher Utility Programs

Although teacher utilities are used by teachers rather than students, they support the delivery of instruction and are thus considered educational software. Word processors and database management programs can be viewed as teacher utilities; however, such programs are usually designed for a general audience. A separate body of software has been created specifically for use by teachers.

Authoring programs are one example. These programs help teachers to create computer-based lessons. They are quite easy to use so that the teacher can develop software programs without becoming a computer programmer. For example, some authoring programs provide a lesson "shell," and the teacher simply answers questions in order to fit the appropriate instructional content into the shell. The system might ask the teacher to supply the name of the lesson, the text to be displayed on the screen, the first question to be asked, the correct answer or answers to that question, the response that should be given if the question is answered cor-rectly (or incorrectly), and so on. The authoring program then transforms this information into a computer-based lesson. See Figure 8–4 for an example of an authoring program.

There are several other types of teacher utility programs, including electronic grade books and programs that assist in the preparation of instructional materials. For instance, the teacher can use a program such as *Crossword Magic* (Mindscape) to generate crossword puzzles in order to provide students with additional practice with new vocabulary or spelling words. One

---

FIGURE 8–4
Player's Choice

Player's Choice is a public domain shell program. Public domain software is not copyrighted; it is typically free or distributed at cost, and users can make unlimited copies. Shell programs are simple authoring systems; the "shell" is the basic structure of the lesson, and teachers add content and may be able to determine some of the instructional parameters. *Player's Choice* is an arcade-type drill and practice program; its screen looks like this:

It is easy to create a computer-based lesson in almost any subject area with *Player's Choice*. For each item, the teacher simply enters the question, the correct answer, and three incorrect answers.

Player's Choice and *Juegos Selectos*, a Spanish-language version of the program, are available from CUE Softswap (4655 Old Ironsides Drive, Suite 200, Santa Clara, CA 95054). CUE Softswap, a project of Computer-Using Educators, distributes public domain software for education.

of the most popular programs with teachers (and students) is *The Print Shop® Deluxe* (Brøderbund Software, Inc.). See "Spotlight on Technology" for more information about this versatile tool.

Sometimes educational programs are a combination of two instructional modes. For example, included in some drills and tutorials is a record-keeping component that collects and stores information on student performance. Comprehensive systems for **computer-managed instruction** provide the teacher with information about each student's progress toward the mastery of specific skills. These systems, sometimes called *integrated learning systems,* are often designed to deliver instruction in broad curriculum areas such as reading, math, or language arts.

Any type of software can be stored on standard computer disks or on CD-ROM. Any type can be multimedia, although voice, music, and video are used most often in tutorials, drills, simulations, and software tools such as electronic encyclopedias. Programs can also be arranged in a linear sequence or use a newer approach called hypertext or hypermedia. In traditional programs, although the learner may be able to make some choices, the overall sequence of the program is fixed. In **hypertext** (i.e., text only) or **hypermedia** programs, the user directs the flow of the program; its sequence is not fixed. For example, the Discis Books series (Discis Knowledge Research) is a set of talking storybooks that make use of hypermedia. The student can skip to any page in the book, hear an entire page or a sentence read aloud (in English or Spanish), select one word in the story to hear it read in syllables or hear its meaning explained, or select an object in one of the pictures that accompany the story to see the word it represents and hear it pronounced. Clearly, in programs such as these, the user is in charge of the instructional sequence.

SELECTING APPROPRIATE SOFTWARE

Good quality software is the key to effective computer use. Without software, a computer is like a VCR with no tapes. Software is what brings the computer to life, what transforms the potential instructional value of this technology into a classroom reality. Thus, selection of appropriate software is one of the most important decisions educators face in the use of computers.

Try Before You Buy

There is no substitute for sitting down at the computer with a program and trying it out. Software cannot be adequately evaluated by reading an advertisement in a magazine or a description in a catalogue, as many disappointed teachers have learned after purchasing a program sight unseen. Computers are an interactive medium, and it is necessary to see how programs respond to and interact with the user.

First, be sure that the software you are previewing is compatible with your computer. Some programs are designed to run on only one type of computer system; others are available in several versions (e.g., an Apple version, an IBM version, a Macintosh version). Pick programs designed for *your* computer. It's not possible to run an Apple program on an IBM computer (or vice versa).

In trying out a program, the teacher should begin by attempting to answer all questions correctly. If the program's directions are unclear or ambiguous, this may not be possible—a sure sign that the program is not of the best quality. Next, the teacher should go through the program giving incorrect responses. For example, if the program directs the user to answer yes or no, the teacher might type 7 and see what happens. Does the program crash? Or is there a gentle reminder about what to type? The wrong response should be given to other questions, too. If the answer is *A* and *B* is typed, what happens? How are errors handled? Is there an unpleasant beep or buzz? A neutral (or nasty) message on the screen? How many times must the user attempt a question before the program moves on?

This type of experience with a program provides the teacher with adequate information to judge the program's worth. Again, there is no substitute for hands-on evaluation. Some software companies allow teachers to preview software before they buy; others do not but permit programs to be returned

The Print Shop® Deluxe: A Versatile Program for Teachers and Students

*T*he Print Shop® Deluxe (Brøderbund® Software, Inc.) is a recent update of one of the most popular software programs of all time. With *The Print Shop®*, teachers (and students) express their creativity by mixing text and graphics. It is quite easy to use (although later versions of the program are a bit more difficult than earlier versions because they offer more options). However, the most important feature of this program is its versatility. Classroom uses of *The Print Shop®* are virtually limitless: signs to remind students of classroom rules, illustrations for class writing projects, covers for reports in science and social studies, calendars of classroom events, and so on. *The Print Shop®* can also be used with young students as an introduction to word processing.

The first menu in *The Print Shop® Deluxe* program for the Macintosh presents the five types of products that can be created: greeting cards, signs, banners, letterhead stationery, and calendars.

Note. ©1992, Brøderbund Software, Inc. All Rights Reserved. Used by Permission. Photo by Dylan Lewis.

When the sign option is chosen, the screen shows a blank sign. At the top of the screen is a menu bar and the mouse is used to pull down the menus to make choices.

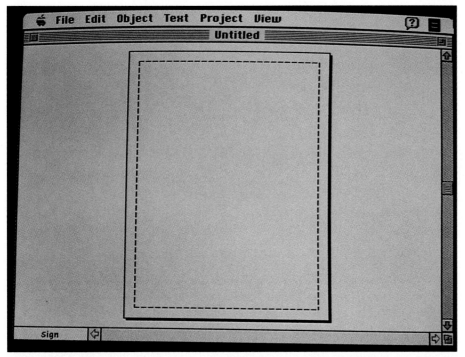

Note. ©1992, Brøderbund Software, Inc. All Rights Reserved. Used by Permission. Photo by Dylan Lewis.

For example, one of the choices on the Object menu is "Add" and there are several possibilities. In the finished sign shown on the next page, the teacher has added a headline ("CONGRATULATIONS!"), a graphic, a text message, and a border.

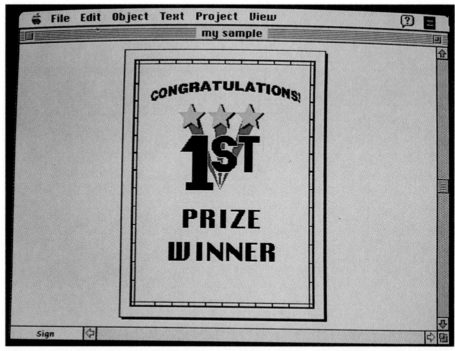

Note. ©1992, Brøderbund Software, Inc. All Rights Reserved. Used by Permission. Photo by Dylan Lewis.

In creating a sign or other product with *The Print Shop® Deluxe,* the teacher can select from a variety of different type styles and sizes. More than 250 graphics are included as well as 35 different borders. Additional sets of graphics can also be purchased; collections are available with themes such as school, celebrations, business, sports, and animals. And, when teachers run out of ideas for using this program, they can consult the book *The Official Print Shop Handbook.*

for a refund if they are found unsatisfactory. Sometimes, publishers will supply a demonstration disk. Teachers may also be able to locate programs in the software collection of another educator, school, district, or instructional materials center.

When previewing a program is simply not possible, published software reviews can provide critical information about a program's value. Reviews are also useful when searching for software because they may help teachers eliminate some programs

from consideration. Reviews are published in many professional journals and by several different agencies. One yearly publication that integrates reviews from a variety of sources is *Only the Best: Annual Guide to Highest-Rated Education Software/Multimedia for Preschool–Grade 12* (available from Education News Service, P.O. Box 1789, Carmichael, CA 95609). The programs it features are those that have been highly rated by a variety of organizations and agencies in the United States and Canada. *Only the*

Best also contains a section on special education software. Another source is *The Latest and Best of TESS; TESS* stands for *The Educational Software Selector* (available from EPIE Institute, 103-3 West Montauk Highway, Hampton Bays, NY 11946).

Evaluate with Particular Students in Mind

Software cannot be evaluated in a vacuum. A program may be appropriate for one group of learners but not for another; for example, it may meet the needs of kindergarten students but be much too juvenile for third graders. The instructional purpose must also be considered; an excellent drill-and-practice program will not suffice if a tutorial is needed.

In reviewing educational software, the teacher needs to keep in mind the student population with which the program will be used and the purposes of instruction. The worksheet for software evaluation, which appears in Figure 8–5, can help in this and other aspects of the review process. The teacher begins by noting the program's name and other descriptive information about the software. Then the target students are described in terms of their current grade in school, their current skill levels (which may differ from school placement), and any special needs they may have.

Look Carefully at the Program's Content and Mode of Instruction

First, the teacher should consider what the software publisher says about the general purpose of the program and its educational objectives. This type of information usually appears in the program's documentation (i.e., the print materials that accompany the software). Then the teacher should review the program to form a personal opinion of its content. The fact that a program is labeled as reading software does not necessarily mean that it teaches reading skills; it could ask students to spell words, not read them. Or a program said to address the curriculum area of writing could cover only one small aspect of this skill, such as capitalization or forming possessives.

The mode of instruction is also a concern. Many programs advertised as tutorials are, in reality, drill programs. When the program's curricular content and type have been identified, the teacher can decide whether the program is worth further review. If its purpose and type are not what the teacher is looking for, the review process can be discontinued.

Determine Whether the Program Makes Use of the Computer's Capabilities

Computers are primarily a visual medium: most of the information presented to learners appears on the screen. That information can be in the form of text (i.e., letters, numbers, and symbols), still or animated graphics, and/or video. Today, most programs are written in color. However, color is apparent to the viewer only if the computer is equipped with a color monitor.

The information presented on the screen should be clear and comprehensible. Text should be legible and easy to read. The text displays in many older programs were crowded and written all in capital letters, giving the appearance of difficulty. Newer programs tend to use large, clear letters in both upper- and lowercase and to space the display so that it is inviting, even to reluctant readers.

Some programs provide auditory information. Sound effects like bells, beeps, buzzers, tones, and rocket blasts make programs seem more like games. In instructional software, sounds are often used as signals. For example, one sound may alert students that it is time to respond, another that the response was correct, and another that the answer was not correct. Music can also be added to programs, as can speech. Multimedia programs often include recordings of music, speech, and other types of auditory information. Speech is also available with some specially designed programs that make use of a computer peripheral called a speech synthesizer.

The hallmark of the computer as an instructional device is its ability to interact with the learner. Programs that appear to be electronic textbooks (or, as some call them, electronic page turners) do not capitalize on the computer's capabilities. A program

FIGURE 8–5
Worksheet for Software Evaluation

Directions: Complete this worksheet as you review the instructional program and its documentation. Fill in the identifying information, complete the description of the program, and then evaluate its usefulness for the students in your classroom.

A. IDENTIFYING INFORMATION

Name of instructional program _____

Publisher _____ Cost _____

Backup copy provided? _____ Available? _____ Cost _____

Network/lab pack available? _____ Cost _____

Computer _____ Other equipment _____

Grade level of your students _____

Skill levels of your students _____

Special needs _____

B. DESCRIPTIVE INFORMATION

1. What is the purpose of the instructional program, as stated by its publisher?

2. What curriculum area or areas does it address?

3. What type of instructional program is it? _____ tutorial _____ drill and practice

_____ arcade-type drill _____ simulation _____ problem solving _____ educational game

_____ teacher utility _____ other (specify) _____

4. For what type of learner was the program designed?

age level _____ grade level _____

ability level _____

interest level _____

5. Are the objectives of the program stated? _____ yes _____ no

If they are, what skills or information does the program attempt to teach or review? (state briefly)

6. How does the program present information? (check all that apply)

_____ text _____ graphics _____ animation _____ color

_____ sound effects _____ music _____ speech _____ video

7. Is the information presented clearly? Is text legible and readable? Are graphics comprehensible? Are sounds audible and intelligible? _____ yes _____ no   If no, explain.

8. Are directions for using the program clearly stated and understandable? _____ yes _____ no
   Where do directions appear? _____ within the program _____ in the program's documentation or manual

9. Is the program under user control? That is, can the user control the program's movement from screen to screen? review directions at any time? exit the program at any time?
   _____ yes _____ no   If no, explain.

10. What *computer use demands* are placed on the learner?
    _____ insert disk and turn on computer   _____ select from menu
    _____ other (specify _____)

11. What *academic demands* are placed on the learner?
    _____ reading (level _____)
    _____ spelling (level _____)
    _____ other (specify) _____ , level _____)
    _____ other (specify) _____ , level _____)

12. What *physical demands* are placed on the learner?
    _____ keyboard must be used to enter responses
        _____ press any key
        _____ press a key from one half or one quadrant of keyboard
        _____ press one specific key
        _____ press several keys in order
    _____ other device(s) used to enter responses (specify_____
    _____)

13. What *speed demands* are placed on the learner?
    _____ presentation of information controlled by program (_____ moderate _____ fast _____ slow)
    _____ presentation of information under user control
    _____ unlimited response time
    _____ response time set by program (_____ moderate _____ fast _____ slow)
    _____ response time varied by user

14. What *accuracy demands* are placed on the learner?
    _____ user can correct typing errors

FIGURE 8–5
continued

_____ program does not allow correction of typing errors

_____ program traps common errors

_____ program requires correct spelling of all responses

_____ program allows only one correct response for most questions

15. Is feedback about response accuracy provided to learners appropriately?

   a. knowledge of results provided after each response? _____ yes _____ no

   b. correct responses confirmed? _____ yes _____ no

   c. learner informed if response incorrect? _____ yes _____ no

   d. another trial provided if response incorrect? _____ yes _____ no

   e. number of trials provided _____

   f. correct response demonstrated if learner fails to answer correctly? _____ yes _____ no

   g. learner allowed opportunity to respond after demonstration of correct response? _____ yes _____ no

16. Does the program use any branching procedures besides differential treatment of correct and incorrect responses? _____ yes _____ no   If yes, explain.

17. What techniques are used for reinforcement and motivation? (check all that apply)

   _____ knowledge of results and confirmation of correct responses

   _____ summary information about learner performance

   _____ text message of praise for correct responses

   _____ graphics display and/or sound for correct responses

   _____ competitive game in which correct responses earn points

   _____ other (specify _____)

   reinforcement is _____ continuous _____ intermittent

18. What user options are available to students and teachers?

   a. Students can select

   _____ activity from menu   _____ difficulty

   _____ number of questions   _____ type of questions

   _____ other (explain _____)

   b. Teachers can select

   _____ sound on or off   _____ difficulty

   _____ number of questions   _____ type of questions

_____ sequence of instruction   _____ number of trials

_____ speed of presentation   _____ speed demands for responses

_____ other (explain _____)

c. Teachers can

     _____ enter own content into program

     _____ review student records

     _____ other (explain _____)

19. Is the program's documentation adequate?

     a. all program features fully and clearly explained? _____ yes _____ no

     b. rationale for program, purpose and objectives, and field test data included? _____ yes _____ no

     c. print materials provided for students? _____ yes _____ no

        if available, are they appropriate? _____ yes _____ no

     d. additional learning activities suggested in documentation? _____ yes _____ no

20. Other comments about the instructional program:

C. OVERALL EVALUATION

Rate the appropriateness of the instructional program for your students in each of the following areas, using this scale:

inadequate	adequate	excellent
1	2	3

a.	Curricular content (program addresses important skills)		1 2 3
b.	Interest level (program is age-appropriate)		1 2 3
c.	Ease of use for learners		1 2 3
d.	Demands on learner (computer use, academic, speed, accuracy, physical)		1 2 3
e.	Instructional procedures		1 2 3
f.	Motivational value		1 2 3
g.	Appropriate use of the medium		1 2 3
h.	Important instructional variables under teacher control		1 2 3
i.	Other (specify _____)		1 2 3

In summary, what is your overall evaluation of the instructional program? Would you recommend its use? If you would, for what purpose(s)? Are there aspects of the program about which you would like to caution other educators?

Note. From _Worksheet for Software Evaluation_ by R. B. Lewis, 1994, San Diego, CA: San Diego State University. Copyright 1983, 1989, 1992, 1994 by Rena Lewis. Adapted by permission.

does not need to take advantage of all features of the medium, but it should be more than a software translation of an instructional material that exists (or should exist) in print form.

Consider the Demands Placed on the Student

The demands that software places on students, over and above the requirements of the instructional content and the questions asked, can prevent students from being able to interact successfully with the program. There are five areas of concern:

1. *Computer use demands.* Before using any type of software, students must be trained to operate the computer. Usually it takes little time before students are running programs independently. However, some software can be difficult to operate. For example, a multidisk program that requires students to insert first one disk, then another, and then another may be quite difficult for a young or inexperienced computer user.
2. *Academic demands.* Reading and spelling skills are needed to profit from many educational programs. Programs may present textual information that must be read by the student, even when the purpose of the program is to teach math skills or introduce content subject information. In addition, spelling skills are required for programs in which students type words or sentences to respond to questions. The reading and spelling levels required for program use are a major consideration, particularly for students with academic learning problems.
3. *Physical demands.* In most educational programs, students respond by typing on the keyboard. The easiest type of keyboard response is pressing any key, a response mode used in discovery programs for preschoolers. More difficult is pressing one of a limited number of keys (e.g., *A, B, C,* or *D*), and most difficult is typing connected text (words, phrases, or sentences). Some programs get away from keyboard and typing demands by having the student respond with a mouse or joystick. However, some manual dexterity is required to operate such devices. There

are also special devices for students with physical disabilities so that they can enter information without using the keyboard or mouse.
4. *Speed demands.* Another important concern is whether the pace of the program is under the control of the user. Some programs present information quickly, and the student cannot regulate the speed with which text appears on the screen. The learner may be reading the first of three paragraphs when the screen changes to a new display. However, with programs that are under user control, it is the student who decides when it is time to move to new information. The pace is controlled by the student so that he or she can spend as much time as needed on any one part of the program. The time allowed for responding to questions can also be under user control, or response time can be controlled by the program, with a limited time allowed for the student to enter the answer.
5. *Accuracy demands.* Programs differ in error handling capabilities. In some, the student can type the response, correct any typing errors, and then signal that the response is complete (e.g., by pressing the Return or Enter key on the keyboard); in others, whatever the student first types is considered the final response. Error trapping is another concern. Some programs are written to "trap" common errors; for example, if the student types *yse* instead of *yes,* the program accepts the response as correct or provides a prompt ("Not quite. Try again."). Programs without this capability simply count the response as incorrect.

Check the Adequacy of Instructional Procedures

The first step here is to evaluate the directions given to students. Are they clear and easy to follow or ambiguous and misleading? Then the content presented in the program is checked for accuracy and clarity of presentation.

Another aspect to consider is how the program provides feedback to students about the accuracy of their responses. At the minimum, students should receive knowledge of results after each response;

the program should tell the student whether the answer was right or wrong.

When students make incorrect responses, how does the program react? Is the student informed and another trial provided? How many trials are given before the program shows the correct answer and moves on to the next question? Some programs do not advance until the student answers correctly; this procedure encourages guessing and then frustration if the student cannot come up with the answer. It is also important to determine whether the consequences of an incorrect response are more attractive than those of a correct response. For instance, in some arcade-type programs, the monster destroys the spaceship when errors occur, whereas the only consequence of correct responses is more questions to answer.

Programs use different techniques to reinforce students for correct responses. Some simply confirm the response; others confirm and add a text message of praise ("Right, Joey. Good job!"). Graphics or sound effects can also be used as reinforcers. Of course, the reward should be appropriate for the student's response. "GREAT!!!!" flashing in color on the screen with bells ringing for 15 seconds is not a suitable reward for success on the third try.

Evaluate the Program's Motivational Value

Perhaps the best way to determine a program's motivational value is to try it out with students to see how they like it. This is not a foolproof method, however, because students may like a program at first but quickly tire of it.

Many programs include game features as motivational devices. For example, the student may receive points for each question answered correctly; the student's score is displayed throughout the program so that he or she can watch it increase. Some programs are designed for two or more players to compete to earn the highest score.

Arcade-type programs put academic content into the format of arcade games. The student "shoots" the correct answer to an addition problem or travels through a maze to find the letters to spell a word. Other programs use games as rewards for successful

performance; if the student answers a certain number of questions correctly in the drill section of the program, he or she can play a game.

The interest level of a program should also be examined. A program that features nursery rhyme characters will be insulting to junior high students, even if the content and skill level of the program are appropriate. Programs that will appeal to learners must suit their age and their interests. With older students who have academic skill problems, it may be necessary to seek out high interest–low skill level instructional programs.

Look for Program Flexibility

One indicator of a flexible program is that it allows users to make choices. For example, at the start of the program, students may be able to select from a range of different activities, determine the number of questions they will attempt, and then choose the difficulty level of those questions. Teachers may also be offered choices. They may be able to turn the program sound on or off, set the number of questions the program will present, and control important instructional variables, such as the number of trials per question and the amount of time allowed for responding.

Another aspect of flexibility is whether instructional software offers record-keeping and authoring features. Some educational programs record data on student performance so that the teacher can review each student's progress at any time to see what skills have been mastered and what types of errors are occurring. Also, teachers may be able to customize a program to the needs of specific students by revising its content or adding new content. For example, *New Math Blaster Plus!* and several other programs by Davidson & Associates have built-in authoring systems, and most spelling programs are designed so that new lists of spelling words can be added.

See Whether the Documentation Is Clear and Complete

The print material that accompanies the program should provide a full, clear explanation of the purpose of the software and its method of operation. Field test data should be reviewed, if these are included, to see whether they support the program's effectiveness. Sometimes documentation suggests ways to use the program in the classroom and recommends learning activities to supplement or extend the program's content. If activity books or other print resources for students are part of the documentation, they should offer clear, complete, and easily understood directions for using the software.

After all these factors have been considered, it is up to the teacher to decide whether the instructional program is worth adding to the classroom software collection. No piece of software will be perfect in every respect. Instead, it is necessary to weigh the advantages and disadvantages to determine whether a program will be a useful addition to the instructional resources already available within the classroom. However, there are certain characteristics that immediately signal an unsatisfactory program. In "Tips for the Teacher" are Lathrop's (1982) 10 reasons for automatically rejecting a program.

■ TECHNOLOGIES FOR SPECIAL STUDENTS

Some special students, like those with severe physical disabilities or those who are blind, cannot interact with a standard computer system unless special adaptations have been made. Several devices are available today that allow such students and others with less serious disabilities to use computers for learning. The two major types of adaptations are alternative input devices (i.e., alternatives to or enhancements of the standard computer keyboard) and alternative output devices (i.e., alternatives to or enhancements of the standard computer monitor). In addition, several types of assistive devices are designed to meet the instructional needs of special learners with physical, sensory, and communication impairments. Special educators report that computers and other technologies can cause dramatic changes in the skills, abilities, and attitudes of students with disabilities (Lewis & Harrison, 1988); see Figure 8–6 for a sampling of success stories.

Alternatives to the Computer Keyboard

Special input devices can be used to enhance or bypass the keyboard for students who are not able to enter information into the computer by typing. These devices are most often used with young children, particularly preschoolers, and persons with physical disabilities that affect control of hand and finger movement.

Sometimes all that is necessary is a simple adaptation to the standard keyboard or an alternative way of typing on that keyboard. For example, a student who is partially paralyzed but has good control of head and neck muscles might be able to type using a headpointer, a device like a hat with a stick attached. The student positions the pointer on the key to be typed and then depresses that key. A keyguard can be used with a student with tremor. Keyguards are covers that fit over the standard keyboard with holes cut out so that a student can reach down and press one key without touching the keys around it. Figure 8–7 illustrates these devices.

Alternate keyboards attach to the computer and bypass the standard keyboard. They may be larger or smaller than the regular keyboard; typically less pressure is required to activate their "keys." Most alternative keyboards are one flat, touch-sensitive surface. Instead of having separate keys, the surface is divided into "key" areas. These areas may be

Ten Reasons for Automatically Rejecting a Program

A few short years ago, we were generally pleased if a program would run. Today we demand much more from the courseware that we purchase. My "Terrible Ten" may differ from yours. Each of us applies our own criteria to the evaluation process. Yet I urge you to reject programs with any of the negative factors outlined here and to communicate to the publisher your reasons for the rejection. Our refusal to purchase courseware that is merely "adequate" can help to upgrade the overall quality of the instructional software market.

1. *Audible response to student errors.* Drill and practice programs are the worst offenders. They are most frequently used by the less able students, and NO student should be forced to advertise to the entire class that s/he has just made another mistake.
2. *Rewarding failure.* Hangman programs are classic examples of making it more fun to fail, by use of clever graphics, than to succeed.
3. *Any sound that cannot be controlled.* Sound can be effective as motivation or reward, but it is often distracting in the classroom or library media center. Constant repetition of the same sound also becomes annoying.
4. *Technical problems.* Programs marketed today MUST run smoothly without errors.
5. *Uncontrolled screen advance.* It is frustrating to have the screen advance while you are still reading it, and it is boring to wait for long seconds after finishing it. It is unnecessary to guess how long a screen should be displayed; let the user control the speed.
6. *Inadequate instructions.* We are no longer willing to guess how to operate a program.
7. *Errors of any kind.* Mistakes in factual content, spelling, grammar, etc., are totally unacceptable.
8. *Insults, sarcasm and derogatory remarks.* Students MUST NOT be attacked or belittled by the program.
9. *Poor documentation.* Instructional objectives, suggested student activities, instructions for teacher modification of the program and other classroom-related information should be standard with good courseware.
10. *Denial of a back-up copy.* If publishers insist on copy-locking their software, they should provide one free back-up copy. We are responsible for showing our good faith by refusing to make or to accept illegal copies of software for classroom use and by using our back-up copy for archival purposes only.

Note. From "The Terrible Ten in Educational Programming (My Top Ten Reasons for Automatically Rejecting a Program)" by A. Lathrop, 1982, *Educational Computer, 2*(5), p. 34. Copyright 1982 by *Educational Computer.* Reprinted by permission.

FIGURE 8–6
Success Stories

Almost every teacher who uses technology has at least one success story to share, one story that shows how powerful a force technology can be in helping students with special needs become less disabled. The following stories were contributed by special educators in California.

- My favorite story concerns a student with very little self confidence in the regular classroom. My program has had our computer much longer than his regular class. He now explains software to the other students, can run the printer, and even finds solutions when minor difficulties arise.

- An 11-year-old, nonoral student participated verbally for the first time in a class project. It was a "Monster Contest," and each student had to make up a monster, write about it, and then recite their description to the class. This student wrote her description on an Apple IIe using a single switch, then programmed it into her Epson Speech Pak. When it was her turn, she recited using her own "voice" for the first time—the Speech Pak.

- One student with mild retardation whose father lives in Hawaii is able to write to him successfully for the first time using a word processing program and the printer.

- For students with hearing impairment, color is like stereo to hearing students. Students' interest levels have increased dramatically with the color monitor on the computer screen.

- One of my students, a quadriplegic young woman with cerebral palsy, told me two years ago that she wanted more than anything else to be a writer. She had a difficult time managing conventional writing tools. Our Title IX Office sponsors a creative writing contest each year and thanks to computer-based word processing my student entered the contest and came in second place among all 11th and 12th grade entries. Incidentally, there were more than 1900 total essays submitted from throughout the district!

- I had a new sixth grade boy reading at first grade level who was my best Terrapin Logo student. He brought his mother and deaf uncle to Open House. First time since first grade.

- A "non-reader" was able to learn a math program without another student or adult sitting by him due to the speech synthesizer. He had completed something *on his own* for the first time!

- It's wonderful seeing students with attention spans of 15 seconds be able to concentrate for 10 minutes at a computer.

Note. From *Special Education Technology in Action: Teachers Speak Out* by R. B. Lewis, S. J. Dell, E. W. Lynch, P. J. Harrison, and F. Saba, 1987, and *Technology in Special Education: California's Exemplary Programs* by P. J. Harrison, E. W. Lynch, R. B. Lewis, F. Saba, and S. J. Dell, 1987, San Diego, CA: San Diego State University, Department of Special Education. Copyright 1987. The development of these books was supported by the State of California, Department of Education, Contract #4175. Adapted by permission.

FIGURE 8–7
Devices to Facilitate Standard Keyboard Use
This student uses a headpointer to type. Note that a keyguard covers the keyboard.

Note.   Photo by Scott Cunningham/Prentice Hall and Merrill.

larger than the keys on a standard keyboard, and/or there may be space between them so that the "keys" are easier to locate.

The "key" areas on alternate keyboards are arranged in different ways. Keys may be in the traditional configuration used on typewriters, they may be in alphabetical order for young children, or the keyboard may feature pictures or words rather than individual letters and numbers. For example, on the Muppet Learning Keys (Sunburst Communications), an alternate keyboard designed for young children, there is a chalkboard with the letters of the alphabet in order, a ruler with numbers, and a paint box with colors. IntelliKeys (IntelliTools) is a more versatile alternate keyboard. It comes with several overlays that are placed on its surface; each overlay features a different selection and arrangement of keys. For example, one overlay contains only number keys, another shows the letters in alphabetical order, and another shows the arrow keys and the command keys needed for interacting with many drill and game software programs. If the standard overlays do not meet the needs of a particular student, the teacher can easily create a new overlay and reprogram the IntelliKeys keyboard.

Other devices bypass the keyboard by allowing students to respond via the screen of the computer monitor. For example, with a touch screen, the student simply touches the area of the screen where the chosen response is shown. Light pens work in a similar fashion; the student places the pen on the screen to select a response. Devices such as these are usually limited to software designed specifically to accept touch or light input.

Students with severe physical limitations can use switches to interact with computers. Switch input is possible if the student is able to make some type of consistent movement: a movement of the head from side to side, movement of a hand or elbow back and forth, movement of a foot up and down, or even a wrinkling of the eyebrow or a sucking motion. Switches come in many forms to accommodate students' movement repertoires. Examples are plate, leaf, brow wrinkle, and "suck-and-puff" switches.

Switches work only with specially designed software unless a special device such as the Adaptive Firmware Card or Ke:nx (Don Johnston Incorporated) is added to the computer. These devices make switch input possible with any program by placing an array of letters and numbers somewhere on the screen display. The letters and numbers are scanned (e.g., first the letter *A* is highlighted, then the letter *B*, and so on), and the student selects one by pressing the switch.

Scanning through a series of letters or other possible responses is a laborious process. A more efficient (but more expensive) mode of interacting with the computer is voice input. With a voice input device, the student simply speaks into a microphone to enter information. First, however, the student must "train" the device to recognize his or her voice; the student's vocabulary is then stored for use with any software. See Figure 8–8 for photos of a voice input device and other methods of bypassing the standard computer keyboard.

Alternatives to the Computer Monitor

Alternative output devices bypass or enhance the visual display on the screen of the computer's monitor. One modification often used with students with vision problems is enlargement of the screen display. The regular monitor is replaced with a large-screen monitor, or a magnification device is used to increase the size of the screen display.

Speech can be added to the computer's output for young nonreaders, older students with reading difficulties, and students who are blind. One common way of adding speech is to install a hardware device called a speech synthesizer; some of the newer computers come equipped with synthesizers. Speech synthesizers use voice chips that store phonemic rules; words are built or synthesized from phonemes as letters are typed in, and mispronunciations can occur when words do not follow phonemic rules. Synthesized speech typically sounds somewhat robotic, although it is usually clear enough to be intelligible to students. Synthesizers work with programs written to take advantage of their speech capabilities; they do not work with all software. Many of the newer multimedia programs use digitized (rather than synthesized) speech. This higher-quality, more natural-sounding speech is produced by recording actual speech and storing it as part of the program.

Special Software

Some software has been designed to accommodate the special needs of students with disabilities. For example, there are "talking" word processing pro-

grams for students who are blind; when the student types in a letter, a speech synthesizer says the name of the letter as it appears on the screen. The student can also direct the synthesizer to read the program's menu and other screen directions and review what has been written, either letter by letter or as words and sentences. Some beginning reading programs also "talk" as do programs designed for students with delayed oral language. In addition, software has been developed to teach everyday living and vocational skills to students with mild cognitive disabilities.

However, most mainstreamed students can benefit from the software intended for average learners, if that software is well designed (Eiser, 1986; Shepard, 1986). In fact, special educators report that the software they use most often with students with mild disabilities is general education software (Lewis & Harrison, 1988). Although teachers of mainstreamed classrooms may need to take extra care in the selection of instructional programs, the range of software available today offers many options appropriate for students with mild learning needs.

Assistive Devices for Students with Physical Disabilities

Mobility is a major need of some students with physical disabilities. Some students use standard wheelchairs, that is, chairs they propel with their hands and arms. Others, with limited strength or movement in their upper bodies, use power chairs (or scooters) equipped with motors and batteries. Power chairs are usually controlled by a joystick that the student operates by moving his or her hand, arm, foot, head, or chin.

Braces and prosthetic devices such as artificial limbs are aids that strengthen or replace portions of the body. In recent years, the design of these devices has improved, and lighter and stronger materials have been used in their construction. These changes have made braces and prosthetic devices more comfortable and better looking, which increases the likelihood that their owners will wear them. Now under development are prostheses that

FIGURE 8–8

Alternatives to the Standard Computer Keyboard

Muppet Learning Keys™

IntelliKeys

TouchWindow

A mouse used as a switch input device

Dragon Dictate voice input device

Note. Photos reprinted with permission of Sunburst Communications *(top left)*, IntelliTools *(top right)*, Edmark Corporation *(middle left)*, Apple Computer, Inc. *(middle right)*, and Dragon Systems *(bottom)*.

use microprocessors (such as those found in computers) to improve mobility and motor control.

In the classroom, students who have difficulty writing may use electric typewriters or computers. These are easier to operate than manual typewriters because less strength is needed to depress the keys. Some students can use their fingers to type; for those with limited hand movement, there are special sticks that are held in the mouth or attached to the head. Electronic calculators, especially those with print output, also assist students for whom writing is difficult. Audiotapes are used for several purposes: recording class lectures, "reading" taped texts, and taping assignments or exams rather than writing them. Pageturners, either manual or electronic, assist students by holding a book in an open position for reading; to turn the page, the student activates the device with a chin or mouth movement.

Communication Aids

Some students are unable to speak, or their speech is very difficult to understand. To bypass this problem, communication aids are used. Communication aids allow students to "talk" by simply pointing or pressing a button. For example, a simple communication board may be a piece of cardboard with pictures, letters, or words on it; a student could point to a picture of a glass to indicate thirst or use an alphabet to spell out greetings or requests. Electronic communication aids are more sophisticated because they "talk." One type of electronic communication device uses prerecorded speech. Spoken messages are recorded by a family member, teacher, or peer; to "speak," the student simply selects one of the available messages. Other communication devices contain speech synthesizers. The student may spell out words by typing on the device's keyboard or messages may be preprogrammed so that they can be activated by pressing a single key or a switch. When a word or phrase has been entered, the synthesizer pronounces it. Figure 8–9 shows one example of a communication aid.

Assistive Devices for Students with Vision Impairments

Audio aids help students with vision impairments learn by listening. For example, students can gain access to printed information by listening to tapes of books, magazines, and textbooks. Sometimes tapes use compressed speech; in this mode, the spoken word is speeded up so that large amounts of information can

FIGURE 8–9
Electronic Communication Aid

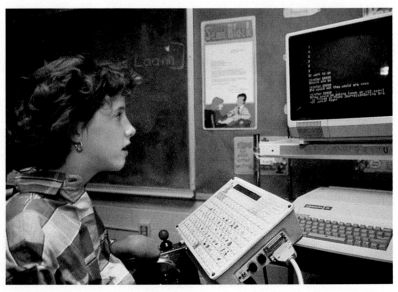

Note.   Photo courtesy of Prentke Romich Company.

be reviewed in less time. Tape recorders can also be used to tape lectures or class notes so that information is available for later access. A talking calculator resembles a regular pocket calculator, but it provides both a visual and an audible display. When a key is pressed or a calculation completed, the calculator speaks.

Magnification devices enlarge visual images for students able to use their residual vision. Devices called low vision aids resemble small telescopes or magnifying glasses; they are used to read print and look at drawings and maps. Closed-circuit television systems are used to enlarge reading materials; the book or paper is placed on a platform and a video camera projects its image to a monitor that looks like a television screen. Print is greatly enlarged, and the student can control the size and brightness of the display and whether the image is black on a white background or white on a dark background. Figure 8–10 shows one example of a magnification device.

Devices that translate print to some other communication mode are designed for students unable to use sight for reading. The Xerox/Kurzweil Personal Reader (Xerox Imaging Systems) is a device that converts printed material to synthesized speech. The Optacon (TeleSensory) converts print to a tactile image. The student moves a small camera across the reading material and places the other hand on a tactile display; this display contains rods that vibrate to form the shape of the text (or other visual information) seen by the camera. The Optacon is portable and can be adapted for use with computer screens, calculators, and typewriters.

Electronic mobility aids have been developed to help persons with vision impairments travel safely and independently. These aids use ultrasonic sound or laser beams to detect environmental obstacles. The user carries or wears the aid, and when an obstacle is detected, the aid produces an auditory and/or tactile signal (Lewis, 1993). For example, one laser cane emits three beams of light to detect obstacles in the user's path, obstacles at head height, and holes or drop-offs (Mellor, 1981). The user moves the cane as he or she travels and listens for the different tones that signal the different types of obstacles.

Assistive Devices for Students with Hearing Impairments

Several technologies assist students with hearing impairments to communicate with each other and the hearing world. Hearing aids have become smaller and more versatile as a result of transistors and

FIGURE 8–10
Print Enlarger

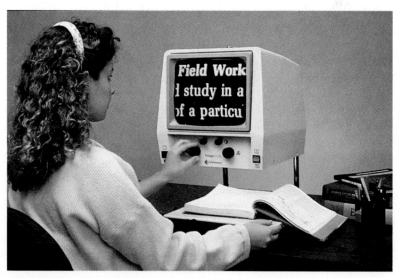

Note.   Photo courtesy of TeleSensory Company.

printed circuits. There are four basic types of hearing aids: (1) the body aid (approximately the size of a portable calculator, it is strapped to the body or carried in the pocket and connected by a wire to an earpiece), (2) the behind-the-ear aid that hangs over the ear, (3) the eyeglass aid, and (4) the all-in-the-ear aid. All aids use an ear mold, a plastic earpiece customized to fit the individual. The in-the-ear aid contains all electronic components within the earpiece; in other types of aids, the ear mold serves to direct the amplified sound into the ear.

Cochlear implants are being attempted with some individuals with serious hearing losses. The implants consist of a tiny external microphone, signal processor, and transmitter that are attached to a receiver implanted in the mastoid bone behind the ear, just under the skin. Electrical signals are transmitted from the receiver to the intact auditory nerve in the inner ear, bypassing the damaged cochlea or sensory organ. This system converts sounds to electrical signals that are transmitted to the brain for interpretation (Lowenbraun & Thompson, 1986). Although this option is not appropriate for all individuals, it does provide an option to many persons with profound hearing losses, particularly adults who have lost their hearing within the past two or three years. However, the use of cochlear implants has not been without controversy (D'Antonio, 1993). Representatives of the Deaf community have objected to the use of implants as a method to "fix" deafness, especially for children who are not yet old enough to decide for themselves if they wish to belong to the Deaf culture or the hearing culture.

Several types of assistive devices are also available. For example, Telecommunication Devices for the Deaf (TDDs) allow persons who are deaf or others who are nonverbal to communicate on the telephone. These devices resemble a portable typewriter or computer; the individual types a message on the keyboard and looks at a visual display for the response. Some TDDs also have printers so that a record can be made of the telephone conversation. TDDs can communicate only with other TDDs. However, the Americans with Disabilities Act required that, by July 1993, all companies providing phone services also provide relay services. Relay services allow TDD users and hearing persons to communicate; in effect, the relay operator acts as a translator. When the hearing person speaks, the operator types the message for the TDD user; when the TDD user types a response, the operator reads it aloud. Devices for individuals who are hard of hearing amplify telephone conversations through the handset of the telephone.

Closed captioning allows students with hearing impairments to enjoy regularly scheduled television programs. Written captions transmitted along with the television signal are decoded by a special device and projected onto the screen. The Americans with Disabilities Act now requires that all televisions sold in the United States contain built-in decoding devices (Goldberg, 1992). Open captioned films and television programs provide captions visible to all viewers and do not require a special decoder. Amplification devices using infrared transmission facilitate television use for viewers who are hard of hearing.

Other types of assistive devices include

■ visual alerting systems for the telephone, door bell, alarm clock, fire alarm, and smoke detector (these use bright strobe lights to attract attention);
■ amplification systems in classrooms, cinemas, theaters, auditoriums, and other public facilities, for use with or without hearing aids; and
■ tactile or vibrating devices for speech therapy, alarm clock systems, and paging systems.

Clearly, classroom computers represent only one of the technologies that can facilitate integration of students with disabilities in school and in the community. Assistive devices such as the ones described in the preceding paragraphs also help students to bypass or compensate for disabilities that could interfere with their ability to succeed in the mainstream classroom. In addition, new technologies continue to emerge. For more information about technologies and their uses in special education, see "Tips for the Teacher" for a list of resources.

Throughout this book, the "Spotlight on Technology" sections highlight applications of technology with special relevance for mainstreamed students and their teachers. Sometimes, as in chapter 7, the technologies are familiar instructional tools like tape recorders. In other cases, the technologies are less well known but equally useful. The focus is usually on technologies for students, but occasionally, as in the "Spotlight" found earlier in this chapter, both teachers and students are the technology users. In all cases, these sections focus on practical suggestions for the use of technology to improve the mainstreaming experience.

STRATEGIES FOR CLASSROOM COMPUTER USE

Obtaining classroom computers and selecting appropriate software are only the first steps in computer use. What must also occur is an integration process, in which the computer is "mainstreamed" into the instructional activities of the classroom. Computers are instructional tools like textbooks and chalkboards, and, if they are to be used effectively, the teacher must consider them as one of the many resources available to assist in the teaching-learning process. Figure 8–11 presents the basic principles to consider when integrating computers and other technologies into the general education classroom. The following paragraphs describe a few of the approaches that teachers can take to make computers a part of the classroom learning environment.

Design an Instructional Unit Around a Software Program

One of the adventure games, simulations, or problem-solving programs can be used as the basis for a series of class activities. For example, the teacher might begin by demonstrating the simulation *The Oregon Trail* (MECC) to the entire class and then breaking the class into several teams, each of which will attempt to survive the trek westward to Oregon. As part of the unit, students can keep a log of their journey, write letters home, keep records of their expenses and the status of their stores of provisions, read about the adventures of actual pioneers, and chart their progress on the map.

Use Software to Enrich and Extend Classroom Instruction

Software can also be used to expand the instructional content to which students are exposed. For example, if students are learning about the political process in the United States, they can extend their knowledge with a computer program that simulates a presidential election. If the subject of instruction is addition and subtraction of decimals, a home budget program or a money management simulation can provide a set of practical problems for students to solve.

Use Computer Drills to Expand Practice Opportunities

Drill-and-practice programs are the most common type of instructional software; although they may be less creative than other types, they serve an important classroom function. All students, particularly those with learning problems, need to practice the skills they are learning, and drill programs provide an additional way for this to occur. Most drills give students immediate feedback, and thus the practice provided is guided practice. In addition, unlike teachers, computers never tire: They can repeat the same questions or problems to one student or 35, provide consistent feedback when students make errors, and reinforce each and every instance of appropriate responding.

Make Free Time with the Computer a Classroom Reward

Because students like to work with computers, computer time can become a free time activity that students work to earn. Possible rewards are playing a computer game of the student's choice, using a graphics program to create a picture, spending time

Resources for Information About Special Education Technology

Books

Special Education Technology: Classroom Applications by R. B. Lewis (1993). A practical book for teachers with information on setting up a classroom technology program and using technology to teach reading, writing, math, and other school subjects. Includes chapters on technologies for preschool children and individuals with severe disabilities, communication disorders, physical disabilities, and sensory impairments. (Brooks/Cole, 511 Forest Lodge Rd., Pacific Grove, CA 93950)

Computers and Exceptional Individuals (2nd ed.) edited by J. D. Lindsey (1993). Discusses computer use with gifted and talented individuals as well as with persons with several types of disabilities (mild, speech and language, severe and physical, and sensory). Also describes administrative applications and interactive videodisc technology. (PRO-ED, 8700 Shoal Creek Blvd., Austin, TX 78758)

Technology for Inclusion (2nd ed.) by M. Male (1994). Covers applications such as word processing, database management, spreadsheets, telecommunications, and multimedia. Other chapters address classroom implementation, social development, partnerships between parents and professionals, and restructuring for inclusion. (Allyn & Bacon, 160 Gould St., Needham Heights, MA 02194)

Beyond Drill and Practice: Expanding the Computer Mainstream by S. J. Russell, R. Corwin, J. R. Mokros, and P. M. Kapisovsky (1989). Describes the ways computers can benefit students in addition to drill-and-practice activities; features chapters on teaching writing, developing problem-solving and critical thinking skills, and improving students' motivation, responsibility, perseverance, and insight. (The Council for Exceptional Children, 1920 Association Dr., Reston, VA 22901)

with a word processor to complete a homework assignment, and having free time to explore any program in the classroom.

Encourage Students to Use Software Tools for Assignments

Computers can assist students in preparing any type of assignment in which text must be written, charts or pictures drawn, or computations performed. If students learn how to use software tools to perform these tasks, they are gaining experience in valuable computer applications that can be used in a variety of situations. For example, when students learn to write with a word processor, they gain a tool that can facilitate all sorts of writing tasks: letters, essays, poems, book reports, lab notes, term papers, shopping lists, memoranda, and so on.

Integrating Computers into the Curriculum edited by M. M. Behrmann (1988). Includes chapters on a variety of topics such as assistive devices, electronic toys and robots, authoring, word processing, and telecommunications. (College-Hill Press, 34 Beacon St., Boston, MA 02108)

Apple Computer Resources in Special Education and Rehabilitation. A comprehensive guide, updated periodically, to resources in technology for children and adults with disabilities. Provides data on computer applications, hardware adaptations, software, and information sources. (DLM Teaching Resources, One DLM Park, P.O. Box 4000, Allen, TX 75002)

Magazines, Journals, and Newspapers

Closing the Gap. A newspaper about applications of technology for persons with disabilities. Published six times yearly. One issue each year includes the *Closing the Gap Resource Directory,* a comprehensive guide to hardware, software, publishers, and organizations related to special education and rehabilitation technology. (*Closing the Gap,* P.O. Box 68, Henderson, MN 56044)

Journal of Special Education Technology. A journal that focuses on research regarding the use of new technologies with students with disabilities. This journal is sponsored by the Technology and Media Division (TAM) of The Council for Exceptional Children. (The Council for Exceptional Children, 1920 Association Dr., Reston, VA 22901)

Electronic Learning. A computer magazine for teachers. Features ideas for classroom uses of computers, reviews of hardware and software, and updates on new technologies. (*Electronic Learning,* P.O. Box 3797, Boulder, CO 80322)

Technology & Learning. Also a computer magazine for teachers. Provides software reviews, suggestions for classroom activities, and feature articles on new developments in technology. (*Technology & Learning,* Peter Li, Inc., 330 Progress Rd., Dayton, OH 45449)

Promote Cooperative Learning by Forming Computer Work Groups

Computer use does not need to be a solitary activity. With many educational software programs, there is no reason that small groups of students cannot work together on one computer. Students can take turns reading the questions and typing in the answers; they can collaborate in arriving at the best response. By grouping students together and structuring the task in this way, the teacher promotes cooperative learning and provides an opportunity for socialization as well.

Experiment!

Computers can contribute to the richness of the learning environment in countless ways. Some of these have just been described; others can be found

FIGURE 8-11

Principles for Integrating Technology

1. Start with the curriculum, not the technology. The needs of individual students and the curriculum designed to meet those needs should drive the selection of technologies and the ways in which they are used.

2. Take advantage of the motivational value of technology, but don't limit its use to that of a reward or a leisure time activity. Technology has too much value as a teaching tool to ignore its use in instruction.

3. Use technology to reinforce skills taught by the teacher. Technology can present guided practice activities, monitor students' responses, and provide students with immediate feedback.

4. Select technology activities that match the goals of instruction and the skill levels of individual students. No matter how dazzling the technology or how superb the instructional strategy, teaching an irrelevant skill is a waste of time.

5. Take advantage of the customization options that some technologies offer. Features such as the ability to control content and instructional parameters make it easier to adapt learning activities to students' needs.

6. Monitor students' work at the computer or with other technologies with the same diligence used to monitor other types of classroom work. If performance data are collected by the technology, use that information in making instructional decisions.

7. Use technology to present new information to students. Although technology is certainly not the only instructional strategy available for this purpose, it does provide teachers with an additional resource for introducing new material.

8. Enrich and extend the curriculum through technology. Technology opens doors to experiences that students can't access in other ways, and these experiences can expand both the depth and breadth of the standard curriculum.

9. Teach students to use technologies as tools, then provide opportunities and encouragement for practice. Technology can help students bypass or compensate for disabilities, enpowering them to achieve greater levels of independence.

10. Extend the benefits of technology to teachers. Technology is truly mainstreamed when it becomes an important tool not only for students but also for teachers.

Note. From *Special Education Technology: Classroom Applications* by R. B. Lewis. Copyright © 1993 by Brooks/Cole Publishing Company, Pacific Grove, CA. Reprinted by permission.

THINGS TO REMEMBER

- Classroom computers are becoming more and more common, and educational software is increasing in both quality and quantity.
- Computers can teach, be taught, or serve as tools for accomplishing other tasks.
- Among the advantages of computers are their capacities for individualizing instruction, motivating students, and allowing new types of learning; with students with special needs, computers can help bypass or compensate for disabilities.
- All computer systems are made up of five parts: input, output, central processing unit, memory, and storage; the most common input and output devices are the keyboard and the computer monitor.
- There are many types of educational programs, including tutorials, drill-and-practice programs, simulations, problem-solving programs, educational games, software tools such as word processors, and teacher utilities.
- In evaluating educational software, teachers should try a program before buying it and evaluate the program's instructional features with particular students in mind.
- Computer adaptations for special students include modified keyboards, input alternatives such as single switches and voice input devices, speech synthesizers that add the spoken word to programs, and special software.
- Assistive devices help students with physical, sensory, and communication impairments.
- Computers can be integrated or "mainstreamed" into the classroom in many ways. For example, educational software can enrich classroom instruction, expand students' opportunities for practice, and promote cooperative learning.
- Teachers are just beginning to explore how classroom computers can be used to assist in the education of special students and their regular class peers.

in magazines such as *Electronic Learning* and *Technology & Learning*. Still others are waiting to be discovered. Experiment! The only limits are the boundaries of your imagination.

This chapter has focused on strategies for the effective use of computers and other technologies in the mainstreamed classroom. The next chapters describe specific techniques for teaching different types of special students. Before turning to chapter 9 and considering students with learning disabilities, consult "Things to Remember" to review the primary concerns in classroom computer use.

ACTIVITIES

1. Visit a school and observe how teachers use computers in instruction. Find out where computers are located (in classrooms, a central computer lab, the library or media center, or a combination of these arrangements), what types of software are available, and what types of learning activities students accomplish with computers. For example, do students use computers for drill and practice? Word processing? Science or social studies simulations?

2. Observe a classroom or lab in which students are using computers. Are students actively involved in the computer-based learning task, or does their attention wander? Do they appear excited about learning? Watch the interactions among students. Is any cooperative learning taking place?

3. Use the worksheet for software evaluation (Figure 8–5) as a guide in reviewing an educational software program. Be sure to consider your student population as you run the program and evaluate its strengths and weaknesses. Also, check to

see whether the program would be appropriate for students with special learning needs.

4. Several professional organizations are concerned with computers in education, but one that focuses on technologies for individuals with disabilities is the Technology and Media (TAM) Division of The Council for Exceptional Children. Write to TAM (1920 Association Drive, Reston, VA 22091) to find out about the services it provides.

5. Look through recent issues of *Electronic Learning, Technology & Learning,* or other educational computing magazines and journals, and select an article that provides suggestions for classroom computer activities. Write a short summary of the article, then add your ideas for adapting the activities for students with special needs.

III

Methods for Mainstreaming Students with Disabilities

257

9 Teaching Students with Learning Disabilities

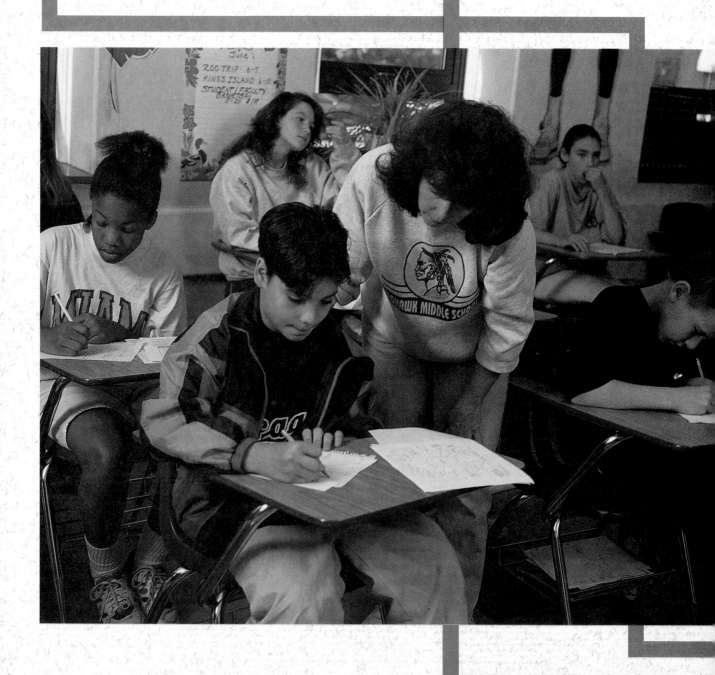

■ *Jane is a seventh grader with a learning disability; she has great difficulty remembering what she has learned, particularly in the area of written language. It took Jane several years to acquire basic reading and spelling skills; now, she can read fourth grade material with adequate word recognition and good comprehension, and in spelling she performs at the third grade level. This year in seventh grade, Jane is mainstreamed for all subjects except English; during that period, she visits the special education resource teacher for reading and spelling instruction. With the help of her seventh grade teacher, Mr. Henry, Jane is earning passing grades in math, science, and social studies. Regular classroom adaptations for Jane include taped textbooks and modified exams and assignments. Portions of Jane's special education assessment report and IEP appear later in this chapter.*

■ *Danny is a student with learning disabilities who is 8 years old and in second grade. Although Danny can read and spell quite well for his age, he has difficulty with handwriting and math. His printing is large and uncoordinated, and he has trouble staying within the lines. Several of his letters and numbers are written incorrectly; for example, he confuses b and d, n and u, and 6 and 9. In math, Danny has learned some of the basic addition facts but has not yet begun subtraction. His math papers are messy and difficult to read; the margins are irregular, and the columns of numbers poorly aligned. Danny visits the resource teacher for an hour each day for special help in math and handwriting. During the rest of the day, Danny participates in the activities of his mainstream classroom. Mrs. Rose, Danny's second grade teacher, provides him with extra practice in math facts to help him progress more quickly. Handwriting assignments are also modified so that Danny can complete them successfully. Later we will see how Danny's mainstreaming teacher assesses his specific educational needs.*

■ A learning disability is a perplexing condition. Students with learning disabilities are of average intelligence and learn some things quickly and easily. However, because of deficits in attention, perception, and memory, they acquire other skills only with extreme difficulty. Students with learning disabilities may read well yet spell poorly. Or they may fail a written test but be able to answer every question correctly on an oral exam. These special students are often members of mainstreamed classes; they can participate successfully if instructional modifications are made.

Students with learning disabilities have special needs in academic, classroom behavioral, physical, and social performance. However, the most common area requiring adaptation of classroom procedures is academic instruction. Students like Danny need extra help in acquiring basic skills; reading, handwriting, spelling, written expression, or math can be trouble areas. Older students, such as Jane, benefit from assistance in content area subjects. Class requirements may need to be modified in science, social studies, and English courses to help students compensate for poor basic skills.

This chapter explores the characteristics of mainstreamed students with learning disabilities and provides methods for the general education teacher to use in gathering data, teaching basic skills, and modifying content area instruction. In addition, the last section of this chapter suggests strategies for instructional modifications for another group of learners who often experience academic difficulties: students with attention deficit disorder (ADD) or attention deficit hyperactivity disorder (ADHD). Books that can help teachers become more familiar with learning disabilities are listed in "Exceptional Literature." Several professional books as well as fictional and biographical accounts of the lives of persons with learning disabilities are included.

■ INDICATORS OF LEARNING DISABILITIES

For students with learning disabilities, the general education teacher is a vital member of the mainstreaming team. Classroom teachers are usually the first to notice signs of learning disabilities and refer students for special education assessment. In addition, general educators assist in gathering assessment information and in coordinating special services.

The legal definitions of learning disabilities and other disabilities were discussed in chapter 3. However, a learning disability is one of the most difficult disabilities to define. Since the passage of PL 94-142, debate over definitional issues has continued, and new definitions of learning disabilities have been proposed. One example is the definition of the National Joint Committee on Learning Disabilities (1981), a coalition of organizations concerned with this disability:

> Learning disabilities is a generic term that refers to a heterogeneous group of disorders manifested by significant difficulties in the acquisition and use of listening, speaking, reading, writing, reasoning, or mathematical abilities. These disorders are intrinsic to the individual and presumed to be due to central nervous system dysfunction. Even though a learning disability may occur concomitantly with other handicapping conditions ... or environmental influences ... it is not the direct result of those conditions or influences.

Common to this and other definitions of learning disabilities is an extreme difficulty in the acquisition of basic school skills despite adequate intellectual ability.

Students may be identified as learning disabled at any age, but most are noticed during the early elementary grades. There are two major indicators of learning disabilities. First, students appear capable but experience extreme difficulty in some area(s) of learning. This is a discrepancy between expected and actual achievement. For example, a young child might be verbal and appear bright but be very slow to learn the alphabet, write his or her name, and count to 20. The second indicator is variation in performance; that is, there is a discrepancy among different areas of achievement. A fourth grader might perform well in math but read and spell poorly. Or a tenth grader might be a good science student except when required to express ideas in writing. In addition to these two main indicators of learning disabilities, teachers should watch for several other signs, including the following:

— ■ Speaks well but reads poorly
— ■ Confuses similar letters and words, such as *b* and *d*, *was* and *saw*

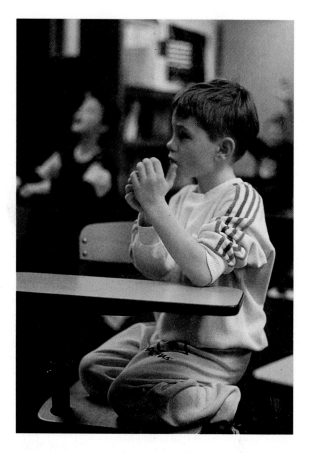

— ■ Guesses constantly when reading
— ■ Has extreme difficulty with math
— ■ Is clumsy; has difficulty with laces, buttons, ball-catching
— ■ Has trouble understanding or following directions
— ■ Has difficulty expressing thoughts
— ■ Has trouble understanding time and distance
— ■ Confuses up/down, left/right, and front/back
— ■ Has a short attention span; is easily distracted
— ■ Is overactive; or inactive, listless
— ■ Is impulsive; cannot wait; cannot foresee consequences (California Association for Neurologically Handicapped Children [now called the Learning Disabilities Association of California], 1980, p. 3)

Although it is a rare individual who displays all these characteristics, most students with learning disabilities exhibit at least one or two.

Research indicates that poor **learning strategies** may also be a sign of learning disabilities (Hallahan &

EXCEPTIONAL LITERATURE
Learning Disabilities

FICTION AND BIOGRAPHY

Reversals, A Personal Account of Victory over Dyslexia by E. Simpson (Boston: Houghton Mifflin, 1979). The autobiography of a woman whose school years were plagued by reading, spelling, and writing disabilities; now a psychotherapist and writer, Eileen Simpson says, "I seemed to be like other children, but I was not like them: I could not learn to read and spell."

Can't Read, Can't Write, Can't Talk Too Good Either: How to Recognize and Overcome Dyslexia in Your Child by L. Clarke (New York: Penguin Books, 1975). A mother's story of her own learning disabilities and the problems faced by her son Mike from preschool through graduate studies. Written as a handbook for parents, this biography describes methods for teaching students

with severe oral and written language problems.

Where's Hannah? An Inspiring Story for Parents and Teachers of Learning Disabled Children by J. Hart and B. Jones (New York: Penguin Books, 1980). The story of Hannah, a child with severe perceptual-motor problems, written by her mother and her teacher. This work traces Hannah's development from birth through age 11 and stresses motor training (rather than academic instruction).

Gideon: A Boy Who Hates Learning by G. Natchez (New York: Basic Books, 1975). An excerpt from this book appears in *The Exceptional Child Through Literature* (pp. 69–79) by E. D. Landau, S. L. Epstein, and A. P. Stone (Englewood Cliffs, NJ: Prentice-Hall, 1978). Gideon is a third grader with a severe reading disability; his failure in the regular classroom and his success in learning to read with special help are described.

There are several books about learning disabilities for young readers:

The Don't-Give-Up Kid and Learning Differences by J. Gehret (Fairport, NY: Verbal Images Press, 1990). The story of Alex, a young boy with reading problems who wants to become an inventor. (appropriate for primary grades)

Shelley, the Hyperactive Turtle by D. M. Moss (Rockville, MD: Woodbine House, 1989). Shelley, unlike other young turtles, cannot sit still. (primary grades)

Eagle Eyes by J. Gehret (Fairport, NY: Verbal Images Press, 1991). Ben's attention problems interfere with his life at school and home. (primary grades)

Josh, a Boy with Dyslexia by C. Janover (Burlington, VT: Waterfront Books, 1988). Josh, a boy with a learning disability, begins fifth grade in a new school. (intermediate grades)

Reeve, 1980; Lewis, 1983; Torgesen, 1980). Learning strategies are the methods students use to plan, begin, and complete learning tasks; students with learning disabilities tend to use less effective strategies than average achievers. For example, with memory tasks, average achievers rehearse the information they are trying to commit to memory, whereas students with learning disabilities do not. This difference in performance has led Torgesen (1977) to call students with learning disabilities inactive learners because they fail to become actively involved in the learning task. In contrast, Swanson (1989) suggests

that these students are not passive but "*actively inefficient* learners" (p. 10).

Many school districts have developed checklists to help general education teachers identify students with learning disabilities, and several commercial measures such as the *Learning Disability Evaluation Scale* (McCarney, 1988) are also available. A teacher can use this rating scale to screen students for learning disabilities in academic areas (e.g., listening, thinking, speaking, reading, writing, spelling, math) and in areas such as attention, auditory discrimination, visual perception, fine-motor skills, and memory.

Trouble with School: A Family Story about Learning Disabilities by K. B. Dunn and A. B. Dunn (Rockville, MD: Woodbine House, 1993). Allison and Allison's mother take turns telling the story of how Allison's learning disability was identified in second grade. (primary/intermediate grades)

When Learning Is Tough: Kids Talk about Their Learning Disabilities by C. Roby (Morton Grove, IL: Albert Whitman & Company, 1994). Eight young people discuss their lives, learning disabilities, and triumphs. (intermediate grades)

What Do You Mean I Have a Learning Disability? by K. M. Dwyer (New York: Walker, 1991). Jimmy, a 10-year-old, learns that he is not stupid and that he can succeed in school. (intermediate grades)

PROFESSIONAL LITERATURE

Learning Disabilities: Theories, Diagnosis, and Teaching Strategies (6th ed.) by J. Lerner (Boston: Houghton Mifflin, 1993). Presents an overview of learning disabilities, the assessment-teaching process, theoretical perspectives, and instructional strategies. Separate chapters describe preschool children and adolescents and adults with learning disabilities.

Students with Learning Disabilities (4th ed.) by C. D. Mercer (New York: Merrill/Macmillan, 1992). An introduction to the field of learning disabilities with information on assessment, educational services, teaching approaches, and disorders in oral and written language, reading, mathematics, and social and emotional behavior.

Teaching Students with Learning Problems (4th ed.) by C. D. Mercer and A. R. Mercer (New York: Merrill/Macmillan, 1993). Describes methods for teaching math, language, reading, spelling, handwriting, and written expression skills; includes chapters on social-emotional development and teaching at the secondary level.

Teaching the Learning Disabled Adolescent: Strategies and Methods by G. Alley and D. Deshler (Denver: Love, 1979). An older book but a classic for secondary educators. Introduces the learning strategy approach and describes methods for teaching academics, speaking and listening, thinking, and social skills to adolescents with learning disabilities.

Academic and Developmental Learning Disabilities by S. A. Kirk and J. C. Chalfant (Denver: Love, 1984). Another classic, this introductory book divides learning disabilities into two types: developmental (disabilities in attention, memory, perception, thinking, and oral language) and academic (deficits in reading, arithmetic, and other school skills).

ASSESSMENT PROCEDURES

When learning disabilities are suspected, the general education teacher refers students for special education assessment. Parents are notified of the reasons for referral and are presented with an assessment plan prepared by the multidisciplinary team. If consent is given for special education evaluation, the team begins to collect information about the student.

Assessment is an information-gathering process that includes both formal testing and informal procedures such as observation, inventories, and work sample analyses. In the assessment of learning disabilities, information is collected about the student's current intellectual functioning, academic achievement, and performance in areas related to the disability: information processing and strategies for learning. Figure 9–1 presents a portion of the special education assessment report for Jane, one of the students introduced at the beginning of this chapter.

Intellectual functioning is assessed by intelligence tests, such as the *Wechsler Intelligence Scale for Children–Third Edition* (*WISC–III*) (Wechsler,

FIGURE 9–1
Special Education Assessment Results

Student: Jane   **Age:** 13 years, 2 months   **Grade:** 7

Intellectual Performance

The *Wechsler Intelligence Scale–Third Edition* was administered to Jane by Ms. Ducharme, the school psychologist. Jane performed within the average range on all Verbal subtests except Digit Span, a measure of short-term memory, attention, and freedom from distractibility. She earned a scaled score of 6 on this subtest, which indicates low average performance. All Performance subtest results were within the average range. Jane's Intelligence Quotient (IQ) scores were as follows:

Verbal IQ	108
Performance IQ	92
Full Scale IQ	101

All IQ scores fell within the average range as did Index scores for Verbal Comprehension, Perceptual Organization, and Processing Speed. One Index score, Freedom for Distractibility, fell within the low average range because of Jane's poor performance on the Digit Span subtest. These results indicate that, overall, Jane shows average capabilities for academic learning. However, short-term memory may be a weak area for Jane.

Academic Performance

Mr. Ross, the resource teacher, administered the *Peabody Individual Achievement Test–Revised.* On this measure, Jane showed average performance in Mathematics, Reading Comprehension, and General Information (a measure of content area knowledge). However, her performance fell within the low average range in Reading Recognition and Spelling. She earned these standard scores:

1991). This is an individual test, appropriate for students from age 6 to 17, that is administered by the school psychologist. Several intelligence quotient (or IQ) scores are obtained. The test average (or mean) is 100; scores between IQ 85 and 115 are considered to be within the average range of performance, and those between IQ 70 and 85 are considered low average (McLoughlin & Lewis, 1994). In this interpretation system, approximately 68% of the population falls within the average range of performance, 14% show low average performance, and 2% show below average performance. Most states require students to achieve an IQ score in the low average range or above to qualify for special education services for learning disabilities.

WISC–III results include a total test score called the Full Scale IQ, and two other global scores, Verbal IQ and Performance IQ. Verbal subtests require students to listen to questions and reply orally; performance subtests are made up of visual-motor tasks. Also available are Index scores that describe performance in the areas of Verbal Comprehension, Perceptual Organization, Freedom from Distractibility, and Processing Speed. IQ scores, Index

General Information	98
Reading Recognition	82
Reading Comprehension	88
Mathematics	101
Spelling	72
TOTAL TEST	84

Jane scored at the fourth grade level in decoding, as measured by the Reading Recognition subtest. Spelling, at grade 3, was her weakest area. These results are consistent with the observations of Mr. Henry, Jane's seventh grade teacher. Despite average intellectual performance, Jane continues to experience difficulty in some academic tasks.

Learning Abilities and Strategies

To find out more about Jane's memory skills, Ms. Ducharme administered portions of the *Woodcock-Johnson Psycho-Educational Battery–Revised, Tests of Cognitive Ability.* Jane's performance was within the low average range on tests of Long-Term Retrieval and tests of Short-Term Memory. Mr. Henry notes that Jane appears to comprehend grade 7 material but has great difficulty committing facts to memory. Mr. Ross, Jane's resource teacher, reports that Jane is beginning to learn strategies for memorizing information but is not yet able to use these strategies consistently. These teacher observations and test results point to a learning disability in the area of memory and the need for continued instruction in strategies for learning and recalling academic information.

scores, and scores on individual subtests are all of interest to professionals in the interpretation of *WISC–III* results. As the report in Figure 9–1 indicates, Jane scored within the average range in most areas. However, her performance fell in the low average range on the Digit Span subtest, a measure of short-term memory, and on the Freedom from Distractibility factor.

After the student's general ability level has been determined, academic achievement is assessed. One commonly used measure is the *Peabody Individual Achievement Test–Revised* (PIAT–R) (Markwardt,

1989). It is administered individually by the school psychologist or the special education resource teacher and is appropriate for students in kindergarten through grade 12. The *PIAT–R* assesses several areas of school achievement, and results include grade scores, age scores, percentile ranks, and standard scores. *PIAT–R* standard scores, like the IQ scores on the *WISC–III*, have a mean of 100; the range of average performance extends from standard score 85 to 115.

Jane's *PIAT–R* results also appear in Figure 9–1. There is a discrepancy between her performance on the *PIAT–R* (Total Test standard score of 84) and her overall intellectual performance (Full Scale IQ of 101). Also, there is variation among the different academic areas: Jane's achievement is average in math, reading comprehension, and general information but low average in reading recognition and spelling.

The third area of assessment is information processing. Several measures are available; examples are the *Motor-Free Visual Perception Test* (Colarusso & Hammill, 1972), the *Auditory Discrimination Test* (Reynolds, 1987; Wepman, 1975), the *Goldman-Fristoe-Woodcock Auditory Skills Test Battery* (Goldman, Fristoe, & Woodcock, 1976), and the *Illinois Test of Psycholinguistic Abilities* (Kirk, McCarthy, & Kirk, 1968). However, the psychometric quality of many information processing measures has been heavily criticized (McLoughlin & Lewis, 1994; Salvia & Ysseldyke, 1991), and in many schools older tests such as these are no longer used.

Instead, newer measures such as the *Woodcock-Johnson Psycho-Educational Battery–Revised* (Woodcock & Johnson, 1989) and the *Detroit Tests of Learning Aptitude* (3rd ed.) (Hammill, 1991) provide information about students' functioning in areas such as memory, processing speed, auditory and visual processing, and attention. Tests are often supplemented with results of informal assessments such as observations of the student's strategies for learning. In Jane's case, a memory problem is indicated by test results and her teachers' observations.

Once it has been established that a student is eligible for special education services for pupils with learning disabilities, the mainstreaming team begins to gather information about educational needs. The general education teacher can provide valuable assistance at this point in the assessment process. For example, for Danny (the second grader described at the beginning of this chapter), specific data about math and handwriting performance must be collected. Formal tests are available, but more specific information is obtained from informal measures. One example is the *BRIGANCE® Diagnostic Comprehensive Inventory of Basic Skills* (Brigance, 1983), a criterion-referenced test that assesses skills in readiness, reading, language arts, and math.

The general education teacher might decide to devise an informal procedure for a particular student. As shown in Figure 9–2, Danny's teacher pre-

FIGURE 9–2
Informal Assessment

Student: Danny   **Age:**   8 years, 4 months   **Grade:**   2

Criterion-Referenced Test of Basic Addition Facts

Objective: When presented with any 20 one-digit plus one-digit basic addition facts problems (e.g., 1 + 1, 4 + 3, 8 + 5), the student will write the correct answer to at least 18 problems within 2 minutes.

Test and Student's Responses:

1 + 4 **5**	5 + 2 **7**	3 + 3 **6**	(9 + 4 **14**)	0 + 7 **7**	(2 + 7 **8**)	4 + 5 **9**
(8 + 1 **10**)	5 + 6 **11**	3 + 5 **8**	7 + 0 **7**	(3 + 8 **12**)	4 + 2 **6**	9 + 7 **16**
6 + 3 **9**	(8 + 9 **16**)	1 + 1 **2**	(6 + 8 **15**)	2 + 8 **10**	(7 + 9 **14**)	

Criterion for Acceptance Performance: 18 correct responses in 2 minutes

Student's Score: 13 correct responses in 2 minutes

pared a criterion-referenced test of addition facts to assess current math skills; results indicate that Danny has not yet mastered the basic facts of addition. The teacher might also wish to obtain a sample of Danny's handwriting and analyze it to locate typical error patterns.

Other assessment procedures available to the classroom teacher are informal inventories, curriculum-based measurement, direct observation, and classroom tests. Also useful are the results from recently administered group achievement measures and placement tests for educational materials and programs. One area of special need for many mainstreamed students with learning disabilities is reading. "Tips for the Teacher" suggests several ways to assess reading in the classroom. These include methods to

TIPS FOR THE
TEACHER

Determining Reading Levels

To ensure effective instruction, the teacher must match reading materials to the skills of special students. There are several ways to accomplish this.

Oral Reading Sample

To check oral reading skills, the teacher can simply have the student read a portion of a textbook or other reading material aloud. If the student can read at least 95% of the words and successfully answer at least 75% of the comprehension questions the teacher asks, it is likely that the text is appropriate for the student (Kirk, Kliebhan, & Lerner, 1978). Oral reading samples should be collected in a private setting so that students are not embarrassed by the errors they make.

Cloze Procedure

With the cloze procedure, students can read silently or orally. This procedure is a valuable (and quick) way to determine whether class textbooks in subjects such as science, history, or shop are written at an appropriate level for students. The student reads a short passage in which every fifth (or seventh or nth word) has been replaced with a blank. The student must insert appropriate words in the blanks. If at least 44% to 57% of the missing words are correctly supplied, the passage is at the student's instructional level (Bormuth, 1968; Burron & Claybaugh, 1977).

Informal Reading Inventories

Another approach is to first determine the instructional reading level of the student and then select materials written at this level. Informal reading inventories (IRIs) are useful for this purpose. These measures contain several reading passages and comprehension questions for each passage. The student reads (usually aloud) and answers the questions; results are used to determine three reading level scores: Independent, Instructional, and Frustration.

According to McLoughlin and Lewis (1994), materials at the student's Independent Level can be read easily without assistance from the teacher, those at the Instructional Level are more difficult but appropriate for classroom reading instruction, and those at the Frustration Level are too difficult for the student. Students are expected to show 90% to 100% accuracy in comprehension at the Independent Level, 75% to 90% accuracy at the Instructional Level, and less than 75% accuracy at the Frustration Level (Kirk, Kliebhan, & Lerner, 1978).

Three popular IRIs that are available commercially are these:

- *Analytical Reading Inventory* (4th ed.) (Woods & Moe, 1989). Appropriate for students reading between the primer and grade 9 levels.
- *Classroom Reading Inventory* (6th ed.) (Silvaroli, 1990). Appropriate for students reading between the preprimer and grade 8 levels.
- *Ekwall Reading Inventory* (2nd ed.) (Ekwall, 1986). Appropriate for students reading between the primer and grade 9 reading levels.

It is important to remember that published IRIs may focus on a different set of reading skills than those emphasized by the classroom reading series or other instructional materials.

If a student achieves an instructional reading level of grade 6 on an IRI, then books at that reading level will generally be appropriate for instruction. However, that student may not be able to read a sixth grade science text. Grade levels of content area texts refer to subject matter, not reading level, and such texts often require above-grade-level reading ability. For example, a fourth grade social studies book can have a reading level of fifth, sixth, or even seventh grade.

Readability Measures

To select instructional materials that are appropriate for mainstreamed students, the teacher must match the reading levels of students with those of texts and other materials. A readability formula or graph can be used to discover the reading level of the books in a classroom. There are many readability measures that teachers can use to determine the reading level of materials such as textbooks (e.g., Dale & Chall, 1948; Flesch, 1951; Spache, 1953).

One relatively quick and easy method is that suggested by Fry (1968). It is appropriate for use with materials that range from first grade to college levels; extended versions are available for preprimer and primer materials (Maginnis, 1969) and reading matter at college and graduate school levels (Fry, 1977). Use the Fry readability graph and the directions on pages 270 and 271 to discover the approximate reading levels of texts, supplementary reading materials, newspapers and magazines, and any other type of reading matter you might use in your classroom. Once potentially appropriate materials have been identified by readability analyses, their suitability for particular students can be determined by oral reading samples or the cloze procedure.

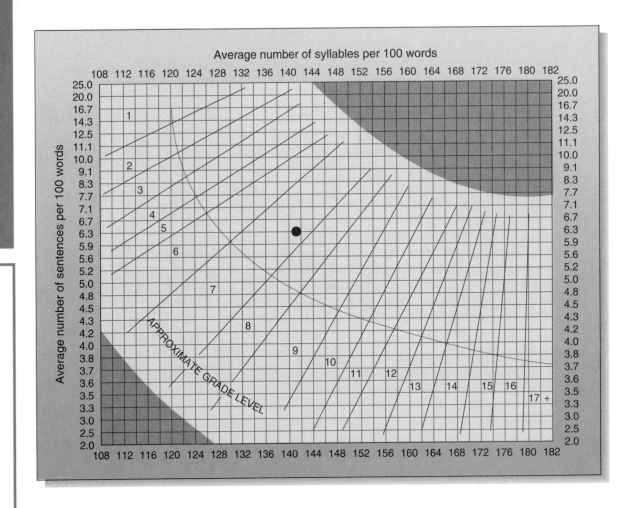

Average number of syllables per 100 words

Average number of sentences per 100 words

determine students' reading levels and to measure the readability of textbooks and other instructional materials.

■ SPECIAL SERVICES

When assessment is complete, the mainstreaming team meets to plan the student's IEP. Figure 9–3 presents portions of the IEP for Jane. Like most students with learning disabilities, she is mainstreamed and leaves the regular classroom for only a short time each day for special education services.

Although the resource room is the most typical placement for students with learning disabilities, some districts provide self-contained special classes for those with comprehensive learning needs. In addi-

DIRECTIONS: Randomly select 3 one hundred word passages from a book or an article. Plot average number of syllables and average number of sentences per 100 words on graph to determine the grade level of the material. Choose more passages per book if great variability is observed and conclude that the book has uneven readability. Few books will fall in gray area [shown here in blue] but when they do grade level scores are invalid.

Count proper nouns, numerals and initializations as words. Count a syllable for each symbol. For example, "1945" is 1 word and 4 syllables and "IRA" is 1 word and 3 syllables.

EXAMPLE:	SYLLABLES	SENTENCES
1st Hundred Words	124	6.6
2nd Hundred Words	141	5.5
3rd Hundred Words	158	6.8
AVERAGE	141	6.3

READABILITY 7th GRADE (see dot plotted on graph)

EXPANDED DIRECTIONS FOR WORKING READABILITY GRAPH

1. Randomly select three (3) sample passages and count out exactly 100 words beginning with the beginning of a sentence. Do count proper nouns, initializations, and numerals.
2. Count the number of sentences in the hundred words estimating length of the fraction of the last sentence to the nearest 1/10th.
3. Count the total number of syllables in the 100-word passage. If you don't have a hand counter available, an easy way is to simply put a mark above every syllable over one in each word, then when you get to the end of the passage, count the number of marks and add 100. Small calculators can also be used as counters by pushing numeral "1", then push the "+" sign for each word or syllable when counting.
4. Enter graph with average sentence length and average number of syllables; plot dot where the two lines intersect. Area where dot is plotted will give you the approximate grade level.
5. If a great deal of variability is found in syllable count or sentence count, putting more samples in the average is desirable.
6. A word is defined as a group of symbols with a space on either side; thus, "Joe," "IRA," "1945," and "&" are each one word.
7. A syllable is defined as a phonetic syllable. Generally, there are as many syllables as vowel sounds. For example, "stopped" is one syllable and "wanted" is two syllables. When counting syllables for numerals and initializations, count one syllable for each symbol. For example, "1945" is 4 syllables and "IRA" is 3 syllables, and "&" is 1 syllable.

Note. From "Fry's Readability Graph: Clarifications, Validity, and Extension to Level 17" by E. Fry, 1977, *Journal of Reading, 21,* 242–252. Reproduction permitted. No copyright.

tion to part- or full-day special education, many students with learning disabilities receive assistance in oral language development from speech-language clinicians. Some receive counseling from the school psychologist, social worker, or counselor; those with motor problems may attend special physical education classes. For the general education teacher, consultant services are available to assist in mainstreaming stu-

dents with learning disabilities. To learn more about this group of students, consult "For Your Information."

ADAPTATIONS FOR MAINSTREAMING

Academic instruction is the primary area in which adaptations are made for students with learning dis-

FIGURE 9–3
IEP Goals and Services for Jane

Annual Goals

1. By the end of the school year, Jane will read sixth grade material with adequate word recognition skills and comprehension.

   Person responsible: Resource teacher

2. By the end of the school year, Jane will correctly spell all words on a high-frequency word list such as the Dolch list.

   Person responsible: Resource teacher

3. By the end of the school year, Jane will correct her spelling errors by using the dictionary.

   Person responsible: Resource teacher

4. Jane will successfully complete all requirements for seventh grade math, science, and social studies.

   Person responsible: Seventh grade teacher

Amount of Participation in Regular Classes

Jane will attend all regular seventh grade classes with the exception of English.

Special Education and Related Services

1. Jane will receive special education services from the resource teacher (annual goals 1, 2, and 3) for one period daily.

2. The resource teacher will provide consultation to Jane's seventh grade teacher as needed.

abilities in the general education classroom; the rest of this chapter focuses on methods of meeting academic needs. Some students with learning disabilities also require assistance in classroom behavior; methods of teaching study skills and controlling disruptive behavior can be found in chapter 11. For students who have difficulty relating to classmates, chapter 6 presents ways to increase social acceptance.

Two approaches are available for the instruction of mainstreamed students with learning disabilities. In the **remediation** approach, the teacher instructs the student in skills that are areas of need. For example, extra assistance in spelling might be provided to a fourth grader who spells at the second grade level. **Compensation,** on the other hand, attempts to bypass the student's weaknesses. For instance, to compensate for the reading and writing problems of a high school student, the teacher might administer class tests orally. Remediation techniques are used to teach basic skills and are most appropriate for elementary-aged mainstreamed students. Compensation techniques bypass deficiencies in basic skills in order to teach content area subjects; they are used most commonly in the late elementary grades, junior high, and high school.

The following sections of this chapter present several remediation techniques and compensatory strategies. Methods of teaching basic skills to younger students and methods for adapting content area instruction are included. In the latter section,

Students with Learning Disabilities

- Students with learning disabilities make up about 5% of the school-aged population (U.S. Department of Education, 1993).
- Learning disabilities are the most common disability; in 1991–1992, 50% of the students served in special education were identified as learning disabled (U.S. Department of Education, 1993).
- There are 2.5 times as many boys with learning disabilities as girls (Lerner, 1993).
- Reading is one of the academic skills in which students with learning disabilities experience difficulty most frequently (Lewis, 1983). Other common problem areas are math, spelling, handwriting, and written expression.
- Among the most typical behavioral characteristics of students with learning disabilities are hyperactivity, impulsivity, and disorders of attention (Tarver & Hallahan, 1976).
- Terms such as *dyslexia* (a difficulty in reading) and *dyscalculia* (a computational difficulty) are sometimes used in reference to learning disabilities. Medical terms such as these do little to describe the learning problem and should be avoided. Instead of calling a student dyslexic, it is better to say he or she has a learning disability in the area of reading.
- Most students with learning disabilities are mainstreamed in regular classrooms and receive part-time special education services in areas of need. For example, in 1990–1991, approximately 76% of the students identified as learning disabled in the United States were served in regular classrooms (U.S. Department of Education, 1993).
- Famous people with learning disabilities include Winston Churchill, Thomas Edison, Albert Einstein, Nelson Rockefeller, Leonardo da Vinci, and Woodrow Wilson.

secondary teachers can find ideas for modifying assignments and exams, using taped texts, and compensating in other ways for the academic difficulties of mainstreamed students.

TEACHING BASIC SKILLS

Reading, handwriting, spelling, written expression, and math are often called basic skills; these "tool" subjects, once acquired, are used in the acquisition of new information and concepts. Although most students learn the rudiments of basic skills in the early elementary grades, special students may not. They may need additional instruction in order to progress. In general, basic skills instruction is provided to special students by the general education teacher if it is a part of the curriculum in the mainstreamed classroom. Some students may receive tutoring in some skills as part of their special education program, but most will take part in at least some of the basic skills instruction in the regular classroom. The general education teacher can enhance the learning of special students by modifying the techniques used to teach basic skills. Three adaptations are recommended: providing prompts, giving additional instruction, and allowing extra guided practice.

Prompts are features added to learning tasks; they are particularly helpful for students with learning disabilities who have difficulty focusing attention on relevant instructional cues. Prompts also structure the task and help the student know exactly what to do. Danny could use the prompts in Figure 9–4 to help improve his printing.

Providing additional direct instruction and allowing extra guided practice are adaptations that aid students with poor recall. To ensure successful learning, the teacher should break down the subject matter into small steps and present it as slowly as necessary. Several practice opportunities should be available; the teacher can monitor performance during practice, enlist the aid of a peer tutor or adult volunteer, or use self-correcting materials. The basic math auto-instructional materials in Figure 9–5 can help Danny learn addition facts.

Reading

Word recognition and comprehension are the two most important subskills of reading. Word recognition is the ability to decode printed symbols; decoding is accomplished by sight if the word is familiar or by analysis of the word's phonetic components or its structure (i.e., roots, prefixes, suffixes, etc.). Reading comprehension—the ability to understand what is read—involves knowing the meanings of individual words, following the sequence of events in a passage, detecting the main ideas, drawing conclusions, and making inferences.

There are two major approaches to teaching reading skills: the code-emphasis approach and the meaning-emphasis approach. According to Mercer and Mercer (1993), code-emphasis programs teach decoding first, then comprehension; instruction in decoding stresses the regular relationships between letters and sounds. In contrast, meaning-based programs emphasize comprehension from the start; students practice decoding by reading common words.

The whole language approach to reading instruction is an example of a meaning-emphasis program.

In this approach, reading is not broken down into separate skill areas; thus, skills such as decoding are not taught separately. Instead, reading is integrated with the other language arts of listening, speaking, and writing (Lapp & Flood, 1992). McLoughlin and Lewis (1994) provide this description:

> In the whole language classroom, language learning takes place in a social context where students use language for real (i.e., authentic) purposes. Students read whole texts, not fragments, and those texts tend to be children's literature rather than stories constructed solely for inclusion in textbooks. Throughout meaning and motivation are emphasized; the development of isolated skills is deemphasized. (p. 285)

Although the whole language approach is currently quite popular, research results suggest that code-emphasis programs are more effective, particularly for students with special needs and those at risk for learning problems (Chall, 1967, 1977, 1983, 1989; Stahl & Miller, 1989). In particular, students with learning disabilities will likely require explicit instruction in skills such as decoding if they are to succeed in whole language classrooms (Lerner, Cousin, & Richeck, 1992; Mather, 1992).

Code-emphasis programs provide beginning readers with a systematic method of decoding unfamiliar words. Students learn decoding strategies and then practice with words that can be read using these strategies. Code-based reading materials feature a controlled vocabulary, that is, one limited to words that can be read by students who have mastered the strategies taught in the program.

Materials based on the phonics method represent the code-based approach to reading; two examples are *Reading Mastery: DISTAR Reading* (Engelmann & Bruner, 1988) and the *Corrective Reading Program* (Engelmann, Becker, Hanner, & Johnson, 1988). Students first learn the sound for each letter (phoneme-grapheme combinations) and practice reading phonetically regular words; later, other types of words are introduced. Linguistic methods are an adaptation of the phonics approach; reading instruction begins with phonetically regular word families such as *at, bat, cat, rat,* and *sat.* The *Merrill Linguistic Reading Program* uses this approach.

FIGURE 9–4
Prompts for Basic Skills Instruction

Faded visual prompts in the instruction of manuscript letter formation

Additional visual cueing devices used in the instruction of handwriting

Directional arrows

Colored start and stop points for each stroke:
o Red
x Green

Color-coded baseline and top line:
Red
Green

Heavy-lined baseline:

Pale vertical lines (or sheet with vertical lines placed under handwriting sheet):

Note. Reprinted with permission of Merrill, an imprint of Macmillan Publishing Company, from *Teaching the Mildly Handicapped in the Regular Classroom* (2nd ed., p. 108) by J. Affleck, S. Lowenbraun, and A. Archer. Copyright © 1980 Merrill Publishing Company, Columbus, Ohio.

FIGURE 9–5
Materials for Independent Practice

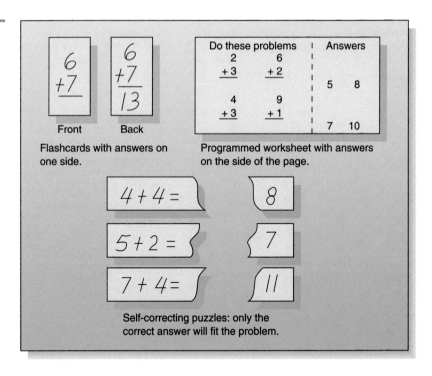

Flashcards with answers on one side.

Programmed worksheet with answers on the side of the page.

Self-correcting puzzles: only the correct answer will fit the problem.

Reading programs that begin with a controlled vocabulary help students acquire skills quickly and gain confidence in their ability to decode print; however, students eventually must make the transition to a more conventional vocabulary selection. One way to accomplish this is to teach students to read common words that appear with high frequency in the English language. Because many of these words are irregular and therefore not readily decodable with phonics strategies, they are often taught as sight vocabulary. The *Dolch Basic Sight Word List* (Dolch, 1953) is one example of a high-frequency word list; an updated version of the Dolch list (Johnson, 1971) is shown in Table 9–1. Simms and Falcon (1987) suggest dividing this word list into categories for instruction. Categories might include self words (e.g., *I, me*), moving words (*come, play*), size words (*big, little*), and question words (*who, when*).

Reading is a problem area for many students with special needs, not only those with learning disabilities. Some have difficulty learning (or applying) word recognition skills; others fail to understand what they have read despite adequate decoding skills. Still oth-

ers require assistance in both word recognition and comprehension. The following suggestions for modifying reading instruction for students with special needs include examples of prompts and ways to enhance the practice of reading skills:

■ Add cues to help students decode troublesome words; for example, mark long vowels (sēed), cross out silent letters (mak¢), and divide words into syllables (dis-crim-i-nāt¢).
■ Provide markers for students who lose their place while reading. They can move their finger along under the line of print or use an index card with an arrow for a guideline; cards with windows can be placed on the page to expose only a few words at a time.

TABLE 9–1
High-Frequency Word List

Preprimer	Primer	First	Second	Third
1. the	45. when	89. many	133. know	177. don't
2. of	46. who	90. before	134. while	178. does
3. and	47. will	91. must	135. last	179. got
4. to	48. more	92. through	136. might	180. united
5. a	49. no	93. back	137. us	181. left
6. in	50. if	94. years	138. great	182. number
7. that	51. out	95. where	139. old	183. course
8. is	52. so	96. much	140. year	184. war
9. was	53. said	97. your	141. off	185. until
10. he	54. what	98. may	142. come	186. always
11. for	55. up	99. well	143. since	187. away
12. it	56. its	100. down	144. against	188. something
13. with	57. about	101. should	145. go	189. fact
14. as	58. into	102. because	146. came	190. through
15. his	59. than	103. each	147. right	191. water
16. on	60. them	104. just	148. used	192. less
17. be	61. can	105. those	149. take	193. public
18. at	62. only	106. people	150. three	194. put
19. by	63. other	107. Mr.	151. states	195. thing
20. I	64. new	108. how	152. himself	196. almost
21. this	65. some	109. too	153. few	197. hand
22. had	66. could	110. little	154. house	198. enough
23. not	67. time	111. state	155. use	199. far
24. are	68. these	112. good	156. during	200. took
25. but	69. two	113. very	157. without	201. head
26. from	70. may	114. make	158. again	202. yet
27. or	71. then	115. would	159. place	203. government
28. have	72. do	116. still	160. American	204. system
29. an	73. first	117. own	161. around	205. better
30. they	74. any	118. see	162. however	206. set
31. which	75. my	119. men	163. home	207. told
32. one	76. now	120. work	164. small	208. nothing
33. you	77. such	121. long	165. found	209. night
34. were	78. like	122. get	166. Mrs.	210. end
35. her	79. our	123. here	167. thought	211. why
36. all	80. over	124. between	168. went	212. called
37. she	81. man	125. both	169. say	213. didn't
38. there	82. me	126. life	170. part	214. eyes
39. would	83. even	127. being	171. once	215. find
40. their	84. most	128. under	172. general	216. going
41. we	85. made	129. never	173. high	217. look
42. him	86. after	130. day	174. upon	218. asked
43. been	87. also	131. same	175. school	219. later
44. has	88. did	132. another	176. every	220. knew

Note. From "The Dolch List Reexamined" by D. D. Johnson, 1971, *The Reading Teacher, 24,* pp. 455–456. Copyright 1971 by the International Reading Association. Reprinted by permission of D. D. Johnson and the International Reading Association.

TABLE 9–2
High Interest–Low Vocabulary Reading Materials

Title	Publisher	Reading Grade Level	Interest Grade Level
Action Series	Scholastic Magazine and Book Services	4–5	7–12
American Adventure Series	Harper & Row	3–6	4–8
Basic Vocabulary Books	Garrard	2	1–6
Breakthrough Series	Allyn & Bacon	2–6	7–12
Checkered Flag Series	Field Educational Publications	2–4	6–12
Childhood of Famous Americans Series	Bobbs-Merrill	4–5	7–9
Cowboy Sam Series	Benefic Press	PP–3	1–6
Dan Frontier Series	Benefic Press	PP–4	1–7
Deep Sea Adventures	Field Educational Publications	2–5	3–11
Everyreader Series	McGraw-Hill	6–8	5–12
Fastback Books	Fearon	4–5	6–12
First Reading Books	Garrard	1	1–4
Focus on Reading	Science Research Associates	1–6	3–12
Folklore of the World Books	Garrard	2	2–8
Interesting Reading Series	Follett	2–3	7–12
Jim Forest Readers	Field Educational Publications	1–3	1–7
Junior Science Books	Garrard	4–5	6–9
Morgan Bay Mysteries	Field Educational Publications	2–4	4–11
Morrow's High Interest/Easy Reading Books	William Morrow	1–8	4–10

- To enhance reading comprehension, tell students the purposes for reading and what to look for in the passage. For example, they might read a story to discover the main characters and the sequence of events, or a textbook chapter to learn important facts and main ideas. **Advanced organizers** that provide an overview of the passage to prepare students for what they will be reading are an effective strategy for increasing comprehension

(Graham & Johnson, 1989). Mercer and Mercer (1993) suggest giving students a list of questions to guide their reading and the page numbers of the text on which answers can be found.

- Use peer tutors and volunteers for sight word drill.
- Provide **high interest–low vocabulary** reading materials to aid in the practice of silent reading. They appeal to students who read at a lower grade

Title	Publisher	Reading Grade Level	Interest Grade Level
Mystery Adventure Series	Benefic Press	2–6	4–9
Pacemaker Classics	Fearon	2	7–12
Pacemaker Story Books	Xerox Education Publications	2	7–12
Pacemaker True Adventure	Fearon	2	5–12
Pal Paperback Kits	Xerox Education Publications	1–5	5–12
Pleasure Reading Books	Garrard	4	3–7
Racing Wheels Series	Benefic Press	2–4	4–9
Reading for Concepts Series	McGraw-Hill	3–8	5–12
Reading Reinforcement Skill-text Series	Merrill	1–5	1–8
Reading Skill Builders	Reader's Digest Services	1–4	2–5
Sailor Jack Series	Benefic Press	PP–3	1–6
Space Science Fiction Series	Benefic Press	2–6	4–9
Sports Mystery Stories	Benefic Press	2–4	4–9
Super Kits	Warner Educational Services	2–5	4–12
Superstars Series	Steck-Vaughn	4–6	7–12
Teen-Age Tales	D. C. Heath	4–6	6–11
Top Picks	Reader's Digest Services	5–7	5–12
What Is It Series	Benefic Press	1–4	1–8

Note. Reprinted with the permission of Macmillan College Publishing Company from *Teaching Students with Learning Problems,* 4/e by Cecil D. Mercer and Ann R. Mercer. Copyright ©1993 by Macmillan College Publishing Company, Inc.

level than expected for their age; examples appear in Table 9–2. Another good resource is *Easy Reading: Book Series and Periodicals for Less Able Readers* (2nd ed.) (Ryder, Graves, & Graves, 1989), which is available from the International Reading Association (800 Barksdale Rd., Newark, DE 19711).

■ Tape texts or stories; students can read the passage while listening to correct word pronunciation and phrasing of sentences.

■ Use computer software to help teach basic reading skills. For example, many multimedia programs "talk," allowing students to develop sight vocabulary as they read and listen to stories, poems, and other texts. (See "Spotlight on Technology" in chapter 10 for more information about reading software.)

■ Provide practice in reading comprehension with materials such as the *Specific Skill Series* (Boning, 1990). This program includes activities for skills such as using context clues, locating facts, following directions, and drawing conclusions. A source of ideas for other activities for comprehension practice is *Locating and Correcting Reading Difficulties* (5th ed.) (Ekwall, 1989).

■ To increase reading fluency, have students reread a passage several times. **Repeated readings** increase both speed and accuracy, which helps students master a selection before attempting more difficult selections. Sindelar (1987) says that "mastery is seldom achieved with a single reading, especially for students experiencing difficulty in learning to read" (p. 59).

■ Teach students strategies for approaching comprehension tasks. In one study (Jenkins, Heliotis, Stein, & Haynes, 1987), students improved their comprehension of stories by learning to name the most important person (*Who?*) and the major event (*What's happening?*) in each paragraph.

■ Another strategy, the SQ3R method (Robinson, 1961), can help students improve their comprehension of expository reading materials such as content area textbooks. (*SQ3R* stands for *survey, question, read, recite,* and *review.*) Expository text is usually more difficult to understand than narrative text (i.e., stories). In the SQ3R method, students begin by surveying the passage to get a general idea of its contents. Students ask questions about the text, then read to find the answers. The answers are recited without reference to the text, and then the entire passage is reviewed.

Handwriting, Spelling, and Written Expression

Writing skills are built on reading skills, and many special students need extra assistance in this area. One important subskill is handwriting, the mechanical process of forming letters and words. The goal in handwriting instruction is for students to write legibly and with sufficient speed. Usually students learn manuscript writing (printing) first, then they are introduced to cursive writing in the middle elementary grades. For students with difficulty in letter formation and spacing, cursive writing may be less demanding. For example, in printing, the letters *b* and

d require a similar motor pattern and are easily confused; in cursive, they are written quite differently.

Students who fail to make a complete transition from printing to cursive writing often continue forming capital letters in manuscript while writing the rest of the word in cursive. If legibility and speed are not affected, this style is acceptable. In fact, many of the special cursive alphabets developed for students with handwriting problems contain print-style capitals; in addition, letters and words are written almost vertically with little slant. One example is found in *D'Nealian Handwriting* (Thurber & Jordan, 1981). In the modified alphabet proposed by Spalding and Spalding (1986), after students learn to form manuscript letters and five connecting strokes, the transition to cursive can be made with ease.

Spelling is the arrangement of letters to form words. Because English is not a completely phonetic language, many words cannot be spelled the way they sound. Although consonants have fairly reliable phoneme-grapheme correspondence, vowel letters take on several different sounds; for example, the letter *a* produces distinct sounds in *at, ate, all,* and *father.* For this reason, teaching spelling solely by phonics is probably not the best practice, particularly for students who learn words slowly. Although phonics skills should be a part of the spelling curriculum, words that appear frequently in written language should also be stressed; see, for example, the high-frequency word list in Table 9–1. Combining basic instruction in phonics (with emphasis on consonant sounds) and instruction in spelling common words as well as words selected by the student is a practice that produces an excellent individualized spelling program.

When basal spelling programs are used, lessons can be modified for special students as necessary; for instance, the number of words to be learned each week can be reduced. Teachers should carefully monitor the words included in each lesson. For example, if lists include similar words, such as *receive* and *piece,* students may become confused and, as a result, acquire few new spelling words.

Written expression is the process of putting one's thoughts down on paper. Several skills are needed: the mechanics of writing, such as handwriting, spelling, punctuation, and capitalization; language skills such as knowledge of word meanings and syntax (grammar); and thinking skills such as organization, sequence, and logic. Although written expression used to be "the neglected basic skill" (Freedman, 1982, p. 34), the whole language movement has resulted in increased emphasis on writing as part of the language arts curriculum. As Lerner, Cousin, and Richeck (1992) comment, "Writing takes on a new role in whole language instruction and is just as important as reading" (p. 227). As in reading, the whole language approach to writing stresses meaning rather than the development of specific skills. However, for many students with special needs, written language skills must be taught directly.

Several ideas for teaching spelling, handwriting, and composition in the mainstreamed classroom are listed here, along with examples of prompts and suggestions for practice activities. Also, see "Spotlight on Technology" later in this chapter for information about using computers to teach writing skills.

■ Help students who are poor spellers begin to use the dictionary as an aid; provide them with a minidictionary that contains high-frequency words and words that they often misspell.

■ Use the test-study-test method for spelling instruction (Graham & Miller, 1979). Begin with a pretest to identify words students have already mastered, then focus study activities on the words they need to learn. Students also should correct their own spelling tests under the teacher's direction. Graham and Miller (1979), in a review of research on strategies for teaching spelling skills, say that this approach is "the single most important factor in learning to spell" (p. 10).

■ Provide handwriting prompts such as those shown in Figure 9–4. Fade the prompts as quickly as possible.

■ Review rules for capitalization and punctuation before students begin writing; post rules on the bulletin board.

■ Use instructional tapes for the practice of high-frequency and phonetically irregular spelling words. Students listen to the word, attempt to write it, and listen again to hear the correct spelling.

■ For students who form letters slowly and laboriously, use newsprint and felt-tip pens for handwriting practice. When students write slowly on newsprint, the ink spreads, making individual letters indecipherable. Students must increase speed in order for their handwriting to be legible.

■ Provide many different opportunities to practice written expression. Have students keep a daily journal, write three-sentence stories, compose a note to a friend each day, and/or describe an event or person. At first, keep writing activities brief; encourage clarity and accuracy.

■ Teach writing as a multistage process. Isaacson (1987) describes three stages: prewriting (or planning), writing, and rewriting (or revising). Mercer (1992) identifies five: prewriting, drafting, revising (making changes in content), editing (correction of errors), and sharing. Whatever process model is used, provide guided practice at each stage. At the prewriting stage, for instance, students can engage in a variety of activities to generate ideas and gather information for writing. Students can think about the topic, read, or research ideas; they can observe or interview others or listen to speakers, watch demonstrations, or take part in field trips (Tompkins & Friend, 1986; Whitt, Paul, & Reynolds, 1988).

■ Give students a format for writing compositions or essays. For example, have them list the main ideas they wish to present and formulate a title. The main ideas are then converted to topic sentences for paragraphs, and supporting sentences are added.

■ **Mapping** is another strategy to help students organize their ideas for writing. Students list the key words and ideas they have identified for the topic they will write about, then draw a map showing the relationship between the main topic and key words (Tompkins & Friend, 1986). Figure 9–6 shows a map developed by a group of students for a report on scorpions.

■ Teach students specific strategies for planning the content of their writing. For narratives, Graham and Harris (1989) suggest the CSPACE strategy:

FIGURE 9–6
Organizational Map for an Essay on Scorpions

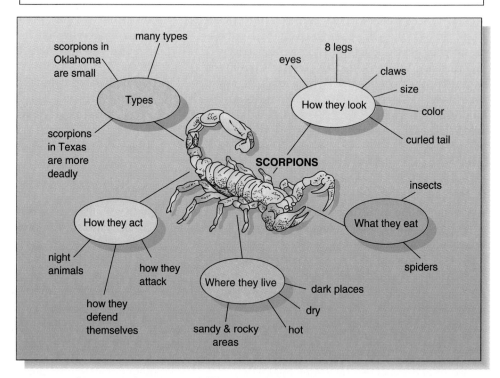

Note. From "On Your Mark, Get Set, Write!" by G. E. Tompkins and M. Friend, 1986, *Teaching Exceptional Children*, *18*(2), p. 86. Copyright 1985 by The Council for Exceptional Children. Reprinted by permission.

C character
S setting
P problem or purpose
A action
C conclusion
E emotion

The TREE strategy (Graham & Harris, 1989) is used when planning opinion essays:

T topic
R reasons
E examples
E ending

■ Include structured activities for the revising stage of writing. One possibility is the formation of writ-ing groups in the classroom. Each student reads his or her composition aloud to the group, and peers comment on specific strengths in the writing; the writer then asks for help (e.g., "Did the ending make sense?") (Tompkins & Friend, 1988). Students can also evaluate their own work using guides like the self-edit think sheet described by Englert and Raphael (1988). With this guide, students

first look back at their papers, star the parts they like best, and anticipate readers' questions by putting question marks next to the unclear parts. Next, they rate the extent (e.g., "yes," "sort of," "no") to which they answered the text structure questions (e.g., Did I . . . "Tell what was being explained?" "Tell what materials you need?" "Make the steps clear?" etc.). (p. 518)

- Also teach strategies for locating and correcting writing errors. Schumaker, Nolan, and Deshler (1985) recommend the COPS strategy:

    C capitalization
    O overall appearance
    P punctuation
    S spelling

    See "Spotlight on Technology" for a strategy students can use when revising essays they have written with a word processor.

Math

Many students with special needs require extra assistance in math. Within the area of math are two important subskills: computation and reasoning. Computation is based on the prerequisite skills of number concepts, reading and writing numerals, and counting. It includes mastery of number facts in the basic operations (addition, subtraction, multiplication, and division) and knowledge of **algorithms**, the procedures for performing operations. For example, in the algorithm for adding two two-digit numbers such as 25 and 48, it is necessary to begin with the right-hand or 1's column ($5 + 8 = 13$); if the sum of the 1's column numbers is more than 9 (in this case 13), then the 1's portion (3) is written in the 1's column, and the 10's portion (1) is carried over to the 10's column.

In math reasoning, computation skills are used to solve problems. A typical classroom example is the word or story problem in which students are presented with a situation and asked to find a solution. Some students find these difficult because poor reading skills interfere with their understanding of the problem; others have trouble separating essential from superfluous information, determining the appropriate algorithm, and computing the answer. Recent educational reform efforts have attempted to make problem solving a more important part of the math curriculum. For example, the National Council of Teachers of Mathematics (1989) recommends that students be actively engaged in authentic problem-solving tasks beginning in the early grades. Students who perform poorly in math reasoning tasks should receive extra instruction and practice in this area.

Ways of modifying math instruction in the general education classroom are presented here. Prompts to aid students in computation and reasoning and suggestions for mainstream practice activities are included.

- Add visual prompts to help students solve computation problems; see the examples presented in Figure 4–11.
- For students who have trouble spacing math problems and writing numbers, use paper that has been marked off in squares, or add guidelines so that students write within boundaries.
- Include only a few problems per page if students appear confused by several problems or if they have difficulty finishing their work.
- Use auto-instructional materials for drill in number facts; see Figure 9–5 for ideas for materials that can be made by teachers. Or select one of the many software programs for math drill and practice. (Several of these programs are described in "Spotlight on Technology" in chapter 11.)
- Work toward automatic recall of number facts. Facts are automatic when students no longer need to rely upon counting strategies; their responses are quick, accurate, and consistent. To develop **automaticity**, Hasselbring, Goin, and Bransford (1987) suggest introducing no more than two or three facts and their reciprocals at a time. Timed drills are used for practice, with the goal being a 1-second response time.
- Manipulative objects help some students learn basic number concepts and relationships; for example, use beans, blocks, or poker chips to teach counting, the relationship of multiplication to addition, and so on.
- Provide verbal prompts to assist in the application of algorithms; for instance, Affleck, Lowenbraun, and Archer (1980) recommend the following for two-digit multiplication: "Multiply by the one's column first. Remember to line up the numbers carefully. Remember to cross multiply" (p. 109).
- Use real situations for word problems. For example, the students' own performance data or the number of points earned for appropriate behavior provide material for practice problems.

Using Word Processors to Improve Writing Skills

Smith (1982) describes writing as a schizophrenic activity because the writer must assume two roles, that of an author and that of a secretary. Students with learning disabilities often have difficulty with the secretarial aspects of writing (spelling, handwriting, usage), and word processing programs may alleviate some of these difficulties (Lewis, 1987, 1993).

One of the major advantages of word processors is that writers can easily manipulate the text to revise and improve it. To assist in the editing process, some programs contain a spelling checker or thesaurus. Another advantage is that the writer's final product is printed so that it is neater and easier to read than a hand-written paper. This is particularly important for students with learning disabilities with poor handwriting. As one teacher commented about a student who had learned to word process, "Now, even with hunt and peck, his written assignments are done willingly, on time, and *I can read them!!!*" (Lewis, Dell, Lynch, Harrison, & Saba, 1987, p. 61).

To use a word processor for writing, however, students must learn a variety of new skills. First, they must be able to operate a computer. Second, they must have some systematic way of interacting with the computer keyboard. Touch typing is the most efficient method, but it is a skill that takes time to learn. Several computer programs are available to help even young children learn keyboarding skills. Examples are *Kids on Keys* (Spinnaker), *Stickybear Typing* (Weekly Reader Software), *MicroType: The Wonderful World of PAWS* (South-Western), *Typing Tutor* (Que Software), and *Mavis Beacon Teaches Typing!* (Software Toolworks).

Third, students must learn to use the word processing program itself. A great many word processors are on the market, and they vary in their complexity and ease of use. Among the programs with special features for students with learning disabilities are these:

- *Magic Slate II* (Sunburst Communications). Advertised as the "word processor that grows with you," this program is available in versions for primary, intermediate, and secondary grades. The versions vary in the size of text and the number of word processing commands available to the student.
- *Bank Street Writer III* (Scholastic). One of the first word processors for education, this version offers three sizes of text, a spelling checker, and a thesaurus. Another feature is "frozen" text; teachers can prepare writing prompts for students and "freeze" the prompts so they cannot be erased.
- *Talking Text Writer* (Scholastic). With this word processor and the Echo speech synthesizer, students can listen to what they have written. The synthesizer will pronounce one word, a line of text, or a full page. A dictionary feature lets students hear words and their definitions read aloud.

- *Write This Way* (Hartley Courseware).   This talking word processor was designed to detect the types of writing errors typically made by students with learning disabilities. The program proofreads the student's document for errors in spelling, capitalization, and grammar and provides corrective feedback.

Some desktop publishing programs (i.e., programs in which writers can mix text and graphics) also offer features that may assist students with learning disabilities:

- *Kid Works 2* (Davidson & Associates).   With this desktop publishing program, students can write a story, then draw a picture to illustrate it. In the word processing portion of the program, students type in words or choose small graphics (called icons) to represent words. In the screen shown here, the student has written "The cat played with the dog." Text can be converted to icons (and vice versa), and the program will read the student's composition aloud.

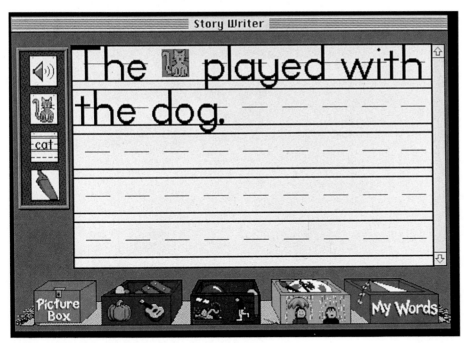

Note.   Photo courtesy of Davidson & Associates, Inc.

- *The Children's Writing and Publishing Center* (Learning Company). An older program for Apple II series and IBM computers, this desktop publisher allows students to produce text in two formats: one-column for reports and stories and two-column for newsletters. Students can write in eight different type styles (called fonts) and choose from more than 150 graphics.
- *The Writing Center* (Learning Company) This is an updated version of *The Children's Writing and Publishing Center* for Macintosh computers. It offers more than 200 color graphics, a built-in spelling checker, and a thesaurus. Students can easily change the size, style, and color of text and alter the size and placement of graphics. The photo shows a report produced by middle school students using *The Writing Center.*

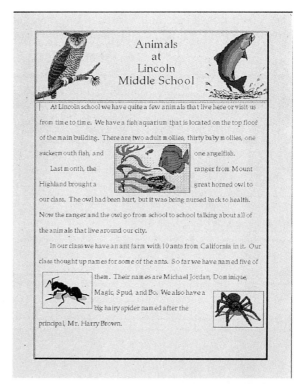

Note. Photo courtesy of the Learning Company.

- *Bank Street Writer for the Macintosh* (Scholastic).   A desktop publishing version of *Bank Street Writer*, this program provides more than 80 graphics, a spelling checker and thesaurus, a frozen text option, and a set of activities to help students in planning, composing, revising, and editing their work.

The research findings to date on the use of word processing with students with learning disabilities are somewhat ambiguous. Writing on a word processor seems to take longer than writing the same amount of text by hand (MacArthur & Graham, 1987; Vacc, 1987); lack of keyboarding skills seems to interfere with students' ability to write quickly. In some studies, word processing resulted in improvements in the quality of students' writing (Graham & MacArthur, 1988; Kerchner & Kistinger, 1984; MacArthur & Schwartz, 1990; Yau, Ziegler, & Siegel, 1990), quantity increased (Graham & MacArthur, 1988; MacArthur & Schwartz, 1990; Outhred, 1987, 1989; Vacc, 1987; Yau et al., 1990), and there were fewer errors in spelling and grammar (Dalton, Winburg, & Morocco, 1990; Fais & Wanderman, 1987; MacArthur & Schwartz, 1990; Outhred, 1987, 1989). However, MacArthur and Graham (1987) found no differences between handwriting and word processing for story length, quality, or number of mechanical errors. Outhred (1989) observed that word processing seems of most benefit to students who write the shortest stories and those with the most severe spelling problems.

One promising approach is described by Graham and MacArthur (1988). In their study, students were taught a strategy for revising essays they composed on a word processor; the quality of their written products increased as well as the length. The revision strategy contained six steps:

1. Read your essay.
2. Find the sentence that tells what you believe—is it clear?
3. Add two reasons why you believe it.
4. SCAN each sentence (Does it make *sense*? Is it *connected* to my belief? Can I *add* more? *Note* errors.).
5. Make changes on the computer.
6. Re-read the essay and make final changes. (Graham & MacArthur, 1988, p. 138)

- Help students begin to analyze story problems by identifying the key words that often (but not always) signal the different operations. Mercer and Mercer (1989) call these "clue words" and give these examples:

  Addition: Altogether, sum, and, plus, finds
  Subtraction: Left, lost, spent, remains
  Multiplication: Rows, groups, altogether
  Division: Share, each, cost per month (p. 254)

- Set up a class store, bank, or stock exchange, and devise different types of activities for practice in math reasoning.

MODIFYING CONTENT AREA INSTRUCTION

In the late elementary grades, the curriculum shifts in emphasis from the acquisition of basic skills to the use of these tool subjects to gain other types of information. Content areas such as English, science, health, history, and social studies begin to dominate the curriculum. In high school, most courses are content subjects, and there is great variety—art, music, business education, shop and woodworking, home economics, physical education and sports, driver education, vocational subjects such as welding and auto mechanics, and so on.

Content area instruction assumes that students have mastered the basic skills of reading, writing, and math. For many special students, this is simply not the case. For these students to benefit from instruction, modifications must be made. Two types of changes are recommended: changing the criteria for task performance and altering the characteristics of content area tasks. Task criteria include speed and accuracy demands and the amount of work required. Task characteristics, in contrast, refer to the basic skills necessary for performance.

Compensatory strategies are used with older special students to enhance their chances of success in the mainstream. The most common strategy is the replacement of written language requirements with oral language requirements. Instead of reading and writing, students listen and speak; they use areas of strength to compensate for poor basic skills.

The following paragraphs describe several of the task demands that cause difficulty for special students in content area instruction; suggestions for modifications are also presented.

Reading Assignments

Students whose reading level is less than expected for their age often find content subjects unmanageable. They may be unable to read textbook assignments, or they may be able to read only slowly and with great effort. To help such students acquire the information presented in assigned readings, teachers can try the following modifications:

- Reduce the amount of reading required. Permit students to read only part of the assignment or to concentrate on the most important elements, such as headings, italicized words, and chapter previews and summaries.
- Substitute materials written on a lower reading level. For example, use a sixth grade history text for tenth graders. Many remedial reading versions of content subject texts are available from commercial publishers.
- Present the information through another medium. Possible methods are lecture; class discussion; visual aids such as photos, maps, slides, and filmstrips; audiovisual aids such as movies, videotapes, television, and interactive videodisc; resource people who can be interviewed; peer tutors and volunteers who act as readers; and audiotapes of reading material. One of the most typical adaptations is the use of taped texts. For more information about preparing and using these aids, see "Tips for the Teacher."

Written Assignments and Exams

Because they may be unable to read directions and questions, students with reading problems find written assignments and exams troublesome. For these students, the adaptations previously suggested can

Taped Texts

*I*n the article "Tape Recording Educational Materials for Secondary Handi-capped Students," Deshler and Graham (1980) present guidelines for the use of tape-recorded materials:

1. Teachers should decide what material is to be taped; it is probably necessary to record only key sections of reading assignments, rather than entire texts or chapters.
2. Tapes can be used not only to present content area information but also to provide instruction in study skills. As Deshler and Graham note,

   While taping a reading assignment, a teacher has an excellent opportunity to demonstrate how to differentiate between main and supportive material within a chapter; how to use illustrations, graphs, charts, etc., to aid comprehension; how to use questions at the end of a section or chapter to determine major points; and how to use chapter titles, section headings, etc. to skim a reading section for main ideas. (p. 53)

3. To facilitate the acquisition of study skills, the teacher can mark the text to indicate important information, less crucial content that will be paraphrased, the point at which to stop the tape to complete activities, and so on.
4. Tapes should be of sufficient quality to ensure comprehension.
5. Principles of learning should guide tape preparation. Deshler and Graham list several important characteristics of an instructional tape:

   - Is well organized
   - Provides a variety of activities
   - Highlights or cues important points
   - Contains a variety of questions designed to facilitate recall and critical analyses
   - Repeats key concepts or ideas
   - Accommodates the assimilation and/or practice of new concepts or ideas
   - Provides immediate and delayed feedback (p. 54)

6. Edwards (1980) adds that it is necessary to determine whether students learn best with or without the text in front of them while listening to the tape. She suggests conducting a quick, informal assessment of all students to see whether they should listen and read simultaneously or simply listen.

---

be used. For students who perform poorly in writing despite adequate reading skills, try the following modifications:

- For students who work slowly, reduce the length of the written task or extend the time limits.
- Allow students with poor handwriting to print, use a typewriter, or write with a word processor.

- Provide poor spellers with a dictionary or a list of commonly misspelled words.
- Consider a dictionary designed for poor spellers, available in most bookstores. In this dictionary, students look up words by their phonetic spellings to find the correct version. The Franklin Spelling Master is an electronic version of a poor speller's dictionary. It is a small, portable device;

---

the student types in a phonetic spelling (e.g., *reseve* for *receive*), and a list of possible options is generated: *resolve, receive, reserve,* and so on.

- Permit students to write using a word processor with a spelling checker program to help identify and correct spelling errors.
- Design assignments and exams so that writing requirements are minimized. For example, use multiple-choice and completion formats rather than essays.
- Have students who are unable to compose and write at the same time compose on a tape recorder and then transcribe what they have dictated.
- Have students respond through a medium other than writing. Two possible methods are telling answers to peer tutors or volunteers who write them for the student and giving oral responses to the teacher.

Math Skills

Content area subjects often require that students have rudimentary math skills. Basic facts and algorithms are necessary for success in algebra, geometry, trigonometry, home economics, woodshop, and auto mechanics. In some areas, such as higher math and vocational classes, computation skills are essential. Classes like English, history, and social studies can demand quantitative reasoning; for instance, graphs and charts are often used to convey important information.

The most common adaptation for students with poor math skills is the use of aids. Students can rely on facts tables for basic computation or use calculators for problems requiring more complex operations. This compensatory strategy is a useful one, and many adults also rely on electronic aids. However, simply providing students with calculators will probably not result in successful performance. Students need to learn how to operate calculators, estimate what the answer should be, and check their results.

By providing special students with compensatory strategies for reading assignments, written work and exams, and math skills, the general education teacher helps bypass basic skills deficits in order to

facilitate content area instruction. Many students with special needs rely on compensatory procedures for their entire lives. Consider the words of Nelson Rockefeller, a former governor of New York and later vice president of the United States, who was learning disabled:

> If it helps a dyslexic child to know that I went through the same thing . . .
>
> But can conduct press conferences today in three languages . . .
>
> And can read a speech on television . . .
>
> (Though I may have to rehearse it six times . . .
>
> (With my script in large type . . .
>
> (And my sentences broken into segments like these . . .
>
> (And long words broken into syllables) . . .
>
> And learned to read and communicate well enough to be elected Governor of New York four times. . . . (Rockefeller, 1976, p. 14)

ADAPTING INSTRUCTION FOR STUDENTS WITH ADD/ADHD

Students with attention deficit disorder or attention deficit hyperactivity disorder have many of the same needs as students with learning disabilities and others with academic learning problems. However, unlike students with learning disabilities, students with ADD/ADHD may experience difficulty in most, if not all, school subjects. Problems with inattention, distractibility, impulsiveness, and hyperactivity affect all areas of learning. For some students with ADD/ADHD, these problems cause serious delays in academic achievement; for others, the effects are less severe.

Students with ADD/ADHD are identified by the behaviors they display. The definition currently accepted by most professionals is that of the American Psychiatric Association. Figure 9–7 presents the major elements of the definition proposed for inclusion in the fourth edition of that organization's *Diagnostic and Statistical Manual of Mental Disorders* (Task Force on DSM-IV, 1993).

Although ADD and ADHD are not recognized as disabilities under IDEA, some students may be eligible for special education services because they

FIGURE 9-7
Definition of ADHD

The American Psychiatric Association (Task Force on DSM-IV, 1993) identifies several characteristics that may indicate attention deficit hyperactivity disorder. These characteristics must appear before age seven, persist for at least six months, be present in more than one environment (e.g., home, school, work), and cause "clinically significant distress or impairment in social, academic, or occupational functioning" (as cited in McBurnett, Lahey, & Pfiffner, 1993, p. 113).

The first set of characteristics relates to inattention and the second to hyperactivity-impulsivity. Three classifications are possible: primarily inattentive, primarily hyperactive, or combined. For example, a student who shows six or more of the Inattention characteristics but fewer than six of the Hyperactivity-Impulsivity characteristics would be identified as having ADHD, Primarily Inattentive Type. The two sets of characteristics, as cited by McBurnett et al. (1993, p. 113), follow.

Inattention: At least six of the following symptoms of inattention have persisted for at least 6 months to a degree that is maladaptive and inconsistent with developmental level:

(a) often fails to give close attention to details or makes careless mistakes in schoolwork, work, or other activities

(b) often has difficulty sustaining attention in tasks or play activities

(c) often does not seem to listen to what is being said to him or her

(d) often does not follow through on instructions and fails to finish schoolwork, chores, or duties in the workplace (not due to oppositional behavior or failure to understand instructions)

(e) often has difficulties organizing tasks and activities

(f) often avoids or strongly dislikes tasks (such as schoolwork or homework) that require sustained mental effort

meet criteria for another disability such as learning disabilities or behavioral disorders. Others may qualify for services under Section 504 of the Rehabilitation Act of 1973. Such services may include special education, related services, and adaptations in general education programs. The U.S. Department of Education (1991) gives these examples of possible classroom modifications:

providing a structured learning environment; repeating and simplifying instructions about in-class and homework assignments; supplementing verbal instructions with visual instructions; using behavioral management techniques; adjusting class schedules; modi-

fying test delivery; using tape recorders, computer-aided instruction, and other audiovisual equipment; selecting modified textbooks or workbooks; and tailoring homework assignments. (p. 7)

Interventions for students with ADD/ADHD are often multimodal (Lerner & Lowenthal, 1993; Reeve, 1990). That is, they include not only instructional adaptations but also behavior management programs and medical treatment. Strategies for modifying instruction are discussed here; chapter 11 describes behavioral and medical interventions.

The major approach to adapting instruction for students with ADD/ADHD is to increase the struc-

(g) often loses things necessary for tasks or activities (e.g., school assignments, pencils, books, tools, or toys)

(h) is often easily distracted by extraneous stimuli

(i) often forgetful in daily activities

Hyperactivity-Impulsivity: At least six of the following symptoms of hyperactivity-impulsivity have persisted for at least six months to a degree that is maladaptive and inconsistent with developmental level:

Hyperactivity:

(a) often fidgets with hands or feet or squirms in seat

(b) leaves seat in classroom or in other situations in which remaining seated is expected

(c) often runs about or climbs excessively in situations where it is inappropriate (in adolescents or adults, may be limited to subjective feelings of restlessness)

(d) often has difficulty playing or engaging in leisure activities quietly

(e) often talks excessively

(f) often acts as if "driven by a motor" and cannot remain still

Impulsivity:

(g) often blurts out answers to questions before the questions have been completed

(h) often has difficulty waiting in lines or awaiting turn in games or group situations

(i) often interrupts or intrudes on others

ture of the classroom learning environment. In addition, the teacher attempts to decrease the sources of distraction within the classroom and, at the same time, make learning materials and activities more powerful so they will attract and sustain students' attention. Lerner and Lowenthal (1993) provide several specific suggestions drawn from the work of Abramowitz and O'Leary (1991) and Ysseldyke, Algozzine, and Thurlow (1992):

■ Place the youngster in the least distracting location in the class. This may be in front of the class, away from doors, windows, air conditioners, heaters, and high traffic areas. It may be necessary for the child to face a blank wall or be in a study carrel to enable the child to focus attention.

■ Surround the student with good role models, preferably peers that the child views as *significant others.* Encourage peer tutoring and cooperative learning.

■ Maintain a low pupil-teacher ratio whenever possible through the use of aides and volunteers.

■ Avoid unnecessary changes in schedules and monitor transitions, because the child with ADD often has difficulty coping with changes. When unavoidable disruptions do occur, prepare the student as much as possible by explaining the situation and what behaviors are appropriate.

- Maintain eye contact with the student when giving verbal instructions. Make directions clear, concise, and simple. Repeat instructions as needed in a calm voice.
- Combine visual and tactile cues with verbal instructions since, generally, multiple modalities of instruction will be more effective in maintaining attention and in increasing learning.
- Make lists that will help the student organize tasks. Have the student check them off when they are finished. Students should complete study guides when listening to presentations.
- Adapt worksheets so that there is less material on each page.
- Break assignments into small chunks. Provide immediate feedback on each assignment. Allow extra time if needed for the student to finish the assignment.
- Insure that the student has recorded homework assignments each day before leaving school. If necessary, set up a home-school program in which the parents help the child organize and complete the homework.
- If the child has difficulty staying in one place at school, alternate sitting with standing and activities which require moving around during the day.
- Provide activities that require active participation such as talking through problems or acting out the steps.
- Use learning aides such as computers, calculators, tape recorders, and programmed learning materials. They help to structure learning and maintain interest and motivation.
- Provide the student opportunities to demonstrate strengths at school. Set up times in which the student can assist peers. (pp. 4–5)

Reeve (1990) adds these recommendations:

- Help the child get started with individual seat work. Have the child verbalize to you what the task is and how he or she is to approach it. Check back periodically to see if the child is still on track.
- Make frequent contact with the child by touching or speaking the child's name. Be sure that you have his or her attention before speaking. . . .
- Give the child extra time to work on assignments or exams, without criticism or fanfare. . . .
- If note taking is a problem, arrange to have a more attentive classmate share notes by photocopying or using carbon paper; or give the child your notes.

- Use multiple choice or one-to-one oral tests to assess the child's mastery of content.
- Give regular feedback and praise successes. (p. 75)

In this chapter, you have learned about ways to adapt classroom instruction for students with learning disabilities and those with ADD/ADHD. In the next chapter, you will meet another group of students who are often members of mainstreamed classes, students with mental retardation. Methods for teaching functional academics and improving general work habits will be presented. But first, check "Things to Remember" to review ways to meet the needs of students with learning disabilities and others with academic learning problems.

ACTIVITIES

1. Visit a special education resource room that serves students with learning disabilities. Observe the students and talk with the teacher. In what school subjects do students experience the most difficulty? What subjects are taught by the special education teacher? Find out how many of the students are mainstreamed for the majority of the school day. In what regular classroom instructional activities do these students participate?

2. Select one of the special education journals that focus on learning disabilities. Choose from the *Journal of Learning Disabilities, Learning Disabilities Quarterly, Learning Disabilities Research and Practice,* and *Learning Disabilities: A Multidisciplinary Journal.* Look through recent issues for articles that present mainstreaming suggestions. Collect ideas for making instructional adaptations in the regular classroom.

3. There are several professional organizations in the field of learning disabilities. One is the Division for Learning Disabilities, which is part of The Council for Exceptional Children (the national headquarters is located at 1920 Association Dr., Reston, VA 22091). Another is the Council for Learning Disabilities (P.O. Box 40303, Overland Park, KS 66204). Write these organizations to find out about their purposes, the journals they publish, and the services they offer to members.

THINGS TO REMEMBER

- The most common area in which adaptations must be made for mainstreamed students with learning disabilities is academic instruction; these students may require assistance in acquiring basic skills and/or learning content area information.
- Major indicators of learning disabilities are a discrepancy between expected and actual achievement and variation in performance.
- In assessment of learning disabilities, information is gathered about intellectual performance, academic achievement, information processing abilities, and strategies for learning; the general education teacher assists by collecting classroom performance data.
- Two approaches to the instruction of mainstreamed students with learning disabilities are remediation and compensation. The goal of remediation is the improvement of weaknesses; compensatory strategies, on the other hand, bypass or make up for weaknesses by using the strengths of the student.
- Remediation is used to teach younger students the basic skills of reading, handwriting, spelling, written expression, and math.
- In basic skills instruction, three adaptations are recommended: prompts, extra instruction, and additional guided practice.
- With older students, compensatory strategies are used to bypass basic skill deficiencies in order to teach content area subjects.
- In content area instruction, reading assignments, written work and exams, and math demands are modified by changing task criteria and characteristics.
- The most common compensatory strategy is the substitution of oral language tasks for reading and writing tasks.
- Inattention, distractibility, impulsiveness, and hyperactivity are indicators of ADHD. Students with ADD show similar characteristics, with the exception of hyperactivity.
- Instruction is modified for students with ADD/ADHD by increasing the structure of the learning environment and by eliminating distractions that compete with academic tasks for students' attention.

4. Choose one of the fiction books or biographies about people with learning disabilities that were described in "Exceptional Literature." Read that book to find out the answers to the following questions: When was the person's learning disability first noticed? What types of services did the person receive? If the book describes the person's school years, note what special education services were available. Was the person mainstreamed? In your opinion, what are the major areas in which the learning disability affects the daily life of the person?

5. Pretend that you are a student with learning disabilities enrolled in a college course. You are doing quite well but anticipate that you will have trouble on the final exam. You fear that you won't be able to finish in the allotted 2 hours. How would you explain this to your instructor? What alternatives or instructional modifications could you suggest?

6. CH.A.D.D. (Children with Attention Deficit Disorders) is an organization for parents and families of persons with ADD or ADHD. Contact CH.A.D.D. to learn about the services it provides. In particular, ask about information resources such as the ADD Fact Sheet, ADD Information Booklet, and ADD Teacher's Guide. CH.A.D.D.'s national headquarters is located at 499 N.W. 70th Ave., Suite 308, Plantation, FL 33317.

10 Teaching Students with Mild Retardation

■ *Judy is a fourth grade student with mild mental retardation. In most areas of academic and social development, 10-year-old Judy performs like a student who is 7 or 8. Her reading and math computation skills are at the second grade level, and her spelling skills are at the first grade level. At home, most of Judy's playmates are younger than she is; she enjoys interacting with first and second graders but doesn't appear interested in the more advanced games and activities of her age mates. At school, Judy spends most of her day in a regular fourth grade classroom and she has made friends with several of her classmates. In the morning, the special education resource teacher comes to Judy's classroom to teach reading to Judy and four other students. In the afternoon, Judy visits the resource room for instruction in spelling, handwriting, and written expression. Judy receives instruction from Mrs. Thomas, her fourth grade teacher, in math, art, music, and physical education. To help Judy succeed in fourth grade math, Mrs. Thomas modifies assignments and exams and provides Judy with extra practice in computational skills. Also, Judy's math program includes practice in the application of basic skills to daily life problems. For instance, she is learning to add and subtract money and to make change. We will see portions of Judy's special education assessment results and her IEP later in this chapter.*

■ *Joe is a high school student with mild retardation who is 15 years old and in the ninth grade. Joe wants to learn a marketable skill in high school so that he can get a job when he graduates. Because his basic academic skills are at approximately the fifth grade level, Joe attends special education classes in Basic English and Basic Math. He is also enrolled in Career Exploration, a special education course that surveys several job options and provides instruction in general vocational skills, such as punctuality, job-related social skills, work completion, and filling out job applications. Joe is mainstreamed for two classes— Auto Mechanics I and Physical Education. With the assistance of his general and special education teachers, Joe is earning passing grades in auto mechanics. Ms. Frye, Joe's reading teacher, provides*

tapes of textbooks so that Joe can keep up with reading assignments. Mr. Nash, the auto mechanics teacher, adapts the written assignments for Joe and allows him to take quizzes and exams orally. In addition, Joe's Career Exploration teacher works closely with Mr. Nash to ensure that Joe acquires the basic work skills important in auto shops. If Joe continues to succeed in his regular vocational class, next year he will advance to Auto Mechanics II.

■ Mental retardation is a comprehensive disability. It affects not only school learning but also the development of language, social, and vocational skills. Students with mental retardation are able to learn, but their learning proceeds slower than that of students with average ability. Consequently, students with retardation often perform at a level expected of younger students. At age 6, pupils with mild retardation may act like average 4-year-olds; at age 10, their school achievement may resemble that of second or third graders. Because it is difficult for these students to learn quickly, it is crucial that instruction focus on important areas that will help them become self-supporting adults. For most students with mild retardation, much of this instruction occurs in the mainstream. With the aid and assistance of general and special educators, students with mild retardation can successfully participate in many of the activities of the regular classroom.

Students with mild retardation have special needs in academic, classroom behavioral, physical, and social performance and may require individualized assistance from special educators in several of these areas. In addition, when students with mild retardation are mainstreamed, the general education teacher must often modify classroom procedures for academic instruction. Younger students, like Judy, may need extra help in basic skills such as reading, math, and spelling; such students may also require help in learning to generalize skills from one situation to another. In junior high and high school, students like Joe often continue their study of basic skills and begin to acquire important career skills;

when mainstreamed, they may participate in vocational education classes. Throughout the school years, instruction for youngsters with mild retardation focuses on the development of basic academic skills and the application of these and other skills to career preparation.

This chapter describes the characteristics of mainstreamed students with mild mental retardation. It also presents methods for the general education teacher to use in gathering data, teaching functional academic skills, and improving students' general work habits. Most students identified as mentally retarded have mild disabilities. Students are considered severely disabled when their retardation is moderate or severe, rather than mild. Students with severe disabilities are often members of special classes located within neighborhood schools; some are mainstreamed in regular classrooms. The final section of this chapter addresses this group of learners; suggested are ways to promote the inclusion of students with severe disabilities as members of the school community and to adapt classroom instruction to meet severe learning needs. To become more familiar with the disability of mental retardation and its effects on development, school learning, and family and social relationships, consult one of the books described in "Exceptional Literature."

■■■ INDICATORS OF MENTAL RETARDATION

The general educator is an important member of the mainstreaming team for students with mild retardation. These special students usually begin their education in the mainstream and are referred for special education assessment when they are slow to acquire basic academic skills. The classroom teacher plays a role in not only instruction but also identification and referral; in addition, general education services are coordinated with the services of special educators such as the resource teacher.

Students are generally identified as having mild retardation during the first few years of school. There are two main indicators of mild mental retardation. First, although such students are able to learn, their rate of learning is slow. Because of this, their level of development resembles that of younger children. For example, a second grade student may be just beginning to learn to say the alphabet, count, and write his or her name. The second indicator is that most areas of development are delayed. Unlike students with learning disabilities, individuals with mild retardation perform poorly on most tasks when compared to age peers. Their disability is comprehensive; it impinges on performance at school, at home, in the neighborhood, and in the community. These students fail to meet age expectations in intellectual and language development, academic achievement, social competence, and prevocational skills.

Students with mild retardation, although characterized by slower learning rates, are able to profit from many of the instructional activities in the regular classroom. These individuals make up the great majority of all persons with retardation, and, according to the Association for Retarded Citizens (n.d.), "Their retardation is not usually apparent until they enter school. And then, as adults, they often lose their identity as retarded when they enter the job market and daily community life" (p. 5).

Students with mild retardation learn in the same ways that average students do. However, some types of learning cause them particular difficulty. For example, reading comprehension skills appear more difficult for students with mild retardation than reading recognition. Similarly, such students are less successful with math problem solving than math computation (Thomas & Patton, 1990). Evidence also suggests that students with mild retardation have memory and attention problems and difficulty applying learned skills to new situations (Forness & Kavale, 1993; Drew, Logan, & Hardman, 1992).

These and other indicators of mild mental retardation can be noticed by the teacher of the regular classroom. Students who learn slowly, perform at a level appropriate for younger individuals, and show consistent delays in several areas are prime candidates for referral for special education assessment. Consult "For Your Information" on page 302 to learn more about students with mild retardation.

EXCEPTIONAL LITERATURE
Mental Retardation

FICTION AND BIOGRAPHY

Like Normal People by R. Meyers (New York: McGraw-Hill, 1978). The true story of two young people with mild retardation who meet, fall in love, and marry. Written by the brother of the groom, this book weaves factual information about the condition of mental retardation with accounts of two individuals who live their lives "like normal people."

A Special Kind of Hero by C. Burke and J. B. McDaniel (New York: Dell, 1991). The autobiography of Chris Burke, the young man with Down syndrome who starred in the hit television show *Life Goes On*. When Chris was born in 1965, the doctor told his parents to place him in an institution. They took him home instead. As Chris says, "My Down syndrome never kept me from doing anything I wanted to do" (p. vii).

Retarded Isn't Stupid, Mom! by S. Z. Kaufman (Baltimore: Paul H. Brookes, 1988). The biography of Nicole, written by her mother, that traces her development from infancy to young adulthood and the issues of renting an apartment, obtaining a driver's license, holding a job, and dating. The book's title comes from Nicole's comment, "Mom, I know I'm retarded, but I'm not stupid."

Flowers for Algernon by D. Keyes (New York: Bantam Books, 1966). The fictional account of Charlie, a man with retardation who undergoes experimental surgery to raise his IQ. The story is told in Charlie's journal, which reveals his thoughts and feelings as a person with retardation and, later, as one with extraordinary intelligence.

Being There by J. Kosinski (New York: Bantam Books, 1970). A novel about Chance the gardener, who, though retarded, achieves fame, power, and wealth by being in the right place at the right time; a story that is humorous while conveying an accurate picture of retardation.

There are several books about mental retardation for young readers:

Charlsie's Chuckles by C. W. Berkus (Rockville, MD: Woodbine House, 1992). The adventures of Charlsie, a 7-year-old boy with Down syndrome. (appropriate for primary grades)

Where's Chimpy? by B. Rabe (Niles, IL: Albert Whitman & Com-

▓ ASSESSMENT PROCEDURES

When mental retardation is suspected, the multidisciplinary team meets and prepares an assessment plan. According to McLoughlin and Lewis (1994), it is important to collect information about at least three areas of current performance: academic achievement, intellectual functioning, and adaptive behavior. However, there is some variation in the specific guidelines that states use to determine eligibility for public school services for students with retardation. States differ in the IQ scores used as cutoffs for determining retardation. Also, although impaired adaptive behavior is generally accepted as an important indicator of retardation, not all states include this area in their definition of mental retardation (Bruininks, Thurlow, & Gilman, 1987; Patrick & Reschly, 1982). Therefore, teachers must become aware of the specific guidelines in force in their states and school districts.

When individuals are referred for consideration for special education services for students with retardation, academic achievement is measured to determine whether there is an educational performance problem. The *Peabody Individual Achievement Test–Revised* (*PIAT–R*) (Markwardt, 1989), which was described in chapter 9, can be administered, or the team can select another individual measure, such as the *Wide Range Achievement Test 3* (*WRAT3*) (Wilkinson, 1993).

The *WRAT3*, which is generally administered by the school psychologist or special educator, is appropriate for students from age 5 through adulthood. It is made up of three subtests that assess basic skills: Spelling, Arithmetic, and Reading. On the *WRAT3* the student writes spelling words from dictation, pany, 1988). Misty, a young girl with Down syndrome, has lost her favorite toy, her stuffed monkey. (primary grades)

Making Room for Uncle Joe by A. B. Litchfield (Niles, IL: Albert Whitman & Company, 1984). Uncle Joe, an adult with Down syndrome, comes to live with Amy, Beth, and Dan. (intermediate grades)

I'm the Big Sister Now by M. Emmert (Niles, IL: Albert Whitman & Company, 1989). Michelle Emmert tells the story of her older sister Amy, a teenager with severe disabilities. (intermediate grades)

PROFESSIONAL LITERATURE

Mental Retardation: A Life Cycle Approach (5th ed.) by C. J. Drew, D. R. Logan, and M. L. Hardman (New York: Merrill/Macmillan,

1992). An introduction to mental retardation that describes the disability throughout the life span: early life and the preschool years, elementary school age, adolescence, and adulthood; also included are chapters on mental retardation and the family, social and ethical issues, and legal and legislative issues.

Mental Retardation (3rd ed.) edited by J. R. Patton, M. Beirne-Smith, and J. S. Payne (New York: Merrill/Macmillan, 1990). An introductory textbook that discusses definition, assessment, etiology, levels of retardation, programming from infancy to adulthood, and continuing concerns such as family issues and legal issues.

Strategies for Teaching Learners with Special Needs (5th ed.) by E. A. Polloway and J. R. Patton (New York: Merrill/Macmillan,

1993). Describes methods for teaching spoken language, reading, written language, mathematics, science, social studies, creative arts (art, music, and drama), physical education, study skills, social skills, and career development and life skills.

Life Centered Career Education: A Competency Based Approach (3rd ed.) edited by D. E. Brolin (Reston, VA: Council for Exceptional Children, 1989). Designed for teachers of students with all types of disabilities, this book presents a model career education curriculum organized around three areas: daily living skills, personal-social skills, and occupational guidance and preparation. Included are specific suggestions for teaching almost 100 skills.

writes answers to arithmetic computation problems, and reads a list of words; unlike the *PIAT–R*, no measure of reading comprehension is included. Grade scores, standard scores, and percentile rank scores are available for each of the three subtests. The mean (or average) standard score on the *WRAT3* is 100, and scores between 85 and 115 are considered to be within the average range of performance. The assessment results in Figure 10–1 show that Judy, introduced at the beginning of this chapter, is performing below grade-level expectations in all academic subjects assessed by the *WRAT3*.

Another major step in assessment is the determination of the student's general ability level. This is particularly important if mild retardation is suspected because below average intellectual performance is one of the criteria for this disability. The *Wechsler Intelligence Scale for Children–Third Edition*

(*WISC–III*) (Wechsler, 1991), which was described in chapter 9, is usually used to assess global ability in school-aged children. Judy's assessment results in Figure 10–1 include *WISC–III* scores; her Verbal, Performance, and Full Scale IQs fall below 70, which indicates current functioning within the below average range.

Adaptive behavior is a third consideration in assessment when mental retardation is suspected. According to the American Association on Mental Retardation's definition of mental retardation, it is important to document not only below average intellectual performance but also impaired adaptive behavior. Measures such as the *AAMR Adaptive Behavior Scale–School* (2nd ed.) (Lambert, Nihira, & Leland, 1993) and the *Adaptive Behavior Inventory for Children* (*ABIC*) (Mercer & Lewis, 1977) can be used to gather information about the student's social competence.

Students with Mild Retardation

- Mental retardation is one of the most common disabilities; in 1991–1992, 12% of the students served in special education programs were identified as mentally retarded (U.S. Department of Education, 1993).
- There is still concern today about the overrepresentation of students from minority groups in special education programs for individuals with mild retardation (Chinn & Hughes, 1987). According to the National Coalition of Advocates for Students (1985), "Black students are more than three times as likely to be in a class for the educable [i.e., mildly] mentally retarded as white students, but only half as likely to be in a class for the gifted and talented" (p. 10).
- Although estimates of the prevalence of mental retardation vary, Kirk and Gallagher (1979) suggest that approximately 0.5% to 1% of the population can be classified as mildly retarded.
- Individuals with mild retardation account for 85% to 90% of the persons identified as retarded (Drew et al., 1992).
- For most persons with mild retardation, the cause of the disability is unknown (Hallahan & Kauffman, 1988).
- According to Kirk and Gallagher (1979), students with mild retardation are those who are able to profit from academic instruction; the IQ range associated with this group is 50 to 70 or 75, which is equivalent to that of adults with mental ages of 7.5 to 11 years (Becker, Engelmann, & Thomas, 1975).
- During their school years, students with mild retardation acquire basic academic skills up to approximately the sixth grade level; as adults they can achieve the necessary social and vocational skills to become at least minimally self-supporting (President's Committee on Mental Retardation, 1975).
- The most typical special education placement for students with mild retardation is part-time service in a resource room or special class. During the remainder of their school day, they are integrated with age peers in the regular classroom (Blake, 1981; Heward & Orlansky, 1992).

On the *AAMR* scale, teachers and others rate the student's performance in areas such as independent functioning, physical development, economic activity, language development, and numbers and time; the scale is appropriate for use with students aged 3 to 21. The *Adaptive Behavior Inventory for Children,* designed for students aged 5 to 11, relies on parents to provide information about the current functioning levels of their children. This inventory contains six subtests that assess different aspects of adaptive behavior: Family, Community, Peer Relations, Nonacademic School Roles, Earner/Consumer, and Self-Maintenance. Two types of scores are available from the *ABIC:* standard scores and percentile ranks. According to the test manual, when students earn scores that fall at or below the third percentile, they are "at risk"; that is, students who perform better than only 3% of their age peers can be consid-

FIGURE 10–1
Special Education Assessment Results

Student: Judy   **Age:** 10 years, 5 months   **Grade:** 4

Academic Performance

Judy was administered the *Wide Range Achievement Test 3* by Mrs. Simeon, the resource teacher. These results were obtained:

Subtest	Grade Score	Standard Score	Percentile Rank
Reading	2	72	3
Spelling	1	66	1
Arithmetic	2	76	5

Judy's skills fall below grade levels in all areas, a result confirmed by her fourth grade teacher, Mrs. Thomas. In reading (decoding), spelling, and math computation, Judy's grade scores indicate performance at the grade 1 to grade 2 level. On the Reading subtest, she earned a percentile rank of 3, which indicates that her performance was equal to or better than that of only 3 percent of her age peers in the test's norm group. On the Spelling subtest, she achieved a percentile rank of 1. Her performance was somewhat better in arithmetic, where she earned a percentile rank of 5. These results indicate serious achievement problems in three basic skill areas, with the most severe problems occurring in decoding isolated words and spelling words from dictation.

Intellectual Performance

The *Wechsler Intelligence Scale–Third Edition* was administered to Judy by Mr. Henry, the school psychologist. Judy's intelligence quotient (IQ) scores were as follows:

---

ered to show adaptive behavior deficits. The case of Judy in Figure 10–1 illustrates a student "at risk" in two areas of adaptive behavior.

If a student is found to perform below age expectations in academic achievement, general intellectual ability, and adaptive behavior, the mainstreaming team may decide that the student is eligible for special education services for students with retardation. The next step is to determine the precise educational needs of the student. All members of the mainstreaming team, including the student's parents, have valuable information to contribute; however, the general education teacher is probably the person most knowl-

edgeable about the student's current academic skill levels. Before an educational program for a student with mild retardation can be planned, information is needed about current school performance and the student's ability to use basic academic skills to solve daily life problems. Also, the prevocational and career skills of the student must be considered. Teachers can develop informal assessments for this purpose, or they can choose from commercially available measures, such as the criterion-referenced tests by Brigance.

BRIGANCE® inventories are available for preschool, elementary, and secondary students: the *Inventory of Early Development–Revised* (Brigance,

FIGURE 10–1
continued

Verbal IQ	64
Performance IQ	61
Full Scale IQ	59

All IQ scores fall within the below average range. These results point to the possibility of mild mental retardation.

Adaptive Behavior

Mrs. Simeon interviewed Judy's parents to learn more about Judy's performance at home and in community situations. The *Adaptive Behavior Inventory for Children* was used for this purpose, with the following results:

Area	Approximate Percentile Rank
Family	15
Community	10
Peer Relations	2
Nonacademic School Roles	2
Earner/Consumer	5
Self-Maintenance	15

On this measure, percentile rank scores of 3 and below are considered to place a student "at risk" for mental retardation. Judy's performance was rated "at risk" by her parents in two areas of adaptive behavior, Peer Relations and Nonacademic School Roles. This finding, along with the results of other measures and the information provided by Judy's classroom teacher, support the conclusion of mild mental retardation. Intellectual performance is below average, adaptive behavior appears to be impaired, and academic achievement falls within the low average and below average ranges.

1991) for children from birth to developmental age 7, the *Comprehensive Inventory of Basic Skills* (Brigance, 1983) for grades kindergarten through 9, and the *Inventory of Essential Skills* (Brigance, 1981) for assessment of grade 4 through grade 11 achievement. A special feature of the secondary *BRIGANCE*® instrument is its coverage of basic skills not only in isolation but also as applied to daily life and vocational areas. Table 10–1 presents a listing of functional skill subtests from which teachers can choose.

The *BRIGANCE*® inventories allow teachers to determine which skills have been mastered by the student and which must still be taught. Each criterion-referenced test includes simple directions for administration and scoring, plus a recommended instructional objective for the skill. For example, on the Warning/Safety Signs subtest the student is asked to read 40 signs, such as *Keep Out* and *High Voltage;* the objective recommended for this skill is

By __(date)__, when presented with a list of 40 words and phrases frequently seen on warning and safety signs, __(student's name)__ will read __(number)__ correctly.

TABLE 10–1
Functional Skills Assessed by the BRIGANCE®
Diagnostic Inventory of Essential Skills

Area	Subtests
Functional Word Recognition	Basic Sight Vocabulary
	Direction Words
	Abbreviations
	Warning/Safety Signs
	Reads Number Words
Schedules and Graphs	Reads Class Schedule
	Reads Television Schedule
	Identifies and Interprets Graphs
Forms	School Information Form
	Computer Base Form
Measurement	Equivalent Values of Coins and the Dollar Bill
	Total Values of Collections of Coins and Bills
	Conversion of Coins
	Time
	Equivalent Units of Time
	Conversion of Units of Time
	Equivalent Calendar Units
	Conversion of Calendar Units
	Calendar
	Dates
	Ruler
	Equivalent Units of Measurement
	Conversion of Units of Measurement
	Meters and Gauges
	Concepts of Fahrenheit Temperature
Health and Safety	Medical Vocabulary
	Medical Labels
	Health Evaluation Form
	Health Practices and Attitude Rating Scale
	Self-Concept Rating Scale
	Warning Labels

TABLE 10–1
continued

Area	Subtests
Vocational	Attitude Rating Scale
	Personality Rating Scale
	Responsibility and Self-Discipline Rating Scale
	Job Interests and Aptitudes
	Health and Physical Problems/Handicaps
	Application for a Social Security Number
	Choosing a Career
	Employment Signs
	Employment Vocabulary
	Employment Abbreviations
	"Help Wanted" Advertisements
	Simple Application for Employment
	Complex Application for Employment
	Job Interview Questions
	Job Interview Preparation Rating Scale
	Job Interview Rating Scale
	W-4 Form
	Future Time on Clock
	Past Time on Clock
	Time Duration on Clock
	Payroll Deductions
	Federal Income Tax Return—Form 1040A
	Unemployment Compensation Form
Money and Finance	Price Signs
	Computes Totals for Amounts of Money
	Making Change
	Comprehends and Computes Purchase Savings
	Computes Expenses Using Charts and Tables
	Banking and Credit Vocabulary
	Manages a Checking Account
	Computes Interest on Loans

Area	Subtests
	Reads and Comprehends a Credit Agreement
	Application for a Credit Card
	Reads and Comprehends Monthly Credit Statement
Travel and Transportation	Traffic Signs
	Traffic Symbols
	Car Parts Vocabulary
	Identifies Car Parts
	Application for Driver's Instruction Permit
	Auto Safety Rating Scale
	Gas Mileage and Cost
	Mileage Table
	Bus Schedule and Map of Route
	Road Map
Food and Clothing	Food Vocabulary
	Food Preparation Vocabulary
	Basic Recipe Directions
	Food Labels
	Conversion of Recipes to Different Servings
	Foods for a Daily Balanced Diet
	Computes Cost of Purchasing Different Quantities
	Food Quantity at Best Price
	Personal Sizes of Clothing
	Clothing Labels
Oral Communication and Telephone Skills	Speaking Skills
	Speaking Skills Rating Scale
	Listening Skills
	Listening Skills Rating Scale
	Telephone
	Telephone Book
	Telephone Yellow Pages

Note. From the BRIGANCE® *Diagnostic Inventory of Essential Skills.* Copyright 1981 by Curriculum Associates. Reproduced by permission of the publisher.

These objectives, if appropriate for the student, can aid the mainstreaming team in preparation of the IEP.

SPECIAL SERVICES

Individualized education programs for students with mild retardation usually contain several annual goals. Typical areas of instruction are reading, math, oral language, written language, and vocational and career education. Special education services can be provided by the resource teacher or, for students with severe delays, the teacher of a special class. Others such as the speech-language clinician and the adapted physical education teacher often provide support services for children and adolescents with mild retardation.

These special students are mainstreamed to the maximum extent appropriate. Some may participate in only nonacademic regular classroom activities such as art, music, and physical education; others, like Judy and Joe, are included in academic programming. A portion of Judy's IEP in Figure 10–2 shows that, although Judy visits the resource room for an hour each afternoon, the majority of her instruction takes place in the regular classroom.

ADAPTATIONS FOR MAINSTREAMING

Classroom instruction is the primary area in which adaptations are made for mainstreamed students with mild retardation; this section focuses on methods for meeting the special academic needs of these students. Some individuals with mild retardation also require assistance in the area of classroom conduct; chapter 11 presents strategies for controlling disruptive behaviors. Chapter 6 contains suggestions for increasing the social acceptance of special students who have difficulty relating to classmates.

Habilitation is the major approach to the education of mainstreamed students with mild retardation. The goal is not to remediate or compensate for skill deficiencies; instead, instruction is directed toward the development of the crucial skills necessary for successful adulthood. Habilitation is the process of becoming capable or qualified; for students with mild retardation, this means the acquisition of skills that are important for daily life, citizenship, and a future career. Because these special students learn more slowly than their age peers, their educational program must concentrate on the most crucial and functional skills.

Career education is one way of conceptualizing the habilitation process for students with mild retardation. According to the Council for Exceptional Children (1978), career education is "the totality of experiences through which one learns to live a meaningful, satisfying work life." Brolin (1986) expands this definition:

> Career education is not simply preparation for a job. It is also preparation for other productive work roles that comprise one's total career functioning. This includes the work of a homemaker and family member, the participation as a citizen and volunteer, and the engagement in productive leisure and recreational pursuits that are of benefit to oneself and others. (p. vii)

Kokaska and Brolin (1985) identify three major curriculum areas necessary in a career education program: daily living skills, personal-social skills, and occupational skills; specific competency areas are listed in Figure 10–3. In the system described by Cronin and Patton (1993), life skills are organized into six major domains: employment-education, home and family, leisure pursuits, personal responsibility and relationships, emotional-physical health, and community involvement.

One important factor to consider in a career education program is the sequence in which competencies are presented. Kokaska (1980) recommends the following progression for special students:

- career awareness (Kindergarten onward)
- career exploration (Grade 6 onward)
- career preparation (Grade 6–7 onward)
- career placement, follow-up, and continuing education (Grade 10 onward) (p. 38)

In the last two stages, career preparation and career placement, students may have the opportunity to participate in supervised job placements on the school campus and in the community. Community-based training is an important component of career

FIGURE 10–2

IEP Goals and Services for Judy

Annual Goals

1. By the end of the school year, Judy will read grade 2 level material with adequate word recognition and comprehension.

   Person responsible: Resource teacher

2. By the end of the school year, Judy will correctly spell a minimum of 100 high-frequency words.

   Person responsible: Resource teacher

3. By the end of the school year, Judy will legibly print all lower- and uppercase manuscript letters.

   Person responsible: Resource teacher

4. By the end of the school year, Judy will write simple sentences and personal information, such as her name, address, and telephone number.

   Person responsible: Resource teacher

5. By the end of the school year, Judy will perform math computation problems at grade 3 level.

   Person responsible: Fourth grade teacher

6. By the end of the school year, Judy will achieve minimum competencies in math application skills such as time, money, and measurement.

   Person responsible: Fourth grade teacher

7. Judy will successfully complete minimum requirements for fourth grade art, music, and physical education.

   Person responsible: Fourth grade teacher

Amount of Participation in the Regular Classroom

Judy will receive instruction in the regular fourth grade class for the entire day except for 1 hour in the afternoon.

Special Education and Related Services

1. The resource teacher will provide special education services to Judy for 1 hour each morning in the regular classroom (goal 1) and for 1 hour each afternoon in the resource room (goals 2, 3, and 4).

2. The resource teacher will provide consultation for Judy's fourth grade teacher as needed.

FIGURE 10–3
Important Career Education
Competencies

Daily Living Skills

Managing family finances

Selecting, managing, and maintaining a home

Caring for personal needs

Raising children—family living

Buying and preparing food

Buying and caring for clothing

Engaging in civic activities

Utilizing recreation and leisure

Getting around the community (mobility)

Personal-Social Skills

Achieving self-awareness

Acquiring self-confidence

Achieving socially responsible behavior

Maintaining good interpersonal skills

Achieving independence

Achieving problem-solving skills

Communicating adequately with others

Occupational Skills

Knowing and exploring occupational possibilities

Selecting and planning occupational choices

Exhibiting appropriate work habits and behaviors

Exhibiting sufficient physical-manual skills

Obtaining a specific occupational skill

Seeking, securing, and maintaining employment

Note. Reprinted with permission of Merrill, an imprint of Macmillan Publishing Company, from *Career Education for Handicapped Individuals* (2nd ed., pp. 46–47) by C. J. Kokaska and D. E. Brolin, Copyright © 1985 Merrill Publishing Company, Columbus, Ohio.

preparation for students with mild retardation because it promotes the generalization of work skills to actual work environments.

Career education can be infused into the general education classroom curriculum in several ways. First, by providing academic skill instruction, the general education teacher emphasizes one important component of career preparation: literacy, which is essential for most work and many life tasks. Second, the classroom teacher can help students by providing instruction and practice in the application of basic school and work skills to life problems. Such assistance is particularly important for students with mild retardation, who often have difficulty generalizing skills and information from one situation to another. Third, a portion of the general education curriculum can be devoted to career awareness and exploration. At the secondary level, much of the curriculum is already career oriented; students learn specific job skills in vocational classes, and in college preparatory courses students acquire skills and information necessary for further training.

The following sections present methods for teaching students with mild retardation in the regular classroom. Included are ways to teach functional academic skills and techniques for improving students' general work habits. Teachers interested in other aspects of career education should consult Brolin (1989), Cegelka and Greene (1993), and Cronin and Patton (1993).

TEACHING FUNCTIONAL ACADEMICS

Students with mild retardation need special help to acquire the basic skills of reading, handwriting, spelling, written expression, and math. Typically, they receive instruction in these areas from the special education teacher; many students also participate in instructional activities in the regular classroom. In teaching basic skills to persons with mild retardation, the general education teacher will find the techniques recommended for students with learning disabilities useful. As described in chapter 9, academic instruction is adapted to special needs by providing prompts, giving additional instruction,

and allowing extra guided practice. Several strategies for adapting basic skills instruction were suggested in chapter 9. For students who learn slowly and require much repetition and practice, computers can be a useful tool for learning academic skills. See "Spotlight on Technology" for information about using "talking" software to teach reading skills.

The need to provide instruction and practice in skill generalization is a major consideration in teaching students with mild retardation. These students have difficulty applying skills and information learned in one situation to a new but similar problem or situation. For example, a student might add and subtract whole numbers easily when given a worksheet of computation problems but be unable to apply this skill to adding and subtracting coins. For this reason, educational programs for students with retardation focus on **functional skills**, that is, skills required for the satisfactory performance of everyday life tasks. Basic skills instruction must go beyond textbooks and workbook pages; it must extend into the real world if special students are to use tool subjects to solve the problems of everyday life.

There are two major strategies for teaching functional academic skills. In one, the **unit approach**, instruction in several basic skill areas is integrated around a central theme of interest and value to the students; this approach is probably best used with younger students. In the other approach, reading, writing, and math are taught as separate subjects, but functional practice activities are designed to promote generalization of skills to life problems.

The Unit Approach

Instructional units allow the teacher to present functional academics in a meaningful context. First, an important life theme is selected; then, basic skills are presented, and practice opportunities related to the theme are provided. In *Developing Instructional Units*, Meyen (1981) provides two sample units for illustration. The first, "Time," is intended for intermediate grade students. Basic skills instruction and practice is included within subtopics such as recreation, seasons, measurement, money, and holidays. The second unit, "Home Safety and Maintenance,"

SPOTLIGHT ON
TECHNOLOGY

"Talking" Software for Reading Instruction

Computers can be used to teach basic reading skills to children just beginning to learn to read and to older students with difficulties in reading. For this to occur, however, it is necessary to use "talking" software. Some "talking" software requires a peripheral device called a speech synthesizer; other programs need no special equipment because prerecorded speech is stored on disk.

The speech produced by speech synthesizers is not as natural sounding as prerecorded speech. However, speech synthesizers are used for talking word processing software because they will attempt to pronounce any word the writer enters. In reading software, prerecorded speech is preferred. This type of speech requires large amounts of memory so programs that contain it are typically stored on several floppy disks or on CD-ROM. The programs described in the following paragraphs all contain prerecorded speech.

"Talking" reading programs teach many types of skills. *Stickybear's Reading Room* (Weekly Reader Software), a program designed for ages 4 to 8, is a sight word program for beginning readers. Speech is available in either English or Spanish, and students can choose from four activities: Word Find, Word Bop, Word Match!, and Sentence Builder. These activities teach recognition of more than 80 nouns and approximately 50 verb phrases. In the Word Find activity (shown here), the student chooses a word to complete a sentence. When the correct word is selected, the program speaks a message of praise and reads the sentence aloud; then, the graphic animates to illustrate the meaning of the sentence.

Note. Photo courtesy of Weekly Reader Software.

In Word Bop, students "shoot" a picture to hear its name pronounced. In Word Match!, they must find a picture that depicts a word. In the Sentence Builder activity, students choose noun and verb phrases to construct a sentence; when they have made their selections, the sentence is read aloud and a graphic performs the action.

Reader Rabbit 1 (Learning Company), for ages 3 to 6, offers a different approach. It teaches phonics skills through practice with regular words. Each of the more than 70 words it presents are cvc words; that is, each begins and ends with a consonant and the medial letter is a short vowel (e.g., hen, bed, top). Four activities are available: Sorter Game, Labeler Game, Word Train Game, and Matchup Game. In the Sorter Game, students match words coming off an assembly line with a model. In the screen shown here, students must find words with a in the middle; words with other medial vowels should be placed in the trash.

Note.   Photo courtesy of The Learning Company.

The Labeler Game is a spelling activity, Word Game is a discrimination task (finding a word different in one letter from the model), and Matchup is a concentration game.

Both comprehension and word recognition skills can be developed with a newer type of software, the talking storybook. In the Living Books® series from Living Books, a Random House/Brøderbund® Company, students hear the story read aloud, watch action on the screen, and then interact with the story. In *Just Grandma and Me,* the student can choose English, Spanish, or Japanese speech. In the screen here, the text is read aloud (with sound effects) and Grandma and her grandson walk down the path to wait for the bus.

Note. ©1992, Mercer Mayer and Living Books, a Random House/Brøderbund Company. All Rights Reserved. Used by Permission. Photo by Dylan Lewis.

The student can hear the text read as many times as desired. Also, clicking on some of the objects in the picture causes sound and action. If the grandson is selected, he asks Grandma if he can sit by the window on the bus. If the cow is selected, it moos. There are several other titles in the Living Books® series including *Arthur's Teacher Trouble, The Tortoise and the Hare,* and *The New Kid on the Block.*

is also for intermediate grade students. It features subtopics such as basic first aid, emergencies, and drugs and poisonous substances.

Many unit themes would be appropriate for mainstreamed special students and other members of mainstreamed classrooms. For example, "Becoming a Consumer" is a topic that could be adapted to

varying skill, age, and interest levels. For younger students, this unit could be used to teach basic money skills, such as identifying coins and bills, adding and subtracting amounts of money, and making change. For older (or more capable) students, appropriate consumer skills are reading advertisements, comparison shopping, and installment buy-

Another set of talking storybooks, the Discis Books Kids Can Read! series (Discis Knowledge Research), offers color illustrations but no animation. However, students can listen to a story read aloud and then choose individual words or sentences to hear them pronounced. Students can also click on a portion of a picture to see (and hear) its label. Other options include hearing words pronounced syllable by syllable and hearing an explanation of a word's meaning. The screen here shows a page from the Discis Book *The Tale of Peter Rabbit.*

Note. Photo courtesy of Discus Knowledge.

This series contains several programs; examples are *Thomas' Snowsuit, Cinderella, Heather Hits Her First Home Run, A Long Hard Day on the Ranch,* and *Scary Poems for Rotten Kids.*

ing. Other flexible unit themes are transportation (e.g., riding the school bus, using public transportation, driving a car), getting a job (e.g., chores at home, the want ads, job applications and interviews), and money management (e.g., budgeting your allowance, using the bank, handling paychecks and taxes).

Functional Practice Activities

The classroom teacher can design practice activities in any basic skill area so that they relate to daily life problems. One source of ideas for functional activities is a career education curriculum, such as the one outlined in Figure 10–3. The key factor to be kept in mind when developing practice tasks is their relevance to life and work activities. Of course, the teacher must also consider the students' skill levels and the amount of supervision required during student practice.

Reading is an excellent skill to practice with everyday materials. Activities can focus on reading for information or reading as a leisure pastime. Some examples of reading materials appropriate for functional activities are listed here:

- Signs commonly found in buildings and in the community (e.g., *Women, Men, Stop, Do Not Enter*)
- Adult and student newspapers and magazines
- Menus for fast-food and regular restaurants
- Schedules for classes, television, movies, buses, and trains
- The phone book
- Advertisements for consumer goods and jobs
- Directions for building models, assembling toys, or completing forms
- Labels on foods, medicines, and clothing

Figure 10–4 lists important career and vocational words suggested by Schilit and Caldwell (1980); practice of words such as these is appropriate for secondary students.

Many daily life activities can be used to practice handwriting, spelling, and written expression. The tasks that follow emphasize writing as a means of communication:

- Making a shopping or a things-to-do list
- Leaving a note for a friend or family member
- Writing a postcard, invitation, or friendly letter
- Completing a job application
- Ordering something by mail by filling in an order blank
- Writing a business letter
- Applying for a social security number or a driver's permit
- Writing down a telephone message for someone

The skill area of math also offers numerous opportunities for functional practice. Computation ability is often required in everyday life, particularly in tasks involving time, money, and measurement. Examples are

- making a purchase;
- budgeting an allowance or paycheck;
- comparison shopping;
- using a checking or savings account;
- using a credit card;
- applying for a loan;
- selecting and preparing food;
- using measurement, as in reading a thermometer, determining a person's weight and height, and measuring the length and width of a room; and
- using time, as in telling time, using a calendar, and computing time (e.g., "If it takes 20 minutes to walk to school, at what time must you leave home to arrive at school at 8:00 A.M.?").

Functional tasks often require more than one basic skill. For instance, in planning and cooking a meal, several skills are needed: reading (ads, labels, cooking and preparation directions), writing (shopping list), and math (buying foods, measuring ingredients, computing cooking times). When tasks such as these are used with special students, the teacher should be sure that the students are proficient in all necessary skills; that is, a math practice activity should be designed so that low reading skills are not an obstacle.

When students with mild retardation are mainstreamed into the regular classroom for basic skills instruction, the assignment of grades is often difficult. Students can be working hard and making progress, but their performance may remain at a lower level than that expected for their grade placement. Alternatives for grading mainstreamed students are suggested in "Tips for the Teacher."

IMPROVING GENERAL WORK HABITS

Work habits can be viewed as the behaviors a person exhibits when presented with a task to perform. Many work behaviors apply to all types of tasks. For example, no matter what type of work is involved, it is necessary to begin work promptly, stay on task, and complete the task. Important not only on the job but also in school and daily life, work habits are a necessary part of the curriculum for children and youth with mild retardation. Kokaska and Brolin

FIGURE 10–4

FIGURE 10–4
Important Career and Vocational Words

1. rules	26. supervisor	51. entrance	76. withholding
2. boss	27. vacation	52. responsibility	77. vote
3. emergency	28. apply	53. hospital	78. break
4. danger	29. fulltime	54. hourly rate	79. cooperation
5. job	30. income	55. schedule	80. dependable
6. social security	31. quit	56. instructions	81. money
7. first-aid	32. check	57. save	82. physical
8. help-wanted	33. careful	58. union	83. hazardous
9. safety	34. dangerous	59. credit	84. net income
10. warning	35. employee	60. elevator	85. strike
11. signature	36. layoff	61. punctuality	86. owner
12. time	37. take-home-pay	62. rights	87. repair
13. attendance	38. unemployed	63. hours	88. alarm
14. absent	39. cost	64. payroll	89. gross income
15. telephone	40. deduction	65. attitude	90. manager
16. bill	41. fired	66. reliable	91. reference
17. hired	42. closed	67. work	92. uniform
18. overtime	43. parttime	68. caution	93. hard-hat
19. punch in	44. correct	69. license	94. authority
20. directions	45. foreman	70. poison	95. training
21. paycheck	46. time-and-a-half	71. office	96. holiday
22. wages	47. worker	72. power	97. late
23. appointment	48. buy	73. qualifications	98. personal
24. income tax	49. raise	74. earn	99. tools
25. interview	50. on-the-job	75. transportation	100. areas

Note. From "A Word List of Essential Career/Vocational Words for Mentally Retarded Students" by J. Schilit and M. L. Caldwell, 1980, *Education and Training of the Mentally Retarded, 15*, p. 115. Copyright 1980 by The Council for Exceptional Children. Reprinted by permission.

(1985) include work habits as a competency area in their career education program and list important work behaviors:

- following directions
- working with others
- working at a satisfactory rate
- accepting supervision
- recognizing the importance of attendance and punctuality
- meeting demands for quality work
- demonstrating occupational safety skills (pp. 157–160)

Several of these skills are just as important for success in the regular classroom as they are for vocational endeavors.

Differential Grading

R eport cards are a major way for teachers to inform parents of their children's progress in school. However, with mainstreamed special students, grading performance is often difficult. How should the teacher grade Judy, who is mainstreamed into the fourth grade class but is successfully completing math assignments at the third grade level? Here are some alternatives:

1. State the student's current grade level in the academic subject, and grade the student's performance at that grade level.

   Judy, Grade 4

   Math grade level __3__

   Math performance at Grade 3 level __B__

2. State the student's current grade level in the academic subject, and grade the student's work behaviors rather than skill performance.

   Judy, Grade 4

   Math grade level __3__

   Works independently __B__

   Completes assignments __B+__

   Neatness __B__

3. State the student's IEP goals and objectives in the academic subject, and indicate which have been met and which still require work.

   Judy, Grade 4

   Goal: By the end of the school year, Judy will perform math computation problems at the 3.5 grade level. __in progress__

   Objectives:

   a. Judy will add and subtract two-digit numbers with regrouping with 90% accuracy. __achieved__
   b. Judy will write multiplication facts with 90% accuracy. __achieved__
   c. Judy will multiply two-digit numbers with regrouping with 90% accuracy. __in progress__
   d. Judy will write division facts with 90% accuracy. __in progress__

   Other options include replacing traditional letter grades with simplified grading systems such as pass/fail or satisfactory/needs improvement (McLoughlin & Lewis, 1994). Teachers also can assign multiple grades in a subject area; for example, the student might earn one grade for reading achievement and another for effort in reading activities (Banbury, 1987).

General education teachers can help their mainstreamed students develop and improve their general work habits in three ways. First, the acquisition of work habits must be accepted as a valuable educational goal. Second, students must receive instruction and practice in specific work behaviors. Third, good work performance must be reinforced. The following paragraphs suggest ways to promote three general work habits.

Attendance and Punctuality

These work habits are key ingredients in successful school and job performance. Students with poor attendance and those who are frequently tardy may fall behind their classmates in important school skills. Adults whose work records show frequent absences and late arrivals may find themselves unemployed. Attendance and punctuality are typically expected by teachers but are not addressed directly in instruction. For many special students, these work habits must become part of the curriculum so that students are taught the behaviors, provided with practice opportunities, and rewarded for successful performance. To teach these work habits, the teacher first communicates to students that attendance and punctuality are important. One way to do this is to incorporate these behaviors into the class rules. For example, the rule for punctuality might be "When the bell rings, be in your seat." It is also necessary to explain why attendance and punctuality are important for students (and for employees). To do this, the teacher might lead the class in a discussion of the disadvantages of being tardy for school (or work).

When students are aware of the teacher's expectations, then appropriate work behaviors can be rewarded. There are several ways to reinforce students for attending class and arriving on time:

■ Keep a record of attendance and punctuality. At the end of each week, allow students with good records to participate in a special free-time activity.
■ Have students keep a log of their own attendance and punctuality. This can be done in the form of a journal or graph or even with a time clock.
■ Present a certificate or award to students with good attendance. Begin gradually by rewarding

students who come to school each day for 1 week.
■ Encourage punctuality by scheduling a favorite activity at the beginning of the class period.
■ Use individual contracts for students who are chronically absent or habitually late. Negotiate the terms of the contract so that acceptable performance is followed by a privilege, activity, or reward that the student values.

Work Completion

A second important work behavior critical for school and job success is task completion. Students and employees are expected to complete their work assignments. In school, the teacher must be sure that learning tasks are appropriate for the skill levels of the student. Kolstoe (1976) offers the following suggestions for teachers of students with retardation:

■ The tasks should be uncomplicated. . . .
■ The tasks should be brief. . . .
■ The tasks should be sequentially presented. . . .
■ Each learning task should be the kind in which success is possible. . . .
■ Learning tasks should be applied to objects, problems, and situations in the learner's life environment. (p. 27)

When tasks are at an appropriate level for the learner, the teacher can concentrate on building work completion skills. Students should first be told that they are expected to finish their work. Then, task completion should be reinforced by the teacher. Ways to encourage and reward work completion are identified here:

■ Make free-time activities contingent on work completion. For example, tell students, "*If you finish your work, then* you may listen to a record or read a magazine."
■ Have students record the number of tasks they complete each day. They can then graph the data and see how they progress from day to day.
■ For students who are overwhelmed by lengthy assignments, break the work into several short tasks. Reward these students after the completion of each short task.

- Begin gradually with students who rarely complete tasks. First, expect and reward one task per day, then two tasks, and so on.

Working with Others

In many situations at school and on the job, people must work closely with one another. This interaction necessitates communication, cooperation, and civility. Job-related social skills are particularly important for youngsters with mild retardation because, as Kokaska and Brolin (1985) note, one of the most common reasons for job failure is the inability to get along with coworkers and supervisors.

Practice in working with others can begin at any age. In most mainstreamed classrooms, students have many opportunities to work with peers. Besides the most typical examples of group instruction and class discussions, the teacher can design special projects to be completed by teams of students: for example, preparing group science reports, writing a class newspaper, putting up a bulletin board, or planning a class field trip.

When students work in groups, the teacher must often provide instruction and guidance in important interpersonal skills. Students need to learn to share work materials, work quietly with others, be polite to coworkers, and complete tasks by working cooperatively. These skills can be practiced in any classroom and, once acquired, are among the most valuable of all general work habits for student and adult workers alike.

By helping special students learn functional academic skills and work habits, the teacher of the mainstreamed classroom is providing them with important tools that they will use for the rest of their lives. Consider the story of Bill Yore, as told by Kokaska and Brolin (1985). Bill, a young man who was in special education programs all his life, graduated from high school at age 19 and was selected by his classmates as one of the commencement speakers. In his speech, Bill said:

It isn't easy competing with other kids, even when you are normal much less handicapped. But, the love and the patience were there for 19 long years. And, tonight

I am proud to stand here and say that I am that boy—almost condemned to an institution. True, I am not an A student. But neither am I a dropout. I may never go to college but I won't be on the welfare rolls either. I may never be a great man in this world, but I will be a man in whatever way I am able to do it. (p. 386)

STRATEGIES FOR WORKING WITH STUDENTS WITH SEVERE DISABILITIES

The educational needs of students with severe disabilities are more complex than those of students with mild retardation. There is a greater degree of retardation, and poor intellectual performance may be accompanied by physical disabilities, sensory impairments, or even emotional disturbance. According to Pumpian (1988), "individuals are typically identified as severely handicapped when the severity and/or multiplicity of their handicap(s) pose major challenges to them, their families, and society in general in nearly all aspects of growth, development, and functioning" (p. 181).

Until quite recently, such students were educated almost exclusively in special schools and residential facilities; prior to the passage of PL 94-142, many were denied the opportunity to participate in public education in any form. However, within the past decade, advances in research and changes in educational philosophy have led to increased integration of students with severe disabilities in public school life. In the 1990–1991 school year, for example, approximately 90% of the students identified as mentally retarded in the United States attended regular schools in which special education services were delivered in a general education classroom, resource room, or special class (U.S. Department of Education, 1993). Although many of these students were mildly retarded, a significant number were those identified as having severe disabilities.

Although many students with severe disabilities now attend regular schools, physical proximity is not sufficient to guarantee their successful integration into the school community. Falvey, Grenot-Scheyer, and Bishop (1989) identify several other factors that must be considered, and these appear in Figure 10–5. In an optimal integration program, students with

1. Placement must be in close (reasonable) geographic *proximity* to the student's home.

2. *Chronological age–appropriate regular schools* must be identified and used as appropriate school settings.

3. Schools that serve a *natural proportion* of students with severe handicaps as compared to the number of nonhandicapped peers (e.g., students with severe handicaps should not represent more than approximately 2% of the entire school population).

4. *Teachers specifically trained* to teach students with severe handicaps must be employed to teach on the regular school site.

5. The necessary *support services* (e.g., speech, orientation and mobility, physical and occupational therapy, adaptive physical education) must be provided to the student on the regular school site.

6. Schools that are *physically accessible* to students with severe handicaps, if necessary (i.e., schools without architectural barriers) must be provided.

7. School buildings that are *socially accessible* (i.e., schools where schedules for nonhandicapped students and students with severe handicaps are compatible and offer opportunities to facilitate interaction opportunities) must be provided.

Note. From "Integrating Students with Severe Handicaps" by M. A. Falvey, M. Grenot-Scheyer, and K. Bishop, 1989, *California State Federation/CEC Journal, 35*(3), 8-10. Reprinted by permission.

severe disabilities would attend neighborhood schools with same-age peers; however, no school would enroll a disproportionate number of students with severe (or other) disabilities. Special educators and support staff would be available to provide students with an appropriate instructional program. And the school would be both physically and socially accessible to students with severe disabilities.

Social accessibility refers to the availability of opportunities for interaction between students with and without disabilities. When students with severe disabilities are members of a special class within a regular school, they should have the same access to school functions and activities as others within the school community. For example, they should arrive at and depart from school at the same times and places as other students, they should attend school assemblies and social events, they should eat lunch at one of the regular lunchtimes, and their recess or

physical education activities should be scheduled similarly to those of other classes.

Research supports the benefits of integration, not only for students with severe disabilities but also for their peers without disabilities. Positive interactions occur between these groups of students, and typical students begin to develop more positive attitudes toward individuals with disabilities (Brinker, 1985). Parents of students with severe disabilities also report satisfaction with integrated programs (McDonnell, 1987). Few reported that their children were mistreated or isolated; most said that their children had made or will make friends at school with peers without disabilities.

In addition to providing opportunities for interaction, it is also possible to set up structured programs that facilitate the building of relationships between students with and without disabilities. One approach is a peer tutoring program in which regular class students are trained as tutors for students with severe disabilities (e.g., Kohl, Moses, & Stettner-Eaton, 1983). Special class students benefit from positive peer models and the additional instructional resources, while regular class peers develop an understanding of and appreciation for individual differences. Tutors may also gain social status among their regular class peers (Sasso & Rude, 1988). A more innovative approach is the "Special Friends" program of Voeltz (1980, 1982). In this program, the relationship between peers with and without disabilities is social rather than pedagogical; the outcome is the building of new friendships and a positive change in the attitudes of regular class students.

Full Inclusion

In the past few years, advocates for students with severe disabilities have taken the position that all students should be members of general education classrooms (Stainback & Stainback, 1988, 1990b, 1992; Stainback, Stainback, & Forest, 1989; Thousand & Villa, 1990). Called *full inclusion,* this movement encourages full-time mainstreaming for students with severe disabilities and others with identified special education needs. The general education teacher becomes responsible for the education of all students, although special educators and other staff are available to support students and teachers as needed. When a student with severe disabilities is fully included, general and special educators collaborate to ensure that the following occur:

(a) The student's natural participation as a regular member of the class
(b) The systematic instruction of the student's IEP objectives
(c) The adaptation of the core curriculum and/or materials to facilitate student participation and learning (Neary, Halvorsen, & Smithey, 1991, p. 1)

One of the major goals of full inclusion is the development of friendships between students with and without disabilities. Opportunities for social interactions increase when students with severe dis-

abilities are full-time members of regular classrooms. Also, students without disabilities can be directly involved in the full inclusion effort. For example, Forest and Lusthaus (1989) recommend two strategies, circles of friends and MAPS. A circle of friends is a network of students who volunteer to offer friendship to a student with disabilities; see "Tips for the Teacher" to see how a circle works.

MAPS stands for Making Action Plans (York, Doyle, & Kronberg, 1992); it was originally called the McGill Action Planning System (Lusthaus & Forest, 1987; Vandercook, York, & Forest, 1989). It is a team approach to planning the inclusion process. Members of the team include the student him- or herself, parents (and perhaps other family members), professionals, and the student's circle of friends. In the MAPS process, the team addresses seven major questions:

1. What is the individual's history?
2. What is your dream for the individual?
3. What is your nightmare?
4. Who is the individual?
5. What are the individual's strengths, gifts, and abilities?
6. What are the individual's needs?
7. What would the individual's ideal day at school look like and what must be done to make it happen? (Vandercook et al., 1989, pp. 207–208)

When students with severe disabilities are included in general education classrooms, it is often necessary to adapt instructional procedures. One concern is the curriculum, and Giangreco, Cloninger, and Iverson (1990) present four alternatives. First, the student with severe disabilities can participate in the same learning activities with the same goals as other students in the class. Second, in a multilevel curriculum, the student can work in the same curriculum area as classmates but at a different level. For example, while peers work on algebraic problems, a student with severe disabilities might practice addition and subtraction skills (York et al., 1992). Third, in curriculum overlapping, all students participate in the same learning activities but pursue goals in different subject areas. Giangreco and colleagues (1990) provide this example:

*F*orest and Lusthaus (1989) provide this example to describe the establishment of a circle of friends for May, a student with disabilities who is going to join a regular seventh grade class.

In September, a few days before May Russell would be attending her new seventh grade classroom, an integration consultant visited the class to speak with the students. She asked them the following series of questions. The students' actual responses are included here, too.

Consultant (C)—	"Hi, I've come to talk to you about May who is coming to your class next week. You met her last week when she visited with her mother. For years May has gone to a segregated school or been in a self-contained life skills class. What does that mean?"
Students (S)—	"Places for retarded people" "Schools for kids who are really bad" "Like the one near my house where all the wheelchairs go"
C—	"Well, May is coming here and I'll tell you a secret. Everyone is really scared. Her mother and father are scared. Mr. Gorman [teacher] is scared. Mr. Cullen [principal] is scared. I'm scared. Why do you think all of us are so scared?"
S—	"You all think we'll be mean to her." "You think we'll tease her and be mean to her." "You think she'll be left out."
C—	"There are some things we don't want you to do when she arrives. What do you think these are?"
S—	"Don't treat her like a baby." "Don't pity her." "Don't ignore her." "Don't feel sorry for her."
C—	"Why are we doing this? Why is May coming to this class?"
S—	"Why not? She's our age, she should be here." "How would you feel if you were 12 and never were with kids your own age?" "It's dumb for her not to be here." "She needs friends." "She needs a boy friend."
C—	"What do you think we want you to do?"
S—	"Treat her like one of us." "Make her feel welcome." "Help her make friends." "Help her with her work." "Call her and invite her to our parties."
C—	"I want to switch gears for a few minutes and ask you to all do an exercise with me called "circle of friends." I do this very same thing

with teachers and parents and I think you are all grown up enough to handle it."

(The consultant handed out a sheet with four concentric circles on it. After the first circle, each circle was a little larger and farther away from the center of page where a stick person was drawn.)

C— "There are four circles. On each circle you are to list people you know. I want you to think about whom you would put in your first circle. These are the people closest to you, people you really love. You can do this privately or in pairs, and you can tell us or keep it private." (The consultant filled in her own circles on the chalkboard while the students did theirs at their seats. When finished, the facilitator shared her circles and then asked for volunteers to share theirs.)

S— "OK. In my first circle I put in my mom, my dad, Matt who is my best friend, and Stacey—that's my Mom's best friend and she often helps me when I have a problem."

C— "Why did you put those people in your first circle?"

S— "They are people I feel close to. I love them."

C— "What do you do with the people in circle one?"

S— "I share my secrets, I can be myself, I go to them when I'm hurt, I trust them, I love them."

C— "Now let's do circle two—these are people you really like but not enough to put in circle one."

S— "I put in my dog and my two best friends Tim and Todd, and my teacher Mr. Gorman. I put them in because I can do everything with them and we have fun together and we visit a lot."

C— "The third circle is groups of people you like or people you do things with, like Scouts, swimming, hockey, etc."

S— "I have lots—I'm in Boy Scouts, my church, my Sunday school, this class, my street hockey group, and my family is like a group.

C— "The last circle is for people you pay to be in your lives, like your doctor, dentist, and so on."

S— "I put in my doctor and my eye glass doctor, that's all."

C— "Now I want you to think about a person's circle. Here's a fantasy person named Sebastian. He's your age (12) and his circle looks like

Suppose students are in science lab learning about properties of electricity. A student with special needs may be involved in these activities for the primary purpose of pursuing objectives from other curriculum areas (e.g., communication, socialization) such as following directions, accepting assistance from others, or engaging in a school job with a nonhandicapped peer. (as cited in Thousand & Villa, 1990, p. 15)

The fourth option is an alternative curriculum. This is recommended for use only when it is impossible to address a student's educational goals within the regular classroom setting.

Vandercook and York (1990) have developed the Regular Classroom Integration Checklist to help teachers assess progress toward full inclusion of students with severe disabilities. As can be seen in Figure 10–6, that checklist is divided into four sections. The first, "Go with the Flow," is used to determine whether all students follow the same classroom routines. "Acting Cool" is concerned with participation this. He only has his Mom in circle one and the rest of his circles are empty except for circle four, which is filled with doctors, social workers, therapists, etc. Think hard for a few minutes because this is real serious. How would you feel if your life looked like Sebastian's?" (This is a list of responses from the seventh grade students in the brainstorming session.)

S— "Lonely, depressed, unwanted, terrible, disgusted, like what's the use of living, I'd want to commit suicide, like dying, awful, crazy, hurt, nobody cares, angry, furious, mad."

C— "How do you think you'd act?"

S— (Again, a list of responses from the brainstorming.) "I'd hide and keep my head down all day, I'd hit people, I'd cry all day, I'd hate everyone, I'd kill myself, I'd want to kill others, I'd steal, I'd curse and spit, I'd fight."

C— "OK, I want to wind this up for today and I'll be back in a few weeks to see what's happening. Remember, I came and we started talking about May who will be in your class soon. Well, right now her life looks a bit like Sebastian's imaginary circle. So why did I do all this?"

S— "To help us understand about all the new kids who are coming into our classes—about how they must feel."

C— "What I'd like is for a group of you to act as a welcome committee and another group to act as a telephone crew. I want a phone caller for each day of the week. Do you think that's a good idea?"

S— "Wow, yeah—what a neat idea!"

C— "Remember, friends don't develop overnight. This is just the start. Not all of you will be May's friends—though all of you can be 'friendly.' My dream and hope is that out of this great class May will have at least six friends who will do things with her in school and most of all after school and on weekends. This won't happen fast, but I bet it will happen. Who wants to help?"

Note. From "Promoting Educational Equity for All Students" by M. Forest and E. Lusthaus in *Educating All Students in the Mainstream of Regular Education* (pp. 47–49) by S. Stainback, W. Stainback, and M. Forest (Eds.), 1989. Copyright 1989 by Paul H. Brookes, P.O. Box 10624, Baltimore, MD 21285-0624. Reprinted with permission.

in class activities, "Talking Straight" with communication, and "Looking Good" with personal appearance. Items receiving a "no" response should be addressed by the mainstreaming team when it meets to discuss ways to improve the integration process.

In this chapter you have learned ways to adapt regular classroom instruction to help students with mild retardation learn functional academic skills and *basic work habits. You have also learned more about students with severe disabilities and strategies for increasing their participation as members of the school community. In the next chapter, you will meet mainstreamed students with behavioral disorders. Methods for teaching study skills and handling disruptive behavior will be presented. First, however, consult "Things to Remember" to review ways to help students with retardation succeed in the mainstream.*

FIGURE 10–6
Integration Checklist

Directions: Record a "y" for yes and an "n" for no on the blank preceding each item. If the answer to any of the items is "no" your team may wish to consider whether any changes should be made and what those changes might be.

Go with the Flow:

_____ Does the student enter the classroom at the same time as classmates?

_____

_____

_____ Is the student positioned so that she or he can see and participate in what is going on? _____

_____

_____ Is the student positioned so that classmates and teachers may easily interact with him or her (e.g., without teacher between the student and his or her classmates, not isolated from classmates)? _____

_____

_____ Does the student engage in classroom activities at the same time as classmates?_____

_____

_____ Does the student make transitions in the classroom at the same time as classmates?_____

_____

_____ Is the student involved in the same activities as his or her classmates?

_____

_____

_____ Does the student exit the classroom at the same time as classmates?

_____

_____

Acting Cool:

_____ Is the student actively involved in class activities (e.g., asks or responds to questions, plays a role in group activities)? _____
_____

_____ Is the student encouraged to follow the same classroom and social rules as classmates (e.g., hugs others only when appropriate, stays in seat during instruction)? _____
_____

_____ Is the student given assistance only as necessary (assistance should be faded as soon as possible)? _____
_____

_____ Is assistance provided for the student by classmates (e.g., transitions to other classrooms, within the classroom)? _____
_____

_____ Are classmates encouraged to provide assistance to the student?
_____
_____

_____ Are classmates encouraged to ask for assistance from the student?
_____
_____

_____ Is assistance provided for the student by classroom teachers? _____
_____
_____

_____ Does the student use the same or similar materials during classroom activities as his or her classmates (e.g., Tom Cruise notebooks, school mascot folders)?_____
_____

FIGURE 10–6
continued

Talking Straight:

_____ Does the student have a way to communicate with classmates? _____

_____

_____

_____ Do classmates know how to communicate with the student? _____

_____

_____

_____ Does the student greet others in a manner similar to that of his or her
classmates?_____

_____

_____ Does the student socialize with classmates? _____

_____

_____ Is this facilitated? _____

_____

_____ Does the student interact with teachers? _____

_____

_____ Is this facilitated? _____

_____

_____ Do teachers (e.g., classroom teachers, special education support staff)
provide the same type of feedback (e.g., praise, discipline) for the student as for his or her classmates?_____

_____

_____ If the student uses an alternative communication system do classmates
know how to use it? _____

_____

_____ If the student uses an alternative communication system do teachers
know how to use it? _____

_____

_____ Is the system always available to the student? _____

_____

Looking Good:

_____ Is the student given the opportunity to attend to his or her appearance as classmates do (e.g., check appearance in mirror between classes)?

_____

_____

_____ Does the student have accessories which are similar to his or her classmates (e.g., oversize tote bags, friendship bracelets, hair jewelry)?

_____

_____

_____ Is the student dressed similarly to classmates? _____

_____

_____ Is clothing that's needed for activities age appropriate (e.g., napkins instead of bibs, 'cool' paint shirts)?_____

_____

_____ Are personal supplies or belongings carried or transported discreetly?

_____

_____

_____ Is the student's equipment (e.g., wheelchair) kept clean? _____

_____

Given the opportunity (and assistance as needed):

_____ Is the student's hair combed?

_____ Are the student's hands clean and dry?

_____ Does the student change clothing to maintain a neat appearance?

_____ Does the student use chewing gum, breath mints, breath spray?

Note. From "A Team Approach to Program Development and Support" by T. Vandercook and J. York in *Support Network for Inclusive Schooling* (pp. 117–118) by W. Stainback and S. Stainback (Eds.), 1990. Copyright 1990 by Paul H. Brookes, P.O. Box 10624, Baltimore, MD 21285-0624. Reprinted with permission.

THINGS TO REMEMBER

- Academic instruction is the most common area in which adaptations must be made for mainstreamed students with mild retardation. They require assistance in acquisition of basic skills and work habits and in the application of these skills to daily life and career situations.
- Major indicators of mild retardation are a slow rate of learning and consistent delays in most areas of development.
- In assessment of mild retardation, information is gathered about academic achievement, intellectual performance, and adaptive behavior. The general education teacher assists by collecting classroom performance data.
- The major approach to the education of mainstreamed

students with mild retardation is habilitation; instruction is directed toward development of the critical skills necessary for successful adulthood.
- Career education is one way to view habilitation of students with mild retardation; in career education, students are prepared for adult life by instruction in functional academic, daily living, personal-social, and vocational skills.
- When students with mild retardation are mainstreamed for basic skills instruction or vocational education, the classroom teacher assists by teaching functional academic skills and improving the general work habits of the students.
- Two approaches to teaching functional academics are instructional units and functional practice activities; both help students generalize learned skills to daily life and vocational situations.

- General work habits important for school and later employment include attendance and punctuality, work completion, and working with others. The general education teacher promotes the development of these skills in mainstreamed students with instruction, guided practice, and reinforcement of appropriate performance.
- Students with severe disabilities may attend special classes within regular schools or be fully included in general education classrooms. Both options offer opportunities for interactions between peers with and without disabilities and participation in age-appropriate school activities.

ACTIVITIES

1. Visit a special education classroom, either a resource room or a special class, that serves students with mild retardation. Observe the students and talk with the teacher. In what school subjects do students experience the most difficulty? What subjects are taught by the special education teacher? Is career education part of the curriculum? Find out how many of the students are mainstreamed for at least part of the school day. Do they participate in academic instruction in the regular classroom? In nonacademic subjects such as music and art? In social activities?

2. Select one of the special education journals that focus on mental retardation. Choose from the *American Journal of Mental Retardation, Education and Training in Mental Retardation,* and *Mental Retardation.* Look through recent issues for articles with suggestions that mainstreaming teachers can use. Collect ideas for teaching functional academics and for incorporating career education into the general education curriculum.

3. There are several professional organizations in the field of mental retardation. Two of the major ones are the American Association on Mental Retardation (1719 Kalorama Rd., NW, Washington, DC 20009) and the Division on Mental Retardation of

The Council for Exceptional Children (1920 Association Dr., Reston, VA 22091). Contact a local, state, or national branch of one of these organizations. What is its purpose? Who may belong? What services are offered to members?

4. Choose one of the fiction books or biographies about people with mental retardation that are described in "Exceptional Literature." Read this book to find out the answers to the following questions: When was the person's disability first noticed? What types of services did the person receive? If the book describes the person's school years, note whether special education services were available. Was the person mainstreamed? In your judgment, what are the major areas in which retardation affects the daily life of this person?

5. Imagine that you are a general education teacher with several students with mild retardation mainstreamed in your class. Design an instructional program to improve the general work habits of all your students. What work habits will you include in your program? How will you explain the program to the class? How will you implement the program? Outline a method to use to evaluate your program.

6. Contact local school districts to find out how students with severe disabilities are served. Do students attend special classes located in regular neighborhood schools? Are students fully included in general education classes? Visit an integrated site and observe how students with severe disabilities participate in school life. If the school has a full inclusion program, use the checklist in Figure 10–6 to guide your observation.

11 Teaching Students with Behavioral Disorders

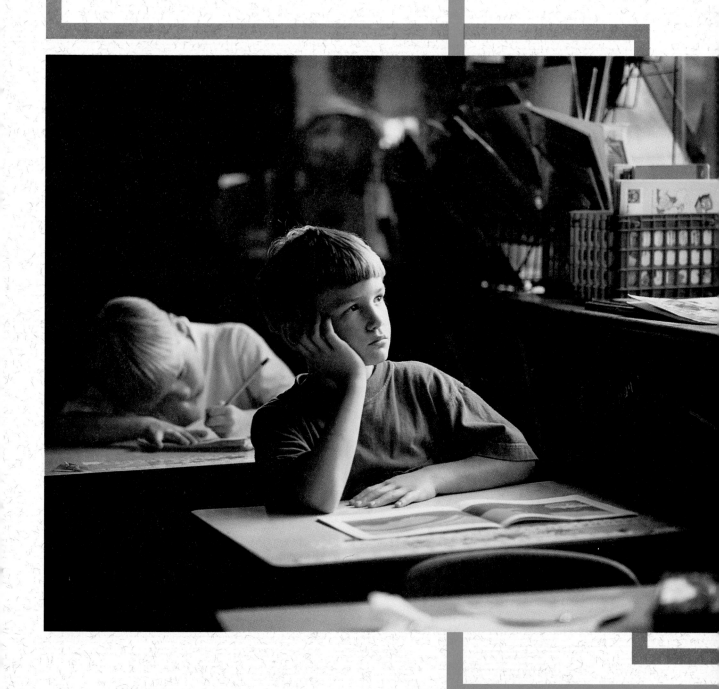

■ Jake is 15 years old, in the eighth grade, and identified as a student with behavioral disorders. He is often late for classes and, as soon as he has arrived, draws attention to himself by his restlessness and constant activity. He frequently argues with teachers, other students, and even the few friends he has in his neighborhood. At present, Jake attends general education classes for social studies, English, physical education, and shop; he also spends two periods a day in the resource room. The special education teacher works with Jake to improve his math and reading performance, study skills, and classroom behavior. Jake's academic progress is adequate when he completes his work; however, Jake often argues with the teacher over the assignment and begins to work only when the class period is almost over. These conduct problems are evident in all classes except shop. Jake is never late to his shop class; he enjoys working on small motors and reading books that will help him build the go-cart that is his project for the year. Observational data and portions of the IEP for Jake will be described later in this chapter.

■ Six-year-old Tina is a first grade student who is small for her age. At school, she seldom talks to other children and withdraws when others try to talk to her. She speaks with the teacher but only in a very soft voice. Tina plays alone during recess; her favorite classroom activity is art, and she enjoys painting. Tina's full-day placement is in the general education classroom; in addition, she visits the speech-language clinician twice a week, and once a week she spends a half hour with the school social worker. Tina's parents are concerned about her lack of social relationships. At home, she spends her time drawing and watching television rather than playing with the neighborhood children. Tina's teacher is also concerned. Although Tina's written classwork is of average quality, she does not participate in class discussions and refuses to respond orally in class.

Even though the problem behaviors of Jake and Tina are quite different, students such as these can be equally perplexing to a classroom teacher. Jake and Tina are both capable of meeting the academic demands of the general education classroom, yet their behaviors interfere. Jake's difficulty is his conduct in the classroom; his tardiness, poor work habits, and argumentativeness prevent successful performance. Tina, on the other hand, is withdrawn; she attends to her work but refuses to engage in social interaction. These students present two examples of the many types of behavioral disorders that can be found in the general education classroom.

As noted in chapter 3, many attempts have been made to define the term *behavioral disorders*; however, there is no common agreement on any one definition. One reason for this is that no single pattern of behaviors identifies a student as having behavioral disorders. Instead, many student behaviors can be indicative of a behavioral disorder, ranging from aggression to extreme withdrawal. In the schools, the mainstreaming team studies the needs of each student, explores all possible adjustments in the general education program, and then decides whether to assess the student to determine eligibility for special education services.

Students with behavioral disorders can have special needs in several areas, such as classroom behavior, social skills, and academic instruction. In classroom behavior, the student's problem can lie in school conduct or the application of appropriate study skills. For example, students with poor conduct may disregard class rules or disrupt instructional activities; those with poor study skills may not pay attention to classroom instruction, may fail to complete assignments, or may work hastily and carelessly. Students with social skill problems may have difficulty getting along with their peers or the teacher and other adults. In academic instruction, students with behavioral disorders, like students with learning disabilities and those with mild retardation, may require extra assistance to learn and apply basic school skills; chapters 9 and 10 offered suggestions for modifying academic instruction. Other students can have more serious problems, such as involvement in drug abuse or severe depression that could lead to suicide. Students with problems such as these, and others at risk for school failure, will be discussed further in chapter 17.

This chapter focuses on the needs of students with behavioral disorders. It includes ways to identify such students in the mainstream, techniques for collecting useful assessment data, and methods for improving both classroom conduct and study skills. "Exceptional Literature" presents a list of books for professionals as well as several suggestions for lighter reading about these special students. Although many of the fictional and biographical works deal with students with emotional disturbances who would typically not be found in mainstreamed classrooms, these stories help to explain the effects of such a disability on the student, school, and family.

INDICATORS OF BEHAVIORAL DISORDERS

Teachers in general education classrooms are typically the first professionals to bring students with behavioral disorders to the mainstreaming team's attention. These students can be identified at any age, but they are most likely to be noticed at the middle or upper levels of elementary school. Male students are more often identified as having behavioral disorders than are female students. Although both males and females can exhibit acting-out or withdrawn behaviors, boys are typically referred for aggressive behaviors and girls for withdrawal.

There are three major indicators of a behavioral disorder. According to Nelson (1993), a student's behavior "may be judged disordered (1) if it deviates from the range of behaviors for the child's age and sex which significant adults perceive as normal; (2) if it occurs very frequently or too intensely; or (3) if it occurs over an extended period of time" (p. 549). These indicators can be used by the classroom teacher and the mainstreaming team to study a student's need for special education services.

Another important sign is academic underachievement. Many students with behavioral disorders experience difficulty in coping with the academic demands of the classroom. They may read poorly and have trouble in math and other basic school subjects. In many cases, there is overlap between this group of students and those with

learning disabilities; inappropriate classroom behaviors can be either the cause or result of poor academic performance.

Other frequently mentioned characteristics of students with behavioral disorders are hyperactivity, distractibility, and impulsivity. **Hyperactivity** refers to excessive activity; students are considered hyperactive when they are constantly in motion and when the amount of movement is inappropriate for their age and the task at hand. For example, 2-year-old children are very active, but their constant motion, directed toward exploration of the environment, is appropriate for their age. Equal activity from a 10-year-old during a classroom discussion would not be considered appropriate.

Distractibility concerns attention to task (or lack of it); when students are easily distracted from school tasks and unable to maintain attention, they can be considered distractible. Again, however, it is necessary to consider the circumstances. A student who has missed breakfast and is hungry may be justifiably distractible in the class period before lunch.

Impulsivity is characterized by actions that occur without careful thought and deliberation. When students act impulsively and do not pause to reflect, their actions are more likely to be inappropriate and their classroom responses inaccurate. Examples of impulsive students are those who shout out answers in class before hearing the entire question and students who rush through the assignment putting down the first response that comes into their heads.

When hyperactivity, distractibility, and impulsivity occur together, the label **attention deficit hyperactivity disorder (ADHD)** is often used to describe the student's difficulty in maintaining attention to task. These characteristics are highly interrelated; the child who is hyperactive is likely also to be distractible and impulsive. These attributes are associated not only with students with behavioral disorders but also with other groups of special students, such as individuals with learning disabilities and those with mild retardation. The school problems of students with these characteristics are sometimes attributed to some sort of internal deviation, such as brain damage. However, this attribution can be misleading and hinder the evaluation of the student's

EXCEPTIONAL LITERATURE
Behavioral Disorders

FICTION AND BIOGRAPHY

Ordinary People by J. Guest (New York: Ballantine Books, 1976). A readable novel about an ordinary family shaken by the death of one son and the emotional problems of the other; an excellent picture of the effects of mental illness on all members of the family constellation.

Dibs in Search of Self by V. M. Axline (New York: Ballantine Books, 1964). The true story of Dibs, a troubled little boy, as told by his psychotherapist; believed to have mental retardation, Dibs emerges from his severe emotional disturbance to become a happy and gifted student.

Lisa, Bright and Dark by J. Neufeld (New York: New American Library, 1969). The fictional account of Lisa, a high school student who believes she is going crazy. Unable to get help from her parents or teachers, Lisa turns to her friends for counseling.

A Circle of Children by M. Mac-Cracken (New York: New American Library, 1973) and ***P.S. You're Not Listening*** by E. Craig (New York: New American Library, 1972). Written by teachers of children with serious emotional disturbances, these books are true accounts of successful educational intervention programs.

Each describes several students and the teacher's role in helping them learn and develop.

This Stranger, My Son by L. Wilson (New York: New American Library, 1968). The biography of Tony, a child with serious emotional disturbances. Written by his mother, this story follows Tony from birth through adulthood and chronicles the family's never-ending search for an effective treatment.

PROFESSIONAL LITERATURE

Characteristics of Emotional and Behavioral Disorders of Children and Youth (5th ed.) by J. M. Kauffman (New York: Merrill/Macmillan, 1993). A comprehensive overview of the field of behavioral disorders with information on prevalence, identification, assessment, origins, causal factors, and facets of behavioral disorders. Included are chapters on attention and activity disorders, conduct disorders involving overt aggression and covert antisocial behavior, anxiety-withdrawal, depression and suicidal behavior, and delinquency and substance abuse.

Teaching Behaviorally Disordered Students: Preferred Practices by D. P. Morgan and W. R. Jenson (New York: Merrill/Macmillan, 1988). Presents information on assessment, behavior management, mainstreaming students, and teaching academic

and social skills. Legal issues and techniques for working with parents are also included.

The Acting-Out Child: Coping with Classroom Disruption by H. M. Walker (Boston: Allyn & Bacon, 1979). Practical suggestions for working with students who call attention to themselves by their acting-out behaviors. Included are procedures for observing and recording behaviors, several case studies, and a chapter on involving parents in the intervention process.

Strategies for Managing Behavior Problems in the Classroom (2nd ed.) by M. M. Kerr and C. M. Nelson (New York: Merrill/Macmillan, 1989). Classroom strategies for teachers working with students with behavioral problems; specific guidelines are provided for implementing interventions to resolve a variety of typical problem behaviors.

Classroom Management for Secondary Teachers (2nd ed.) by E. T. Emmer, C. M. Nelson, and D. L. Lambert (New York: Merrill/Macmillan, 1987). For secondary educators, this book includes strategies for assessing and improving classroom and academic behaviors; postsecondary school adjustment is featured in a separate chapter, as are drug abuse, sexual maturation, and understanding the juvenile justice system.

abilities and the development of an appropriate intervention strategy. As Kauffman (1993) notes, there is empirical evidence that the behavior of students considered hyperactive, distractible, and impulsive can be improved by the use of systematic instructional/management techniques.

As with most educational problems, speculation about the medical etiology does not contribute useful information to educators for planning instructional programs. However, many students with ADHD can benefit when they receive an appropriate type and dosage of psychostimulant medication such as Ritalin (methylphenidate), Dexedrine (dextroamphetamine), or Cylert (pemoline). While these medications do not remediate academic problems or teach new behaviors, it has been demonstrated that they can help improve behavior and facilitate learning by making the student more teachable. As noted in chapter 5, when students are receiving medication, it is best if their physician seeks information from the teacher about how the medication is influencing behavior and whether any side effects are apparent in the school setting; an inappropriate dosage may actually impair learning.

It is important to note that ADHD is not considered to be a disability under IDEA; students are eligible for special education services under IDEA only if they qualify for one of the existing disability categories. Some students with ADHD may meet criteria for learning disabilities or behavioral disorders; others may qualify as other health impaired if they are determined to have a "chronic or acute health problem resulting in limited alertness, which adversely affects educational performance" (U.S. Department of Education, 1991). In addition, if the ADHD limits a major life activity (e.g., learning) and interferes with school performance, students may be protected by the provisions of Section 504 of the Vocational Rehabilitation Act. If this is the case, the local education agency must make an individualized determination of the student's educational needs and provide appropriate adaptations and interventions in the general education classroom (Task Force on Children with Attention Deficit Disorder, 1992). Many of the adaptations and interventions discussed in this chapter are appropriate for

meeting the unique educational needs of students considered to have ADHD.

The great many indicators of behavioral disorders do not provide one hard-and-fast rule that tells teachers when to refer a student for consideration for special services; teachers, therefore, are sometimes understandably confused. Several guidelines may be useful. First, all students exhibit inappropriate behavior at some time during their school careers. Such behavior should be considered a possible problem only when it interferes with a student's academic performance, relationships with teachers or peers, or the operation of the instructional program. Second, the behaviors of concern should occur consistently over an extended period of time. In most cases, one instance of an unacceptable behavior is not sufficient to warrant the attention of the teacher. However, if the behavior in question is extreme (e.g., one that could lead to the injury of another student), then just one occurrence may be justification for a referral.

Several other indicators of behavioral disorders appear regularly in the professional literature. These include descriptors such as *disobedient, defiant, attention seeking, irritable, anxious, timid, preoccupied,* and *passive.* Although these terms suggest student behaviors that may concern teachers, they have limited value because they are subjective and can be interpreted differently. Before clear communication can occur, there must be a careful definition of terms; what one teacher considers "hyper" or attention seeking may be perfectly acceptable to another. It is also important to look at the reasons for student behaviors that suggest such labels: A student who is passive may be tired, and one who is anxious and irritable may be concerned about the illness of a family member.

Another guideline suggests that the nature of the inappropriate behavior be considered. The actions of students with behavioral disorders will differ from what teachers expect of normal students. The difference can lie in the frequency of the inappropriate behavior; such students may talk out in class not once or twice a period but once or twice a minute. They may have more intense reactions; a student may become extremely upset over an incident that most students would treat lightly. Or behaviors may be of longer duration; instead of quickly calming down after a disagreement, a student may remain upset throughout the school day.

Different professionals hold different views on what constitutes normal and disordered behavior. Such behavioral expectations influence teachers' decisions about which students should be referred for consideration for special services. If a teacher prefers a quiet and orderly classroom in which students remain seated at their desks, an active student may be perceived as a problem. However, this student may fit quite well in a classroom in which student activity, movement, and interaction are encouraged by the teacher. Prior to initiating a referral, the teacher should attempt all possible interventions in the general education class. Often this is accomplished with the assistance of a special education consultant.

The problems of substance abuse and suicide are gaining increased attention from educators. **Substance abuse** is the voluntary intake of chemicals with adverse social and physical consequences. Alcohol and various other drugs (e.g., narcotics, depressants, marijuana, cocaine) can cause side effects that have a detrimental impact on the student's ability to perform appropriately in the school environment. For example, teachers may observe changes in the student's ability to attend to instruction; temperament; work quality; attitudes toward school, parents, or peers; or self-concept (Coleman, 1986; Kerr & Nelson, 1989). Suicide is one of the leading causes of death in adolescents; it occurs more frequently in males, although females have a much higher rate of suicide attempts (Kauffman, 1993). It is often associated with feelings of depression and hopelessness and is more likely to occur among active drug and alcohol abusers. Educators should not attempt to deal with such students without outside assistance. However, teachers should be alert to the problem and aware of resources within the school and community for suicide prevention and crisis intervention. Additional information on these and other related topics is provided in chapter 17.

Students with severe behavioral disorders are less likely to be found in general education classroom programs. Disorders such as **autism** (extreme withdrawal and poorly developed communication or language skills) and **psychosis** (lack of contact with reality) are typically identified in the preschool years or early grades. School districts generally provide special programs in which these students spend the majority of their time in special classes or special schools. If students with severe behavioral disorders are returned to the mainstream, they and their teachers receive a great deal of support from special educators.

ASSESSMENT PROCEDURES

When behavioral disorders are suspected, and the behavior problems exhibited by a student do not respond to the interventions available in the general education classroom, the student is referred to the mainstreaming team for possible special education services. Parents are notified of the referral and the team's plans for special education assessment. When parents grant permission, the team can begin to collect formal assessment information.

As with students with learning disabilities and mild retardation, several major areas are addressed in the special education assessment of students with behavioral disorders. Academic performance is one; measures such as the *Peabody Individual Achievement Test–Revised* (Markwardt, 1989) and the *Woodcock-Johnson Psycho-Educational Battery–Revised* (Woodcock & Johnson, 1989) help determine whether reading, spelling, and math are areas of need. Intellectual ability is another area of concern; tests such as the *Wechsler Intelligence Scale for Children–Third Edition* (Wechsler, 1991) provide information about intellectual functioning. In many states, students must perform within an average IQ range to be considered for programs for individuals with behavioral disorders.

A third major concern is classroom behavior. Information about the student's typical patterns of behavior is gathered from teachers and parents. Interviews can be conducted, or the team can consider results from behavior checklists and rating scales. The *Behavior Rating Profile* (2nd ed.) (Brown & Hammill, 1990) uses the input of teachers, parents, peers, and students themselves to determine whether students have significant difficulty in home behavior, school conduct, or relationships with peers. With the

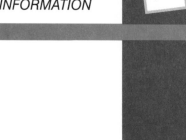

- From 1955 to 1980, the U.S. Office of Education estimated that 2% of school-aged students had behavioral disorders; it lowered its estimate to a range of 1.2% to 2.0% in the mid-1980s. Research literature in the field suggests that 3% to 6% is a more realistic estimate, although current programs for students with behavioral disorders serve slightly under 1% of the school age population (Kauffman, 1993).
- Students with behavioral disorders are found in both elementary and secondary schools; at least 50% of the public school programs for students with behavioral disorders are at the secondary level (Grosenick & Huntze, 1980).
- Nelson (1993) states that "although studies do not consistently find more boys than girls with behavior problems, boys tend to be overrepresented in programs for behaviorally disordered children as much as ten to one" (p. 542).
- The majority of students with behavioral disorders spend most of their school day in the general education classroom.
- Most students with behavioral disorders encounter problems in the general education classroom because they lack appropriate social and study skills. Instruction in these areas will lead to skill improvement that will enhance their chances for success in the mainstream (Morgan & Jenson, 1988).
- The intelligence level of students with behavioral disorders does not vary significantly from that of the general school population. However, these students fall behind their peers in academic achievement, and the gap seems to widen as the students progress through school, unless they receive high-quality academic instruction.

Behavior Evaluation Scale–2 (McCarney & Leigh, 1990), teachers rate the frequency of five types of behaviors: Learning Problems, Interpersonal Difficulties, Inappropriate Behavior, Unhappiness/Depression, and Physical Symptoms/Fears. Other measures such as projective tests are sometimes used; however, the information they provide is of little use to the teacher and the mainstreaming team in planning an appropriate intervention plan. On projective tests, students are asked to describe ambiguous stimuli such as inkblots, and the students' personality traits are inferred from their responses.

Direct observation, as described in chapter 5, is the best source of data for planning behavioral change programs. Observation gives the teacher specific information about the current behavior of the student and later serves as a basis for evaluation of student progress. Because a variety of measurement systems are available, the teacher can select or design one to generate the type of information that will be useful for any particular student.

Assessment of student behavior is most effective when specific behaviors are pinpointed and accurate information is collected about the occurrence of these behaviors. In the case of Jake, the eighth grader described at the beginning of this chapter, Mr. Johnson, Jake's English teacher, was particularly concerned about two of Jake's problem behaviors: tardiness and failure to complete assignments on time. To gather more data on these behaviors, Mr. Johnson set up the observation system shown in Figure 11–1. Each day Mr. Johnson noted the number of minutes that Jake was late to class (duration recording), the number of assignments that were due, and the number of assignments that Jake completed on time (event recording). The results of this observation were then used as a basis for developing and evaluating the intervention plan for Jake.

In some cases, it is not necessary to collect new assessment information. For example, Tina's first grade teacher was also concerned about specific behaviors. The teacher considered gathering data on the fre- quency of Tina's interactions with other students and her participation in class discussions. However, an observation period was not really necessary because Tina never exhibited these behaviors. Instead, the teacher decided to begin the intervention program at once.

SPECIAL SERVICES

If assessment results indicate that an individual is eligible for services for students with behavioral disorders, the mainstreaming team meets to design the

---

FIGURE 11–1
Observational Data

Student: Jake

Behaviors Observed: Number of minutes late to class
Number of assignments completed on time/number of assignments due

Setting: English 8, Period 3

Day	Number of Minutes Late	Assignments Completed/ Assignments Due	Percentage of Assignments Completed
1	10	0/5	0
2	5	1/4	25
3	2	1/2	50
4	7	0/3	0
5	11	0/4	0
6	4	2/6	33
7	4	1/4	25
8	6	0/2	0
9	3	0/2	0
10	8	0/3	0

IEP. Most students identified as having behavioral disorders remain in the general education classroom for at least a portion of the school day. As shown in Figure 11–2, Jake will participate in four general education classes and receive special education services from the resource teacher for two periods each day. In addition, consultation services are available to Jake's general education teachers.

Other professionals can also provide support to students with behavioral disorders. In addition to the special instruction provided for the student by the resource teacher, the resource teacher or another consultant may be available to assist the student's general education classroom teacher. Students can also visit the school psychologist, school counselor, or school social worker for regular counseling sessions. Some students and their families can be referred to community agencies that offer family counseling or other appropriate services.

Although most students with behavioral disorders are educated in the general education class, those with severe disabilities may attend special classes or

---

FIGURE 11–2
IEP Goals and Services for Jake

Annual Goals

1. By the end of the school year, Jake will complete and return to the teacher all assignments at the time they are due.

    Persons responsible: Resource teacher, eighth grade teachers

2. By the end of the school year, Jake will arrive on time to classes at least four out of five days per week.

    Persons responsible: Resource teacher, eighth grade teachers

3. By the end of the school year, Jake will remain in his seat during class time unless he is given permission to leave.

    Persons responsible: Resource teacher, eighth grade teachers

4. By the end of the school year, Jake will reduce the number of his arguments with teachers and other students to less than two per week.

    Persons responsible: Resource teacher, eighth grade teachers

5. Jake will continue to perform at the eighth grade level or above in reading and math.

    Person responsible: Resource teacher

Amount of Participation in the Regular Classroom

Jake will attend regular eighth grade social studies, English, physical education, and shop classes.

Special Education and Related Services

1. Jake will receive special education services from the resource teacher (annual goals 1, 2, 3, 4, and 5) for two periods daily.

2. The resource teacher will provide consultation to Jake's eighth grade teachers as needed to accomplish annual goals 1, 2, 3, and 4.

---

special schools. In extreme cases, residential or hospital settings may be the most appropriate placement.

■ ADAPTATIONS FOR MAINSTREAMING

When students with behavioral disorders are mainstreamed, the general education teacher may find it necessary to make program adaptations in three areas: classroom behavior, social skills, and academic instruction. Suggestions for classroom modifications to meet academic needs were presented in the previous two chapters; the techniques and strategies described for students with learning disabilities and mild retardation are also applicable to students with behavioral disorders. See the "Spotlight on Technology" for additional ideas for teaching math skills, an area in which students with behavioral disorders often experience difficulty.

Techniques for social skills training were discussed in chapter 6. The current chapter provides additional suggestions for improving social skills as well as methods for improving classroom conduct and teaching study skills. Although these strategies are suggested for students with behavioral disorders, they can be used with equal success with any student, special or typical, who disrupts classroom activities or has not yet acquired effective study skills.

Several types of approaches have been advocated for use with students with behavioral disorders. Some of these strategies assume that it is necessary to determine what is wrong with the student and study the student's past for possible causes; for example, the history of the student's family and his or her early childhood experiences might be investigated. This type of approach offers little aid to the classroom teacher in dealing with problem behaviors encountered daily in the classroom. As chapter 5 has explained, the teacher is most effective in controlling behavior problems if the emphasis is on the current status of the student and if information is gathered about the student's observable behaviors. This chapter adopts the same viewpoint.

In systematic management of behavior, the teacher first identifies the behavior(s) of interest, collects data on their current status, designs and institutes an intervention program, and then collects additional data to evaluate the effectiveness of the intervention and determine whether it should be continued, modified, or abandoned. There are three possible instructional goals: to increase the occurrence of an appropriate behavior, decrease the occurrence of an inappropriate behavior, or teach a new behavior that is presently absent from a student's repertoire. Examples of these goals are increasing the number of times Johnny comes to class on time, decreasing the number of times Harvey leaves his seat during class, and teaching Esther a new study strategy, such as skimming a chapter for major ideas before reading it.

Teachers must assume that students with behavioral disorders can learn the appropriate behaviors expected of all students in the mainstreamed classroom. The teachers who work directly with special students hold the primary responsibility for planning and carrying out interventions to change problem behaviors. Although others, such as the psychologist or counselor, can provide some assistance, the general education teacher spends the majority of the school day with the student and is therefore responsible for bringing about improvement in classroom behavior.

Many students who exhibit behavioral disorders at school may also display some of these behaviors at home. It can be very helpful to involve parents by informing them of the interventions that are being implemented at school and to consider providing them with suggestions regarding activities they may use at home. Concerned parents are generally open to suggestions regarding dealing with difficult behaviors. These recommendations can be communicated at conferences, through written suggestions, at specific training meetings, or through suggested readings. Publications such as *Attention Deficit Hyperactivity Disorder: Questions and Answers for Parents* (Greenberg & Horn, 1991) can help parents understand the problem behaviors and also provide specific recommendations regarding strategies they can use at home.

The remainder of this chapter presents several ways to handle disruptive behavior in the classroom and help students acquire effective study skills. Before selecting one of these interventions (or designing an alternative), the teacher should carefully consider each of the following questions:

1. Can the intervention be carried out in the classroom? That is, is it feasible? Consider the type of problem (e.g., tardiness vs. drug abuse), the age of the students involved, the resources within the classroom (e.g., availability of an aide, the experience and training of the teacher), and the structure of the classroom.
2. Can the intervention be implemented consistently? If it cannot, another strategy should be selected.
3. How will data be collected to assess student progress? Can this be done consistently?
4. Do students have the prerequisite skills necessary to learn the appropriate behavior? If not, what skills must be taught?
5. Are there dangerous behaviors involved that require immediate elimination or remediation? If not, which intervention being considered is the most positive and the least intrusive?
6. How can students be involved in the intervention? Can they record their own performance data? Help to develop contingency contracts? Serve as models or recorders for other students?

7. What reinforcers are meaningful to the student(s) for whom the program is designed? Is it possible to use these reinforcers with the program?
8. What resources are needed? Does the intervention require teacher time? Aide time? Reinforcers? Are these available?
9. What other factors must be considered? For example, must the physical arrangement of the classroom be changed? Must peer tutors be recruited and trained?
10. What criteria, and evidence, will be used to determine the success or failure of the program? What alternative interventions can be used if the original program fails?

CONTROLLING DISRUPTIVE BEHAVIORS

One of the most common concerns of classroom teachers is the student who disrupts the instructional process. Whether typical or special, students with conduct problems call attention to themselves by arriving late, talking out in class, moving about the classroom, and interacting poorly with others. These inappropriate behaviors indicate poor social skills or poor general work habits. Whereas chapters 6 and 10 have discussed methods for developing good social and work skills, the following sections concentrate on what to do with students who have acquired inappropriate work habits or social skills that interrupt classroom activities.

Tardiness

Students who arrive late begin the school day or class period at a disadvantage. Tardiness affects the performance of these students and interrupts and distracts the teacher and other students. Most students are late occasionally; however, frequent tardiness is an inappropriate behavior that must be resolved so that the student can become an active classroom participant. Suggestions for decreasing tardiness are presented next. Before implementing one of these plans, though, the teacher must be sure to collect data on current performance.

Math Software

*T*here is a large collection of math software. In fact, more programs are available for math than any other academic subject (Lewis, 1993). Most common are programs for math computation, although software is available for math readiness, problem solving, and everyday math skills such as time, money, and measurement.

Math and Me (Davidson & Associates), for ages 3 to 6, includes 12 different readiness activities to teach young children about shapes, numbers, patterns, and addition. In the addition activities, students begin by counting objects, then progress to number sentences such as $3 + 2 = \_\_$.

Millie's Math House (Edmark) is a readiness program for students in preschool through grade 2. This program "talks" so no reading is required. It introduces young children to shapes, patterns, counting skills, and math concepts such as size. For example, in the activity shown here, students must find shoes to fit the Big, Middle, and Little characters:

Note. Reprinted with permission of Edmark Corporation; photo by Dylan Lewis.

New Math Blaster Plus! (Davidson & Associates) is a versatile program for drill and practice in math computation skills. Students can choose different types of problems—basic operations (addition, subtraction, multiplication, division), fractions, decimals, and percentages—and can vary the level of difficulty. This program contains more than 750 math facts for practice. Teachers can also create their own sets of problems, and problem sets can be printed for use as a worksheet or quiz.

Four activities are available: Rocket Launcher, Trash Zapper, Recycler, and Math Blaster. In Rocket Launcher, students study math facts (the answer appears on the screen) or solve problems. In Trash Zapper, shown here, students complete number sentences (6 + __ = 7):

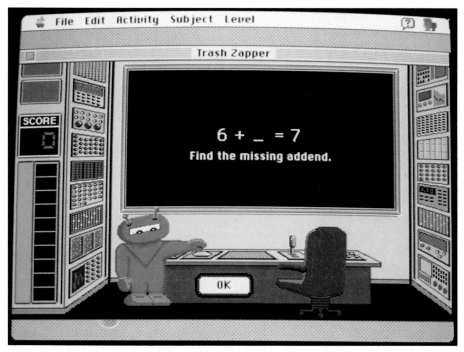

Note. By permission of Davidson & Associates, Inc.; photo by Dylan Lewis.

In Recycler, students evaluate several number sentences and make corrections in those with errors. The fourth activity, Math Blaster, is an arcade-type game.

MECC, one of the first developers of educational programs in the United States, offers a wide variety of math software. For example, the Mastering Math series for grades 1 to 4 includes programs for each of the four basic operations (e.g., *Early Addition, Space Subtraction, Multiplication Puzzles, Quotient Quest*). The Conquering Math series, grades 3 to 8, offers programs to teach fractions, ratios and proportions, percentages, and decimals. MECC also produces software for math applications such as time, money, and measurement (*Clock Works, Money Works, Measure Works*). For more information, contact MECC at 6160 Summit Dr. North, Minneapolis, MN 55430, 800-865-MECC.

Math Word Problems (Weekly Reader Software) is designed to give students practice in problem-solving skills. The program presents a word problem and students can use an on-screen calculator to help with computations. One feature of this program is the feedback it provides when students make errors. In the correction sequence, the program highlights each important number in the word problem, constructs the appropriate equation, then solves the equation. *Stickybear Word Problems* (Weekly Reader Software) is a similar program for younger students.

- Reward students for arriving on time. For example, students who arrive before the late bell rings can get tickets for a raffle or have the opportunity to copy answers from the board for a couple of quiz questions. More structured programs may provide points or tokens redeemable for reinforcers. Criteria can be set up to encourage improvement in arrival time. For example, students can earn 5 points if they arrive on time and 2 points if they arrive less than 5 minutes late. Gradually reduce the number of minutes students are allowed to arrive late until it is possible to earn points only by being on time.

- Help students analyze the skills or steps required to arrive on time. For example, determine the times they should leave home, arrive at school, and be in the area of the classroom. Use this task analysis to establish a program to help students gradually master the skills needed for punctuality.

- Place a sign-in sheet at the door so students can record their name and time of arrival. Students who are late can leave tardy slips or excuses in an envelope attached to the sign-in sheet. The teacher can review these at a time that does not disrupt other classroom activities (Emmer, Evertson, Sanford, Clements, & Worsham, 1989).

- Schedule activities that students enjoy at the start of the class period. Allow only those students who are on time to class to participate.

- Set up contracts with students to specify the consequences of tardiness and punctuality. Be sure to identify clearly the criteria for success, who will keep the records, and the reinforcers that the students can earn. Students can record their own data if teachers periodically verify their accuracy.

- Discuss student tardiness with parents. Alert them to the extent of the problem, and encourage them to support the school's rules and to require, and reinforce, punctuality at home.

- Encourage parents to give their children watches so that students can keep track of time. If this is not possible, help students locate public clocks that they can consult.
- Arrange with parents to provide rewards at home. When students meet the prespecified punctuality criteria, they receive the rewards.
- Set up a system in which tardy students lose an equal number of minutes in a favorite activity.
- Group students into teams, and provide special reinforcers each week for the team with the best punctuality record.
- Assign peer tutors to help students get from class to class or from playground to classroom on time. As students develop appropriate skills, reduce the amount of assistance.
- Provide additional grade points for on-time arrival. For example, a student might earn 5 bonus points on an assignment if the assignment is started at the beginning of class.
- When students arrive on time, allow them to choose where they will sit. That is, use classroom seating preferences as reinforcers.

When any one of these interventions is implemented in the classroom, the teacher must continue to collect data on student performance to assure that the program is effective. An alternative should be selected only after the intervention has been consistently implemented over a period of time, modifications have been made, and collected data have proved that the intervention is not working.

Verbal Outbursts

When students talk out in class, they disrupt the orderly flow of classroom activities. The teacher is distracted, and the work of other students is interrupted. Examples of verbal outbursts considered inappropriate by most teachers are answering out of turn, making irrelevant comments, arguing with the teacher or peers, and chatting with classmates during instruction. The following strategies are used to decrease the occurrence of this problem behavior:

- Establish clearly stated classroom rules regarding student verbal interactions. State the specific cir-

cumstances under which students are permitted to talk (e.g., when asked a question by the teacher, when asking the teacher a question after being called on, during assigned group work), and model the acceptable and unacceptable voice levels for each occasion. Teach these rules and provide students with opportunities to practice with teacher supervision and to obtain feedback that provides recognition for appropriate interactions and correction of inappropriate behaviors.
- Reinforce students who are good behavioral models for others, that is, those who speak out in class only at appropriate times or when teacher permission has been granted. Make the reinforcers strong enough so that students with problem behaviors will consider changing their ways. Teachers might try reinforcers such as early departure for recess or lunch, first place in line, or a certain number of minutes in a special activity.
- Recognize and reinforce problem students when they exhibit an appropriate behavior that is incompatible with the inappropriate verbal behavior, such as raising their hands and gaining recognition before answering questions in class. Clearly identify why the reinforcer is provided. For example, the teacher might say, "I like the way you raised your hand before you talked. You may take this book to the office for me." A statement such as this identifies the appropriate behavior and provides both a social reward and an activity reinforcer. Often these students are used to gaining recognition only when they exhibit inappropriate behaviors.
- Set up a system in which a loss of points results if students talk out. List the cost of talking out on the reinforcement menu or the student contract.
- Have students record the number of times they talk out in class each day. They can graph the data each day for a week and then compute the weekly total. Their goal for the next week is to decrease the number of times they talk out. Provide reinforcers if they meet their targets.
- Set up time periods in which students receive reinforcers for not talking out. Start with short time segments and gradually increase these to longer periods. The teacher might begin with 5-

minute periods, then 10-minute, and so on until students are able to refrain from making verbal outbursts for an entire class period or activity.

- If classroom noise (caused by several loud students) becomes a problem, use an obvious signal such as "Stop talking!" or briefly turning off the classroom lights to alert students to be quiet.

Moving About the Classroom

A familiar conduct problem is the active student who moves about the classroom at inappropriate times. Such students leave their seats during instruction and interrupt the teacher's attempt to present information. They also move about when they have been assigned independent work tasks at their desks, interfering with their own academic progress and also disturbing the work of others. Some students remain at their desks but are constantly in motion; they wiggle and squirm in their seats, bounce up and down, tap their desks with their fingers, and kneel on their chairs.

Active behaviors such as these are described by some as hyperactivity. However, this label does not specify an observable behavior that can be counted or measured in any way. "Hyper" behaviors can be improved, but first they must be pinpointed and described in appropriate, observable terms. Consult the suggestions here for ways to decrease the occurrence of inappropriate activity in the classroom:

- Find out whether students fully understand the class rules about when they should remain in their seats and when they can move about the room. Demonstrate appropriate "in seat" and transition behaviors, and clarify any misinterpretations the students may have. Reteach and provide practice for any rules the students do not remember. Briefly remind students of the rules before a transition time. As needed, provide reinforcement and correction.
- Provide frequent reinforcers for appropriate behavior; for example, students might receive rewards for remaining in their seats during instruction. If students are permitted to share reinforcers with other students seated nearby,

these peers will often encourage the target students to behave appropriately.

- Record the amount of time the student is out of his or her seat; reduce time in a favorite activity by an equal amount or provide for a loss of points for each minute away from the desk.
- Allow opportunities for movement. Set up a system in which students can earn the chance to move about the room or travel to other parts of the school. For example, running errands to the office can serve as a reinforcer.
- Use extinction to reduce the occurrence of inappropriate movement. That is, provide no attention or reinforcement for inappropriate behaviors, but reward appropriate ones.
- Anticipate student movement and arrange to be near students when they are most likely to leave their seats. Often the proximity of the teacher, or a reminder provided by the teacher, will prevent inappropriate movement.
- Have students record their own in-seat behavior. They can begin with 5- or 10-minute intervals and note whether they remain seated during this time; if they leave their seats during the interval, they do not receive a checkmark for that time period. At first, students can be reinforced for each successful interval. Then requirements are gradually increased so that students must perform successfully in 8 out of 10 intervals to earn reinforcers. The requirements are increased until expectations are consistent with those for all students in the class.
- Use a timing device to check student behavior. This can be a timer or a tape recording with preset random signals. When the signal is heard, reinforce students only if they are exhibiting appropriate behavior. Be sure to vary the number of minutes between signals so that students are not aware of when their behavior will be observed.

Social Relationships

Many students have difficulty getting along with others. This type of classroom conduct problem can be characterized by either aggressive behaviors or withdrawal; in either case, students do not establish and maintain satisfactory social relationships with teachers and peers. Examples of aggressive behaviors are fighting, swearing, arguing, refusing to follow directions, and antagonizing others. Withdrawn students, in contrast, may have limited interactions with teachers and peers and may avoid both physical proximity and verbal communication.

Many of the programs mentioned in chapter 6 provide specific problem-solving strategies and lessons for teaching the behaviors associated with appropriate social skills. The following suggestions can also help improve the social behaviors of students in the classroom:

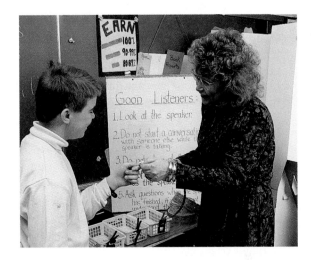

- Provide students with examples of nonaggressive behaviors that can be used in situations that might lead to aggression. One way to do this is with good models; these can be adults, peers such as classmates or peer tutors, or films and videotapes.
- Use role playing to help students practice nonaggressive responses. Simulations provide students with an opportunity to learn appropriate behaviors before encountering difficult situations in daily life.
- Teach students acceptable responses to verbal or physical attacks. Options include calling for assistance, leaving the area, or saying something nonaggressive, such as "You played well in the softball game yesterday" or "I like the car I saw you driving after school." If students have not learned options such as these, they may react by fighting back or verbally attacking the aggressor. They need to learn a range of alternative responses and know which are appropriate for use in which situation.
- Reinforce students who substitute appropriate, nonaggressive responses for the aggressive behaviors they previously exhibited. For example, provide a special reinforcer when students spend the lunch period or recess playing a game rather than arguing, fighting, or name calling.
- Use extinction for inappropriate verbal behaviors such as swearing, arguing, and teasing. Supply reinforcers for other students in the classroom to encourage them to ignore this type of problem behavior.

- Provide a penalty or punisher when a student exhibits an inappropriate behavior. This action might be removing the student to a setting without reinforcement (time-out), taking away activity time or other reinforcers earned, or introducing an aversive such as scolding or notification of parents. This type of intervention should be used sparingly, but it is sometimes necessary to stop a problem behavior quickly. Punishment, when used, should be administered immediately each time the inappropriate behavior occurs. Punishment is most effective when used in conjunction with positive reinforcement of appropriate behaviors.
- Carefully review the social skills of withdrawn students, and determine their specific strengths and weaknesses. Provide instruction in important areas of need, such as how to greet others or what to do to start and participate in a conversation with others.
- Encourage the social interaction of withdrawn students with reinforcement techniques. Reinforcers can be used with the withdrawn student to encourage interaction, but, especially at first, it may be better to reinforce the student's peers. Focusing a great deal of attention on the withdrawn student at the start of the intervention may cause further withdrawal and avoidance of interactions.

- Include the withdrawn student in a classroom group assigned to complete a project or activity. Furnish specific activities that lead to interactions. For example, in completing worksheets, each student can be given a different portion of the materials needed to answer the questions. Provide reinforcers to the entire group when the target student is an active participant.
- Pair a withdrawn student with a peer tutor, cross-age tutor, or adult volunteer. The tutor or volunteer should model appropriate social interactions and reinforce the target student for like behaviors.

Many of the techniques suggested here for controlling disruptive behaviors involve the use of reinforcers. Rossett and Glassman (1979) maintain that one very effective reinforcer for improving classroom behavior is technology. Consult "Spotlight on Technology" for ideas on how to use technology to change behaviors.

TEACHING STUDY SKILLS

Students with poor study habits are at a distinct disadvantage in the general education classroom (Archer, 1988; Gleason, 1988; Heron & Harris, 1993). They may have difficulty maintaining attention in class, staying on task, organizing their work, or producing accurate responses. These problems have grave effects on academic performance and hinder a teacher's instructional effort. With students who fail to complete assignments, assessing current skill levels and progress is difficult because few work samples are available. As these students fall further and further behind their classmates, teachers become frustrated, and the probability increases that classroom conduct problems will occur.

Teachers have not typically taught study skills in a systematic fashion. However, new programs such as *Skills for School Success* (Archer & Gleason, 1989b) provide teachers with a method, and the materials, to teach students a wide range of school and study skills such as organizing a notebook, keeping a calendar, writing neat papers, and completing assignments. Skills such as these should be included as part of the school curriculum; they should be taught directly with opportunities for guided and independent practice.

The sections that follow discuss strategies to promote several important study skills; included are ideas to help students increase their ability to maintain attention, organize their work, and respond accurately.

Maintaining Attention

Students with classroom behavior problems often spend a great deal of instructional time engaging in off-task behavior; their attention is not directed toward the appropriate classroom activity. They may stare into space, watch other students, doodle on their papers, or attend to stimuli that are irrelevant to the instructional task. These students are often referred to as distractible; they do not attend to the appropriate task for an adequate time period. The task in question can be any classroom activity: a worksheet, text chapter, class discussion, teacher lecture, or oral directions. Such students do not make effective use of independent study time. Instead of maintaining attention on the specific task, they attend to other features of the environment. Or their attention span is brief, and they shift attention from the instructional task to some other aspect of the classroom. Some engage in disruptive behaviors and interrupt the concentration of others. One of the following strategies might help students improve their on-task behavior:

- Before presenting important verbal information to students, use a cue to alert them, such as "Listen," "Ready?" or "It's time to begin the lesson!" Establish a standard way of beginning lessons, and use the signal word or phrase only at times when you wish to obtain everyone's attention.
- Make teacher attention or other reinforcers contingent on attending behavior. Students with severe attention problems will need strong reinforcers provided immediately. This approach is much more effective than scolding students for not attending.
- When presenting information to students, seat them in a semicircle or U-shaped formation to assure that all students can maintain visual contact with the teacher.
- Provide clear directions. Students with attention problems may be unable to follow long sets of

Technology as a Reinforcer

A consideration in any intervention program designed to change the behavior of students is the selection of reinforcers. One option is technology. Most students enjoy media as consumers; they may also be enthusiastic about becoming producers. Listed here are several ways in which classroom technological aids can be transformed into reinforcers.

Consuming Media

Students can earn the right to

- listen to instructional tapes;
- listen to music tapes or CDs;
- listen to the radio;
- view a music videotape;
- rent tapes, CDs, or videotapes to play at home;
- play electronic learning games;
- view instructional films or videotapes;
- view films or videotapes for entertainment;
- watch television either at school or at home;
- use the computer to practice in an instructional area such as spelling or math; and
- use a word processing program on the computer to write a story or complete an assignment.

Malouf (1987–1988) points out that computer activities are motivating to students with disabilities, particularly when academic tasks are presented in a game format. He reports the results of a study comparing two language arts programs, one incorporating arcade game features and the other an identical program without game features. Students showed equal gains under both conditions but the game resulted in higher levels of continuing motivation. Semmel and Lieber (1986) warn that the game features in software can distract students' attention from the academic task. However, that is not a concern if the program is used primarily as a reinforcer rather than an instructional tool.

Producing Media

Students can earn the right to

- make an audiotape of a story they have read or written,
- tape-record a message to a friend,
- produce a videotape of a class skit,
- take photographs for a bulletin board or a class book or project,
- use a video camera to create a film,
- create an overhead transparency of a favorite poem or drawing,
- write a simple program for the computer, and
- use a computer graphics program to create a sketch or drawing.

directions with several steps. Simplify the directions and provide reinforcement when students complete each step. Avoid directions such as "Everyone return to your seat, get out your science book, turn to page 28, and answer the first five questions." Instead, start with the first step ("Everyone return to your seat") and provide reinforcement when students comply.

- Present lessons at a brisk pace. Time spent on unimportant points or skills already mastered by the group can contribute to student inattention.
- Continually monitor whether students are attending to the lesson. Be prepared to modify your instructional approach if students seem confused or inattentive or if the material is too difficult.
- Use physical proximity to encourage attention. When students start to shift attention from the task, move closer to them.
- Reduce the predictability of your actions by varying the presentation of lessons. Ask different kinds of questions, vary the intonation of your voice, and let students know that they may be asked questions at any time.
- Provide students with individual work areas in which there are few distractions. These can be cubicles, carrels, or study booths. Be sure to consider both visual and auditory distractions when selecting an appropriate place for student offices.
- Hold students accountable for attending to the lesson and learning the material presented. Periodic teacher checks of students' understanding with techniques such as random questioning can increase student involvement.
- Simplify instructional materials so that only relevant information remains. For example, pictures or drawings can be distracting in reading materials.

Organizational Skills

Some students lack the ability to plan ahead. They are unorganized and use class time poorly. Such students can miss the important parts of task directions; fail to ask appropriate questions about assignments; and neglect to bring pens, pencils, and other necessary equipment to class. At test time, they are not prepared and have difficulty using the time allotted for the test effectively. The following suggestions may help students learn to plan ahead and become more organized:

- To help students budget their time, develop a schedule that divides the class period into short segments, each a few minutes in length. Make a list of activities to be finished during each time period, and reinforce students when these tasks are completed. Gradually allow students to help in devising the daily schedule until this is an independent activity. As students learn to complete their work, make the reinforcers more difficult to earn. For example, reinforcement might be delivered only after the satisfactory completion of work for two intervals rather than one.
- State directions for assignments and classroom work clearly and concisely; include only essential information. Alert students well ahead of time to work that is due and provide older pupils with a weekly schedule of assignments.
- Assist students in organizing their materials. This may involve teaching them how to organize their desk or how to set up a notebook. Student notebooks should contain a calendar, a place for recording assignments due, and sections for notes and assignments for each subject or class; they can also hold materials such as paper, pencils, pens, and rulers. The teacher should check notebooks periodically and reinforce or reinstruct students as necessary. Parents should be informed of the notebook requirements and encouraged to compliment students for organizing their work.
- Present directions for assignments and classwork both verbally and in writing. Students can practice by first listening to directions and taking notes and later checking their accuracy with written directions.
- Begin with work directions that have only a few steps. Reinforce students for following each step. Gradually increase the standards for success; the time period allowed for task completion can be shortened, or the accuracy criterion raised. When students are able to follow simple directions, then introduce ones that are more complex.

- Teach students to ask appropriate questions about directions and assignments by providing a model. The model can be a demonstration by the teacher or a written set of questions to ask when a task is unclear. Allow students to practice asking questions about hypothetical assignments.
- Group students together for completing individual assignments. Reinforce the group if all members finish their work and meet the criterion for accuracy.
- Make a list of materials needed to complete an assignment, and have students assemble these before beginning work. Later, require that students prepare such a list before they start an assignment. Grade both the list and the assignment itself.
- Encourage parents to set aside quiet time—with no television, radio, or telephone—each evening for their children to study and complete assignments.
- Work with parents in setting up a home program to reinforce studying. Parents can talk with the teacher each week or sign a checksheet to report whether the student has spent the appropriate time studying at home.

Several other sources of information are available about teaching organizational skills to special students, particularly those in junior high and high school. Examples are *Teaching Students with Learning Problems* by Mercer and Mercer (1993), *Teaching Students with Learning and Behavior Problems* by Hammill and Bartel (1993), and *Teaching Students with Mild Disabilities* by Smith, Finn, and Dowdy (1993). Woodward (1981) also presents many useful ideas; Figure 11–3 lists Woodward's sugges-

FIGURE 11–3
Study Techniques for Secondary Students

1. The student should first obtain an overview of the assignment. He should begin by writing exactly the assignment task the teacher has given—is he to read? to answer questions? to outline?

2. With a definitive purpose in mind, the student can more efficiently address the task. He should write what he hopes to gain as a result of his effort so that he has a clear and concrete goal to serve as a guide.

3. The student should use the aids provided through the structure of the text. Chapter titles, subheadings, summaries are valuable to the student taking notes of "important" information. Further they provide "cues" to the student of the information that is important.

4. The next step is actually outlining or noting information in an organized manner. The teacher can assist here by asking the student to write only the information he feels is the most important and using this as a basis for comparing with the teacher's notes. (A tendency of many students is to copy verbatim or to take excessive notes without really assimilating the information.)

5. The student should attempt to summarize the material in the assignment (with the goal he has established for the reading in mind). He should ask himself the following questions: have I the necessary information to meet the goal? am I able to discuss the main points in my own words? what does this material really mean?

Note. From *Mainstreaming the Learning Disabled Adolescent* (p. 33) by D. M. Woodward, 1981, Austin, TX: PRO-ED. Copyright 1981 by PRO-ED, Inc. Reprinted by permission.

tions for helping secondary students learn study techniques.

Increasing Accuracy

Inaccurate responses occur for many reasons. For students with behavioral disorders, a rapid response rate is one common cause. In this instance, students work quickly, without taking time to think about their answers or check them for accuracy. In class discussions, these students may blurt out a response before carefully considering the question. Such students are characterized by the speed with which they work and the resulting high number of incorrect responses; a term used to describe this behavior is *impulsivity*. To help hasty students increase the accuracy of their work, teachers can try one of the strategies described here:

■ When giving assignments, remind students that part of the task is checking for accuracy, and reinforce students for completing this step. Teachers can observe students to see whether they are checking their work, or reinforcement can be contingent upon a continual decrease in the number of errors.

■ Provide reinforcement for accurate responses. For example, students might earn tokens for each correct response.

■ Model appropriate proofreading procedures. Show the class examples of work containing errors, and review how to make corrections. Students may be taught to use a proofreading strategy such as COPS, in which students check Capitalization, Overall appearance, Punctuation, and Spelling (Schumaker, Nolan, & Deshler, 1985).

■ Carefully design instructional materials to achieve high rates of student success, which is associated with higher levels of student learning. Poorly designed instruction leads to student frustration and poor levels of performance.

■ Teach students strategies for taking tests and examinations. An example of a program to improve test-taking skills appears in Figure 11–4; teachers might also be interested in the article "Improving Test-Taking Skills of LD Adolescents" by Markel (1981).

■ Encourage students to think before they speak. For example, after asking a question, require students to observe a short 5- to 10-second "thinking time" before making a response. As students learn to deliberate before answering, gradually reduce the structure of this requirement.

■ Use a cognitive behavior modification technique to help students learn to direct their own problem solving. Consult "Tips for the Teacher" for information about the self-instructional training program described by Finch and Spirito (1980).

■ Kauffman (1993) suggests that careless student errors can be reduced through the use of response cost procedures. That is, when errors are made, students lose something, such as part of their recess time. The procedure can be made more effective by adding a provision that students must complete an additional question or problem correctly for each error made.

■ Use peer tutors to help students correct work or practice correct responses. For instance, the teacher might provide tutors with questions likely to be asked in class, and the tutor and student could then practice those questions. Tutors should be reminded to encourage students to think before they respond.

In this chapter, you have learned ways to handle disruptive behavior in the classroom and improve the study skills of students with behavioral disorders and others with similar needs. Techniques for teaching mainstreamed students with communication disorders will be described next. Before proceeding, check "Things to Remember" to review strategies used to meet the behavioral needs of students identified as having behavioral disorders.

FIGURE 11–4

How to Be a Better Test-Taker

To the Student:

If you have ever studied for a test only to find your efforts didn't pay off in a good grade because you didn't study efficiently, this packet can help. Follow the suggestions in the order presented. Read each item carefully. Review wherever you feel necessary. Begin!

1. When taking a test, don't panic! Be prepared with a pencil (with eraser), pen, and paper.

2. Carefully examine the entire test before starting to answer any questions. It is very important that you understand what you are to do in response to the test. Knowing whether the teacher wants one word answers or discussion responses, for example, makes a difference in the correctness of your response.

3. After you have looked at the number of questions and the type of response required, estimate how much time you are going to devote to each question or area. Pay particular attention to the weight each question carries. An essay question worth 25 points out of a 100 possible points must be given more time than two multiple-choice questions of 2 points each.

4. Answer first those questions you feel most confident of the answers.

5. When you are responding to an essay question, it is a good idea to write down the key ideas or main points in brief form. This will help you include everything you feel is of importance in your answer.

6. It is a good idea to try to answer all the questions in a test (unless you're told that you could be penalized for wrong answers). If you are really stumped on a question, go on to another. Sometimes another question will help you to remember the answer to the question you have been struggling with.

7. Write clearly. You are likely to lose points if the teacher has great difficulty reading your writing.

8. Leave time to reread your paper before you hand it in. Pay attention to punctuation and spelling. Most importantly, ask yourself if you wrote what you intended.

9. In objective tests, don't waste time on questions that are confusing to you.

10. Once you have made a guess to a question you are unsure of, you should not change it; first guesses are usually best.

Note. From *Mainstreaming the Learning Disabled Adolescent* (p. 35) by D. M. Woodward, 1981, Austin, TX: PRO-ED. Copyright 1981 by PRO-ED, Inc. Reprinted by permission.

TIPS FOR THE TEACHER

Self-Instructional Training

*A*ccording to Finch and Spirito (1980), self-instructional training is a procedure in which students learn a step-by-step system for attacking a problem by means of specific verbalizations. That is, students learn specific strategies to talk themselves through problem situations; they themselves give the instructions.

Finch and Spirito (1980) describe the four general types of verbal messages used in the program:

1. Problem definition ("What is it I should do in this situation?")
2. Focusing of attention ("I have to concentrate and do what I'm supposed to do.")
3. Coping statements ("Even though I made a mistake, I can continue more slowly.")
4. Self-reinforcement ("Great! I did it! That was good.")

Students learn this strategy by observing the teacher, who models completion of a task using the verbalization procedures. Then the students perform the task and begin by instructing themselves out loud. Next, they perform the task using only whispered instructions. Eventually, the instructions are internalized, and students are able to direct their own problem-solving behavior.

■ ACTIVITIES

1. Observe a mainstreamed special student who has been identified as having behavioral disorders. Describe how this student's behavior differs from that of his or her typical class peers. How does the teacher treat this student? How do classmates react? For this student and one or two "normal" students, try to get a count of the number of positive and negative interactions with the teacher and with other students; compare your data. Look back through this chapter for intervention ideas that might be appropriate for the student. Select one and defend your choice.

2. Interview a special educator who works with students with behavioral disorders. Ask that teacher for recommendations of appropriate techniques to use in the general education classroom. In the teacher's view, what are the important differ-

ences between students with behavioral disorders who succeed in the mainstream and those who require a special class? Write a summary of your interview, and discuss any of the teacher's points with which you disagree.

3. Read two articles that discuss techniques for working with students with behavioral disorders. *Behavioral Disorders, Teaching Exceptional Children, Education and Treatment of Children, The Pointer,* and *Behavior Therapy* are journals in which such articles often appear. Think about the articles you have read, and describe how these techniques could be used in a general education class.

4. Survey your local community for agencies that provide services to students with behavioral disorders. These agencies may deal with acting-out or withdrawn students, drug abuse, or suicide prevention. Local school districts or mental

- The most common areas in which adaptations must be made for mainstreamed students with behavioral disorders are social skills and classroom behavior. Although these students usually require assistance in academic instruction, the most urgent needs are generally control of disruptive behaviors and acquisition of appropriate social and study skills.
- The major indicators of behavioral disorders are actions that deviate significantly in frequency, intensity, and duration from those expected of the student's normal peers of the same age and sex.
- Many students with behavioral disorders have academic needs that closely resemble those of students with learning disabilities and require the use of similar instructional interventions.
- Assessment of behavioral disorders is most useful when data are gathered about the current status of students' problem behaviors.
- Typical disruptive behaviors of students include tardiness, verbal outbursts, inappropriate physical activity, and poor social relationships.
- In the area of study skills, students with behavioral disorders experience difficulty maintaining attention, organizing work, and responding with accuracy.
- Students with behavioral disorders are capable of learning to act appropriately; their school conduct and work habits can be improved with proper instructional and behavioral management techniques.

health organizations may be able to provide the names of some appropriate agencies. Contact two agencies and find out what types of services they offer. How do these programs differ from school programs? Are services offered to parents? In your view, how useful are these programs?

5. Presume that you have been selected to explain behavioral disorders to another teacher. Make an outline of your presentation, including the benefits of mainstreaming for these students. Formulate four questions that you anticipate the teacher is likely to ask, and prepare answers for these questions.

6. Watch a movie that includes information about individuals who have unusual or disordered behavior (such as *To Sir With Love, Rain Man,* or *Blackboard Jungle*). Describe their behaviors in terms that would be meaningful in planning for their educational needs. Explain how a general education teacher could accommodate a school-aged individual with similar needs in his or her classroom. What type(s) of special support or services might be needed by the student? By the teacher? Discuss any questions you would have about the feasibility and appropriateness of the placement.

12 Teaching Students with Communication Disorders

■ *There are three children with communication problems in Ms. Ranson's first grade class. Despite their speech and language difficulties, these students are mainstreamed for all regular class activities. Each receives individual help twice each week from the speech-language pathologist. We will look more closely at the special education needs of two of these children—Elaine and Rocky—later in the chapter.*

Elaine speaks clearly and distinctly but has difficulty producing the r sound. Because of this articulation problem, she calls her teacher Ms. Wanson.

Jeff's speech is like that of a much younger child. He mispronounces sounds, omits some, and speaks hurriedly and indistinctly. Jeff's teacher and classmates often find it difficult to understand what he is saying.

Rocky speaks intelligibly but makes many grammatical errors. He uses incomplete sentences and may mix plural nouns with singular verbs ("boys runs"). In addition, his speaking vocabulary is limited, and his knowledge of word meanings is poor for his age.

■ *Willy stutters. He is in 10th grade and is a good student. On written reports, assignments, and exams, Willy excels. However, because of his dysfluency in speech, he is reluctant to answer questions in class, participate in discussions, or give oral reports. Willy has several close friends around whom he is comfortable speaking, but he is hesitant to talk with persons he does not know well. Although mainstreamed for all his academic work, Willy receives special education services from the speech-language pathologist. This special teacher is working with Willy to reduce his dysfluency and to overcome his embarrassment in speaking. She also consults with Willy's general education teachers to help them provide a nonthreatening classroom environment in which Willy will feel comfortable and will practice speaking in front of others.*

■ When children enter school, they are expected to be able to communicate. This expectation may not be realized in students with speech and language impairments. Communication disorders, one of the most common of all disabilities, affect a student's ability to interact with teachers and classmates. Students with speech problems may mispronounce words or sounds, speak with **dysfluency,** or have an unusual voice quality; as a result, their speech is difficult for the listener to understand. Students with language problems may fail to understand the speech of others and may have trouble expressing their own thoughts in words. Although communication disorders can accompany other disabilities such as learning disabilities, mental retardation, and hearing impairment, most students with speech and language problems remain in the mainstream. Special services are provided to them on a part-time basis by professionals such as speech-language pathologists.

The special needs of students with communication problems fall in the areas of academic and social performance. In instruction, the general education teacher may need to make minor adaptations in order to stress language, listening, and speaking skills for such students. Creating an accepting classroom environment is also important. Students with communication impairments are more likely to practice verbal interactions with others if their classmates and teacher are tolerant, accepting, and supportive.

This chapter describes the characteristics of mainstreamed students with communication disorders and suggests methods for the general education teacher to use in gathering data, teaching listening and speaking skills, and creating an accepting classroom environment. To become more familiar with speech and language disorders and their impact on communication, try one of the simulations described in Table 12–1.

■ INDICATORS OF COMMUNICATION DISORDERS

Because students with communication disorders typically remain members of mainstreamed classrooms for their entire educational careers, the general education teacher is an important professional on the mainstreaming team. It is the general education teacher who notes signs of communication difficulties, refers individual students for special education assessment, helps gather assessment information, and later coordinates students' classroom instruction with special speech and language services.

TABLE 12-1
Simulations of Speech and Language Disorders

Communication Situation	Type of Disorder	Suggested Simulation
You are speaking to a group of teachers and parents. Describe the instructional program in your classroom.	Delayed speech	Deliver your speech without talking. You may gesture.
You have just met your new principal. Introduce yourself and welcome him or her to your school.	Articulation	Introduce yourself after you have placed one or two saltine crackers in your mouth. Don't chew.
You are reporting to the school board about the new parent involvement program at your school.	Poor voice quality	Tape record your speech and then play it back at the wrong speed.
You are chatting with the parents of several of your students about the upcoming school play.	Dysfluency or stuttering	S-say th-the f-first s-sound o-of e-each w-word, th-then th-the w-word i-itself.

Communication disorders are of two types: those that affect language and those that affect speech. **Language** is the ability to communicate using symbols; it includes both oral and written communication and requires both expression and reception of ideas. **Speech** is one aspect of oral language; it is the vehicle by which thoughts are expressed in oral communication.

According to the American Speech-Language-Hearing Association (ASHA) (n.d.), language and speech disorders can be differentiated as follows:

> A *language disorder* is characterized by an inability to use the symbols of language through (a) proper use of words and their meanings, (b) appropriate grammatical patterns, and (c) proper use of speech sounds.
>
> A *speech disorder* is characterized by difficulty in (a) producing speech sounds (articulation), (b) maintaining speech rhythm (fluent speech), and (c) controlling vocal production (voice). (p. 1, italics added)

Thus, students with difficulty understanding or expressing ideas appropriate to their age may be experiencing language problems. Those with adequate language but poor speech sound production, fluency, or voice quality may be candidates for special services in the area of speech.

Most speech problems are detected at an early age; articulation disorders are most commonly found among children in the first few grades of school. Language disorders are also identified in young children but can persist throughout the elementary and secondary years. Speech disorders are usually obvious to the listener. In fact, Van Riper (1978) maintains that one criterion for identifying a communication disorder is speech unusual enough to bring attention to itself. *Unusual*, however, is not a very precise description of a possible problem. The questions in "Tips for the Teacher" can assist in obtaining more specific information.

TIPS FOR THE TEACHER

Recognizing Speech Disorders

*P*erhaps the best way to determine whether a person has a speech problem is to ask yourself the following questions:

1. *Can I understand this person?* This is the simplest judgment you will have to make. If you cannot understand or can understand only with difficulty what a person is saying, she has a communication disorder.
2. *Does this person sound strange?* If you can understand someone, but he doesn't sound like you expect him to, he has a problem. An adult who sounds like Elmer Fudd, a 200-pound adult male who sounds like a nine-year-old girl, and a person who has a flat, expressionless manner of speaking all have communication problems.
3. *Does this person have any peculiar physical characteristics when speaking?* A person who has distracting mannerisms that interfere with his message has a problem. These mannerisms might include unnecessary or unexpected movements of the lips, tongue, nostrils, arms, legs, or posture.
4. *Is the communication in a style inappropriate to the situation?* We do not expect the president of the United States to greet Congress before his annual State of the Union address by saying, "Hey, baby, what's happenin'? It's cool at my pad, what's goin' down here?". . . . Our point is that we normally shift our style of communication to fit a given situation. A speaker unable to do this may have a problem.
5. *Do I enjoy listening to this speaker?* This is a judgment we all feel comfortable making. If the reason we don't enjoy a speaker is that we don't like her message, the speaker doesn't have a problem. If, on the other hand, we don't enjoy a speaker for one of the reasons mentioned here, she probably does have a problem. . . . Speakers who can alienate people merely by introducing themselves need help.
6. *Is the speaker damaging his communication mechanisms?* Like most other parts of the body, the organs used in communication can be misused. Although diagnoses of physiological abuse can only be made by specialists, listeners can often detect signs of strain in a speaker. Teachers should always refer to professionals children they think may be injuring their voices. An unnecessary referral hurts no one, but overlooking a symptom can have disastrous consequences.
7. *Does the speaker suffer when attempting to communicate?* This is difficult to judge, because a listener cannot usually determine how a person feels about her efforts to communicate. Many people considered normal communicators by their peers suffer emotionally as a result of shortcomings they imagine. Communication problems such as these that do not have obvious symptoms are among the most difficult to treat.

Note. From *An Introduction to Special Education* 2nd ed. by William H. Berdine and Edward Blackhurst. Copyright © 1985 by William H. Berdine and A. Edward Blackhurst. Reprinted by permission of HarperCollins College Publishers.

ASSESSMENT PROCEDURES

When communication disorders are suspected, the mainstreaming team meets to prepare an assessment plan. One important consideration is the student's hearing; the school nurse is consulted to determine whether a hearing loss is contributing to poor speech or language performance. If the problem appears to be a minor speech disorder, the speech-language pathologist takes primary responsibility for assessment. If more serious difficulties are suspected, several specialists participate in gathering assessment information. Formal assessment begins when the parents of the referred student have given written consent.

In evaluating a student's speech, the speech-language pathologist can administer a standardized measure such as the *Goldman-Fristoe Test of Articulation* (Goldman & Fristoe, 1986). The specialist also talks with the student in an informal setting in order to evaluate speech fluency and voice quality. The classroom teacher may be asked to contribute observations concerning the usual speech patterns of the student.

Figure 12–1 presents a checklist that the teacher may use to evaluate the speech of young elementary children. Voice quality, speech fluency, and sound production are included. The checklist also provides the ages at which students are expected to produce the various speech sounds; these are general guidelines and should be used with caution when evaluating the performance of an individual child.

Most children have mastered the sounds of the English language by the age of eight. Some, however, progress more slowly. Consider Elaine, the first grader introduced at the beginning of this chapter who has yet to master the *r* sound. Her articulation error is one of substitution; she replaces the *r* sound with the *w* sound. Other types of articulation errors are omissions, distortions, and additions of sounds.

The assessment of language disorders requires the expertise of several disciplines. In addition to the general education teacher and the speech-language pathologist, the mainstreaming team may include the school nurse, an audiologist or other specialist in the detection of hearing losses, the school psychologist, and the special education teacher. The student is evaluated in many areas: hearing, intellectual performance, academic achievement, and language skills.

Language assessment typically focuses on both reception and expression. The student's ability to receive and understand information from language is evaluated; likewise, the student's skill in using the symbols of language to express thoughts is assessed. One standardized measure that looks at both of these dimensions is the *Test of Language Development–2, Primary* (Newcomer & Hammill, 1988), an individual test appropriate for students aged 4 to 9. This test assesses three important features of language: **semantics**, the meaningful aspects of language; **syntax**, the grammatical aspects of language; and **phonology**, the sound system of language.

Figure 12–2 presents a portion of the assessment report for Rocky, the first grader with grammar and vocabulary problems who was described at the beginning of this chapter. The results of the *Test of Language Development–2, Primary* show that Rocky understands language well but has difficulty in expression, particularly in semantics and syntax.

Many other measures are available to the speech-language pathologist or special education teacher responsible for language assessment. Examples include the *Test of Language Development–2, Intermediate* (Hammill & Newcomer, 1988) for students aged 8 to 13, the *Clinical Evaluation of Language Fundamentals–Revised* (Semel, Wiig, & Secord, 1987) for students aged 5 to 17, and the *Test of Adolescent Language–2* (Hammill, Brown, Larsen, & Wiederholt, 1987) for students aged 12 to 19. These measures concentrate on semantics, syntax, and phonology.

To assess the fourth dimension of language, pragmatics, professionals often rely on informal procedures. **Pragmatics** is the use of language, that is, how language functions in the various situations in which communication occurs. Clearly, language use varies according to the purpose of communication, audience, and setting. For example, when the message to be communicated is that today's homework

FIGURE 12–1
Speech Checklist

Student _____ Age _____ Grade_____

Teacher _____ Date of Evaluation _____

1. **Voice Quality** (check all that are appropriate)

    The student's *usual* voice quality is

    _____ pleasant to listen to   _____ monotone

    _____ unpleasant to listen to   _____ very high-pitched

    _____ hoarse or husky   _____ very low-pitched

    _____ like a whisper   _____ very loud

    _____ nasal   _____ very soft

2. **Speech Fluency** (check one)

    The student's *usual* speech is

    _____ very fluent

    _____ generally fluent with occasional hesitations, repetitions, and/or prolonga-
          tions of sounds and syllables

    _____ frequently dysfluent and characterized by hesitations, repetitions, and/or
          prolongations of sounds and syllables

has not been completed, the language a student uses to communicate that message to the teacher is likely to differ from that used with a classmate.

In addition, a student's parents and general education teacher are valuable sources of information about language performance. These team members have observed the student over long time periods and can comment on the student's usual facility with language tasks. By observing typical classroom activities, the teacher can gather data about the student's performance of language skills such as

■ understanding oral directions,
■ speaking in complete sentences,
■ using age-appropriate vocabulary in oral communication, and
■ using correct grammar in speech.

Of course, the teacher can also rely on commercially available instruments such as the *BRIGANCE*® inventories (Brigance, 1981, 1983, 1987, 1991) for assistance in gathering information about skill development in language.

3. **Sound Production** (check each sound that the student *usually* produces clearly and correctly)*

Sounds expected by age 5[†]

___ /p/ as in *pal*   ___ /g/ as in *goat*   ___ /n/ as in *not*   ___ /t/ as in *tap*

___ /m/ as in *map*   ___ /d/ as in *dog*   ___ /b/ as in *ball*   ___ /ng/ as in *ring*

___ /f/ as in *fat*   ___ /h/ as in *hit*   ___ /k/ as in *kill*   ___ /y/ as in *year*

___ /w/ as in *water*

Sounds expected by age 6[†]

___ /r/ as in *rag*   ___ /l/ as in *lad*

Sounds expected by age 7[†]

___ /ch/ as in *church*   ___ /sh/ as in *ship*   ___ /j/ as in *junk*

___ /th/ (voiceless) as in *thank*

Sounds expected by age 8[†]

___ /s/ as in *son*   ___ /z/ as in *zoo*   ___ /v/ as in *very*

___ /th/ (voiced) as in *this*

Sounds expected after age 8[†]

___ /zh/ as in *azure* or *pleasure*

* Only consonant sounds are listed because most children are able to produce vowel and diphthong sounds upon entry to school.
[†] Age norms derived from Sander (1972).

▩ SPECIAL SERVICES

As with all individuals with disabilities, the special services provided to students with communication disorders depend on the severity and extent of the students' educational needs. For many students with speech problems, only minor educational adaptations are necessary. Such students are members of mainstreamed classrooms and fully capable of participation in instructional activities. They leave the classroom only for short periods of time to receive special services from the speech-language pathologist on a daily or weekly basis. Elaine, the first grader introduced earlier, is an example of a student with a speech disorder who is successfully mainstreamed. Elaine's problem was identified early in her school career, and she is receiving the special help she needs to overcome her problem.

Other types of communication disorders may require more extensive special programming. Rocky,

Student: Rocky   **Age:** 6 years, 2 months   **Grade:** 1

Classroom Performance

Ms. Ranson, Rocky's first grade teacher, reported that Rocky is experiencing difficulty in classroom language tasks. According to Ms. Ranson's observations, Rocky appears to be a bright child but one who has not yet learned the grammatical rules and vocabulary expected of a first grade student. Rocky's progress in math is adequate, but he makes mistakes in oral reading that reflect his problems with grammar. Also, he has difficulty expressing his thoughts when speaking in class and in play situations with the other children.

Hearing

Results of a routine hearing screening at the beginning of the school year indicated that Rocky's hearing is adequate.

Intellectual Performance

Mr. Scott, the school psychologist, administered the *Wechsler Intelligence Scale for Children–Third Edition* to Rocky. All subtest and IQ scores were within the average range, which indicates adequate intellectual performance.

Oral Language Skills

To learn more about Rocky's oral language skills, Mrs. Putnam, the speech-language pathologist, administered the *Test of Language Development–2, Primary* to Rocky. This test includes measures of both receptive and expressive language. On the receptive language tests, Rocky scored within the average range; he shows adequate skills in understanding the semantic, syntactical, and phonological aspects of language.

Expressive language tasks were more difficult for Rocky, as the following results indicate. (Average performance is indicated by standard scores 85 to 115.)

Language Area	Subtest	Standard Score
Expressive Semantics	Oral Vocabulary	78
Expressive Syntax	Sentence Imitation	80
Expressive Syntax	Grammatic Completion	76
Expressive Phonology	Word Articulation	95

Expressive phonology, assessed by the Word Articulation subtest, was within the average range. However, other expressive skills fell within the low average range of performance. Rocky's major areas of need are expressive semantics and syntax. Rocky's oral vocabulary is more typical of a 4- or 5-year-old child than a first grader, and his command of grammatical structures is limited for his age.

the first grader with difficulty in expressive language, requires special help to learn better language skills. Figure 12–3 shows that his IEP goals focus on improvement of expressive vocabulary and grammar. However, Rocky remains with his first grade class for instruction in all academic subjects.

Some students with communication disorders also have social needs. Because of their speech or language problems, they have difficulty interacting with others and may feel isolated or disliked. Willy, the 10th grade student described at the beginning of this chapter, is keenly aware of his dysfluent speech and, as a result, remains silent throughout most of the school day. The IEP for Willy stresses not only more fluent speech but also an increased number of interactions with teachers and classmates.

The regular classroom is the most typical placement for students with speech and language impairments. If communication problems are related to other disabilities such as learning disabilities, resource services may be provided. If more severe disabilities such as mental retardation or hearing impairment are present, the intensive services available in a special class setting may be needed. Most students, however, remain in the regular classroom and receive special services only on a part-time basis. The general education teacher provides all academic instruction and receives consultant help from the speech-language pathologist as necessary. To learn more about people with communication disorders who remain in the mainstream of school and life, consult "For Your Information."

 FIGURE 12–3
IEP Goals and Services for Rocky

Annual Goals

1. By the end of the school year, Rocky will speak in grammatically correct sentences with agreement in number between nouns and verbs.

   Person responsible: Speech-language pathologist

2. By the end of the school year, Rocky will increase his speaking vocabulary by at least 100 words.

   Person responsible: Speech-language pathologist

3. Rocky will successfully complete all requirements for first grade reading, language arts, math, and other academic subjects.

   Person responsible: First grade teacher

Amount of Participation in Regular Classes

Rocky will attend the general education first grade class for all academic instruction.

Special Education and Related Services

1. Rocky will receive special education services from the speech-language pathologist (annual goals 1 and 2) for 30 minutes daily.

2. The speech-language pathologist will provide consultation to Rocky's first grade teacher as necessary.

FOR YOUR INFORMATION

Students with Communication Disorders

- It is estimated that students with communication disorders make up about 2% of the school-aged population. Communication disorders are the second most prevalent disability, accounting for approximately one-fifth of the students served in special education (U.S. Department of Education, 1993).
- Articulation problems are the most usual type of communication disorder in school-aged children, although the number of students with language disorders is increasing (Heward & Orlansky, 1992).
- Speech and language problems are most often found in young children. According to Kirk and Gallagher (1979), the prime time for identification of communication disorders is the first and second grades.
- Expectations for communication skills are related to the age of the child. For example, young preschool children are expected to pass through a developmental stage in which dysfluencies are common (Swift, 1988).
- The great majority of school-aged children with communication disorders remain in the regular class, and only a very few receive special services in a special class or school; in 1990–1991, over 90% of students with speech or language impairments were educated in the regular classroom for the majority of the school day (U.S. Department of Education, 1993).
- Every child and adult who speaks makes articulation errors, and everyone's speech at one time or another is marked by dysfluencies. Deviations in speech are considered communication disorders only when they become frequent and severe enough to interfere with the ability to communicate.
- Speech characterized by an accent or dialect is different but is *not* considered disordered.

ADAPTATIONS FOR MAINSTREAMING

The general education teacher usually does not have to make major classroom adaptations in order to meet the special needs of mainstreamed students with communication disorders. Even though characterized by speech or language problems, these students are generally able to participate in all aspects of the general education curriculum. Special attention is needed in only two areas: speech and language skills, and social acceptance.

Students with speech disorders may need to improve articulation, voice quality, or fluency. To meet these needs, an individualized special education program is provided by the speech-language pathologist. The major goal in the regular classroom becomes practice of oral communication. Students require a nonthreatening environment in which to try out the new speech skills they are learning in special education. By collaborating with the speech-language pathologist, the general education teacher can target these skills for reinforcement in the regular classroom. The classroom teacher assists by encouraging the students' participation and ensuring that their attempts at oral communication are accepted with tolerance and support by classmates.

Students with language disorders experience difficulty in the reception and expression of oral communication. Again, although the speech-language pathologist takes primary responsibility for instruction in the areas of educational need, students should have opportunities within the regular classroom to practice the new language skills they are learning. The general education teacher also assists by modeling appropriate grammar, stressing vocabulary development in all curriculum areas, and modifying the language aspects of classroom activities and assignments. "Exceptional Literature" provides resources for learning more about communication disorders.

The following sections include methods for teaching mainstreamed students with communication disorders, ways to encourage practice of oral communication by mainstreamed students with speech disorders, and suggestions for teaching language skills to students with grammar and vocabulary needs.

▮▮ ENCOURAGING ORAL COMMUNICATION

For students with speech disorders, the regular classroom should be a place where they can hear correct speech and feel comfortable enough to practice their newly learned communication skills. In order to accomplish this, the general education teacher must provide good speech models, an accepting environment, and opportunities for practicing oral communication skills.

Special students need to have good models of oral communication. The teacher is the primary model and should be careful to speak clearly, fluently, and with appropriate articulation. Classmates are also able to help. By demonstrating appropriate speech, they, too, serve as important models for special students.

How the teacher and regular classroom peers react to speech errors made by special students is a major factor in encouraging oral communication. It is crucial that the communication attempts of students with speech disorders be treated with respect and tolerance. If the teacher and peers are accept-

ing listeners, then special students will feel comfortable enough to practice oral communication. Guidelines for establishing a tolerant classroom climate are identified here:

- When students with speech problems speak, the teacher should listen with full attention and ensure that other students listen.
- Speech errors should not be criticized by teacher or classmates. However, the teacher may wish to demonstrate correct speech for the special student by repeating what was said. For example, if the student says, "The story was about a wittle wabbit," the teacher might say, "Right! The story was about a little rabbit."
- The teacher should not call attention to speech errors. If the teacher accepts misarticulations and dysfluencies and attends to the content of what the special student is saying, peers are more likely to do the same. This approach is particularly important with dysfluency problems that may become much more serious if attention is called to them.
- Peers should not be allowed to ridicule or make fun of speech errors. The teacher should make it clear that this is not appropriate behavior. One way to help regular class peers understand the problems of special students is by using simulations. Table 12–1 presents ways to experience simulated oral communication problems.
- The teacher should take care when placing students with speech problems in situations in which their communication difficulties might interfere. For example, if class members are reading tongue twisters aloud, "six silly snakes" should be reserved for the student who can articulate the *s* sound. In other words, the teacher should carefully consider which oral classroom activities are appropriate to assign to students unsure of their communication abilities or embarrassed by speaking.
- Changing the nature of the communication situation can sometimes improve stuttering problems. Shames and Ramig (1994) report that dysfluencies often decrease (or, in some cases, disappear) when students sing, read aloud in unison with

EXCEPTIONAL LITERATURE
Communication Disorders

FICTION AND BIOGRAPHY

There are fewer fictional and biographical accounts of persons with communication disorders than there are of persons with other types of disabilities. However, descriptions of speech and language problems can be found in books about other disabilities because communication disorders often accompany mental retardation, cerebral palsy, and even learning disabilities. For example, Louise Clark (1973) discusses her son's language and learning disabilities in *Can't Read, Can't Write, Can't Talk Too Good Either*. In addition, both *Like Normal People* (Meyers, 1978) and *I Raise My Eyes to Say Yes* (Sienkiewicz-Mercer & Kaplan, 1989) include descriptions of communication problems. See the "Exceptional Literature" sections in chapters 9, 10, and 13 for further suggestions.

PROFESSIONAL LITERATURE

Human Communication Disorders (4th ed.) by G. H. Shames, E. H. Wiig, and W. A. Secord (Eds.) (New York: Merrill/Macmillan, 1994). A comprehensive introduction to the field of communication disorders, which discusses the bases of human communication; language differences and disorders; disorders of articulation, voice, and fluency; and the communication disorders of special populations.

Language and Communication Disorders in Children (3rd ed.) by D. K. Bernstein and E. Tiegerman (Eds.) (New York: Merrill/Macmillan, 1993). An introductory textbook that covers the social and cognitive bases of language, stages of language development, strategies for language assessment and instruction, and special populations such as children with autism.

"Students with Communication Problems" by B. K. Culatta and R. Culatta in *An Introduction to Special Education* (3rd ed., pp. 238–269) by A. E. Blackhurst and W. H. Berdine (Eds.) (New York: HarperCollins, 1993). An introduction to communication disorders; describes basic concepts of speech and language, specific disorders, and the role of the classroom teacher in educating children with communication disorders.

"Communication Disorders" by C. A. Swift in *Exceptional Children and Adults* (pp. 318–351) by E. W. Lynch and R. B. Lewis (Eds.) (Glenview, IL: Scott, Foresman, 1988). An introduction to disorders of speech and language; describes the types of communication disorders, etiology and prevention, student characteristics, assessment techniques, and typical intervention strategies.

Language Instruction for Students with Disabilities (2nd ed.) by E. A. Polloway and T. E. C. Smith (Denver: Love, 1992). Describes the language needs of students with disabilities and techniques for language instruction; included are chapters on cultural diversity and language differences, development of initial language skills, and strategies for teaching oral language skills.

Language Arts by G. Wallace, S. B. Cohen, and E. A. Polloway (Austin, TX: PRO-ED, 1987). Discusses the development of language and strategies for assessment and instruction of listening, speaking, and written language skills; features chapters on preschool children, variant language speakers, and gifted and talented students.

Language Assessment and Intervention for the Learning Disabled (2nd ed.) by E. H. Wiig and E. M. Semel (New York: Merrill/Macmillan, 1984). A survey of language disabilities in school-aged children and youth, describing methods of assessment and remediation of deficits in semantics, morphology and syntax, and pragmatics; includes suggestions for adapting and enhancing the language components of the curriculum.

another person, whisper, speak in a monotone, speak in a higher or lower pitch than usual, or speak in time to a metronome.

- For some students with communication problems, speech is slow and labored. A stutterer make take a long time to produce a single sentence, a student with cerebral palsy may make facial grimaces as he or she struggles to articulate each word, and a person who communicates by means of a communication board or an electronic communication aid may require several seconds to select the message he or she wants to convey to the listener. Such students require patient listeners. Attempts to hurry them will likely result in slower, not faster, communication; finishing their sentences for them will discourage and frustrate them further.

The teacher should model appropriate listening skills for the class as well as attempt to sensitize students to the need to wait quietly and listen while others speak. In some situations, the teacher may want to speed communication by phrasing questions to students with speech problems so that only short responses are required. In other situations, these students should be encouraged to express their thoughts and opinions more fully. See "Spotlight on Technology" for more information on alternative methods of communication such as electronic communication devices.

In addition to providing good speech models and an accepting environment, the classroom teacher should ensure that students with speech disorders have frequent opportunities to practice their communication skills. McCormick (1986) recommends that practice take place in a variety of contexts throughout the school day. Oral communication can be incorporated into most areas of the curriculum. Whether the subject is reading, math, or social studies, students can practice speaking with the teacher, in small work groups, and during class discussions. Lunchtime, work breaks, and recess create natural opportunities for socialization and talking with others, as do many free-time activities in the classroom. Culatta and Culatta (1993) provide these suggestions for creating communication opportunities:

- *Do not anticipate needs.* A child who is given paper without crayons or who is provided with only a small amount of juice at a time is encountering the need to communicate.
- *Arrange for unusual or novel events to occur.* A child who sees a box of cereal taped to the wall is likely to want to share that event and seek information about it. Language can also be evoked by engaging in such actions as "inadvertently" throwing away toys, wearing clothes that are too big, and trying to eat soup with a fork.
- *Arrange for the child to convey information to others.* In the cafeteria the child may be asked to direct others to their seats, describe the menu, convey the location of utensils, and report the acceptability of the food to the cook. Many opportunities to convey experiences to others can be created throughout the day.
- *Provide the child with choices.* During a snack activity, the child can decide what to drink, where to sit, whether to use a napkin or a paper plate, and who should be responsible for cleaning up. Each decision requires communication. (pp. 251–252)

An important goal of any mainstreaming program is the inclusion of special students in as many classroom activities as possible. For students with speech

SPOTLIGHT ON TECHNOLOGY   *Augmentative Communication*

When students do not talk or their speech is not intelligible, an **augmentative communication** system may be used to increase their ability to communicate. There are many types of augmentative communication systems. For example, if you have a cold and find it difficult to talk, you might augment your usual means of communication by using more gestures or even writing notes rather than speaking. In classrooms, two types of systems are used most often with students with communication disorders: communication boards and electronic communication devices.

Communication Boards

Communication boards are considered a "low" technology. According to Lewis (1993),

> A communication board can be as simple as a piece of paper or cardboard with two photographs pasted on it, or as elaborate as a notebook filled with pages of messages for a variety of different communication situations. The essential elements are the "board" itself, which may be composed of paper or a sturdier material, and the choices depicted on the board by photos, drawings, or some kind of symbol system. (p. 383)

To use a communication board, the student simply points to one of the choices. For some students, all choices are depicted by photos or drawings. Other students are able to use communication boards with letters, words, and phrases.

Computers can be used to make communication boards with programs such as *The Communication Board-Builder* (Mayer-Johnson). This program contains more than 3,000 picture symbols from the Mayer-Johnson picture communication symbol collection (Johnson, 1985).

---

problems, both social and academic activities should be considered. One way to promote acceptance while maximizing communication opportunities is to seat the special student in the midst of several regular class peers. In traditional classrooms, students with special needs are usually seated near the teacher in an arrangement that does not encourage student interaction (see Figure 12–4 on page 376). Instead, the classroom environment should be modified so that the special student is surrounded by good speech models and has natural opportunities for communication.

■ TEACHING LANGUAGE SKILLS

Students with language problems receive individualized help from the speech-language pathologist. They may require assistance in the development of receptive language skills and/or expressive language skills; instruction focuses on the area of need, whether it be grammatical constructions (syntax) or vocabulary development (semantics). The general education teacher can help mainstreamed students with language disorders by modeling appropriate grammar,

As the screen here shows, it is possible to select symbols from several categories: social, people, verbs, and so on. This board was designed for Yvonne; her best friend, Tammy, is also included.

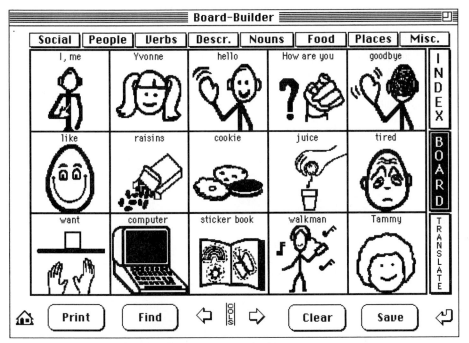

Note. Used by permission of Mayer-Johnson Company.

by helping expand their listening and speaking vocabularies, and by modifying classroom activities and assignments that require language skills.

For students with difficulty in the area of syntax, the classroom teacher must provide a consistent model of grammatically correct speech. The teacher should correct students' grammatical errors by demonstrating the proper construction. If, for instance, a student comments, "It's funner to swim than to water ski," the teacher can respond, "It's more fun to swim? Why?" With this approach, the student hears the grammatically correct version of the statement without being criticized for poor language.

Some students with language disorders need help in vocabulary development. They may not be familiar with the words their classmates and teachers use; they may fail to express themselves in the vocabulary expected of their age level. The classroom teacher can help these special students increase their receptive and expressive vocabularies by following these suggestions:

Electronic Communication Devices

Electronic communication devices "talk." Because of this capability, they are sometimes called *voice output communication aids,* or VOCAs. Some electronic devices use prerecorded speech, others contain speech synthesizers, and still others use both technologies.

The SpeakEasy (AbleNet), shown below, is an example of an inexpensive VOCA. On its surface are 12 touch-sensitive "keys"; the student presses a key to play back a prerecorded message. Each key is covered by a photo, drawing, word, or phrase that illustrates its message. The SpeakEasy can store up to 2 minutes of prerecorded speech, and it is very easy to record new messages. Thus, as students move from one activity to another during the school day, the teacher (or a peer) could replace the messages needed for math class with those needed for science.

Note. Photo courtesy of AbleNet Inc.

Devices such as the SpeakEasy, although inexpensive, may not be appropriate for a more advanced student because they can store only a limited number of messages. More sophisticated (and more expensive) devices such as the DynaVox (Sentient Systems), Liberator (Prentke Romich), RealVoice (acs Technologies), or System 2000 (Words+) may be needed. The Liberator Versa (shown at the top of the next page) contains a speech synthesizer, and its keyboard can be configured so that it contains 8, 32, or 128 keys.

Note. Photo courtesy of Prentke Romich Company.

The System 2000 Versa, shown below, offers both prerecorded voice and synthesized speech. Also, its "keyboard" resembles a computer screen. That "screen" presents choices and, when the student has made a selection, new choices may appear. For example, as the photo shows, the student may see a menu with choices such as food, needs, letters, and school. If the student selects food, he or she would then see choices relating to food and drinks.

Note. Photo courtesy of Words+, Inc.

FIGURE 12–4
Traditional and Modified Classroom Environments

Traditional Classroom Environment

Modified Classroom Environment

△ = Mildly handicapped child

Note. Reprinted with permission of Merrill, an imprint of Macmillan Publishing Company, from *Language Arts for the Mildly Handicapped* (pp. 201, 203) by S. B. Cohen and S. P. Plaskon. Copyright © 1980 Merrill Publishing Company, Columbus, Ohio.

- Encourage students to ask about the meanings of words they do not understand.
- Use demonstration to teach the meanings of some words. Because prepositions and action verbs are often hard to explain in words, *show* students their meanings.
- Use definitions, explanations, and examples to teach other words. For example, define *container* as something that holds something else; then give examples of objects that are containers and objects that are not.
- Provide multiple examples of word meanings. For example, if students are learning the word *break*, they might "break cookies and crackers, encounter objects that keep falling apart, break spaghetti in order to glue the pieces on a picture,

and break carrot sticks for lunch" (Culatta & Culatta, 1993, p. 252).

- Include vocabulary instruction in all curriculum areas. Teach the meanings of new reading words, new math terms, and new vocabulary in science, social studies, and art.
- Teach students to use regular or picture dictionaries to discover the meanings of unfamiliar words.
- Give students opportunities throughout the school day to practice the new vocabulary they are learning.

In addition to helping students with language disorders acquire correct grammar and new word meanings, the general education teacher may need to make adaptations in classroom activities and assignments. With students who have difficulty listening with understanding, directions for school tasks should be brief, to the point, and in simple language. With students who find it hard to express themselves, questions that require a yes or no response are easier to answer than open-ended questions. For example, "Is the platypus a mammal?" may be an easier question for a student with language disorders than "What type of animal is the platypus?"

Some students may require direct instruction in listening skills. Bauwens and Hourcade (1989) suggest teaching the LISTEN strategy to improve students' ability to attend and listen to oral directions. *LISTEN* is an acronym for a six-step procedure: "Look, Idle your motor, Sit up straight, Turn to me, Engage your brain, Now . . . " (p. 61). The teacher models this strategy, and students practice it to mastery. The goal is for students to internalize the strategy so that they follow each step automatically whenever the teacher says, "Listen."

Older students may benefit from instruction in the skills needed for listening to lectures in content area classes. One activity for developing these skills uses tape recordings of news broadcasts (Forster & Doyle, 1989). The teacher prepares an outline of the news items, including major points but leaving space for students to add supporting details; the outline also lists background concepts and vocabulary with which students may be unfamiliar. Students begin the activity by reviewing the outline, and the teacher explains any terms or concepts that students do not recognize or understand. As students listen to the tape, they underline key points on the outline and add details. Students have the opportunity to ask questions before taking a quiz on the information presented in the news broadcast.

The general education teacher plays an important role in the education of students with communication disorders. When these students are provided with a classroom environment that encourages the learning and practice of speech and language skills, their chances for successful performance in school (and in life) increase. Many speech and language problems are developmental in nature; they appear in young children and, with maturation and appropriate treatment, may disappear. The special education program is only part of the appropriate treatment for students with communication disorders. Another important component is the instruction and support received from the general education teacher in the mainstreamed classroom.

Special students who leave the classroom to visit the speech-language pathologist or resource teacher may return to discover that the class has moved on to a different activity. To help these students feel more a part of their classroom, see "Tips for the Teacher."

When Students Leave the Classroom for Special Services

*M*any mainstreamed special students leave the general education classroom for a short time each day to visit a special education teacher. While they are gone, the activities of the classroom continue. When they return, they may feel lost, confused, and unsure of what they should be doing. To help special students reenter the classroom and regain their bearings quickly and easily, try these suggestions:

1. Work with the special education teacher to arrange the best time for each student to leave the regular classroom. Usually, it is better for students to receive special education services when their class is working on
   - independent practice rather than direct instruction
   - the student's best rather than worst subject
   - the student's least liked rather than favorite activity
2. Maintain a regular daily schedule so that you and the student know what will be missed each day.
3. Help the student take responsibility for leaving the classroom for special education services at the appropriate time. One method is to provide the student with a drawing of a clock showing the time to leave.
4. Arrange a communication system so that when the student returns, he or she knows how to find out what to do. The student might
   - go directly to the teacher for instructions
   - look for a note on the board
   - check in the work folder on his or her desk
   - consult a classmate who has been assigned as a buddy
5. Do not penalize the student for leaving the class for special education help. Avoid scheduling treats and special activities during the time the student is out of the room. Do not double the work load by requiring the student to keep up with the current class activity as well as make up what was missed during his or her absence.

SPECIAL CONSIDERATIONS FOR STUDENTS WITH AUTISM

Autism is usually considered a severe disability, and many students with autism have special needs in a number of areas, including communication. Some children with autism are nonverbal. Others have echolalic speech; that is, they repeat the words of other speakers. When students with autism are included in general education classrooms, special educators and other professionals should be available to assist the classroom teacher in adapting instruction and, when necessary, developing alternative learning activities.

Wood, Lazzari, and Reeves (1993) offer these suggestions for working with students with autism in mainstreamed settings:

- Structure the learning environment so that it is predictable and consistent. This includes the physical structure of the classroom as well as routines, schedules, and teacher behavior.

- Design instructional programs to provide ways to help children learn to communicate. Remember that verbal communication is but one way to communicate; provide students with alternatives such as signing, writing, using the computer or facilitated communication. . . .
- Since students with autism have difficulty managing their own behavior without structure, develop individual and group behavior plans that stress positive behavior management and set forth clear instructions, rules, and consequences. . . .
- Work closely with the family to ensure consistency between school and home and other settings in approaches, methods of interaction, and response to students. (p. 115)

The second suggestion of Wood et al. mentions several alternative modes of communication. One of these, **facilitated communication**, is a controversial technique developed in Australia by Rosemary Crossley and popularized in the United States by Douglas Biklen (1990). In facilitated communication, the nonverbal person points to letters or types while another individual, the facilitator, provides some type of physical support. For example, the facilitator may help the nonverbal person isolate his or her index finger for pointing; hold the hand, wrist, forearm, or elbow of the nonverbal person; and then help the nonverbal person move his or her arm away from the letterboard or keyboard after a selection has been made (Lehr, 1992).

Biklen and his associates provide numerous examples of the successful use of facilitated communication with students identified as autistic and others without verbal communication skills. For example, Biklen and Schubert (1991) report the results of one study in which 18 of 21 students were able to produce sentences via facilitated communication. In their writings, students "revealed unexpected literacy, typing, for example, 'IM NOT RETARDED' and "I WANT TO GO TO THE OFFICE AND TELL MRS. H. IT WANT TO TELL HER THAT THE KIDS ARE BAD. THE KIDS TOLD ME THAT I AM STUPID'" (Biklen, Morton, Gold, Berrigan, & Swaminathan, 1992, p. 5). According to

Biklen (1990), facilitated communication is effective because it helps students overcome the verbal expression problems associated with autism.

At present, however, facilitated communication is a controversial technique that has received much criticism (e.g., Prior & Cummins, 1992). As Calculator (1992) comments, "This communication technique remains one that is characterized by its ambiguity (e.g., lack of specific teaching principles), mystique, recurring anecdotes and spiritual underpinnings" (p. 18). One concern is the lack of experimental research supporting the effectiveness of facilitated communication (the studies of Biklen and his colleagues have been case studies, not experiments). In one experimental study (Wheeler, Jacobson, Paglieri, & Schwartz, 1993), students using facilitated communication were able to type the names of familiar objects correctly only when both they and their facilitators saw identical objects. When facilitators were shown one object and students another, students were unable to answer correctly.

One possible conclusion from these results is that the facilitator, perhaps unconsciously, is conveying his or her own message in facilitated communication by providing physical support to the nonverbal student. Another concern is the large number of sexual abuse allegations that have been made by students being facilitated; the evidence to date indicates that the majority of these charges are untrue (Chideya, 1993). Given these concerns, it appears best to continue to conduct carefully designed experimental studies of the effects of facilitated communication— and to postpone widespread implementation efforts until more data become available.

In this chapter, you have learned ways to teach language skills to students with communication disorders. You have also learned methods for creating a classroom climate that encourages the practice of speaking skills. In chapter 13, you will meet mainstreamed students with physical and health impairments. Before going on, check "Things to Remember" to review ways to help students with speech and language disorders succeed in the mainstream.

THINGS TO REMEMBER

- The primary areas of need for students with communication disorders are speech and language; because of their communication difficulties these students may also require assistance in social interactions.
- Major indicators of speech disorders are misarticulations of speech sounds, dysfluent speech, and unusual voice quality.
- Major indicators of language disorders are problems in reception or expression of grammatical constructions and vocabulary.
- In assessment of communication disorders, information is gathered about a possible hearing loss, current performance in speech and language, and, for serious problems, general intellectual performance.
- Students with communication disorders receive individualized special education from the speech-language pathologist. These students remain in the regular class and take part in special services for only short periods each day or several times each week.
- Major instructional adaptations are usually not necessary to accommodate the needs of students with communication disorders in the regular classroom.
- For mainstreamed students with speech disorders, the general education teacher provides an accepting classroom environment in which students can feel comfortable practicing newly acquired communication skills.
- For mainstreamed students with language disorders, the classroom teacher assists their acquisition of language skills by modeling appropriate grammar and helping them expand their listening and speaking vocabularies. Classroom activities and assignments that require language skills may need to be modified.
- Students with autism have challenging communication needs; when these students are mainstreamed, teachers should receive support from special educators and other professionals.

ACTIVITIES

1. Interview a speech-language pathologist to find out more about students with communication disorders. Ask this professional to describe his or her caseload. How many students does he or she serve? What are their ages and typical problems? Are most students mainstreamed for the majority of the day? If so, what effects do their speech and language disorders have on their performance in the regular classroom?

2. Locate one of the journals that deals primarily with communication disorders. You might select the *Journal of Speech and Hearing Disorders, Journal of Speech and Hearing Research,* or *Language, Speech, and Hearing Services in the Schools.* Look through recent issues for articles that present suggestions for encouraging oral communication and teaching language skills. Do you find any ideas that could be used in the regular classroom?

3. The major professional organization in the field of communication disorders is the American Speech-Language-Hearing Association (ASHA). Its national headquarters are located at 10801 Rockville Pike, Rockville, MD 20852. Write to ASHA to find out more about this organization. Or talk with a speech-language pathologist or audiologist who is an ASHA member.

4. Communication disorders can be found in persons of any age. Survey your community to locate agencies that provide services to adults with

speech and language problems. What types of services are available? How do these differ from the services offered by the public schools to children and adolescents?

5. In a group, try one or more of the simulations of communication disorders described in Table 12–1. Afterward, discuss your reactions to the following questions: What were the feelings of the person with the simulated speech or language disorder? Did he or she feel frustrated? Anxious? Angry? How did the listeners feel? Were they sympathetic? Impatient? Embarrassed? What recommendations can the group make to teachers of students with communication disorders?

13

Teaching Students with Physical and Health Impairments

■ Tim is a 16-year-old high school sophomore with spastic cerebral palsy. He is quite mobile with the aid of his braces and crutches; he is able to get from class to class, use the rest room, and eat in the lunchroom without assistance. Tim attends all general education classes during the day (except for adapted physical education) and is maintaining a B average this semester. He does not receive resource services, but the special education teacher is available to assist Tim's teachers when necessary. In class, Tim is allowed to use a portable computer and word processing program because his handwriting is poor; however, he is expected to complete assignments and exams within the usual time limits. Tim has been in general education classes since the first grade and has several friends at his high school. This semester he is taking the driver's education course, and he's very excited about getting his driver's license.

■ Maxine is 10 years old and in the fourth grade. She enjoys school and has many friends both at school and in her neighborhood. Every day Maxine must take the medication that has helped to control her epileptic seizures for the past 3 years. Despite this medication, she has grand mal seizures at school about once a month. Mrs. Emerick, Maxine's teacher, knows what to do when a seizure occurs, and she and the school nurse have explained the nature of Maxine's problem to the other students in the class. Although her classmates are quite understanding, Maxine worries about what they think when seizures occur. In the past year she has become more concerned about this problem, and she visits the school counselor once a week to talk about her feelings. In all other respects, Maxine is typical. She is a good student. She performs well in all school subjects and is particularly interested in science and math.

■ Hank is 13 years old and attends Madison Junior High School. When he was in the first grade, he suffered a spinal injury in a bike accident and now travels by wheelchair. He is able to get to all of his classes because some of the school's architectural barriers have been removed; for instance, a ramp has been built so that he can bypass the three steps up to the door of his English classroom. Hank missed much school during his elementary years and had difficulty acquiring reading skills. At present, he attends general education classes for the majority of the school day but continues to visit the special education teacher for assistance in reading. Hank is a sports enthusiast who keeps up with all the high school and professional teams. He attends an adapted physical education class but is often frustrated because he is not able to participate in many of the athletic activities in which he is interested. Hank has a small circle of close friends, and he is well liked by his teachers. He's an active participant in class discussions and usually maintains at least a C average. This semester he has had several medical appointments that have caused him to miss school at least one day each week; his grades have not yet suffered, but he is beginning to fall behind in some of his classes. We will take a look at a portion of Hank's IEP later in this chapter.

■ Students with physical and health impairments are an extremely heterogeneous group with a wide variety of conditions and diseases; **cerebral palsy**, paralysis, **epilepsy**, clubfoot, asthma, polio, **diabetes**, and allergies are just a few. Some physical and health impairments are **congenital**, that is, present at birth; others are acquired after birth through disease or injury. Physical and health problems can have grave, little, or no effect on school performance. Some students with physical and health impairments require no special adaptations; others need only modification of the physical environment. For others, it is necessary to adapt instructional activities in the general education classroom or to provide special instruction in areas of need, such as mobility, communication, and basic skills. Students with similar impairments may have very different special needs; one student with lower-limb paralysis may be active and outgoing, whereas another may be withdrawn and unwilling to interact with others.

Teachers often believe that it is necessary to create a protective environment for students with physical and health impairments. However, such an environment discourages the development of skills necessary for independence. Dependency is one of the greatest problems of these special students, and teachers must take care not to add to this difficulty. Expectations for students with physical and health impairments should be realistic and geared toward the actual capabilities of the individual students. The goal for these students is the same as that for any other students: the development of skills that lead to independence.

This chapter describes the characteristics of mainstreamed students with physical and health impairments and presents methods for the general education teacher to use in gathering assessment data and modifying classroom procedures and activities to meet special needs. "Exceptional Literature" includes fictional, biographical, and professional books to help teachers and students become more familiar with the problems encountered by individuals with health disorders and physical impairments.

INDICATORS OF PHYSICAL AND HEALTH IMPAIRMENTS

The general education teacher is an important member of the mainstreaming team for those with physical and health impairments. Depending on the nature of the student's problem, the general education teacher may be involved in a variety of activities. He or she can help identify a physical or health impairment, provide the mainstreaming team with information about the student's current classroom performance, or take primary responsibility for the education and management of the student. In the general education classroom, a range of possible adaptations may be necessary; these include additional instruction for students with frequent absences, modification of the physical environment to allow mobility, and adaptations of instructional materials and activities.

Some students with physical and health impairments begin their school careers with an identified disability. With others, the problem is first noted after they enter school, or it may result from an accident or disease that occurs during the school years. Because students in this group may have many different physical disabilities and health problems that

EXCEPTIONAL LITERATURE
Physical and Health Impairments

FICTION AND BIOGRAPHY

Mornings on Horseback by D. McCullough (New York: Simon & Schuster, 1981). A biographical account of the childhood and youth of Theodore Roosevelt, who was plagued by recurrent asthma attacks; a sensitive picture of the effects of asthma on the child and his family.

Death Be Not Proud: A Memoir by J. Gunther (New York: Harper & Row, 1949). A father's story of the death of his teenage son from a brain tumor; the boy himself speaks in letters to friends and in the diary he kept throughout his illness.

I Raise My Eyes to Say Yes by R. Sienkiewicz-Mercer and S. B. Kaplan (New York: Avon Books, 1989). The autobiography of Ruth Sienkiewicz-Mercer, a young woman with cerebral palsy who spent most of her school years institutionalized in a state hospital. She tells of her many frustrations in this situation and her eventual success in bridging the communication gap by means of communication boards and electronic devices.

Mark by J. Hoyle (South Bend, IN: Diamond Communications, 1988). Mark was a hemophiliac who developed acquired immune deficiency syndrome (AIDS) from a transfusion and died as a teenager. This story, written by Mark's uncle, describes Mark's bravery in dealing with his disease and how the community reacted to his situation in a reasonable fashion and grew to accept his condition.

Nicholas and Alexandra by R. K. Massie (New York: Dell, 1967) and ***Journey*** by R. Massie and S. Massie (New York: Warner Brooks, 1975). *Nicholas and Alexandra* is the account of the last czar and empress of Russia and their firstborn son, who had hemophilia. In *Journey* Robert and Suzanne Massie tell about their own life and the effect of their only son's hemophilia.

A Brief History of Time: From the Big Bang to Black Holes by S. W. Hawking (New York: Bantam Books, 1988). Stephen Hawking is a world-renowned theoretical physicist who speaks and writes using a small personal computer mounted on his wheelchair. Although Professor Hawking speaks briefly in this book of his battle with Lou Gehrig's disease, his major purpose is to convey to a general audience his theories about the nature of the universe and its origins. In his view, his disability has not been a serious handicap because theoretical physics "is all in the mind" (p. vii).

There is a plentiful supply of children's literature about physical disabilities and health impairments. These books feature heroes and heroines who travel by wheelchair:

- ***Nick Joins In*** by J. Lasker (Chicago: Albert Whitman & Company, 1980), primary grades
- ***Howie Helps Himself*** by J. Fassler (Chicago: Albert Whitman & Company, 1975), primary grades
- ***Arnie and the New Kid*** by N. Carlson (New York: Viking, 1990), primary grades
- ***Princess Pooh*** by K. M. Muldoon (Chicago: Albert Whitman & Company, 1989), primary grades

can serve as impairments, it is not possible to make a single list of signs or symptoms that identify this group. The glossary of terms in "For Your Information" describes several of the most common physical and health impairments.

Knowledge about a student's physical or health problem does not provide educators with much information about instructional programming. As Reynolds and Birch (1988) point out:

a. The names of the medical conditions give few clues to individual special education needs;

b. only a minority of children with these conditions have any special education needs at all; and

c. there is no educational justification for grouping these children in school by their medical diagnoses. (p. 269)

As with other special students, it is necessary to go beyond the label and consider the individual needs of the student.

FIGURE 13–3
IEP Goals and Services for Hank

Annual Goals

1. By the end of the school year, Hank will demonstrate the basic skills necessary to participate in two group-oriented recreational activities.

    Person responsible: Adapted physical education teacher

2. By the end of the school year, Hank will participate in 4 hours of self-directed recreational activity each week.

    Person responsible: Adapted physical education teacher

3. By the end of the school year, Hank will read materials at the sixth grade level with adequate word recognition and comprehension.

    Person responsible: Resource teacher

4. Hank will successfully complete eighth grade math, English, social studies, and science.

    Persons responsible: Eighth grade teachers

Amount of Participation in Regular Classes

Hank will attend regular eighth grade classes in math, English, social studies, and science.

Special Education and Related Services

1. Hank will receive special education services from the adapted physical education teacher (annual goals 1 and 2) for one period per day.

2. Hank will receive special education services from the resource teacher (annual goal 3) for one period per day.

3. The resource teacher, adapted physical education teacher, and school nurse will provide consultation to Hank's eighth grade teachers as needed.

ADAPTATIONS FOR MAINSTREAMING

When students with physical and health impairments enter the general education classroom, one of the teacher's first tasks is to learn about their disabilities. Other students must also become aware of the problems of special students and learn about possible ways of helping these students function as independently as possible. In addition, it may be necessary to adapt portions of the general education program to allow full participation of students with physical and health impairments. The areas in which modifications are usually required are the arrangement of the physical environment and the format and structure of instructional activities and assignments.

The following sections of this chapter describe methods for meeting physical and health needs in the general education classroom, modifying the physical environment, and adapting instructional activities. For students with specific needs in academic instruction, the teacher should refer to the

FOR YOUR INFORMATION

Students with Physical and Health Impairments

- The U.S. Department of Education (1993) indicated that 51,690 students (aged 3 to 21) with orthopedic impairments and 58,880 with other health impairments received special education services in the 1991–1992 school year.
- According to Reynolds and Birch (1982) "for every 20 children with medically significant conditions, perhaps 4 or 5 of them will be in need of special educational programming" (p. 301).
- Over 50,000 children between the ages of 1 and 14 are permanently crippled and disabled by accidents each year (Telford & Sawrey, 1981).
- In the school-aged population, 1 in 500 students is hospitalized each year because of a head injury; head injuries are most common in males and in students between the ages of 15 and 24 (Mira & Tyler, 1991). Approximately 16% of hospital admissions in pediatrics are due to head trauma (Tucker & Colson, 1992).
- It is estimated that students with physical and health impairments make up less than 1% of the school-aged population; they account for only about 2.4% of the students with disabilities who receive special education services (U.S. Department of Education, 1993).
- Cerebral palsy is one of the most complex of all physical disabilities; because it results from damage to the brain, other areas of functioning including speech, vision, hearing, and intelligence can also be affected. However, there is no relationship between the extent of physical impairment and intellectual performance; individuals with severe motor involvement may be intellectually gifted.
- At the end of 1991 over 3,420 children under the age of 13 had been diagnosed as having AIDS in the United States (Seidel, 1992). About 80% of these children were infected by their mothers during pregnancy and about 19% received contaminated blood products during transfusions (Byrom & Katz,

methods suggested for students with learning disabilities and mild retardation. If classroom behavior is a concern, the suggestions provided for students with behavioral disorders might prove helpful.

Reynolds and Birch (1988) point out that students with physical and health impairments "seldom need to be taught material that is outside the curriculum for all other pupils" (p. 281). That is, the general education curriculum with its emphasis on academic skills is appropriate. However, several additional curriculum areas may benefit students

with physical and health impairments. Mobility training (instruction in planning travel within the school building) may help some students conserve their limited energy. For secondary students, continued instruction in writing skills (handwriting, typing, or using computers and word processors) may be necessary. Other possible areas of benefit are driver's training, recreation and use of leisure time, and sex education. In many cases, these additions to the general education curriculum are offered as part of the student's special education program.

1991). While their educational needs are very similar to other students of similar age and ability, some interesting challenges are presented to educators serving this population of students because their right to participate alongside their peers in an educational program has often been questioned. The rights of these students to an appropriate education have been protected by the due process provisions of PL 94-142 and the courts (Zirkel, 1989) as well as the provisions of Section 504 of the Rehabilitation Act.

- Different, and relatively new, diseases such as Lyme disease, Tourette's syndrome, or Reyes syndrome appear periodically (Sklaire, 1989). Lyme disease, which results from the bite of a deer tick, was first noticed in the 1970s. It starts with a rash and can lead to swollen joints and stiffness; complications can affect the heart and nervous system. Tourette's syndrome is a rare motor disorder that typically affects children between the ages of 2 and 15. While its cause is not known, it appears to be related to a chemical imbalance; youngsters with Tourette's syndrome are characterized by involuntary movements and behavior similar to students with ADHD. Reyes syndrome can result from administering aspirin to children and youth with flu or chicken pox, and it can be fatal. Education regarding the use of alternates to aspirin has led to a reduction in the number of cases of Reyes syndrome.

- Most students with physical and health impairments spend the majority of the school day in the regular classroom; many of these students also receive special education services from a resource teacher or other specialist(s), such as a physical therapist, occupational therapist, or adapted physical education teacher.

- Many famous people have had physical and health impairments, including several presidents of the United States: Theodore Roosevelt was asthmatic, Franklin Delano Roosevelt suffered from polio, and John F. Kennedy was plagued by back problems.

MEETING PHYSICAL AND HEALTH NEEDS

Students' physical and health needs are an important area of concern to any teacher. Students with identified physical and health impairments often require special diets, have restrictions placed on their physical activities, or take medication during the school day. The teacher's first step in meeting special physical and health needs is to learn as much as possible about each student's limitations and capabilities. One source of information is the assessment data collected by the mainstreaming team. Recent evaluations will describe the current functioning levels of the student in important areas such as mobility, communication, academic achievement, classroom behavior, and social skills. Cross (1993) suggests that teachers contact a student's parents and the professionals who have worked with that student in the past to find out the best ways to meet physical and health needs. Figure 13–4 lists questions that teachers can ask to find out more about a student's specific requirements.

FIGURE 13–4
Questions to Ask About Physical and Health Needs

Medical Concerns

- In addition to the child's primary disorder, does the child have additional problems such as seizures or diabetes? Does the child have any sensory disorders?
- Does the child take medication? How frequently, and in what amounts?
- If medication is taken, is the school authorized to administer the medication during school hours?
- What are the expected side effects of the medication? What are the other possible side effects?
- What procedures should be followed in the event of a seizure, insulin shock, diabetic coma, or other problem, with regard to contacting the child's parents or medical personnel?
- Should the child's activities be restricted in any way?

Travel

- How will the child be transported to school?
- Will the child arrive at the usual time?
- Will someone need to meet the child at the entrance to the school to provide assistance in getting the child on and off the vehicle?
- Will the child need special accommodations to travel within the school building or the classroom?

Transfer and Lifting

- What methods are used to get the child on and off the school bus?
- What is the preferred way to lift and transfer the child out of a wheelchair and onto a chair or to the floor?
- What cautions or limitations are there regarding transfer and lifting?
- How much help does the child really need with movement and transfer?

Communication

- If the child does not communicate verbally, what particular or unique means of communication does the child use?
- Does the child have a speech or language problem?

- Does the child use gestures? If so, what are they? Is a pointer used? Does the child use the same signal consistently for *yes, no,* or other common words?
- Can the child write? Type? How?
- Is an electronic communication aid used? If so, are there any special instructions necessary for the child to use it or for the teacher to understand and maintain it? Are fresh batteries or a charger needed?
- Can the child make his or her needs known to the teacher? How?

Self-Care

- What types of help does the child need with self-care activities such as feeding, dressing, toileting, and so forth?
- What equipment, such as a special feeding tray, does the child need?

Positioning

- What positioning aids or devices (braces, pillows, wedges, etc.) does the child use?
- What particular positions are the most useful for specific academic activities? What positions for resting?
- What positions are best for toileting, feeding, dressing, and other activities?
- Are there any other special aids or devices that I should know about?

Educational Needs

- What is the child's current level of achievement and of developmental and vocational functioning?
- What are the child's strengths and weaknesses?
- To what extent is achievement in school affected by physical disabilities?
- What medical considerations must be taken into account (that is, to what extent is the child able to participate in classroom activities)?
- What physical modifications to the classroom need to be made?
- What special equipment must be acquired?
- What related services will be needed?

Note. From *An Introduction to Special Education* 3rd ed. by William H. Berdine and Edward Blackhurst. Copyright © 1993 by HarperCollins College Publishers. Reprinted by permission.

Medical personnel such as the school nurse and the student's physician are another excellent source of information. Typically the school nurse helps the mainstreaming team interpret medical reports and translate medical findings into educationally relevant information. The nurse might explain why certain students have activity restrictions, how different medications affect students' classroom behavior, and what the reasons are for medical treatments and procedures. The nurse can also help teachers learn to deal with unusual medical situations, such as epileptic seizures in the classroom. If teachers are aware of the proper procedures to follow should a seizure occur, they will face the situation more calmly and be of more assistance to the student and the student's peers. To learn about what to do in case of a seizure, see "Tips for the Teacher."

When teachers are fully aware of the physical and health needs of special students, the next step is consideration of what information to provide to other students in the class. This issue should be discussed with the mainstreaming team, including the student's parents and, if appropriate, the student. In some cases, parents and students may be reluctant to have teachers inform students in the general education class about the specific nature of the problem. However, with disabilities and conditions that are obvious to a student's peers, the general education teacher or the school nurse should prepare the class by explaining the impairment and the ways in which it will affect the student's participation in class activities. Older special students may want to give this explanation themselves. This approach should be encouraged because these students, as adults, will often have occasion to explain their disabilities to friends, acquaintances, and potential employers.

Information about physical and health needs should be presented factually, with emphasis not only on the student's problems but also the student's abilities. Any questions peers might have should be answered openly and accurately. This sharing of information is particularly important with young students, who may wonder whether needing to ride in a wheelchair is contagious or whether being naughty causes seizures. The teacher should anticipate such concerns and attempt to quell apprehensions with a matter-of-fact explanation.

One subject that many teachers find difficult to discuss with their students is death. If there is a child or adolescent in the class with a terminal illness, this discussion may become necessary. Some thoughts on death education are presented in Figure 13–5. Other sources of information that may also be of interest are "Death in My Classroom?" by Postel (1986) or *Death Education: A Concern for the Living* by Gibson, Roberts, and Buttery (1982).

To accommodate the physical and health needs of mainstreamed special students, alterations in some classroom routines and procedures may be necessary. These students should not be automatically excused from classroom activities simply because they have a disability. However, if there are medical restrictions that prevent participation or if their disabilities truly impose limits, then classroom standards should be changed. Examples of appropriate modifications appear here:

- If students in wheelchairs or those with mobility problems travel slowly, they can be dismissed a few minutes early from class so that they can arrive at their next class or activity on time.
- Students should be allowed to take breaks during the day if these are necessary for rest, a visit to the bathroom, medication, or a special diet.
- There should be classroom procedures for emergency situations. For example, in the case of a fire drill, someone should be assigned the responsibility of making certain that students with mobility problems are assisted in leaving the classroom quickly.
- For some students, it is hard to follow dietary or activity restrictions. The student who is on a low-carbohydrate diet may want to eat candy; one who is restricted to short exercise periods may want to join the others playing football at recess. These students should be provided with attractive alternatives to help them adhere to their medical regimens. For instance, instead of snacks for classroom rewards, activities can be used as reinforcers; or if students are unable to play sports, they can be appointed coaching assistants to the teacher.

Students with physical and health impairments may require some assistance, but it is equally important that these students be offered opportuni-

What to Do for Seizures

When tonic-clonic (also known as grand mal) seizures occur in the classroom, the teacher should remain calm, assist the child with the seizure, and assure the other students that their classmate is not in pain and that the seizure will last only a few minutes.

The Epilepsy Foundation of America (1987) suggests that the teacher take the following steps to safeguard the student having a tonic-clonic seizure:

- Keep calm. Reassure the other students that the child will be fine in a minute.
- Ease the child to the floor and clear the area around him of anything that could hurt him.
- Put something flat and soft (like a folded coat) under his head so it will not bang on the floor as his body jerks.
- You cannot stop the seizure. Let it run its course. Do not try to revive the child and do not interfere with his movements.
- Turn him gently on his side. This keeps his airway clear and allows saliva to drain away.
    DON'T try to force his mouth open.
    DON'T try to hold his tongue.
    DON'T put anything in his mouth.
- When the jerking movements stop, let the child rest until he regains consciousness.
- Breathing may be shallow during the seizure, and may even stop briefly. In the unlikely event that breathing does not begin again, check the child's airway for obstruction and give artificial respiration.

Some students recover quickly after this type of seizure; others need more time. A short period of rest is usually advised. If the student is able to remain in the classroom afterwards, however, he or she should be encouraged to do so. Staying in the classroom (or returning to it as soon as possible) allows for continued participation in classroom activity and is psychologically less difficult for the student. If a student has frequent seizures, handling them can become routine once the teacher and classmates learn what to expect.

---

ties to learn to function independently. Often it is quicker and easier for the teacher or peers to do things for these students rather than allow them to do things for themselves. For example, a student may take 5 minutes to put on a jacket, whereas, with assistance, only a few seconds are required. However, such skills are acquired only with practice, and another's help may really hinder learning.

MODIFYING THE PHYSICAL ENVIRONMENT

One major consideration in the education of students with physical and health impairments is the physical environment of the classroom and school. For some students with mobility problems, this may be the prime area in which modifications must be

A child once wrote a letter to God:

> Dear God,
> What is it like to die?
> Nobody ever told me.
> I just want to know.
> I don't want to do it.
>   Your friend, Harry

This letter points out two important needs of children: (1) "nobody ever told me," people are reluctant to talk about death, and (2) "I don't want to do it," children feel anxiety about death.

- A challenge to teachers and parents is to put the thought and experience of death into the context of living. In this way, much of the child's fears and anxiety may be alleviated.

- Proper death education enhances the child's joy of life. Death education can reduce the child's fear of death thereby increasing the joy of living.

- Death education works to improve the quality of the child's total life span, birth, living, process of dying and death . . . .

What Can Teachers Do?

- The role of the teacher in death education is to disseminate the results of scientific studies and to facilitate the child's acceptance of death.

- What a teacher should do in any specific situation cannot be known for there are too many variables. The best thing one can bring to a terminally ill student is one's self. Every teacher, therefore, needs to clarify an individual philosophy for working with terminally ill students . . . .

made. The following guidelines should help ensure that the physical environment is suitably arranged to accommodate students with disabilities:

- Evaluate the school and classroom for accessibility. Architectural barriers that restrict the travel of students in wheelchairs or students with physical limitations may prevent their full participation in the educational program. The most brilliant student cannot benefit from the best of programs if stairs are the only route to the classroom and the student uses a wheelchair. Use the checklist in "Tips for the Teacher" to evaluate the accessibility of your school building. If problems are evident, bring these to the attention of the school principal and the mainstreaming team.

What Teachers Need to Know

The dying child goes through a number of stages before accepting death. These stages may be experienced simultaneously; not every child experiences all of them. It is important that the child experience some of them if death is to be accepted. The stages and conjectured positive contributions are as follows:

1. *Shock and disbelief*—This serves as a temporary anesthesia holding the child's sense of self-esteem together for a brief time.

2. *Crying (sometimes hysterical)*—This usually provides the needed emotional release.

3. *Feelings of isolation and loneliness*—This may help the child feel the need for others and to experience the discomfort which alienation brings. A degree of personal untidiness may be observed at this stage.

4. *Psychosomatic symptoms*—This may momentarily deviate the child's attention from the fatal prognosis to lesser conditions.

5. *Panic*—This pushes the child to explore all possibilities and to eventually accept the fact that the dying process is occurring.

6. *Guilt feelings*—This eventually enables the child to accept the fact that nobody is to blame and that the process of dying is unlikely to be reversed.

7. *Hostility-resentment*—The child attempts to defend and protect his ego by projecting these negative feelings onto teachers, parents and friends.

8. *Resists usual routine*—The child questions the worth and complains of the difficulty in doing everyday activities in an effort to come to terms with the requirements for continued living.

9. *Reconciliation*—This very positive stage enables the child to avoid feelings of hopelessness and to begin the process of accepting the inevitability of death.

10. *Acceptance*—The child struggles to adjust to the reality that death is happening and that there is living and work yet to be accomplished. The child becomes a deeper more profound person—young in years but old in experience.

Note. From "What Parents and Teachers Should Know about Death Education" by R. Berner, 1977, *DOPHHH Journal, 3*, pp. 17–21. Copyright 1977 by DOPHHH, The Council for Exceptional Children. Reprinted with permission.

- Arrange the classroom to facilitate mobility. Be sure sufficient room is allowed for students in wheelchairs or those who use crutches to travel from one work area to another.
- Make all areas and activities within the general education classroom accessible to students with mobility problems. This includes chalkboards, bookcases, storage cupboards, coat racks, art supplies, bulletin boards, display cases, computers, audio visual equipment, activity centers, and so on.
- Consider the seating arrangements for special students. Those in wheelchairs may need a special table or lapboard to write on. Others may require special chairs that provide extra support; for instance, arm- or footrests can help students maintain an upright position for reading and writ-

TIPS FOR THE TEACHER

Checking Your School for Accessibility

Sidewalks

Are there curb cuts which provide access?

Is there a width of at least 48"?

Are they level, without irregular surfaces?

Is there a level area 5' by 5' if the door swings in?

Ramps

Are handrails present (32" high)?

Is the grade of the ramp [less] than a 1" rise in every 12' length?

Does it have a non-slip surface in all types of weather?

Doors (including elevator)

Is there an opening of at least 32" when door is open?

Are floors level for 5' in both directions of the door?

Are the thresholds navigable (1/2")?

Floor

Do hallways, stairs, and class areas have carpeting or some other non-slip surface?

Toilets

Is one stall 3' wide by 4'8" deep with handrails 33" high?

Is the toilet seat 20" high and urinals 19" from floor?

Are sinks, towel dispensers, mirrors, etc. 36–40" from floor?

Water fountains

Are the controls hand operated?

Is the spout in the front of the unit?

Are they mounted 26–30" from the floor?

Note. From "Environmental Alternatives for the Physically Handicapped" by B. B. Greer, J. Allsop, and J. G. Greer in *Implementing Learning in the Least Restrictive Environment* (pp. 128–129) by J. W. Schifani, R. M. Anderson, and S. J. Odle (Eds.), 1980, Austin, TX: PRO-ED. Copyright 1980 by PRO-ED. Reprinted by permission.

ing activities. Check with the school nurse, special education teacher, or physical therapist for specific information about the positioning needs of each student.

- Provide storage space for students' aids and equipment. For example, crutches should be within their owner's easy reach without presenting a hazard to others moving about the classroom. One method is to use crutch holders on the back or sides of a student's chair.
- Be sure that special equipment is kept in good working order. Check wheelchairs periodically for proper fit, comfort, and good repair. Figure 13–6 presents a checklist from *Wheelchair Prescriptions* (1968, 1976) that can be used for regular inspections. If there is need for modification or repair, notify the student's parents or the special educator who works with the student.
- For students with crutches, Glazzard (1982) suggests chairs with wheels to facilitate movement about the classroom; an office chair on rollers is appropriate. In rooms without carpets, crutches can slip when students use them to help themselves up from a sitting position. If assistance is needed, show their peers in the general education class how to use their foot as a brace to prevent the crutch from slipping.
- Students with limited strength or poor coordination may need easy access to work equipment. Desks with open storage space are preferable to those with a lid that must be raised. Pencil grooves on the desk top or a small box to hold pencils, pens, and erasers can help keep work materials close at hand.

ADAPTING INSTRUCTIONAL ACTIVITIES

In addition to meeting physical and health needs and modifying the classroom environment, it may also be necessary to adapt instructional activities and procedures. Glazzard (1982) suggests several ideas for assisting students with poor coordination or inadequate muscle control:

- Tape the student's paper to the desk with a piece of masking tape applied to the top and bottom of the paper.
- Attach one end of a string to a pencil and the other end to the desk with a thumbtack or masking tape so that a student can easily retrieve a dropped pencil.
- Appoint a student to bring teacher handouts to the student's desk.
- Allow students to answer questions orally, or have them record answers for later evaluation. It is often laborious for some...students [with disabilities] to write their answers. If they have poor muscle control in their hands they must exert much more energy than the...[typical] students to write their answers.
- Make a copy of your lecture notes for the child with disabilities who writes slowly or with difficulty. It would also be simple for a classmate to insert a sheet of carbon paper under his or her paper so that a duplicate set of notes can be supplied to the . . . student [with disabilities].
- Provide . . . students [with disabilities] with plastic or wooden rulers to use as bookmarks. They are easier to manipulate than paper markers.
- A . . . child [with disabilities] may use a shoulder bag to carry books and supplies from class to class. The book bag leaves arms free to handle crutches. (pp. 7–8)

Be creative, but remember that simple modifications are sometimes all that's necessary. Don't use clamps and tape if a paperweight will work just as well.

Many of the technological aids available to assist mainstreamed students with physical and health impairments have been described in chapter 8. These devices help students compensate for the effects of their disabilities on mobility, communication, and academic learning. See "Spotlight on Technology" for more information about switches and how these simple devices can provide access to a wide variety of activities in the classroom, at home, and in the community.

Some mainstreamed students may require further adaptations in instruction in order to keep pace in the general education classroom. When students miss school because of illness or medical treatment,

FIGURE 13–6
Wheelchair Checklist

	No	Yes	Comments
I. With the student out of the wheelchair			
A. Arms			
1. Are the armrests and side panels secure and free of sharp edges and cracks?			
2. Do the armlocks function properly?			
B. Backs			
1. Is the upholstery free of rips and tears?			
2. Is the back taut from top to bottom?			
3. Is safety belt attached tightly and not frayed?			
C. Seat and frame			
1. Is the upholstery free of rips and tears?			
2. Does the chair fold easily without sticking?			
3. When the chair is folded fully are the front post slides straight and round?			
D. Wheel locks			
1. Do the wheel locks securely engage the tire surfaces and prevent the wheel from turning?			
E. Large wheels			
1. Are the wheels free from wobble or sideplay when spun?			
2. Are the spokes equally tight and without any missing spokes?			
3. Are the tires free from excessive wear and gaps at the joined section?			
F. Casters			
1. Is the stem firmly attached to the fork?			
2. Are the forks straight on sides and stem so that the caster swivels easily?			
3. Is the caster assembly free from excessive play both up and down as well as backward and forward?			
4. Are the wheels free of excessive play and wobble?			
5. Are the tires in good condition?			
G. Footrest/Legrest			
1. Does the lock mechanism fit securely?			
2. Are the heel loops secure and correctly installed?			
3. Do the footplates fold easily and hold in any position?			
4. Are the legrest panels free of cracks and sharp edges?			

	No	Yes	Comments
II. With the student sitting in the chair			
A. Seat width			
1. When your palms are placed between the patient's hip and the side of the chair (skirtguard), do the hands contact the hip and the skirtguard at the same time without pressure?			
2. Or, is the clearance between the patient's widest point of either hips or thigh and the skirtguard approximately 1 inch on either side?			
B. Seat depth			
1. Can you place your hand, with fingers extended, between the front edge of the seat upholstery and to the rear of the knee with a clearance for three or four fingers?			
2. Or, is the seat upholstery approximately 2 to 3 inches less than the student's thigh measurement?			
C. Seat height and footrest			
1. Is the lowest part of the stepplates no closer than 2 inches from the floor?			
2. Or, is the student's thigh elevated slightly above the front edge of the seat upholstery?			
D. Arm height			
1. Does the arm height not force the shoulders up or allow them to drop significantly when in a normal sitting position?			
2. Is the elbow positioned slightly forward of the trunk midline when the student is in a normal sitting position?			
E. Back height			
1. Can you insert four or five fingers between the patient's armpit area and the top of the back upholstery touching both at the same time?			
2. Is the top of the back upholstery approximately 4 inches below the armpit for the student who needs only minimum trunk support?			
III. With the student pushing or riding in the wheelchair			
A. Is the wheelchair free from squeaks or rattles?			
B. Does the chair roll easily without pulling to either side?			
C. Are the large wheels and casters free of play and wobble?			

Note. From *Wheelchair Prescriptions: Measuring the Patient* and *Wheelchair Prescriptions: Care and Service* by Everest and Jennings, Los Angeles: Author. Copyright 1968 and 1976 by Everest and Jennings. Adapted by permission.

Switch Access

*B*ecause of physical impairments, some students cannot grip a pencil or pen, hold a book or turn its pages, or play with toys designed for typical children. However, students can access these activities if they have voluntary control over at least one type of motor movement. That movement can involve any part of the body: lifting a finger, raising an eyebrow, moving a hand outward from the body, pressing downward with a foot, or blowing through a tube. Movements such as these allow students to operate a switch, and switches can control a number of different types of devices.

There are many types of switches, but each requires only a single action. With some switches, the student pushes or pulls; with others, he or she pinches or squeezes, sucks or blows, changes the position of a body part, or makes a small muscle movement such as flexing the muscles in a hand. Switches requiring a pushing motion are most common:

Note.   Photo courtesy of AbleNet Inc.

Students who are switch users can control toys, appliances, and even the lights in their home or classroom (Lewis, 1993). Here are some examples:

- *Battery-operated toys* can be converted for switch use by adding a device called a battery adapter. Also, companies such as Toys for Special Children sell toys adapted for switch users.
- *Electrical appliances* can be accessed by switch with a device such as the AbleNet PowerLink2 Control Device. The appliance and the switch are plugged into the control device and it in turn is plugged into a wall socket. With this configuration, a student could press the switch to turn on a radio or television, blender, hair dryer, or fan.
- *Slide projectors* can be operated by switch with a special adapter. By pressing the switch, the student moves to the next slide.

- *Automatic pageturners* hold a book or magazine, then turn its pages when the reader presses a switch.
- Some *environmental control devices* can be operated by switch. Options these devices offer include turning on lights and appliances, automatically dialing the telephone, and automatically releasing a door lock.
- Some *electronic communication devices* accept switch input. To select a message, the student presses the switch rather than a key on the device's keyboard.
- *Computers* can also be adapted for switch users.

Computer Adaptations

Students who respond by switch can interact with computers in one of two ways. The first method requires a switch, a switch interface device (used to connect the switch to the computer), and special software. This software must be specifically designed to accept switch input. For example, Don Johnston Incorporated offers a number of switch-operated programs for young students and those with severe disabilities. However, switch programs are not available in all subject areas for all ages; in fact, the collection is quite small compared to the number of programs on the market for typical learners.

The second method allows switch users to access any software, including that designed for typical learners. This method requires a switch, any software program, and a special control device such as the Adaptive Firmware Card (AFC) (Don Johnston Incorporated) for Apple II series computers or Ke:nx (Don Johnston Incorporated) for the Macintosh. These devices allow the switch to control the computer in the same way that the keyboard and mouse do.

Ke:nx allows students to "type" letters by pressing a switch.

Note.   Photo courtesy of Don Johnston Incorporated.

With the AFC or Ke:nx, a small window containing an array of choices is added to the computer screen. For example, if a student was using Ke:nx with a word processor, this array might appear at the bottom of the screen:

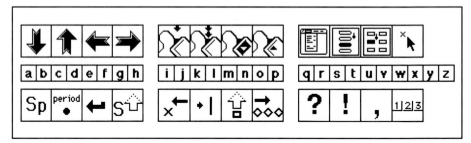

Note. By permission of Don Johnston Incorporated.

The array contains the letter keys (in the middle row), mouse commands, special keys, punctuation marks, and numbers. The student makes choices through a process called scanning. The first row of the array is highlighted, then the second, then the third. The student presses the switch when the desired row is high-lighted. For example, to type the word *dog*, the student would press the switch when the second row was highlighted. Then, each of the three blocks of letters is highlighted in turn (first the block beginning with *abcd,* then that beginning with *ijkl,* etc.). When a block of letters has been selected, each of the letters within that block is highlighted (e.g., first *a,* then *b,* etc.).

Although scanning is a slow process, it is a powerful one because it allows students with severe physical disabilities to access any software program. The array that the student sees can be changed. Both Ke:nx and the AFC come with several preprogrammed arrays, and teachers can create new ones to meet the needs of individual students. For example, with Ke:nx, it is possible to create arrays with graphics for young children.

Word prediction programs are designed to speed up the writing process for students who word process by switch or those who tire easily when interacting with a keyboard. These programs attempt to predict what the writer will say next. The student starts the program, a small word prediction window appears on the screen, and the student types the first letter of the first word of the sentence. For example, the window shown at the top of the next page is from the *Co:Writer* program (Don Johnston Incorporated), and the sentence the student wants to write is "I went to the zoo last Saturday." To do this, the student types a lowercase *i* and the program predicts these choices:

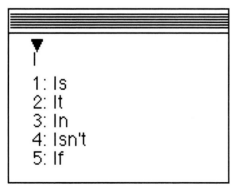

To accept the first choice (uppercase *I*), the student presses the switch. The first letter of the second word in the sentence *(w)* is then typed, and these choices appear:

To select *went* (choice number 2), the student waits until the program scans to that choice, then presses the switch. This process continues until the entire sentence is entered. If the program fails to predict the desired word, the student must enter the second letter of the word, then the third, and so on until his or her choice appears in the window. Many word prediction programs offer other short-cuts. For example, when a student selects one of the words the program predicts, the program adds a space at the end of the word. Also, common word endings (e.g., *-ing, -s, -er, -est, -ly*) are easily added. Some programs have the ability to remember students' word choices and store frequently used words in their prediction dictionaries.

extra instruction should be provided so that they do not fall far behind. For those who work slowly, the teacher can alter requirements for assignments and exams; more time can be allowed, or the amount of work can be reduced. If students have difficulty speaking or writing, other response modes can be substituted. For example, instead of writing, a student might type, tape-record, or dictate a response to a peer. By adapting instruction in these ways, the general education teacher creates a learning environment in which special students have every chance for success. For more information about adaptations for one group of students with physical and health impairments, those with traumatic brain injuries, see "Tips for the Teacher."

When a child or adolescent receives a head injury, the first interventions will be medical. It is likely that the student will be hospitalized for some period of time, then continue rehabilitation on an out-patient basis with professionals such as occupational and physical therapists. Depending on the length of hospitalization, the student may attend hospital school; once back at home, he or she may receive educational services from a teacher who visits several times a week. Planning the student's return to school requires a team approach; Mira and Tyler (1991) recommend collaboration between hospital staff, school personnel, and the student and his or her family. Consider, for example, the reentry plan developed for Barbara, a 16-year-old who sustained a severe head injury in an auto accident:

1. *Reduce course load:* Barbara enrolled in a limited number of academic courses with the understanding that others could be added.
2. *Special scheduling:* Barbara took her most taxing courses early in the day, when she was most alert.
3. *Resource room:* Barbara would begin and end the day in the resource room with an aide present to provide assistance.
4. *Rest breaks:* Barbara was allowed to rest in the nurse's office when she became fatigued.
5. *Adaptive physical education:* Barbara would receive adaptive PE with an aide present to assist her at all times, because of the danger of her falling.

6. *Student aide:* One of her friends would assist her in moving from one class to the next.
7. *Extra set of books:* Barbara was given an extra set of books to keep at home, to avoid having to carry them back and forth.
8. *Lunch room provisions:* Because Barbara was still physically unsteady, someone would carry her lunch tray and have her seated before the lunchroom crowds arrived.
9. *Counseling:* Meetings were scheduled with the school counselor, and she was given the option for other meetings as needed.
10. *Other modifications:* Barbara would be allowed to have someone take notes for her in her class and tape her lectures, and she would be able to take her exams in a setting other than the regular classroom, with extra time allowed. She also would have use of a computer to complete assignments.[*]

In this chapter, you have learned about the special needs of students with physical and health impairments. Methods for accommodating their disabilities within the general education classroom, modifying the physical environment, and adapting instructional activities have been suggested. The next chapter describes ways to mainstream students with sensory disabilities— those with vision and hearing impairments.

▬ ACTIVITIES

1. Use the checklist provided in "Tips for the Teacher" on page 402 to check the accessibility of one of your local public schools. Also consider whether instructional activities within the classroom are accessible. Can a student in a wheelchair write on the chalkboard? Remove a book from the bookcase? Hang up a coat? Use the classroom computer? If possible, borrow a wheelchair and

---

[*] From "Students with Traumatic Brain Injury: Making the Transition from Hospital to School" by M. P. Mira and J. S. Tyler, 1991, *Focus on Exceptional Children*, 23(5), p. 7. Copyright 1991 by Love Publishing Company. Reprinted with permission.

Working with Students with Traumatic Brain Injury

Students with traumatic brain injuries (TBIs) may have special needs in a variety of areas including physical, academic, social-emotional, and behavioral performance. Although teachers expect students who have received serious head injuries to experience difficulty with learning tasks (and, depending on the injury, with tasks requiring physical skills), they often do not anticipate the social-emotional consequences that can accompany this disability. Tucker and Colson (1992) describe the types of behaviors that some students with TBI may show:

- *Overestimates abilities*—Student brags to friends that he or she is still the fastest runner or will win the spelling bee.
- *Lowered social inhibition and judgment*—Student tries to touch and hug everyone.
- *Lowered impulse control*—Student interrupts teachers and peers at inappropriate times.
- *Faulty reasoning*—Student confronts peers and teachers with unfair accusations.
- *Lowered initiative*—Student will not begin a task without a reminder or assistance.
- *Depression*—Student appears uninterested and passive, even in activities once considered highly enjoyable. The emotional stress of the injury may be prolonged and can be overwhelming.
- *Fatigue*—This can be a result of both the injury and medication. Sleep disorders are common.
- *Acting-out behavior*—Student may yell or curse about being asked to do a task he or she doesn't want to do. He or she may walk out of class or knock over a desk.
- *Impulsivity*—Student may be unable to wait his or her turn at a drinking fountain or in the cafeteria. He or she may talk out during a test or speak before being called on.
- *Rigidity*—Student may be unable to adapt to changes in schedule or routine. Student may be unwilling to go to an assembly if it is scheduled during the regular math period.
- *Flat affect*—Student seems to have no voice inflections. Face seems expressionless, eyes seem vacant, he or she doesn't laugh or smile appropriately.
- *Low motivation*—What appears as low motivation may be confusion and inability to conceptualize and plan how to do the task.
- *Agitation and irritability*—Varying degrees of agitation and irritability may manifest themselves, such as becoming annoyed over picky things to becoming aggressive toward self or teachers.

Note. From "Traumatic Brain Injury: An Overview of School Re-Entry" by B. F. Tucker and S. E. Colson, 1992, *Intervention in School and Clinic, 27,* p. 201. Copyright 1992 by PRO-ED, Inc. Adapted with permission.

THINGS TO REMEMBER

■ The special needs of students with physical and health impairments are diverse and vary with each individual. Some students require no educational adaptations, some require modification of the physical environment because they have limited energy or mobility, and others require modification of instructional activities. However, the major goal for all of these students is circumvention of the restrictions imposed by their physical or health impairments.

■ There are a great many conditions that can produce special physical and health needs. Among the most common are traumatic brain injuries, epilepsy, cerebral palsy, diabetes, and asthma.

■ Some physical and health impairments are congenital, whereas others occur after birth and are due to injury, accident, or disease.

■ The primary purpose of assessing physical and health impairments is to gather information about the impact of the disabilities on educational performance and participation in instructional activities. It is also important to consider the effect of the disabilities on the development of social, vocational, and leisure skills. Medical information is useful only when it is interpreted in relation to classroom functioning.

■ One primary need of students with physical and health impairments is the opportunity to develop independence. Students should be encouraged to learn the skills necessary to assume responsibility for their own needs.

■ In the general education classroom, the teacher provides for physical and health needs, ensures an environment that is accessible, and accommodates learning difficulties by adapting instruction.

travel through the school and several classrooms to gain a better understanding of what environmental features can impose barriers.

2. Visit a school with a special education program for students with physical and health impairments. Talk with the teacher and find out what types of disorders the students have. Are most of the students mainstreamed? How are these students accepted by their peers? What adaptations are necessary in the general education classroom?

3. Interview a young person or adult with a physical or health impairment. What impact does this condition have on daily life? That is, how does it affect routine tasks such as eating, dressing, shopping, traveling, and working? How do others react to the disability, and how does the person with disabilities deal with these reactions?

4. Learn more about agencies and organizations in your community that provide services to those with physical and health impairments. You might consult the United Cerebral Palsy Association, Epilepsy Foundation of America, American Cancer Society, or National Easter Seal Society. What services do these agencies provide? How does one go about obtaining services?

5. Locate journal articles that present suggestions for mainstreaming students with physical and health impairments. Good places to look include special education journals and writings in the field of rehabilitation; try, for example, the *Journal of Rehabilitation* or *Rehabilitation Literature*.

14 Teaching Students with Vision and Hearing Impairments

■ Beverly is a 17-year-old junior in high school who has been blind since birth. She has attended general education classes since the first grade. She also has been active in choir, plays the guitar, and is in the drama club. This year, she attends general education classes for all of her academic subjects. In the regular physical education class, she excels in swimming and gymnastics. Beverly uses an electronic device to take class notes in braille, transfers those notes to her computer, and completes her assignments with a talking word processor. In math, she uses a talking calculator and, when materials for her classes are not available in tape-recorded or braille formats, two of her fellow students act as readers so that she can keep up with her reading assignments. Beverly receives special services from a mobility instructor who is helping her develop the skills needed to use public transportation to travel around town. An itinerant teacher of students with vision impairments provides assistance and special instructional materials to Beverly and also to her teachers when needed.

■ Morris is a third grader who is partially sighted; he spends the majority of his school day in a general education class. He is able to read large-print material if it is further enlarged through magnification. During the school day, Morris visits the resource room for an hour to use special magnification equipment and to obtain help in math. He has some social problems with other students, especially when they call attention to his thick glasses or call him "four eyes." The resource teacher provides special materials to the general education teacher, enlarges classroom worksheets and other papers, and is on call to assist with special needs as they arise. Goals and services from Morris's IEP will be presented later in this chapter.

■ Beatrice is a 10-year-old student who is hard of hearing and in the fourth grade. She acquired her moderate hearing loss two years ago as the result of an accident. Beatrice spends one period a day in the resource room getting help in speech, speechreading, and language. In the general education class, she is assisted by a careful seating arrangement, the teacher's awareness of her need to see him speaking, and her hearing aid. Beatrice had developed excellent speech before the accident and currently has little trouble communicating information to others. The students in her class accept Beatrice's hearing loss and have learned to talk directly and clearly to her.

■ Max is a high school sophomore who has a congenital hearing impairment that has resulted in a severe bilateral hearing loss. Max wears hearing aids that provide some assistance to him in understanding the speech of others. Although Max's reading and math skills are quite good, his speech, oral language, and written work are poor; his writing is characterized by incomplete sentences, errors in punctuation and word usage, and word omissions. Max attends general education classes; during two periods each day he works with the resource teacher of students with hearing impairments to improve his speechreading, oral and written language, and sign language skills. He is also learning to use a word processing program on a computer for written assignments. Max has an interpreter who attends general education classes with him; the interpreter helps Max understand lectures and class discussions and communicate with teachers and peers. Several of Max's friends have learned enough sign language to carry on simple conversations. Max hopes to graduate in two more years and then attend college. We will look at portions of Max's IEP later.

Each of the students just introduced has a specific and different hearing or vision impairment. They all, however, share a sensory loss. Such students can exhibit a wide range of abilities and can experience a variety of problems in school. Their vision and hearing impairments can be mild, moderate, or severe. Although their performance in most areas falls within a range similar to that of typical students, their school achievement is generally poorer than that expected for their age and grade. Students with vision impairments have difficulty with mobility and with reading print or other visual materials (Hazekamp & Huebner, 1989); those with hearing impairments experience problems in language development and oral communication (Luetke-Stahlman & Luckner, 1991). Both the degree of the disability and the specific characteristics of the student influence the nature and extent of the impairment.

Special education for students with sensory impairments may be provided in a special class or resource room; in many cases, students remain in the general education class and receive special instruction, materials, or equipment to supplement or enrich their educational program. The goal of special education for students with vision and hearing impairments is the same as it is for other students with disabilities—facilitation of learning. This may require teaching students to make use of remaining sensory abilities and/or helping them learn to use other abilities to compensate for their disabilities.

Students with vision impairments are taught to rely on unaffected senses, such as hearing and touch. For example, they may learn to read **braille**, to develop their listening skills, and to travel using **orientation** and **mobility** skills. For students with vision impairments with some usable vision, the educational program may include instruction in the use of **low vision aids**, such as magnification devices, large-print reading materials, and new technological devices. Students with hearing impairments may require instruction in speech and language, training in other communication systems such as **speechreading** and **sign language**, or assistance in learning to use and care for **amplification devices** such as hearing aids. It is generally necessary to provide **auditory training** to students with hearing impairments in order for them to develop listening skills by learning to use their residual hearing. In addition to the specific sensory needs of these students, adaptations in the general education classroom may be needed to give them the opportunity to participate in instructional activities and social interactions.

The characteristics of students with vision and hearing impairments, methods for gathering data and adapting the classroom environment, and instructional procedures for the general education teacher are described in this chapter. The publications described in "Exceptional Literature" can help familiarize teachers and students with the problems encountered by individuals with sensory impairments.

INDICATORS OF VISION AND HEARING IMPAIRMENTS

For students with vision and hearing impairments, the general education teacher plays an important role on the mainstreaming team. Many of these students are initially identified and referred for consideration for special education services by the general education classroom teacher. In addition, general education teachers assist in collecting information about their students' classroom performance and in coordinating the services provided by various specialists.

Vision and hearing impairments can be congenital or **adventitious**. An adventitious impairment is one that is acquired as a result of illness or accident. Students with severe impairments are generally identified by parents or a physician prior to entrance into school; those with impairments that are milder or that result from illness or accident may be identified during the school years. Students who acquire impairments after they have experienced normal vision or hearing (with normal development of speech and language) are usually affected less adversely than those whose impairments are present at birth.

The extent of a vision or hearing loss is determined only after all possible corrections have been made. If a sensory impairment can be corrected so that the student has adequate vision or hearing, then the student is not considered disabled and in need of special education. If impairments remain after

EXCEPTIONAL LITERATURE
Vision and Hearing Impairments

FICTION AND BIOGRAPHY

In This Sign by J. Greenberg (New York: Avon, 1970). This powerful novel about Abel and Janice Ryder, a couple who are deaf in a hearing world, clearly conveys the communication problems encountered by individuals who are deaf.

The Miracle Worker by W. Gibson (New York: Bantam, 1956). This play tells the story of Helen Keller (who was blind and deaf) and her teacher, Annie Sullivan; an excellent account of the effects of a child with disabilities on the family.

If You Could See What I Hear by T. Sullivan and D. Gill (New York: New American Library, 1975). Tom Sullivan was blinded as an infant by the oxygen in the incubator that saved his life; in this autobiography he tells of his experiences in school and college, as an athlete and musician, and as a husband and father.

Emma and I by S. Hocken (New York: New American Library, 1977). Sheila Hocken is a woman who is blind, and Emma is her seeing-eye dog; this book describes Sheila's childhood and schooling, her relationship with Emma, and the changes in her life when successful eye surgery gave her the ability to see.

Books for young readers include:

Handtalk Birthday by R. Charlip, M. B. Miller, and G. Ancona (New York: Aladdin Books, 1991). A storybook in words, photos, and sign language that includes the signs for numbers. (appropriate for primary grades and up)

A Cane in Her Hand by A. B. Litchfield (Chicago: Albert Whitman & Company, 1977). The story of Valerie, a young girl with low vision who learns to use a cane to help her travel from place to place. (primary/intermediate grades)

I'm Deaf and It's Okay by L. Aseltine, E. Mueller, and N. Tait (Chicago: Albert Whitman &

Company, 1986). A young boy tells about his life and the problems he experiences because he is deaf. (primary/ intermediate grades)

Words in Our Hands by A. B. Litchfield (Chicago: Albert Whitman & Company, 1980). Michael, Gina, and Diane's mother and father are deaf. Michael tells about the family's move to a new town. (intermediate grades)

Finding a Common Language by T. Bergman (Milwaukee, WI: Gareth Stevens Children's Books, 1989). Lina is a young girl who attends a special school for deaf children in Sweden; this book uses words and photos to describe a typical day in Lina's life. (intermediate grades)

Special Parents, Special Children by J. E. Bernstein and B. J. Fireside (Chicago: Albert Whitman & Company, 1991). Includes the story of Lisa whose father is blind and that of Angela, Vanessa, and Ryan whose mother and father are deaf. (primary/intermediate grades)

---

corrections have been made (e.g., eyeglasses, hearing aids, and all possible medical treatments, including surgery), then the student is considered to have a disability.

Students with vision impairments may be **blind** or **partially sighted**. These designations are based on measures of visual acuity and may have little educational relevance, just as an IQ score is not always an accurate predictor of academic achievement. Students who are blind are defined legally as (1) those whose visual acuity is 20/200 or less in the better eye with the best possible correction or (2) those whose

field of vision is restricted to an angle subtending an arc of 20 degrees or less (American Foundation for the Blind, 1961). A larger group is made up of students who are partially sighted, whose vision in the best eye is between 20/70 and 20/200 after correction. The designation of 20/200 roughly indicates that the individual can see at 20 feet what a person with normal vision can see at 200 feet. Grayson (n.d.) indicates that "the American Foundation for the Blind prefers that the term blindness be reserved for a complete loss which can accurately be determined by ophthalmic measurements" (p. 1).

PROFESSIONAL LITERATURE

Effectively Educating Students with Hearing Impairments by B. Luetke-Stahlman and J. Luckner (White Plains, NY: Longman, 1991). This textbook describes the characteristics and educational needs of students with hearing impairments. Included is information on working with the various professionals that serve individuals with hearing impairments and suggestions for teaching students with hearing impairments who are mainstreamed and working with their parents.

"Students with Hearing Loss" by W. W. Green and J. E. Fischgrund in *An Introduction to Special Education* (3rd ed., pp. 271–311) by A. E. Blackhurst and W. H. Berdine (Eds.) (New York: HarperCollins, 1993). This introductory chapter explains the way the ear works, types of hearing impairments and methods of evaluating them, and the effects of hearing impairments on students' performance and adjustment; it also provides an overview of the educational needs of students with hearing impairments and considerations for the teacher.

Educational Audiology across the Lifespan: Serving All Learners with Hearing Impairment by K. M. English (Baltimore: Brookes, 1995). This book describes the educational issues related to hearing impairment and provides suggestions for appropriate modifications for young children, students in grades K through 12, and college students and adults. It also includes information on students who have hearing losses in addition to other disabilities.

Mainstreaming and the American Dream: Sociological Perspectives on Parental Coping with Blind and Visually Impaired Children by H. L. Nixon II (New York: American Foundation for the Blind, 1991). Directed towards both parents and professionals, this book discusses important elements of programs serving students with vision impairments in mainstream settings.

Visual Handicaps and Learning (3rd ed.) by N. Barraga and J. N. Erin (Austin, TX: PRO-ED, 1992). An introduction to the problems of students with vision impairments; information is provided for both general and special education teachers on designing appropriate instructional settings and programs to accommodate the needs of these students.

When You Have a Visually Handicapped Child in Your Classroom: Suggestions for Teachers by I. Torres and A. L. Corn (New York: American Foundation for the Blind, 1990). Strategies and techniques to be used when mainstreaming students with vision impairments is the focus of this book. Included are answers to questions frequently asked by general education teachers and suggestions for planning and running an effective mainstreaming program. Single copies of this book are available free from the American Foundation for the Blind (15 W. 16th St., New York, NY 10011, 800-AFBLIND).

Legal terminology to describe vision impairments often lacks meaning for the educator. Instead, teachers are primarily concerned with assessing and developing a child's functional use of residual vision. Teachers need to know whether the student's remaining vision will allow learning with visually presented material, whether learning must be through other senses, or what combination of these approaches will be most beneficial. Many students who are legally blind are not considered **educationally blind**. Some are able to read regular print; others can read print that is enlarged typographically or viewed through a magnifying device. Because of the limited educational relevance of the legal terms and acuity scores, teachers should be aware that it is important to acquire information on the visual functioning of mainstreamed students; assumptions regarding their ability to use their vision should not be based on a label or acuity score.

Students with vision impairments who have not been identified before entering school are often located in the periodic vision screening conducted for all students in a school. The general education teacher can play an important role by carefully

Students with Sensory Impairments

- About 1 student in 1,000 has a highly significant, noncorrectable vision impairment, but only about 3 out of 10 of these students are considered blind for educational purposes (Reynolds & Birch, 1988).
- The loss of vision can slow the pace of intellectual and concept development because it limits access to the normal range and variety of experiences (Caton, 1993).
- Students with vision impairments may be somewhat below grade level in school because of factors such as school absences for medical reasons and the difficulty of acquiring adequate instructional materials in braille or large print (Caton, 1993).
- Fewer than 1 out of 100 students has a hearing impairment severe enough to warrant special education services (Reynolds & Birch, 1988).
- Hearing losses are measured in decibels (dB) and can be categorized by severity; individuals with losses in the speech range may have a mild (20–40 dB), moderate (40–60 dB), severe (60–80 dB), or profound (80 dB or greater) hearing impairment.
- Amplification of unintelligible sounds may do nothing for the person with a hearing impairment except make the unintelligible sound louder.
- American Sign Language (called Ameslan or ASL) is the fourth most used language in the United States (after English, Spanish, and Italian). It employs both fingerspelling and signs, with its own system and rules for formation of signs; it is not merely a manual form of English (Cartwright, Cartwright, & Ward, 1989).
- Speechreading (or lipreading) is a system of interpreting a speaker's words and message without hearing the speaker's voice. The speechreader watches the lips, mouth, tongue, gestures, and facial movements of the speaker in order to decode the message. This approach is difficult because many words are identical in appearance. For example, the words *pie* and *buy* appear the same on the lips. According to Green and Fischgrund (1993), "only 30 to 40 percent of the sounds in our language are produced with visible lip movements, so the speechreader has many gaps to fill in" (p. 293).
- The majority of students with vision and hearing impairments spend most of their school day in the general education classroom.

observing students in the classroom. The signs and symptoms of vision problems listed in Figure 14–1 can alert the teacher to students in need of further investigation.

Students with hearing impairments may be **deaf** or **hard of hearing**. Students who are deaf are not able to use their hearing to understand speech, even with a hearing aid. Students who are hard of hearing have a significant hearing loss that requires some special adaptations; they are able to use hearing to understand speech, often through the use of a hearing aid (Heward & Orlansky, 1992).

Conductive hearing losses are caused by interference with the transmission of sound from the outer ear to the inner ear; this interference can occur in either the outer or the middle ear. Individuals with this type of loss are usually treated by medication or surgery, but occasionally hearing aids are prescribed. An impairment to the auditory nerve or inner ear results in a **sensorineural hearing loss**. Surgery and medication are generally less effective in treating this type of loss; most individuals with a sensorineural loss will benefit from the use of hearing aids. A mixed hearing loss involves both conduc-

---

 FIGURE 14–1
Signs of Possible Vision Problems

The National Society to Prevent Blindness (1977) urges teachers and parents to watch for these signs that a child might be experiencing vision problems.

Behavior
- Rubs eyes excessively
- Shuts or covers one eye, tilts head or thrusts it forward
- Has difficulty reading or doing other work requiring close use of the eyes
- Blinks more than usual or is irritable when doing close work
- Is unable to see distant things clearly
- Squints eyelids together or frowns

Appearance
- Crossed eyes
- Red-rimmed, encrusted, or swollen eyelids
- Inflamed or watery eyes
- Recurring sties

Complaints
- Itching, burning, or scratchy feeling in eyes
- Inability to see well
- Dizziness, headaches, or nausea following close work
- Blurred or double vision

If students exhibit any of these problems for a period of time, they should be referred to the school nurse or appropriate special education personnel.

---

tive and sensorineural impairments. Functional hearing losses have no known organic origin, can be due to emotional factors, and are generally not improved by sound amplification.

Frequency and intensity are two of the physical characteristics of sound used in measuring hearing loss. Frequency, or pitch, is expressed in a unit called hertz (Hz). An example of pitch is the musical scale; as the voice ascends the scale, pitch or frequency increases. Intensity, or loudness, is measured in decibels (dB). These symbols often appear on reports of students' hearing losses, with a loss indicated in dB at each Hz level. It is important for the educator to consider a hearing loss in relation to speech sounds. Most speech is between 500 and 2,000 Hz in frequency and between 40 and 65 dB in intensity (Green & Fischgrund, 1993). A student with a 75 to 80 dB loss in the 1,000 to 4,000 Hz range would have a severe loss that would affect his or her ability to understand speech.

Hearing losses not identified during the preschool years by parents or physicians are often detected during annual school hearing screenings. By also carefully observing the behaviors of students, the classroom teacher can be alert to signs and symptoms that indicate possible hearing impairments. Warning signals to watch for are listed in Figure 14–2; these and other indicators of vision or hearing impairments may be noticed by the teacher. Students who do not respond normally to visual or auditory stimuli are potential candidates for special education assessment.

ASSESSMENT PROCEDURES

When students are suspected of having vision or hearing impairments, they are referred to the mainstreaming team for special education assessment. An assessment plan is then developed and presented to the parents, who must grant permission before it is implemented. This assessment should determine the student's intellectual functioning, academic achievement, and communicative status. It must be conducted in an appropriate mode of communication (e.g., braille or sign language when appropriate) and must assess all areas that relate to the suspected

sensory impairment. The assessment should determine the student's capabilities and identify factors that are interfering with school performance.

Assessments of students with vision and hearing impairments can be conducted by a variety of professionals. Several—such as special teachers of students with vision or hearing impairments, ophthalmologists, and audiologists—may assess only this type of special student. Many instruments commonly used to evaluate the ability or achievement of other students with disabilities may be inappropriate for students with sensory impairments. To obtain accurate and reliable information about these individuals, measures must be selected carefully and, if necessary, adapted to allow students to circumvent their disabilities.

The intellectual functioning of pupils with vision and hearing impairments can be assessed with adapted, modified, or specially designed measures. The verbal section of the *Wechsler Intelligence Scale for Children–Third Edition (WISC-III)* has been used to assess students with vision impairments. The *Perkins-Binet Intelligence Scale* (Davis, 1980) is designed for students with vision impairments who are ages 2 to 22. This adaptation of the *Stanford-Binet Intelligence Scale* has two forms, one for those with nonusable vision and another for those with usable vision. Approximately 25% to 30% of the items are performance based, and the test yields both mental age and intelligence quotients. The *Nebraska Test of Learning Aptitude (NTLA)* (Hiskey, 1966) is a measure of the learning aptitude of individuals between the ages of 3 and 16 who are deaf. Each of the measures identified here is specifically designed to provide an indication of the capability of students with vision or hearing impairments.

Many academic assessment instruments for sighted or hearing students can be administered with little or no modification to individuals who are partially sighted or hard of hearing. Students with more severe impairments may require adaptations, such as communicating in sign language or transcribing portions of the test into braille. In addition, students can be allowed extra time to finish portions of a test if this is necessary to reflect their skill levels adequately. However, if modifications have been

FIGURE 14–2
Signs of Hearing Problems

Ear Problems

- Draining ears.
- Infected outer ear.
- Unpleasant odor in ears.
- Cotton in ears.
- Continuous mouth breathing.
- Consistent pulling or tugging of ears.

Hearing Defects

- Persistent inattentiveness.
- More awareness of movement or action than of sound.
- Extremely watchful of the teacher (lip reading).
- Turns head to one side in an effort to hear.
- Consistently asks that questions be repeated.
- Seems to confuse words that have similar sounds.
- Constantly interrupts conversations without awareness of interruption.
- Finds it difficult to follow verbal directions.
- Fails to locate source of sound in class.
- Has difficulty with articulation.
- Has a monotonous voice pitch.
- Mumbles without being aware of it.
- Speaks very quietly.

Note. From *School Health Problems* (p. 34) by J. Smolensky, L. R. Bonvechio, R. E. Whitlock, and M. A. Girard, 1968, Palo Alto, CA: Fearon. Copyright 1968 by Fearon. Reprinted by permission.

made in the administration procedures of standardized tests, they must be noted in the assessment report.

Vision and hearing assessments are normally conducted by specially trained individuals. These assessments can be useful in indicating the extent of an impairment and determining possible remedies (e.g., glasses, low vision aids, hearing aids) that can reduce the impact of the impairment on the student's educational performance. Students who are partially sighted should be encouraged to have their vision rechecked frequently because their visual efficiency may improve and adjustments may be needed in their optical aids or the type size used for their materials (Harley & Lawrence, 1984). Ophthalmologists are medical doctors who specialize in the diagnosis and treatment of defects and diseases of the eye. An optometrist is a nonmedical practitioner licensed to measure refractive errors and eye muscle disturbances. Both of these professionals measure vision and prescribe corrective lenses, but only the ophthalmologist may perform surgery, prescribe medication, and administer other medical treatments. Medical doctors concerned with hearing

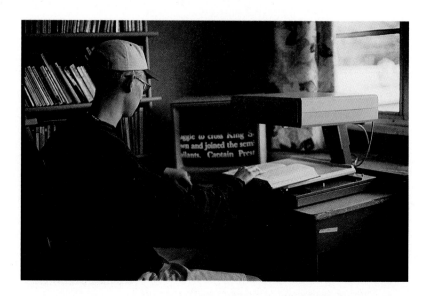

impairments are the otolaryngologist (who diagnoses and treats ear, nose, and throat disorders) and the otologist (who specializes in the treatment of ear diseases and disorders).

The **Snellen Chart** is commonly used for vision screening of students; its purpose is to identify students with possible visual acuity problems who are in need of a more thorough evaluation by a vision specialist. The chart is composed of rows of letters of various sizes, which students must identify from a preset distance. For young children, the Snellen Chart contains only the letter *E* in various sizes and orientations; this allows the child to point in the direction the *E* is facing rather than name various letters. Hearing is assessed with a device called an **audiometer**. The student listens to tones or speech delivered via air or bone conduction at a variety of frequencies and intensities.

A mobility specialist may meet with students with vision impairments to assess their orientation and mobility skills and to determine their need for training in these areas. Other specialists may evaluate students' ability to use low-vision aids or read printed material. For students with hearing impairments, the speech-language pathologist is the professional who determines current functioning in oral communication and language development. The educational audiologist is responsible for ensuring that hearing aids and other amplification systems are functioning properly.

Direct observation and informal assessment by the teacher can provide a great deal of information for the mainstreaming team. Much of the data needed to determine a student's requirements for special services and to prepare the goals and objectives for the IEP can most effectively be gathered by the teacher or specialists while the student is performing under typical conditions in the general education classroom.

◼ SPECIAL SERVICES

Information gathered through the assessment process is used by the mainstreaming team to develop a student's IEP. The IEPs of students with vision and hearing impairments usually contain several goals. Students with vision impairments often have goals in the use of vision aids, improvement of listening skills, development of braille reading and writing ability, note taking, mobility, and academic skill areas. Figure 14–3 shows portions of an IEP for Morris, one of the students introduced at the beginning of this chapter. Morris is a third grader who is partially sighted.

FIGURE 14-3
IEP Goals and Services for Morris

Annual Goals

1. By the end of the school year, Morris will increase his reading rate for print material enlarged through magnification.

   Person responsible: Resource teacher

2. By the end of the school year, Morris will decrease his math errors by correcting his work with a talking calculator.

   Person responsible: Resource teacher

3. By the end of the school year, Morris will decrease the number of inappropriate reactions to comments of other students about his glasses.

   Persons responsible: Resource teacher and grade 3 teacher

4. Morris will successfully complete third grade requirements.

   Person responsible: Grade 3 teacher

Amount of Participation in Regular Classes

Morris will spend the entire day in the third grade classroom with the exception of 1 hour per day in the special education program.

Special Education and Related Services

1. Morris will receive special education services from the resource teacher (annual goals 1, 2, and 3) for 1 hour daily.

2. The resource teacher will provide consultation to Morris's third grade teacher and special materials such as large-print books as needed.

Students with hearing impairments may have goals in speechreading, speech and language, auditory training, sign language, and the use of amplification devices. Max, the high school student described at the start of this chapter, has a severe bilateral hearing loss that resulted from a congenital hearing impairment. A portion of Max's IEP appears in Figure 14–4.

The majority of students with sensory impairments spend some portion of their school day in a mainstreamed setting. Many receive services from an itinerant special education teacher to supplement the activities provided in the general education class. For those spending the entire day in the general education classroom, teacher consultants may work with the general education teacher to help design needed classroom adaptations and provide special materials or equipment. Other students may attend a resource room. Very young students or those with multiple or more severe disabilities may spend the majority of their school day in a special class and participate in general education classroom activities only when there is some assurance that they can be successful. Students with sensory impairments receive services from a variety of specialists, such as speech-language pathologists, adapted physical education teachers, and vocational rehabilitation counselors. The school system or outside agencies may offer these students special programs, such as instruction in daily living skills or

FIGURE 14–4
IEP Goals and Services for Max

Annual Goals

1. By the end of the school year, Max will use a word processor to write a 300-word composition with complete sentences, correct punctuation, and appropriate paragraph structure.

    Persons responsible: Resource teacher and English teacher

2. By the end of the school year, Max will use speechreading accurately for short lectures.

    Person responsible: Resource teacher

3. By the end of the school year, Max will be able to conduct an oral conversation with an adult.

    Person responsible: Resource teacher

4. By the end of the school year, Max will complete all requirements in English, math, chemistry, and driver's education.

    Person responsible: General education teachers

5. By the end of the school year, Max will be able to carry on a complete conversation with a person competent in sign language.

    Person responsible: Resource teacher

Amount of Participation in Regular Classes

Max will attend all regular classes with the exception of two class periods.

Special Education and Related Services

1. Max will receive special education services from the resource teacher (annual goals 1, 2, 3, and 5) for two periods each day.

2. The resource teacher will provide consultation services to Max's classroom teachers as needed.

---

recreational activities. The special services required for different students with similar impairments may vary considerably.

In making decisions about mainstreaming students with disabilities, it is necessary to consider the views of parents and those of students themselves. In the past few years, for example, many members of the Deaf community have become advocates for special schools for students who are deaf. This position reflects a growing awareness of Deaf culture and the Deaf community's pride in that culture. For example, in 1988, students at Gallaudet University, a university for students who are deaf, staged a protest until trustees named a person who was deaf as president. Another example is the testimony given by Jesse Thomas, a 15-year-old who is deaf, before the National Council on Disabilities:

> I think I have to explain that I am not disabled, I'm just deaf. Deaf persons are a minority group. They use American Sign Language (ASL) and are part of the Deaf Culture. One of the main reasons that mainstreaming is not good is because mainstreaming lacks

Deaf Culture and ASL. I can't really explain Deaf Culture. I do know that Deaf Culture makes me proud of who I am—DEAF. (as cited in Heward & Orlansky, 1992, p. 295)

ADAPTATIONS FOR MAINSTREAMING

Students with vision or hearing impairments who are in the general education program frequently require adaptations in the arrangement of the learning environment and in the structure of instructional procedures. Extensive curricular adaptations are typically not needed. Although additional hands-on experiences may be beneficial for students with sensory impairments, other adjustments correspond to those generally provided for typical students.

The idea of adapting instruction for students with vision and hearing impairments is not new. In 1900, for example, Helen Keller wrote specifications for her own classroom adaptations. Much has been written about the obviously gifted Helen Keller, who had severe impairments in both hearing and vision. Her familiar story and struggle to adapt to a world she could neither see nor hear is captured in the letter she wrote to the chairman of the academic board at Radcliffe College. In this letter, she asks for adaptations to the regular, not special, college classroom.

Dear Sir:

As an aid to me in determining my plans for study the coming year, I apply to you for information as to the possibility of my taking the regular courses in Radcliffe College.

Since receiving my certificate of admission to Radcliffe last July, I have been studying with a private tutor, Horace, Aeschylus, French, German, Rhetoric, English History, English Literature and Criticism, and English Composition.

In college I should wish to continue most, if not all, of these subjects. The conditions under which I work require the presence of Miss Sullivan, who has been my teacher and companion for thirteen years, as an interpreter of oral speech and as a reader of examination papers. In college, she, or possibly in some subjects someone else, would of necessity be with me in the lecture room and at recitations. I should do all my written work on a typewriter, and if a Professor could not understand my speech, I could write out my answers to his questions and hand them to him after the recitation.

Is it possible for the College to accommodate itself to these unprecedented conditions, so as to enable me to pursue my studies at Radcliffe? I realize that the obstacles in the way of my receiving a college education are very great—to others they may seem insurmountable; but, dear Sir, a true soldier does not acknowledge defeat before the battle. (Keller, 1965, p. 151)

The classroom adaptations described in chapter 13 are similar to those required for students with vision and hearing impairments. The teacher should be sure to explain the special student's impairment(s) to the other students in the general education class. A careful explanation facilitates the acceptance of students with disabilities by their peers. However, teachers and students should be careful not to become overprotective of students with disabilities; they must be encouraged to develop independence.

ARRANGING THE LEARNING ENVIRONMENT

Students with sensory impairments may require adaptations in the arrangement of the classroom, seating patterns, and other factors related to lighting, sound transmission, and proximity to activities. The following are suggestions for general education classroom teachers working with students with vision impairments:

- Be sure students' tables or desktops are large enough for braillewriters and other equipment (Maron & Martinez, 1980).
- Copyholders, easels, and adjustable tops on desks help students to maintain good posture for close-eye activities (Harley & Lawrence, 1984).
- Provide an accessible storage area with adequate space for large pieces of equipment such as optical devices or reading stands and braille or large-print books (Torres & Corn, 1990).
- Do not place students who are partially sighted where they must face the glare of a primary source of light, such as a window (Pasanella &

Volkmor, 1981). However, lighting should be adequate; some students may need additional light from a source such as a desk lamp or a window.

■ Seat students so that they are able to participate in activities with other class members. A flexible seating arrangement will allow students to be close to different classroom activities or to adjust the amount of light available as needed. For example, a student might relocate to obtain a better view of the teacher, the chalkboard, or the projection screen, or to obtain a greater amount of light for a particular activity.

■ Use copy machines to enlarge print materials for students with vision impairments (Torres & Corn, 1990).

■ Allow students to become oriented to the classroom; permit them to explore (Maron & Martinez, 1980). Other suggestions for developing the mobility skills of students with vision impairments are listed in "Tips for the Teacher."

Students with hearing impairments require other types of adaptations to facilitate their successful mainstreaming:

■ The student's seat should be away from noise and close to the area where instruction takes place.

■ Seating arrangements should permit the student to face the teacher and other students. Teachers should take care not to turn their back to students with hearing impairments while speaking. During a class discussion, it may be necessary to allow the student to move around the room to be able to see individuals who are speaking (Reynolds & Birch, 1988).

■ If an interpreter is provided, that individual should be seated near the student. The student and the interpreter should have some flexibility in where they choose to sit.

■ Speakers should avoid standing with a direct light behind them; if the teacher stands in front of a window, it may not be possible to see what he or she is saying.

■ Keep classroom and background noise to a minimum; when students wear hearing aids, *all* sounds are amplified (Reynolds & Birch, 1988).

■ Label items in the classroom to help in the development of vocabulary for the young student. This practice can also help other students in learning to read (Glazzard, 1980).

For many students with sensory impairments, special assistive aids and equipment (such as those described in chapter 8) are helpful, and students should be encouraged to use the special devices that have been provided. Become acquainted with one type of device designed to help students with vision impairments communicate with others by consulting "Spotlight on Technology" on pages 430 and 431.

Other adaptations are often required to meet the individual needs of students. Special educators, the students' parents, and often the students themselves can give suggestions for such adaptations. Careful observation of students in a classroom setting provides information on how the educational environment can best be modified.

■ MODIFYING INSTRUCTIONAL PROCEDURES

When students with vision or hearing impairments are present in the general education classroom, it may be necessary for the teacher to modify instructional procedures. These adaptations depend on the individual needs and capabilities of the mainstreamed students and vary from minimal to extensive. Specialists are generally available to assist the teacher in developing and implementing modified instructional strategies.

Students with vision impairments who are mainstreamed may require instruction from a specialist to acquire the skills needed to use low vision aids or to read and write braille. In addition, some students need special materials or equipment; others use only those materials available in the classroom. Suggestions for teachers working with students with vision impairments in a mainstreamed setting are listed here:

■ Change instructional procedures only when absolutely necessary. Curricular goals should remain the same for typical and special students (Blankenship & Lilly, 1981).

Orientation and Mobility

*F*or students who are blind, or those with limited vision, the orientation and mobility specialist provides instruction in how to travel from one place to another. According to Mandell and Fiscus (1981), "*Orientation* refers to the ability to understand the relationship between self and environment through intact sensory input. *Mobility* refers to one's ability to travel safely and independently through the physical environment" [emphasis added] (p. 209). Independent travel is an important skill for individuals who are blind, and several types of travel aids are available: a long cane, a guide dog (for older students and adults), and electronic devices that signal the presence of obstacles in the path of travel. The general education teacher can support and supplement the training provided by the mobility specialist, as Craig and Howard (1981) suggest:

- Eliminate unnecessary obstacles; inform students of changes in room arrangement or of any temporary obstacles, such as a portable movie screen.
- Keep doors completely closed or completely open to eliminate the possibility of the student running into a partially open door.
- Initially, allow the student to travel with a companion to frequently used rooms, such as the library, restroom, and auditorium. Discuss the route, pointing out right and left turns and any distinguishing landmarks.
- Allow the student to move about freely until he has familiarized himself with the room or route.
- Discourage reliance upon sighted guides once the student has demonstrated the ability to travel independently.
- If necessary, make provisions for a sighted guide for fire drills, field trips, assemblies, and seating in rooms that ordinarily have unassigned seating. (p. 191)

Recommendations for persons who will act as sighted guides are provided by the Arkansas Enterprises for the Blind (n.d.):

- When offering assistance to a . . . person [who is blind], be direct. Speak in a normal tone. Simply ask: "May I be of help?" Address him directly; this helps him locate you.
- Never "grab" . . . [the] arm [of a person who is blind]; he can't anticipate your movements if you do. Permit him to take your arm and say: "Here's my left arm" or the right, as the case may be. He knows, then, how to take your arm and he will respond to your motion much as a dancer follows a partner.
- In walking with a . . . person [who is blind] proceed at a normal pace; hesitate slightly before stepping up or down; don't drag him over the curb. After crossing a street, see that he is started in the direction he wants to take, and caution him of any unusual obstructions ahead.
- In showing a . . . person [who is blind] to a chair, place his hand upon the back of it; don't try to push him into it. His touch will tell him the type, width and height of the chair. (p. 2)

SPOTLIGHT ON TECHNOLOGY

Braille Personal Notetakers

*B*raille personal notetakers are portable electronic devices that allow students who are blind to take notes in class, complete written assignments, and write answers to exam questions. One example is BrailleMate (TeleSensory). It is light (1 pound), quite small (8" by 3" by 1.25"), and powered by battery. Its eight-key keyboard is designed for typing braille, not standard text. Two keys are used solely for word processing. The other six correspond to the six dots found in braille; the student presses one, two, three, or more keys depending on the braille character he or she wants to type.

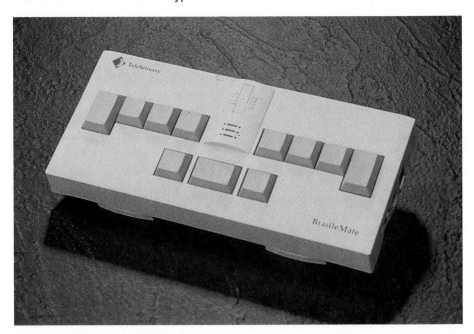

Note. Photo courtesy of TeleSensory.

■ Many of the print materials used in the general education classroom may be available in other formats. Work with the student's special teacher to locate large-print, braille, or tape-recorded texts. Start looking well ahead of the time materials are needed, to ensure their availability. For information about sources of materials for students with vision (and hearing) impairments, see Figure 14–5.

■ When descriptive language is used to interpret events that involve facial expressions or gestures, students are less likely to be off-task (Spenciner, 1992).

■ Allow adequate time for students with vision impairments to complete reading assignments; some students may need some extra time to locate their materials and to find the starting place (Spenciner, 1992).

BrailleMate contains a built-in speech synthesizer so that it can read the student's text aloud. It also converts braille to standard text that can be edited with the full range of standard word processing features on the BrailleMate. The student can also use the built-in filing system, talking calendar, talking calculator, and talking address and appointment books.

Another feature of the BrailleMate is its dynamic braille display. This is a tactile display; small reeds corresponding to the dots in the braille cell are raised electronically to form braille characters. One braille cell is displayed at one time on the BrailleMate. This type of braille is called paperless or refreshable braille. It does not need to be printed on paper, and it can be reused (or refreshed) by lowering the reeds and then arranging them to form a different braille character.

When the students are ready to print their work, they can connect the personal notetaker to a braille printer, a standard printer, or a printer that produces pages with text in both braille and print formats. Printers with both braille and print output are very useful in mainstreamed settings because a student who is blind and a teacher who is sighted can both read from the same copy. It is also possible to connect personal notetakers to computers. This allows the student to edit and spell check the text he or she has produced using a talking word processor designed for writers with vision impairments. These word processors "speak" everything on the screen (including instructions and menu choices), not just the text the student has written.

With assistive devices such as personal notetakers, students who are blind can participate in regular classroom activities without having to rely on others for note taking or the production of written assignments. For example, when writing a paper, a student might draft the outline on the personal notetaker, print it in braille to review it, use the notetaker's talking word processing program to expand the outline into the final paper, then transfer it to a computer for a spelling check before printing the final draft.

- Encourage students to use a word processor or to type communications that must be read by sighted individuals; examples include written reports, homework assignments, and personal correspondence. The special education teacher may provide word processing and typing instruction; the general education teacher can help by allowing students access to a computer or a typewriter in the classroom.

- Say aloud material that is being written on the chalkboard or on the overhead projector (Spenciner, 1992).
- Provide students with instruction and experiences that develop critical listening skills; individuals with vision impairments do not automatically have better listening skills (Blankenship & Lilly, 1981).
- Occasionally provide tape-recorded materials to students who read braille or large print in order

---

FIGURE 14–5
Sources of Materials for Students with Sensory Impairments

Large-Print Materials

- American Printing House for the Blind, Inc., P.O. Box 6085, Louisville, KY 40206, 800-223-1839

- National Association for Visually Handicapped, 22 West 21st Street, New York, NY 10010

Braille Materials

- American Printing House for the Blind, Inc. (address above)

- Library of Congress National Library Service for the Blind and Physically Handicapped, 1291 Taylor Street, NW, Washington, DC 20542, 800-424-9100

Tape-Recorded Materials

- American Printing House for the Blind, Inc. (address above)

- Library of Congress National Library Service for the Blind and Physically Handicapped (address above)

- Recording for the Blind, 20 Roszel Road, Princeton, NJ 08540, 800-221-4792

Captioned Films and Videos

- Captioned Films/Videos for the Deaf, Modern Talking Picture Service, Inc., 5000 Park Street North, St. Petersburg, FL 33709, 800-237-6213

---

to vary the presentation of reading material (Spenciner, 1992).

- Vigorous physical exercise is recommended for students with vision impairments. Encourage them to compete with sighted peers whenever possible (Reynolds & Birch, 1988).
- Become familiar with the various types of special equipment used by the students with vision impairments in your class. Let the special teacher know immediately of any necessary replacement or repairs. Perkins **braillewriters** are small machines that are often used to write (type) material in braille; the **slate and stylus** is a small hand-held device also used to write braille. Devices such as an abacus, braille ruler, or raised relief map are also useful for students. To learn more about the braille system, consult Figure 14–6.

In addition to the special equipment available for students with vision impairments, the teacher can use regular classroom materials more effectively by adapting them. Glazzard (1980) suggests several ideas for modification of materials:

- Use a heavy black marking pen on dittoed worksheets. It makes them easier to see.
- Use a marking pen to delineate lines on writing paper or purchase heavy-lined paper.
- Write chalkboard directions on a separate piece of paper for the child with poor vision. Keep copying work for the . . . student to a minimum.
- Ask parents or other students to read reference material or lengthy reading assignments to the . . . student [with vision impairments].
- Record reading material or other assignments for the . . . child [with vision impairments]. Aides, par-

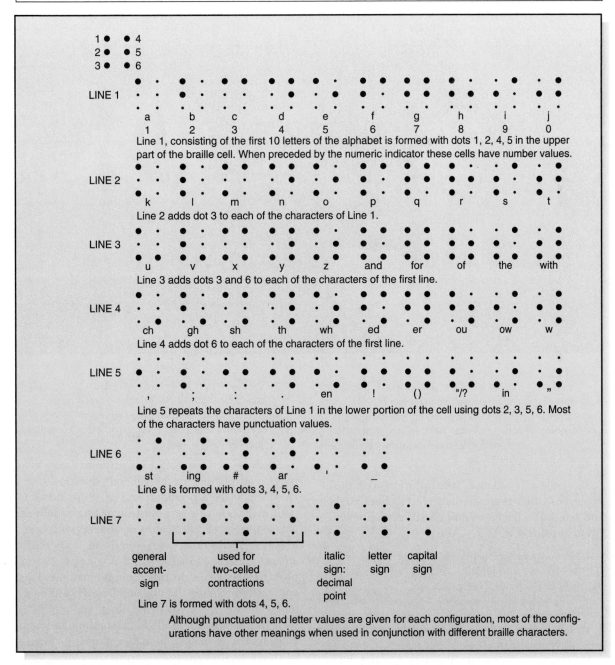

1 ● ● 4
2 ● ● 5
3 ● ● 6

LINE 1
a b c d e f g h i j
1 2 3 4 5 6 7 8 9 0

Line 1, consisting of the first 10 letters of the alphabet is formed with dots 1, 2, 4, 5 in the upper part of the braille cell. When preceded by the numeric indicator these cells have number values.

LINE 2
k l m n o p q r s t

Line 2 adds dot 3 to each of the characters of Line 1.

LINE 3
u v x y z and for of the with

Line 3 adds dots 3 and 6 to each of the characters of the first line.

LINE 4
ch gh sh th wh ed er ou ow w

Line 4 adds dot 6 to each of the characters of the first line.

LINE 5
, ; : . en ! () "/? in "

Line 5 repeats the characters of Line 1 in the lower portion of the cell using dots 2, 3, 5, 6. Most of the characters have punctuation values.

LINE 6
st ing # ar ' _

Line 6 is formed with dots 3, 4, 5, 6.

LINE 7
general accent-sign | used for two-celled contractions | italic sign: decimal point | letter sign | capital sign

Line 7 is formed with dots 4, 5, 6.

Although punctuation and letter values are given for each configuration, most of the configurations have other meanings when used in conjunction with different braille characters.

Note. From *Understanding Braille* by the American Foundation for the Blind, n.d., New York: Author. Reprinted by permission.

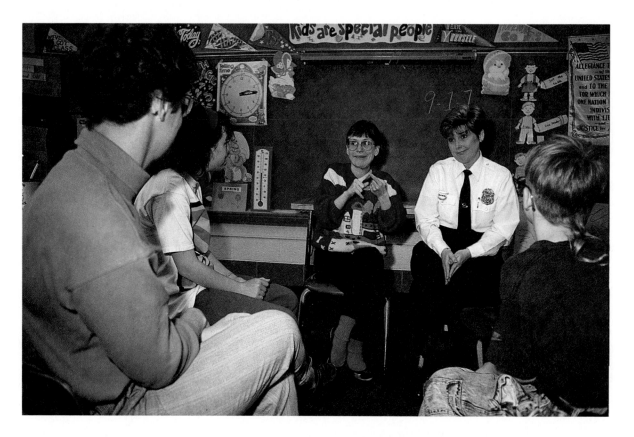

ents, volunteers, or other students are possible sources of help for recording assignments.

■ A magnifying glass may be helpful for enlarging the print of regular class materials. It is less tiring for some . . . students [with vision impairments] to use such an aid. (pp. 27–28)

Pasanella and Volkmor (1981) provide additional suggestions that general education teachers might find helpful in communicating with students with vision impairments:

■ Use a vocabulary that is related to sight, such as the words *see* and *look*. . . . [P]ersons [with vision impairments] use those words, too.

■ Call the student by name when you are speaking to him.

■ Talk directly to the student. Look him in the face and remind classmates to do the same.

■ Some . . . students [with vision impairments] develop unusual mannerisms. Gently remind them about more appropriate behaviors.

■ Tell the student who you are when you approach him or her and tell him when you leave.

■ Encourage the student to use any adaptive aids s/he needs and to explain their use to other classmates. (pp. 186–187)

Students with hearing impairments may also require adaptations in the general education classroom. Specialists provide many of these students with instruction in speechreading, fingerspelling, and sign language. Educators of students with hearing impairments do not agree on the most appropriate communication method for this group, but many professionals advocate **total communication**. This approach combines the oral/aural method of communication (speech, speechreading, and audition) with the manual method (fingerspelling and sign language). The manual alphabet, shown in Figure 14–7, allows students to fingerspell names and technical terms that are not available in sign language. The following suggestions can help the general edu-

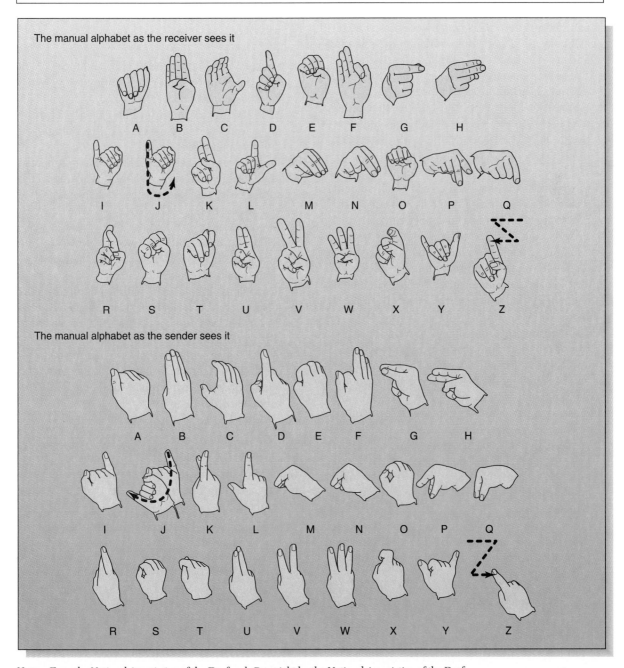

The manual alphabet as the receiver sees it

A B C D E F G H
I J K L M N O P Q
R S T U V W X Y Z

The manual alphabet as the sender sees it

A B C D E F G H
I J K L M N O P Q
R S T U V W X Y Z

Note. From the National Association of the Deaf, n.d. Copyright by the National Association of the Deaf. Reprinted by permission.

cation teacher work with mainstreamed students with hearing impairments:

- Teachers and students should speak naturally, use natural gestures, and maintain face-to-face contact when speaking with a student with a hearing impairment (Reynolds & Birch, 1988).
- Encourage students with hearing impairments to use their hearing aids at all times.
- Find out the best seating position for the student to speechread the teacher's verbal presentations to the class by discussing this with the student (Rees, 1992).
- Use an overhead projector; it permits a teacher to write material that can be seen by all students while the teacher continues to face the class. It is best to use a projector with a quiet fan.
- Provide copies of the teacher's notes or those of two other students when material is presented in lecture format; it is not possible to speechread and take notes simultaneously. Write assignments and outlines of lectures on the board (Reynolds & Birch, 1988).
- Use **captioned films** whenever possible. Many films and videotapes used in the classroom are available in a captioned version. (See Figure 14–5 for information about the source for captioned films and videos.)
- Hearing aids should be checked daily. Consult with an educational audiologist or speech-language pathologist to determine who will assume this responsibility. "Spotlight on Technology" describes the use of hearing aids and classroom amplification devices with students with hearing impairments.
- Question students with hearing impairments to determine whether they understand information presented in class. Do not assume that students understand the material.
- Clearly explain concepts being taught. Use visual examples whenever possible, and keep terminology consistent.
- Do not talk when distributing handouts as the student with a hearing impairment cannot look for papers and watch the teacher at the same time (Rees, 1992).

- Talk in full sentences. Avoid the use of single words, and rephrase the entire sentence if it was not understood; content and meaning are easier to grasp in context (Reynolds & Birch, 1988).
- Provide assignments both orally and in writing to avoid confusion (Rees, 1992).
- Speechreading and attending to auditory stimuli with deficient hearing can be tiring tasks; watch for student fatigue.
- Start lectures with an outline of material to be presented and end the lecture with a summary of the key points (Rees, 1992).
- During class discussions, allow only one person to speak at a time and signal who is talking so the student with hearing impairment knows where to look (Rees, 1992).
- The academic problems of many students are related to their language impairments, not to a lack of intelligence. Closely monitor their achievement (Blankenship & Lilly, 1981).
- Classmates of a student with a hearing impairment may wish to learn sign language. Arrange for instruction in this area if it is appropriate (Blankenship & Lilly, 1981).
- Work closely with specialists to assure that students with hearing impairments are provided with appropriate experiences in the general education classroom.

Specific suggestions for working with students who are hard of hearing are presented in "Tips for the Teacher" on pages 440 and 441. In addition, Harrington (1976) makes the following recommendations about communicating with a student with a hearing impairment:

(a) If you have difficulty understanding the child ask him to repeat; (b) Do not call attention to the child's speech errors in the classroom. Record and share them with the speech clinician; (c) Realize that the child may have limited vocabulary and syntax, both receptively and expressively. His/her failure to understand may be related to this language deficit as well as the inability to hear normally. (p. 25)

General education teachers ordinarily are not required to become proficient in specialized techniques, such as braille or sign language. However,

Classroom Amplification Devices

S tudents with hearing impairments benefit from technological devices that amplify sounds in order to optimize residual hearing. Some amplification systems also overcome the problem of trying to hear in noisy situations.

Hearing aids differ in shape and style (see chapter 8), but all operate on the same principles. Sound is picked up by a microphone, amplified, and delivered to a receiver in the canal of the ear. Unfortunately, *all* sounds are amplified, making it difficult for the user to discriminate between conversation and all other noises in the background. In the classroom, a student with a hearing impairment will likely find it difficult to follow a teacher's instructions in the presence of competing noise (rustling paper, shuffling feet, pencil sharpeners, aquarium motors, heating systems, etc.).

The hearing aid user is also affected by two other factors: distance and direction. As distance between the speaker and the hearing aid user increases, the intensity of the speaker's voice decreases. To a person with a hearing impairment, this decrease has a significantly negative impact on speech perception. As a speaker turns away from a hearing aid user, the speech signal again becomes weaker and sometimes distorted. In order to overcome these limitations of a hearing aid, a teacher would need to directly face the student with a hearing impairment at all times, and speak at a distance of approximately 12 inches from the hearing aid microphone.

A device designed specifically to address the problems of noise, distance, and direction is the auditory trainer, or FM classroom amplification system (Flexer, Wray, & Ireland, 1989; Maxon, Brackett, & van den Berg, 1991). To use an FM system, the classroom teacher wears a wireless microphone, and the student wears a wireless receiver. Some receivers look and operate like personal stereos. Recently, receivers have also been designed to be worn as behind-the-ear hearing aids. This new type of receiver is a preferred choice among students if cosmetic concerns become an issue.

The FM system has three advantages: (1) the teacher's voice is amplified 12 to 15 decibels above the classroom noise; (2) the teacher's voice is transmitted at an even intensity across a distance of up to 100 feet; and (3) the teacher's voice is not affected by direction. This "FM advantage" has helped make the FM system standard equipment in special classrooms for students with hearing impairments for many years. Because the FM system is easy to use, it has been introduced into

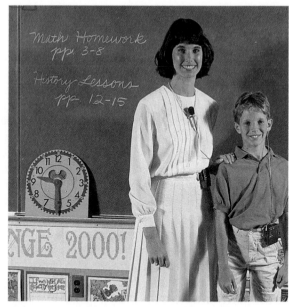

Phonic Ear Personal FM System

Note. Photo courtesy of Phonic Ear, Inc.

mainstreamed and inclusion settings with much success. Because there is a real risk of overamplification, FM systems must be fit and monitored by an audiologist.

Another type of amplification system used in classrooms is called sound field amplification. FM technology is used to transmit the teacher's voice by a microphone to a few speakers placed around the classroom. The teacher's voice is slightly amplified and conveyed to the whole room (that is, the sound field); students in the back hear the teacher's voice as loudly as the students in front. If there is a student in the classroom with a hearing impairment, he or she may wear either an FM receiver or his or her personal hearing aids, depending on the audi-

they must be aware of students' needs and be familiar with the specialists who provide assistance in adapting instructional procedures for students with sensory impairments. Many such students are fully capable of spending the majority of the school day in the general education classroom when appropriate adaptations are introduced.

This chapter has presented information on adapting the classroom environment and instructional pro-

cedures for students with vision and hearing impairments. In the next chapter, you will meet students who are gifted and talented and will learn methods for promoting the achievement of these individuals.

ACTIVITIES

1. Observe the classroom behavior of a student with a vision or hearing impairment. Keep a record of the adaptations made by the student and by oth-

Sound Field System from Phonic Ear
Note. Photo courtesy of Phonic Ear, Inc.

ologist's recommendation. Research indicates that all members in the class can benefit from sound field amplification: for example, students have demonstrated significant academic gains and an increase in on-task behavior. Teachers also report a noticeable reduction in vocal fatigue (Berg, 1987; Sarff, 1981).

Note. Developed by Kris English, Ph.D., CCC-A, educational audiologist and assistant professor at the University of Pittsburgh.

ers. What problems, if any, are encountered? Can the student adjust as unexpected events occur? What reactions do you observe from other students? From teachers? Write a brief summary of your observations.

2. Interview the parents of a student with a sensory impairment. When were they first aware of the disability? How did they react? Does the student encounter any difficulties at home or in the neighborhood? Has mainstreaming been a posi-

tive experience for the student? Are the parents apprehensive about the student's eventual adulthood? How do they encourage their child to become independent? Describe your impressions of the interview.

3. Read two articles about students with sensory impairments, one about vision impairments and one about hearing losses. The *Journal of Visual Impairment and Blindness* and *The Sight-Saving Review* provide articles related to vision impair-

TIPS FOR THE TEACHER

Students Who Are Hard of Hearing

Hearing Aid Basics

- Do not expect a hearing aid to "correct" hearing impairments like glasses correct vision impairments. The instrument will make sounds louder but not necessarily clearer. In addition, a hearing aid amplifies all sounds; it cannot sort out the teacher's instruction from the general background noise.
- If the aid "whistles" or produces feedback while in the child's ear, check the earpiece (or earmold) to see whether it has been inserted properly. Feedback will naturally occur if the aid is covered with a hand or a hat, or if the student leans close to a wall or turns the volume too high. However, if the earmold is fully in the ear, if the aid is not covered, and if the volume is at the appropriate setting, the earmold may be too small and need to be replaced. Inform the parent of the situation. Reducing the volume is only a temporary solution.
- Obtain a battery tester and a hearing aid stethoscope from the school audiologist and request training in conducting a hearing aid check. Hearing aids must be checked every day.
- Ask parents to provide spare batteries to keep at school, and let them know when dead batteries are replaced.

Classroom Acoustic Considerations

Because noise has a negative effect on the listening abilities of students with hearing impairments, it is advisable to evaluate the acoustic environment of the classroom. The following environmental modifications significantly reduce noise and reverberation problems:

- Carpeting, acoustic ceiling tile, and walls covered with bulletin board or similar materials, which absorb rather than reflect noise
- Acoustic treatments for noise sources such as rumbling plumbing, rattling window blinds, and buzzing fluorescent lights

Acoustic modifications to a classroom can generally be accomplished by the site custodial staff and will result in an environment conducive for learning for students with normal hearing as well as those with hearing impairments.

Strategies to Optimize Visual Information

Students with hearing impairments need as much visual cueing as possible. Comprehension increases significantly when a student can watch the teacher's face in order to lipread, or more accurately, speechread. Here are some suggestions to improve speechreading conditions:

- Speak in a normal fashion, without exaggeration or an increase in volume. Speak in phrases, at a normal pace. If there is a misunderstanding, rephrase rather than repeat.
- As often as possible, the teacher should directly face a student with hearing impairment, at eye level. Proximity is also very important: it is too difficult to speechread beyond 10 feet.
- When the room is darkened for films or slides, the student will not be able to speechread the teacher. Ask another student to take notes.
- Be aware that some people are naturally better speechreaders than others and that, even for the best speechreaders, only one-third of English speech sounds are visible. Speechreading becomes more difficult when the speaker has a foreign accent or a mustache that covers the mouth.

Other Teaching Strategies

- Students with hearing impairments often have some language deficits as a result of inconsistent auditory input. Pretutoring helps a student develop familiarity with new vocabulary and concepts before they are presented in class. Have the student read ahead on a subject to allow for extra time to consider new material. This can be accomplished as a homework assignment or with a resource teacher.
- As often as possible, write page numbers, homework assignments, public address announcements, key vocabulary, and so forth, on the chalkboard.
- Routinely check comprehension with questions that require more than yes or no answers. When simply asked, "Do you understand?" a student with a hearing impairment may prefer to nod his or her head rather than volunteer that he or she does not fully understand.
- For older students, it is helpful to have another student act as a notetaker. If the notes are made on NCR (no carbon required) paper, a copy can also be provided for a notebook available to any class member who may have missed information during class lectures. A student with a hearing impairment will then have a copy without conspicuously requiring special assistance.

_____

Note. Developed by Kris English, Ph.D., CCC-A, educational audiologist and assistant professor at the University of Pittsburgh.

THINGS TO REMEMBER

- Students with vision or hearing impairments commonly require modification of the learning environment and adaptation of instructional procedures to facilitate their performance in the general education classroom.
- Students with severe vision and hearing impairments are typically identified before they enter school. Milder impairments may be identified as a result of school screening programs or teacher observation and referral.
- Sensory impairments may be congenital, or they may occur as a result of illness or accident.
- Legal definitions of vision impairment have little educa-tional relevance. Educators need to know whether students can use their remaining vision to learn or whether they must rely on other senses.
- An educator needs to know the effects of a hearing loss on a student's ability to use and understand speech. Speech and language are the most significant areas in which hearing impairments affect students educationally.
- Students with vision or hearing impairments can learn to use other senses to compensate for their disabilities. Individuals who are blind can develop tactile reading skills and improve their listening skills; persons with hearing impairments can learn to speechread and to communicate manually. Students with vision impairments may also need orientation and mobility training to facilitate independent travel in the school and community.
- Many technological developments have improved the opportunities for students with sensory impairments to communicate with others; examples include FM classroom amplification systems for students with hearing impairments and braille notetakers and talking computer programs for students who are blind.
- Special educators are generally available to assist general education teachers in making classroom adaptations and obtaining appropriate materials for students with sensory impairments who are main-streamed.

ments; *American Annals of the Deaf, Volta Review*, and *Language, Speech, and Hearing Services in Schools* discuss hearing impairments. Summarize each article's relevance for the general education teacher.

4. Contact a large and a small school district to determine what services they offer for students with vision and hearing impairments. Are all the services needed by these students provided within the district, or must services be contracted from another district? What personnel are employed to provide instruction for these students? Is the percentage of students with sensory impairments about the same in both districts? What services are provided for general education teachers?

5. Write a short report describing one of the new electronic devices being used by persons who are blind or deaf. Explain the way in which the device works, its advantages and disadvantages, cost, and special benefits to the user. If possible, interview an individual who actually uses the device. Find out how this person evaluates the device and include this information in your report. Determine whether the device is available for students in a local school district.

IV

Methods for Mainstreaming Students with Other Special Needs

443

15 Teaching Students Who Are Gifted and Talented

■ *Kay is a high school junior who was identified in the second grade as gifted. Since that time, special adaptations have been provided in much of her education, especially in the area of mathematics. Her current program allows her to complete a 3-year high school curriculum in 2 years, and she plans to enroll as a full-time college student at age 16. At present, she is taking courses in calculus and computer programming at the local junior college, in addition to her regular high school program. In her after-school hours, she plays on the school golf team, serves as president of the math club, and has helped with set designs for several of the drama club's plays.*

■ *Luis is a 6-year-old first grader who has recently been identified as gifted. He was able to read when he entered kindergarten and now is in an advanced reading group in the school's resource program for students who are gifted. The resource teacher assists the general education teacher by providing Luis with individualized assignments in most academic areas; much of the material appropriate for Luis's classmates he has already mastered. Math is an exception; Luis's performance in this area is only average. Although assessment results indicate that Luis is quite capable, his interest in math is low. As a result, his teacher is providing an individualized program in which Luis can earn extra reading time for each math development step. Luis is very interested in music and has learned to play both the piano and the guitar; he takes music lessons twice a week at the local recreation center. Later in this chapter we will take a look at the goals and services from Luis's IEP.*

■ *Johnny is a sixth grader with special talent in writing. Although he did not learn to read until he entered school, he began to write short stories and poems in first grade. Several of his pieces have been published in children's magazines. Although his spelling is not always the best, his vocabulary and ability to use words are far beyond those expected of a 12-year-old student. Johnny's school has no special programs for students who are talented, and he does not qualify for the gifted program because his achievement is average in all areas except writing.*

Despite the lack of special services, Johnny's teacher is interested in helping him progress and maintain his interest in writing. She allows him to select his own topics for classroom writing assignments, reads and critiques any poems or stories he brings to her, and is investigating ways to help Johnny enroll in the creative writing course offered at the high school in the summer.

Students who are gifted and talented are found at all ages and grade levels within the school system. They are "a minority distinguished not by race, socioeconomic background, ethnic origin, or impaired powers, but by its exceptional ability . . . members come from all levels of society, from all races and nationalities, and from both sexes in about equal numbers" (Lyon, 1981, pp. 15–16). Many believe that gifted and talented individuals are one of the most neglected and underserved of all special student groups (Gallagher, 1988) because their special learning needs are neither universally recognized nor provided for.

Many teachers and parents do not clearly understand the needs of students who are gifted and talented. Some educators continue to believe that these students, because of their exceptional abilities, are capable of realizing their maximum potential without the benefit of specially designed educational adaptations or programs. Some teachers are somewhat in awe of gifted and talented pupils; others resent their probing minds and seemingly endless questions. There is also the question of resource allocation. In a supposedly egalitarian society, should monies be spent to promote the achievement of those who are already in some way superior (Mann & McIntyre, 1992)?

Many educators do not realize that students who are gifted and talented often have special learning needs that are not fully met by the general education program. Such students should be identified in order to adapt the general education program or provide special educational services. In this way, it is possible to help them achieve at a level commensurate with their potential (Parker, 1989).

This chapter examines the characteristics of mainstreamed students with special gifts and talents and also describes methods for the general education teacher to use in gathering data and designing and implementing program adaptations. To learn more about individuals who are gifted and talented, review the references presented in "Exceptional Literature."

■ INDICATORS OF TALENT AND GIFTEDNESS

Some students who are gifted and talented have highly unusual abilities that are identified early in life by their parents. For most students, however, it is the classroom teacher who first notices their special abilities. Students who are gifted and talented can be identified at any time during their school careers, but they are most likely to come to their teachers' attention during the elementary school years.

Giftedness and talent have several indicators that teachers might look for. However, Heward and Orlansky (1992) caution that general descriptions of group characteristics are not always effective in the identification of individuals; students may be gifted or talented and display several or none of the specific characteristics included on a list. As with all special individuals, the student's unique needs must be considered.

Although there is not universal agreement concerning a definition of this group of students, the description included in the Gifted and Talented Children's Act of 1978 (PL 95-561, Section 902) is often cited:

> The term *gifted and talented children* means children and, whenever applicable, youth who are identified at the preschool, elementary, or secondary level as possessing demonstrated or potential abilities that give evidence of high performance capabilities in areas such as intellectual, creative, specific academic, or leadership ability, or in the performing and visual arts, and who by reason thereof, require services or activities not ordinarily provided by the school.

In contrast to earlier definitions, this statement includes not only those who are intellectually gifted but also those with specific gifts or talents in the arts

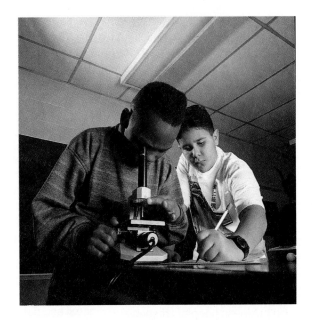

or in leadership. In general, **giftedness** is characterized by above average intellectual ability, which may be accompanied by superior academic achievement and creative capability. **Talented** individuals, in contrast, excel in one or more specific areas of endeavor: drama, art, music, leadership, and so on. This distinction between giftedness and talent is expanded by Gardner (1987) who identifies seven different types of intelligence: linguistic, logical-mathematical, spatial, musical, bodily-kinesthetic, interpersonal, and intrapersonal.

Giftedness and talent may occur in combination or separately; that is, students may be either gifted or talented or both. It is also possible for an individual to be intellectually gifted and yet experience difficulty in school learning; the special problems of underachieving students who are gifted pose a real challenge to a classroom teacher.

"Tips for the Teacher" summarizes some of the major indicators of giftedness and talent that can be observed in the general education classroom. Although special students do not generally display all these signs, the presence of one or two of them is cause for a teacher to consider further assessment.

Heward and Orlansky (1992) point out that even though descriptions of students who are gifted usually

EXCEPTIONAL LITERATURE
Individuals Who Are Gifted and Talented

FICTION AND BIOGRAPHY

There is a plentiful supply of biographies of gifted and talented individuals. In fact, most biographies chronicle the lives of persons found noteworthy either by their contemporaries or history. Included among biographical accounts of gifted and talented people are the life stories of artists, writers, musicians, generals, politicians, actors, sculptors, and business people. Of special interest are the lives of gifted and talented persons who also have disabilities. See, for example, **Mornings on Horseback** by D. McCullough (New York: Simon & Schuster, 1981) for the story of the young Theodore Roosevelt, who suffered from asthma, or **The Miracle Worker** by W. Gibson (New York: Bantam, 1956) for an account of the early years of Helen Keller.

In addition to biography, several fictional works describe gifted and talented individuals:

Flowers for Algernon by D. Keyes (New York: Bantam Books, 1966). The story of a man with mental retardation named Charlie who undergoes experimental surgery to raise his IQ; Charlie's journal reveals his progression from retardation to giftedness.

The Child Buyer by J. Hersey (New York: Bantam Books, 1960). In this novel Wissey Jones is the child buyer who attempts to purchase gifted children for educational and patriotic purposes; the book includes an excellent description of a gifted boy, Barry Rudd.

PROFESSIONAL LITERATURE

Handbook of Gifted Education edited by N. Colangelo and G. A. Davis (Boston: Little, Brown, 1991). A text that focuses on the educational, psychological, and social perspectives of giftedness and includes information on instructional strategies that can be used by teachers. Definitions, characteristics of students who are gifted, working with parents, counseling students, ethnic and cultural issues, students who are both gifted and disabled, and educational programs are described as well as techniques for modification of content area instruction and enhancement of inductive, creative, and evaluative thinking.

"Students with Unique Gifts and Talents" by E. D. Pendarvis in *An Introduction to Special Education* (3rd ed.; pp. 563–599) by A. E. Blackhurst and W. H. Berdine (Eds.) (New York: HarperCollins, 1993). An introductory chapter on giftedness and talent that presents information about definition, prevalence, educational programs, and current issues. Also included is information about etiology, identification, characteristics, intervention issues at all age levels, and new trends in gifted programs.

Growing Up Gifted (4th ed.) by B. Clark (New York: Merrill/Macmillan, 1992). A book about students who are gifted that features school programs, identification procedures, classroom strategies, and suggestions for parents. Also provided are strate-

---

emphasize only positive characteristics, these students can also display less attractive behaviors. Figure 15–1 presents both sides of the giftedness coin.

Several techniques are used to identify students who are gifted and talented. These include referrals from teachers, parents, peers, or students themselves; group measures of achievement or intellectual performance; and observation of special academic or creative achievements. Although teachers are the most common source of referrals, their accuracy as identifiers is questionable, especially with younger children and classes with many students from diverse ethnic, cultural, or linguistic groups (Baldwin, 1991; Kitano, 1989). Even with training, teachers tend to look for the stereotypical student who is gifted—who is highly motivated and adjusted to school—and often overlook the unique student with a set of unusual skills and abilities.

gies for understanding gifted individuals, techniques for teaching gifted preschool children to read, methods for serving students who are gifted at the middle and secondary school levels, and descriptions of standardized tests appropriate for this population.

Gifted Students in Regular Classrooms by B. N. Parke (Boston: Allyn & Bacon, 1990). A book directed at providing information for teachers trying to meet the educational needs of students who are gifted in general education classroom settings. Information is presented on characteristics, interests, and educational needs of gifted pupils. Development and selection of an appropriate curriculum, procedures for maintaining programs in the general education classroom, and services outside the general education classroom are also covered.

Creative Thinking and Problem Solving in Gifted Education (3rd ed.) by J. F. Feldhusen and D. J. Treffinger (Dubuque, IA: Kendall/Hunt, 1985). Provides a valuable guide for teachers interested in developing lessons for teaching creative thinking and problem solving to students who are gifted. Background information on instruction in these areas is discussed, but the most important features of the book are the specific suggestions provided for teachers and the extensive reviews and recommendations regarding instructional materials and books.

Comprehensive Curriculum for Gifted Learners (2nd ed.) by J. VanTassel-Baska (Boston: Allyn & Bacon, 1994). This book is designed to provide educators with information on both the theoretical aspects and practical applications of curriculum for gifted pupils. It seeks to provide specific procedures to follow and concepts to consider in creating curricular experiences for these learners, including adapting curriculum in traditional content areas.

"Literature for Students Who Are Gifted" by C. L. Schlichter in the Spring 1989 issue of *Teaching Exceptional Children*. This article presents an excellent review of books that are appropriate for students who are gifted in grades K–6. The citations for each book are accompanied by abstracts and are grouped into four categories that parallel the needs of students who are gifted. The books cited are ones that (1) encourage language development through the use of rich and challenging vocabulary, (2) stimulate creative and imaginative powers, (3) provide nonstereotyped role models that help students gain accurate perspectives on the world, and (4) furnish how-to skill training in interest areas such as conducting research or structuring a report.

"Counseling Students Who Are Gifted Through Bibliotherapy" by M. Adderholdt-Elliott and S. H. Eller in the Fall 1989 issue of *Teaching Exceptional Children*. The article provides teachers with suggestions for using novels to help students deal with personal problems by reading stories about characters who have problems similar to the ones they experience. Specific examples of novels are provided, as well as procedures teachers should use to implement this technique for elementary and middle school students.

Behavior checklists or rating scales can prove helpful to the teacher. For example, the *Scales for Rating the Behavior Characteristics of Superior Students* (Renzulli, Smith, White, Callahan, & Hartman, 1976) is used by a teacher to rate a student's performance in the areas of learning, motivation, and creativity. This type of scale provides information on a student's strengths and is useful for both identification and educational planning.

Stephens and Wolf (1978) suggest that identification of special students should be tied directly to the goals of the program in which they will be placed. To assure a better match between student and program, these authors recommend the following steps:

1. Establish Program Goals
2. Develop Objectives
3. Specify Requisite Student Characteristics

Signs of Giftedness and Talent

*T*here are numerous lists of characteristics or distinguishing features and attributes of gifted and talented children. Teachers and parents should interpret any single list, including this one, as only an example of possible traits.

Few gifted children will display all of the characteristics in a given list; however, when clusters of these characteristics are present, they do serve as fairly reliable indicators. Giftedness may exist in only one area of academic learning, such as mathematics, or may be quite general across the school curriculum. . . . These characteristics are signals to indicate that a particular child might warrant closer observation and could require specialized educational attention, pending a more comprehensive assessment.

General Behavioral Characteristics

- Many typically learn to read earlier with a better comprehension of the nuances of the language. As many as half of the gifted and talented population have learned to read before entering school. They often read widely, quickly, and intensely and have large vocabularies.
- They commonly learn basic skills better, more quickly, and with less practice.
- They are frequently able to pick up and interpret nonverbal cues and can draw inferences which other children have to have spelled out for them.
- They take less for granted, seeking the "hows" and "whys."
- They display a better ability to work independently at an earlier age and for longer periods of time than other children.
- They can sustain longer periods of concentration and attention.
- Their interests are often both widely eclectic and intensely focused.
- They frequently have seemingly boundless energy, which sometimes leads to a misdiagnosis of "hyperactive."
- They are usually able to respond and relate well to parents, teachers, and other adults. They may prefer the company of older children and adults to that of their peers.
- They are willing to examine the unusual and are highly inquisitive.
- Their behavior is often well organized, goal directed, and efficient with respect to tasks and problems.
- They exhibit an intrinsic motivation to learn, find out, or explore and are often very persistent. "I'd rather do it myself" is a common attitude.
- They enjoy learning new things and new ways of doing things.
- They have a longer attention and concentration span than their peers.

Learning Characteristics

- They may show keen powers of observation, exhibit a sense of the significant, and have an eye for important details.

- They may read a great deal on their own, preferring books and magazines written for youngsters older than themselves.
- They often take great pleasure in intellectual activity.
- They have well developed powers of abstraction, conceptualization, and synthesizing abilities.
- They generally have rapid insight into cause-effect relationships.
- They often display a questioning attitude and seek information for the sake of having it as much as for its instrumental value.
- They are often skeptical, critical, and evaluative. They are quick to spot inconsistencies.
- They often have a large storehouse of information regarding a variety of topics which they can recall quickly.
- They show a ready grasp of underlying principles and can often make valid generalizations about events, people, and objects.
- They readily perceive similarities, differences, and anomalies.
- They often attack complicated material by separating it into its components and analyzing it systematically.

Creative Characteristics

- They are *fluent* thinkers, able to produce a large quantity of possibilities, consequences, or related ideas.
- They are *flexible* thinkers able to use many different alternatives and approaches to problem solving.
- They are *original* thinkers, seeking new, unusual, or unconventional associations and combinations among items of information. They also have an ability to see relationships among seemingly unrelated objects, ideas, or facts.
- They are *elaborative* thinkers, producing new steps, ideas, responses, or other embellishments to a basic idea, situation, or problem.
- They show a willingness to entertain complexity and seem to thrive in problem situations.
- They are good guessers and can construct hypotheses or "what if" questions readily.
- They often are aware of their own impulsiveness and the irrationality within themselves and show emotional sensitivity.
- They have a high level of curiosity about objects, ideas, situations, or events.
- They often display intellectual playfulness, fantasize, and imagine readily.
- They can be less intellectually inhibited than their peers in expressing opinions and ideas and often exhibit spirited disagreement.
- They have a sensitivity to beauty and are attracted to aesthetic dimensions.

Note. From "Characteristics of Intellectually Gifted Children" (Digest 344) by J. R. Whitmore, 1985, *Digests on the Gifted* (Reston, VA: The Council for Exceptional Children), pp. 1–2. Material is in the public domain.

List A: Positive Aspects	List B: Not-So-Positive Aspects
1. Expresses ideas and feelings well	1. May be glib, making fluent statements based on little or no knowledge or understanding
2. Can move at a rapid pace	2. May dominate discussions
3. Works conscientiously	3. May be impatient to proceed to the next level or task
4. Wants to learn, explore, and seek more information	4. May be considered nosey
5. Develops broad knowledge and an extensive store of vicarious experiences	5. May choose reading at the expense of active participation in social, creative, or physical activities
6. Is sensitive to the feelings and rights of others	6. May struggle against rules, regulations, and standardized procedures
7. Makes steady progress	7. May lead discussions "off the track"
8. Makes original and stimulating contributions to discussions	8. May be frustrated by the apparent absence of logic in activities and daily events
9. Sees relationships easily	9. May become bored by repetitions
10. Learns material quickly	10. May use humor to manipulate
11. Is able to use reading skills to obtain new information	11. May resist a schedule based on time rather than task
12. Contributes to enjoyment of life for self and others	12. May lose interest quickly
13. Completes assigned tasks	
14. Requires little drill for learning	

Note.   Reprinted with the permission of Macmillan College Publishing Company from *Exceptional Children*, 4/e by William L. Heward and Michael D. Orlansky. Copyright ©1992 by Macmillan College Publishing Company, Inc.

4. Locate Students
5. Assign Students (p. 390)

Kitano (1989) provides several suggestions to teachers to assist them in improving their accuracy in identifying gifted children:

■ Consider all children as potential candidates for giftedness. For example, a hyperactive, disruptive, or unkempt child may also be gifted.

■ Recognize that "negative" traits [e.g., List B in Figure 15–1] . . . do not disqualify a child from consideration as gifted. Although gifted and average children may display negative behaviors, gifted children will also demonstrate their strengths when provided with opportunities to do so.

■ Look for and analyze the strengths exhibited by all children, including those who do not display stereotypical achieving, cooperating, and conforming behaviors. For example, the child who touches expensive equipment after being admonished not to touch may be exhibiting extreme curiosity rather than defiance.

■ Provide opportunities for and encourage children to express their abilities. For example, the teacher can informally assess reading and writing skills by inviting children individually to read to them at the book center and encouraging volunteer efforts to write their names and other words.

■ Use parents as informants. Parents serve as effective identifiers of gifted children. . . . Moreover, they can provide accurate observations about what their children can and cannot do. (p. 60)

Special attention should be paid to the inclusion of qualified students from diverse ethnic, cultural, or linguistic groups and those with disabilities in programs for students who are gifted and talented (Karnes & Johnson, 1991; Klein, 1989). Total reliance on standardized tests should be avoided; norm-referenced measures can lead to the exclusion of many such students who are excellent candidates for programs for students who are gifted and talented. Educators should use several different measures, rather than only one or two, and stress procedures that reduce cultural bias to identify students from these populations (Kitano & Kirby, 1986).

ASSESSMENT PROCEDURES

When a student is identified as a potential candidate for special education services for students who are gifted and talented, the next step is a comprehensive assessment. The purpose is to gather information about the learning needs and abilities of the student in order to assist in planning appropriate educational modifications. Both formal and informal measures are used; examples of possible informal procedures are direct observation, inventories, checklists, and analysis of various types of work samples. In some states, there are specific guidelines for determining eligibility for special education programs for gifted and talented pupils; in others, this decision is left to the discretion of the local school district. Care should be taken to gather only information that will be used in the actual identification process. It is inappropriate to collect a variety of data and then determine eligibility solely on the basis of an intelligence test score (Reis & Renzulli, 1985; Sternberg, 1991).

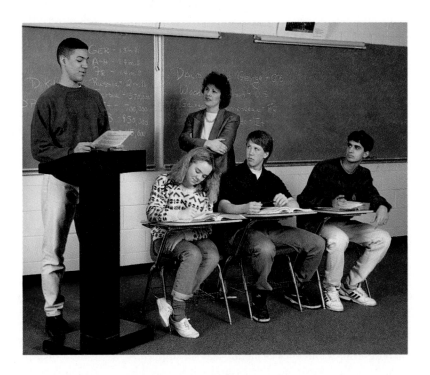

In the past, many programs for students who are gifted relied almost exclusively on norm-referenced tests of intelligence for assessment. Measures such as the *Wechsler Intelligence Scale for Children–Third Edition* (Wechsler, 1991) and the *Stanford-Binet Intelligence Scale* (4th ed.) (Thorndike, Hagen, & Sattler, 1986) remain in use today, particularly for identification of students who are academically talented. Practices vary widely regarding minimum scores for eligibility for services for students who are gifted; a *WISC-III* score of IQ 115 may qualify a student in one state or school district, whereas a score of 130 or 135 is necessary in another.

Although individual IQ tests such as the *WISC-III* and the *Stanford-Binet* are considered the single most reliable indicator of intellectual giftedness, they have many drawbacks. They are expensive to use and can be administered only by special personnel. They are biased in favor of middle- and upper-class students and discriminate against those students who have disabilities or come from diverse ethnic, cultural, or linguistic groups. In addition, they fail to assess such important abilities as creativity, leadership, and specific talents.

Measures such as the *Torrance Tests of Creative Thinking* (Torrance, 1966) can be used to assess creativity. Such tests help identify divergent thinkers who may be overlooked on intelligence tests. In describing these instruments, Gay (1981) notes that

> one such test asks the individual to list as many uses as he or she can think of for an ordinary brick. Think about it and list a few. If you listed uses such as build a school, build a house, build a library, etc., then you are not very creative; all of those uses are really the same, namely, you can use a brick to build something. Now, if you are creative, you listed different uses such as break a window, drown a rat, and hit a robber on the head. (p. 128)

Creativity test results should be supplemented with information from other sources, such as analysis of students' creative products and performances and direct observation of student behavior.

Observation techniques help to objectively assess and describe a student's academic and social performance in the classroom. For example, it is possible to observe the amount and reading levels of material the student reads each week, the number of social interactions per class period, or the time taken to complete an assignment. Information such as this not only helps to determine the student's current performance levels but also assists in the development of program modifications.

Analysis of work samples is conducted somewhat differently with students who are gifted and talented. Instead of searching for error patterns, the purpose is to discover a student's strengths and potential for further achievement. In the area of academics, a teacher looks for advanced school skills or competence in a subject matter not normally taught in the general education curriculum. Examples include the precocious kindergartner who reads and understands fourth grade material and the second grader who has special knowledge in botany and zoology. For information about specific talents, the teacher should consider a wide variety of student products, such as writings, artwork, musical compositions, and inventions; other possibilities are dramatic or musical performances. A teacher can analyze these work samples or ask for assistance from others. Subject matter experts and practicing artists, musicians, or writers may be better able to judge whether students' work is exceptional and whether students have potential to benefit from advanced study in the area.

In addition to the strengths of students who are gifted and talented, areas of relative weakness must also be considered. This is particularly important for students with major discrepancies between ability and achievement and those who excel in one or two areas but not in others. The assessment procedures suggested for students with learning disabilities and behavioral disorders are appropriate for gathering information about academic achievement and school conduct. The procedures suggested in chapter 6 can be helpful if social acceptance problems are suspected.

■ SPECIAL SERVICES

When the assessment data have been collected, the mainstreaming team meets to plan an appropriate educational program for the student. If special education services for students who are gifted and tal-

Students Who Are Gifted and Talented

- It is estimated that, under the current U.S. Office of Education definition of gift-edness and talent, 3% to 5% of the school-aged population is eligible for special services. "This percentage includes talented children who might be excluded under a definition that is based only on general intellectual ability" (Pendarvis, 1993, p. 566).

- A study conducted by The Council for Exceptional Children found that, between 1970 and 1980, there was a 100% increase in the number of students identified as gifted and talented and provided with special services. Between 1975 and 1980, funding for programs for students who are gifted increased 112% (Thomason, 1981).

- The Council of State Directors of Programs for the Gifted found that there was an increase in the number of public school students served in gifted programs from 2.7% in 1984 to 4.5% in 1987. Program growth is also illustrated by the fact that $289 million is currently allocated to local districts by 41 states, Puerto Rico, and Guam (Reis, 1989).

- A nationwide poll (Gallup & Elam, 1988) indicates a reversal in the recent trend of increased support for spending more public school funds on students who are gifted and talented than on average students. Between 1982 and 1985, public support for allocating more funds to programs for students who are gifted increased from 19% to 30%, but in 1988 this level of support fell to 25%.

- "Between 39 and 63% of the potentially gifted and talented [students] of our country are still not identified or not receiving specialized instruction" (Thomason, 1981, p. 102).

- Many students who are gifted may have high levels of activity in the classroom because of boredom or intense interest in an activity and may be considered to be hyperactive (e.g., have ADHD) and in need of special education services. This possibility should be carefully evaluated before decisions are made regarding changes in their programs (Webb & Latimer, 1993).

- Teachers of children and adolescents who are gifted do not necessarily have to be gifted themselves, but they "must be flexible, curious, tolerant, competent, and self-confident" (Heward & Orlansky, 1988, p. 437).

- Males and females do not differ in intellectual ability, but there have traditionally been significant differences in their achievement. Girls tend to achieve better than boys until puberty, when boys begin to excel, especially in math and science. In the adult years, the expectations of society continue to have a negative effect on the achievement of many women (Kerr, 1991; Pendarvis, 1993). Females are frequently found to disguise their abilities and limit their achievement to "socially acceptable" levels (Parke, 1989).

ented are not available, the team may be composed of only the general education teacher and the student's parents. In districts where appropriate services are offered, the team may include a full complement of specialists; possible team members are teacher-consultants, special class teachers, psychologists, administrators, and subject matter experts or professionals practicing in a student's area of talent. Even if IEPs are not required for students who are gifted and talented, it is good practice to develop a written educational plan. Figure 15–2 presents portions of the individualized plan for Luis, the first grader introduced at the beginning of this chapter.

Special services for students who are gifted and talented can be provided in many ways. As shown in Figure 15–3, these approaches span a continuum from mainstreamed programs to complete segregation (Reynolds & Birch, 1988). The most appropriate placement is selected for each student on the basis of individual learning needs. As with students with disabilities, the least restrictive environment is an important consideration; the appropriate placement closest to the mainstream of education is judged the least restrictive.

ADAPTATIONS FOR MAINSTREAMING

Educational adaptations are made for students who are gifted and talented who fail to attain their full

FIGURE 15–2
IEP Goals and Services for Luis

Annual Goals

1. By the end of the school year, Luis will read fifth grade material with adequate comprehension.
    Person responsible: Resource teacher
2. By the end of the school year, Luis will successfully complete all requirements for first grade math.
    Person responsible: First grade teacher
3. By the end of the school year, Luis will write short reports (with correct spelling and sentence structure) on topics of his choice.
    Persons responsible: First grade teacher and resource teacher
4. By the end of the school year, Luis will successfully play a series of songs on both the guitar and the piano.
    Person responsible: Parent

Amount of Participation in Regular Classes

Luis will attend the regular first grade class for all subjects except reading.

Special Education and Related Services

1. Luis will receive special education services from the resource teacher for students who are gifted (annual goals 1 and 3) for 1 hour daily.
2. The resource teacher will provide consultation to Luis's first grade teacher as needed.

FIGURE 15–3
Placement Alternatives for Students Who Are Gifted

Full Mainstreaming   Complete Segregation

- Special summer programs
- Special schools
- Clustered special classes in regular schools
- Limited enrollment seminars and courses
- Resource rooms and clinical centers
- Limited participation field trips and events on school time

- Cluster groups within the regular class

- Limited participation in before and after school groups

- Tutoring carried on in regular class

- Independent and individualized study in the context of the regular class

Note. From: *Adaptive Mainstreaming: A Primer for Teachers and Principals* 3/e by Maynard C. Reynolds and Jack W. Birch. Copyright © 1988 by Longman Publishers USA. Reprinted with permission.

potential in the general education program. According to Stephens and Wolf (1978):

> Bright students should receive systematically differentiated instruction throughout their school lives because they learn differently. While the objectives for the gifted are similar to those for other students, the ways to meet them differ. Emphasis should be on creativity, intellectual initiative, critical thinking, social adjustment, responsibility, and leadership. (pp. 398–399)

Instruction is the most typical area in which classroom adaptations must be made for students who are gifted and talented. For those who excel, advanced instruction is appropriate; for those with achievement problems, additional help with basic school subjects may be needed. The following sections of this chapter address ways in which the general education teacher can select appropriate educational options, promote the development of creativity and problem solving, and assist underachieving students in better realizing their capabilities.

EDUCATIONAL OPTIONS FOR STUDENTS WHO ARE GIFTED AND TALENTED

Individualized programs can be delivered in several ways to students who are gifted and talented. In many of these options, the student remains in the general education classroom with age peers. Special instruction can be provided within this class by the general education teacher, on a part-time basis by a special teacher in a special class or resource room, or in a setting outside the school when school is not in session.

The selection of an appropriate method for providing service depends on many factors. One important consideration is the relationship between student needs and program goals. According to Pendarvis (1993), educational modifications for students who are gifted and talented can be designed to accomplish the following things:

- Quicken the pace of learning by moving the student through activities faster than would be appropriate for children of average ability.

- Broaden the range of experiences and knowledge of gifted children by teaching subjects not offered in the general education curriculum at the children's grade level.
- Develop skills of analysis and expression in academic or artistic disciplines.
- Provide opportunity for concentrated, in-depth study of areas in which the students are especially interested or able. (p. 587)

Enrichment and **acceleration** are the two most typical ways in which the general education program is altered to meet the needs of students who are gifted and talented (Heward & Orlansky, 1992). In enrichment, something is added to the general education program. Students may study the same subjects as their peers but in greater depth. Or the curriculum may be broadened to include areas of study not generally covered; examples include after-school instruction in chess for first and second graders or the investigation by junior high students of finance policies in state government.

In acceleration, students progress through the general education curriculum at a faster rate than that in the regular classroom. They may be admitted to school at a younger-than-usual age or be allowed to skip one or more grades. Another way to accelerate is the telescoping of grades; for instance, the course of study for two grades might be compressed into one school year. Research conducted on acceleration programs establishes that students enrolled in these programs achieved at a much higher rate than their talented same-age peers who were not accelerated and as well as talented older peers in the same classes, while experiencing no negative effects on social-emotional development (VanTassel-Baska, 1994).

One of the primary advantages of enrichment is that students remain with age peers in the general education classroom. Acceleration, in contrast, requires either removal from the general education class to a special setting or placement in a regular class with students of older chronological ages. To learn more about the available educational options for providing enrichment and acceleration, consult the list of programs described in Figure 15–4.

Not only the needs of the student but also the resources of the school and community must be considered in determining the most appropriate instructional adaptation for individual students. Kirk and Gallagher (1979) present specific guidelines for selecting a suitable option:

1. When a child's pattern of growth in physical, social, mental, and educational areas . . . [is] accelerated beyond the chronological age . . . acceleration in grade placement should be considered.
2. When the physical, social and emotional areas are equal to chronological age, but the educational achievement is advanced, a special class or resource room can be considered.
3. When the school system is too small (not providing sufficient numbers of gifted children of a particular kind for a special class), enrichment, tutoring, or itinerant teachers for the gifted children in the regular classroom may be necessary.
4. When the class in which a gifted child is placed contains a preponderance of children of superior intelligence, even though it is not designated as a class for the gifted, enrichment of the program is probably more desirable than special classes or acceleration, neither of which may be necessary.
5. When the child is gifted but underachieving, special attention to social and emotional problems or to possible areas of weakness is called for. Intensive counseling and parent education or even remedial instruction may be more important for the child than classroom placements.
6. When inner discrepancies in growth are quite marked, as we often find in children with extremely high IQs, a tutorial or individualized method of instruction may be necessary, especially when the child is found to be unable to adjust to existing educational situations.
7. When school systems feel that enrichment in the regular grades is the most feasible plan, a special teacher or coordinator for gifted children is advisable. (pp. 95–96)

■ PROMOTING CREATIVITY AND PROBLEM SOLVING

When students who are gifted and talented are mainstreamed, the general education teacher is responsible for making program adaptations that facilitate maximum growth and development. Reynolds and Birch (1982) present six principles to help the teacher provide appropriate educational experiences for this group of special students:

1. Teach pupils to be efficient and effective at independent study, instilling and polishing the skills called for in self-directed learning and in analyzing and solving problems on one's own.
2. Help pupils to invoke and apply complex cognitive processes such as creative thinking, critiques, and pro and con analyses.
3. Encourage pupils to press discussions of questions or issues all the way to the culminating activity of decision making and to clear communication to others of plans, status reports, or solutions based on the decisions.
4. Establish the human interaction skills necessary to work smoothly with groups of all ages and of all levels of cognitive development.
5. Aid pupils in acquiring respect for all other humans whatever their gifts or talents and in understanding themselves in relation to all others.
6. Build pupils' positive expectations about careers and about lives as adults that optimize their talents and gifts. (p. 185)

Creativity and problem solving are two important areas in which students who are gifted and talented may require special attention and instruction. **Creativity**, according to Kirk and Gallagher (1979), is the production of "a unique product (from the child's point of view) from the available data or information" (p. 81). Creativity can also be conceptualized as the ability to generate novel solutions to specific problems.

One component of creativity is **divergent thinking**. In divergent thinking, several solutions to one problem are suggested. Four factors are important:

- *Fluency*—the ability to generate many responses.
- *Flexibility*—the ability to change the form, modify information, or shift perspectives.
- *Originality*—the ability to generate novel responses.
- *Elaboration*—the ability to embellish an idea with details. (Silverman, 1988, p. 276)

For ideas about ways to encourage creative thinking in mainstreamed students, consult the following suggestions:

- Provide regular opportunities for creative thinking. Creativity can be incorporated into most school subjects as soon as basic skills are acquired. Do not, however, accept novelty when accuracy is the goal. For example, spelling is one of the areas in which creativity should not be encouraged.
- Develop fluency with brainstorming sessions. Present a problem and see how many possible solutions can be suggested within a certain period of time. Do not evaluate the proposed solutions; instead, encourage a high rate of response. Younger students can practice with problems such as how to finance a trip to the toy store; older students may wish to suggest solutions for societal problems, such as how to provide proper health care for senior citizens or funding for public education.
- Encourage flexibility. For students who tend to generate one solution and remain with it loyally, require two suggestions. Keep increasing the number of solutions required until the student is able to generate several spontaneously.

FIGURE 15–4

Options for Providing Enrichment and Acceleration

Acceleration

- Subject matter acceleration—remaining at grade level while advancing in specific subject areas (e.g., advanced placement classes).
- Telescoping—covering more than a full year's work in a given year (e.g., multi-age grouping).
- Grade skipping—bypassing at least one year of instruction (e.g., early graduation).
- Early entrance—entering school at least one year younger than the norm (e.g., early admission to kindergarten or college).

Enrichment in the Regular Classroom

- Individualized programming
- Independent study
- Ability grouping
- Cluster grouping—all students who are gifted at a grade level are placed with one teacher to facilitate differentiated instruction.
- Flexible scheduling—students attend class less often than peers, perhaps for only 4 days each week.
- Use of faster-paced, higher-level materials
- Field trips
- Use of community resource persons at school

Special Classes

- Honors classes and seminars
- Extra course work
- Special course offerings (e.g., Junior Great Books)
- Use of a resource room or itinerant teacher on a weekly basis
- Segregated "pull-out" program for part of the day or week
- Full-time placement in a special class

- Special study centers
- Magnet schools—one may specialize in science, another in language arts. Students choose to enroll in a school that will serve them best.
- School within a school—a portion of the school is reserved for specialized classes for students who are gifted.
- Specialized school for students who are gifted (e.g., Bronx High School of Science)

Flexible Scheduling [i.e., Offerings Outside the School Day]
- Extracurricular clubs
- Early-bird classes—special classes held before school
- Extended day
- Extended school year
- Saturday or after-school workshops, classes, excursions
- Summer courses
- Evening courses

Off-Campus Options
- Mentorships
- Individual study with a community member
- Internships—working in the field with a specialist
- Outreach activities—programs developed for students who are gifted at local museums, colleges, businesses, etc.
- Residential summer institutes
- Community-based career education
- Student exchange programs
- Credit for educational experiences outside school (e.g., travel)

Note. From "Gifted and Talented" by L. K. Silverman in *Exceptional Children and Youth* (3rd ed., pp. 281–283) by E. L. Meyen and T. M. Skritic (Eds.), 1988, Denver: Love. Copyright 1988 by Love. Adapted by permission.

- Flexibility also involves the ability to change one's perspective. Have students list solutions to a school problem from their own point of view. Then, have them adopt the viewpoint of the teacher, the principal, the school board, or their parents.
- Originality is the creation of new solutions. As Kirk and Gallagher (1979) suggest, this means that the solution must be new to its creator, not necessarily new to society. For instance, the student who discovers an old idea or invents an existing device should be given credit for originality. Develop original thinking by providing opportunities for its occurrence. Suggest problems or needs, and direct students to come up with novel solutions. For example, ask students to suggest new ways of solving everyday problems, such as how to keep the toothpaste container and its cap together or how to prevent injuries caused by falls in the bathtub. Better yet, have students think of important problems and then generate novel solutions. One possibility is to challenge students to invent assistive devices to help bypass some of the limitations imposed by disabilities such as physical impairments, blindness, and deafness.
- In elaboration, ideas are expanded and made more detailed. Give students practice in elaborative thinking by presenting simple statements that they must expand. Use quotations or sayings, such as "All's well that ends well" and "All people are created equal." Or consider one of the novel responses produced in an original thinking exercise; have students expand the idea to include directions for implementation, ways of evaluating effectiveness, potential advantages, and possible disadvantages.

Problem solving is an extension of divergent thinking. It is important for students to become sensitive to the fact that problems exist and that they possess the skills required to develop appropriate solutions for these problems (Feldhusen, 1989). Guilford (1967), in his structure of intellect model, describes five types of mental operations: cognition,

memory, divergent production, convergent production, and evaluation. Cognition and memory relate to the gathering of information about a specific problem. In divergent thinking, several solutions are proposed; in convergent thinking, one "best" solution is selected. The final step is evaluation, in which the success of the selected solution is assessed; if the result is unsatisfactory, another solution can be chosen.

These different types of mental operations relate closely to the problem-solving model suggested by Gordon (1974). In this approach, conflicts are resolved by means of a six-step process:

1. Defining the problem
2. Generating possible solutions
3. Evaluating the solutions
4. Deciding which solution is best
5. Deciding how to implement the solution
6. Assessing how well the solution solved the problem (p. 228)

In the second step, all possible solutions are specified (divergent production). Then the solutions are considered, and one is selected (convergent production). The process ends with implementation and evaluation of the chosen alternative.

The Gordon model is one that can be taught to students who are mainstreamed and then used for the solution of classroom problems. It is also useful as a general strategy for attacking any problem situation. To students who are gifted and talented, it represents a powerful tool to guide analysis, synthesis, and evaluation activities.

"Spotlight on Technology" describes two ways for students to use technology to practice their problem-solving skills. These are Logo, the computer programming language designed for children, and simulation programs in which students practice making decisions in simulated situations.

ASSISTING STUDENTS WHO ARE UNDERACHIEVING

Underachieving students who are gifted and talented are one of the great tragedies of education. Because their potential for achievement is so great,

Software for Practice in Problem Solving

*SPOTLIGHT ON
TECHNOLOGY*

Logo

Logo is a programming language that is often used to develop problem-solving
skills in young students. Introduced by Papert in the book *Mindstorms* (1980),
Logo gained popularity as a way to encourage computer-based discovery learning (Bull, Lough, & Cochran, 1987). Logo is a very accessible language; with just
a few commands, students can begin to create graphics. It is also a powerful language that advanced students can use for sophisticated applications.

Students begin their exploration of Logo's graphic capabilities with some of the
simple commands built into the program. For example, typing the word FORWARD
(or FD) and a number moves the triangle-shaped cursor forward on the screen;
typing BACK (or BK) and a number moves it backward. To turn, the student types
RIGHT (RT) or LEFT (LT) and a number. The screen here shows a simple program
for drawing a square:

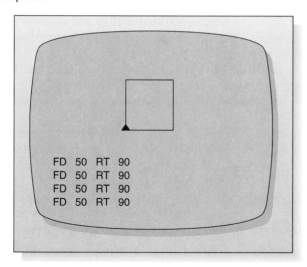

```
FD  50  RT  90
FD  50  RT  90
FD  50  RT  90
FD  50  RT  90
```

This program can be simplified by the use of a REPEAT statement:

REPEAT 4[FD 50 RT 90]

One major feature of Logo is that simple commands can be combined to form
new commands called *procedures*. In effect, the student is teaching the computer
new ways to act. To create a procedure to draw a square, the student might type:

463

```
TO SQUARE
REPEAT 4[FD 50 RT 90]
END
```

Then, whenever the command SQUARE is given, the program draws a square. Procedures can also be grouped together. For example, a procedure to draw a house might include procedures for SQUARE and for TRIANGLE.

In teaching Logo, the teacher acts as a facilitator. Students should be allowed to discover their own answers to problem situations, not told the "right" answer. As Male (1988) suggests, a teacher should say "'I wonder what would happen if . . .' rather than 'This is the way to fix it'" (p. 113).

Simulations

There are a number of software programs where students can practice their problem-solving skills in simulated situations related to topics in social studies, science, and other academic subjects. One of the best known examples is *The Oregon Trail* (MECC). In this simulation, the year is 1848 and students attempt to travel by wagon train from Independence, Missouri, to Oregon. Students must make several decisions throughout the journey, and each decision has the potential to affect the outcome of their trip. For example, if students decide to ford a river that is too deep, they may lose one of their oxen. Random events also occur; for instance, they may happen upon an abandoned wagon filled with supplies that they need.

In the Macintosh version of this program, the screen display includes several "buttons" that students can select to get further information about a variety of topics. For example, along the left side of the screen are the choices Map, Guide, Status, Rations, and Buy. In the screen shown on the next page, the student pioneers have encountered a snowstorm. The text window (below the wagon) displays the Trail Log, a running record of what has happened thus far on the journey. The contents of this log can be transferred to a word processing program for use in writing activities.

Wagon Train 1848 is a version of *The Oregon Trail* for computers that are networked together. In this "groupware" program, each computer represents one wagon, and students sitting at different computers join together to form a wagon train. Decisions about the journey are made over the network through cooperative group problem solving.

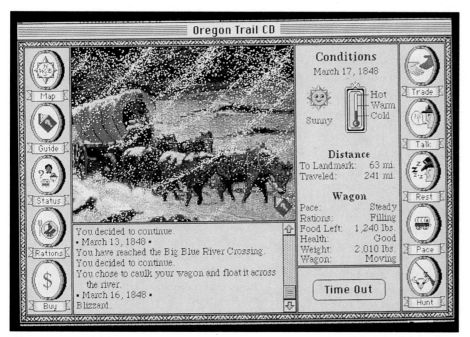

Left side menu: Map, Guide, Status, Rations, Buy

Trade, Talk, Rest, Pace, Hunt

Conditions
March 17, 1848

Sunny — Hot, Warm, Cold

Distance
To Landmark: 63 mi.
Traveled: 241 mi.

Wagon
Pace: Steady
Rations: Filling
Food Left: 1,240 lbs.
Health: Good
Weight: 2,010 lbs.
Wagon: Moving

Text box: You decided to continue.
• March 13, 1848 •
You have reached the Big Blue River Crossing.
You decided to continue.
You chose to caulk your wagon and float it across the river.
• March 16, 1848 •
Blizzard.

Time Out

Note. Photo courtesy of MECC.

Another popular set of simulation programs is the Carmen Sandiego series (Brøderbund® Software, Inc.). Carmen is a thief and leader of the V.I.L.E. gang, and students must play detective to track her down. Each program in the series includes a reference book. For example, in *Where in the World Is Carmen Sandiego?,* students consult *The World Almanac.* Other programs featuring Carmen and her band of thieves are *Where in the U.S.A. Is Carmen Sandiego?, Where in America's Past Is Carmen Sandiego?, Where in Time Is Carmen Sandiego?,* and *Where in Space Is Carmen Sandiego?*

their failure to thrive in school is doubly disappointing. The reasons for underachievement are many and complex. Some, particularly students from diverse ethnic, cultural, or linguistic groups and those with disabilities, may simply be overlooked. Hallahan and Kauffman (1988) address this issue and others in their recommendations to general education teachers:

1. The teacher should periodically review the characteristics of all the pupils in the class in order not to overlook any child who may be gifted. Which students in the class show particular ability, creativity, and task commitment? Are there pupils in the class, especially pupils who are economically disadvantaged or . . . [from a diverse ethnic, cultural, or linguistic] group, whose abilities may be less obvious according to white middle-class standards or who may be masking their abilities because of peer pressure for conformity?

2. The teacher must analyze and adjust his or her educational requirements for gifted pupils. Is the gifted child turned off to education because the work is not challenging or is not suitable for his superior intellectual powers? Is the gifted child underachieving simply because he is not being given appropriate work? Especially with the disadvantaged or culturally different gifted, it is important to present specific educational tasks in a structured environment with the firm and consistent expectation that they will be completed. . . .

3. The teacher must seek out and employ the resources of the school and community that can be used to the advantage of gifted children. Are there other teachers or older students with knowledge of the problems and methods of inquiry in a field of special interest who can help the child in independent study or small-group activities? Are there residents of other communities with special expertise who are willing to tutor the child or use him as an assistant?

4. The teacher should support whatever movement there may be in the school system toward establishing special programs for the gifted. Are there parents of gifted children whose pleas for special programs should be encouraged? Are there workshops for teachers? Does the school system employ resource teachers or specialists who will help . . . [general education] teachers find methods, materials, community resources? (pp. 453–454)

Another factor in underachievement is motivation. When students are uninterested in academic pursuits or bored with school activities, poor performance can result. Several suggestions for whetting students' appetites for learning appear in "Tips for the Teacher." Hallahan and Kauffman (1988) also recommend the *Handbook of Instructional Resources and References for Teaching the Gifted* by Karnes and Collins (1980).

Pendarvis (1993) adds several ideas gleaned from various sources for removing the barriers to achievement:

■ Don't give the students lectures or "pep talks" to get them to try harder. This has been shown to have detrimental effects on achievement.
■ Show support and respect for the student's efforts.
■ Establish appropriate standards and provide the instruction, guidance, and support to help students meet them.
■ Encourage cooperation, rather than competition, in the classroom.
■ Reward small gains in achievement, and don't expect quick success. (p. 583)

Levy (1981) also discusses ways to meet the needs of students who are gifted and talented. Three of these suggestions are particularly appropriate for the teacher of underachievers:

■ Let them teach you what they need. By listening to them and observing them, you can make guesses about what is needed . . . these students are articulate. They also appreciate a good listener. I constantly experience delight in my encounters with them.
■ Let them teach each other. Often my students teach each other content and processes that are way beyond my comprehension. As the teacher, I am not responsible to be the sole source of knowledge. I see myself as a facilitator of student learning . . . [two students] taught each other more in 5 months of computer instruction than I could have in a year, considering my other teacher responsibilities. They also provided each other with more minutes of instruction than I could have done in several years of being their classroom teacher.
■ Enjoy them. They are interesting people who are fun to have in class. (p. 142)

M any bright students need little encouragement. Some, however, have not yet developed the motivation to learn. With these individuals Stephens and Wolf (1978) suggest the following tactics:

- Provide recognition for their efforts
- Provide extra credit for novel ideas or products
- Stress positive comments in all teacher-pupil exchanges
- Offer special privileges for specified performances
- Permit high-achieving students to be "teacher"
- Encourage student-initiated projects and activities for those who have completed assignments
- Make special arrangements for high-achieving students to take selected subjects in higher grades
- Introduce elementary age students to research methods
- Teach debating skills and encourage students to sponsor and participate in debates on topics of their choice
- Have high-achieving math students create mathematical puzzles
- Encourage students to write scripts for TV and radio programs and "participate in" the programs
- Have students present a synopsis of a magazine or newspaper article to the class in a way that is interesting and understandable
- Have a "crazy idea" session where only unusual notions can be discussed
- Conduct a traditional brain-storming session
- Let them express themselves in art forms such as drawings, creative writing, and role playing
- Have them dramatize their readings
- Have a great books seminar to introduce students to the classics

Note. Reprinted with permission of Merrill, an imprint of Macmillan Publishing Company, from "The Gifted Child" by T. M. Stephens and J. S. Wolf in *Behavior of Exceptional Children* (2nd ed., pp. 403-404) by N. G. Haring (Ed.), Copyright © 1978 Merrill Publishing Company, Columbus, Ohio.

In this chapter, you have learned about some of the characteristics of students who are unusually bright and those with special gifts and talents. Methods for identifying appropriate educational options, promoting creativity and problem solving, and assisting underachievers have been suggested. In the next chapter, you will meet another group of special students—those from culturally and linguistically diverse backgrounds.

ACTIVITIES

1. Observe a general education classroom in which there are one or more students identified as gifted or talented. Are these pupils involved in any special programs outside the classroom or school? What special provisions are made in the general education classroom? Do the behaviors of these students differ in any way from those of

THINGS TO REMEMBER

- For achievement to be commensurate with potential, students who are gifted and talented require special educational adaptations in the general education class or in separate programs.
- Students who are gifted and talented are characterized by their above-average ability. Their gift or talent can be in intellectual performance, creativity, academic achievement, leadership potential, or special areas of endeavor such as art or music.
- This group of special students is composed of both males and females and individuals representing all socioeco-

nomic strata and cultures. As a group, students who are gifted and talented are more verbal, learn more rapidly, and are better adjusted than their typical class peers.
- The major educational adaptations for students who are gifted and talented are enrichment and acceleration. In the general education class, enrichment opportunities are offered to expand both the depth and breadth of study.
- One important goal in the education of this group of special students is the development of creativity and problem-solving skills. Divergent thinking is encouraged, and appropriate solutions to problems are sought through convergence and evaluation.

- Students who are gifted and talented do not all excel in school; some, considered underachievers, remain unidentified and/or lack sufficient motivation to perform near their potential.
- Most students who are gifted and talented remain in the mainstream for the majority of their school careers. To meet their special learning needs, educators must adapt the instructional procedures in the general education classroom.
- It is not necessary to be gifted or talented to be an effective teacher of such students. It is more important to be an adept facilitator of learning than an expert in all subject matter areas.

their peers? Are they well accepted by their classmates and teacher?
2. Interview children or young adults who have been identified as gifted or talented. What are their current interests? What do they like and dislike about school? Ask them to suggest ways in which the school experience could be made more valuable to them.
3. Locate articles that discuss education of pupils who are gifted and talented. *G/T/C* (Gifted/Talented/Creative), *Roeper Review, Journal of Creative Behavior, Journal for the Education of the Gifted*, and *The Gifted Child Quarterly* are possible sources. Do you find suggestions for general education class adaptations? For assisting underachievers? For students from diverse ethnic, cultural, or linguistic groups?

4. Contact local schools to find out what services are available for youngsters who are gifted and talented. Are there special classes? Early admission? Resource services? Enrichment programs to augment the general education classroom? What assistance is available to the general education teacher?
5. Ask several members of your community to define the terms *gifted* and *talented*. You might select teachers, students, school administrators, parents of school-aged children, and others with no current connection with the public school system. Compare their definitions to see whether there is any consensus. Use the information you have collected to prepare a set of local definitions meaningful to the persons in your community. Be clear and concise, and use language understandable to both educators and the general public.

16 Teaching Students from Culturally and Linguistically Diverse Backgrounds

■ *Let's begin with the case of Juanito, or Pablo, or Pedro, who is attending school for the first time. He comes to school with a language that has served him quite well for his first five years and with possibly some knowledge of English. He has grown up in a Mexican American family with traditional values unique to his culture and has been socialized in this culture. He goes to a school which reflects the values of the dominant society. This child comes in having a different language and a different culture from that of the school. He finds himself in a strange and threatening situation, not only with the need to master a new language, but to make immediate use of it in order to function as a student. Moreover, many of the social relationships and cultural attitudes on which the total school program is based are completely outside his experience. (Sierra, 1973, p. 43)*

■ *Chau became an honor student this year. Seventeen years old and a tenth grader, she is enrolled in a college prep curriculum with plans for becoming a counseling psychologist. . . . Born to a privileged Vietnamese family, Chau was six years old when the North Vietnamese entered Saigon as victors. She remembers hiding for hours with relatives in a cellar until the shooting stopped and then walking home over, and on, the bodies of those massacred. She remembers the government troops replacing a picture of her grandparents with one of Ho Chi Minh and then removing all furniture, clothes, and other belongings from her home. . . . And she remembers her first attempt to flee Vietnam with two brothers. Discovered by roving government troops, one brother escaped, one was killed, and Chau was shot and left for dead. (Cegelka, 1988, p. 547)*

■■ The United States is a culturally diverse
■■ nation, and the composition of many mainstreamed classrooms reflects this diversity. Students may differ from one another and from their teachers in culture and in language. These differences, when encouraged and fostered by society, are known as **cultural pluralism** (Rueda & Prieto, 1979).

Although each person is an individual with distinct characteristics, each is influenced by the culture in which he or she is reared and in which he or she lives. Aragon (1973) describes five major components that define a culture:

> First is a common pattern of communication, sound system or language which is unique to that group. Second is a common basic diet and method of preparing food. If the group adorns and protects their bodies with the same kinds of dress, or if the group has common costuming, they meet the third criterion of culture. And if the relationships within the group—woman-man, mother-child, uncle-niece—are predictable, or if there are common socialization patterns within the group, they have met the fourth. And finally, the group must subscribe to a common set of values and beliefs or have a common set of ethics. (p. 26)

Students in schools in the United States represent many different cultures. The dominant culture, or *macroculture*, has its roots in western European traditions. According to Gollnick and Chinn (1990), "the major cultural influence on the United States, particularly on its institutions, has been white, Anglo-Saxon, and Protestant" (p. 12). Persons living in the United States are influenced by the macroculture whether or not they choose to adopt all of its values and belief systems.

Each individual is also influenced by his or her membership in several microcultures. A *microculture* is a group of individuals who share some, but not all, of the cultural patterns of the macroculture *and* a common set of cultural patterns distinct from those of the macroculture (Gollnick & Chinn, 1990). Microcultures may be based on factors such as ethnicity or national origin, socioeconomic class, religion, gender, age, disability, or the area of the country in which a person lives (Gollnick & Chinn, 1990). Consider, for example, the differences between the customs and mores of New England and those of the Deep South or the differences in cultural patterns among Irish Americans, Mexican Americans, and Chinese Americans.

The term *minority* is used to describe groups with fewer members than the "majority" group. In the United States, census data and other sources of demographic information often define these groups as minorities: (a) Native Americans (including Alaskan Natives), (b) Asian Americans and Pacific Islanders, (c) African Americans, and (d) Hispanics (or Latinos). It is important to recognize that each of these groups is itself heterogeneous. For example, among people with Asian roots are those who identify themselves as Chinese, Vietnamese, Laotian, Hmong, Cambodian, Filipino, Korean, and Japanese (Cheng, 1991). Also, the Native American population is made up of more than 500 tribes with over 200 different languages (McDonald, 1989).

Many consider *minority* to be a pejorative term. In addition, in some parts of the country, it is inaccurate. Consider these statistics about the changing nature of the U.S. population:

- America's racial profile is rapidly changing. While the rate of increase for white Americans is 3.2 percent, the rate of increase for racial and ethnic minorities is much higher: 38.6 percent for Hispanics, 14.6 percent for African-Americans, and 40.1 percent for Asians and other ethnic groups.
- By the year 2000, this Nation will have 260,000,000 people, one of every three of whom will be either African-American, Hispanic, or Asian-American.

- Taken together as a group, it is a more frequent phenomenon for minorities to comprise the majority of public school students. Large city school populations are overwhelming minority, e.g., Miami, 71 percent; Philadelphia, 73 percent; Baltimore, 80 percent. . . .
- The limited English proficient population is the fastest growing in our Nation, and the growth is occurring in many parts of our Nation. In the Nation's 2 largest school districts, limited-English students make up almost half of all students initially entering school at the kindergarten level. (PL 101-476, Individuals with Disabilities Act, 1990, Sec. 610 (j)(1))

There have been many approaches to the education of students from culturally and linguistically diverse groups. Kitano (1991), however, describes the two major philosophical positions underlying these approaches: assimilation and pluralism. In assimilation, the goal is to move students away from their original culture and teach them the skills needed to compete in the macroculture. In pluralism, students are encouraged to retain their original culture and, to promote educational success, schools

---

FIGURE 16–1
Evaluating the Educational Context

For each of the items below, circle "Yes" if the statement is characteristic of your school (or your district, if you prefer). Circle "No" if the statement is not characteristic of your school or district.

Yes   No   1. My school/district supports cultural pluralism.

Yes   No   2. The curriculum incorporates students' contemporary culture, not only history, customs and holidays.

Yes   No   3. The curriculum helps students strike a balance between cultural pride and identity on one hand and appreciation of cultures different from their own on the other.

Yes   No   4. The curriculum teaches certain humanistic values such as the negative effects of prejudice and discrimination.

Yes   No   5. My school/district is integrated (or facilitates opportunities for cross-cultural interaction).

Yes   No   6. Inservices *routinely* incorporate considerations in teaching linguistically/culturally diverse students.

Yes   No   7. Children are encouraged to use their native language.

Yes   No   8. The administration supports bilingual education.

Yes   No   9. Minority parents are actively encouraged to participate in school activities.

Yes   No   10. Training is provided to facilitate involvement of minority parents in their children's education.

Yes   No   11. The regular classroom curriculum is appropriate for the diverse student populations served.

Yes   No   12. Regular classroom (not only bilingual education or ESL) teachers understand how limited English proficient students acquire English competence and incorporate language development activities in subject matter instruction.

---

make accommodations based upon students' experiential backgrounds.

Multicultural education is an instructional approach based on the pluralistic perspective. According to the policy statement, "No One Model American," of the American Association of Colleges for Teacher Education (1973):

Multicultural education is education which values cultural pluralism. Multicultural education rejects the view that schools should seek to melt away cultural differences or the view that schools should merely tolerate cultural pluralism. To endorse cultural pluralism is to endorse the principle that there is no one model American. To endorse cultural pluralism is to understand and appreciate the differences that exist among

Yes	No	13. Minority students do as well on achievement tests as do Anglo students.
Yes	No	14. Poor students do as well as middle- and upper-income students on tests of academic achievement.
Yes	No	15. As much emphasis is given to developing higher cognitive skills as is given to basic skill attainment.
Yes	No	16. Teachers are facilitators of learning as opposed to transmitters of information and facts.
Yes	No	17. Teachers adjust instructional approaches and activities to accommodate culturally-conditioned learning styles.
Yes	No	18. Informal assessment is given as much emphasis as is formal assessment in psychoeducational evaluations of linguistically/culturally different students.
Yes	No	19. Teachers are trained in informal assessment procedures.
Yes	No	20. Reading and writing instruction is characterized by student control and an emphasis on meaningful communication and creativity.
Yes	No	21. There is a well-articulated prereferral process in place to assure that students receive appropriate educational opportunities *before* they are referred to special education.
Yes	No	22. The emphasis of assessment is on gleaning information to guide intervention.
Yes	No	23. Students participate in school governance.
Yes	No	24. Teachers are involved in planning and selecting inservice training topics and activities.
Yes	No	25. My school/district would be described as a "happy" place by minority students and parents.

Note. This questionnaire was developed by Alba A. Ortiz, Department of Special Education, The University of Texas at Austin; it appeared in the Bilingual Special Education Newsletter (Vol. 7, Spring 1988) published by The University of Texas at Austin. The questionnaire may be reproduced without special permission when appropriate credit is given to the author.

the nation's citizens. It is to see these differences as a positive force in the continuing development of a society which professes a wholesome respect for the intrinsic worth of every individual. (p. 264)

When this viewpoint is adopted, the general education classroom begins to meet the needs of students from diverse cultural and linguistic backgrounds.

Figure 16–1 presents a checklist developed by Ortiz (1988) for evaluating a school or district's educational environment and its effectiveness for culturally diverse learners. Among the factors to consider are the relevance of the curriculum, parental participation, student involvement, and opportunities for teachers to continue to refine their skills.

DIVERSITY IN THE GENERAL EDUCATION CLASSROOM

Students are considered culturally diverse when their home culture is at variance with that of the school. According to Hodgkinson (1993):

> ... the population of American schools today truly represents the world. Children come to school today with different diets, different religions (there were more Moslems than Episcopalians in the U.S. in 1991), different individual and group loyalties, different music, different languages. (p. 620)

Some students from culturally diverse backgrounds were born in the United States and have lived there all their lives; others are recent immigrants still experiencing the shock of adapting to an entirely new culture. Immigrants come from all parts of the world, but in recent years the majority have been Latin Americans and Asians (Hodgkinson, 1993; Kellogg, 1988). Some are refugees who were forced to flee their homelands. The article "Educating Refugees: Understanding the Basics" (1989) reports that "in many cases, refugees have had to abruptly leave their home culture, language, family and friends, and may never be able to return to their countries" (p. 1).

Some students differ from their peers in not only cultural background but also language. They may speak with an accent or in a dialect; some may know little English and may feel more comfortable speaking the language of their home. Heward and Orlansky (1992) estimate that there are now more than 10 million U.S. students whose first language is not English. The population of a single school may reflect several of the more than 3,000 languages spoken in the world (Cheng, 1991). Cegelka (1988) provides examples of schools in California that serve 25 to 38 different language groups.

Some culturally diverse students have special learning needs, and others do not. Some have disabilities, some are gifted, and others are average achievers. Like their peers, most are best served in the regular classroom. However, the general education teacher must recognize the impact of cultural and linguistic diversity on the performance of these students. Knowledge of and respect for differences among cultural groups will help the teacher of the mainstreamed classroom provide a more successful educational experience for all students.

CULTURAL DIVERSITY

Culture influences behavior. Within each culture is a set of values and beliefs that guide the members of that culture in social interactions. However, what is accepted as desirable conduct in one culture may be considered inappropriate in another. The mainstream teacher must be aware of such differences in order to understand the behavior of students from diverse groups.

However, before proceeding, it is important to point out that descriptions of cultures are necessarily generalizations. As such, they provide some guidance in understanding the customs and beliefs of a *group* of persons but little information about specific individuals within that group. As Lynch (1992) warns:

> Culture is only one of the characteristics that determine individuals' and families' attitudes, values, beliefs, and ways of behaving. ... Assuming that culture-specific information ... applies to all individuals from the cultural group is not only inaccurate but also dangerous—it can lead to stereotyping that diminishes rather than enhances cross-cultural competence. When applying culture-specific information to an individual or family, it is wise to proceed with caution. (p. 44)

Pepper (1976) observes that there are many differences between the values of the dominant culture in the United States and those of the Native American culture; several of these differences appear in Table 16–1. For example, whereas the macroculture emphasizes competition and individual achievement, Native American culture stresses cooperation and group achievement. Also, in contrast to the dominant culture, in which words are the primary mode of communication, Native American students are more likely to express themselves through actions. These cultural differences can affect a student's ability to conform to the expectations of the school. In discussing points of divergence between the two cultures, Walker (1988) notes:

Cultural and Linguistic Diversity in the United States

- Asian Americans include (but are not limited to) Japanese, Chinese, Filipino, Korean, Vietnamese, Cambodian, Laotian, Guamanian, Indian, Pakistani, Burmese, Thai, Marshallese, Saipanese, Ponapean, and Yapese individuals (Cheng, 1991; Decano, 1979; Garcia, 1978). Asian Americans are the fastest-growing "minority" group, now numbering more than 7 million (Chan, 1992).
- Native Americans number more than 2 million and show great diversity in culture and language, as evidenced by the more than 200 different Native American languages in use today (Garcia, 1978; Joe & Malach, 1992; McDonald, 1989; Pepper, 1976).
- African Americans are the largest "minority"; the more than 30 million African Americans make up 12% of the U.S. population (Willis, 1992).
- The second largest group (and the largest bilingual group) is Latinos; numbering more than 19 million persons, they are largely concentrated in New York and Florida and the southwestern states of Arizona, California, New Mexico, Colorado, and Texas (Baca & Cervantes, 1989a; Garcia, 1978; Smith, 1979; U.S. Department of Commerce, 1989; Zuniga, 1992).
- More than 31 million people in the United States speak languages other than English at home (Schmidt, 1992).

- Family or cultural expectations for child behavior may differ from the expectations of the educational setting. For example, levels of independence in decision making might be greater for American Indian children.
- Identification of a child with his or her peer group may be more important than selection or recognition as an individual, thus inhibiting performance [by] noncompetitiveness.
- Cultural and family expectations for verbal interactions with adults may be contradictory to teacher expectations. (pp. 50–51)

Other cultures also have value systems that may be in conflict with the expectations of the dominant culture school. Kitano (1973) describes several characteristics of Asian culture that may affect student behavior:

- The Asian doesn't do anything that would make him stand out from the group. . . .

- The Asian culture utilizes a much more indirect or subtle means of communication than we usually find here in this country. . . .
- The Asian family structure is based on the traditional agrarian family model; males are considered more desirable than females. . . .
- Very few Asians engage in free participation in group discussions. Generally, they feel that if they say something, it must be profound and important. (p. 14)

Teachers' expectations for student performance often come into conflict with the expectations of Asian parents, as Table 16–2 illustrates.

Several authors have addressed the effects of Latino culture on student behavior (Aragon & Marquez, 1973; Condon, Peters, & Sueiro-Ross, 1979; Rodriguez, Cole, Stile, & Gallegos, 1979; Sierra, 1973; Zuniga, 1992). Cultural characteristics frequently mentioned are the existence of close family ties and strong family loyalties, preference for cooperative

TABLE 16–1
Native American and Dominant Culture Values

Native American	Dominant Culture
Excellence is related to a contribution to the group—not personal glory.	Competition and striving to win or to gain status is emphasized.
Cooperation is necessary for group survival.	Competition is necessary for individual status and prestige.
Good relationships and mutual respect are emphasized.	Success, progress, possession of property and rugged individualism are valued above mutual respect and maintaining good relationships.
People express their ideas and feelings through their actions.	People express themselves and attempt to impress others through speech.
People are usually judged by what they do.	People are usually judged by their credentials.
Time is present oriented—this year, this week—NOW—a resistance to planning for the future.	Time is planning and saving for the future.
Clocktime is whenever people are ready—when everyone arrives.	Clocktime is exactly that.
Work is when necessary for the common good. Whatever Indian people have, they share. What is mine is ours.	Work is from 9–5 (specified time) and to obtain material possessions and to save for the future. What is mine, stays mine.
Going to school is necessary to gain knowledge. Excelling for fame is looked down upon by the Indian.	Going to school is necessary to gain knowledge and to compete for grades.

Note. Adapted from "Teaching the American Indian Child in Mainstream Settings" by F. C. Pepper in *Mainstreaming and the Minority Child* (pp. 135–136) by R. L. Jones (Ed.), 1976, Reston, VA: The Council for Exceptional Children. Reprinted by permission.

rather than competitive activities, emphasis on interpersonal relationships rather than tasks, and a relaxed sense of time (in relation to that of the macroculture).

Likewise, values of the African American culture can influence students' classroom behavior. Teachers expect students to speak one at a time and to listen quietly while others are speaking. However, African American culture emphasizes general audience participation and spontaneity, not taking turns (Ratleff, 1989). Schools value verbal expression over other modes of communication. In contrast, African American culture encourages not only speech but also other forms of expression as well, including body language, nonverbal communication, and visual and dramatic expression (Ratleff, 1989). Franklin (1992) adds that African American students prefer student-centered classrooms with multiple opportunities for interpersonal interactions.

TABLE 16–2
*Incongruities Between American Teachers' Expectations
and Asian Parents' Expectations*

American Teachers' Expectations	Asian Parents' Expectations
Students need to participate in classroom activities and discussion.	Students are to be quiet and obedient.
Students need to be creative.	Students should be told what to do.
Students learn through inquiries and debate.	Students learn through memorization and observation.
Asian students generally do well on their own.	Teachers need to teach; students need to "study."
Critical thinking is important. Analytical thinking is important.	It is important to deal with the real world.
Creativity and fantasy are to be encouraged.	Factual information is important; fantasy is not.
Problem solving is important.	Students should be taught the steps to solve problems.
Students need to ask questions.	Teachers are not to be challenged.
Reading is a way of discovering.	Reading is the decoding of new information and facts.

Note. From Assessing Asian Language Performance (p. 14) by L. L. Cheng, 1991, Oceanside, CA: Academic Communication Associates. Reprinted by permission.

Although all persons are influenced by their cultures, they remain individuals; no group of people is homogeneous. However, it is worthwhile for teachers to attempt to gain insight into the cultural backgrounds of their students—and to identify their own values and belief systems. Lynch (1992) identifies three components of cross-cultural competence for teachers and other professionals: awareness of one's own culture, awareness and understanding of students' cultures, and development of cross-cultural communication skills. One way to begin to develop cultural understanding is through reading, and "Exceptional Literature" provides several suggestions.

LINGUISTIC DIVERSITY

Language is another important consideration in the education of students from diverse backgrounds.

Although some students are quite competent in English, others enter school speaking little or no English. The language of a student's family also concerns the teacher. Even if a child is fluent in English, the parents may not feel comfortable conversing in that language. For many (but certainly not all) culturally diverse students, the language spoken in the home is not English. Their parents and siblings may speak Spanish, one of many Asian languages, or one of many Native American tongues. Students who enter school with few English language skills are at a distinct disadvantage; as noted by Sierra (1973), the school expects these students not only to speak English but also to use that language to acquire other school skills.

At present, Spanish speakers make up the largest group of bilingual individuals in the United States. Much has been written regarding the overlap

EXCEPTIONAL LITERATURE
Cultural and Linguistic Diversity

PROFESSIONAL LITERATURE

Developing Cross-Cultural Competence by E. W. Lynch and M. J. Hanson (Eds.) (Baltimore: Brookes, 1992). Although written for professionals who work with young children with special needs and their families, this book is a valuable resource for any professional interested in cultural diversity. Includes informative chapters on several major U.S. cultures: Native American, African American, Latino, Asian, Pilipino, Native Hawaiian and Pacific Island, Middle Eastern, and Anglo-European.

Multicultural Education in a Pluralistic Society by D. M. Gollnick and P. C. Chinn (New York: Merrill/Macmillan, 1990). An introduction to multicultural education that explores influences such as ethnicity and race, language, class, gender, religion, age, and exceptionality. Ends with a chapter on strategies for promoting pluralism through multicultural education.

Cultural Awareness in the Human Services by J. W. Green (Ed.) (Englewood Cliffs, NJ: Prentice-Hall, 1982). Designed for social workers, this book discusses cross-cultural learning, language and world view, and the provision of services within cultural contexts. Includes descriptions of several cultural groups.

Several journals have published special issues with series of articles on students from various cultural groups. Examples are:

- **Exceptional Children** (October/November 1992, Vol. 59, No. 2)—African American youth
- **Phi Delta Kappan** (November 1988, Vol. 70, No. 3)—students who are recent immigrants to the United States
- **Teaching Exceptional Children** (Summer 1988, Vol. 20, No. 4)—students from culturally and linguistically diverse backgrounds

- **Exceptional Children** (October 1989, Vol. 56, No. 2)—Hispanic students

The Bilingual Special Education Interface (2nd ed.) by L. M. Baca and H. T. Cervantes (Eds.) (New York: Merrill/Macmillan, 1989). This text discusses the special educational needs of bilingual students who have disabilities. Of particular interest to general educators are the chapters on bilingualism and bilingual education, mainstreaming, consultation, and parent and community involvement.

Assessing Asian Language Performance by L. L. Cheng (Oceanside, CA: Academic Communication Associates, 1991). This book provides practical information on Asian cultural and linguistic values, factors in second language acquisition, and intervention issues and procedures. Chapters are devoted to Chinese, Indochinese (Vietnamese, Laotian, Hmong, and Cambodian), and other Asian peoples (Filipino, Korean, Japanese, Hawaiian, Guamanian, and Micronesian).

between language and culture and the difficulties this overlap presents in the education of students whose dominant language is Spanish. Condon, Peters, and Sueiro-Ross (1979) cite the examples of Lado (1968), which identify communication problems that can occur among speakers of Spanish and speakers of English:

- The Spanish compliment "Qué grueso estás," which is translated literally as "how fat you are," becomes an insult in English.

- The use of the name "Jesús" for a boy is quite common in Hispanic society, but not in the Anglo-Saxon community, where it is regarded as inappropriate, if not sacrilegious.
- To be "informal" in Spanish is "to be neglectful," but to be so in English simply conveys the notion of "casual" behavior.
- "Compromiso" as it applies to negotiations carries a negative connotation in Hispanic culture which is not found in its English counterpart "compromise." (Condon, Peters, & Sueiro-Ross, 1979, p. 82)

Evans and Guevara (1974) discuss other problems of communication that result from the interdependence of language and culture. Several of their examples are presented in Figure 16–2 on page 482.

When children acquire English as a second language, their speech may sound somewhat different from that of students who are native speakers of English. A teacher may note that they speak with an accent. One reason for this is the nonequivalence of speech sounds between languages. Taylor (1986) points out that Spanish speech sounds can interfere with English pronunciation. For instance, a Spanish speaker may substitute *chair* for *share* and *watch* for *wash* in English. These and other examples appear in Table 16–3.

It should be noted that not all culturally diverse students are bilingual; for many, English is the language of their home, and it is the only language that they know. However, they may speak a dialect of English rather than the standard English of the public school. One example is Black English, considered by many experts to be a dialect of standard English. As shown in Table 16–4, Black English is characterized by its own formal rules and structures.

ASSESSMENT AND SPECIAL SERVICES

Although most students from culturally diverse backgrounds receive their education in the regular classroom, some may be referred for assessment if they appear to have special learning needs. If students are identified as disabled, gifted, or talented, they may be provided with appropriate special education services. Others may qualify for bilingual education services, if these are available within the district. According to Gonzalez (1978), students are in need of bilingual instruction if (1) their primary or home language is other than English and (2) their school performance indicates academic underachievement.

Bilingual education is concerned with both language and culture, and programs take many forms

---

TABLE 16–3
Examples of Spanish Interference with English Speech Sounds

English Sound	Sound Substituted	Examples
initial sound of *ship*	initial sound of *chip*	*chair* for *share* *watch* for *wash*
initial sound of *zoo*	initial sound of *see*	*sip* for *zip* *racer* for *razor*
final sound of *ring*	final sound of *in*	*sin* for *sing*
initial sound of *voice*	initial sound of *boy*	*bat* for *vat*
initial sound of *thing*	initial sound of *see* or initial sound of *top*	*tin* or *sin* for *thin*
initial sound of *that*	initial sound of *do*	*den* for *then* *ladder* for *lather*
initial sound of *in*	initial sound of *eat*	*cheap* for *chip*

Note. Reprinted with permission of Merrill, an imprint of Macmillan Publishing Company, from "Language Differences" by O. L. Taylor in Human Communication Disorders (2nd ed., p. 400) by G. H. Shames and E. H. Wiig (Eds.), Copyright © 1986 Merrill Publishing Company, Columbus, Ohio.

FIGURE 16–2
Relationships Between Language and Culture

■ **It is sometimes not possible to translate a word from one language to another.**

Example: In studying a unit on animals, young English speakers understand *pet.* However, translation into Spanish results in *animal doméstico* (a domesticated animal) or perhaps *animalito* (a little animal), neither of which . . . [carries] the same meaning. The word *pet* is an English culture concept and the difficulty lies in the impossibility of translating the culture.

■ **Translation may result in misinformation.**

Example: For many English speakers, the word *tools* is a general category label indicating objects which are used in different occupations or tasks. At the end of a study unit on community helpers, the child may be asked to subcategorize tools on the basis of occupation (those used by a carpenter, janitor, gardener, etc.). In Spanish, there is no single general term for *tools* and translation may result in *fierros* (objects made of iron or steel), *herramientas* (implements), *instrumentos* (instruments), *equipo* (equipment), or *útiles* (utensils). Tools used by a carpenter are *fierros* while those used by a janitor may be referred to as *equipo.* It is impossible to teach a child to subdivide a category label that does not exist.

■ **A word specifying one concept in one language may specify several concepts in another.**

Example: The positional terms *in, on,* and *over* carry distinct concepts in English. However, in Spanish *en* is the equivalent of both *in* and *on*; *sobre* may mean *on* or *over*; and *encima* and *arriba de* can also mean *on* or *on top of.* To translate an activity written in English in which *in, on* and *over* are taught as contrasting concepts is not only confusing but may result in teaching erroneous concepts.

Example: In English *hot* or the phrase "it is hot" may be used in multiple ways such as describing the weather, a heated object, or degree of food seasoning. For example:

1.   "It (stove) is hot."
2.   "It (weather temperature) is hot."
3.   "It (highly seasoned chili) is hot."

However, in Spanish, these ideas must be expressed in a completely different manner. For example:

1.   "Está caliente."
2.   "Hace calor."
3.   "(El chile) pica."

TABLE 16–4
Characteristics of Black English

Linguistic Categories	Characteristics	Examples	
		Standard English	Black English
Phonological differences			
Initial position	Merging of /f/ with /th/	thigh	fie
	Merging of /v/ with /th/	Thou	vow
Medial position	Deletion of /r/	Carol	cal
	Merging of /i/ and /e/	pen	pin
	Merging of /v/ with /th/	mother	movver
	Merging of /f/ with /th/	birthday	birfday
Final position	Deletion of /r/	sore	saw
	Deletion of /l/	Saul	saw
	Simplification of consonant clusters:		
	/st/	past	pass
	/ft/	left	leff
	/nt/	went	wen
	/nd/	wind	wine
	/zd/	raised	raise*
	/md/	aimed	aim*
	/ks/	six	sick
	/ts/	it's	it*
	/lt/	salt	saught

* These items also are morphological differences.

TABLE 16–4
continued

		Examples	
Linguistic Categories	*Characteristics*	*Standard English*	*Black English*
Morphological differences			
Future	Loss of final /l/	you'll	you
Past tense	Simplification of final consonants such as:		
	/st/	passed	pass
	/nd/	loaned	loan
Plural	Deletion of final /s/ and /z/	50 cents	50 cent
		3 birds	3 bird
Syntactical differences			
Auxiliary verb	Deletion of auxiliary	He is gone.	He goin.
Subject expression	Repetition of subject	John lives in NY.	John, he live in NY.
Verb form	Substitution of past participle for simple past form	I drank the milk.	I drunk the milk.
Verb agreement	Deletion of /s/ for third person singular present tense	He runs home.	He run home.
Future form	Substitution of a variation of present progressive tense	I will go home.	I'ma go home.
Negation	Use of double negative	I don't have any.	I don't got none.
Indefinite article	Deletion of /n/	I want an apple.	I want a apple.
Pronoun form	Substitution of objective for nominative case	We have to do it.	Us got to do it.
Preposition	Difference in preposition	He is over at his friend's house.	He is over to his friend's house.
Copula ("be")	Use of durative be for is	He is here all the time.	He be here.

Note. From "Special Education and the Linguistically Different Child" by D. N. Bryen, 1974, *Exceptional Children*, 40, p. 593. Copyright 1974 by The Council for Exceptional Children. Reprinted by permission.

depending on their goals. According to Baca and Cervantes (1989b), *transitional* bilingual education programs utilize the student's native language and culture to facilitate the acquisition of English. The goal is to integrate the student into the general education curriculum as quickly as possible. *Maintenance* programs, in contrast, are designed to develop the student's native language skills and cultural competence as well as to teach English; the goal is to maintain the first language and augment (not replace) it with English.

Cummins (1989) maintains that educators should encourage students to develop proficiency in their first language (L1), even if bilingual education programs are not available. To do this, teachers should follow these suggestions:

■ Encourage students to use their L1 around the school.
■ Provide opportunities for students from the same ethnic group to communicate with one another in their L1 where possible (e.g., in cooperative learning groups on at least some occasions).
■ Recruit people who can tutor students in their L1.
■ Provide books written in the various languages in both classrooms and the school library.

■ Incorporate greetings and information in the various languages in newsletters and other official school communications. (Cummins, 1989, p. 113)

Like bilingual education, ESL (English as a second language) and ESOL (English for speakers of other languages) programs are concerned with the acquisition of English skills. However, instruction takes place only in English, and no effort is made to maintain or develop proficiency in the student's first language. Schools often use an ESL approach when there are insufficient numbers of non-English-speaking students to form a bilingual education class or when students represent a number of different language groups. Thus, when students are identified as limited in English proficiency (LEP), they may take part in ESL/ESOL classes, or bilingual education services may be provided in self-contained bilingual education classrooms or on a part-time basis by bilingual education resource teachers. See "Spotlight on Technology" for examples of software designed for students learning English language skills.

When students from culturally diverse backgrounds are evaluated either for special education

SPOTLIGHT ON TECHNOLOGY

Word Processors for Students Learning English

The Bilingual Writing Center

This program from Learning Company is a bilingual version of *The Writing Center* described in chapter 9. In effect, it is two programs in one: an English-language word processor almost identical to *The Writing Center* and a Spanish-language equivalent. In the Spanish portion of the program, all the directions, menus, and choices are in Spanish. There is a Spanish spelling checker and thesaurus and, if a student selects "Ayuda," he or she sees help messages in Spanish. The graphics that accompany this program are bicultural; for example, the graphics for special days include not only Christmas and Hanukkah but also Three Kings Day. The program also contains suggestions for classroom activities and sample word processing files for teachers. The photo here shows a school newsletter created by students:

Note.   Photo courtesy of The Learning Company.

ESL Writer

This word processor from Hartley Courseware is designed for students of English. Students write in English, and the program provides feedback on spelling, grammar, and capitalization. What is interesting about this program is that feedback is tailored to the specific language needs of different groups of students. Thus, there is a Spanish dictionary for ESL students who speak Spanish; an Asian dictionary for students whose language background is Vietnamese, Cambodian, Hmong, Filipino, Laotian, Chinese, Japanese, or Korean; and a generic dictionary for speakers of other languages.

When a student's work is checked for spelling, words not found in the dictionary are highlighted on the computer screen. Then, the spelling hints provided to the student are based on the typical errors made by native speakers learning English. For example, because native Spanish speakers often substitute *b* for *v,* the spelling hints for the misspelled word *bery* would include both *very* and *berry.*

Capitalization errors are identified for the student by highlighting the first letter of the word in question. Grammar errors are flagged by a highlighted square that appears in the sentence containing the mistake. Twelve types of grammar errors are identified, including subject/verb agreement, sentence fragment, helping verb problem, and missing word. As in spelling, feedback is based on typical errors of native speakers and students can request grammar hints. For example, if a word is missing, as in the sentence *I ice cream,* the student sees this hint: <?> ice cream. If necessary, the student can request additional help; the help screens define each type of error and provide examples.

or bilingual education services, it is necessary to ensure that assessment procedures are nonbiased. That is, measurement devices must not discriminate on the basis of race, culture, or language (McLoughlin & Lewis, 1994). The language of the student is an obvious consideration. If the student has limited proficiency in English, it is futile to use an English-language test to assess aptitude or school achievement. In fact, if the student's primary language is Spanish, Navajo, or Tagalog, the only justification for testing in English is to determine the student's facility in this second language.

The cultural background of the student is another important concern. If a measure has been designed for use with dominant culture students, those who differ in experiential background are unjustly penalized. Consider the example of Williams (1974) that is cited by Alley and Foster (1978):

> "When is Washington's birthday?" If you are of the majority culture, you probably would answer "February 22." This response would be scored correct according to the Wechsler Adult Intelligence Scale scoring criteria. . . . If, however, you were to respond "April 5," your response would be scored as incorrect, using that scoring criteria. The implication is that you must associate George rather than Booker T. with Washington. This item could be classified as culture-biased. (p. 1)

In the general education classroom, the teacher should also take care in assessing students from various cultural backgrounds. Many typical classroom measures are in opposition to the values held by some cultures. For instance, students who are not influenced by clock time will fare poorly on tests of speed or timed assignments. Those who prefer cooperation to competition may feel threatened by class contests. Individuals who are reluctant to stand out from the group may not respond to awards, prizes, and recognition as incentives.

ADAPTATIONS FOR MAINSTREAMING

Most students from culturally and linguistically diverse backgrounds are full-time members of regular classes. Although some students with special needs may receive services from a special education resource teacher or from an expert in bilingual education, most of their school career is typically spent in mainstreamed settings. Therefore, the general education teacher must be aware of cultural and linguistic differences and their effects on performance in academics, classroom conduct, and social interactions.

Multicultural education is the major approach to instruction of students from diverse backgrounds. According to Gonzales (1979), multicultural education includes five major components:

1. Staffing composition patterns throughout the organization hierarchy that reflect the pluralistic nature of American society;
2. Curricula that are appropriate, flexible, and unbiased, and that incorporate the contributions of all cultural groups;
3. Affirmation of the languages of cultural groups as different rather than deficient;
4. Instructional materials that are free of bias, omissions, and stereotypes; that are inclusive rather than supplementary; and that show individuals from different cultural groups portraying different occupational and social roles;
5. Educational evaluation procedures, which assess not only the content of the curricula and instructional materials, but also how well the experience and materials help encourage better understanding and respect for humankind. (p. 15)

These principles help guide the development of instructional programs that promote not only the acceptance of students who differ from their peers in culture and language but also their academic success.

In addition, teachers can use several strategies to adapt instruction to better meet the needs of students from diverse groups. One approach recommended by experts is **cooperative learning** (e.g., Baca & Almanza, 1991; Franklin, 1992; Ruiz, 1989). Many cultures value cooperation over competition and prefer interpersonal interactions to interactions with tasks. Cooperative learning, in which students work together to accomplish a common goal, is therefore more congruent with the values of these cultures than individualistic or competitive learning situations. See chapter 6 for descriptions of several types of cooperative learning strategies and the research supporting this approach.

Franklin (1992) discusses the major characteristics of culturally sensitive instruction for African-American students, which include:

■ Presenting instruction at a faster pace, with greater verve and rhythm
■ Increasing the amount of stimulation in the classroom by combining media (e.g., speech, singing, music, print, movement, visuals) and by providing a variety of different types of activities
■ Using several types of verbal activities such as rap, choral reading, chants, and responsive reading
■ Encouraging divergent thinking
■ Considering students' experiential backgrounds when choosing instructional materials and activities

■ Incorporating real-life tasks into the curriculum
■ Increasing the "people focus" of instruction so there are many opportunities for person-to-person interactions
■ Frequently using small groups for cooperative learning and peer tutoring

Ruiz's (1989) work focuses on another group of students: those who enter school less proficient in English than in Spanish. Ruiz presents the following guidelines for planning instruction for students learning English. Although these guidelines address the language arts curriculum in the elementary grades, many are also applicable to other subjects and other age groups.

■ Take into account students' sociocultural backgrounds and their effects on oral language, reading and writing, and second-language learning. . . .

- Follow developmental processes in literacy acquisition.
- Locate curriculum in a meaningful context where the communicative purpose is clear and authentic.
- Connect curriculum with the students' personal experiences.
- Incorporate children's literature into reading, writing, and English-as-a-second language (ESL) lessons.
- Involve parents as active partners in the instruction of their children.
- Give students experience with whole texts in reading, writing, and ESL lessons.
- Incorporate collaborative learning whenever possible. (p. 134)

Sheltered instruction is another strategy often used with students who are learning English. In sheltered instruction, the goal is to teach English language skills at the same time that students are learning specific content area knowledge (Northcutt & Watson, 1986). To do this, the teacher analyzes the content of the lesson to identify key concepts and vocabulary. Then, he or she systematically teaches those concepts and vocabulary by using instructional techniques designed to maximize students' ability to comprehend English language input (Krashen, 1987). These techniques include linking new information to students' background knowledge; use of clear, consistent language with many repetitions; and incorporation of extralingual cues such as visual aids, media, props, realia (i.e., real objects), demonstrations, dramatizations, and so forth (Freeman & Freeman, 1988; Gersten, Taylor, & Graves, in press; Ratleff, 1989; Towell & Wink, 1993). If the teacher or aide speaks the language of the student, key concepts can be pretaught in that language prior to the start of the lesson.

PROMOTING ACCEPTANCE OF DIVERSITY

Peer acceptance is a special need for many students from culturally and linguistically diverse groups. Students who appear different by virtue of language, dress, or customs may find interactions with classmates difficult. One way to overcome this problem is through instruction. When students learn about the language and culture of groups other than their own, differences become less frightening and easier to understand. When students learn about cultural pluralism, diversity is more likely to be treated not only with tolerance but also with respect. McCormick (1990) lists 10 suggestions to assist the teacher of the mainstreamed classroom; these appear in "Tips for the Teacher."

It is also important that the school curriculum and instructional materials such as textbooks reflect the contributions of all cultural groups. That is not always the case, as these examples provided by the National Coalition of Advocates for Students (1985) show:

> Witnesses told us of Native American children sitting through lessons about "taming the frontier" and of Columbus "discovering America"; of world history texts which devote no more than a few paragraphs to Africa; of Asian history courses that treat "all Japanese, Chinese, and Filipino people, whose histories are all different and all need to be told" as if they were one; of schools in the Southwest which teach the history of their region with little more than a cursory look at its rich pre-Anglo culture. (p. 17)

Garcia (1978) has compiled a set of techniques for promoting acceptance of diversity. Some of Garcia's suggestions are appropriate for all ages of students, whereas others are particularly useful in the secondary grades.

- Students can study and discuss their ethnic heritages.
- Ethnic minority group parents can be invited to school to visit and talk with students.
- Students can study the contributions that all ethnic groups have made to the community.
- Students can conduct surveys of their own ethnic group's geographic distribution and develop charts to record the information.
- Students can make a multi-ethnic map of U.S. society using pictures from old magazines.
- Any special ability of ethnic minority students, such as bilingualism, may be used to build their sense of belonging to the class. Sharing folktales, ethnic games, or songs are examples.
- Playground activities can be monitored so that students practice cooperation and fair play.
- Field trips to other schools with diverse student populations can be planned so that students of dif-

Teaching Students from Diverse Groups

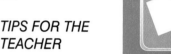

1. As you identify the different ethnic groups in your classroom, become informed about their characteristics and learning styles.
2. Encourage and assist students in sharing their culture in the classroom; you can start the process by sharing your own cultural values and traditions.
3. Avoid textbooks and materials that present cultural stereotypes.
4. Know as much as possible about minority students' home and community, interests, talents, skills, and potentials and develop an instructional program accordingly.
5. Find out how the minority students in your class wish you to refer to their ethnic group; for example, some Mexican Americans prefer to be called Chicanos while others may take offense at the term.
6. Include ethnic studies in the curriculum to help minority students gain a more positive self-image.
7. Make parents your partners in educating minority students.
8. Treat all students equally; do not fall into the trap of reverse racism.
9. Be sure assessment techniques used are appropriate and take into account cultural differences.
10. Avoid imitating speech patterns of minority students; rather than an aid in education, this may be viewed as mockery.

Note. Reprinted with permission of Merrill, an imprint of Macmillan Publishing Company, from "Cultural Diversity and Exceptionality" by L. McCormick in *Exceptional Children and Youth* (5th ed., p. 75) by N. G. Haring and L. McCormick (Eds.), Copyright © 1990 by Merrill Publishing Company, Columbus, Ohio.

ferent ethnic backgrounds can have one-to-one cultural exchanges.

- A multi-ethnic reading table or reading shelf can be maintained by the teacher and student. It might contain ethnic magazines, newspapers, and books. . . .
- Students and teachers may work with P.T.A. groups to conduct activities, such as a multi-ethnic song fest, that are cultural exchanges designed to improve community group relations.
- A multi-ethnic student welcoming committee can be organized to greet all new students, teachers, and school personnel.
- Role playing can be used to help students learn to take the role of out-groups as well as in-groups.

- A multi-ethnic bulletin board can be maintained by the students to display reports, pictures, and other items about persons from various ethnic groups.
- Students can work out a code covering sports, games, elections, and classroom behavior in which all students are treated as equals.
- Students and teachers can discuss frankly instances in which namecalling, prejudice, or discrimination are practiced by students or teachers.
- A teacher can use an intergroup incident that occurs in the school or community for helping students acquire a sound perspective.
- A science teacher might demonstrate the similarities of racial groups by studying the blood samples of blacks, Asians, etc.

- Teachers in all subject areas can make an effort to incorporate a study of ethnic groups as they relate to the curriculum, e.g., Chinese math discoveries, black scientists, and American inventions.
- Schoolwide activities, Chicano dramas, blues festivals, and dances should be planned and conducted to offer students positive multi-ethnic experiences.
- Students should not be encouraged to develop fraternities, sororities, clubs, or cliques that would divide students along racial, ethnic, or socioeconomic lines. Instead, multi-ethnic clubs should be encouraged. (pp. 35–36)

The suggestions that follow are designed to help refugee students adjust to their new culture and school environment ("Educating Refugees: Understanding the Basics," 1989). However, several of these strategies apply equally well to all culturally diverse students:

Adjusting to a New Culture

- Enhance students' self-esteem by focusing on their positive qualities and the progress they have already made.
- Help students develop realistic expectations for adjustment to the United States.
- Help students develop coping skills such as not overreacting to stressful situations and making the best of difficult situations.

Culture and Family

- Learn about cultural differences and be sensitive to these differences when working with students.
- Provide opportunities for students to share information about their culture during social studies, geography, and other classes.
- Familiarize yourself with different cultural, medical, and religious practices, such as fasting or holiday celebrations, that might affect students' school attendance and participation.
- Learn to correctly pronounce students' names in the proper order and how to address students' parents. For example, the order of Vietnamese names is family name, middle name, and first name. Vietnamese people are usually addressed using their first name.

Educational Concerns

- When new students arrive, have students from the same linguistic and cultural background who have been at the school longer become "buddies" to help the new students become oriented.
- During class, pose questions related to the content of instruction to check if students have understood; do not assume they understand simply because they appear to have understood.
- Use nonverbal gestures to supplement your instruction.
- Make sure newly arrived students meet and interact with American students, especially in classes that do not require much English proficiency, such as art, physical education, and music.
- Write out class assignments and important instructions to reinforce your oral statements. (p. 1)

Another important consideration for the mainstream teacher is communication with parents of culturally diverse students. Lynch (1981), in a study of parents' views of special education services, identified several barriers to parents' participation in the public school programs of their children. Two major roadblocks were language and cultural barriers. Suggestions for overcoming these barriers are presented in "Tips for the Teacher."

In summary, multicultural education is an attempt to affirm the value and worth of cultural diversity. In many ways, the mainstreaming movement echoes this ideal: Mainstreaming is an attempt to integrate but not obliterate differences. This point is well made by McLaughlin-Williams (1977):

> Mainstreaming can become a force for the valuing of individual differences, a process to foster acceptance of varying physical, psychological, educational, and racial characteristics, and a futuristic model to celebrate variance as a desirable state. (as cited in Fuchigami, 1980, p. 640)

■ ACTIVITIES

1. Write a short paper that describes your cultural background. Include your family's traditions for holidays, foods, ceremonies such as weddings, child-rearing practices, and so on. Exchange papers with one of your classmates. What similarities do you find? What differences?

Overcoming Language and Cultural Barriers

Overcoming Language Barriers

■ If you are not bilingual, have someone available who is when you talk to parents. Better yet, encourage them to bring a bilingual friend or relative. Make an attempt to learn words, phrases, and to say something positive about the child in the family's preferred language.

■ Be sure that printed materials for parents are available in their preferred language.

■ Provide a sign language interpreter for parents who are deaf or hard of hearing.

Overcoming Cultural Barriers

■ Learn as much as you can about the cultures that your students represent through talking with the parents and other staff, reading books, attending in-service sessions, and viewing films. Family structures, values, and child-rearing practices vary greatly. You can then use the cultural differences as strengths rather than working at cross-purposes.

■ Instead of lumping all groups together, recognize the many differences that exist within groups of Hispanics, Anglos, blacks, Pan-Asians. Each country, each region, and most important, each individual has unique ways of interpreting their cultural experience.

■ Weed out the stereotypes and prejudices that have been acquired through your own cultural roots. Try to approach people individually and openly.

■ Use cultural differences to bring schools and families together. Utilize celebrations and the special traditions that go with them as ways of learning and working together.

■ Never feel that you have to apologize for your own culture or ethnicity. We all have something special to contribute.

Note. From *But I've Tried Everything! A Special Educator's Guide to Working with Parents* (pp. 37–39) by E. W. Lynch, 1981, San Diego, CA: San Diego State University. The development of this book was supported by the State of California, Department of Education, Project Number 37-3062-80-3293-7100. Reprinted by permission.

THINGS TO REMEMBER

- Mainstreamed classrooms may reflect the cultural and linguistic diversity of the United States.
- Several important cultural groups live in the United States today, including African Americans, Latinos, Asian Americans, and Native Americans.
- African Americans make up the largest minority group whereas Latinos represent the largest bilingual culture.
- Cultural pluralism is the belief that cultural and linguistic diversity is a strength, not a weakness.

- A student's language and culture can affect school behavior and academic success; if the student's background is discrepant from the culture of the school, the student may fail to meet scholastic expectations.
- Students who enter school with few English-language skills are at a distinct disadvantage; however, not all students from culturally diverse backgrounds have limited English proficiency.
- Most students from culturally and linguistically diverse backgrounds are educated in general education classes. Those with special learning needs may receive special education

services or bilingual education services.
- Assessment of students from diverse groups must be nonbiased; measures must not discriminate on the basis of race, culture, or language.
- The major approach to instruction of students from diverse backgrounds is multicultural education; students who learn about the language and culture of others are more likely to accept diversity.
- Mainstreaming and multicultural education share the same goal: to teach students to appreciate the value of individual differences.

2. Interview someone who learned English as a second language. Ask that person to describe some of the problems that occur in translating from one language to another. Are there some concepts that cannot be expressed in the English language?

3. Look through several of the textbooks used in elementary or secondary classrooms. Do these texts include information about the contributions of several cultures? Do the illustrations depict a multicultural society?

4. Observe in a classroom that serves students from culturally and linguistically diverse backgrounds. Can you identify any special needs? In what ways does the teacher adapt instruction to meet the needs of diverse students? How are social interactions among students encouraged?

5. It was noted that mainstreaming is an attempt to integrate but not obliterate differences. Discuss this statement in relation to the "No One Model American" policy statement of the American Association of Colleges for Teacher Education.

17 Teaching Students at Risk for School Failure

■■■ The kindergartner who comes to school hungry, the 15-year-old who is two months pregnant, the young boy who seeks solace from drugs when his stepfather beats him, the lonely adolescent who sees little reason for living: these are students at risk. The factors that place them at risk—substance abuse, delinquency, abusive caregivers, and so on—interfere with their ability to benefit from the school experience.

A Phi Delta Kappa study considered children at risk "if they are likely to fail—either in school or in life" (Frymier & Gansneder, 1989, p. 142). The inclusion of failure "in life" in the definition considers the individual's involvement in areas such as drug abuse, suicide, physical or sexual abuse, delinquency, or other factors that may contribute to future problems. Although these students usually have not been identified as individuals with disabilities (and may never be considered eligible for special education services), it is important that educators provide them with educational experiences appropriate to their special needs.

Ogden and Germinario (1988) describe the problem as follows:

> All children are at times students-at-risk and there is a portion of every school population that consistently shows a lack of the necessary intellectual, emotional and/or social skills to take full advantage of the educational opportunities available to them. Often these students become disenchanted, and ultimately openly or passively reject school—they are then students-at-high-risk.
>
> The purpose of school is to maximize learning for all students. The most obvious way in which schools attempt to carry out their mission is through direct instruction in the curriculum areas. However, another way of maximizing learning is by controlling or eliminating the effects of those factors which limit the learning and potential of children. (p. xvii)

Although educators generally agree that many students are at risk, they do not necessarily agree on who these students are or how to deal with their problems. All 50 states have made some attempt to consider the question; only 25 states have formally defined the at-risk population. These definitions vary widely, from limiting the group to only dropouts to associating students at risk with a long list of adverse social and economic conditions (e.g., truancy, absenteeism, drug abuse, delinquency, teenage pregnancy, poverty). The states have had a similar piecemeal approach to providing programs that attempt to remedy the problems of students at risk. At this point, only pilot programs that provide limited interventions have been introduced (Mirga, 1988a, 1988b).

According to various sources, from 25% to 35% (Frymier & Gansneder, 1989; Hodgkinson, 1993) to as many as 35% to 40% (Siegel & Senna, 1994; "Technology," 1988) of the K–12 school population can be considered at risk. High numbers of students at risk can be found in schools in urban (Cuban, 1989), suburban, and rural (Helge, 1991) communities. The potential for being identified as at risk is higher for students raised in disadvantaged or impoverished home settings. These students are often not able to meet the academic demands of the school because of their delayed physical and psychological development (Butler, 1989). The longer students live under poverty conditions, the more likely they are to be underachievers in school (Reeves, 1988) and to experience emotional or behavioral problems (Recer, 1989). Many other factors such as drug or alcohol abuse, child abuse or neglect, eating disorders, suicide, delinquency, single parent homes, and teenage pregnancy are thought to be related to a student's potential inclusion in the at-risk population.

School personnel encounter a number of unique challenges in providing appropriate educational programs for students at risk. First, this group does not generally benefit from the equal access provisions of laws and policies designed to ensure that appropriate educational programs or special services are provided for other students, such as those with disabilities or students who are bilingual. Second, students at risk require an adequate education to ensure that they will be contributors to society rather than future recipients of welfare or institutional services. Third, schools are being given the responsibility to teach life and social skills needed by many of these students that were once the domain of the family. Finally, if the educational needs of these students are not met, their negative attitudes are likely to deleteriously affect the behavior, achievement, and attitudes of other stu-

EXCEPTIONAL LITERATURE
Students at Risk for
School Failure

FICTION AND BIOGRAPHY

Young Alcoholics by T. Alibrandi (Minneapolis: Comp-Care, 1978). A highly readable discussion of alcoholism among children and youth, what fosters it, signs to watch for, and one approach to treatment. Informative reading for both high school students and adults.

The Best Little Girl in the World by S. Levenkron (New York: Warner, 1981). A novel about a teenage girl's descent into anorexia nervosa and her successful participation in a hospital-based program and therapy.

PROFESSIONAL LITERATURE

The At-Risk Student: Answers for Educators by E. H. Ogden and V. Germinario (Lancaster, PA: Basel, 1988). The book provides information on prevention and intervention strategies with students at risk for failure at all grade levels. It deals with information on the role of teachers, administrators, and school board members in developing programs that respond to the needs of students at risk.

Effective Programs for Students at Risk by R. E. Slavin, N. L. Karweit, and N. A. Madden (Boston:

Allyn & Bacon, 1989). Improving the academic achievement of at risk and special education students is the primary focus of this book. It describes the educational needs of these students and provides specific information on the most appropriate school programs to reduce the chance of these students experiencing school failure.

Youth Suicide: What the Educator Should Know by E. C. Guetzloe (Reston, VA: The Council for Exceptional Children, 1989). This book is designed to help teachers, principals, and counselors become more alert to the danger signs and adolescent crises that trigger suicide. It includes information that will assist in assessing suicide potential, establishing communication, and developing prevention programs.

Adolescent Suicide: A School-Based Approach to Assessment & Intervention by W. G. Kirk (Champaign, IL: Research Press, 1993). A text that provides an overview of child and adolescent suicide, the extent of the problem and probable causes, and a careful examination of contributing factors. Also included is information that will assist educators in identifying the signals and symptoms of suicidal behavior, and in assessing suicide risk factors.

Guidelines are provided for interventions in the school setting and for establishing a school crisis team. Information on dealing with the problem of suicide with special populations of adolescents (e.g., students from culturally diverse groups, gay and lesbian youth, youth with eating disorders) is also provided.

The National Education Association publishes a series of books for educators interested in students at risk:

- **How Schools Can Help Combat Student Drug and Alcohol Abuse** by R. L. Towers (1987)
- **How Schools Can Help Combat Student Eating Disorders** by M. P. Levine (1987)
- **How Schools Can Help Combat Child Abuse and Neglect** (2nd ed.) by C. C. Tower (1987)
- **How Schools Can Help Combat Student Pregnancy** by N. Compton, M. Duncan, and J. Hruska (1987)

Each of these books provides background information on the problem, ways of identifying the problem, prevention and educational programs, instructional materials, and so on. NEA also publishes other books on topics related to at-risk issues.

dents currently in school and those of their own children in the future (Ogden & Germinario, 1988; Reeves, 1988; Stevens & Price, 1992).

Members of every community should carefully review the potential consequences of not responding to the special needs of students at risk. Failing to

respond to these needs can increase both dropout rates and the likelihood that students at risk will fail. Additional information about students at risk can be found in "For Your Information."

Many of the techniques and classroom strategies mentioned earlier in this text are highly appropriate

---

Students at Risk for School Failure

■ Close to one-third of the children born in 1992 will become students who are at the greatest risk for school failure and should be the focus of the energies and talents in education in the United States (Hodgkinson, 1993).

■ Of the children entering school in the fall of 1987, 14% were the children of teenage mothers, as many as 15% were non-English-speaking immigrants, and in many states almost 25% of the children lived below the poverty line (Olson, 1988).

■ "Each year, nearly 1 million students drop out of the nation's public schools" (Butler, 1989, p. 50).

■ "In 1993 more than 23% of America's children were living below the poverty line and thus were at risk of failing to fulfill their physical and mental promise" (Hodgkinson, 1993, p. 620).

■ More than one out of five teachers working with students at risk in urban schools do not believe that all students are capable of learning; these low expectations can become a self-fulfilling prophecy. Many teachers now believe that the responsibility for working with these students belongs to someone else, such as a specialist (Reeves, 1988).

■ Although the practice of retention is often considered appropriate, its effective-ness is open to question (Frymier & Gansneder, 1989). According to Gastright (1989), "80% of the dropouts had been retained at least once; 16% of these had been retained two or more times. A study of ninth-grade students showed that almost 90% of the students who had never been retained later received a diploma. The probability of graduating decreased to 41% for students who were retained once and less than 19% for students who were retained twice" (p. 2).

■ Poor basic skills are characteristic of disadvantaged youth; in a survey of 19- to 23-year-old disadvantaged persons, results indicated that 85% were dropouts, 72% were unemployed, 79% were welfare dependents, 68% had been arrested, and 85% of the women were unwed mothers (Berlin & Sum, 1988).

■ Businesses and corporations spend from $25 to $40 billion a year on remedial education to supplement that currently provided by the educational system (Reeves, 1988; "Technology," 1988).

■ Students at risk will continue to be served primarily by general education pro-grams; only 5% of state education funds are being used specifically for pro-grams for these students, and such programs serve only between 4% and 10% of those in need (Mirga, 1988a).

- It is estimated that approximately 1,000 teens attempt suicide every day (Patros & Shamoo, 1989).
- The 25th Gallup Poll on Education reports that 81% of the population believes that it is very important to improve the nation's inner-city schools; 60% indicate that they would be willing to pay more federal taxes to improve the quality of these schools (Elam, Rose, & Gallup, 1993).
- A majority of the public (59%) expresses a willingness to spend more tax money to expand childcare centers for all preschool children as part of the public school system. A majority (61%) also indicated they would be willing to pay more taxes to fund these programs for children whose parents were unable to pay (Elam et al., 1993).
- "High-quality preschool education for three- and four-year-olds helped reduce by about half later dropout behavior, criminal involvement, teen pregnancy, welfare dependency, and the need for remedial education" (Butler, 1989, p. 51).
- Poverty and the child-raising methods associated with it contribute to the number of youth identified as emotionally and behaviorally troubled (over 20% of some inner-city populations) (Recer, 1989).
- The reduction in later delinquency that results from preschool programs, prenatal care, and nutrition programs for women and infants provides taxpayers with a saving of $3 to $6 for every $1 spent (Butler, 1989).
- Cohen (1992) reports that $4.75 would be saved for every $1 spent on preschool programs by reducing special education, crime, and welfare costs; yet, in 1990, half the states spent less than $25 per child on early childhood care and education.
- Some states have begun to deny driver's licenses to dropouts. Advocates of such an approach believe that it will encourage students to complete school. Opponents feel that this program does not consider the many other factors that strongly influence the student's lack of achievement and eventual dropping out of school (Russell & Fessenden, 1989).
- Dropping out of high school is not an irrevocable action. Many dropouts later complete high school, often within a short period after dropping out. Nearly half (46%) of the dropouts from the sophomore class of 1980 had completed high school by 1986, that is, within four years of the expected date of their graduation (Frase, 1989).
- "A substantial number of today's young people from low-income ethnic and racial minorities are unequipped to find jobs when they leave school" (Cuban, 1989, p. 782).

for use with students at risk because they are similar to other students with special needs in many of their characteristics and educational requirements. Innovative techniques, such as interactive videodisc technology (which is described in "Spotlight on Technology" on pages 504–506), can also prove useful with this population of students. Students at risk require appropriate educational interventions as well as optimum behavior management and instruction in academics and social skills. If these components are provided as part of their educational program, it is likely that students will experience gains in achievement and develop an overall sense of confidence and personal worth. However, teachers and other school personnel are not expected to become therapists. Their primary role is to work on the learning problems of the student as part of their daily instructional responsibilities, and, when it is appropriate, they should help identify other more serious problems (e.g., addiction, suicide, child abuse) and refer these cases to experts (Ogden & Germinario, 1988).

Educators working with students at risk must be aware of specific information about and techniques used with people in the at-risk categories. The importance of this need is cited in a study (Frymier & Gansneder, 1989) indicating that professionals "lacked skill with or confidence about particular approaches to working with at risk students" (p. 145). The remainder of the chapter will present information about the at-risk categories of dropouts, suicide, drug and alcohol abuse, teenage pregnancy and sexually transmitted diseases, child abuse and neglect, eating disorders, and delinquency. Information included about each category will note the extent of the problem, contributing factors, potential prevention and intervention techniques, and alternative services available outside the school setting.

▬ *DROPOUTS*

▬ *By his sophomore year, Bill had become so disenchanted with his monotonous school program that he began cutting class regularly. He recalls that the year he dropped out he went to school no more than 60 days. Bill explains that since both his parents worked, "It was easy; I'd cut out and go home to watch TV, get high with friends, or sleep all day. Nobody did anything about it." Bill's family had moved six times since kindergarten, and he reported that he had not yet found a school he considered worth going to. The times he was in school were, in his opinion, "a waste of time." He often asked, "Why are we learning this?" He thought about going to see his counselor but decided, "why bother?" In his two years of high school, Bill saw his counselor for one 10-minute interview, despite failing several classes each semester. "At the end they called twice to tell me to come in and sign out, but I didn't." No one tried to talk Bill out of dropping out. In fact, it was easy; he just never came back. (Grossnickle, 1986, p. 11)*

Although educators and researchers agree that the number of students dropping out of school is a major problem, they currently do not agree on who should be considered as dropouts. The U.S. Census Bureau provides the most concise definition; it considers a **dropout** to be anyone over the age of 18 who is no longer enrolled in and has not graduated from high school. The current national dropout rate, using this definition, is reported to be 14% (Woodring, 1989). Other figures from the National Center for Education Statistics (Frase, 1989) indicate that 13% of 16- to 20-year-olds had not completed high school and that, between 1985 and 1988, a total of 4.4% of the students in grades 10 to 12 dropped out of school each year. Dropout rates in inner-city schools are often cited as being over 50% ("Technology," 1988) and sometimes as high as 80% (Bowen, 1988); rates may be as high as 40% to 50% in small or rural schools (Phelps & Prock, 1991).

Reeves (1988) reported that an examination of the 17-year-olds in school determined that 13% of the students are functionally illiterate and 44% are marginally literate; also, 60% of the dropouts at this age are functionally illiterate. In addition, the "rate of delinquency is significantly higher for those who drop out of school than among those who do not" (Siegel & Senna, 1994, p. 356). It is estimated that the costs to the nation resulting from dropouts alone is at least $60 billion annually—possibly as high as $228 billion—in the cost of welfare, crime prevention, unemployment, and lost tax revenues; this is a cost of at least $60,000 per dropout (McNergney & Haberman, 1988). These figures make the importance of providing for the educational needs of this group of students at risk readily apparent.

Assumptions based solely on the data on current dropout rates may be somewhat misleading because over the past 90 years there has actually been a reduction in the dropout rate and an increase in the number of students completing high school. In 1900, only 17% of school-age children graduated from high school. By the 1920s, this figure had increased to 25% and later to 35% in 1935, 59% in 1950, 66% in 1965, and 74% in 1989 (Kunisawa, 1988; MacMillan, 1991; Woodring, 1989). The major problem is the fact that during this period there have been an overall decline in the skill levels of those leaving school and a decrease in the probability that the dropout will be a contributing member of society.

In discussing the results of a 1986 longitudinal study of high school students, Kunisawa (1988) described the general characteristics of the contemporary dropout in this way:

> Dropouts are usually from low-income or poverty settings, often from a minority group background (although not often Asian-American), and have very low basic academic skills (especially in reading and math). Their parents are not high school graduates, are generally uninterested in their child's progress in school, and do not provide a support system for academic progress. English is often not spoken in the home, and many dropouts are children of single parents. Dropout rates are higher among males than females. Males are more likely to leave school to get a job (which usually turns out to be a failure), while females tend to drop out in order to have a child. Dropouts are generally bored in school; they perceive themselves accurately as failures in the school culture and are usually very alienated from school. (p. 62)

Reducing the dropout rate is a major challenge for educators. The call to raise the standards for student performance as part of the movement to reform educational programs has created additional problems for students at risk. The increase in standards has not been accompanied by an increase in assistance for the students who had difficulty meeting the old standards (Hill, 1989; Woodring, 1989). Although the dropout rate has decreased over the past 90 years, the ability of the dropout to assimilate into society has also decreased. The number of jobs available for workers lacking basic skills is much smaller (Slavin, 1989), and the dropouts can no longer "go West" or return to the farm as they did earlier in the century (Woodring, 1989).

The school can play an important role in helping reduce the numbers of dropouts. Information gathered from other studies can do little more than provide a general framework for a prevention program; educators must examine their own local setting to identify their specific needs as part of the development of the components of this program (Gastright, 1989). A variety of recommendations are provided here for preventing students from dropping out of school:

■ Early prevention programs are needed that provide services such as prenatal and postnatal care for young mothers, day care and preschool programs,

SPOTLIGHT ON TECHNOLOGY

Interactive Videodisc

*I*nteractive videodisc technology has the capacity to add high-quality, full-motion video to computer programs. One way to think about this technology is to visualize a computer with a videotape or a television program running on its monitor (although, at present, the video display typically is shown on one monitor and the computer program on another). Videodiscs, which are played on videodisc players, store both visual and auditory information. One disc can hold 54,000 frames of still video per side (approximately 30 minutes of continuous-play video), and any of these images can be accessed within 1 or 2 seconds (Hofmeister & Thorkildsen, 1993; Holzberg, 1991).

Archival videodiscs are collections of photographs or video segments; these don't appear in any special order and there is no built-in instructional framework (Hofmeister, 1989). Examples are the *National Gallery of Art* videodisc (Voyager), which contains photos of the National Gallery's painting and sculpture collections,

Note. Photo courtesy of Videodiscovery.

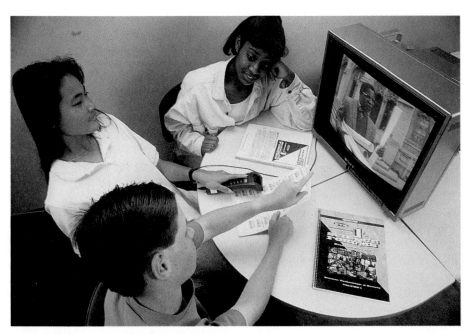

Note. Photo courtesy of Videodiscovery.

and *Bio Sci II* (Videodiscovery), a videodisc with still images and video sequences related to biology. Instructional videodiscs, on the other hand, are designed for classroom or individual learning. Some instructional videodiscs require only a player, a monitor, and a hand-held controller or a barcode reader (Lewis, 1993; Phillipo, 1988). For group instruction, the teacher uses the control device to direct the disc to branch to new activities based on students' performance. Individual students can also interact with videodiscs with hand-held controllers or barcode readers as shown in the photo above. In more elaborate applications, a computer controls the operation of the videodisc player.

Interactive video may be particularly useful for students at risk for school failure. As Bialo and Sivin (1989) comment, "...in this day of television, rock videos, and movies, video-based lessons are one way of gaining the interest and attention of young people who have been turned off to school" (p. 51). As members of the MTV generation, these students may find interactive video more appealing than traditional computer activities.

Instructional videodiscs are available in many different content areas. One promising application for students at risk is the use of interactive video to teach basic school skills. Examples are *PALS* (*Principle of the Alphabet Literacy System*) (IBM), a literacy program for adolescents and adults, and *English Express* (Davidson & Associates), a program that teaches English to speakers of other languages.

Videodisc simulations also offer promise for this group of students. With simulations, students can practice solving real-life problems under controlled conditions. For example, in *What's Next*, a high school student is trying to decide whether to drop out of school; in *TIP* (*TARGET Interactive Project*), students attend a simulated party where they help various characters make decisions about drug and alcohol use (Bialo & Sivin, 1989). Other examples are *You Can Say No to a Drink or Drugs* and *Never Say Yes to a Stranger.*

The Videodisc Compendium for Education and Training is a good source of information about videodiscs (and CD-ROMs) that are currently available. Updated three times each year, this guide provides descriptions of thousands of multimedia applications. Included are videodiscs on topics such as career guidance (e.g., *Making It On Your First Job*), driver training (*Defensive Driving Tactics*), and health (*AIDS: Everything You Should Know*).

and health care programs for students at risk. Such programs are the most promising and cost-effective interventions (Butler, 1989; Hill, 1989; Kunisawa, 1988).

■ Teachers can play an important role by developing an interest in the progress of all students and establishing a level of personal interaction that communicates this interest to the students (Barone, 1989).

■ "Prevention and early intervention are much more promising than waiting for learning deficits to accumulate and only then providing remedial and special education services" (Slavin, Madden, & Karweit, 1989, p. 355).

■ Although teachers and administrators seem to have a good basic knowledge of the characteristics and attributes of potential high school dropouts, they appear to have a negative outlook regarding their own ability to encourage a dropout to return to school (Soderberg, 1988).

■ Teachers must communicate a feeling that the student is capable of achieving and be accountable for providing the type of instruction designed to ensure that achievement will occur (Gajar, Goodman, & McAfee, 1993; Ogden & Germinario, 1988).

■ Effective programs for students at risk accommodate instruction to individual needs while maximizing direct instruction and following models such as mastery learning and cooperative learning. Quality instruction that improves students' skills increases the likelihood that they will achieve and benefit from their school experiences (Cuban, 1989; Slavin et al., 1989).

■ Consistent attendance is critical if students are to benefit from the educational program, and students missing a great deal of school are more likely to drop out. Strong attendance policies should be established and enforced. Teachers and staff should be involved in following up on student absences and should reinforce students for attendance (Gajar et al., 1993; Kerr, Nelson, & Lambert, 1987).

■ Job training programs that provide for the development of specific job skills and work behaviors (e.g., reporting on time, following directions) are needed to initiate and support the employment of students at risk because they are likely to be a group with a high rate of unemployment ("Project," 1988; Snider, 1988).

The importance of involving parents in their children's education is stressed by many experts. Parents need to be informed of their child's progress and encouraged to be supportive of their child's education and attendance at school. It may be necessary to provide parents with assistance in order for them to gain the skills and attitudes necessary for supporting the educational opportunities provided by the school. School personnel may also need to assist parents in obtaining services from social or health agencies in the community. It is critical that every available resource be directed at reducing the risk factors that potentially lead students to drop out of school. The school's efforts should focus on making the student a success in school and in life.

■ SUICIDE

■ *To the casual observer, Jimmy was a fairly typical teenager—reticent, especially around adults, and a moderate achiever in school. He had few close friends, all of them quiet and unassuming around the tougher kids at school. According to his homeroom teacher, Jimmy kept mostly to himself. These traits are typical of adolescents and aren't necessarily reason for special concern or attention. That's why Jimmy's death was initially thought to be an accident. One dark weekday morning, while delivering papers on his bike, Jimmy suddenly swerved into the path of an oncoming truck and was killed instantly. At first police thought that the unsafe conditions—darkness and light drizzle that made the road slippery—caused Jimmy to lose control of his bike. That was until a note describing his feelings of hopelessness and rejection was found in his school locker. Part of his note read, "Why me, why always me? They make fun of everything I do, everything that I am. It's such a cruel punishment."*

■ *Jeanine was an ebullient 16-year-old. Her grades were good, and she was popular enough to be elected to homecoming court. She was regarded by the faculty as a model student and a fine representative of her school. Then, gradually, she became apathetic. Parents and teachers thought the change was only a temporary emotional "phase" that many young women go through. Her death by drug overdose shocked everyone. How could this lovely, popular young lady with a promising future do such a terrible thing? She left no note to explain the confusion. However, subsequent investigations uncovered the apparent cause: Jeanine had been rejected by three of her friends who became jealous of her success and popularity. They apparently started a rumor that Jeanine was promiscuous and had contracted a venereal disease. Feeling overwhelmed and isolated, Jeanine took what she thought was the only way out. (Kirk, 1993, p. 5)*

Suicide is the second leading cause of death among 15- to 24-year-olds (second to vehicle fatalities). The rate of suicide for this group has increased dramatically over the past 35 years, 300% among males and 230% among females (Edwards, 1988; Garfinkel et al., 1988; Pfeifer, 1986). Suicides account for over 5,000 deaths of young people each year (Guetzloe, 1993). While the rate of suicides is much lower for children under 14, the suicide rate for this age group increased notably in the 1980s (Kirk, 1993). Some experts would argue that it is the leading cause of death in this age range, but they contend that it is difficult to get an accurate count because the stigma placed on suicide often leads suicides to be labeled as a type of accident (Kauffman, 1993).

A recent study of young people in the United States (Centers for Disease Control, 1991) estimated that during 1990 there were 3.6 million in this group that considered suicide and that actual plans to take their own lives were devised by 2.1 million students (in grades 9 to 12). Among high school students, as many as 350 suicides are attempted for every 1 completed. As many as 3% of students in this age group attempt suicide each month (Garfinkel et al., 1988) and, in the 14 and under group, "suicide attempts lead to the hospitalization of an estimated 12,000 youngsters" (Guetzloe, 1993, p. 34) each year.

Males are four to five times as likely to complete the act of suicide, yet females are three to nine times more likely to attempt suicide (Kirk, 1993). It should be noted that special education students, especially those with severe behavioral disorders, often have a disproportionately high representation in the group attempting suicide (Guetzloe, 1988, 1989).

Teachers can play an important role in identifying students who may be suicide candidates, although suicide attempts often occur without warning. As part of a prevention program, school staff should be provided with training on identifying warning signs and procedures to follow after these signs are noted. Information on warning signs is provided in Figure 17–1.

Adolescent suicide is usually precipitated by a combination of factors. Depression, impulsivity, stress, physical or sexual abuse, or involvement with drug and alcohol abuse are frequently associated with suicide attempts.

Another factor that often contributes to suicide among students is the death of another adolescent from suicide or an accident (Dismuke, 1988; Garfinkel et al., 1988). Such an event often causes a contagion effect that leads to cluster suicides (i.e., a series of suicide attempts by friends or acquaintances). Specific suggestions for dealing with suicide threats and with potential cluster suicides are included in "Tips for the Teacher."

Teachers and other school personnel can be involved in a variety of activities that can potentially reduce the number of suicides. Social skills training programs (such as those mentioned in chapter 6) can contribute to the development of skills that will permit students to establish a network of social relationships and reduce their vulnerability to social isolation and possible depression (Patros & Shamoo,

1989). Providing experiences that lead to the development and reinforcement of personal self-worth is important in programs designed to prevent suicide (Guetzloe, 1989).

Schools serving adolescents should consider their legal responsibilities regarding the physical and psychological safety of students (such as those noted in Figure 17–2), develop a plan for dealing with suicide, and communicate this to all staff members. In addition, it is essential that mental health clinics, crisis centers, counseling agencies, suicide hotlines, and other community resources in the area of suicide prevention be identified and information provided to the entire staff describing how these services supplement those provided by the school. It is also important that the staff be aware of the referral process that must be used for each of these agencies; often there is not a great deal of time available to search for this information. School personnel should not assume responsibilities for follow-up or long-term counseling if they do not have the expertise or time available. The responsibility for this care should be delegated to the appropriate agency in the community (Capuzzi, 1988).

■ DRUG AND ALCOHOL ABUSE

■ *They started young, usually with pot, and moved on to coke—sometimes snorted, sometimes injected, sometimes freebased. Now they're patients at Phoenix House, a residential treatment center in Orange County, Calif. "When I first smoked rock I fell in love," says Samantha. "I wanted to do more right away. I would lie, steal—anything for a hit off the pipe. It gets hold of you real fast." To Amy, "coke was the wonder drug, and freebasing was better than sex. I had no morals: I'd do anything with my body for coke." Dan, a bleached-blond 15-year-old from Orange County stole from his parents, from his employer and from neighbors. "I used all the cash for drugs," he says. "I didn't care about food, I didn't care about a bed. It was scary on the street, but the cocaine made it all right." Dan says about half the kids at his old high school now use coke. (Morganthau, 1986, p. 63)*

At-Risk Adolescent Checklist

Listed below are several factors associated with at-risk adolescents. None of these factors alone is an indication of suicidal tendencies; but educators should be alert to clusters of these factors, which could indicate potential problems.

1. Inability to compete in school, failing grades.
2. Family instability (divorce, blended family, neglect, and abuse).
3. Death or chronic illness of a loved one or pet, or the anniversary of such an event.
4. Failure to communicate feelings of unhappiness.
5. Health problems.
6. Major disappointment or humiliation (real or imagined).
7. Economic insecurity.
8. Parental role failure.
9. Desire for revenge against a girl friend, boy friend, or significant other.
10. Sense of not belonging to anyone (family, community, school).
11. Family history of suicide or suicide attempts.

Symptoms of Suicidal Youth Checklist

1. Extreme mood swings (violent or rebellious behavior, sudden cheerfulness).
2. Difficulty concentrating.
3. Sudden lifestyle changes.
4. Withdrawal or isolation from peers, family, or school activities.
5. Neglect of personal appearance.
6. Previous suicide attempts.
7. Loss of friends (boy friend, girl friend, best friend).
8. Giving away possessions, pulling affairs together, voluntarily cleaning room, or throwing things out.
9. Decline in school work, failing grades, cheating.
10. Noticeable change in sleeping habits and energy level.
11. Frequent suicidal talk (revealed through writing, drawings, or indirect verbal expression).
12. Drug use (half of suicidal youngsters are involved in substance abuse).
13. Many unexplained absences.

*TIPS FOR THE
TEACHER*

Dealing with Potential Suicides

Suicide Threat Checklist

Do these things:

1. Remain calm. Stay with the student. Remember, the student is overwhelmed, confused, as well as ambivalent.
2. Get vital information if possible (name, address, home phone number, parent's work number). Send another teacher or student to get help.
3. Clear other students from the scene. Direct them to return to class.
4. Assure the student that he or she has done the right thing by talking to you. Try to win the student's trust. Assure the student that emergency help is coming. Tell the student that there are options available.
5. Get the student to talk. Listen! Listen! Listen! Repeat back what you hear the student saying (help the student define the problem). Acknowledge the student's feelings ("You are really angry." "You must feel humiliated.").
6. Establish direct eye contact with the student. Speak in a calm, low voice. If student is about to commit suicide, buy time. Say, "Don't jump. Stand there. Talk with me. I'll listen." Show that you are not shocked by discussing suicide.
7. Try to get the student to agree to a verbal "no suicide" contract ("No matter what happens, I will not kill myself.").
8. Monitor the student's behavior constantly.
9. Make a mental note at the time of the incident of what the student says.
10. Ask the principal or another administrator to contact the parents with the message that their child is hurt and they will be called back immediately with the name of the hospital where they can join their child. Tell them to keep the telephone line clear.

Do not do these things:

1. Do not ignore your intuitions if suicide is suspected.
2. Do not minimize the student's threat. Take it seriously.
3. Do not be concerned about long periods of silence. Give the student time to think.
4. Do not leave the student. Do not let him or her go to the restroom.
5. Do not lose patience with the student.
6. Do not argue with the student about whether suicide is right or wrong.

7. Do not promise confidentiality. Instead promise help and promise privacy.
8. Do not discuss the incident in the teacher's lounge or with another student. (Garfinkel et al., 1988, p. 26)

Reducing the Effects of a Suicide

The following are recommendations to help communities prevent young people from killing themselves and, when a young person does commit suicide, to help communities handle the situation as well as possible.

1. Plan community action to deal with any event or situation that might cause a suicide cluster before trouble starts.
2. Appoint a committee of community representatives and a community agency to coordinate a response to suicide among the young.
3. Identify people and groups in the community who can help prevent suicide clusters or respond when one occurs.
4. Put the response plan into action when a suicide cluster occurs—or when one is suspected.
5. When such a situation arises, immediately prepare the groups that are key to the community response to take up their assigned responsibilities.
6. Avoid any action that could be interpreted as glorifying suicide, and minimize any sensational aspects of suicides or suicide attempts.
7. Identify people who may be especially likely to kill themselves and put them in touch with a counselor.
8. Arrange for a timely flow of accurate, appropriate information to the news media after a suicide.
9. Identify elements in the environment—school, home and community—that might increase the likelihood of suicide. Change those elements—or get rid of them.
10. If a group of youngsters do kill themselves, find out whether their deaths are connected to any long-term issue—and, if so, deal with it. (Dismuke, 1988, p. 21)

Note. From *Responding to Adolescent Suicide* (p. 26) by B. D. Garfinkel, E. Crosby, M. R. Herbert, A. L. Matus, J. K. Pfeifer, and P. L. Sheras (The Phi Delta Kappa Task Force on Adolescent Suicide), 1988, Bloomington, IN: The Phi Delta Kappa Educational Foundation and from "Reducing Suicides" by D. Dismuke, November 1988, *NEA Today* (Washington, DC: National Education Association), p. 21. Reprinted by permission.

FIGURE 17–2
Liability Issues in Dealing with Suicide

Guidelines for determining what to do with a student when psychological impairment is suspected are not always clear. What is clear is that when a life is in jeopardy, the school system must provide every available resource to save that life. How that responsibility translates into legal risk is the focus of . . . [this section].

The basic concern must be the life of the student. As a society, we seem reasonably aware of the need to protect children and adolescents, but obviously suicidology is not an exact science. Administrators and educators need to know, as do all professionals, what their legal obligations are in the case of a suicidal student. The following points are generally accepted legal guidelines, but each state, and even certain school districts within states, may have different statutes or guidelines. [It is important that each educator determine the specific policies and procedures that apply to his or her own school assignment.]

- School personnel are not responsible for the suicide death of a student unless they aided and abetted the student in death or during a period of obvious suicidality. This is interpreted as specifically assisting the student in attempting or completing the act of suicide by providing the means or by intentionally doing nothing, knowing that the suicide was going to occur.

- When a student is assessed as or suspected of being suicidal, the parents or guardians must be informed about the assessment and the actions being taken to alleviate or treat the vulnerability. This should be done as quickly as possible without jeopardizing the life of the student.

- When an employee or consultant to the school system becomes aware of the possibility of suicidal ideation in a student, he or she should consider immediate assessment and intervention. If this is not possible, immediate referral to an appropriate professional within or outside the school system should be made while the safety of the student is simultaneously ensured. The specific school administrator responsible for the student, such as the building principal, should always be apprised of suicide vulnerability and what staff and faculty are doing to counter the process with any student.

From 1986 to 1992, a series of national Gallup polls found that the general public considered the use of drugs as the major problem faced by the public schools (Elam et al., 1993). Another national poll identified drug abuse as the top problem in the nation ("News Beat," 1989). Other figures (Newcomb & Bentler, 1989) indicate that the most prevalent drug use activities in the early adolescent group are drinking alcohol (56%) and smoking (45%), although nearly 30% had tried at least one illicit controlled substance or drug (marijuana was tried most frequently—24%).

Alcohol and tobacco appear to be the most abused drugs because they are the most readily available and the most highly visible due to the amount of advertising they receive (Horton, 1985). Data reported by Rosenthal (1994) indicate that, in a 12-month period prior to being polled, 31% of the students in the 12th grade group had used an illicit

- The rules of confidentiality can be broken when information that suggests that a student is suicidal is obtained. The suspicion need only be slight, but it must be concrete. The statement or behavior that leads the educator to suspect a suicidal process needs to be documented. It is always prudent to err on the side of safety. Thus, breaking confidentiality to consult with a professional when suicidal ideation is suspected will result in a more effective assessment process.

- All communications, conversations, and actions taken with regard to the assessment, intervention, and referral of a suicidal (or suspected suicidal) student should be documented and recorded. These records should be kept in the student's confidential file. Some teachers and school clinicians keep what is known as "working files," which are not necessarily subject to legal seizure. However, if information regarding suicidal vulnerability remains only in a working file, the information does little to facilitate suicide prevention or intervention.

- When the suicide process is accurately assessed, regardless of risk level, the student should be referred to a therapist or clinic specializing in the evaluation and treatment of depression and suicide. Referral to professionals saves lives and provides educators with a measure of legal protection.

 If all faculty, pupil personnel specialists, and administrators are trained in suicide assessment and referral, they might not be as hesitant to intervene with students for fear of legal troubles. Stated simply, educators are responsible for taking all signals and threats seriously and for acting professionally, effectively, and quickly on the information available. Following these guidelines should keep intervention in the school setting on firm legal footing. When all educators have access to the information and training they need in order to handle these types of situations, we will surely see a reduction in the loss of life.

Note. From *Adolescent Suicide: A School-Based Approach to Assessment and Treatment* (pp. 105–107) by W. G. Kirk, 1993, Champaign, IL: Research Press. Copyright 1993 by W. G. Kirk. Reprinted by permission.

drug, and 87% had tried alcohol; 28% admitted to binge drinking (five or more drinks in a row) during the past two weeks. Marijuana had been used at some time by 35% of this group, and 2% used it daily. In 1988–1989, 4.6% of high school students used cocaine, 24.9% of the students in grades 6–8 stated that they used liquor ("Student Drug Use," 1989), and the average age at which students first used alcohol was 12.8 years (Needham, 1989).

The data on **drug and alcohol abuse** for students are not completely surprising when considered next to statistics on the adult population. For example, alcohol consumption is at its lowest level in 30 years, and still 56% of Americans drink alcoholic beverages ("Alcohol Use," 1989). Individuals who abuse drugs or alcohol are very much at risk for failure in school and in other aspects of their lives (Elmquist, 1991).

FIGURE 17–3
Signs of Alcohol and Other Drug Use

Signs of alcohol and other drug use [AOD] vary, but there are some common indicators of AOD problems. Look for changes in performance, appearance, and behavior. These signs may indicate AOD use, but they may also reflect normal teenage growing pains. Therefore, look for a series of changes, not isolated single behaviors. Several changes together indicate a pattern associated with use.

Changes in Performance:

- Distinct downward turn in grades—not just from Cs to Fs, but from As to Bs and Cs
- Assignments not completed
- A loss of interest in school; in extracurricular activities
- Poor classroom behavior such as inattentiveness, sleeping in class, hostility
- Missing school for unknown reasons
- In trouble with school, at work, or with the police
- Increased discipline problems
- Memory loss

Changes in Behavior:

- Decrease in energy and endurance
- Changes in friends (secrecy about new friends, new friends with different lifestyles)
- Secrecy about activities (lies and avoids talking about activities)
- Borrows lots of money, or has too much cash

Factors such as having friends who provide drugs and encourage their use, low socioeconomic status, disturbed families, adult family members using drugs, poor school performance, stressful life events, deviant behaviors, depression, or anxiety can all contribute to the possibility that an individual will be at risk for use or abuse of alcohol and drugs. The greater the number of these factors influencing a specific student, the more likely that student is to abuse alcohol and other drugs (Newcomb & Bentler, 1989). Listed in Figure 17–3 is a series of symptoms that can help educators to identify students involved in drug and alcohol abuse.

A variety of programs directed at preventing and/or treating drug and alcohol abuse have been developed, and many of these programs have had limited success. These programs have often attempted to reduce the use of milder drugs such as cigarettes, alcohol, and marijuana on the theory that their use will lead to the use of harder drugs. Prevention programs whose sole purpose is to provide information on drug and alcohol abuse have not been highly successful. Programs that

- Mood swings; excessive anger, irritability
- Preferred style of music changes (pop rock to heavy metal)
- Starts pulling away from the family, old friends, and school
- Hostile or argumentative attitude; extremely negative, unmotivated, defensive
- Refusal or hostility when asked to talk about possible alcohol or other drug use

Changes in Appearance and Physical Changes:
- Weight loss or gain
- Uncoordinated
- Poor physical appearance or unusually neat. A striking change in personal habits
- New interest in the drug culture (drug-related posters, clothes, magazines)
- Smells of alcohol, tobacco, marijuana
- Frequent use of eye drops and breath mints
- Bloodshot eyes
- Persistent cough or cold symptoms (e.g., runny nose)
- Always thirsty, increased or decreased appetite, rapid speech
- AOD paraphernalia (empty alcohol containers, cigarettes, pipes, rolling papers, baggies, paper packets, roach clips, razor blades, straws, glass or plastic vials, pill bottles, tablets and capsules, colored stoppers, syringes, spoons, matches or lighters, needles, medicine droppers, toy balloons, tin foil, cleaning rags, spray cans, glue containers, household products)

Note. From "School-Based Alcohol and Other Drug Prevention Programs: Guidelines for the Special Educator" by D. L. Elmquist, 1991, *Intervention in School and Clinic, 27*(1), p. 14. Copyright 1991 by PRO-ED, Inc. Reprinted by permission.

involve improving peer interactions and enhancing social skills and assertiveness or refusal skills have been the most effective in reducing the use of drugs, but they have had less impact on individuals currently abusing drugs. Interventions that involve individuals in alternative activities, build their confidence, broaden their experiences, and improve social competence were the most successful in reducing the abuse of drugs (Newcomb & Bentler, 1989).

Studies on the effectiveness of various types of treatment programs are needed so that programs can become more accountable to the students they serve and their families. Problems have occurred when programs have placed individuals into the wrong type of program (sometimes because of an error and other times because of a need to fill that program's beds). For example, if parents agree to have a mildly involved adolescent (i.e., one who has used a drug infrequently as a result of normal experimentation or social pressure) "thrown in" with youth who are truly drug abusers, the adolescent may be alienated from his or her family and exposed to an environment that

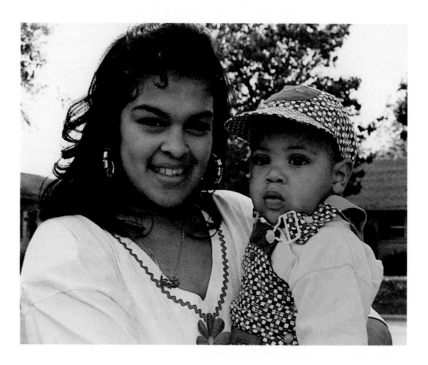

may actually encourage further drug abuse (New-comb & Bentler, 1989). Any recommended treatment must be matched to the individual needs of the student. Also, treatments should include attempts to provide for family involvement because programs tend to be more effective if they involve other members of the family. Miksic (1987) has outlined the essential elements of a prevention program for drug abuse; see "Tips for the Teacher."

Many aspects of the treatment program for students who are drug or alcohol abusers will incorporate the services of public or private community agencies. Teachers should not expect to be counselors or investigators; their responsibility is to make appropriate referrals when there are signs of drug use or abuse. In addition, teachers may be called on to assist in managing suspected drug abuse episodes involving intoxication or withdrawal crises. At these times, they should remain calm and nonconfrontational because demonstrating control is not as important as ensuring safety (Kauffman, 1993).

The long-term effects of the use and abuse of drugs are not yet known. It is well documented that drug and alcohol abuse impairs the ability of stu-

dents to function effectively in school and in their interactions with others. Educators can play an important role in decreasing the number of students who use and abuse alcohol and other drugs by including accurate information on drug and alcohol use in the school curriculum, being aware of the signs of potential problems, and helping to refer students to the appropriate professional resources.

■■■ TEENAGE PREGNANCY AND SEXUALLY TRANSMITTED DISEASES

■ *At age 15, Barbara quit school in the fourth month of her pregnancy. She was afraid that the baby might be "damaged" due to heavy drug use at the time of conception, but she has decided to keep the baby rather than have an abortion. Her boyfriend had denied that the baby is his. Barbara suspects it was her boyfriend who smashed the windshield of her mother's car as a threat to leave him out of this "mess." Barbara's mother is unemployed and on welfare. Their plan is to have the mother babysit and Bar-*

Elements of a Successful Drug Abuse Prevention Program

*L*isted here are a series of elements that are considered essential in developing a school drug abuse prevention program:

1. Establish a clear, well-defined policy for teachers and students spelling out how teachers and administrators will deal with apparent or substantiated drug use or possession.
2. Encourage teachers to establish a basic drug education curriculum for their grade levels—keeping it simple, brief, and nonjudgmental and emphasizing the teachers' concern for the students' physical and psychological welfare.
3. Help teachers increase their awareness of local drug problems and use community service agencies.
4. Provide an atmosphere in which the teacher can develop the skills and sensitivity for resolving classroom and individual problems and for leading group discussions about topics such as adolescent development and drug use.
5. Develop an intervention program that involves families as well as students by offering both one-to-one and group counseling centers and drop-in centers within the school. (A drop-in center could be staffed by an education counselor with some training in drug abuse counseling.)
6. Try to get all teachers to review their role perceptions. If they feel their jobs are basically unfulfilling and that they are unable to empathize with students and deal with affective as well as cognitive training, this may lead to constructive career reorientation.
7. Develop peer-group approaches with positive role models for group or individual support. Different types of peer programs are discussed in the National Institute on Drug Abuse publication, "Adolescent Peer Pressure" (NIDA Publication No. ADM 83-1152).
8. Promote understanding of the emotional structure and perceptions that often accompany drug use. Many drug-using students feel they are incompetent and unreasonably rejected by adults and peers. They need an understanding approach rather than a disciplinary and judgmental attitude that confirms their belief that teachers and administrators are only concerned about keeping order, not about helping students.

Note. This list is reprinted with permission of Merrill, an imprint of Macmillan Publishing Company, from "Drug Abuse Management in Adolescent Special Education" by S. Miksic in *Helping Adolescents with Learning and Behavior Problems* (p. 245) by M. M. Kerr, C. M. Nelson, and D. L. Lambert, Copyright © 1987 Merrill Publishing Company, Columbus, Ohio.

bara will get a job to support the three of them. Barbara does not see returning to school as an option for her. She feels that her problems with school were mostly her fault and does not blame her teachers or the school. (Grossnickle, 1986, pp. 13–14)

■ *Joshua is a 17-year-old teenager from a typical American family. He has been diagnosed with AIDS. He contracted the virus through sexual experimentation. He has been prevented from attending school. His mother and father cry and feel helpless in the battle to keep him alive. He now weighs 86 pounds. He is often too sick to go out of the house. He will die soon. He is very frightened. (Gray & House, 1989, p. 231)*

Each year, 12 to 13 million teen and preteen girls are sexually active (Cartwright, Cartwright, & Ward, 1989). Adolescents in the United States have pregnancy rates that are "dramatically higher than those of other developed countries (21% compared to 14-15% elsewhere)" (Muccigrosso, Scavarda, Simpson-Brown, & Thalacker, 1991, p. 1). Every day, 2,740 teenagers become pregnant, and 1,293 have babies ("Data Bank," 1989). Of the nearly 1 million teenage girls who become pregnant each year, (a) 50% never complete high school (Woodring, 1989), (b) 40% of the pregnancies end in abortion (Furstenberg, Brooks-Gunn, & Chase-Lansdale, 1989), and (c) 90% of the babies that are born are kept and raised by the teenage mothers (Mathes & Irby, 1993). Recent figures indicate that 23.9% of all women become pregnant before the age of 18 and 43.5% before the age of 20 (Furstenberg et al., 1989); about 13% of all babies are born to teenagers (Mathes & Irby, 1993). Sixty percent of white males are sexually active by age 18, and 60% of African American males are sexually active by age 16.

The high level of sexual activity reported in teenagers also increases the possibility of contracting **sexually transmitted diseases** (STDs) such as acquired immune deficiency syndrome (AIDS), herpes, syphilis, or gonorrhea (Brooks-Gunn & Furstenberg, 1989). Males (1993) estimates that the rate of STDs among teenage girls is 2.5 times higher than that of boys in the same age group.

When a teenage mother plans to raise her baby, a number of potential problems arise. She is generally unprepared for this role and is very likely to terminate her education by failing or dropping out of school. Many of the babies born to teenage mothers are likely to be premature and/or have medical problems and a higher than average risk of poor cognitive development. These difficulties may occur because many of the mothers do not have appropriate nutrition or health care during pregnancy, and it is not likely that they will be able to provide these essentials for their child. The teenager's child is apt to be at high risk for failure because of potential health, nutritional, and emotional problems, and it is probable that he or she will need special attention at school (Bonjean & Rittenmeyer, 1987; Cartwright et al., 1989; Mathes & Irby, 1993).

Many factors contribute to the level of teenage sexual activity and pregnancy. Social attitudes and the attitudes of peers often encourage sexual activity. Many teenagers have not been exposed to sex education or the use of contraceptives, and they lack knowledge about pregnancy prevention and the consequences of their sexual behavior. Lack of close relationships with parents or friends may contribute to a need to participate in sexual activities in order to be "accepted" by others (Brooks-Gunn & Furstenberg, 1989; Cartwright et al., 1989).

The school must play several roles in dealing with this issue. First, educational programs must provide information on sex education and STDs to assure that students are aware of the possible ramifications of sexual activity. Second, because Title IX of the Education Amendments of 1972 protects the teenage mother from discrimination, schools are obligated to continue to provide educational programs for these students (Bettinger, 1989). Finally, because children of teenage mothers are more likely to be at risk for potential failure, the school can improve the probability of their success by supporting the development of infant and preschool programs and attending to their risk status and their needs when they enter the general education program (Furstenberg et al., 1989).

While many educators believe that the school can play an important role in the areas of teenage pregnancy and AIDS education, only about 35% to 40% of the public indicate that they have confidence in the school's ability to deal with these topics (Gallup & Elam, 1988). Prevention programs introduced in schools typically provide general information on sexuality and contraception, attempt to modify attitudes in order to discourage early sexual activity, or provide specific information on family planning or contraception. These primary prevention programs have had limited success and "may promote healthier—but probably not less—childbearing by teenagers" (Males, 1993, p. 568). At present, many experts believe that actually providing family planning and contraception is most likely to reduce the early childbearing rate. A sex education curriculum should be carefully developed to provide information on the "social, health and economic risks related to sex and teen pregnancies" (Ogden & Germinario, 1988, p. 150).

In addition to informing students about all STDs, Yarber (1987) recommends that students should be specifically taught about how AIDS is transmitted (i.e., via sexual intercourse or exchange of blood) and the ways in which the transmission of this deadly disease can be prevented. After carefully reviewing many AIDS education programs, Popham (1993) indicates that in order for programs to teach students to "avoid behavior that places them at risk of HIV infection, students need to be *knowledgeable* about HIV and AIDS, *skilled* in avoiding behaviors that place them at risk of infection, and *motivated* to use their HIV-relevant skills and knowledge" (p. 561).

Students must be provided with the information they will need to make their own decisions regarding their sexual activity. In some communities, the school must approach this topic with a great deal of care. Teachers must take into account the values of parents, students, and the community, and they must carefully examine their own values when they provide instruction and guidance in this area. Cartwright and others (1989) provide teachers with an important reminder:

> A teacher may be the one person a girl who thinks or knows she is pregnant approaches for advice or for help. It is essential that teachers be aware of their own reactions to this situation and be able to control their own feelings in order to provide the assistance requested or to arrange for referrals to appropriate health-care agencies. (pp. 430–431)

CHILD ABUSE AND NEGLECT

■ *Kara, age 5, always presented a neat, well-ordered picture. Although not expensive, her clothes were well-chosen, clean, and pressed. Her long-sleeved blouses and colorful tights seemed a bit strange in warmer weather, but the teacher made no comments about them. The child was very affectionate, almost to the point of smothering; her endearing ways made her an easy candidate for teacher's pet. It was not until Kara unexplainably wet her pants and the teacher helped her remove her tights to clean up, that anything seemed amiss. Kara's small legs revealed numerous bruises in various stages of healing. An examination by the school nurse attested to the abuse Kara had suffered over her entire body. (Tower, 1987, p. 24)*

Identifying Suspected Child Abuse

School personnel need assistance in determining if a situation they have observed is a case of child abuse that should be reported. The following list of descriptions of abuse, and the indicators for each will be useful in helping educators recognize child abuse.

Physical Abuse

Physical abuse is characterized by inflicting physical injury by punching, beating, kicking, biting, burning, or otherwise harming a child. Although the injury is not an accident, the parent or caretaker may not have intended to hurt the child.

Physical Abuse—Physical Indicators
Child shows evidence of unexplained or repeated injury or injuries in the form of:
a. lacerations, punctures, or missing teeth
b. fractures, sprains, or dislocations
c. rope burns, immersion burns, or cigarette or cigar burns (especially on soles of feet, palms, back, or buttocks—these are seldom self-inflicted)
d. bruises or welts reflecting shape of object used to inflict the injury or injuries on several different surface areas
e. new injuries before old injuries have healed

Physical Abuse—Behavioral Indicators
The child is or may be:
a. wary of adult contacts
b. consistently on the alert for danger
c. subject to frequent and severe mood changes
d. frightened of parents and avoids home (consistently arrives at school early or leaves late)
e. apprehensive when other children cry
f. demonstrating behavioral extremes (aggressive, disruptive, or destructive; or unusually shy, withdrawn, passive, or overly compliant)

Child Neglect

Child neglect is characterized by failure to provide for the child's basic needs. Neglect can be physical, educational, or emotional. Physical neglect includes refusal of or delay in seeking health care, abandonment, expulsion from home or not allowing a runaway to return home, and inadequate supervision. Educational neglect includes permission of chronic truancy, failure to enroll a child of mandatory school age, and inattention to a special educational need. Emotional neglect includes such actions as chronic or extreme spouse abuse in the child's presence, permission of drug or alcohol use by the child, and refusal of or failure to provide needed psychological care.

Neglect—Physical Indicators
Child shows evidence of:
a. constant fatigue or listlessness
b. unattended physical problems or medical needs
c. consistent hunger (begs for food, undernourished)
d. poor hygiene, unbathed, filthy clothing, or inappropriate dress for the weather
e. abandonment

Neglect—Behavioral Indicators
Child is or may be:
a. constantly hungry, begs for food
b. rejected by other children because of offensive body odor
c. constantly falling asleep in class
d. constantly arriving at school early and leaving late
e. left alone for substantial periods of time

Sexual Abuse

Sexual abuse includes fondling a child's genitals, intercourse, incest, rape, sodomy, exhibitionism, and sexual exploitation. To be considered child abuse, these acts have to be committed by a parent responsible for the care of a child.

Sexual Abuse—Physical Indicators
Child shows evidence of:
a. difficulty in walking or sitting
b. torn, stained, or bloody underclothes
c. pain or itching in genital area
d. semen around the genitals or on clothing
e. lacerations, bruises, or bleeding in external genitalia, vaginal, or anal area
 f. venereal disease (especially in young children)
g. pregnancy

Sexual Abuse—Behavioral Indicators
Child shows evidence of:
a. bizarre, sophisticated, or unusual sexual behavior or knowledge
b. regression (Some sexually abused children, especially younger ones, will retreat into a fantasy world, or exhibit infantile behaviors, which may be interpreted as retardation.)

c. delinquency or aggression (The anger and hostility these children, particularly teenagers, feel toward the perpetrator may cause them to adopt aggressive behavior toward others.)

d. poor peer relationships (Because of guilt feelings the child cannot form relationships with peers.)

e. running away to escape from the home situation (Running away may be an indirect manner of asking for help in a situation in which they feel powerless.)

f. unwillingness to participate in physical activities (Young children who have been highly stimulated sexually or have had forced sexual intercourse may find it painful to sit during school or to play at active games.)

g. drug use/abuse (The use of alcohol and other drugs may be the child's method of handling his/her guilt and anxieties.)

h. indirect allusion (Sometimes sexually abused children confide in someone they feel may be helpful by using vague or indirect allusions to the home situation; e.g., "I'm afraid to go home tonight," "I'd like to come and live with you," or "I want to live in a foster home.")

i. seductive behavior (If a child views sexual contact as a positive source of attention, he/she may adopt seductive behaviors with peers or adults.)

Emotional Maltreatment

This form of child abuse and neglect includes acts or omissions by the parents that have caused, or could cause, serious behavioral, cognitive, emotional, or mental disorders. Examples include: refusal to acknowledge the child's worth and needs, depriving them of normal social experiences, verbally terrorizing them and creating a climate of fear, ignoring them, or corrupting them through encouragement to engage in destructive behavior and reinforcing the deviance.

Child abuse and neglect can occur in many forms. It is legally defined by the Child Abuse Prevention and Treatment Act of 1974 as "the physical or mental injury, sexual abuse or exploitation, negligent treatment, or maltreatment of a child under the age of eighteen or the age specified by the child protection law of the State in question, by a person who is responsible for the child's welfare, under circumstances which indicate that the child's health or welfare is harmed or threatened" (PL 93-247 as amended by PL 95-266, April 24, 1978, Sec. 3). Reports indicate that each year there are approximately 1 million reported cases of child abuse and neglect (Emery, 1989) and over 55,000 cases of child

sexual abuse (Tower, 1987). Bauer and Shea (1989) indicate that abused and neglected children may not relate well with peers or adults and are likely to have "deficits in measured intelligence, academic performance, and readiness to learn" (p. 303).

No single set of characteristics can be associated with those who abuse children. The abusive behavior commonly can occur as the result of various types of stress (e.g., marital stress), lack of basic knowledge of appropriate child-rearing practices, a low tolerance for child behaviors such as crying or whining, or an inaccurate assessment of the motivation for the child's misbehavior (Emery, 1989). London and Stile (1982) indicate that the following

Emotional Maltreatment—Physical Indicators

Child shows evidence of:

a. habit disorders (sucking, biting, rocking)
b. conduct disorders (hyper- or hypo-activity, antisocial, destructive)
c. neurotic traits (sleep disorders, speech, enuresis, inhibition of play)
d. psychoneurotic reactions (hysteria, obsessions, depression, compulsion, phobias, hypochondria)
e. physical manifestations of nervous disorders (overweight, skin rashes)

Emotional Maltreatment—Behavioral Indicators

Child shows evidence of:

a. low self-esteem
b. behavior extremes (compliant and passive or aggressive, demanding, disruptive)
c. overly compliant behavior
d. developmental lags (physical, mental, emotional)
e. seeking affection
f. attempting suicide
g. excessive temper tantrums

_____

Note. From *The School's Role in the Prevention of Child Abuse* (pp. 19–22) by S. B. London and S. W. Stile, 1982, Bloomington, IN: The Phi Delta Kappa Educational Foundation. Copyright 1982 by The Phi Delta Kappa Educational Foundation. Also from *Abuse and Neglect of Exceptional Children* (pp. 3–4) by C. L. Warger, S. Tewey, and M. Megivern, 1991, Reston, VA: The Council for Exceptional Children. Adapted by permission.

characteristics are often found in child abusers:

- A history of being abused and/or neglected as a child.
- Uses physical punishment as the primary method of disciplining a child.
- Has unrealistic expectations that are inconsistent with the developmental age of the child.
- Has had no models of successful family relationships and, therefore, has little notion of parenting skills.
- Does not have friends or family to help with the heavy demands of caring for small children.
- Reports that there was not much love or emotional support from adults during his/her childhood.
- Has poor impulse control.
- Has an undue fear of "spoiling" the child by "giving in" to the child or allowing the child to "get away with" anything. (p. 11)

It is possible that abuse is more likely to occur with students with special needs than with their "typical" peers (Warger, Tewey, & Megivern, 1991). Some students with special needs are more difficult to control in the home, or they may exhibit high levels of inappropriate and/or irritating behaviors. Others may lack the skills required to respond as appropriately as the parent would like them to in social situations, or they are "easy marks" because they are incapable of defending themselves. "Tips for the

Teacher" on pages 520–523 provides information on identifying suspected child abuse.

The actual number of cases of child abuse and neglect is hard to determine because experts estimate that only 20% of the cases are reported. It is difficult to obtain accurate statistics in this area because (a) definitions and reporting requirements vary across states and agencies, (b) people are not trained to recognize abuse, (c) individuals are unwilling to report cases because they do not want to get involved, and (d) agencies assigned to protect children have a difficult time obtaining evidence that maltreatment has occurred.

Educators have legal, ethical, and professional responsibilities to report cases of abuse and neglect and assist these children at school. It is their obligation to obtain the information necessary to report these cases accurately and provide for the needs of these students in the school setting (London & Stile, 1982). Educators are legally responsible for reporting child abuse, and "every state provides immunity by law from civil suit and criminal prosecution that might arise from the reporting of suspected child abuse or neglect" (Fischer & Sorenson, 1985, p. 188). Guidelines for a school's reporting policy and a set of suggested procedures for teachers to follow in preparing reports on child abuse and neglect are presented in Figure 17–4. It is important, however, that each teacher know the required guidelines and timelines for reporting abuse in their own school assignment.

In the area of child abuse and neglect, the responsibilities of educators do not end with identifying and reporting suspected cases of abuse or neglect. Educators should also (a) model appropriate adult-pupil interactions; (b) support positive pupil-pupil interactions; (c) include opportunities for students to develop parenting skills as part of the school's curriculum; (d) support and participate in the development of prevention activities that involve parents; (e) encourage the development of programs that respond to the specific needs of students at risk; and (f) assure that cases are monitored, reported, investigated, and that the school is informed of the disposition of the case (London & Stile, 1982).

Students need to be informed (a) that all individuals have basic human needs (i.e., for food, shelter, safety, and affection); (b) of acceptable ways that adults interact with children so that they would be able to tell whether they were being abused or exploited; (c) that an adult should be contacted if they are confused or concerned about something that is occurring in their life; (d) how they should deal with others to protect themselves from possible abuse; (e) of resources available to them in the community; and (f) who should be notified in the case of an emergency situation, such as someone approaching them on the street or attempting to enter their home when their parents are away (Tower, 1987). These topics should be covered at each appropriate grade level and may be included as part of the programs for sex education or the teaching of parenting skills.

EATING DISORDERS

■ *Julie is a pretty, intelligent 15-year-old who has been hospitalized twice for anorexia nervosa. She is the youngest of three children in an intact family. Her father is a professor at a prominent university and her mother is an artist with her studio in the home. The two older children are also bright and successful. The oldest, a son, has graduated from one of the Ivy League schools and is now in medical school. The older sister is currently attending a small, private, liberal arts school and earning almost straight As. She, too, expects to do graduate work. Julie has always been a good student and, according to her parents, after numerous food allergies as a baby, was the easiest to raise. Julie, however, thinks she is ugly, fat, not well-liked by her peers, and not as competent as her siblings. She also thinks her parents think the two older siblings are brighter and more productive. When she was 13, Julie started overeating and then gagging herself afterwards. This quickly led to strict dieting and strenuous exercise. Julie had a boyfriend, Nick, but shortly before the second hospitalization, they quit dating. There had been much conflict between them: Nick wanted more sexual intimacy than Julie. She finally acquiesced, but felt much*

FIGURE 17–4
Reporting Child Abuse and Neglect

School Reporting Policy

Although educators are responsible for reporting child abuse and neglect, it is important that the school system has an established reporting procedure. Such a policy should include specific information such as:

1. At what point should the teacher report child abuse? Suspicion? Reasonable cause to believe? (This may be based not only on school policy but also on state law.)

2. Whom does the teacher notify? Nurse? Principal? School social worker?

3. What specific information does the teacher need to know to report?

4. What actions should the teacher have taken before reporting to validate suspicions?

5. What other school personnel should be involved?

6. Who makes the report to the appropriate authorities? How?

7. What information should be included in the report? (This may be dictated by state law or protective agency policy.)

8. What follow-up is expected on reported cases?

9. What role will the school play in possible community/child protection teams?

10. What commitment does the school have to inservice training or community programs?

Teacher's Checklist for Preparing to Report

Certainly reporting child abuse is neither easy or clear-cut. But the potential benefit for the abused child is worth every effort you are able to expend. Consider the following points when preparing to report:

1. Have you documented your data and written down the information to organize it in your own mind?

2. Have you analyzed your data? What causes you to suspect abuse/neglect? List the symptoms—physical or behavioral.

---

ambivalence and guilt afterward. She feels Nick broke up with her because he thought she was promiscuous. (Epanchin, 1987, p. 175)

About 25% of all adolescents exhibit symptoms of anorexia nervosa, bulimia, or obesity (Maloney & Klykylo, 1985). Problems related to their condition can contribute to their risk for failure in school and in their interactions with others. Although these students may require services provided by professionals outside the school setting, it is important that educators be aware of the symptoms of these disorders and be able to identify and refer these students for the appropriate treatment.

FIGURE 17–4
continued

3. Have you been able to observe the parent/child interaction? Does the parent see the child as worthwhile or different and/or hard to handle?

4. Have you spoken with other professionals within the school? Do they have reason to suspect abuse/neglect? Why?

5. Do you know the reporting policy of your school? Do you know the answers to the questions listed above (i.e., in **School Reporting Policy**)? To whom do you report?

6. Do you have the necessary information required for a report? State law usually requires the following information:
   - names of the child and parents
   - address
   - age and sex of the child
   - type and extent of the child's injuries or complaints
   - evidence of prior injuries
   - explanation of the injuries given by the child
   - name and telephone number of the reporter
   - actions taken by the reporter (such as detaining the child, photographs)
   - other pertinent information

7. Do you (or does the school) have the exact telephone number and address of the agency to which you should report?

8. Have you talked with your administrator about the support you will receive once the report is made? What if the parents try to remove the child from your class? Will you have the support of the administration?

9. Does the school have on hand the necessary report forms?

10. Have you set up a support system for yourself with other teachers or administrators? (After the report is made, you may feel vulnerable and need to talk.)

Now you should be ready to report, knowing that you are providing a chance for both the child and the family to receive much-needed help.

Note. From *How Schools Can Help Combat Child Abuse and Neglect* (2nd ed., pp. 50–51, 53, 67–68) by C. C. Tower, 1987, Washington, DC: National Education Association. Copyright 1987 by National Education Association of the United States. Adapted by permission.

Individuals with **anorexia nervosa** choose to restrict their intake of food to such an extent that they lose 20%–25% of their appropriate body weight. Approximately 90% of the cases occur in young women who are overly concerned about being overweight and have a distorted idea of their body appearance (often thinking they are fat when they are actually underweight). Anorexia is most likely to occur in girls in the 14- or 15-year-old age range and usually begins with dieting that turns into an obsession with weight loss. At one time, approximately 10%–20% of anorexic individuals died from starvation or from complications arising from the disorder; this number has dropped sharply as awareness of the disorder has increased (Coleman, 1986).

Bulimia involves primarily young women who have recurrent episodes of binge eating that are followed by induced vomiting and the use of laxatives, fasting, or drugs to reduce weight. Bulimics tend to go on a food binge when they are under stress, angry, depressed, or lonely and then try to remove the food from their body before it can be digested. They are preoccupied with both eating and losing weight. Frequently these individuals hide their disorder from others (Levine, 1987).

Obesity occurs when body weight exceeds ideal weight by 20% or more. It may occur because of inappropriate eating habits, family eating behaviors and attitudes, or genetic factors (Maloney & Klykylo, 1985).

The school's health curriculum should include information on eating disorders and provide a forum for developing knowledge and skills in (a) how to deal with stress, depression, and anxiety; (b) the role of society in setting specific expectations for physical appearance; (c) normal growth and development; and (d) appropriate nutrition. Educators who identify students who are at risk because of a potential eating disorder should consider contacting the school nurse or a counselor or referring the student to local mental health support services. Individuals with anorexia have responded well to behavioral interventions that provide positive reinforcement for weight gain, and bulimics often respond positively to treatment for depression or to participation in support groups with other bulimics (Coleman, 1986). Obesity can often be treated through behavioral approaches (e.g., self-monitoring and reinforcement) and the teaching of appropriate eating habits (Doleys & Bruno, 1982).

■ DELINQUENCY

■ *The child, nicknamed "Scarface" because of the cuts and scars on his face, was ten years old, only five feet tall, and weighed just 90 pounds. His spindly legs barely touched the floor as he sat in detention, waiting for his court-appointed lawyer. He was accused of molesting a ten-year-old girl on the school grounds while one of his friends held her down. The judge released him into the custody of his parents. Over the next ten weeks, he was arrested five more times—more times than any other juvenile in Washington, D.C. in that year, 1985. His other arrests were for holding up and robbing two men, threatening a woman with an iron pipe, participating in a brawl, illegally entering a car, and roughing up a woman and snatching her purse. (Kauffman, 1993, p. 370)*

Of the 2.3 million juveniles arrested in 1986, 1.4 million were arrested for crimes such as vandalism, drug abuse, or running away; 900,000 were arrested for more serious crimes such as larceny-theft, robbery, or forcible rape. These figures may represent a very small percentage of the actual delinquent acts (Siegel & Senna, 1994), perhaps as few as 2% of the violations that are actually committed by delinquents (Patterson, DeBaryshe, & Ramsey, 1989).

Delinquents are much more likely to be boys. Those who show early signs of delinquent behavior and are initially arrested before they are 12 are more likely to continue their antisocial behavior as adults (Kauffman, 1993). Those initially arrested later in their teens are more likely to be one-time offenders. About 50% of the children who are antisocial become adolescent delinquents and approximately 50% to 75% of the adolescent delinquents become adult offenders (Patterson et al., 1989). Each year, about 450,000 delinquents are placed in juvenile detention centers and state training schools, while 300,000 are sent to adult jails (Leone, Rutherford, & Nelson, 1991).

Many factors have been noted as contributing to **delinquency**. Low intelligence, constitutional differences, location of the community (urban vs. rural), cultural forces, community attitudes, failure in school, drug or alcohol abuse, poor self-concept, poor impulse control, and emotional problems have all been identified as contributing to the occurrence of delinquency (Cartwright et al., 1989). Patterson and others (1989) suggest that ineffective parenting (lack of appropriate discipline and monitoring) is a major contributor to the antisocial behavior of children. Antisocial behaviors eventually contribute to failure in academic areas and rejection by peers, and these failures can in turn lead to seeking acceptance in a deviant peer group and eventually to delinquency. The peer group is thought to provide the adolescent with antisocial attitudes and an opportunity to commit delinquent acts. Usually peers shape behavior by positively reinforcing deviant acts and punishing socially conforming behavior. Families with a history of antisocial behavior, low socioeconomic status, divorce, marital conflict, low educational level of the parent(s), unemployment, and the use of physical discipline have also been found to be related to the likelihood of delinquent behavior.

When interventions such as academic remediation, parent training, or social skills training have been attempted independently, they have at best had limited success that generally did not endure over time. The most receptive candidates for effective interventions are likely to be elementary students identified as lacking social and academic skills and exhibiting antisocial behaviors. Potential interventions that show the most promise combine specific training for the parents to improve their child management practices (e.g., effective, positive, and consistent discipline; appropriate supervision and monitoring) with training in social skills and academic remediation for the students (Kauffman, 1993; Patterson et al., 1989). Educators should be actively involved in developing programs that identify these students early in their school years, and they should

work to coordinate the efforts and resources of the school and those of appropriate community agencies that can assist in working with the parents.

The material presented in this chapter should help you identify students at risk and understand the difficulties they experience that are likely to interfere with their success in school, at home, and in the community. Many of the specific educational techniques described in earlier chapters will prove to be helpful in working with students at risk because their skills and educational needs in some areas are often similar to those of other students with special needs. When educators work to provide educational experiences that are appropriate for these students, their opportunities for success increase and the likelihood that they will experience failure in school and life decreases.

■ ACTIVITIES

1. Write a short paper that establishes your position on providing mandatory educational programs tailored to meet the needs of students at risk. Tell how students would be identified, how eligibility for these services would be determined, and who would be responsible for providing the services.

2. Contact a local school district, and determine the types of programs they offer for students at risk. Establish who supervises these programs (e.g., special education, remedial services), the specific programs offered, the type of training required for the personnel who deliver the services, and any agencies they work with in the community. From what you know about both the community and students at risk, does the program seem to be adequate? Be prepared to describe your findings and state what changes you would recommend.

3. Identify a student you are familiar with who would fit into one of the at-risk groups described in the chapter. Write a brief description of the student's background as well as his or her current progress (or lack of it) in school. Explain how you would use specific methods or techniques discussed in this chapter, or earlier in the book, to

THINGS TO REMEMBER

- The factors that place students at risk—substance abuse, delinquency, abusive caregivers, and so on—interfere with their ability to benefit from the school experience.
- Definitions of students at risk vary greatly from state to state and sometimes from district to district within the same state.
- Students at risk do not belong exclusively to any one group, community, or population.
- The potential for being identified as at risk is higher for students raised in disadvantaged or impoverished home settings.
- Students at risk do not generally benefit from the equal access provisions of laws and policies designed to ensure that appropriate educational programs or special services are provided for other students, such as those with disabilities or students who are bilingual.
- Educators can increase the probability that many students at risk will be contributors to society.

- The attitudes that students at risk take with them as they leave school will affect the attitudes of their younger siblings and later of their own children.
- Students at risk require appropriate educational interventions as well as optimum behavior management and instruction in academics and social skills.
- Teachers and other school personnel are not expected to become therapists for students at risk, but they can assist in referring them to appropriate services.
- A dropout is anyone over the age of 18 who is no longer enrolled in and has not graduated from high school.
- Suicide is the second leading cause of death among 15- to 24-year-olds.
- Teachers and other school personnel can be involved in a variety of activities that can potentially reduce the number of suicides among students.
- Drug abuse is viewed by the general population as one of the top problems in our schools and the nation at large.

- Both the teenage mother and her children are at high risk for failure.
- The high level of sexual activity reported among teenagers increases the possibility that they will contract sexually transmitted diseases.
- No single set of characteristics is associated with those who abuse children.
- The actual number of cases of child abuse and neglect is difficult to determine because experts estimate that only 20% of the cases are reported.
- About one-fourth of adolescents show symptoms of eating disorders such as anorexia nervosa, bulimia, and obesity.
- The most promising interventions for delinquents combine specific training in child management practices for the parents with training in social skills and academic remediation for the students.
- It is important that educators be aware of the symptoms and characteristics of students at risk and be able to identify and refer these students for the appropriate treatment.

reduce the likelihood that the student would experience failure.

4. Locate community agencies that serve individuals who are at risk. Consider agencies such as telephone hotlines for suicide prevention, child abuse, or drug abuse. Determine the types of services they provide and whether their services are readily available to school-age students.

5. Obtain information that will help you to determine the policy and procedures for identifying and reporting child abuse and neglect in a local school or school district. If possible, also include specific information on the state laws and the penalties for not reporting cases of abuse or neglect in a timely fashion. Prepare a written description of these, with information on the agencies that work with the school to investigate the reports and enforce the laws related to abuse and neglect.

6. Write a letter to a legislator in which you describe what you consider to be the types of societal changes that would reduce the number of students at risk for failure in school, and tell how legislation could produce or influence those changes. Explain the types of losses that we currently experience (in both human and financial terms) as a result of the high number of students at risk.

V

The Future of
Mainstreaming

18 Mainstreaming Today . . . and Tomorrow

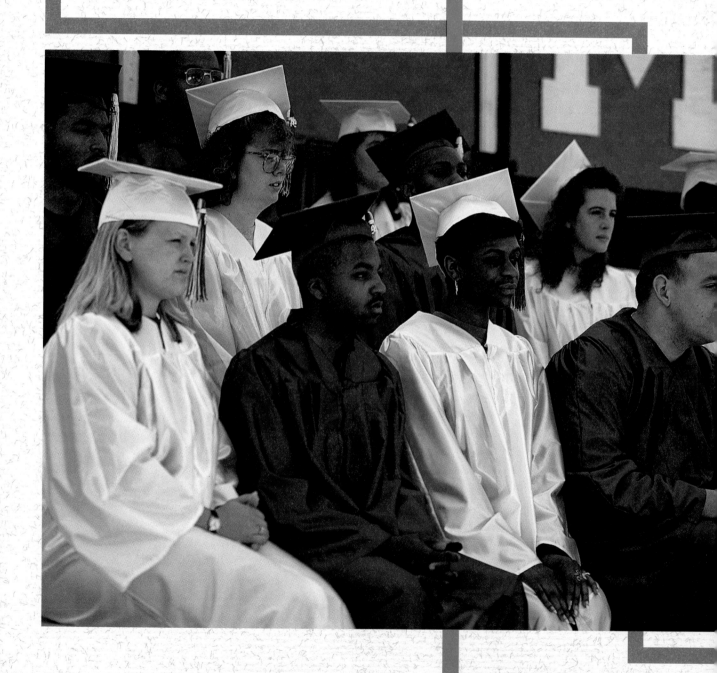

Today, mainstreaming is part of the reality of public schooling in the United States. Although it is not possible to fix an exact date for the birth of this movement, the passage of the Education for All Handicapped Children Act in 1975 stands out as one of the critical starting points. With this law, students with disabilities were guaranteed the right to a free, appropriate public education. That education was to take place in the Least Restrictive Environment (LRE); to the maximum extent appropriate, youngsters with disabilities were to be educated alongside their peers without disabilities. To many educators, this exhortation for placement in the LRE became a mandate for mainstreaming.

What has happened as a result of the implementation of PL 94-142 and its amendments? As countless teachers and administrators have asked, is mainstreaming working? What have we learned, what mistakes have we made, and what issues face us today? This chapter addresses these questions and one other, the most important: How can we make it better? In other words, what can be done to improve the effectiveness of mainstreaming?

PRESENT PRACTICES

In 1990–1991, almost 70% of the students identified as disabled in the United States were mainstreamed for the major portion of their education (U.S. Department of Education, 1993). According to the U.S. Department of Education in its 15th annual report to Congress on the implementation of PL 94-142 and its amendments, the Individuals with Disabilities Education Act, only about 6% of all students with disabilities were educated in segregated programs located outside the regular school building. As Figure 18–1 shows, approximately one-third of all students with disabilities (ages 6 to 21) were placed in regular classes and received special edu-

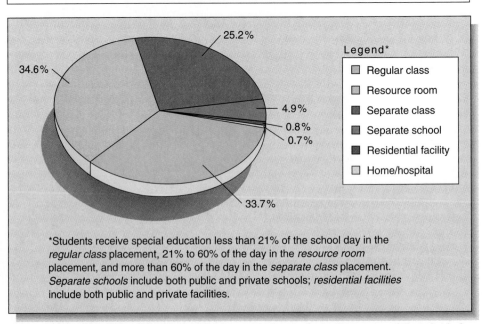

FIGURE 18–1
Educational Environments for Students with Disabilities, Ages 3–21, 1990–1991

25.2%

34.6%

4.9%

0.8%

0.7%

33.7%

Legend*
- Regular class
- Resource room
- Separate class
- Separate school
- Residential facility
- Home/hospital

*Students receive special education less than 21% of the school day in the *regular class* placement, 21% to 60% of the day in the *resource room* placement, and more than 60% of the day in the *separate class* placement. *Separate schools* include both public and private schools; *residential facilities* include both public and private facilities.

Note. From data provided in *Fifteenth Annual Report to Congress on the Implementation of The Individuals with Disabilities Education Act* by U.S. Department of Education, 1993, Washington, DC: Author.

cation no more than 20% of the school day. One-third received resource room services, and one-fourth were educated in separate special classes located within regular schools. The remaining students were served in separate schools (5%), residential facilities (less than 1%), and homebound or hospital environments (less than 1%).

However, not all disabilities are equally represented in the regular classroom. As Figure 18–2 illustrates, students with more severe and comprehensive disabilities (such as mental retardation and multiple disabilities) are less likely to be mainstreamed. In addition, even for groups such as students with learning disabilities and those with speech or language impairments for whom mainstreaming was the most common practice, some students required the more intensive, specialized services available in settings such as special classes.

Students with disabilities whose primary educational placement is the regular class most typically receive part-time special education services in a resource room setting. With the expansion of resource services in the 1970s and 1980s came increased reliance on the regular classroom as the placement of choice for students with disabilities, particularly those with mild disabilities. Soon, however, critics of the mainstreaming movement began to make themselves heard, and among the most insistent were general education teachers. Changes in educational policy and practices had come before the preparation of professionals to implement those changes. General education teachers had long been

FIGURE 18–2

Special Education Services for Students with Different Types of Disabilities

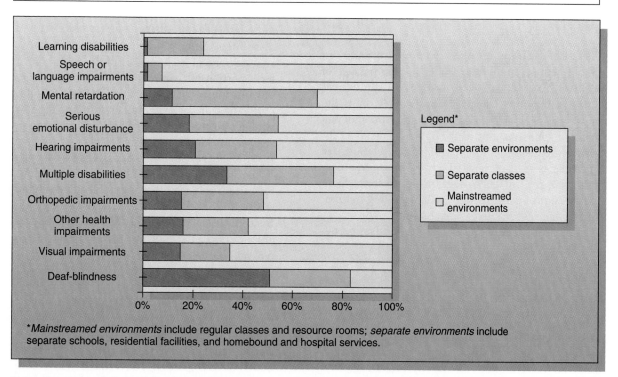

Mainstreamed environments include regular classes and resource rooms; *separate environments* include separate schools, residential facilities, and homebound and hospital services.

Note. From data provided in *Fifteenth Annual Report to Congress on the Implementation of The Individuals with Disabilities Education Act* by U.S. Department of Education, 1993, Washington, DC: Author.

exempt from responsibility for educating students with disabilities and suddenly were asked to accept these students back into their classrooms.

In an effort to alleviate this problem, many states began requiring the inclusion of some special education training in the preparation of all beginning teachers (Smith & Schindler, 1980). Federal monies from PL 94-142 were deployed to update practicing professionals through inservice training programs. At present, approximately 80% of the states require beginning teachers to have training in mainstreaming strategies (Allinder & Peterson, 1992). Although no universal agreement has been reached about the critical skills needed by teachers of mainstreamed classrooms, the competencies proposed by Redden and Blackhurst (1978) appear comprehensive and have the added advantage of an empirical base. These competencies, derived from a survey of general education teachers with experience in mainstreaming, appear in Figure 18–3.

■ PAST MISTAKES

As mainstreaming became a common practice in public schools in the years following the passage of PL 94-142, mistakes were made, and the educational community learned from them. Perhaps the most critical error was the overenthusiastic endorsement of mainstreaming as the optimal placement for all children and youth with disabilities. The evils of special classes as segregated settings that perpetuate labeling and misclassification of students from minority groups were well publicized (e.g., Dunn, 1968). The alternative—placement in the mainstream with special education services as support—appeared a better approach.

In a conscientious attempt to right past wrongs, educators in the late 1970s rushed to place a massive mainstreaming program into operation. However, along the way, many mistakes were made.

■ *Inadequate preparation of mainstreaming participants.* Many mainstreaming programs began without attempts to inform and prepare general education teachers, other school personnel, students without disabilities, and concerned parents

of the changes that would occur in the regular classroom. Such preparation is vital not only to counteract negative attitudes toward individuals with disabilities (Alexander & Strain, 1978) but also to provide skills and information to the professionals responsible for the education of mainstreamed students.

■ *Misunderstanding of the principle of Least Restrictive Environment.* In many cases, the mandate for placement in the LRE was equated with integration into regular classes. The term "Least Restrictive Environment," however, presupposes a continuum of service alternatives for students with disabilities; the mainstream is only one option, albeit the one deemed least restrictive. In the selection of placements, although the restrictiveness of the educational environment should be considered, the primary goal is an appropriate match between the services provided and the student's needs.

■ *Inappropriate selection of students for mainstreaming.* Regular class placement simply is not appropriate at all times for all students with disabilities. Some students require more intensive services, at least for part of the school day or for a portion of their school career. In the early days of mainstreaming, this reality was often overlooked in an overzealous attempt to serve students in a more normalized (and less expensive) educational setting.

■ *Insufficient support to mainstreamed students.* When students with disabilities are mainstreamed for certain subjects, those areas are typically not addressed in the special education program. Instead, special education services concentrate on areas of need: the subjects in which students are not yet able to meet the demands of the regular classroom. For many students, successful performance in reading or math in the resource room has not always led to equivalent performance in the regular class. Mainstreamed students usually require ongoing support and assistance from special education to perform adequately and independently in the general education environment. Early mainstreaming programs devoted little effort to this crucial stage of transition.

FIGURE 18–3

Competencies for Mainstreaming Teachers

In order to effectively teach mildly handicapped students who are integrated with regular students in a mainstream elementary classroom setting, the teacher must be able to

Function 1.0: Develop Orientation Strategies for Mainstream Entry

1.1 Participate in schoolwide planning for mainstreaming activities.
1.2 Set up a training plan that will provide supplementary instruction in areas necessary to teach effectively in a mainstream setting.
1.3 Participate in parent and community orientation programs on mainstreaming.
1.4 Seek out consultative relationships with specialists or school staff.
1.5 When appropriate, develop a program to prepare the special student for entry into a regular class.
1.6 Prepare members of the regular class for the entry of special students into the class.

Function 2.0: Assess Needs and Set Goals

2.1 Gather information to determine the educational needs of each student.
2.2 Evaluate each student's present level of functioning.
2.3 Determine for each student in the class individual goals that are appropriate, realistic, and measurable.
2.4 Determine group goals for the class as a whole and for subsets within the class.
2.5 Involve parents in setting goals for their child and for the class as a whole.

Function 3.0: Plan Teaching Strategies and Use of Resources

3.1 Design a system of teaching procedures that provides for individual differences in students.
3.2 Specify and prepare a variety of activities that will involve the entire class in grouping patterns that are varied and flexible.
3.3 Develop and design a variety of alternate teaching strategies.
3.4 Develop a plan for use of human and material resources.
3.5 Develop a flexible time schedule that provides for the learning, physical, and social needs of each student.
3.6 Provide an optimal classroom climate through appropriate arrangement and adaptation of the physical properties of the classroom.

FIGURE 18–3
continued

Function 4.0: Implement Teaching Strategies and Use Resources

4.1   Select and use a variety of individualized teaching methods to instruct each student within the student's level or capability of functioning.

4.2   Develop, schedule, and maintain on a regular basis a variety of grouping patterns that provide opportunities for students to reach class goals, both social and academic.

4.3   Use the efforts of the special education resource staff with the special students' classroom activities.

4.4   Acquire, adapt, and develop materials necessary to achieve learning goals.

4.5   Plan and maintain a system to use the assistance of volunteers (other students, parents, etc.) to reinforce and supplement classroom activities.

4.6   Develop a plan to use the talents of parents in supporting the learning activities of their child and those of other students in the class.

Function 5.0: Facilitate Learning

5.1   Identify and differentiate between a variety of behavior management techniques and develop skills in selecting appropriate techniques to manage individual and/or group behavior.

5.2   Select and apply adequate behavior management techniques and measures to meet the learning goals set for the class and each individual student.

5.3   Acknowledge appropriate behaviors in each student in order to stimulate continued effort.

5.4   Conduct class activities in a way to encourage interaction between and among students.

5.5   Provide ample instruction and practice for each child to develop and refine adequate coping strategies.

5.6   Plan with class for systematic appraisal and improvement of the psychological climate of the class.

Function 6.0: Evaluate Learning

6.1   Organize a system to collect and record data by which to evaluate student progress toward goal attainment.

6.2   Develop a feedback system that will furnish continuous data to student, teacher, and parents on goal attainment.

6.3   Use evaluation data to assess goal attainment in order to measure terminal outcomes and set new goals.

Note.   From "Mainstreaming Competency Specifications for Elementary Teachers" by M. R. Redden and A. E. Blackhurst, 1978, *Exceptional Children, 44,* pp. 615-617. Copyright 1978 by The Council for Exceptional Children. Reprinted by permission.

- *Insufficient support for general education teachers.* In many cases, when students with disabilities are mainstreamed for part of the school day, some adaptation of regular class practices is needed. Although the classroom teacher holds major responsibility for ensuring that appropriate modifications are made, general educators often require aid and assistance from special educators, particularly when mainstreaming is a new venture and general education teachers are not yet trained. This support has not always been available. Special educators, committed to a variety of other duties, have often lacked the time (and, in some cases, the expertise) to provide appropriate and ongoing consultation services.
- *Inadequate communication among team members.* One component of mainstreaming is the complex network of communication among team members: general education teachers talking with special education teachers, educators building communication links with the home, and older students with disabilities being allowed a voice in their own education. This team approach has not always proved successful. At worst, it has resulted in acrimony as professionals haggle over territorial rights and parents are relegated to the role of passive observers. At best, it has required enormous amounts of time and energy as professionals and parents have learned to work together.

The mistakes of early mainstreaming efforts should not be used as an indictment of the entire movement. Many of the errors made were developmental in nature, a result of hasty implementation in the light of unforeseen contingencies. Mainstreaming remains one of the appropriate options for educating students with disabilities. Our past experiences serve best as a guide for the improvement of present programs and the launching of better efforts in the future.

IS MAINSTREAMING WORKING?

Determining the effectiveness of mainstreaming is a complex task. Mainstreaming affects several constituent groups, and expected benefits vary from group to group. Some of the questions that arise in the evaluation of mainstreaming are identified here:

1. What effects does placement in the regular classroom have on *students with disabilities?* Are such students accepted by peers and teachers? If not, what are the consequences in terms of lowered self-esteem? Is regular class instruction (even when augmented by part-time special services) sufficient to bring about the satisfactory progress of learners with disabilities in crucial academic, social, and vocational skill areas? What are the lifelong effects of mainstreaming? That is, does integration in the classroom result in integration in the community?

2. How does the inclusion of special students impinge on the educational experience of *students without disabilities?* What are the social and personal benefits that accrue from association with individuals with disabilities in the mainstreamed setting? How does instruction change when mainstreaming occurs? Does instructional quality decline when teachers are forced to divide attention between able and less able students? Or does the overall quality of instruction improve as teachers learn new techniques for the solution of educational problems?

3. Is mainstreaming a positive experience for *general education teachers* or only another claim placed on the time and energy of overworked professionals? Do teachers become more tolerant of individual differences with the integration of students with disabilities? Are sufficient support services available, and do teachers know how and when to use these services? How does mainstreaming affect the teacher's ability to present instruction, provide practice, ensure mastery, and manage classroom behavior?

4. How has mainstreaming affected *special education teachers?* How has the role of special educators changed as the duties of consultation, assessment, IEP writing, and so on, have been added to the central function of instruction? Have special education resource programs become tutorial services, acting only as an adjunct to the general education program? Is the consultant function one that most special educators perform effectively?

Even though the central questions about mainstreaming revolve around benefits to individuals with disabilities, it is not possible to ignore the effects on other populations. The impact on students with disabilities must be evaluated in relation to the effects on other students who are members of mainstreamed classes, both general and special educators, school administrators and other professionals, and parents of children with disabilities as well as parents of the other children in mainstreamed classes.

Is mainstreaming working? Although this is much too simplistic a question, it can be answered. The answer is yes; mainstreaming is working very well for some students and some teachers in some schools. The answer is also no; it is not working perfectly everywhere for everyone. Evidence of some current concerns comes from the National Council on Disability (1989) in its report *The Education of Students with Disabilities: Where Do We Stand?* This report identifies several major problems in the delivery of educational services to students with disabilities:

■ Some parents have difficulty finding appropriate services for their children.
■ Parents and students report that some schools have low expectations for students with disabilities and establish inappropriate learning objectives and goals.
■ Services often are not available to meet the needs of disadvantaged, minority, and rural families who have children with disabilities.
■ Families in the military are not universally entitled to the services or the protections guaranteed under P.L. 94-142.
■ Most school reform initiatives appear to be a response to declining academic achievement rather than efforts to find ways for schools to meet the diverse needs of all students.
■ School reform efforts have not specifically addressed the diverse needs of students with disabilities. (pp. 16–28)

Much of the research on the effectiveness of mainstreaming predates the federal mandate for service in the LRE. In large part this literature is composed of comparisons of regular class versus special class placement for students with mild retardation (for reviews of this research, see MacMillan, 1982; Strain & Kerr, 1981; Zigler & Muenchow, 1979). Studies of

effects on the academic achievement of students with disabilities and their acceptance by peers do not consistently favor either placement. According to Zigler and Muenchow (1979), "The data on the merits of educating retarded children with their nonretarded peers are simply inconclusive" (p. 994).

More recent analyses shed new light on this issue. Using a technique called meta-analysis, Carlberg and Kavale (1980) synthesized the results of 50 studies of special versus regular class placement. These authors reported negative effects of special class placement on pupils with low IQs but more positive effects on students with learning disabilities and those with behavioral disorders. Leinhardt and Pallay (1982) reviewed the results of research on a range of educational environments, including special classes, resource programs, regular classes with support services, and regular classes with no support services. They concluded:

> There were several examples of successful programs for mildly handicapped students that used isolated environments. Among the two isolated environments, resource rooms and self-contained classes, there is weak evidence that the less restrictive of the two, the resource room, may be superior. There are also examples of successful programs which help nonachieving students in the mainstream without removing them from the regular class. (p. 564)

Madden and Slavin (1983) present a somewhat different perspective. Their conclusions from a review of the literature are that "research favors placement in regular classes using individualized instruction or supplemented by well-designed resource programs for the achievement, behavior, and social emotional adjustment of academically handicapped students" (p. 519).

Differences in the interpretation of research results can be attributed to two major factors. First, there is no one optimal placement for all students with disabilities; the search for such a panacea in efficacy research is an impossible quest. For some students with disabilities, the regular class with resource support is most appropriate; for others, the more intensive intervention of a special class is necessary. Second, studies of the relative effectiveness of a range of educational placements are asking the wrong question. As Forness and Kavale (1984) point out, *"Where we teach may not be as important as what and how we teach"* (p. 242). That is, it is not the location of the teaching act that is critical but the quality of the curriculum taught and the instructional procedures used to teach it.

Leinhardt and Pallay (1982) share this view, identifying several curricular and instructional factors that promote the achievement of students with disabilities:

- Small class size
- Consistency between curricular goals and instructional activities
- Mastery learning and a formal management system
- Increased time for cognitive activities
- Increased instructional time

These factors are the same as those identified by teacher effectiveness research as important for the achievement of students without disabilities (Brophy & Good, 1986). Good teaching is good teaching, whatever the setting and whoever the audience.

More recently, research has focused on describing the mainstreaming process and identifying factors that lead to its success. One descriptive study examined the school schedules of elementary grade mainstreamed students to determine the extent to which students participated in regular class activities (Sansone & Zigmond, 1986). On the average, the students with mild disabilities in this study spent 15% of the school day in regular classes; mainstreaming occurred most often in nonacademic subjects such as physical education, music, and art. Other researchers have compared the regular class with other settings for students with mild disabilities. The time allocated to various school subjects does not vary between special and general education, but a greater proportion of allocated time is devoted to academic instruction in special education settings (Ysseldyke, Thurlow, Christenson, & Weiss, 1987). Students spend more time on task in resource rooms than in mainstreamed classrooms (Rich & Ross, 1989); at-risk students, after being identified as learning disabled and provided special education services, show an increase in the rate at which their reading skills improve (Marston, 1987-1988). These results suggest that instruction in the resource room is more academically focused than regular classroom instruction. This makes sense because resource services concentrate on the areas in which students with mild disabilities experience the most difficulty: academic skills.

Several studies have examined factors that influence the probability of success for mainstreaming efforts. General education teachers report that the disability of the student is an important factor. Students with learning disabilities or physical impairments are perceived as the easiest to mainstream, whereas those with behavioral disorders or mental retardation are considered the most difficult (Leyser & Bursuck, 1986).

This finding is supported, at least in part, by results of a follow-up study of more than 1,000 elementary grade students with disabilities (Walker, Singer, et al., 1988). After 2 years, 17% of the students no longer required special education services. Those most likely to leave special education were students classified as speech impaired or learning disabled; rarely were special education services terminated for students with hearing impairments, physical/multiple disabilities, or mental retardation. The transition from self-contained special classes to regular class settings appears easiest for students in the elementary grades (Schneider & Byrne, 1984). Eighty-one percent of elementary grade general education teachers were satisfied with the mainstreaming placement of students with mild disabilities, compared with 53% of teachers in grades 7 and above. In the secondary grades, the social skills of students are a critical factor in their ability to succeed in the mainstream. According to secondary teachers, the most important social skills are appropriate work habits (e.g., attending class regularly), respect for others and their property, and ability and willingness to follow school rules (Salend & Salend, 1986).

Effective general education teachers tend to hold high expectations for achievement and classroom behavior (Gersten, Walker, & Darch, 1988). Although highly skilled, these teachers have low tolerance for maladaptive behavior and therefore resist the placement of students with disabilities in their classrooms. However, when mainstreaming occurs, effective teachers are the most willing to receive technical assistance to help them work with their students' learning and behavior problems. Teachers have definite preferences for the types of modifications that should occur when students are mainstreamed (Myles & Simpson, 1989). Most desired are support services from professionals such as special educators and reading specialists, a decrease in class size, and consultation in areas such as behavior management and instructional techniques. Least wanted is inservice training.

Mainstreamed students also have preferences (Jenkins & Heinen, 1989). Special education students in the elementary grades prefer pull-out services (i.e., for which they leave the regular classroom for assistance in the resource room) to in-class services (for which the special teacher comes to the regular class to provide instruction). The most typical reasons students give for this preference are that they receive more or better help in the resource room and that having a specialist come to the regular class would be embarrassing. However, when asked who should provide the special service, students selected their classroom teacher rather than the specialist. Among their reasons were that the classroom teacher knows what they need, they like the classroom teacher, and they know and are used to him or her.

Another avenue for research has been the development of model mainstreaming programs. One well-known program is the Adaptive Learning Environments Model (ALEM) of Wang and her colleagues (Wang, 1981; Wang & Birch, 1984; Wang, Peverly, & Randolph, 1984; Wang & Walberg, 1988). In this model, students with mild disabilities are integrated full-time in regular classrooms. According to Wang (1981), these classrooms are adaptive learning environments characterized by prescriptive learning, exploratory learning, a classroom management system, a family involvement program, and a multi-age and team-teaching organization. Although studies of ALEM programs have documented their success in promoting the achievement of students with mild disabilities (e.g., Wang, Peverly, & Randolph, 1984), there has been criticism of the ALEM research. Critics have pointed out methodological weaknesses in the studies (Fuchs & Fuchs, 1988; Hallahan, Keller, McKinney, Lloyd, & Bryan, 1988) and a lack of information about the characteristics of students described as disabled (Anderegg & Vergason, 1988).

Affleck, Madge, Adams, and Lowenbraun (1988) describe another model for serving students with disabilities in the mainstream. In their approach, one-third of the students in an integrated classroom have mild disabilities. The teacher is an experienced special educator or an experienced general educator who meets state criteria for a special education credential; instructional aides are also available. Results indicate that students with disabilities achieve as well in integrated classrooms as in resource rooms; students without disabilities achieve as well as those in traditional regular classes.

A third model involves providing special education consultation services to general education teachers when students with disabilities are mainstreamed. In one version of this model, both teachers and students receive services; for example, a special educator provides instruction to a student in the resource room or regular classroom *and* consults with that student's teacher. In another version of the model, only the classroom teacher receives services.

Schulte, Osborne, and McKinney (1990) compared the academic progress of students with learning disabilities in three different instructional arrangements: (a) consultation with the student's classroom teacher but no direct services to students, (b) consultation with the teacher and direct services delivered by the special educator in the regular classroom, and (c) resource room services for the students but no consultation. Students showed academic growth in all conditions but were most successful when special educators provided both consultation and direct instructional services. Zigmond and Baker (1990) report contradictory results. In their study, students with learning disabilities were mainstreamed on a full-time basis. General education teachers participated in a year of planning and training prior to the beginning of mainstreaming. Once the project began, special educators provided consultation and served as co-teachers in the regular classroom. At the end of the first year of implementation, students with learning disabilities had made no discernible academic progress. Zigmond and Baker (1990) attributed the project's lack of success to the general educators' failure to make changes in their instructional programs to accommodate the academic needs of mainstreamed students.

Results of current research indicate that, in many cases, students with disabilities can profit from inclusion in mainstreamed classes. They also point to the usefulness of special education services, particularly consultation for teachers and direct instruction for students, as a support for mainstreaming efforts. As would be expected, not all students experience equal success in regular classes. However, a majority of students with disabilities in the United States do spend a substantial portion of their school careers in classrooms alongside their peers without disabilities. Thus, research should continue to seek out new ways to increase the effectiveness of mainstream education for students with disabilities.

CURRENT DIRECTIONS AND DEBATES

Although 20 years have passed since the enactment of PL 94-142, debate continues over the role of mainstreaming in the education of students with disabilities. As the 1990s began, the issue under debate was the Regular Education Initiative (REI). This movement advocates collaboration between special and general education, provision of special services within the regular classroom, and a commitment to serve all students with learning problems, not just those with identified disabilities.

In the article considered the position statement for the REI, "Educating Children with Learning Problems: A Shared Responsibility," Will (1986b) called the current service delivery system a "flawed vision of education for our children" (p. 412). She pointed to the large number of students not eligible for special education who experience difficulty in school and exhorted special educators to "establish a partnership with regular education to cooperatively assess the educational needs of students with learning problems and to cooperatively develop effective educational strategies for meeting those needs" (p. 415).

This viewpoint was endorsed by Reynolds, Wang, and Walberg (1987) in their call for a restructuring of special and general education. Greer (1988), the executive director of The Council for Exceptional Children, also spoke in favor of the REI, saying that "exceptional children cannot succeed as well if they are required to learn with their noses pressed to the glass, from the outside looking in" (p. 295). In Greer's words, *Special education should be carried on as an integral part of the total educational enterprise, not separately* (p. 294).

The REI is concerned primarily with learners with mild disabilities. A parallel movement, full inclusion, is concerned with all students, including those with severe disabilities. The full inclusion movement began in the field of severe disabilities, and its proponents advocate full-time regular class placement for all students, regardless of the severity of their disability (Biklen, 1985; Lipsky & Gartner, 1989; Thousand & Villa, 1990; York & Vandercook, 1991). Full inclusion (or *inclusive education,* as it is sometimes called) is based on the premise that all students have the right to be members of the school community and that no student should be excluded. Stainback and Stainback (1990a) provide this definition:

> An inclusive school is one that educates all students in the mainstream. Educating all students in the mainstream means that every student is in regular education and regular classes (Lusthaus & Forest, 1989). It also means providing all students within the mainstream appropriate educational programs that are challenging yet geared to their capabilities and needs as well as any support and assistance they and/or their teachers may need to be successful in the mainstream (Stainback & Stainback, 1988)... An inclusive school is a place where everybody belongs.... (p. 3)

In support of this position, Taylor (1988) points out that the concept of Least Restrictive Environment may be a faulty one for students with severe disabilities. LRE legitimizes restrictive environments and confuses the intensity of service needed with the amount of segregation. According to Taylor, it is not necessary to segregate students with severe disabilities in order to meet their many educational needs.

Brown and others (1991) offer a more moderate view. Although the "homeroom" of all students should be a general education classroom, students

FIGURE 18–4
Position Statements on Full Inclusion

Council for Learning Disabilities

The Board of Trustees of the Council for Learning Disabilities (CLD) SUPPORTS school reform efforts that enhance the education of all students, including those with learning disabilities (LD). The Council SUPPORTS the education of students with LD in general education classrooms *when deemed appropriate* by the Individual Education Program (IEP) team. Such inclusion efforts require the provision of needed support services in order to be successful.

One policy that the Council CANNOT SUPPORT is the indiscriminate full-time placement of ALL students with LD in the regular classroom, a policy often referred to as "full inclusion." CLD has grave concerns about any placement policy that ignores a critical component of special education service delivery: Program placement of each student should be based on an evaluation of that student's individual needs. The Council CANNOT SUPPORT any policy that minimizes or eliminates service opportunities designed to enhance the education of students with LD and that are guaranteed by the Individuals with Disabilities Education Act. (Council for Learning Disabilities, 1993, p. 595)

National Joint Committee on Learning Disabilities

The National Joint Committee on Learning Disabilities (NJCLD) supports many aspects of school reform. However, one aspect of school reform that the NJCLD cannot support is the idea that *all* students with learning disabilities must be served only in regular education classrooms, frequently referred to as *full inclusion*. **The Committee believes that *full inclusion,* when defined in this way, violates the rights of parents and students with disabilities as mandated by the Individuals with Disabilities Education Act (IDEA).**

with severe disabilities should have the opportunity to spend time in other educational environments, depending on their individual needs.

The REI and full inclusion movements have caused much controversy within the field of special education. The major issue appears to be the need for a continuum of special education services, as required in PL 94-142 and IDEA. Proponents of REI and full inclusion endorse full-time mainstreaming; critics of these movements point to the need for a range of service options. As Braaten, Kauffman, Braaten, Polsgrove, and Nelson (1988) comment, "Research clearly does not support the assertion that all students can be managed and taught effectively in regular classrooms" (p. 23).

According to Wiederholt (1989), "A range of services from programs of total segregation to full-time integration appears as appropriate for the 1990s as it has been for past decades" (p. 189). Several of the professional organizations concerned with the education of students with mild disabilities have expressed similar views, as Figure 18–4 shows. The position statements from these organizations argue that no one placement option is appropriate for all students with disabilities.

One of the major fears of special educators who oppose the REI and full inclusion is that students with disabilities will be placed in regular classrooms on a full-time basis without adequate support. Although provision of special services within the

Because each student with learning disabilities has unique needs, an individualized program must be tailored to meet those needs. For one student, the program may be provided in the regular classroom; yet for another student, the regular classroom may be an inappropriate placement. Therefore, the NJCLD supports the use of a continuum of services and rejects the arbitrary placement of all students in any one setting . . . (National Joint Committee on Learning Disabilities, 1993, p. 596)

Learning Disabilities Association of America

. . . The Learning Disabilities Association of America does not support "full inclusion" or any policies that mandate the same placement, instruction, or treatment for *ALL* students with learning disabilities. Many students with learning disabilities benefit from being served in the regular classroom. However, the regular classroom is not the appropriate placement for a number of students with learning disabilities who may need alternative instructional environments, teaching strategies, and/or materials that cannot or will not be provided within the context of a regular classroom placement.

LDA believes that decisions regarding educational placement of students with disabilities must be based on the needs of each individual student rather than administrative convenience or budgetary considerations and must be the results of a cooperative effort involving the educators, parents, and the student when appropriate . . . (Learning Disabilities Association of America, 1993, p. 594)

regular class is a viable model for some students, others require more intensive intervention. For example, as Schumaker and Deshler (1988) point out, full-time mainstreaming faces many barriers at the secondary level. In junior high and high school, there are large gaps between the skills of students with mild disabilities and the demands of the instructional setting, and instruction tends to be teacher centered rather than student centered. Bringing about the systems changes needed to implement either the REI or full inclusion in secondary schools would be a difficult and lengthy process.

Another consideration is the already difficult task facing the general education teacher as he or she attempts to meet the needs of the diverse group of learners who make up a regular class. The regular classroom of the 1990s includes an increasing number of students at risk for school failure, as chapter 17 has described. It is the view of Kauffman, Gerber, and Semmel (1988) that "more variability than now exists in most regular classrooms is not a reasonable option without additional protected resources for the teacher" (p. 10). In a challenge to advocates of full inclusion, Fuchs and Fuchs (1994) pose these questions:

Why do full inclusionists believe general education can respond appropriately to all students heretofore receiving special education (as well as Chapter 1 and

English as a second language [ESL] instruction)? How can the mainstream improve so dramatically to incorporate an increase in diversity when it has such obvious difficulty accommodating the student diversity it already has . . . ? (p. 302)

Compounding the increased variability in the regular classroom are the current educational reform movements that have resulted in a flurry of new state legislation related to education (Timar & Kirp, 1989). Trends in reform include higher academic standards, increased graduation requirements, more rigorous evaluation of student achievement, and improved discipline (Braaten & Braaten, 1988). Such reforms have direct implications for learners with disabilities and students at risk. According to Braaten and Braaten (1988), "the increased demand for greater skill development in mathematics, science, foreign language, and technology may benefit the general population but further burden students with special needs who are having difficulty coping with current requirements" (p. 46).

Gerber (1988) describes classrooms as systems with resources and instructional technologies. However, if the resources and technologies remain fixed, the teacher's instructional effort can do one of two things. The teacher can increase the average achievement of the class as a whole by maximizing the accomplishments of average and high achievers. Or the teacher can decrease the variability within the classroom by maximizing the achievement of low-performing students so there is less of a gap between low and high achievers. Obviously, neither of these goals is desirable; the aim is to increase the performance of all students. Among the strategies that Gerber (1988) suggests for accomplishing this goal are obtaining more resources, employing more effective instructional technologies, and transferring the responsibility for the achievement of low-performing students to others such as special educators.

Proponents of the REI and full inclusion have suggested a range of instructional options to serve as supports to general education teachers in full-time mainstreaming programs. These include instructional approaches such as mastery learning, individualized learning, and cooperative learning; applied behavior analysis; and peer tutoring (Nevin & Thousand, 1986). However, in a review of research on techniques such as cooperative learning, prereferral teams, consulting teachers, and peer tutoring, Lloyd, Crowley, Kohler, and Strain (1988) advise proceeding with caution. They conclude that, while these strategies hold promise, more research is needed, particularly about the applicability of these approaches to mainstreamed settings.

As in most debates, both advocates and critics of REI and full inclusion have made several valid points. More collaboration is needed between general and special education, and the regular classroom is an appropriate full-time placement for many students with disabilities as long as adequate support is provided to those students and their teachers. However, the regular classroom should remain one of a set of placement options for students with disabilities. As Will (1986a) describes it, the basic principle underlying the concept of least restrictive environment "is that placement decisions must be made on an individual basis and that various alternative placements must be available in order to ensure that each handicapped child receives an education which is appropriate to his or her individual needs" (p. 1).

The federal Office of Special Education and Rehabilitative Services ("OSERS," 1986) amplifies this view by defining integration as:

1. Educating all disabled children in regular schools regardless of the degree of severity of their disabling condition(s).
2. Providing special services within the regular schools.
3. Supporting regular teachers and administrators.
4. Having students with disabilities follow the same schedules as nondisabled students.
5. Involving disabled students in as many academic classes and extracurricular activities as possible, including music, art, gym, field trips, assemblies, and graduation exercises.
6. Arranging for disabled students to use the school cafeteria, library, playground, and other facilities at the same time as nondisabled students.
7. Encouraging helper and buddy relationships between nondisabled and disabled students.

8. Arranging for disabled students to receive their education in regular community environments when appropriate.
9. Teaching *all* children to understand and accept human differences.
10. Placing disabled children in the same schools they would attend if they did not have disabilities.
11. Taking parents' concerns *seriously*.
12. Providing an appropriate, individualized education program. (p. 7)

The last point is a key one. Special education is individualized education, with instruction tailored to the unique needs of each and every student with a disability.

CRITICAL ISSUES FOR THE FUTURE

Mainstreaming is but one of the critical issues that face the field of education at present. Shrinking resources and burgeoning enrollments, the shortage of trained teachers, continuing problems in the maintenance of school discipline, the growing diversity of the school-aged population, the push for quality education and excellence—all are important concerns facing education today. In meeting these challenges, it would be easy to neglect the impressive gains of the recent past, notably the progress toward educational equity.

Mainstreaming is basically an equity issue; it is an expression of belief that all students, including those with disabilities, have an equal right to participate in the educational experience. Mainstreaming is also an integration issue, promoting the concept that students should not be excluded from the normal educational program solely on the basis of a physical, cognitive, or emotional disability. The mainstreaming movement has its critics and has met with resistance from both the general education community and the ranks of special education. This movement, however, has forced U.S. education to reconsider one of its basic issues: Is education designed to serve only those who learn quickly and easily when placed in the standard instructional environment, or is the goal to educate all students, even those who learn with difficulty?

One of the important functions of mainstreaming has been to focus attention on students who, although not identified as disabled, encounter failure in the educational system. As students with disabilities joined the ranks of the regular classroom, it soon became apparent that some of their peers without disabilities had similar needs and benefited from similar instructional modifications. As we progress through the nineties, let us attempt to improve the quality of education for all students who are members of mainstreamed classrooms—students with disabilities and those without, students who represent the U.S. macroculture and those from diverse cultural and linguistic backgrounds, gifted students and students at risk for school failure. To this end, the following recommendations are offered:

■ **Continue to evaluate the practice of mainstreaming and to identify effective approaches to educating students with disabilities in the regular classroom.** Research should continue to examine the effects of mainstreaming on all participants. In addition, it is necessary to document effective mainstreaming strategies and seek out or develop promising new approaches. Determining what has gone wrong can prevent the recurrence of past mistakes; identifying effective practices can increase the probability of future successes.

■ **Increase the use of technology and nonprofessional personnel in the regular classroom.** The teacher need not be the only instructional resource in the regular classroom. With proper training, instructional aides, adult volunteers, and peer tutors can substantially increase a given classroom's capability to provide students with opportunities to learn. For this to occur, educators must recognize that direct delivery of instruction is not the only valid role of the teacher. Management of instruction delivered by others is also appropriate and may be the more efficient method to guarantee appropriate educational experiences for all students in a mainstreamed setting. Also often overlooked as aids to the classroom teacher are computers and other technologies. When educators overcome their reluctance to deal with hardware, they discover the potential of such devices not only in the delivery of instruction but also in the management of classroom information.

- **Search out ways to predict the success of regular class placement before students with disabilities are mainstreamed.** One pressing need in mainstreaming is the development and refinement of a set of criteria or indicators to determine when mainstreaming is likely to be successful for a particular student. However, such judgments cannot be based solely on the student's characteristics; the nature of the classroom environment in which the student is to function must also be considered (Dardig, 1981; Wood & Miederhoff, 1989). To determine the probability of successful mainstreaming, it is necessary to take into account the characteristics of the general education classroom, the instructional techniques in use, the capabilities of the general education teacher and his or her skills in adapting instruction to meet individual needs, and the kinds of special education services and personnel required to support the student's and teacher's efforts.

- **Develop strategies to assist students with disabilities in the generalization and maintenance of important functional skills.** Students with disabilities are often plagued by difficulty in transferring information learned in one setting to another situation or environment. This problem becomes critical when students acquire skills under the tutelage of the special education teacher in the resource room and then are expected to generalize and maintain those skills in the regular classroom setting. This problem has begun to interest researchers (e.g., Anderson-Inman, 1987). Steps toward a solution will benefit mainstreamed students, particularly when emphasis is placed on functional skills that are both currently relevant and important to successful adulthood.

- **Increase efforts to ensure nonbiased assessment.** In an attempt to safeguard against the misidentification of students from minority groups as disabled, PL 94-142 and IDEA mandate procedures for nondiscriminatory assessment. Evaluation measures are to be administered by trained personnel; validated for the purpose for which they are used; in the student's native language; and nondiscriminatory in terms of race, culture, and disability. Although the requirements of law are clear, they have been difficult to implement because of the lack of appropriate assessment tools (McLoughlin & Lewis, 1994). Many measures in widespread use lack adequate validation, appropriate instruments have not been developed for all purposes in all languages, and the problem of measuring skills and abilities without cultural bias has not been solved (Bailey & Hardin, 1980; Duffey, Salvia, Tucker, & Ysseldyke, 1981; McLoughlin & Lewis, 1994; Oakland, 1981). Work must continue to assure the fair and unbiased assessment of students from culturally and linguistically diverse backgrounds.

- **Examine current practices in the labeling and classification of students with disabilities.** One unfortunate result of the current system of labeling and classifying special students on the basis of disability has been the erroneous conclusion that students with different labels require totally different treatments (Lovitt, 1982). Although there may be different curriculum concerns for various groups of students, instructional techniques remain the same across different areas of exceptionality. That is, the skills appropriate for students with mild retardation may be different from those appropriate for students with learning disabilities, but the ways in which teachers go about skill instruction do not vary across groups (Hallahan & Kauffman, 1976). To put it simply, good teaching has the same characteristics whether it occurs in science instruction in the regular class, vocational training in the special class, or individualized reading instruction in the resource room. The ideal classification system for students with disabilities would reflect both the salient differences in curriculum and the universality of instructional techniques.

- **Increase the use of direct instruction and other educational approaches with empirical**

support. In the past decade and a half, research studies on instructional factors affecting student achievement have produced important results, and the teacher's role is quite clear. Students learn when they spend time engaged in the learning process, when learning activities are related to the goals of instruction, and when they have ample opportunity to respond and receive feedback on their responses. Because it promotes these conditions, direct instruction has emerged as an effective strategy for teaching basic academic skills. Although research must continue, educators should begin to discard unsubstantiated teaching methodologies (Arter & Jenkins, 1979) and employ in their stead those approaches with empirical support.

■ **Increase the meaningful involvement of parents and students in the mainstreaming process.** The right to make educational decisions does not belong exclusively to educators. Parents and students are also concerned; and their interest is more immediate, more personal, and more enduring than that of professionals. Education will command higher regard from its constituents when it begins to welcome and not merely permit the continuous participation of these involved individuals.

■ **Transform mainstreaming from a school-based practice to a lifelong condition for individuals with disabilities.** The ultimate test of the mainstreaming movement is its effect on the adulthood of today's children and adolescents. If students with disabilities mature into competent adults and if the community permits and facilitates their social and vocational integration, then mainstreaming has been a success. Although the regular classroom is only the first step, it is a crucial one. If we are successful today, the next generation of teachers and students will regard inclusion of individuals with disabilities in the mainstream of education as an expected, ordinary, and unexceptional occurrence.

APPENDIX
Sources of Software and Assistive Technologies

AbleNet Inc.
1081 Tenth Ave. S. E.
Minneapolis, MN 55414
800-322-0956

acs Technologies Inc.
1400 Lee Dr.
Coraopolis, PA 15108
800-227-2922

Brøderbund Software
P.O. Box 6121
Novato, CA 94948
800-521-6263

Claris Corporation
5201 Patrick Henry Dr.
Santa Clara, CA 95052
800-3-CLARIS

CUE SoftSwap
4655 Old Ironsides Dr., Suite 200
Santa Clara, CA 95054

Davidson & Associates
19840 Pioneer Ave.
Torrance, CA 90503
800-545-7677

Discis Knowledge Research Inc.
P.O. Box 66
Buffalo, NY 14223
800-567-4321

Don Johnston Incorporated
1000 N. Rand Rd., Building 115
P.O. Box 639
Wauconda, IL 60084
800-999-4660

Edmark Corporation
P.O. Box 3218
Redmond, WA 98073
800-362-2890

Hartley Courseware, Inc.
133 Bridge St., Box 419
Dimondale, MI 48821
800-247-1380

IBM Eduquest Resource Center
101 Union St.
P.O. Box 1000
Plymouth, MI 48170
800-426-4338

IntelliTools
5221 Central Ave., Suite 205
Richmond, CA 94804
800-899-6687

Learning Company
6493 Kaiser Dr.
Fremont, CA 94555
800-852-2255

Mayer-Johnson
P.O. Box 1579
Solana Beach, CA 92075
619-550-0084

MECC
6160 Summit Dr. North
Minneapolis, MN 55430
800-685-MECC

Microsoft Corporation
One Microsoft Way
Redmond, WA 98052
800-426-9400

Mindscape Educational Software
55 E. Monroe
Chicago, IL 60603
800-829-1900

Prentke Romich Company
1022 Heyl Rd.
Wooster, OH 44691
800-262-1984

Que Software
201 W. 103rd St.
Indianapolis, IN 46290
800-992-0244

Scholastic Inc.
2931 East McCarty St.
P.O. Box 7502
Jefferson City, MO 65102
800-541-5513

Sentient Systems Technology, Inc.
2100 Wharton St., Suite 630
Pittsburgh, PA 15203
800-344-1778

Software Toolworks
60 Leveroni Ct.
Novato, CA 94949

South-Western Publishing
5101 Madison Rd.
Cincinnati, OH 45227
800-543-8440

Spinnaker Software
201 Broadway, 6th Floor
Cambridge, MA 02139
800-323-8088

Sunburst Communications/WINGS for learning
101 Castleton St.
Pleasantville, NY 10570
800-321-7511

TeleSensory
455 North Bernardo Ave.
P.O. Box 7455
Mountain View, CA 94039

Toys for Special Children, Inc.
385 Warburton Ave.
Hastings-on-Hudson, NY 10706
800-832-8697

Videodiscovery, Inc.
1700 Westlake Ave. North, Suite 600
Seattle, WA 98109
800-548-3472

Voyager Company
1 Bridge St.
Irvington, NY 10533
800-446-2001

Weekly Reader Software
Optimum Resource, Inc.
5 Hiltech Lane
Hilton Head, SC 29926
800-327-1473

Words+, Inc.
40015 Sierra Highway, B-145
Palmdale, CA 93550
800-869-8521

Xerox Imaging Systems, Inc.
9 Centennial Dr.
Peabody, MA 01960
800-343-0311

Glossary

Academic problems. Difficulties encountered in the acquisition, maintenance, and generalization of basic school skills and content area subjects.

Acceleration. Progress through the curriculum at an increased rate.

Access. Ease of entry to and travel from place to place within a building or location.

Acquisition. The initial learning of information or skills.

Adapted physical education teacher. A specialist who modifies physical education instruction to meet the needs of special students.

Adaptive behavior. The individual's ability to change in order to cope with the demands of the environment; also called *social competence.*

Advanced organizers. Information presented to students prior to an instructional task as a preview or overview.

Adventitious. Acquired after birth, for example, as a result of illness or accident.

Algorithm. A procedure used to perform an operation in mathematics.

Amplification device. Anything that increases the volume of sound.

Anorexia nervosa. The disorder in which individuals (usually young women) choose to restrict their intake of food to such an extent that they lose 20%-25% of their appropriate body weight.

Antecedent. Anything that precedes or comes before a behavior; it can be manipulated to control the behavior.

Architectural barriers. Obstructions in the physical environment that prevent access.

Assessment. The process by which information is gathered about students in order to make educational decisions.

Assistive device. A device designed to enhance the performance of individuals with disabilities (typically does not include computer equipment). See also *Assistive technology.*

Assistive technology. Any technology designed specifically for individuals with disabilities; includes add-ons to computer systems and stand-alone devices.

At risk. See *Students at risk for school failure.*

Attention deficit disorder (ADD). A term used in psychiatric classification systems to describe individuals who show poor attention due to distractibility and impulsivity. See also *Attention deficit hyperactivity disorder (ADHD).*

Attention deficit hyperactivity disorder (ADHD). A term used in psychiatric classification systems to describe individuals who show poor attention due to distractibility, impulsivity, and hyperactivity. See also *Attention deficit disorder (ADD).*

Audiologist. A specialist trained in the evaluation of hearing and detection of hearing losses.

Audiometer. A device to assess hearing ability.

Auditory training. Instruction to improve listening skills by teaching individuals with hearing impairments to use as much of their residual hearing as possible.

Augmentative communication. Any system or device designed to enhance the communication abilities of individuals who are nonverbal or whose speech is difficult to understand.

Authoring program. A type of computer program designed to facilitate the teacher's authoring (i.e., writing) of computer-based lessons.

Autism. A disability characterized by extreme withdrawal and poorly developed communication/language skills.

Auto-instructional learning materials. Instructional materials that provide feedback to students and thus allow independent practice.

Automaticity. In skill learning, the ability to perform a skill both accurately and quickly without thought.

Baseline data. Information collected about a behavior before an intervention is implemented.

BASIC. A programming language used to prepare computer programs; *BASIC* stands for Beginner's All-Purpose Symbolic Instruction Code.

Basic skills. The "tool" subjects of listening, speaking, reading, writing, spelling, and mathematics.

Behavioral disorder. A disability in which students are characterized by inappropriate school behavior.

Bilingual. Able to speak two languages.

Bit. With computers, a unit of measurement for quantifying amounts of information. See also *Byte, Kilobyte, Megabyte.*

Blind. A legal designation, often with little educational relevance, that indicates (a) visual acuity of 20/200 or less in the better eye with the best possible correction or (b) a field of vision restricted to an angle subtending an arc of 20 degrees or less.

Blindness. The condition in which so little information is received through the eye that other senses must be used for learning.

Braille. A system of raised dots that can be decoded by touch.

Braillewriter. A machine used to type material in braille.

Bulimia. The disorder in which individuals (primarily young women) have recurrent episodes of binge eating that are followed by induced vomiting, using laxatives, fasting, or taking drugs to reduce weight.

Byte. With computers, a unit of measurement for quantifying amounts of information; eight bits make up a byte, and a byte can express one letter, number, or symbol. See also *Kilobyte, Megabyte.*

Captioned film. A film adapted for viewers who are deaf; dialogue appears in print superimposed on the screen.

Career education. Instruction in the application of basic skills and content area information to problems of daily life, independent living, and vocational independence.

CD-ROM. With computers, a large capacity storage system; *CD-ROM* stands for compact disc read-only memory.

Central processing unit (CPU). The computer component that controls the flow of information and interprets and carries out instructions; the computer's "brain."

Cerebral palsy. A motor impairment due to damage to the brain.

Child abuse and neglect. The physical or mental injury, sexual abuse or exploitation, negligent treatment, or maltreatment of a child under the age of 18 or the age specified by the child protection law of the state in question, by a person who is responsible for the child's welfare, under circumstances which indicate that the child's health or welfare is harmed or threatened.

Choral responding. An instructional technique in which groups of students answer the teacher's question in unison.

Classroom conduct problems. Inappropriate school behaviors that interfere with classroom instruction, impede social interaction with teachers and peers, or endanger others.

Clinical teaching. An instructional technique in which data are gathered both before and during the implementation of an intervention in order to evaluate the effectiveness of that intervention.

Cloze procedure. A method used to determine whether reading material is appropriate for a particular student.

Cognitive behavior modification. The behavior change method that attempts to teach students new thinking strategies for controlling their own behavior; also called *cognitive training.*

Compensation. The instructional technique in which a student's weaknesses are bypassed.

Computer-assisted instruction. The delivery of instruction to learners via computers.

Computer-managed instruction. The use of computers to collect information about student performance in order to manage the sequence and pace of instruction.

Conductive hearing loss. A hearing loss caused by interference with the transmission of sound by air or by bone conduction.

Congenital. Present at birth.

Consequence. Anything that follows a behavior; it can be manipulated to control the behavior.

Content area subjects. Bodies of knowledge in the academic curriculum; for example, English and other languages, the sciences, mathematics, and the social sciences.

Contingency contract. A written agreement between a student and a teacher that states what the student must do to earn a specific reward.

Contingent observation. A type of time-out procedure in which a student is removed from a reinforcing event and can watch but not participate.

Cooperative learning. The instructional model in which students work together as a team to complete activities or assignments (in contrast to *competitive learning*, in which each student works alone).

Creativity. The ability to generate novel solutions to specific problems.

Criterion-referenced test. An informal assessment device that measures whether students have mastered the educational goals stated in instructional objectives.

Cultural pluralism. The belief that cultural and linguistic diversity is a strength.

Curriculum-based assessment. The use of current classroom performance as the basis for determining students' educational needs.

Curriculum-based measurement. A type of curriculum-based assessment in which the teacher takes frequent, brief samples of student performance in important skill areas to evaluate progress toward curricular goals. See also *Curriculum-based assessment*.

Database management program. A type of computer program that facilitates the storage of information and its retrieval.

Deaf. See *Deafness*.

Deafness. The condition in which so little information is received through the sense of hearing that other senses must be used for learning.

Delinquency. Offenses against the legal and social standards of society. The term refers to unacceptable behavior on the part of young people, classified by law as underage, that causes them to be charged as law breakers.

Demonstration. The instructional procedure in which a new skill is modeled.

Desktop publishing program. A computer program that allows the user to manipulate both text and graphics.

Diabetes. A disorder of metabolism.

Direct teaching. The teacher's demonstration of appropriate strategies for the performance of a learning task, encouragement of maximal student response opportunities, and provision of frequent systematic feedback on task performance; also called *direct instruction* or *active teaching*.

Disability. A physical, cognitive, or emotional state or condition that results in an impairment of functioning.

Discovery learning. An instructional technique in which the teacher presents students with opportunities for learning; skills are not taught directly.

Disk. A device for storing information to be read by the computer; computer programs are stored on disks; also called *floppy disks*.

Disk drive. A device that reads information from a disk and communicates that information to the computer. Information can also be sent from the computer to the disk drive and saved on the disk.

Distractibility. Difficulty in maintaining attention.

Divergent thinking. The production of several solutions to one problem.

Dropout. Any individual over the age of 18 who is no longer enrolled in and has not graduated from high school.

Drug and alcohol abuse. Use of alcohol or other drugs that cause negative reactions or other adverse consequences to the individual user, others, or property.

Duration recording. The system of recording observation data in which the length of time a behavior occurs is noted.

Dysfluency. Difficulty in the production of fluent, rhythmic speech; for example, stuttering.

Educationally blind. Having vision impaired to the extent that tactile or auditory materials must be used for reading.

Educational technology. Any technology that has instructional applications.

Engaged time. The actual time during which students are actively involved and participating in instruction.

Enrichment. The instructional technique in which something is added to the regular school program in order to enrich it.

Epilepsy. A convulsive disorder of the central nervous system.

Error analysis. The technique in which student work samples are scanned for patterns of errors.

Etiology. Cause.

Event recording. The system of recording observation data in which the number of times a behavior occurs is noted.

Extinction. A procedure used to decrease the occurrence of a behavior by removing reinforcers that have previously followed the behavior.

Facilitated communication. A controversial augmentative communication strategy in which a facilitator provides physical support to a nonverbal person as he or she types or points to letters. See also *Augmentative communication.*

Full inclusion. See *Inclusion.*

Functional skills. Important skills selected for instruction because of their usefulness in everyday life.

Generalization. The application or transfer of learned material to similar situations and problems.

Gifted and talented students. Exceptional students with intellectual gifts or special abilities in areas such as the arts and leadership.

Giftedness. Superior intellect; it can be accompanied by creative ability.

Group contingencies. Reinforcement provided to members of a group dependent on whether the entire group has reached a criterion level established by the teacher.

Guided practice. The performance of a task under supervision; feedback, correction, and confirmation are immediate.

Habilitation. The instructional approach directed toward the development of the critical skills necessary for successful adulthood.

Handicap. A disability that interferes with an individual's ability to function in a specific situation.

Hard drive. A computer component (or peripheral) used for storing large amounts of information; also called *hard disk drive.*

Hard of hearing. Characterized by a condition in which hearing, although impaired, can be used as one of the senses for learning.

Hardware. Computer equipment such as the computer itself, the monitor, and the disk drive.

Hearing impairment. A disability characterized by a decrease in the ability to hear; see also *Deafness* and *Hard of hearing.*

High interest–low vocabulary. Reading materials that appeal to students who read at a lower grade level than that expected for their age.

Hyperactivity. Excessive activity.

Hypermedia. A computer program in which the user, not the program, determines the sequence of events; the user decides which media (text, voice, video, etc.) to access and when to access them. See also *Hypertext.*

Hypertext. A computer program in which the user, not the program, determines the sequence of events; the user decides which portions of text to read and when to read them. See also *Hypermedia.*

Impulsivity. Lack of reflectivity; activity without careful thought and reflection.

Inclusion. Integration of students with disabilities in general education programs; *full inclusion* refers to full-time mainstreaming for all students, regardless of their special needs.

Independent practice. The performance of a skill without supervision; feedback is delayed.

Individualized Education Program (IEP). A written educational plan that specifies a special student's current levels of educational performance, annual goals, and short-term instructional objectives; prepared by a team that includes the student's parent(s), teacher(s), and, if appropriate, the student.

Individualized instruction. Instruction designed to meet the needs of each student; it can be group instruction or tutorial as long as a high proportion of correct responses is maintained.

Informal assessment. The process of gathering information about students with measures and techniques such as inventories, criterion-referenced tests, and observation; teachers often design their own informal assessment strategies.

Informal reading inventory. An informal assessment device that aids in determining a student's instructional reading level.

Information processing. The method by which persons receive, store, and express information; also called *psychological processing.*

Instruction. The teaching process. See also *Direct teaching* and *Individualized instruction.*

Instructional environment. In the context of the classroom, the procedures, materials, and equipment used by the teacher to increase student performance.

Interval recording. The system of recording observation data in which the occurrence or nonoccurrence of a behavior within a specific time interval is noted.

Inventory. An informal assessment device that samples a variety of skills within a subject matter area; for example, an informal reading inventory.

Itinerant teacher. A professional who travels from school to school rather than providing instruction at one school site.

Keyboard. The most common way people communicate with computers; the computer keyboard resembles a typewriter keyboard with a few additional keys.

Kilobyte. With computers, a unit of measurement for quantifying amounts of information; 1 kilobyte is equal to approximately 1,000 bytes. See also *Byte, Megabyte.*

Knowledge of results. Information provided to students about the accuracy of their responses.

Language. The ability to communicate using symbols.

Learning center. An area of the classroom designed for use of auto-instructional materials for independent practice.

Learning disability. A disorder in the ability to process information that can result in attention, perception, or memory deficits. Students with learning disabilities experience difficulty in school learning despite adequate hearing, vision, and intelligence.

Learning strategies. Methods students use to acquire, rehearse, organize, and recall information.

Least Restrictive Environment (LRE). The most appropriate educational placement that is closest to the mainstream.

Logo. A computer programming language for children in which simple programs can be written to produce designs.

Low vision. The condition in which vision, although impaired, can be used as one of the senses for learning.

Low-vision aid. Any device that aids vision by magnification.

Mainstreaming. The inclusion of special students in the general educational process for any part of the school day.

Mainstreaming team. The group of professionals and parents concerned with the successful integration of special students in the mainstream of education; the team plans, implements, and evaluates the mainstreaming experience.

Maintenance. The recall of information previously learned.

Mapping. An instructional strategy to help students organize ideas for writing; students draw a map showing the relationship between the main topic and key words.

Mediated instruction. Any instructional procedure that includes the use of media.

Megabyte. With computers, a unit of measurement for quantifying amounts of information; 1 megabyte is equal to approximately 1,000,000 bytes. See also *Byte, Kilobyte.*

Memory. The computer component that stores information; *read-only memory* (ROM) stores information permanently (whether the computer is turned on or off), and *random access memory* (RAM) stores information only for the duration of the work session (until the computer is turned off).

Mental retardation. A disability in which subaverage general intellectual functioning is associated with deficits in adaptive behavior.

Mobility. The ability to move from place to place.

Modeling. The reinforcement of another individual, the model, for exhibiting the desired behavior in the presence of the target student. When the target student imitates the desired behavior, he or she is then reinforced.

Modem. A peripheral device that links one computer to another over telephone lines. Modems are used to link home or school computers with electronic bulletin boards and information services.

Monitor. A computer component resembling a television screen. Monitors are the principal way that computers display information to people.

Mouse. A computer input device used in conjunction with the keyboard. The user moves the mouse along a flat surface to change the position on the monitor's screen of a marker called a *cursor.*

Multicultural education. The instructional approach that emphasizes the value of diverse cultures.

Multimedia. Computers and computer software that present information to the user through a variety of media such as photos, video, voice, and music.

Narrative recording. A system of observation in which the observer describes all behaviors that occur.

Negative attention. Use of a negative verbal or nonverbal response (e.g., "Stop" or a frown) that indicates disapproval of a student's behavior. The procedure attempts to reduce the behavior quickly without interfering with ongoing classroom activities.

Negative reinforcement. A procedure used to increase the occurrence of a behavior by following it with the removal of an aversive event or condition.

Network. A system for connecting computers so that they can communicate with each other; often called a *local area network* or *LAN.*

Norm-referenced test. A test designed to compare the performance of one student with that of students in the norm group of the same age or grade; used to determine whether students have significant problems in relation to peers.

Obesity. The condition in which the body weight of an individual exceeds the ideal weight by 20% or more.

Occupational therapist. A specialist who provides therapy and instruction to students with motor disabilities.

Operant behavior. A behavior that is learned and therefore under the voluntary control of the individual.

Orientation. The determination of one's position in space, especially in relation to objects or reference points in the environment.

Partially sighted. Having vision that is impaired but can be used as one of the senses for learning.

Peer tutor. A student who provides instruction to another student.

Peripheral. A device used with a computer but not essential to its operation. The most common peripheral is the printer.

Permanent product recording. The system of recording observation data in which permanent products (such as written assignments, videotapes, and audiotapes) are evaluated.

Phonology. The sound system of language.

Physical and health impairments. Physical disabilities and medical conditions that result in chronic health problems.

Physical environment. In the context of the school, the classroom and its furnishings.

Physical therapist. A specialist who provides treatment under the supervision of a physician to students with motor disabilities.

Portfolio assessment. The process of gathering information about students by assembling samples of their work over time.

Positive reinforcement. A procedure used to increase the occurrence of a behavior by following it with a pleasant or positive event.

Practice. The performance of a learned skill. See also *Guided practice* and *Independent practice*.

Pragmatics. The use of language; language within the context of communication.

Premack Principle. The practice of providing a reinforcement after the completion of a less desired task; for example, if Joan takes out the garbage, then she may watch television.

Prereferral interventions. Modifications of the general education program designed to promote a student's success in the regular classroom and prevent referral for services such as special education.

Problem solving. The process of gathering information about a problem, proposing solutions, selecting a solution, and evaluating the result.

Program. In relation to technology, a set of instructions to be carried out by a computer. Computer programs can be purchased or created using a programming language.

Programmed instruction. A method of instruction in which learners progress at their own pace through small incremental steps that provide immediate feedback about response accuracy.

Prompt. Any feature added to learning tasks that assists students in task performance. Prompts can be verbal, visual, or physical.

Prosthetic device. An aid used to replace a portion of the body; for example, an artificial limb.

Psychosis. A type of emotional disturbance characterized by lack of contact with reality.

Punishment. A procedure used to decrease the occurrence of a behavior by following it with the presentation of an aversive event.

Readability measure. A method of determining the reading level of a given material.

Referral. The process by which a student is identified for study; it can result in consideration for special education services.

Reinforcement. Anything that increases the probability of occurrence of a behavior. See also *Positive reinforcement* and *Negative reinforcement*.

Reinforcement menu. A listing of reinforcers and the number of points or tokens needed to purchase each; it is used in a token economy system.

Related services. Auxiliary services such as psychological services for assessment, transportation, or physical therapy that are available to help students with disabilities derive maximum benefit from special education.

Remediation. The instructional approach that focuses on correcting the weaknesses of the student.

Repeated readings. An instructional technique in which students read a passage several times to increase comprehension.

Resource room. A service arrangement in which special education is provided to students for a portion of the school day. Typically the student is placed in a regular classroom and visits the resource room only for short periods.

Response cost. A mild form of punishment in which an inappropriate behavior is followed by the loss or withdrawal of earned reinforcers or privileges.

Seizure. The loss or alteration of consciousness due to a convulsive disorder.

Self-correcting materials. Instructional materials that provide the student with the correct response so that answers can be checked for accuracy.

Self-instruction. A procedure in which students learn specific strategies to talk themselves through problem situations.

Self-monitoring. Observing, recording, and evaluating one's own behavior; for example, students might observe/record the number of times they leave their chairs, graph the data, and review the graph daily to determine whether they are improving.

Semantics.   The aspects of language related to meaning.

Sensorineural hearing loss.   A hearing loss caused by impairment of the auditory nerve.

Sequence analysis.   A system of observation in which the observer describes each behavior and attempts to identify its antecedent and consequence.

Severe disability.   A severe cognitive disability often accompanied by physical, health, communication, and sensory impairments.

Sexually transmitted diseases (STDs).   Diseases such as gonorrhea, syphilis, herpes, and acquired immune deficiency syndrome (AIDS) that are transmitted most frequently through sexual contact with an individual who has the disease, although newborns may be infected *in utero* or during passage through the birth canal.

Shaping.   The reinforcement of successive approximations or small progressive steps toward a desired behavior.

Sheltered instruction.   A teaching technique for students learning English in which content area lessons include systematic instruction in English language skills.

Sign language.   The system of manual communication in which gestures express thoughts.

Simulation.   A type of computer program that allows students to participate in an experience resembling a real-life or historic event.

Skill-specific group.   A homogeneous instructional group made up of students who require instruction in the same area.

Slate and stylus.   A small hand-held device used to write braille.

Snellen Chart.   A measure used in screening for visual acuity problems.

Sociometric measure.   An assessment device used to determine how students perceive their peers.

Special class.   A service arrangement in which students with special needs are grouped together in a self-contained class; students may leave the special class for short periods to participate in mainstream activities.

Special education.   Instruction that is specially designed to meet the unique educational needs of students with disabilities.

Special students.   Those students with special learning needs who require instructional adaptations in order to learn successfully; includes students with disabilities, gifted and talented students, students from diverse cultural and linguistic backgrounds, and students at risk for school failure.

Special teacher.   A professional educator trained to meet the instructional needs of special students; usually, a special educator who serves students with disabilities or gifted and talented students.

Speech.   The vehicle by which thoughts are expressed in oral communication.

Speech and language impairments.   Disabilities characterized by deficits in speech, receptive language, and/or expressive language.

Speech-language pathologist.   A specialist who serves students with speech and language impairments.

Speechreading.   The process of decoding speech by watching the speaker's face.

Students at risk for school failure.   General education students who show poor achievement and/or are likely to drop out of school.

Students from culturally and linguistically diverse backgrounds.   Students whose home cultures (and perhaps languages) differ from that of the school. Such students may require special assistance to succeed in the mainstream.

Students with disabilities.   Students with special learning needs due to physical, sensory, cognitive, or emotional impairments. Included are students with learning disabilities, mental retardation, behavioral disorders, speech and language impairments, physical and health impairments, vision impairments, hearing impairments, autism, traumatic brain injury, and multiple disabilities.

Study skill problems.   Inappropriate classroom behaviors that interfere with the student's own academic performance or with the teacher's ability to assess academic progress.

Substance abuse.   The voluntary intake of chemicals (e.g., alcohol, narcotics) that can produce adverse social and physical consequences.

Syntax.   The grammatical aspects of language.

Talented.   Having a special ability in an area such as music or leadership.

Task analysis.   The process of breaking down a task into smaller subtasks.

Team-based contingencies.   Reinforcement provided to team members based on the performance of their team; teams can compete against each other or against a preset criterion level.

Telecommunications.   The process of transmitting information from one computer to another over telephone lines; see also *Modem.*

Time management. The organization and scheduling of time for its most effective use.

Time-out. A mild form of punishment in which either the individual is removed from an event that is reinforcing or reinforcement is withdrawn for a specified period of time.

Token economy. A behavior change system in which students are presented with tokens rather than reinforcers after the occurrence of a desired behavior; the tokens can be cashed in for reinforcers at a later time.

Total communication. A method of communication combining oral techniques (speech and speechreading) and manual techniques (fingerspelling and sign language).

Traumatic brain injury. A disability caused by injury or accident involving damage to the brain.

Unit approach. A method of organizing the curriculum by important life themes.

Videodisc. With computers, a large-capacity storage system often used to store video information.

Vision impairment. A limitation in the ability to see.

Vocational rehabilitation counselor. A specialist who assists individuals with disabilities in obtaining employment.

Volunteer. A classroom assistant from the community.

Word prediction program. A computer program that attempts to predict the word a person wants to type based on the first letter(s) of the word; used most often in word processing.

Word processing program. A type of computer program that facilitates written composition by making it easy to manipulate text.

References

Abramowitz, A. J., & O'Leary, S. G. (1991). Behavior interventions for the classroom: Implications for students with ADHD. *School Psychology Review, 20,* 221–235.

Affleck, J. Q., Lowenbraun, S., & Archer, A. L. (1980). *Teaching the mildly handicapped in the regular classroom* (2nd ed.). Columbus, OH: Merrill Publishing Company.

Affleck, J. Q., Madge, S., Adams, A., & Lowenbraun, S. (1988). Integrated classroom versus resource model: Academic viability and effectiveness. *Exceptional Children, 54,* 339–348.

Aiello, B. (1979). Hey, what's it like to be handicapped? *Education Unlimited, 1*(2), 28–31.

Aiello, B., & Shulman, J. (1989). *The Kids on the Block series.* Frederick, MD: Twenty-First Century Books.

Alcohol use. (1989, September 27). *Los Angeles Times,* p. A1.

Alexander, C., & Strain, P. S. (1978). A review of educators' attitudes toward handicapped children and the concept of mainstreaming. *Psychology in the Schools, 15,* 390–396.

Algozzine, B., Christenson, S. L., & Ysseldyke, J. E. (1982). Probabilities associated with the referral to placement process. *Teacher Education and Special Education, 5*(3), 19–23.

Alley, G., & Deshler, D. D. (1979). *Teaching the learning disabled adolescent.* Denver: Love.

Alley, G., & Foster, C. (1978). Nondiscriminatory testing of minority and exceptional children. *Focus on Exceptional Children, 9*(8), 1–14.

Allinder, R. M., & Peterson, R. L. (1992). Readability, interest, and content of current mainstreaming textbooks. *Teacher Education and Special Education, 15,* 202–210.

Alves, A. J., & Gottlieb, J. (1986). Teacher interactions with mainstreamed handicapped students and their nonhandicapped peers. *Learning Disability Quarterly, 9,* 77–83.

America 2000. (1990). Washington, DC: U.S. Department of Education.

American Association of Colleges for Teacher Education, Commission on Multicultural Education. (1973). No one model American. *Journal of Teacher Education, 24,* 264–265.

American Association on Mental Retardation. (1992). *Mental retardation: Definition, classification, and systems of supports* (9th ed.). Washington, DC: Author.

American Foundation for the Blind. (1961). *A teacher education program for those who serve blind children and youth.* New York: Author.

American Psychiatric Association. (1987). *Diagnostic and statistical manual of mental disorders* (3rd ed., revised). Washington, DC: Author.

American Speech-Language-Hearing Association. (n.d.). *Speech and language disorders and the speech-language pathologist.* Rockville, MD: Author.

Anderegg, M. L., & Vergason, G. A. (1988). An analysis of one of the cornerstones of the regular education initiative. *Focus on Exceptional Children, 20*(8), 1–7.

Andersen, M., Nelson, L. R., Fox, R. G., & Gruber, S. E. (1989). Integrating cooperative learning and structured learning: Effective approaches to teaching social skills. *Focus on Exceptional Children, 20*(9), 1–8.

Anderson-Inman, L. (1987). Consistency of performance across classrooms: Instructional materials versus setting as influencing variables. *Journal of Special Education, 21*(2), 9–29.

Aragon, J. (1973). Cultural conflict and cultural diversity in education. In L. A. Bransford, L. M. Baca, & K. Lane (Eds.), *Cultural diversity and the exceptional child* (pp. 24–31). Reston, VA: The Council for Exceptional Children.

Aragon, J., & Marquez, L. (1973). Highlights of Institute on Language and Culture: Spanish-speaking component. In L. A. Bransford, L. M. Baca, & K. Lane (Eds.), *Cultural diversity and the exceptional child* (pp. 20–21). Reston, VA: The Council for Exceptional Children.

Archer, A. L. (1988). Strategies for responding to information. *Teaching Exceptional Children, 20*(3), 55–57.

Archer, A. L., & Gleason, M. M. (1989a). *Design and delivery of lessons.* Paper presented at the annual meeting of The Council for Exceptional Children, San Francisco.

Archer, A. L., & Gleason, M. M. (1989b). *Skills for school success.* North Billerica, MA: Curriculum Associates.

Arkansas Enterprises for the Blind. (n.d.). *10 rules of courtesy to the blind.* Little Rock: Author.

Arter, J. A., & Jenkins, J. R. (1979). Differential diagnosis-prescriptive teaching: A critical appraisal. *Review of Educational Research, 49*, 517–555.

Asher, S. R., & Taylor, A. R. (1981). Social outcomes of mainstreaming: Sociometric assessment and beyond. *Exceptional Education Quarterly, 1*(4), 13–30.

Association for Retarded Citizens. (n.d.). *The truth about mental retardation.* Arlington, TX: Author.

Axelrod, S., & Bailey, S. A. (1979). Drug treatment for hyperactivity: Controversies, alternatives, and guidelines. *Exceptional Children, 45*, 544–550.

Axelrod, S., Hall, R. V., & Tams, A. (1972). *A comparison of common seating arrangements in the classroom.* Paper presented at the meeting of the Kansas Symposium on Behavior Analysis in Education, Lawrence.

Baca, L. M., & Almanza, E. (1991). *Language minority students with disabilities.* Reston, VA: The Council for Exceptional Children.

Baca, L. M., & Cervantes, H. T. (1989a). Background and rationale for bilingual special education. In L. M. Baca & H. T. Cervantes (Eds.), *The bilingual special education interface* (2nd ed., pp. 1–21). New York: Merrill/Macmillan.

Baca, L. M., & Cervantes, H. T. (1989b). Bilingualism and bilingual education. In L. M. Baca & H. T. Cervantes (Eds.), *The bilingual special education interface* (2nd ed., pp. 23–41). New York: Merrill/Macmillan.

Bacon, E. H., & Schulz, J. B. (1991). A survey of mainstreaming practices. *Teacher Education and Special Education, 14*, 144–149.

Bailey, D. B., & Hardin, G. L. (1980). Nondiscriminatory evaluation. *Exceptional Children, 46*, 590–596.

Baldwin, A. Y. (1991). Ethnic and cultural issues. In N. Colangelo & G. A. Davis (Eds.), *Handbook of gifted education* (pp. 416–427). Boston: Allyn & Bacon.

Banbury, M. (1987). Testing and grading mainstreamed students in regular education subjects. In A. Rotatori, M. Banbury, & R. A. Fox (Eds.), *Issues in special education* (pp. 177–186). Mountain View, CA: Mayfield.

Barone, T. (1989). Ways of being at risk: The case of Billy Charles Barnett. *Phi Delta Kappan, 71*, 147–151.

Bauer, A. M., & Shea, T. M. (1989). *Teaching exceptional students in your classroom.* Boston: Allyn & Bacon.

Bauwens, J., & Hourcade, J. J. (1989). Hey, would you just LISTEN. *Teaching Exceptional Children, 21*(4), 61.

Becker, W. C., Englemann, S., & Thomas, D. R. (1975). *Teaching 2: Cognitive learning and instruction.* Chicago: Science Research Associates.

Berdine, W. H., & Blackhurst, A. E. (Eds.). (1985). *An introduction to special education* (2nd ed.). Boston: Little, Brown.

Berdine, W. H., & Cegelka, P. T. (1980). *Teaching the trainable retarded.* Columbus, OH: Merrill Publishing Company.

Berg, F. (1987). *Facilitating classroom listening: A handbook for teachers of normal and hard of hearing students.* Austin, TX: PRO-ED.

Berlin, G., & Sum, A. (1988). *Toward a more perfect union: Basic skills, poor families, and our economic future.* New York: Ford Foundation.

Bettinger, M. M. (1989). Educating the pregnant teen. *CTA Action, 28*(2), 9.

Bialo, E. R., & Sivin, J. P. (1989). Computers and at-risk youth: Software and hardware that can help. *Classroom Computer Learning, 9*(5), 48–55.

Biklen, D. (1985). *Achieving the complete school.* New York: Teachers College Press.

Biklen, D. (1990). Communication unbound: Autism and praxis. *Harvard Educational Review, 60*, 291–314.

Biklen, D., Morton, M. W., Gold, D., Berrigan, C., & Swaminathan, S. (1992). Facilitated communication: Implications for individuals with autism. *Topics in Language Disorders, 12*(4), 1–28.

Biklen, D., & Schubert, A. (1991). New words: The communication of students with autism. *Remedial and Special Education, 12*(6), 46–57.

Binkard, B. (1985). A successful handicap awareness program—run by special parents. *Teaching Exceptional Children, 18*(1), 12–16.

Blake, K. A. (1981). *Educating exceptional pupils.* Reading, MA: Addison-Wesley.

Blankenship, C., & Lilly, M. S. (1981). *Mainstreaming students with learning and behavior problems.* New York: Holt, Rinehart & Winston.

Boning, R. A. (1990). *Specific skill series* (4th ed.). Baldwin, NY: Barnell Loft.

Bonjean, L. M., & Rittenmeyer, D. C. (1987). *Teenage parenthood: The school's response.* Bloomington, IN: Phi Delta Kappa Educational Foundation.

Bormuth, J. R. (1968). The cloze readability procedure. *Elementary English, 45,* 429–436.

Bossert, S. T., & Barnett, B. G. (1981). *Grouping for instruction. A catalog of arrangements.* San Francisco: Far West Laboratory for Educational Research and Development. (ERIC Document Reproduction Service No. ED 201 052)

Bowen, E. (1988, February 1). Getting tough. *Time,* pp. 52–58.

Bower, E. M. (1969). *Early identification of emotionally handicapped children in school* (2nd ed.). Springfield, IL: Thomas.

Braaten, B., & Braaten, S. (1988). Reform: For everyone? *Teaching Exceptional Children, 21*(1), 46–47.

Braaten, S., Kauffman, J. M., Braaten, B., Polsgrove, L., & Nelson, C. M. (1988). The regular education initiative: Patent medicine for behavioral disorders. *Exceptional Children, 55,* 21–27.

Brady, M. P., & McEvoy, M. A. (1989). Social skills training as an integration strategy. In R. Gaylord-Ross (Ed.), *Integration strategies for students with handicaps* (pp. 213–231). Baltimore: Brookes.

Brigance, A. H. (1981). *BRIGANCE® diagnostic inventory of essential skills.* North Billerica, MA: Curriculum Associates.

Brigance, A. H. (1983). *BRIGANCE® diagnostic comprehensive inventory of basic skills.* North Billerica, MA: Curriculum Associates.

Brigance, A. H. (1987). *BRIGANCE® K & 1 screen for kindergarten and first grade.* North Billerica, MA: Curriculum Associates.

Brigance, A. H. (1991). *BRIGANCE® diagnostic inventory of early development—Revised.* N. Billerica, MA: Curriculum Associates.

Brinker, R. P. (1985). Interactions between severely mentally retarded students and other students in integrated and segregated public school settings. *American Journal of Mental Deficiency, 89,* 587–594.

Brolin, D. E. (Ed.). (1983). *Life centered career education.* Reston, VA: The Council for Exceptional Children.

Brolin, D. E. (1986). *Life centered career education: A competency based approach* (rev. ed.). Reston, VA: The Council for Exceptional Children.

Brolin, D. E. (1989). *Life-centered career education: A competency based approach* (3rd ed.). Reston, VA: The Council for Exceptional Children.

Brooks-Gunn, J., & Furstenberg, F. F., Jr. (1989). Adolescent sexual behavior. *American Psychologist, 44,* 249–257.

Brophy, J. E., & Good, T. L. (1986). Teacher behavior and student achievement. In M. C. Wittrock (Ed.), *Handbook of research on teaching* (3rd ed., pp. 328–375). New York: Macmillan.

Brown, L., & Hammill, D. D. (1990). *Behavior rating profile* (2nd ed.). Austin, TX: PRO-ED.

Brown, L., Schwarz, P., Udvari-Solner, A., Kampschroer, E. F., Johnson, F., Jorgensen, J., & Gruenewald, L. (1991). How much time should students with severe intellectual disabilities spend in regular education classrooms and elsewhere? *Journal of The Association for Persons with Severe Handicaps, 16*(1), 39–47.

Bruder, I. (1993). Technology in the USA: An educational perspective. *Electronic Learning, 13*(2), 20–28.

Bruininks, R. H. (1977). *Manual for the Bruininks-Oseretsky test of motor proficiency.* Circle Pines, MN: American Guidance Service.

Bruininks, R. H., Thurlow, M. L., & Gilman, C. J. (1987). Adaptive behavior and mental retardation. *Journal of Special Education, 21*(1), 69–88.

Bryan, T. H., & Bryan, J. H. (1977). The social-emotional side of learning disabilities. *Behavioral Disorders, 2,* 141–145.

Bryan, T. H., & Pflaum, S. (1978). Social interactions of learning disabled children: A linguistic, social, and cognitive analysis. *Learning Disability Quarterly, 1*(3), 70–79.

Bryan, T. H., Pearl, R., Donahue, M., Bryan, J. H., & Pflaum, S. (1983). The Chicago Institute for the Study of Learning Disabilities. *Exceptional Education Quarterly, 4*(1), 1–22.

Bulgren, J. A., & Carta, J. J. (1992). Examining the instructional contexts of students with learning disabilities. *Exceptional Children, 59,* 182–191.

Bull, G., Lough, T., & Cochran, P. (1987). LOGO and exceptional individuals. In J. D. Lindsey (Ed.), *Computers and exceptional individuals (pp. 169–187). New York: Merrill/Macmillan.

Burron, A., & Claybaugh, A. L. (1977). *Basic concepts in reading instruction* (2nd ed.). Columbus, OH: Merrill Publishing Company.

Butler, O. B. (1989). Early help for kids at risk: Our nation's best investment. *NEA Today, 7*(6), 50–53.

Byrne, C. E. (1981, September). Diabetes in the classroom. *ECO*, pp. 5, 19. (Available from the National Education Association)

Byrom, E., & Katz, G. (Eds.). (1991). *HIV prevention and AIDS education: Resources for special educators*. Reston, VA: The Council for Exceptional Children.

Calculator, S. N. (1992). Perhaps the emperor has clothes afterall: A response to Biklen. *American Journal of Speech Language Pathology, 1*(2), 18–20.

California Association for Neurologically Handicapped Children. (1980). *If they aren't learning, don't write them off.* Sacramento: Author.

California Governor's Committee for Employment of Disabled Persons. (1990). *Language guide on disability.* Sacramento: State of California, Employment Development Department.

Campbell, N. J., Dodson, J. E., & Bost, J. M. (1985). Educator perceptions of behavior problems of mainstreamed students. *Exceptional Children, 51*, 298–303.

Campbell, P. H. (1989). Students with physical disabilities. In R. Gaylord-Ross (Ed.), *Integration strategies for students with handicaps* (pp. 53–76). Baltimore: Brookes.

Capuzzi, D. (1988). Adolescent suicide: Prevention and intervention. In J. Carlson & J. Lewis (Eds.), *Counseling the adolescent: Individual, family, and school interventions* (pp. 41–56). Denver: Love.

Carlberg, C., & Kavale, K. A. (1980). The efficacy of special versus regular class placement for exceptional children: A meta-analysis. *Journal of Special Education, 14*, 295–309.

Carter, J., & Sugai, G. (1989). Survey of prereferral practices: Responses from state departments of education. *Exceptional Children, 55*, 298–302.

Cartledge, G., Frew, T., & Zaharias, J. (1985). Social skill needs of mainstreamed students: Peer and teacher perceptions. *Learning Disability Quarterly, 8*, 132–140.

Cartledge, G., & Milburn, J. F. (Eds.). (1986). *Teaching social skills to children: Innovative approaches* (2nd ed). New York: Pergamon.

Cartwright, G. P., Cartwright, C. A., & Ward, M. E. (1989). *Educating special learners* (3rd ed.). Belmont, CA: Wadsworth.

Casto, G., & Mastropieri, M. A. (1986). The efficacy of early intervention programs: A meta-analysis. *Exceptional Children, 52*, 417–424.

Caton, H. R. (1993). Students with visual impairments. In A. E. Blackhurst & W. H. Berdine (Eds.), *An introduction to special education* (3rd ed., pp. 313–349). New York: HarperCollins.

Cegelka, P. T. (1988). Multicultural considerations. In E. W. Lynch & R. B. Lewis (Eds.), *Exceptional children and adults* (pp. 545–587). Glenview, IL: Scott, Foresman.

Cegelka, P. T., & Greene, G. (1993). Transition to adulthood. In A. E. Blackhurst & W. H. Berdine (Eds.), *An introduction to special education* (3rd ed., pp. 136–175). New York: HarperCollins.

Centers for Disease Control. (1991). *Morbidity and Mortality Weekly, 39*(13).

Chalfant, J. C., & Pysh, M. (1989). Teacher assistance teams: Five descriptive studies on 96 teams. *Remedial and Special Education, 10*(6), 49–58.

Chall, J. S. (1967). *Learning to read: The great debate.* New York: McGraw-Hill.

Chall, J. S. (1977). *Reading 1967–1977: A decade of change and promise.* Bloomington, IN: Phi Delta Kappa Educational Foundation.

Chall, J. S. (1983). *Learning to read: The great debate* (updated ed.). New York: McGraw-Hill.

Chall, J. S. (1989). *Learning to Read: The Great Debate* 20 years later—A response to "Debunking the great phonics myth." *Phi Delta Kappan, 70*, 521–538.

Chan, S. (1992). Families with Asian roots. In E. W. Lynch & M. J. Hanson (Eds.), *Developing cross-cultural competence* (pp. 181–257). Baltimore: Brookes.

Cheng, L. L. (1991). *Assessing Asian language performance.* Oceanside, CA: Academic Communication Associates.

Chideya, F. (1993, February 28). The language of suspicion. *Los Angeles Times Magazine*, pp. 34–36, 52, 54.

Chinn, P. C., & Hughes, S. (1987). Representation of minority students in special education classes. *Remedial and Special Education, 8*(4), 41–46.

Christenson, S. L., & Ysseldyke, J. E. (1986). *Academic responding time as a function of instructional arrangements.* Paper presented at the annual meeting of the American Educational Research Association, San Francisco. (ERIC Document Reproduction Service No. ED 271 917)

Close, D. W., Irvin, L. K., Taylor, V. E., & Agosta, J. (1981). Community living skills instruction for mildly retarded persons. *Exceptional Education Quarterly, 2*(1), 75–85.

Cochran, C., Feng, H., Cartledge, G., & Hamilton, S. (1993). The effects of cross-age tutoring on the academic achievement, social behaviors, and self-perceptions of low-achieving African-American males with behavioral disorders. *Behavioral Disorders, 18,* 292–302.

Cohen, D. L. (1992, March 11). Inadequate state funding seen impeding school readiness. *Education Week,* p. 13.

Cohen, S. B., & Hart-Hester, S. (1987). Time management strategies. *Teaching Exceptional Children, 20*(1), 56–57.

Colarusso, R. P., & Hammill, D. D. (1972). *Motor-free visual perception test.* San Rafael, CA: Academic Therapy Publications.

Coleman, M. C. (1986). *Behavior disorders.* Englewood Cliffs, NJ: Prentice-Hall.

Condon, E. C., Peters, J. Y., & Sueiro-Ross, C. (1979). *Special education and the Hispanic child: Cultural perspectives.* Philadelphia: Temple University, Teacher Corps Mid-Atlantic Network.

Council for Exceptional Children. (1976). *Policy statement of the delegate assembly.* Reston, VA: Author.

Council for Exceptional Children. (1978). *Position paper on career education.* Reston, VA: Author.

Council for Exceptional Children. (1993). CEC policy on inclusive schools and community settings. *Teaching Exceptional Children, 25*(4), supplement.

Council for Learning Disabilities. (1993). Concerns about the full inclusion of students with learning disabilities in regular education classrooms. *Journal of Learning Disabilities, 26,* 595.

Craig, R., & Howard, C. (1981). Visual impairment. In M. L. Hardman, M. W. Egan, & D. Landau (Eds.), *What will we do in the morning?* (pp. 180–209). Dubuque, IA: Brown.

Cronin, M. E., & Patton, J. R. (1993). *Life skills for students with special needs.* Austin, TX: PRO-ED.

Cross, D. P. (1993). Students with physical and health-related disabilities. In A. E. Blackhurst & W. H. Berdine (Eds.), *An introduction to special education* (3rd ed., pp. 350–397). New York: HarperCollins.

Cuban, L. (1989). The "at-risk" label and the problem of urban school reform. *Phi Delta Kappan, 70,* 780–784, 799–801.

Cuenin, L. H., & Harris, K. R. (1986). Planning, implementing, and evaluating timeout interventions with exceptional students. *Teaching Exceptional Children, 18,* 272–276.

Culatta, B. K., & Culatta, R. (1993). Students with communication problems. In A. E. Blackhurst & W. H.

Berdine (Eds.), *An introduction to special education* (3rd ed., pp. 238–269). New York: HarperCollins.

Cummins, J. (1989). A theoretical framework for bilingual special education. *Exceptional Children, 56,* 111–119.

D'Alonzo, B. J., D'Alonzo, R. L., & Mauser, A. J. (1979). Developing resource rooms for the handicapped. *Teaching Exceptional Children, 11,* 91–96.

Dale, E., & Chall, J. S. (1948). A formula for predicting readability. *Educational Research Bulletin, 27,* 11–20.

Dalton, B., Winburg, N. E., & Morocco, C. C. (1990). "If you could just push a button": Two fourth grade boys with learning disabilities learn to use a computer spelling checker. *Journal of Special Education Technology, 10,* 177–191.

D'Antonio, M. (1993, November 21). Sound & fury. *Los Angeles Times Magazine,* pp. 44–48, 60–63.

Dardig, J. C. (1981). Helping teachers integrate handicapped students into the regular classroom. *Educational Horizons, 59,* 124–130.

Data bank: Every day. . . . (1989). *NEA Today, 8*(3), 12.

Davis, C. (1980). *Perkins-Binet intelligence scale.* Watertown, MA: Perkins School for the Blind.

Davis, W. E. (1989). The regular education initiative debate: Its promises and problems. *Exceptional Children, 55,* 440–446.

de Grandpre, B. B., & Messier, J. M. (1979). Helping mainstreamed students stay in the mainstream. *The Directive Teacher, 2*(2), 12.

Decano, P. (1979). Asian and Pacific-American exceptional children: A conversation. *Teacher Education and Special Education, 2*(4), 33–36.

Deno, S. L. (1985). Curriculum-based measurement: The emerging alternative. *Exceptional Children, 52,* 219–232.

Deno, S. L. (1987). Curriculum-based measurement. *Teaching Exceptional Children, 20*(1), 41–42.

Deno, S. L., & Fuchs, L. S. (1987). Developing curriculum-based measurement systems for data-based special education problem solving. *Focus on Exceptional Children, 19*(8), 1–16.

Deshler, D. D., & Graham, S. (1980). Tape recording educational materials for secondary handicapped students. *Teaching Exceptional Children, 12,* 52–54.

Diana v. State Board of Education. Civ. No. C-70 37 RFP (N. D. Cal. 1970, 1973).

Dinkmeyer, D., & Dinkmeyer, D., Jr. (1982). *DUSO—Revised: Developing understanding of self and others.* Circle Pines, MN: American Guidance Service.

Dismuke, D. (1988). Reducing suicides. *NEA Today, 7*(3), 21.

Division for Learning Disabilities. (1993). *Inclusion: What does it mean for students with learning disabilities?* Reston, VA: Author.

Dolch, E. W. (1953). *The Dolch basic sight word list.* Champaign, IL: Garrard.

Doleys, D. M., & Bruno, J. (1982). Treatment of childhood medical disorders. In A. S. Bellack, M. Hersen, & A. E. Kazdin (Eds.), *International handbook of behavior modification and therapy* (pp. 997–1016). New York: Plenum.

Donaldson, J. (1980). Changing attitudes toward handicapped persons: A review and analysis of research. *Exceptional Children, 46,* 504–514.

Donaldson, J., & Martinson, M. C. (1977). Modifying attitudes toward physically disabled persons. *Exceptional Children, 43,* 337–341.

Doorlag, D. H. (1989a). Students with learning handicaps. In R. Gaylord-Ross (Ed.), *Integration strategies for students with handicaps* (pp. 33–52). Baltimore: Brookes.

Doorlag, D. H. (1989b, May). *Getting along better with others: How parents and professionals can improve the social skills of special students.* Paper presented at the Fifth Annual California Parent-Professional Collaboration Conference, San Diego, CA.

Doyle, W. (1986). Classroom organization and management. In M. C. Wittrock (Ed.), *Handbook of research on teaching* (3rd ed., pp. 392–431). New York: Macmillan.

Drabman, R. S., & Patterson, J. N. (1981). Disruptive behavior and the social standing of exceptional children. *Exceptional Education Quarterly, 1*(4), 45–56.

Drew, C. J., Logan, D. R., & Hardman, M. L. (1992). *Mental retardation* (5th ed.). New York: Merrill/Macmillan.

Duffey, J. B., Salvia, J., Tucker, J., & Ysseldyke, J. E. (1981). Nonbiased assessment: A need for operationalism. *Exceptional Children, 47,* 427–434.

Dunn, L. M. (1968). Special education for the mildly retarded—Is much of it justifiable? *Exceptional Children, 35,* 5–22.

Dunn, R., & Dunn, K. (1978). *Teaching students through their individual learning styles: A practical approach.* Reston, VA: Reston.

Dunn, R., & Dunn, K. (1979). Learning styles—Practical applications of research. *Practical Applications of Research, 1*(3), 2–3.

Eaton, M. D., & Hansen, C. L. (1978). Classroom organization and management. In N. G. Haring, T. C. Lovitt, M. D. Eaton, & C. L. Hansen (Eds.), *The fourth R: Research in the classroom* (pp. 191–217). Columbus, OH: Merrill Publishing Company.

Edgar, E., & Davidson, C. (1979). Parent perceptions of mainstreaming. *Education Unlimited, 1*(4), 32–33.

Educating refugees: Understanding the basics. (1989). *NCBE Forum, 12*(3), 1, 3.

Edwards, L. L. (1980). Curriculum modification as a strategy for helping regular classroom behavior-disordered students. *Focus on Exceptional Children, 12*(8), 1–11.

Edwards, T. K. (1988). Providing reasons for wanting to live. *Phi Delta Kappan, 70,* 296–298.

Ehly, S. W., & Larsen, S. C. (1980). *Peer tutoring for individualized instruction.* Boston: Allyn & Bacon.

Eiser, L. (1986). "Regular" software for special ed. kids? Yes! *Classroom Computer Learning, 7*(2), 26–30, 35.

Ekwall, E. E. (1986). *Ekwall reading inventory* (2nd ed.). Boston: Allyn & Bacon.

Ekwall, E. E. (1989). *Locating and correcting reading difficulties* (5th ed.). New York: Merrill/Macmillan.

Elam, S. M., Rose, L. C., & Gallup, A. M. (1993). The 25th annual Phi Delta Kappa/Gallup poll of the public's attitudes toward the public schools. *Phi Delta Kappan, 75,* 137–152.

Ellett, L. (1993). Instructional practices in mainstreamed secondary classrooms. *Journal of Learning Disabilities, 26,* 57–64.

Elmquist, D. L. (1991). School-based alcohol and other drug prevention programs: Guidelines for the special educator. *Intervention in School and Clinic, 27*(1), 10–19.

Emery, R. E. (1989). Family violence. *American Psychologist, 44,* 321–328.

Emmer, E. T. (1981). *Effective management in junior high math classes* (Report No. 6111). Austin: University of Texas, Research and Development Center for Teacher Education.

Emmer, E. T., Evertson, C. M., Sanford, J. P., Clements, B. S., & Worsham, M. E. (1989). *Classroom management for secondary teachers* (2nd ed.). Englewood Cliffs, NJ: Prentice-Hall.

Engelmann, S., Becker, W., Hanner, S., & Johnson, G. (1988). *Corrective reading-decoding.* Chicago: Science Research Associates.

Engelmann, S., & Bruner, E. C. (1988). *Reading mastery: DISTAR reading.* Chicago: Science Research Associates.

Englert, C. S. (1984). Measuring teacher effectiveness from the teacher's point of view. *Focus on Exceptional Children, 17*(2), 1–14.

Englert, C. S., & Raphael, T. E. (1988). Constructing well-formed prose: Process, structure, and metacognitive knowledge. *Exceptional Children, 54,* 513–520.

Epanchin, B. C. (1987). Anxiety and stress-related disorders. In B. C. Epanchin & J. L. Paul (Eds.), *Emotional problems of childhood and adolescence: A multidisci-*

plinary perspective (pp. 165–190). New York: Merrill/Macmillan.

Epilepsy Foundation of America. (1974). *Epilepsy school alert.* Washington, DC: Author.

Epilepsy Foundation of America. (1987). *Epilepsy school alert.* Washington, DC: Author.

Epilepsy Foundation of America. (n.d.). *Teacher tips about the epilepsies.* Washington, DC: Author.

Evans, J., & Guevara, A. E. (1974). Classroom instruction for young Spanish speakers. *Exceptional Children, 41,* 16–19.

Evertson, C. M., Sanford, J. P., & Emmer, E. T. (1981). Effects of class heterogeneity in junior high school. *American Educational Research Journal, 18,* 219–232.

Fais, L., & Wanderman, R. (1987). *A computer-aided writing program for learning disabled adolescents.* Litchfield, CT: The Forman School. (ERIC Document Reproduction Service No. ED 293 273)

Falvey, M. A., Grenot-Scheyer, M., & Bishop, K. (1989). Integrating students with severe handicaps. *California State Federation/CEC Journal, 35*(3), 8–10.

Feldhusen, J. F. (1989). Thinking skills for the gifted. In J. F. Feldhusen, J. Van Tassel-Baska, & K. Seeley (Eds.), *Excellence in educating the gifted* (pp. 239–259). Denver: Love.

Fiedler, C. R., & Simpson, R. L. (1987). Modifying the attitudes of nonhandicapped students toward handicapped peers. *Exceptional Children, 53,* 342–349.

Finch, A. J., & Spirito, A. (1980). Use of cognitive training to change cognitive processes. *Exceptional Education Quarterly, 1*(1), 31–39.

Fischer, L., & Sorenson, G. P. (1985). *School law for counselors, psychologists, and social workers.* New York: Longman.

Flesch, R. (1951). *How to test readability.* New York: Harper & Row.

Flexer, C., Wray, D., & Ireland, J. C. (1989). Preferential seating is not enough: Issues in classroom management of hearing-impaired students. *Language, Speech, and Hearing in Schools, 20,* 11–21.

Forest, M., & Lusthaus, E. (1989). Promoting educational equality for all students. In S. Stainback, W. Stainback, & M. Forest (Eds.), *Educating all students in the mainstream of regular education* (pp. 43–57). Baltimore: Brookes.

Forness, S. R., & Kavale, K. A. (1984). Education of the mentally retarded: A note on policy. *Education and Training of the Mentally Retarded, 19,* 239–245.

Forness, S. R., & Kavale, K. A. (1993). Strategies to improve basic learning and memory deficits in mental retardation: A meta-analysis of experimental studies. *Education and Training in Mental Retardation, 28,* 99–110.

Forster, P., & Doyle, B. A. (1989). Teaching listening skills to students with attention deficit disorders. *Teaching Exceptional Children, 21*(2), 20–22.

Fox, C. L. (1989). Peer acceptance of learning disabled children in the regular classroom. *Exceptional Children, 56,* 50–59.

Foyle, H. C., & Lyman, L. (1990). *Cooperative learning: What you need to know.* Washington, DC: National Education Association.

Franklin, M. E. (1992). Culturally sensitive instructional practices for African-American learners with disabilities. *Exceptional Children, 59,* 115–122.

Frase, M. J. (1989). *Dropout rates in the United States: 1988.* Washington, DC: U.S. Department of Education, Office of Educational Research and Improvement, National Center for Education Statistics.

Freedman, S. W. (1982). Language assessment and writing disorders. *Topics in Language Disorders, 2*(4), 34–44.

Freeman, D., & Freeman, Y. (1988). *Sheltered English instruction. ERIC Digest.* Washington, DC: ERIC Clearinghouse on Languages and Linguistics. (ERIC Document Reproduction Service No. ED 301 070)

Fry, E. (1968). A readability formula that saves time. *Journal of Reading, 11,* 513–516, 575–577.

Fry, E. (1977). Fry's readability graph: Clarifications, validity, and extension to level 17. *Journal of Reading, 21,* 242–252.

Frymier, J., & Gansneder, B. (1989). The Phi Delta Kappa study of students at risk. *Phi Delta Kappan, 71,* 142–146.

Fuchigami, R. Y. (1980). Teacher education for culturally diverse exceptional children. *Exceptional Children, 46,* 634–641.

Fuchs, D. S., & Fuchs, L. S. (1988). Evaluation of the Adaptive Learning Environments Model. *Exceptional Children, 55,* 115–127.

Fuchs, D. S., & Fuchs, L. S. (1994). Inclusive schools movement and the radicalization of special education reform. *Exceptional Children, 60,* 294–309.

Fuchs, L. S. (1986). Monitoring progress among mildly handicapped pupils: Review of current practice and research. *Remedial and Special Education, 7*(5), 5–12.

Fuchs, L. S. (1987). Program development. *Teaching Exceptional Children, 20*(1), 42–44.

Furstenberg, F. F., Jr., Brooks-Gunn, J., & Chase-Lansdale, L. (1989). Teenaged pregnancy and childbearing. *American Psychologist, 44,* 313–320.

Gable, R. A., Laycock, V. K., Maroney, S. A., & Smith, C. R. (1991). *Preparing to integrate students with behav-*

ioral disorders. Reston, VA: The Council for Exceptional Children.

Gable, R. A., Strain, P. S., & Hendrickson, J. M. (1979). Strategies for improving the status and social behavior of learning disabled children. *Learning Disability Quarterly, 2*(3), 33–39.

Gajar, A., Goodman, L., & McAfee, J. (1993). *Secondary schools and beyond: Transition of individuals with mild disabilities.* New York: Merrill/Macmillan.

Gallagher, J. J. (1988). National agenda for educating gifted students: Statement of priorities. *Exceptional Children, 55,* 107–114.

Gallup, A. M., & Elam, S. M. (1988). The 20th annual Gallup Poll of the public's attitudes toward the public schools. *Phi Delta Kappan, 70,* 33–45.

Gans, K. D. (1985). Regular and special educators: Handicap integration attitudes and implications for consultants. *Teacher Education and Special Education, 8,* 188–197.

Garcia, R. L. (1978). *Fostering a pluralistic society through multi-ethnic education.* Bloomington, IN: Phi Delta Kappa Educational Foundation.

Gardner, H. (1987). Beyond the IQ: Education and human development. *Harvard Educational Review, 57,* 187–193.

Garfinkel, B. D., Crosby, E., Herbert, M. R., Matus, A. L., Pfeifer, J. K., & Sheras, P. L. (1988). *Responding to adolescent suicide. A report of the Phi Delta Kappa Task Force on Adolescent Suicide.* Bloomington, IN: Phi Delta Kappa Educational Foundation.

Garrett, M. K., & Crump, W. D. (1980). Peer acceptance, teacher preference, and self-appraisal of social status of learning disabled students. *Learning Disability Quarterly, 3*(3), 42–48.

Gartner, A., & Riessman, F. (1977). *How to individualize learning.* Bloomington, IN: Phi Delta Kappa Educational Foundation.

Gastright, J. F. (1989, April). Don't base your dropout program on somebody else's problem. *Phi Delta Kappa Research Bulletin,* pp. 1–4.

Gay, L. R. (1981). *Educational research* (2nd ed.). Columbus, OH: Merrill Publishing Company.

Gearheart, B. R., Weishahn, M. W., & Gearheart, C. J. (1988). *The exceptional student in the regular classroom* (4th ed.). New York: Merrill/Macmillan.

Gerber, M. M. (1988). Tolerance and technology of instruction: Implications for special education reform. *Exceptional Children, 54,* 309–314.

Gersten, R., & Dimino, J. (1993). Visions and revisions: A special education perspective on the whole language controversy. *Special Education and Remedial Education, 14*(4), 5–13.

Gersten, R., Taylor, R., & Graves, A. (in press). Direct instruction and diversity. In C. Utley (Ed.), *Strategies for improving assessment and service delivery with multicultural students with mild disabilities.* Baltimore: Brookes.

Gersten, R., Walker, H. M., & Darch, C. B. (1988). Relationship between teachers' effectiveness and their tolerance for handicapped students. *Exceptional Children, 54,* 433–438.

Giangreco, M., Cloninger, C., & Iverson, V. (1990). *C.O.A.C.H.—Cayuga-Onondaga assessment for children with handicaps* (6th ed.). Stillwater: Oklahoma State University.

Gibson, A. B., Roberts, P. C., & Buttery, T. J. (1982). *Death education: A concern for the living.* Bloomington, IN: Phi Delta Kappa Educational Foundation.

Gickling, E. E., & Thompson, V. P. (1985). A personal view of curriculum-based assessment. *Exceptional Children, 52,* 205–218.

Gillung, T. B., & Rucker, C. N. (1977). Labels and teacher expectations. *Exceptional Children, 43,* 464–465.

Glass, G. V., & Smith, M. L. (1978). *Meta-analysis of research on class size and achievement.* Boulder: University of Colorado, Laboratory of Educational Research.

Glazzard, P. (1980). Adaptations for mainstreaming. *Teaching Exceptional Children, 13,* 26–29.

Glazzard, P. (1982). *Learning activities and teaching ideas for the special child in the regular classroom.* Englewood Cliffs, NJ: Prentice-Hall.

Gleason, M. M. (1988). Teaching study strategy. *Teaching Exceptional Children, 20*(3), 52–53.

Goldberg, L. (1992). *Adapted interactive media (AIM).* Paper presented at the 1992 Closing the Gap Microcomputer Technology in Special Education and Rehabilitation Conference, Minneapolis.

Goldman, R. M., & Fristoe, M. (1986). *Goldman-Fristoe test of articulation.* Circle Pines, MN: American Guidance Service.

Goldman, R. M., Fristoe, M., & Woodcock, R. W. (1976). *Goldman-Fristoe-Woodcock auditory skills test battery.* Circle Pines, MN: American Guidance Service.

Goldstein, A. P., Sprafkin, R. P., Gershaw, N. J., & Klein, P. (1980). *Skillstreaming the adolescent: A structured learning approach to teaching prosocial skills.* Champaign, IL: Research Press.

Gollnick, D. M., & Chinn, P. C. (1990). *Multicultural education in a pluralistic society* (3rd ed.). New York: Merrill/Macmillan.

Gonzales, E. (1979). Preparation for teaching the multi-cultural exceptional child: Trends and concerns. *Teacher Education and Special Education, 2*(4), 12–18.

Gonzalez, J. (1978). The status of bilingual education today: Un vistazo y un repaso. *National Association for Bilingual Education, 2*(1), 13–20.

Goodman, L. (1978). Meeting children's needs through materials modification. *Teaching Exceptional Children, 10,* 92–94.

Gordon, T. (1974). *Teacher effectiveness training.* New York: Wyden.

Gottlieb, J., & Leyser, Y. (1981). Facilitating the social mainstreaming of retarded children. *Exceptional Education Quarterly, 1*(4), 57–70.

Graden, J. L., Casey, A., & Christenson, S. L. (1985). Implementing a prereferral intervention system: Part I. The model. *Exceptional Children, 51,* 377–384.

Grady, E. (1992). *The portfolio approach to assessment.* Bloomington, IN: Phi Delta Kappa Educational Foundation.

Graham, S., & Harris, K.R. (1989). Improving learning disabled students' skills at composing essays: Self-instructional strategy training. *Exceptional Children, 56,* 201–214.

Graham, S., & Johnson, L. A. (1989). Teaching reading to learning disabled students: A review of research-supported procedures. *Focus on Exceptional Children, 21*(6), 1–12.

Graham, S., & MacArthur, C. A. (1988). Improving learning disabled students' skills at revising essays produced on a word processor: Self-instructional strategy training. *Journal of Special Education, 22,* 133–152.

Graham, S., & Miller, L. (1979). Spelling research and practice: A unified approach. *Focus on Exceptional Children, 12*(2), 1–16.

Gray, L. A., & House, R. M. (1989). No guarantee of immunity: AIDS and adolescents. In D. Capuzzi & D. R. Gross (Eds.), *Youth at risk: A resource for counselors, teachers and parents* (pp. 231–263). Alexandria, VA: American Association for Counseling and Development.

Grayson, D. (n.d.). *Facts about blindness and visual impairment.* New York: American Foundation for the Blind.

Green, W. W., & Fischgrund, J. E. (1993). Students with hearing loss. In A. E. Blackhurst & W. H. Berdine (Eds.), *An introduction to special education* (3rd ed., pp. 271–311). New York: HarperCollins College Publishers.

Greenberg, G. S., & Horn, W. F. (1991). *Attention deficit hyperactivity disorder: Questions and answers for parents.* Champaign, IL: Research Press.

Greer, J. V. (1988). No more noses to the glass. *Exceptional Children, 54,* 294–296.

Gresham, F. M. (1984). Social skills and self-efficacy for exceptional children. *Exceptional Children, 51,* 253–261.

Grosenick, J. K., & Huntze, S. L. (1980). *National needs analysis in behavior disorders: Adolescent behavior disorders.* Columbia: University of Missouri at Columbia, Department of Special Education.

Grossman, H. J. (Ed.). (1983). *Classification in mental retardation* (1983 revision). Washington, DC: American Association on Mental Retardation.

Grossnickle, D. R. (1986). *High school dropouts: Causes, consequences, and cure.* Bloomington, IN: Phi Delta Kappa Educational Foundation.

Guetzloe, E. C. (1988). Suicide and depression: Special education's responsibility. *Teaching Exceptional Children, 20*(4), 25–28.

Guetzloe, E. C. (1989). *Youth suicide: What the educator should know.* Reston, VA: The Council for Exceptional Children.

Guetzloe, E. C. (1993). Answering the cries for help—Suicidal thoughts and actions. *Journal of Emotional and Behavioral Problems, 2*(2), 34–38.

Guilford, J. P. (1967). *The nature of human intelligence.* New York: McGraw-Hill.

Guralnick, M. J. (1981). Programmatic factors affecting child-child social interactions in mainstreamed preschool programs. *Exceptional Education Quarterly, 1*(4), 71–92.

Hallahan, D. P., & Kauffman, J. M. (1976). *Introduction to learning disabilities.* Englewood Cliffs, NJ: Prentice-Hall.

Hallahan, D. P., & Kauffman, J. M. (1988). *Exceptional children* (4th ed.). Englewood Cliffs, NJ: Prentice-Hall.

Hallahan, D. P., Keller, C. E., McKinney, J. D., Lloyd, J. W., & Bryan, T. H. (1988). Examining the research base of the regular education initiative: Efficacy studies and the Adaptive Learning Environments Model. *Journal of Learning Disabilities, 21,* 29–35.

Hallahan, D. P., & Reeve, R. E. (1980). Selective attention and distractibility. In B. K. Keogh (Ed.), *Advances in special education* (Vol. 1, pp. 141–181). Greenwich, CT: J.A.I. Press.

Hammill, D. D. (1991). *Detroit tests of learning aptitude* (3rd ed.). Austin, TX: PRO-ED.

Hammill, D. D., & Bartel, N. R. (1986). *Teaching students with learning and behavior problems* (4th ed.). Austin, TX: PRO-ED.

Hammill, D. D., & Bartel, N. R. (1993). *Teaching students with learning and behavior problems* (5th. ed.). Boston: Allyn & Bacon.

Hammill, D. D., Brown, V. L., Larsen, S. C., & Wieder-holt, J. L. (1987). *Test of adolescent language–2*. Austin, TX: PRO-ED.

Hammill, D. D., & Newcomer, P. L. (1988). *Test of language development–2, Intermediate*. Austin, TX: PRO-ED.

Hamre-Nietupski, S., McDonald, J., & Nietupski, J. (1992). Integrating elementary students with multiple disabilities into supported regular classes: Challenges and solutions. *Teaching Exceptional Children, 24*(3), 6–9.

Handlers, A., & Austin, K. (1980). Improving attitudes of high school students toward their handicapped peers. *Exceptional Children, 47*, 228–229.

Harley, R. K., & Lawrence, G. A. (1984). *Visual impairment in the schools.* Springfield, IL: Thomas.

Harrington, J. D. (1976). Hard-of-hearing pupils in the mainstream: Educational needs and services. In *Serving hard-of-hearing pupils: Alternative strategies for personnel preparation* (pp. 16–31). Minneapolis: University of Minnesota, Leadership Training Institute/Special Education.

Hasselbring, T. S., Goin, L. I., & Bransford, J. D. (1987). Developing automaticity. *Teaching Exceptional Children, 19*(3), 30–33.

Hazekamp, J., & Huebner, K. M. (Eds.). (1989). *Program planning and evaluation for blind and visually impaired students: National guidelines for educational excellence.* New York: American Foundation for the Blind.

Helge, D. (1991). *Rural, exceptional, at risk*. Reston, VA: The Council for Exceptional Children.

Henker, B., Whalen, C. K., & Hinshaw, S. P. (1980). The attributional contexts of cognitive intervention strategies. *Exceptional Education Quarterly, 1*(1), 17–30.

Heron, T. E., & Harris, K. C. (1993). *The educational consultant* (3rd ed.). Austin, TX: PRO-ED.

Heron, T. E., Heward, W. L., & Cooke, N. L. (1980). *A classwide peer tutoring system.* Paper presented at the Sixth Annual Meeting of the Association of Behavior Analysis, Dearborn, MI.

Heward, W. L., Courson, F. H., & Narayan, J. S. (1989). Using choral responding to increase active student response. *Teaching Exceptional Children, 21*(3), 72–75.

Heward, W. L., & Orlansky, M. D. (1988). *Exceptional children* (3rd ed.). New York: Merrill/Macmillan.

Heward, W. L., & Orlansky, M. D. (1992). *Exceptional children* (4th ed.). New York: Merrill/Macmillan.

Hill, D. (1989, September/October). Fixing the system from the top down. *Teacher Magazine*, pp. 50–55.

Hiskey, M. (1966). *Hiskey-Nebraska test of learning aptitude.* Lincoln, NE: Union College Press.

Hobbs, N. (1975). *The futures of children.* San Francisco: Jossey-Bass.

Hobbs, N. (1976). *Issues in the classification of children.* San Francisco: Jossey-Bass.

Hodgkinson, H. (1993). American education: The good, the bad, and the task. *Phi Delta Kappan, 74*, 619–623.

Hofmeister, A. M. (1989). Teaching with videodiscs. *Teaching Exceptional Children, 21*(3), 52–54.

Hofmeister, A. M., & Thorkildsen, R. (1984). Microcomputers in special education: Implications for instructional design. *Exceptional Education Quarterly, 4*(4), 1–8.

Hofmeister, A. M., & Thorkildsen, R. (1993). Interactive videodisc and exceptional individuals. In J. D. Lindsey (Ed.), *Computers and exceptional individuals* (2nd ed., pp. 87–107). Austin, TX: PRO-ED.

Hollinger, J. D. (1987). Social skills for behaviorally disordered children as preparation for mainstreaming: Theory, practice, and new directions. *Remedial and Special Education, 8*(4), 17–27.

Holzberg, C. S. (1991). Sound and image: The world on a disc. *inCider/A+, 9*(11), 30–34.

Horton, L. (1985). *Adolescent alcohol abuse.* Bloomington, IN: Phi Delta Kappa Educational Foundation.

Howell, K. W., Fox, S. L., & Morehead, M. K. (1993). *Curriculum-based evaluation* (2nd ed.). Pacific Grove, CA: Brooks/Cole.

Hunter, B. (1984). *My students use computers.* Reston, VA: Reston.

Idol, L. (1993). *Special educator's consultation handbook* (2nd ed.). Austin, TX: PRO-ED.

Idol, L., & West, J. F. (1991). Educational collaboration: A catalyst for effective schooling. *Intervention in School and Clinic, 27*(2), 70–78, 125.

Isaacson, S. L. (1987). Effective instruction in written language. *Focus on Exceptional Children, 19*(6), 1–12.

Israelson, J. (1980). I'm special too—A classroom program promotes understanding and acceptance of handicaps. *Teaching Exceptional Children, 13*, 35–37.

Jackson, N. F., Jackson, D. A., & Monroe, C. (1983). *Getting along with others: Teaching social effectiveness to children.* Champaign, IL: Research Press.

Jenkins, J. R., & Heinen, A. (1989). Students' preferences for service delivery: Pull-out, in-class, or integrated models. *Exceptional Children, 55*, 516–523.

Jenkins, J. R., Heliotis, J. D., Stein, M. L., & Haynes, M. C. (1987). Improving reading comprehension by using paragraph restatements. *Exceptional Children, 54,* 54–59.

Jenkins, J. R., & Jenkins, L. (1985). Peer tutoring in elementary and secondary programs. *Focus on Exceptional Children, 17*(6), 1–12.

Joe, J. R., & Malach, R. S. (1992). Families with Native American roots. In E. W. Lynch & M. J. Hanson (Eds.), *Developing cross-cultural competence* (pp. 89–119). Baltimore: Brookes.

Johnson, D. D. (1971). The Dolch list reexamined. *The Reading Teacher, 24,* 455–456.

Johnson, D. W., & Johnson, R. T. (1980). Integrating handicapped students into the mainstream. *Exceptional Children, 47,* 90–98.

Johnson, D. W., & Johnson, R. T. (1984). Classroom learning structure and attitudes toward handicapped students in mainstream settings. In R. L. Jones (Ed.), *Attitudes and attitude change in special education* (pp. 118–142). Reston, VA: The Council for Exceptional Children.

Johnson, D. W., & Johnson, R. T. (1989). Cooperative learning and mainstreaming. In R. Gaylord-Ross (Ed.), *Integration strategies for students with handicaps* (pp. 233–248). Baltimore: Brookes.

Johnson, L. J., & Pugach, M. C. (1990). Classroom teachers' views of intervention strategies for learning and behavior problems: Which are reasonable and how frequently are they used? *Journal of Special Education, 24,* 69–84.

Johnson, R. (1985). *The Picture Communication Symbols: Book II.* Solana Beach, CA: Mayer-Johnson.

Jones, F. H., & Eimers, R. C. (1975). Role playing to train elementary teachers to use a classroom management "skill package." *Journal of Applied Behavior Analysis, 8,* 421–433.

Jones, F. H., & Miller, W. H. (1974). The effective use of negative attention for reducing group disruption in special elementary school classrooms. *Psychological Record, 24,* 435–448.

Kameenui, E. J., & Simmons, D. C. (1990). *Designing instructional strategies.* New York: Merrill/Macmillan.

Karnes, F. A., & Collins, E. C. (1980). *Handbook of instructional resources and references for teaching the gifted.* Boston: Allyn & Bacon.

Karnes, M. B., & Johnson, L. J. (1991). Gifted handicapped. In N. Colangelo & G. A. Davis (Eds.), *Handbook of gifted education* (pp. 428–437). Boston: Allyn & Bacon.

Karweit, N. L., & Slavin, R. E. (1981). Measurement and modeling choices in studies of time and learning. *Educational Research Journal, 18*(2), 157–171.

Kauffman, J. M. (1977). *Characteristics of children's behavior disorders.* Columbus, OH: Merrill Publishing Company.

Kauffman, J. M. (1993). *Characteristics of emotional and behavioral disorders of children and youth* (5th ed.). New York: Merrill/Macmillan.

Kauffman, J. M., Gerber, M. M., & Semmel, M. I. (1988). Arguable assumptions underlying the regular education initiative. *Journal of Learning Disabilities, 21,* 6–11.

Kaufman, M. J., Gottlieb, J., Agard, J. A., & Kukic, M. D. (1975). Mainstreaming: Toward an explication of the construct. In E. L. Meyen, G. A. Vergason, & R. J. Whelan (Eds.), *Alternatives for teaching exceptional children* (pp. 35–54). Denver: Love.

Keefe, C. H., & Keefe, D. R. (1993). Instruction for students with LD: A whole language model. *Intervention in School and Clinic, 28,* 172–177.

Keilitz, I., Zaremba, B., & Broder, P. (1979). The link between learning disabilities and juvenile delinquency: Some issues and answers. *Journal of Learning Disabilities, 12,* 2–11.

Keller, H. (1965). *The story of my life.* New York: Airmont.

Kellogg, J. B. (1988). Forces of change. *Phi Delta Kappan, 70,* 199–204.

Kerchner, L. B., & Kistinger, B. J. (1984). Language processing/word processing: Written expression, computers, and learning disabled students. *Learning Disabilities Quarterly, 7*(4), 329–335.

Kerr, B. (1991). Educating gifted girls. In N. Colangelo & G. A. Davis (Eds.), *Handbook of gifted education* (pp. 402–415). Boston: Allyn & Bacon.

Kerr, M. M., & Nelson, C. M. (1989). *Strategies for managing behavior problems in the classroom* (2nd ed.). New York: Merrill/Macmillan.

Kerr, M. M., Nelson, C. M., & Lambert, D. L. (1987). *Helping adolescents with learning and behavior problems.* New York: Merrill/Macmillan.

Kinnaman, D. E. (1992). 2.5 million strong—and growing. *Technology & Learning, 13*(1), 67.

Kirk, S. A., & Gallagher, J. J. (1979). *Educating exceptional children* (3rd ed.). Boston: Houghton Mifflin.

Kirk, S. A., Kliebhan, J. M., & Lerner, J. W. (1978). *Teaching reading to slow and disabled readers.* Boston: Houghton Mifflin.

Kirk, S. A., McCarthy, J. J., & Kirk, W. D. (1968). *Illinois test of psycholinguistic abilities* (rev. ed.). Urbana: University of Illinois Press.

Kirk, W. G. (1993). *Adolescent suicide: A school-based approach to assessment and treatment.* Champaign, IL: Research Press.

Kitano, H. (1973). Highlights of Institute on Language and Culture: Asian component. In L. A. Bransford, L. M. Baca, & K. Lane (Eds.), *Cultural diversity and the exceptional child* (pp. 14–15). Reston, VA: The Council for Exceptional Children.

Kitano, M. K. (1989). The K–3 teacher's role in recognizing and supporting young gifted children. *Young Children, 44*(3), 57–63.

Kitano, M. K. (1991). A multicultural educational perspective on serving the culturally diverse gifted. *Journal for the Education of the Gifted, 15*(1), 4–19.

Kitano, M. K., & Kirby, D. E. (1986). *Gifted education: A comprehensive view.* Boston: Little, Brown.

Klein, E. (1989). Gifted and talented. In G. P. Cartwright, C. A. Cartwright, & M. E. Ward, *Educating special learners* (3rd ed., pp. 315–341). Belmont, CA: Wadsworth.

Kohl, F. L., Moses, L. G., & Stettner-Eaton, B. A. (1983). The results of teaching fifth and sixth graders to be instructional trainers with students who are severely handicapped. *Journal of the Association for the Severely Handicapped, 8*(4), 32–40.

Kokaska, C. J. (1980). A curriculum model for career education. In G. M. Clark & W. J. White (Eds.), *Career education for the handicapped: Current perspectives for teachers* (pp. 35–41). Boothwyn, PA: Educational Resources Center.

Kokaska, C. J., & Brolin, D. E. (1985). *Career education for handicapped individuals* (2nd ed.). New York: Merrill/Macmillan.

Kolstoe, O. P. (1976). *Teaching educable mentally retarded children* (2nd ed.). New York: Holt, Rinehart & Winston.

Krashen, S. D. (1987). *Principles and practice in second language acquisition.* New York: Prentice-Hall.

Kroth, R. (1981). Involvement with parents of behaviorally disordered adolescents. In G. Brown, R. L. McDowell, & J. Smith (Eds.), *Educating adolescents with behavior disorders* (pp. 123–139). Columbus, OH: Merrill Publishing Company.

Krouse, J., Gerber, M. M., & Kauffman, J. M. (1981). Peer tutoring: Procedures, promises, and unresolved issues. *Exceptional Education Quarterly, 1*(4), 107–115.

Kunisawa, B. (1988). A nation in crisis; The dropout dilemma. *NEA Today, 6*(6), 61–65.

Lambert, N., Nihira, K., & Leland, H. (1993). *AAMR adaptive behavior scale–School* (2nd ed.). Austin, TX: PRO-ED.

Lance, W. D. (1977). Technology and media for exceptional learners: Looking ahead. *Exceptional Children, 44*, 92–97.

Lapp, D., & Flood, J. (1992). *Teaching reading to every child* (3rd ed.). New York: Macmillan.

Larry P. v. Riles. C-71-2270-RFP (N. D. Cal. 1972), 495 F. Supp. 96 (N. D. Cal. 1979) Aff'r (9th Cir. 1984), 1983-84 EHLR DEC. 555:304.

Lathrop, A. (1982). The terrible ten in educational programming (My top ten reasons for automatically rejecting a program). *Educational Computer, 2*(5), 34.

Learning Disabilities Association of America. (1993). Position paper on full inclusion of all students with learning disabilities in the regular education classroom. *Journal of Learning Disabilities, 26*, 594.

Lehr, S. (1992). *If you look in their eyes, you know: Parents' perspectives on facilitated communication.* Syracuse: Institute on Facilitated Communication, Syracuse University.

Leinhardt, G., & Pallay, A. (1982). Restrictive educational settings: Exile or haven? *Review of Educational Research, 52*, 557–578.

Leone, P. E., Rutherford, R. B., & Nelson, C. M. (1991). *Special education in juvenile corrections.* Reston, VA: The Council for Exceptional Children.

Lerner, J. W. (1993). *Learning disabilities* (6th ed.). Boston: Houghton Mifflin.

Lerner, J. W., Cousin, P. T., & Richeck, M. (1992). Critical issues in learning disabilities: Whole language learning. *Learning Disabilities Research & Practice, 7*, 226–230.

Lerner, J. W., & Lowenthal, B. (1993). Attention deficit disorders: New responsibilities for special educators. *Learning Disabilities: A Multidisciplinary Journal, 4*(1), 1–8.

Levine, M. P. (1987). *How schools can help combat student eating disorders: Anorexia nervosa and bulimia.* Washington, DC: National Education Association.

Levy, P. S. (1981). The story of Marie, David, Richard, Jane, and John: Teaching gifted children in the regular classroom. *Teaching Exceptional Children, 13*, 39–43.

Lewis, R. B. (1980). Performance technologists and the needs of special learners. *NSPI Journal, 19*(4), 20–21.

Lewis, R. B. (1983). Learning disabilities and reading: Instructional recommendations from current research. *Exceptional Children, 50*, 230–240.

Lewis, R. B. (1987, October). *FrEdWriter: A public domain word processor with a prompted writing feature.* Paper presented at Closing the Gap's Fifth Annual International Conference on Microcomputer Technology in Special Education and Rehabilitation, Minneapolis.

Lewis, R. B. (1989). Educational assessment of learning disabilities: A new generation of achievement measures. *Learning Disabilities: A Multidisciplinary Journal, 1*, 49–55.

Lewis, R. B. (1993). *Special education technology: Classroom applications.* Pacific Grove, CA: Brooks/Cole.

Lewis, R. B., Dell, S. J., Lynch, E. W., Harrison, P. J., & Saba, F. (1987). *Special education technology in action: Teachers speak out.* San Diego, CA: San Diego State University, Department of Special Education.

Lewis, R. B., & Harrison, P. J. (1988, April). *Effective applications of technology in special education: Results of a statewide study.* Paper presented at The Council for Exceptional Children's 66th Annual Convention, Washington, DC.

Leyser, Y., & Bursuck, W. (1986). A follow-up study of regular education students trained in mainstreaming competencies. *Teacher Education and Special Education, 9*, 136–144.

Lipsky, D. K., & Gartner, A. (1989). *Beyond separate education: Quality education for all.* Baltimore: Brookes.

Lloyd, J. W., & Carnine, D. W. (Eds.). (1981). Foreword to structured instruction: Effective teaching of essential skills. *Exceptional Education Quarterly, 2*(1), viii–ix.

Lloyd, J. W., Crowley, E. P., Kohler, F. W., & Strain, P. S. (1988). Redefining the applied research agenda: Cooperative learning, prereferral, teacher consultation, and peer-mediated interventions. *Journal of Learning Disabilities, 21*, 43–52.

Lloyd, J. W., Kauffman, J. M., Landrum, T. J., & Roe, D. L. (1991). Why do teachers refer pupils for special education? An analysis of referral records. *Exceptionality, 2*, 115–126.

Lloyd, J. W., & Keller, C. E. (1989). Effective mathematics instruction: Development, instruction, and programs. *Focus on Exceptional Children, 21*(7), 1–10.

London, S. B., & Stile, S. W. (1982). *The school's role in the prevention of child abuse.* Bloomington, IN: Phi Delta Kappa Educational Foundation.

Lovaas, O. I., & Newsom, C. D. (1976). Behavior modification with psychotic children. In H. Leitenberg (Ed.), *Handbook of behavior modification and behavior therapy* (pp. 303–360). Englewood Cliffs, NJ: Prentice-Hall.

Lovitt, T. C. (1982). What does the direct in directive teacher mean? [Interview with T. C. Lovitt]. *The Directive Teacher, 4*(1), 24–25, 27.

Lowenbraun, S., & Thompson, M. D. (1986). Hearing impairments. In N. G. Haring & L. McCormick (Eds.), *Exceptional children and youth* (4th ed., pp. 357–395). New York: Merrill/Macmillan.

Luetke-Stahlman, B., & Luckner, J. (1991). *Effectively educating students with hearing impairments.* White Plains: NY: Longman.

Luftig, R. L. (1989). *Assessment of learners with special needs.* Boston: Allyn & Bacon.

Lusthaus, E., & Forest, M. (1987). The kaleidoscope: A challenge to the cascade. In M. Forest (Ed.), *More education integration* (pp. 1–17). Downsview, Ontario: G. Allan Roeher Institute.

Lynch, E. W. (1981). *But I've tried everything! A special educator's guide to working with parents.* San Diego, CA: San Diego State University.

Lynch, E. W. (1992). Developing cross-cultural competence. In E. W. Lynch & M. J. Hanson (Eds.), *Developing cross-cultural competence* (pp. 35–59). Baltimore: Brookes.

Lyon, H. C. (1981). Our most neglected natural resource. *Today's Education, 70*(1), 14–20.

MacArthur, C. A., & Graham, S. (1987). Learning disabled students' composing under three methods of text production: Handwriting, word processing, and dictation. *Journal of Special Education, 21*(3), 22–42.

MacArthur, C. A., & Schwartz, S. S. (1990). An integrated approach to writing instruction: The Computers and Writing Instruction Project. *LD Forum, 16*(1), 35–41.

MacMillan, D. L. (1982). *Mental retardation in school and society* (2nd ed.). Boston: Little, Brown.

MacMillan, D. L. (1991). *Hidden youth: Dropouts from special education.* Reston, VA: The Council for Exceptional Children.

Madden, N. A., & Slavin, R. E. (1983). Mainstreaming students with mild handicaps: Academic and social outcomes. *Review of Educational Research, 53*, 519–569.

Madsen, C. H., Becker, W. C., & Thomas, D. R. (1968). Rules, praise, and ignoring: Elements of elementary classroom control. *Journal of Applied Behavior Analysis, 1*, 139–151.

Mager, R. F. (1984). *Preparing instructional objectives* (rev. ed.). Belmont, CA: Pitman Learning.

Maginnis, G. (1969). The readability graph and informal reading inventories. *The Reading Teacher, 22*, 534–538.

Maheady, L., Sacca, M. K., & Harper, G. F. (1988). Classwide peer tutoring with mildly handicapped high school students. *Exceptional Children, 55*, 52–59.

Male, M. (1988). *Special magic: Computers, classroom strategies, and exceptional students.* Mountain View, CA: Mayfield.

Males, M. (1993). Schools, society, and 'teen' pregnancy. *Phi Delta Kappan, 74,* 566–568.

Maloney, M. J., & Klykylo, W. M. (1985). An overview of anorexia nervosa, bulimia, and obesity in children and adolescents. In S. Chess & A. Thomas (Eds.), *Annual progress in child psychology and child development–1985* (pp. 436–453). New York: Bruner Mazel.

Malouf, D. B. (1987–1988). The effect of instructional computer games on continuing student motivation. *Journal of Special Education, 21*(4), 27–38.

Mandell, C. J., & Fiscus, E. (1981). *Understanding exceptional people.* St. Paul, MN: West.

Mann, A., & McIntyre, M. (1992, October). Debate: Should schools eliminate gifted and talented programs? *NEA Today,* p. 39.

Markel, G. (1981). Improving test-taking skills of LD adolescents. *Academic Therapy, 16,* 333–342.

Markwardt, F. C. (1989). *Peabody individual achievement test-Revised.* Circle Pines, MN: American Guidance Service.

Maron, S. S., & Martinez, D. H. (1980). Environmental alternatives for the visually handicapped. In J. W. Schifani, R. M. Anderson, & S. J. Odle (Eds.), *Implementing learning in the least restrictive environment* (pp. 149–198). Baltimore: University Park Press.

Marston, D. (1987-1988). The effectiveness of special education: A time series analysis of reading performance in regular and special education settings. *Journal of Special Education, 21*(4), 13–26.

Martin, E. W. (1974). Some thoughts on mainstreaming. *Exceptional Children, 41,* 150–153.

Mather, N. (1992). Whole language reading instruction for students with learning disabilities: Caught in the cross fire. *Learning Disabilities Research & Practice, 7,* 87–95.

Mathes, P. G., & Irby, B. J. (1993). *Discussion guide: Teen pregnancy and parenting handbook.* Champaign, IL: Research Press.

Maxon, A., Brackett, D., & van den Berg, S. (1991). Classroom amplification use: A national long-term study. *Language, Speech, and Hearing Services in Schools, 22,* 242–253.

McBurnett, K., Lahey, B. B., & Pfiffner, L. J. (1993). Diagnosis of attention deficit disorders in DSM-IV: Scientific basis and implications for education. *Exceptional Children, 60,* 108–117.

McCarney, S. B. (1988). *The learning disability evaluation scale.* Columbia, MO: Hawthorne Educational Services.

McCarney, S. B., & Leigh, J. E. (1990). *Behavior evaluation scale-2.* Columbia, MO: Hawthorne Educational Services.

McCormick, L. (1986). Keeping up with language intervention trends. *Teaching Exceptional Children, 18*(2), 123–129.

McCormick, L. (1990). Cultural diversity and exceptionality. In N. G. Haring & L. McCormick (Eds.), *Exceptional children and youth* (5th ed., pp. 46–75). New York: Merrill/Macmillan.

McDonald, D. (1989). A special report on the education of Native Americans: "Stuck in the horizon" [Special Report insert]. *Education Week, 7*(4), 1–16.

McDonnell, J. (1987). The integration of students with severe handicaps into regular public schools: An analysis of parents' perceptions of potential outcomes. *Education and Training in Mental Retardation, 22,* 98–111.

McGinnis, E., & Goldstein, A. P. (1984). *Skillstreaming the elementary school child.* Champaign, IL: Research Press.

McIntosh, R., Vaughn, S., & Zaragoza, N. (1991). A review of social interventions for students with learning disabilities. *Journal of Learning Disabilities, 24,* 451–458.

McLoughlin, J. A., & Lewis, R. B. (1994). *Assessing special students* (4th ed.). New York: Merrill/Macmillan.

McNergney, R., & Haberman, M. (1988). Dropouts: Time for solutions. *NEA Today, 6*(10), 27.

Medley, D. M. (1982). Teacher effectiveness. In H. E. Mitzel (Ed.), *Encyclopedia of educational research* (5th ed., pp. 1894–1903). New York: Free Press.

Meisgeier, C. (1981). A social/behavioral program for the adolescent student with serious learning problems. *Focus on Exceptional Children, 13*(9), 1–13.

Mellor, C. (1981). *Aids for the 80's.* New York: American Foundation for the Blind.

Mercer, C. D. (1992). *Students with learning disabilities* (4th ed.). New York: Merrill/Macmillan.

Mercer, C. D., & Mercer, A. R. (1989). *Teaching students with learning problems* (3rd ed.). New York: Merrill/Macmillan.

Mercer, C. D., & Mercer, A. R. 1993). *Teaching students with learning problems* (4th ed.). New York: Merrill/Macmillan.

Mercer, C. D., Mercer, A. R., & Bott, D. A. (1984). *Self-correcting learning materials for the classroom.* New York: Merrill/Macmillan.

Mercer, J. R. (1973). *Labeling the mentally retarded.* Berkeley: University of California Press.

Mercer, J. R., & Lewis, J. F. (1977). *Adaptive behavior inventory for children.* San Antonio, TX: Psychological Corporation.

Meyen, E. L. (1981). *Developing instructional units* (3rd ed.). Dubuque, IA: Brown.

Miksic, S. (1987). Drug abuse management in adolescent special education. In M. M. Kerr, C. M. Nelson, & D. L. Lambert, *Helping adolescents with learning and behavior problems* (pp. 225–253). New York: Merrill/Macmillan.

Mills, P. J. (1979). Education within the mainstream: Suggestions for classroom teachers. *The Directive Teacher*, 2(2), 16.

Mira, M. P., & Tyler, J. S. (1991). Students with traumatic brain injury: Making the transition from hospital to school. *Focus on Exceptional Children*, 23(5), 1–12.

Mirga, T. (1988a, September 21). States and the "at risk" issues: Said aware but still "failing." *Education Week*, pp. 1, 14, 15.

Mirga, T. (1988b, September 21). The first step: Some states' working definitions of students "at risk." *Education Week*, p. 14.

Montgomery, M. D. (1978). The special educator as consultant: Some strategies. *Teaching Exceptional Children*, 10, 110–112.

Morgan, D. P., & Jenson, W. R. (1988). *Teaching behaviorally disordered students: Preferred practices.* New York: Merrill/Macmillan.

Morganthau, T. (1986, March 17). Kids and cocaine. *Newsweek*, pp. 57, 59–62, 63, 65.

Morsink, C. V., & Lenk, L. L. (1992). The delivery of special education programs and services. *Remedial and Special Education*, 13(6), 33–43.

Muccigrosso, L., Scavarda, M., Simpson-Brown, R., & Thalacker, B. E. (1991). *Double jeopardy: Pregnant and parenting youth in special education.* Reston, VA: The Council for Exceptional Children.

Munson, S. M. (1986). Regular education teacher modifications for mainstreamed mildly handicapped students. *Journal of Special Education*, 20, 489–502.

Myklebust, H. R. (1981). *The pupil rating scale revised.* New York: Grune & Stratton.

Myles, B. S., & Simpson, R. L. (1989). Regular educators' modification preferences for mainstreaming mildly handicapped children. *Journal of Special Education*, 22, 479–491.

National Advisory Committee on Handicapped Children. (1968). *Special education for handicapped children* [First annual report]. Washington, DC: U.S. Department of Health, Education, and Welfare.

National Coalition of Advocates for Students. (1985). *Barriers to excellence: Our children at risk.* Boston: Author.

National Commission on Excellence in Education. (1983). *A nation at risk: The imperative for educational reform.* Washington, DC: U.S. Government Printing Office.

National Council of Teachers of Mathematics. (1989). *Curriculum and evaluation standards for school mathematics.* Reston, VA: Author.

National Council on Disability. (1989). *The education of students with disabilities: Where do we stand?* Washington, DC: Author.

National Joint Committee on Learning Disabilities. (1981). *Learning disabilities: Issues on definition.* Position paper of the National Joint Committee on Learning Disabilities, January 30, 1981.

National Joint Committee on Learning Disabilities. 1993). A reaction to full inclusion: A reaffirmation of the right of students with learning disabilities to a continuum of services. *Journal of Learning Disabilities*, 26, 596.

National Society to Prevent Blindness. (1977). *Signs of possible eye trouble in children* (Pub. G-112). New York: Author.

NEA survey investigates teacher attitudes, practices. (1980). *Phi Delta Kappan*, 62, 49–50.

Neary, T., Halvorsen, A., & Smithey, L. (1991). *Inclusive education guidelines.* Sacramento, CA: California Department of Education, PEERS Project.

Needham, N. (1989). Meet C. Everett Koop: Gruff, tough, and no bluff. *NEA Today*, 7(7), 10–11.

Nelson, C. M. (1988). Social skill training for handicapped students. *Teaching Exceptional Children*, 20(4), 19–23.

Nelson, C. M. (1993). Students with behavioral disorders. In A. E. Blackhurst & W. H. Berdine (Eds.), *An introduction to special education* (3rd ed., pp. 528–561). New York: HarperCollins.

Nevin, A., & Thousand, J. (1986). What research says about limiting and avoiding referrals to special education. *Teacher Education and Special Education*, 9, 149–161.

Newcomb, M. D., & Bentler, P. M. (1989). Substance use and abuse among children and teenagers. *American Psychologist*, 44, 242–248.

Newcomer, P. L., & Hammill, D. D. (1988). *Test of language development-2, Primary.* Austin, TX: PRO-ED.

News beat: Drug abuse. (1989). *NEA Today*, 8(3), 3.

Nirje, B. (1969). The normalization principle and its human management implications. In R. B. Kugel & W. Wolfensberger (Eds.), *Changing patterns in residential services for the mentally retarded* (pp. 231–240). Washington, DC: U.S. Government Printing Office.

Norris, W. C. (1977). Via technology to a new era in education. *Phi Delta Kappan*, 58, 451–453.

Northcutt, L., & Watson, D. (1986). *Sheltered English teaching handbook.* San Marcos, CA: AM Graphics & Printing.

Oakland, T. (1981). Nonbiased assessment of minority group children. *Exceptional Education Quarterly, 1*(3), 31–46.

Odom, S. L., McConnell, S. R., & Chandler, L. K. (1994). Acceptability and feasibility of classroom based social interaction interventions for young children with disabilities. *Exceptional Children, 60,* 226–236.

Oehring, S. (1992). Adventures with grandparents. *Instructor, 102* (2), 90, 102.

Office of Technology Assessment. (1988). *Power on! New tools for teaching and learning.* Washington, DC: U.S. Government Printing Office.

Ogden, E. H., & Germinario, V. (1988). *The at-risk student: Answers for educators.* Lancaster, PA: Technomic.

Olson, J. L., & Platt, J. M. (1992). *Teaching children and adolescents with special needs.* New York: Merrill/Macmillan.

Olson, L. (1988, September 21). Despite years of rhetoric, most still see little understanding, inadequate efforts. *Education Week,* pp. 1–16.

Ortiz, A. A. (1988, Spring). Evaluating educational contexts in which language minority students are served. *Bilingual Special Education Newsletter, 7,* 1, 3–4, 7.

OSERS answers questions about LRE. (1986). *OSERS News in Print, 1*(2), 6–7.

Osguthorpe, R. T, & Scruggs, T. E. (1986). Special education students as tutors: A review and analysis. *Remedial and Special Education, 7*(4), 15–26.

Outhred, L. (1987). To write or not to write: Does using a word processor assist reluctant writers? *Australia and New Zealand Journal of Developmental Disabilities, 13*(4), 211–217.

Outhred, L. (1989). Word processing: Its impact on children's writing. *Journal of Learning Disabilities, 22,* 262–264.

Papert, S. (1980). *Mindstorms.* New York: Basic Books.

Parke, B. N. (1989). *Gifted students in regular classrooms.* Boston: Allyn & Bacon.

Parker, J. P. (1989). *Instructional strategies for teaching the gifted.* Boston: Allyn & Bacon.

Parson, L. R., & Heward, W. L. (1979). Training peers to tutor: Evaluation of a training package for primary learning disabled students. *Journal of Applied Behavior Analysis, 12,* 309–310.

Pasanella, A. L., & Volkmor, C. B. (1981). *Teaching handicapped students in the mainstream* (2nd ed.). Columbus, OH: Merrill Publishing Company.

Patrick, J. L., & Reschly, D. J. (1982). Relationship of state educational criteria and demographic variables to school-system prevalence of mental retardation. *American Journal of Mental Deficiency, 86,* 351–360.

Patros, P. G., & Shamoo, T. K. (1989). *Depression and suicide in children and adolescents: Prevention, intervention, and postvention.* Boston: Allyn & Bacon.

Patterson, G. R., DeBaryshe, B. D., & Ramsey, E. (1989). A developmental perspective on antisocial behavior. *American Psychologist, 44,* 329–335.

Pendarvis, E. D. (1993). Students with unique gifts and talents. In A. E. Blackhurst & W. H. Berdine (Eds.), *An introduction to special education* (3rd ed., pp. 563–599). New York: HarperCollins.

Pepper, F. C. (1976). Teaching the American Indian child in mainstream settings. In R. L. Jones (Ed.), *Mainstreaming and the minority child* (pp. 133–158). Reston, VA: The Council for Exceptional Children.

Perske, R., & Perske, M. (1988). *Circles of friends: People with disabilities and their friends enrich the lives of one another.* Nashville, TN: Abington.

Petreshene, S. S. (1978). *Complete guide to learning centers.* Palo Alto, CA: Pendragon House.

Pfeifer, J. K. (1986). *Teenage suicide: What can the schools do?* Bloomington, IN: Phi Delta Kappa Educational Foundation.

Phelps, M. S., & Prock, G. A. (1991). Equality of educational opportunity in rural America. In A. DeYoung (Ed.), *Rural education issues and practice* (pp. 269–312). New York: Garland.

Phillipo, J. (1988). Videodisc players: A multi-purpose audiovisual tool. *Electronic Learning, 8*(3), 50–52.

Platt, J. M., & Platt, J. S. (1980). Volunteers for special education: A mainstreaming support system. *Teaching Exceptional Children, 13,* 31–34.

Polloway, E. A., & Patton, J. R. (1993). *Strategies for teaching learners with special needs* (5th ed.). New York: Merrill/Macmillan.

Popham, J. P. (1993). Wanted: AIDS education that works. *Phi Delta Kappan, 74,* 559–562.

Postel, C. A. (1986). Death in my classroom? *Teaching Exceptional Children, 18,* 139–143.

Prasad, S. (1994). Assessing social interactions of children with disabilities. *Teaching Exceptional Children, 26*(2), 23–25.

President's Committee on Mental Retardation. (1969). *The six hour retarded child.* Washington, DC: U.S. Department of Health, Education, and Welfare.

President's Committee on Mental Retardation. (1975). *The problem of mental retardation.* Washington, DC: U.S. Department of Health, Education, and Welfare.

Prior, M., & Cummins, R. (1992). Questions about facilitated communication and autism. *Journal of Autism and Developmental Disorders, 22,* 331–337.

Project seen helping "disconnected" young. (1988, September 21). *Education Week,* p. 17.

Pumpian, I. (1988). Severe multiple handicaps. In E. W. Lynch & R. B. Lewis (Eds.), *Exceptional children and adults* (pp. 180–226). Glenview, IL: Scott, Foresman.

Putnam, J. M. (1992). Teaching students with severe disabilities in the regular classroom. In L. G. Cohen (Ed.), *Children with exceptional needs in regular classrooms* (pp. 118–142). Washington, DC: National Education Association.

Quality Education Data, Inc. (1985). *Microcomputer usage in schools, 1984–1985.* Denver: Author.

Quay, H. C. (1979). Classification. In H. C. Quay & J. S. Werry (Eds.), *Psychopathological disorders of childhood* (2nd ed.). New York: Wiley.

Raison, S. B. (1979). Curriculum modification for special needs at the secondary level. *Education Unlimited, 1*(3), 19–21.

Ratleff, J. E. (1989). *Instructional strategies for crosscultural students with special education needs.* Sacramento, CA: Resources in Special Education.

Ray, B. M. (1985). Measuring the social position of the mainstreamed handicapped child. *Exceptional Children, 52,* 57–62.

Recer, P. (1989, June 8). 12% of kids mentally troubled, study says. *Associated Press,* pp. 1–2.

Redden, M. R., & Blackhurst, A. E. (1978). Mainstreaming competency specifications for elementary teachers. *Exceptional Children, 44,* 615–617.

Rees, T. (1992). Students with hearing impairments. In L. G. Cohen (Ed.), *Children with exceptional needs in regular classrooms* (pp. 98–117). Washington, DC: National Education Association.

Reeve, R. E. (1990). ADHD: Facts and fallacies. *Intervention in School and Clinic, 26,* 70–78.

Reeves, M. S. (1988, April 27). "Self-interest and the commonweal": Focusing on the bottom half. *Education Week,* pp. 14–21.

Reis, S. M. (1989). Reflections on policy affecting the education of gifted and talented students: Past and future perspectives. *American Psychologist, 44,* 399–408.

Reis, S. M., & Renzulli, J. S. (1985). *Identification of the gifted and talented* (ERIC Digest, Clearinghouse on Handicapped and Gifted Children, No. 360). Reston, VA: The Council for Exceptional Children.

Renzulli, J. S., & Smith, L. H. (1978). *Learning styles inventory: A measure of student preference for instructional techniques.* Mansfield Center, CT: Creative Learning Press.

Renzulli, J. S., Smith, L. H., White, A. J., Callahan, C. M., & Hartman, R. K. (1976). *Scales for rating the behavior characteristics of superior students.* Mansfield Center, CT: Creative Learning Press.

Reschly, D. J., & Lamprecht, M. J. (1979). Expectancy effects of labels: Fact or artifact? *Exceptional Children, 46,* 55–58.

Research and Training Center on Independent Living. (1990). *Guidelines for reporting and writing about people with disabilities* (3rd ed.). Lawrence, KS: Author.

Reynolds, M. C., & Birch, J. W. (1982). *Teaching exceptional children in all America's schools* (rev. ed.). Reston, VA: The Council for Exceptional Children.

Reynolds, M. C., & Birch, J. W. (1988). *Adaptive mainstreaming* (3rd ed.). New York: Longman.

Reynolds, M. C., Wang, M. C., & Walberg, H. J. (1987). The necessary restructuring of special and regular education. *Exceptional Children, 53,* 391–398.

Reynolds, M. C., Zetlin, A. G., & Wang, M. C. (1993). 20/20 analysis: Taking a close look at the margins. *Exceptional Children, 59,* 294–300.

Reynolds, W. M. (1987). *Wepman's auditory discrimination test manual* (2nd ed.). Los Angeles: Western Psychological Services.

Rich, H. L., & Ross, S. M. (1989). Students' time on learning tasks in special education. *Exceptional Children, 55,* 508–515.

Rieth, H., & Evertson, C. M. (1988). Variables related to the effective instruction of difficult-to-teach children. *Focus on Exceptional Children, 20*(5), 1–8.

Rinn, R. C., & Markle, A. (1979). Modification of social skill deficits in children. In A. S. Bellack & M. Hersen (Eds.), *Research and practice in social skills training* (pp. 107–130). New York: Plenum.

Robinson, F. P. (1961). *Effective study.* New York: Harper & Row.

Rockefeller, N. A. (1976, October 16). Don't accept anyone's verdict that you are lazy, stupid, or retarded. *TV Guide,* pp. 12–14.

Rodriguez, R. C., Cole, J. T., Stile, S. W., & Gallegos, R. L. (1979). Bilingualism and biculturalism for the special education classroom. *Teacher Education and Special Education, 2*(4), 69–74.

Roland, P. (1989, August). A parent speaks to special educators. *Exceptional Times,* p. 3.

Rosenkoetter, S. E., & Fowler, S. A. (1986). Teaching mainstreamed children to manage daily transitions. *Teaching Exceptional Children, 19*(1), 20–23.

Rosenshine, B., & Stevens, R. (1986). Teaching functions. In M. C. Wittrock (Ed.), *Handbook of research on teaching* (3rd ed., pp. 376–391). New York: Macmillan.

Rosenthal, H. F. (1994, February 1). Teen-age drug use, smoking on rise again, survey reports. *The San Diego Union-Tribune*, pp. 1, 15.

Rossett, A., & Glassman, B. O. (1979). Technology and desirable school behavior. *Journal of Technological Horizons in Education, 6*(2), 37–39.

Rubin, R. A., & Balow, B. (1978). Prevalence of teacher identified behavior problems: A longitudinal study. *Exceptional Children, 45,* 102–111.

Rueda, R., & Prieto, A. G. (1979). Cultural pluralism: Implications for teacher education. *Teacher Education and Special Education, 2*(4), 4–11.

Ruiz, N. T. (1989). An optimal learning environment for Rosemary. *Exceptional Children, 56,* 130–144.

Russell, B., & Fessenden, B. (1989). Debate: Should dropouts be denied driver's licenses? *NEA Today, 8*(3), 39.

Ryder, R. J., Graves, B. B., & Graves, M. F. (1989). *Easy reading: Book series and periodicals for less able readers* (2nd ed.). Newark, DE: International Reading Association.

Sabornie, E. J., & Kauffman, J. M. (1985). Regular classroom sociometric status of behaviorally disordered adolescents. *Behavioral Disorders, 10,* 268–274.

Sailor, W., Gee, K., & Karasoff, P. (1993). Full inclusion and school restructuring. In M. E. Snell (Ed.), *Instruction of students with severe disabilities* (4th ed., pp. 1–30). New York: Merrill/Macmillan.

Salend, S. J. (1987). Group-oriented behavior management strategies. *Teaching Exceptional Children, 19*(1), 53–55.

Salend, S. J., & Salend, S. M. (1986). Competencies for mainstreaming secondary level learning disabled students. *Journal of Learning Disabilities, 19,* 91–94.

Salpeter, J. (1988). Answers to your questions about CD-ROM. *Classroom Computer Learning, 8*(6), 18.

Salvia, J., & Ysseldyke, J. E. (1991). *Assessment* (5th ed.). Boston: Houghton Mifflin.

Sander, E. K. (1972). When are speech sounds learned? *Journal of Speech and Hearing Disorders, 23*(1), 55–63.

Sansone, J., & Zigmond, N. (1986). Evaluating mainstreaming through an analysis of students' schedules. *Exceptional Children, 52,* 452–458.

Sarff, L. (1981). An innovative use of free field amplification in regular classrooms. In R. Roesser & M. Downs (Eds.), *Auditory disorders in school children* (pp. 263–272). New York: Thieme Stratton.

Sasso, G., & Rude, H. A. (1988). The social effects of integration on nonhandicapped children. *Education and Training in Mental Retardation, 23,* 18–23.

Schilit, J., & Caldwell, M. L. (1980). A word list of essential career/vocational words for mentally retarded students. *Education and Training of the Mentally Retarded, 15,* 113–117.

Schlosser, L. Y., & Algozzine, B. (1980). Sex, behavior, and teacher expectancies. *Journal of Experimental Education, 48,* 231–236.

Schmidt, P. (1992). Census data find more are falling behind in school. *Education Week, 11*(38), 1, 9.

Schneider, B. H., & Byrne, B. M. (1984). Predictors of successful transition from self-contained special education to regular class settings. *Psychology in the Schools, 21,* 375–380.

Schubert, M., Glick, H., & Bauer, D. (1979). *The least restrictive environment and the handicapped student.* Dayton, OH: Wright State University.

Schulte, A. C., Osborne, S. S., & McKinney, J. D. (1990). Academic outcomes for students with learning disabilities in consultation and resource programs. *Exceptional Children, 57,* 162–172.

Schultz, J. B., & Torrie, M. (1984). Effectiveness of parenthood education materials for mainstreamed vocational Home Economics classes. *Journal of Vocational Education Research, 9*(1), 46–56.

Schulz, J. B., & Turnbull, A. P. (1983). *Mainstreaming handicapped students* (2nd ed.). Boston: Allyn & Bacon.

Schumaker, J. B., & Deshler, D. D. (1988). Implementing the regular education initiative in secondary schools: A different ball game. *Journal of Learning Disabilities, 21,* 36–42.

Schumaker, J. B., & Hazel, J. S. (1984). Social skills assessment and training for the learning disabled: Who's on first and what's on second? Part I. *Journal of Learning Disabilities, 17,* 422–431.

Schumaker, J. B., Nolan, S. M., & Deshler, D. D. (1985). *Learning strategies curriculum: The error monitoring strategy.* Lawrence: University of Kansas.

Scrogan, L. (Ed.). (1988). The OTA report: New technologies *are* making a difference. *Classroom Computer Learning, 9*(2), 33–42.

Seidel, J. F. (1992). Children with HIV-related developmental difficulties. *Phi Delta Kappan, 74,* 38–40, 56.

Semel, E., Wiig, E. H., & Secord, W. (1987). *Clinical evaluation of language fundamentals-Revised.* San Antonio, TX: Psychological Corporation.

Semmel, M. I., & Lieber, J. A. (1986). Computer applications in instruction. *Focus on Exceptional Children, 18*(9), 1–12.

Shames, G. H., & Ramig, P. R. (1994). Stuttering and other disorders of fluency. In G. H. Shames, E. H. Wiig, & W. A Secord (Eds.), *Human communication disorders* (4th ed., pp. 336–386). New York: Merrill/Macmillan.

Shepard, D. H. (1986, November). Special students and regular software. *The Computing Teacher,* pp. 18–19.

Shinn, M. R., & Hubbard, D. D. (1993). Curriculum-based measurement and problem-solving assessment: Basic procedures and outcomes. In E. L. Meyen, G. A. Vergason, & R. J. Whelan (Eds.), *Educating students with mild disabilities* (pp. 221–253). Denver: Love.

Siegel, L. J., & Senna, J. J. (1994). *Juvenile delinquency: Theory, practice and law.* St. Paul: West.

Sierra, V. (1973). Learning style of the Mexican American. In L. A. Bransford, L. M. Baca, & K. Lane (Eds.), *Cultural diversity and the exceptional child* (pp. 42–49). Reston, VA: The Council for Exceptional Children.

Silvaroli, N. J. (1990). *Classroom reading inventory* (6th ed.). Dubuque, IA: Brown.

Silver, L. B. (1987). The "magic cure": A review of the current controversial approaches for treating learning disabilities. *Journal of Learning Disabilities, 20,* 498–504, 512.

Silverman, L. K. (1988). Gifted and talented. In E. L. Meyen & T. M. Skrtic (Eds.), *Exceptional children and youth: An introduction* (3rd ed., pp. 263–291). Denver: Love.

Simms, R. S., & Falcon, S. C. (1987). Teaching sight words. *Teaching Exceptional Children, 20*(1), 30–33.

Simpson, R. L. (1980). Modifying the attitudes of regular class students toward the handicapped. *Focus on Exceptional Children, 13*(3), 1–11.

Sindelar, P. T. (1987). Increasing reading fluency. *Teaching Exceptional Children, 19*(2), 59–60.

Sirvis, B. (1982). The physically disabled. In E. L. Meyen (Ed.), *Exceptional children and youth* (2nd ed., pp. 382–405). Denver: Love.

Sirvis, B. (1988). Physical disabilities. In E. L. Meyen & T. M. Skrtic (Eds.), *Exceptional children and youth: An introduction* (3rd ed., pp. 387–411). Denver: Love.

Sivin, J. P., & Bialo, E. R. (Eds.). (1988). The OTA report: Educational software quantity, quality, and the marketplace. *Classroom Computer Learning, 9*(3), 54–57.

Sklaire, M. (1989). Today's kids face different diseases. *NEA Today, 7*(8), 9.

Slate, J. R., & Saudargas, R. A. (1986). Differences in learning disabled and average students' classroom behaviors. *Learning Disability Quarterly, 9*(1), 61–67.

Slavin, R. E. (1987). *Cooperative learning: Student teams.* Washington, DC: National Education Association.

Slavin, R. E. (1989). Students at risk of school failure: The problem and its dimensions. In R. E. Slavin, N. L. Karweit, & N. A. Madden (Eds.), *Effective programs for students at risk* (pp. 3–19). Boston: Allyn & Bacon.

Slavin, R. E. (1990). *Cooperative learning: Theory, research, and practice.* Englewood Cliffs, NJ: Prentice-Hall.

Slavin, R. E., Madden, N. A., & Karweit, N. L. (1989). Effective programs for students at risk: Conclusions for practice and policy. In R. E. Slavin, N. L. Karweit, & N. A. Madden (Eds.), *Effective programs for students at risk* (pp. 355–372). Boston: Allyn & Bacon.

Slavin, R. E., Madden, N. A., & Leavey, M. (1984). Effects of cooperative learning and individualized instruction on mainstreamed students. *Exceptional Children, 50,* 434–443.

Smith, F. (1982). *Writing and the writer.* New York: Holt, Rinehart & Winston.

Smith, J. (1979). The education of Mexican-Americans: Bilingual, bicognitive, or biased? *Teacher Education and Special Education, 2*(4), 37–48.

Smith, J. E., & Schindler, W. J. (1980). Certification requirements of general educators concerning exceptional pupils. *Exceptional Children, 46,* 394–396.

Smith, R. M., Neisworth, J. T., & Greer, J. G. (1978). *Evaluating educational environments.* Columbus, OH: Merrill Publishing Company.

Smith, T. E. C., Finn, D. M., & Dowdy, C. A. (1993). *Teaching students with mild disabilities.* Fort Worth, TX: Harcourt Brace Jovanovich.

Snell, M., & Brown, F. (1993). Instructional planning and implementation. In M. Snell (Ed.), *Instruction of students with severe disabilities* (4th ed., pp. 99–151). New York: Merrill/Macmillan.

Snider, W. (1988, September 21). Hispanic students require income to remain in school, study finds. *Education Week,* p. 17.

Soderberg, L. J. (1988). Educators' knowledge of the characteristics of high school dropouts. *The High School Journal, 71,* 108–115.

Spache, G. (1953). A new readability formula for primary-grade reading materials. *The Elementary School Journal, 53,* 410–413.

Spalding, R. B., & Spalding, W. T. (1986). *The writing road to reading* (3rd rev. ed.). New York: Morrow.

Spenciner, L. J. (1992). Mainstreaming the child with a visual impairment. In L. G. Cohen (Ed.), *Children with exceptional needs in regular classrooms* (pp. 82–97). Washington, DC: National Education Association.

Stahl, S. A., & Miller, P. D. (1989). Whole language and language experience approaches for beginning reading: A quantitative research synthesis. *Review of Educational Research, 59,* 87–116.

Stainback, S., & Stainback, W. (1988). Educating students with severe disabilities. *Teaching Exceptional Children, 21*(1), 16–19.

Stainback, S., & Stainback, W. (Eds.). (1985). *Integrating students with severe handicaps into regular schools.* Reston, VA: The Council for Exceptional Children.

Stainback, S., & Stainback, W. (1990a). Inclusive schooling. In W. Stainback & S. Stainback (Eds.), *Support networks for inclusive schooling* (pp. 3–23). Baltimore: Brookes.

Stainback, S., & Stainback, W. (1992). *Curriculum considerations in inclusive classrooms.* Baltimore: Brookes.

Stainback, S., Stainback, W., & Forest, M. (1989). *Educating all students in the mainstream of regular education.* Baltimore: Brookes.

Stainback, S., Stainback, W., & Slavin, R. (1989). Classroom organization for diversity among students. In S. Stainback, W. Stainback, & M. Forest (Eds.), *Educating all students in the mainstream of regular education* (pp. 131–142). Baltimore: Brookes.

Stainback, W., & Stainback, S. (Eds.). (1990b). *Support networks for inclusive schooling.* Baltimore: Brookes.

Stainback, W., Stainback, S., & Froyen, L. (1987). Structuring the classroom to prevent disruptive behaviors. *Teaching Exceptional Children, 19*(4), 12–16.

Stainback, W., Stainback, S., & Wilkinson, A. (1992). Encouraging peer supports and friendships. *Teaching Exceptional Children, 24*(2), 6–11.

Stephens, T. M. (1978). *Social skills in the classroom.* Columbus, OH: Cedars.

Stephens, T. M. (1980). Teachers as managers. *The Directive Teacher, 2*(5), 4.

Stephens, T. M., & Wolf, J. S. (1978). The gifted child. In N. G. Haring (Ed.), *Behavior of exceptional children* (2nd ed., pp. 387–405). Columbus, OH: Merrill Publishing Company.

Sternberg, R. J. (1991). Giftedness according to the triarchic theory of human intelligence. In N. Colangelo & G. A. Davis (Eds.), *Handbook of gifted education* (pp. 45–54). Boston: Allyn & Bacon.

Stevens, L. J., & Price, M. (1992). Meeting the challenge of educating children at risk. *Phi Delta Kappan, 74,* 18–20, 22–23.

Stevens, R., & Rosenshine, B. (1981). Advances in research on teaching. *Exceptional Education Quarterly, 2*(1), 1–9.

Stitt, B. A., Erekson, T. L., Hofstrand, R. K., Loepp, F. L., Minor, C. W., Perreault, H. R., & Savage, J. G. (1988). *Building gender fairness in schools.* Carbondale: Board of Trustees, Southern Illinois University.

Stone, B., Cundick, B. P., & Swanson, D. (1988). Special education screening system: Group achievement test. *Exceptional Children, 55,* 71–75.

Stowitschek, J. J., Gable, R. A., & Hendrickson, J. M. (1980). *Instructional materials for exceptional children.* Germantown, MD: Aspen Systems.

Stowitschek, J. J., & Stowitschek, C. E. (1984). Once more with feeling: The absence of research on teacher use of microcomputers. *Exceptional Education Quarterly, 4*(4), 23–39.

Strain, P. S. (1981a). Peer-mediated treatment of exceptional children's social withdrawal. *Exceptional Education Quarterly, 1*(4), 93–105.

Strain, P. S. (Ed.). (1981b). *The utilization of peers as behavior change agents.* New York: Plenum.

Strain, P. S., & Kerr, M. M. (1981). *Mainstreaming of children in schools.* New York: Academic Press.

Strickland, B. B., & Turnbull, A. P. (1990). *Developing and implementing individualized education programs* (3rd ed.). New York: Merrill/Macmillan.

Student drug use drops but users of cocaine get higher, survey finds. (1989, September 27). *Los Angeles Times,* p. A18.

Sugai, G. M., & Tindal, G. A. (1993). *Effective school consultation: An interactive approach.* Pacific Grove, CA: Brooks/Cole.

Sulzer-Azaroff, B., & Mayer, G. R. (1977). *Applying behavior-analysis procedures with children and youth.* New York: Holt, Rinehart & Winston.

Swanson, H. L. (1989). Strategy instruction: Overview of principles and procedures for effective use. *Learning Disabilities Quarterly, 12,* 3–14.

Swift, C. A. (1988). Communication disorders. In E. W. Lynch & R. B. Lewis (Eds.), *Exceptional children and adults* (pp. 318–351). Glenview, IL: Scott, Foresman.

Taber, F. M. (1983). *Microcomputers in special education.* Reston, VA: The Council for Exceptional Children.

Tarver, S., & Hallahan, D. P. (1976). Children with learning disabilities: An overview. In J. M. Kauffman & D. P. Hallahan (Eds.), *Teaching children with learning disabilities: Personal perspectives* (pp. 2–57). Columbus, OH: Merrill Publishing Company.

Task Force on Children with Attention Deficit Disorder. (1992). *Children with ADD: A shared responsibility.* Reston, VA: The Council for Exceptional Children.

Task Force on DSM-IV. (1993). *DSM-IV draft criteria, 3-1-93.* Washington, DC: American Psychiatric Association.

Taylor, O. (1986). Language differences. In G. H. Shames & E. H. Wiig (Eds.), *Human communication disorders* (2nd ed., pp. 385–413). New York: Merrill/Macmillan.

Taylor, R. P. (Ed.). (1981). *The computer in the school: Tutor, tool, tutee.* New York: Teachers College Press.

Taylor, S. J. (1988). Caught in the continuum: A critical analysis of the principle of the least restrictive environment. *Journal of the Association for Persons with Severe Handicaps, 13*(1), 41–53.

Technology and the at-risk student. (1988, November/December). *Electronic Learning,* pp. 35–49.

Telford, C. W., & Sawrey, J. M. (1981). *The exceptional individual* (4th ed.). Englewood Cliffs, NJ: Prentice-Hall.

Thomas, C. H., & Patton, J. R. (1990). Mild and moderate retardation. In J. R. Patton, M. Beirne-Smith, & J. S. Payne (Eds.), *Mental retardation* (3rd ed., pp. 197–226). New York: Merrill/Macmillan.

Thomason, J. (1981). Education of the gifted: A challenge and a promise. *Exceptional Children, 48,* 101–103.

Thorndike, R. L., Hagen, E., & Sattler, J. (1986). *Stanford-Binet intelligence scale: Fourth edition.* Chicago: Riverside.

Thousand, J. S., & Villa, R. A. (1990). Strategies for educating learners with severe disabilities within their local home schools and communities. *Focus on Exceptional Children, 23*(3), 1–24.

Thurber, D. N., & Jordan, D. R. (1981). *D'Nealian handwriting.* Glenview, IL: Scott, Foresman.

Timar, T. B., & Kirp, D. L. (1989). Education reform in the 1980s: Lessons from the states. *Phi Delta Kappan, 70,* 505–511.

Tompkins, G. E., & Friend, M. (1986). On your mark, get set, write! *Teaching Exceptional Children, 18*(2), 82–89.

Tompkins, G. E., & Friend, M. (1988). After your students write: What's next? *Teaching Exceptional Children, 20*(3), 4–9.

Torgesen, J. K. (1977). The role of nonspecific factors in the task performance of learning disabled children: A theoretical assessment. *Journal of Learning Disabilities, 10,* 27–34.

Torgesen, J. K. (1980). Conceptual and educational implications of the use of efficient task strategies by learning disabled students. *Journal of Learning Disabilities, 13,* 364–371.

Torrance, E. P. (1966). *Torrance tests of creative thinking.* Princeton, NJ: Personnel.

Torres, I., & Corn, A. L. (1990). *When you have a visually handicapped child in your classroom: Suggestions for teachers.* New York: American Foundation for the Blind.

Towell, J., & Wink, J. (1993). *Strategies for monolingual teachers in multilingual classrooms.* Turlock, CA: California State University, Stanislaus. (ERIC Document Reproduction Service No. ED 359 797)

Tower, C. C. (1987). *How schools can help combat child abuse and neglect* (2nd ed.). Washington, DC: National Education Association.

Tucker, B. F., & Colson, S. E. (1992). Traumatic brain injury: An overview of school re-entry. *Intervention in School and Clinic, 27,* 198–206.

Turnbull, A. P., & Schulz, J. B. (1979). *Mainstreaming handicapped students.* Boston: Allyn & Bacon.

U.S. Department of Commerce. (1989). *Statistical abstract of the United States 1989.* Washington, DC: U.S. Government Printing Office.

U.S. Department of Education. (1991, September 16). *Memorandum: Clarification of policy to address the needs of children with attention deficit disorders within general and/or special education.* Office of Special Education and Rehabilitative Services.

U.S. Department of Education. (1993). *Fifteenth annual report to Congress on the implementation of The Individuals with Disabilities Education Act.* Washington, DC: Author.

Vacc, N. N. (1987). Word processor versus handwriting: A comparative study of writing samples produced by mildly mentally handicapped students. *Exceptional Children, 54,* 156–165.

Van Riper, C. (1978). *Speech correction.* Englewood Cliffs, NJ: Prentice-Hall.

Vandercook, T., & York, J. (1990). A team approach to program development and support. In W. Stainback & S. Stainback (Eds.), *Support networks for inclusive schooling* (pp. 95–122). Baltimore: Brookes.

Vandercook, T., York, J., & Forest, M. (1989). The McGill Action Planning System (MAPS): A strategy for building the vision. *Journal of The Association for Persons with Severe Handicaps, 14,* 205–215.

VanTassel-Baska, J. (1994). *Comprehensive curriculum for gifted learners* (2nd ed.). Boston: Allyn & Bacon.

Vergason, G. A., & Anderegg, M. L. (1991). Beyond the Regular Education Initiative and the resource room controversy. *Focus on Exceptional Children, 23*(7), 1–7.

Voeltz, L. M. (1980). Children's attitudes toward handicapped peers. *American Journal of Mental Deficiency, 84,* 455–464.

Voeltz, L. M. (1982). Effects of structured interactions with severely handicapped peers on children's attitudes. *American Journal of Mental Deficiency, 86,* 380–390.

Walker, D. K., Singer, J. D., Palfrey, J. S., Orza, M., Wenger, M., & Butler, J. A. (1988). Who leaves and who stays in special education: A 2-year follow-up study. *Exceptional Children, 54,* 393–402.

Walker, H. M. (1979). *The acting out child: Coping with classroom disruption.* Boston: Allyn & Bacon.

Walker, H. M., McConnell, S., Holmes, D., Todis, B., Walker, J., & Golden, N. (1983). *The Walker social skills curriculum: The ACCEPTS program.* Austin, TX: PRO-ED.

Walker, H. M., Todis, B., Holmes, D., & Horton, G. (1988). *The Walker social skills curriculum: The ACCESS Program.* Austin, TX: PRO-ED.

Walker, J. L. (1988). Young American Indian children. *Teaching Exceptional Children, 20*(4), 50–51.

Wang, M. C. (1981). Mainstreaming exceptional children: Some instructional design and implementation considerations. *The Elementary School Journal, 81,* 195–221.

Wang, M. C., & Birch, J. W. (1984). Effective special education in regular classes. *Exceptional Children, 50,* 391–399.

Wang, M. C., Peverly, S., & Randolph, R. (1984). An investigation of the implementation and effects of a full-time mainstreaming program. *Remedial and Special Education, 5*(6), 21–32.

Wang, M. C., & Walberg, H. J. (1988). Four fallacies of segregationism. *Exceptional Children, 55,* 128–137.

Warger, C. L., Tewey, S., & Megivern, M. (1991). *Abuse and neglect of exceptional children.* Reston, VA: The Council for Exceptional Children.

Webb, J. T., & Latimer, D. (1993). ADHD and children who are gifted. *Exceptional Children, 60,* 183–184.

Wechsler, D. (1991). *Wechsler intelligence scale for children-Third edition.* San Antonio, TX: Psychological Corporation.

Weil, M. L., & Murphy, J. (1982). Instruction processes. In H. E. Mitzel (Ed.), *Encyclopedia of educational research* (5th ed., pp. 890–917). New York: Free Press.

Weinstein, C. S. (1979). The physical environment of the school: A review of research. *Review of Educational Research, 49,* 577–610.

Wepman, J. M. (1975). *Auditory discrimination test* (rev. 1973). Palm Springs, CA: Research Associates.

Westby, C. E. (1992). Whole language and learners with mild handicaps. *Focus on Exceptional Children, 24*(8), 1–16.

Wheelchair prescriptions: Care and service. (1976). Los Angeles: Everest & Jennings.

Wheelchair prescriptions: Measuring the patient. (1968). Los Angeles: Everest & Jennings.

Wheeler, D. L., Jacobson, J. W., Paglieri, R. A., & Schwartz, A. A. (1993). An experimental assessment of facilitated communication. *Mental Retardation, 31,* 49–60.

White, K. R., Bush, D., & Casto, G. (1986). Let the past be prologue: Learning from previous reviews of early intervention efficacy research. *Journal of Special Education, 19,* 417–428.

Whitmore, J. R. (1985). *Characteristics of intellectually gifted children* (ERIC Digest, Clearinghouse on Handicapped and Gifted Children, No. 344). Reston, VA: The Council for Exceptional Children.

Whitt, J., Paul, P. V., & Reynolds, C. J. (1988). Motivate reluctant learning disabled writers. *Teaching Exceptional Children, 20*(3), 37–39.

Wiederholt, J. L. (1989). Restructuring special education services: The past, the present, the future. *Learning Disability Quarterly, 12,* 181–191.

Wiedmeyer, D., & Lehman, J. (1991). "The House Plan" approach to collaborative teaching and consultation. *Teaching Exceptional Children, 23* (10), 7–10.

Wilkinson, G. S. (1993). *Wide range achievement test 3.* Wilmington, DE: Jastak Associates.

Will, M. C. (1986a). Clarifying the standards: Placement in a least restrictive environment. *OSERS News in Print, 1*(2), 1.

Will, M. C. (1986b). Educating children with learning problems: A shared responsibility. *Exceptional Children, 52,* 411–415.

Willis, W. (1992). Families with African American roots. In E. W. Lynch & M. J. Hanson (Eds.), *Developing cross-cultural competence* (pp. 121–150). Baltimore: Brookes.

Winget, P., & Kirk, J. (1991). *California programs and services for students with serious emotional disturbances.* Sacramento, CA: Resources in Special Education.

Winston, S. (1991). *Getting organized* (rev.). New York: Warner Books.

Wolfensberger, W. (1972). *The principle of normalization in human services.* Toronto: National Institute on Mental Retardation.

Wood, J. W., Lazzari, A., & Reeves, C. K. (1993). Educational characteristics and implications. In J. W. Wood (Ed.), *Mainstreaming* (2nd ed., pp. 78–120). New York: Merrill/Macmillan.

Wood, J. W., & Miederhoff, J. W. (1989). Bridging the gap. *Teaching Exceptional Children, 21*(2), 66–68.

Woodcock, R. W., & Johnson, M. B. (1989). *Woodcock-Johnson psycho-educational battery-Revised.* Chicago: Riverside.

Woodring, P. (1989). A new approach to the dropout problem. *Phi Delta Kappan, 70,* 468–469.

Woods, M. L., & Moe, A. J. (1989). *Analytical reading inventory* (4th ed.). New York: Merrill/Macmillan.

Woodward, D. M. (1981). *Mainstreaming the learning disabled adolescent.* Rockville, MD: Aspen Systems.

Worthen, B. R. (1993). Critical issues that will determine the future of alternative assessment. *Phi Delta Kappan, 74,* 444–454.

Yarber, W. L. (1987). *AIDS education: Curriculum and health policy.* Bloomington, IN: Phi Delta Kappa Educational Foundation.

Yau, M., Ziegler, S., & Siegel, L. (1990). *Lap top computers and the learning disabled student. A study of the value of portable computers to the writing progress of students with fine motor problems.* Toronto, Canada: Toronto Board of Education, Library Services Department. (ERIC Document Reproduction Service No. ED 320 342)

York, J., Doyle, M. B., & Kronberg, R. (1992). A curriculum development process for inclusive classrooms. *Focus on Exceptional Children, 25*(4), 1–16.

York, J., & Vandercook, T. (1991). Designing an integrated program for learners with severe disabilities. *Teaching Exceptional Children, 23*(2), 22–28.

York, J., Vandercook, T., MacDonald, C., Heise-Neff, C., & Caughey, E. (1992). Feedback about integrating middle-school students with severe disabilities in general education classes. *Exceptional Children, 58,* 244–258.

Ysseldyke, J. E., Algozzine, B., & Thurlow, M. L. (1992). *Critical issues in special education* (2nd ed.). Boston, MA: Houghton Mifflin.

Ysseldyke, J. E., Thurlow, M. L., Christenson, S. L., & Weiss, J. (1987). Time allocated to instruction of mentally retarded, learning disabled, emotionally disturbed, and nonhandicapped elementary students. *Journal of Special Education, 21*(3), 43–55.

Ysseldyke, J. E., Thurlow, M. L., Wotruba, J. W., & Nania, P. A. (1990). Instructional arrangements: Perceptions from general education. *Teaching Exceptional Children, 22*(4), 4–8.

Zaragoza, N., Vaughn, S., & McIntosh, R. (1991). Social skills interventions and children with behavior problems: A review. *Behavioral Disorders, 16,* 260–275.

Zentall, S. S. (1983). Learning environments: A review of physical and temporal factors. *Exceptional Education Quarterly, 4*(2), 90–115.

Zigler, E., & Muenchow, S. (1979). Mainstreaming: The proof is in the implementation. *American Psychologist, 34,* 993–996.

Zigmond, N., & Baker, J. (1990). Mainstream experiences for learning disabled students (Project MELD): Preliminary report. *Exceptional Children, 57,* 176–185.

Zirkel, P. A. (1989). AIDS: Students in glass houses? *Phi Delta Kappan, 70,* 646–648.

Zirpoli, T. J., & Melloy, K. J. (1993). *Behavior management: Applications for teachers and parents.* New York: Merrill/Macmillan.

Zuniga, M. E. (1992). Families with Latino roots. In E. W. Lynch & M. J. Hanson (Eds.), *Developing cross-cultural competence* (pp. 151–179). Baltimore: Brookes.

Author Index

Bishop, K., 175, 320, 321
Blackhurst, A. E., 13, 362, 370, 397, 419, 448, 536, 538
Blake, K. A., 302
Blankenship, C., 48, 149, 428, 431, 436
Bleck, E., 387
Bliss, E. C., 210
Boning, R. A., 279
Bonjean, L. M., 518
Bonvechio, L. R., 423
Bormuth, J. R., 268
Bossert, S. T., 201
Bost, J. M., 162
Bott, D. A., 216
Bowen, E., 502
Bower, E. M., 69, 70
Braaten, B., 544, 546
Braaten, S., 544, 546
Brackett, D., 437
Brady, M. P., 165
Brady, R. C., 387
Bransford, J. D., 283
Brigance, A. H., 266, 303–304, 307, 364
Brinker, R. P., 321
Broder, P., 68
Brolin, D. E., 93, 301, 308, 310, 311, 316, 320
Brooks-Gunn, J., 518
Brophy, J. E., 94, 201, 541
Brown, F., 174
Brown, G., 182
Brown, L., 338, 543
Brown, V. L., 363
Bruder, I., 223
Bruininks, R. H., 73, 300
Bruner, E. C., 274
Bruno, J., 527
Bryan, J. H., 68, 161
Bryan, T. H., 23, 68, 161, 542
Bryen, D. N., 484
Bulgren, J. A., 102
Bull, G., 463
Burke, C., 300
Burron, A., 268
Bursuck, W., 541
Bush, D., 82
Butler, J. A., 541
Butler, O. B., 498, 500, 501, 506
Buttery, T. J., 398

Byrne, B. M., 541
Byrne, C. E., 391
Byrom, C. E., 394

Calculator, S., 379
Caldwell, M. L., 316, 317
Calhoun, M. L., 148
California Association for Neurologically Handicapped Children, 261
California Governor's Committee for Employment of Disabled Persons, 24
Callahan, C. M., 449
Campbell, N. J., 162
Campbell, P. H., 175
Capuzzi, D., 508
Carlberg, C., 540
Carlson, N., 386
Carlson, N. A., 97
Carnine, D. W., 94
Carta, J. J., 102
Carter, J., 40
Cartledge, G., 125, 163, 165, 166, 175, 178
Cartwright, C. A., 5, 420, 518, 519, 528
Cartwright, G. P., 5, 420, 518, 519, 528
Casey, A., 42
Casto, G., 82
Caton, H. R., 420
Caughey, E., 163, 165
Cegelka, P. T., 110, 193, 202, 311, 472, 476
Centers for Disease Control, 507
Cervantes, H. T., 477, 480, 485
Chalfant, J. C., 42, 263
Chall, J. S., 269, 274
Chan, S., 477
Chandler, L. K., 160
Charles, C. M., 203
Charlip, R., 418
Chase-Lansdale, L., 518
Cheng, L. L., 72, 473, 476, 477, 479, 480
Chideya, F., 379
Chinn, P. C., 302, 472, 480
Christenson, S. L., 40, 42, 103, 541
Clark, B., 448
Clark, L., 370
Clarke, L., 262
Claybaugh, A. L., 268

Clements, B. S., 346
Cloninger, C., 322
Close, D. W., 100
Cochran, C., 175
Cochran, P., 463
Cohen, D. L., 501
Cohen, S. B., 211, 370, 376
Colangelo, N., 448
Colarusso, R. P., 266
Cole, J. T., 477
Coleman, M. C., 337, 527
Collins, E. C., 466
Colson, S. E., 74, 394, 411
Compton, N., 499
Condon, E. C., 477, 480
Cooke, N. L., 214
Corn, A. L., 419, 427, 428
Corwin, J. R., 252
Council for Exceptional Children, 5, 6, 23, 308
Council for Learning Disabilities, 544
Courson, F. H., 104
Cousin, P. T., 96, 274, 281
Craig, E., 336
Craig, R., 429
Cronin, M. E., 308, 311
Crosby, E., 507, 508, 509, 511
Cross, D. P., 395
Crowley, E. P., 23, 47, 546
Crump, W. D., 162, 163
Cuban, L., 498, 501, 506
Cuenin, L. H., 132
Culatta, B. K., 370, 371, 376
Culatta, R., 370, 371, 376
Cummins, J., 485
Cummins, R., 379
Cundick, B. P., 111

D'Alonzo, B. J., 192
D'Alonzo, R. L., 192
D'Antonio, M., 250
Dale, E., 269
Dalton, B., 287
Darch, C. B., 541
Dardig, J. C., 185, 548
Data bank, 516
Davidson, C., 181
Davis, C., 422
Davis, G. A., 448
Davis, W. E., 22

DeBaryshe, B. D., 527, 528
Decano, P., 477
de Grandpre, B. B., 202
Dell, S. J., 244, 284
Deno, S. L., 84, 113, 114
Deshler, D. D., 66, 263, 282, 289, 354, 545
Diana v. *State Board of Education,* 10
Dimino, J., 96
Dinkmeyer, D., 178
Dinkmeyer, D., Jr., 178
Dismuke, D., 508, 511
Division for Learning Disabilities, 23
Dodson, J. E., 162
Dolch, E. W., 276
Doleys, D. M., 527
Donahue, M., 68
Donaldson, J., 164, 171
Doorlag, D. H., 42, 175, 178
Dowdy, C. A., 125, 149, 353
Doyle, B. A., 377
Doyle, M. B., 322
Doyle, W., 143, 192, 196
Drabman, R. S., 161, 162, 175
Drew, C. J., 299, 301, 302
Duffey, J. B., 548
Duncan, M., 499
Dunn, A. B., 263
Dunn, K., 190
Dunn, L. M., 10, 536
Dunn, M. B., 263
Dunn, R., 190
Dwyer, K. M., 263

Eaton, M. D., 203
Edgar, E., 181
Educating refugees, 492
Edwards, L. L., 289
Edwards, T. K., 507
Ehly, S. W., 214
Eimers, R. C., 145
Eiser, L., 246
Ekwall, E. E., 269, 280
Elam, S. M., 125, 501, 512, 519
Eller, S. H., 449
Ellett, L., 47, 63
Elmquist, D. L., 515
Emery, R. E., 522
Emmer, E. T., 125, 190, 336, 346
Emmert, M., 301

Engelmann, S., 274, 302
Englert, C. S., 101, 104, 105, 145, 155, 156, 210, 282
English, K. M., 419, 439, 441
Epanchin, B. C., 525
Epilepsy Foundation of America, 390, 391, 399
Epstein, S. L., 262
Erekson, T. L., 162
Erin, J. N., 419
Evans, J., 481, 482
Evertson, C. M., 94, 101, 104, 121, 190, 196, 346

Fais, L., 287
Falcon, S. C., 276
Falvey, M. A., 175, 320, 321
Fanning, R., 210
Fanning, T., 210
Fassler, J., 386
Feldhusen, J. F., 449, 462
Feng, H., 175
Fessenden, B., 501
Fiedler, C. R., 164, 171
Finch, A. J., 354, 356
Finn, D. M., 125, 149, 353
Fireside, B. J., 387, 418
Fischer, L., 524
Fischgrund, J. E., 419, 420, 422
Fiscus, E., 429
Flesch, R., 269
Flexer, C., 437
Flood, J., 201, 274
Forest, M., 322, 323, 325
Forness, S. R., 299, 540
Forster, P., 377
Foster, C., 488
Fowler, S. A., 104
Fox, C. L., 164
Fox, R. G., 174
Fox, S. L., 113
Foyle, H. C., 174
Franklin, M. E., 478, 488, 489
Frase, M. J., 501, 502
Freedman, S. W., 281
Freeman, D., 490
Freeman, Y., 490
Frew, T., 163, 165
Friend, M., 281, 282
Fristoe, M., 266, 363

Froyen, L., 195, 196, 198
Fry, E., 269, 271
Frymier, J., 498, 500, 502
Fuchigami, R. Y., 492
Fuchs, D. S., 23, 542, 545
Fuchs, L. S., 23, 113, 114, 542, 545
Furstenberg, F. F., Jr., 518

Gable, R. A., 175, 180, 193, 202, 214
Gajar, A., 506, 507
Gallagher, J. J., 6, 14, 72, 302, 368, 446, 458, 459, 462
Gallegos, R. L., 477
Gallup, A. M., 125, 501, 512, 519
Gans, K. D., 162
Gansneder, B., 498, 500, 502
Garcia, R. L., 477, 490
Gardner, H., 447
Gardner, W. I., 130
Garfinkel, B. D., 507, 508, 509, 511
Garrett, M. K., 162, 163
Gartner, A., 190, 543
Gastright, J. F., 500, 503
Gay, L. R., 454
Gearheart, B. R., 5
Gearheart, C. J., 5
Gee, K., 60
Gehret, J., 262
Gerber, M. M., 23, 175, 214, 545, 546
Germinario, V., 498, 499, 502, 506, 519
Gershaw, N. J., 179
Gersten, R., 96, 490, 541
Giangreco, M., 322
Gibson, A. B., 398
Gibson, W., 418, 448
Gickling, E. E., 109
Gill, D., 418
Gillung, T. B., 162
Gilman, C. J., 300
Girard, L. W., 387
Girard, M. A., 423
Glass, G. V., 201
Glassman, B. O., 350
Glazzard, P., 402, 428, 432
Gleason, M. M., 100, 350
Glick, H., 190, 202
Goin, L. I., 283
Gold, D., 379
Goldberg, L., 250

Karnes, M. B., 453
Karweit, N. L., 102, 499, 506
Katz, G., 394
Kauffman, J. M., 23, 40, 69, 76, 82, 127, 128, 133, 175, 214, 302, 336, 337, 338, 339, 354, 466, 507, 516, 527, 528, 544, 545, 548
Kaufman, M. J., 4, 5
Kaufman, S. Z., 300
Kavale, K. A., 299, 540, 541
Keefe, C. H., 96
Keefe, D. R., 96
Keilitz, I., 68
Keller, C. E., 23, 98, 542
Keller, H., 427
Kellogg, J. B., 476
Kelly, D. L., 110
Kerchner, L. B., 287
Kerr, B., 455
Kerr, M. M., 336, 338, 507, 517, 540
Keyes, D., 300, 448
Kinnaman, D. E., 220
Kirby, D. E., 453
Kirk, J., 178
Kirk, S. A., 6, 14, 72, 263, 266, 268, 269, 302, 368, 458, 459, 462
Kirk, W. D., 266
Kirk, W. G., 499, 507, 508, 513
Kirp, D. L., 546
Kistinger, B. J., 287
Kitano, H., 477
Kitano, M. K., 448, 452, 453, 473
Klein, E., 543
Klein, P., 179
Kliebhan, J. M., 268, 269
Klykylo, W. M., 525, 527
Kohl, F. L., 322
Kohler, F. W., 23, 47, 546
Kokaska, C. J., 308, 310, 316, 320
Kolstoe, O. P., 319
Koorland, M. A., 136
Kosinski, J., 300
Krashen, S. D., 490
Krementz, J., 387
Kronberg, R., 322
Kroth, R., 181, 182
Krouse, J., 175, 214
Kruse, C. G., 110
Kukic, M. D., 4, 5
Kunisawa, B., 503, 506

Lahey, B. B., 291
Lakein, A., 210
Lambert, D. L., 336, 507, 517
Lambert, N., 301
Lamprecht, M. J., 162
Lance, W. D., 220
Landau, E. D., 262
Landrum, T. J., 40
Lapp, D., 201, 274
Larsen, S. C., 214, 363
Lasker, J., 386
Lathrop, A., 242, 243
Latimer, D., 455
Lawrence, G. A., 423, 427
Laycock, V. K., 180
Lazzari, A., 378, 379
Learning Disability Association of America, 23, 545
Leavey, M., 174
LeBoeuf, M., 210
Lehman, J., 58
Lehr, S., 379
Leigh, J. E., 339
Leinhardt, G., 12, 540, 541
Leland, H., 301
Lenk, L. L., 96
Leone, P. E., 528
Lerner, J. W., 96, 263, 268, 269, 273, 274, 281, 291, 292
Levenkron, S., 499
Levine, M. P., 499, 527
Levy, P. S., 466
Lewis, J. F., 301
Lewis, R. B., 22, 66, 82, 83, 84, 137, 166, 168, 190, 207, 225, 239, 242, 244, 248, 249, 252, 254, 262, 264, 266, 268, 273, 274, 284, 300, 318, 344, 370, 372, 387, 406, 488, 505, 548
Leyser, Y., 162, 174, 541
Lieber, J. A., 351
Lilly, M. S., 48, 149, 428, 431, 436
Lindsey, J. D., 221, 252
Lipsky, D. K., 543
Litchfield, A. B., 301, 418
Lloyd, J. W., 23, 40, 47, 94, 98, 546
Loepp, F. L., 162
Logan, D. R., 299, 301, 302
London, S. B., 522, 523, 524

Lough, T., 463
Lovaas, O. I., 76
Lovitt, T. C., 548
Lowenbraun, S., 54, 118, 201, 203, 213, 250, 275, 283, 542
Lowenthal, B., 291, 292
Luckner, J., 417, 419
Luetke-Stahlman, B., 417, 419
Luftig, R. L., 166
Lusthaus, E., 322, 323, 325
Lyman, L., 174
Lynch, E. W., 244, 284, 370, 387, 476, 479, 480, 493
Lyon, H. C., 466

MacArthur, C. A., 287
MacCracken, M., 336
MacDonald, C., 163, 165
MacMillan, D. L., 503, 540
Madden, N. A., 12, 174, 499, 506, 540
Madge, S., 542
Mager, R. F., 98
Maginnis, G., 269
Maheady, L., 175
Malach, R. S., 477
Male, M., 229, 252, 464
Males, M., 518, 519
Maloney, M. J., 525, 527
Malouf, D. B., 351
Mandell, C. J., 429
Mann, A., 446
Markel, G., 354
Markle, A., 178
Markwardt, F. C., 265, 300, 338
Maron, S. S., 427, 428
Maroney, S. A., 180
Marquez, L., 477
Marston, D., 541
Martin, E. W., 162
Martinez, D. H., 427, 428
Martinson, M. C., 164
Massie, R., 386
Massie, R. K., 386
Massie, S., 386
Mastropieri, M. A., 82
Mather, N., 96, 274
Mathes, P. G., 518
Matus, A. L., 507, 508, 509, 511
Mauser, A. J., 192

Maxon, A., 437
Mayer, G. R., 134
McAfee, J., 506, 507
McBurnett, K., 291
McCarney, S. B., 262, 339
McCarthy, J. J., 266
McConnell, S., 178
McConnell, S. R., 160
McCormick, L., 371, 387, 490, 491
McCullough, D., 386, 448
McDaniel, J. B., 300
McDonald, D., 473, 477
McDonald, J., 58
McDonnell, J., 321
McDowell, R. L., 182
McEvoy, M. A., 165
McGinnis, E., 178
McIntosh, R., 161, 165, 175
McIntyre, M., 446
McKinney, J. D., 23, 542
McLoughlin, J. A., 22, 82, 83, 84, 137,
    166, 168, 264, 266, 268, 274, 300,
    318, 488, 548
McNergney, R., 503
Medley, D. M., 94
Megivern, M., 523
Meisgeier, C., 160, 178
Mellor, C., 249
Melloy, J. K., 125, 129, 179
Mercer, A. R., 193, 195, 197, 201, 202,
    204, 209, 210, 214, 216, 263, 274,
    278, 279, 288, 353
Mercer, C. D., 193, 195, 197, 201, 202,
    204, 209, 210, 214, 216, 263, 274,
    278, 279, 281, 288, 353
Mercer, J. R., 10, 301
Messier, J. M., 202
Meyen, E. L., 198, 311, 461
Meyers, R., 300, 370
Miederhoff, J. W., 548
Miksic, S., 516, 517
Milburn, J. F., 125, 166, 178
Miller, L., 281
Miller, M. B., 418
Miller, P. D., 274
Miller, W. H., 145
Mills, P. J., 16
Minor, C. W., 162
Mira, M. P., 74, 394, 410
Mirga, T., 498, 500

Moe, A. J., 269
Mokros, J. R., 252
Montgomery, M. D., 93
Morehead, M. K., 113
Morgan, D. P., 336, 339
Morganthau, T., 508
Morocco, C. C., 287
Morsink, C. V., 96
Morton, M. W., 379
Moses, L. G., 322
Moss, D. M., 262
Muccigrosso, L., 518
Mueller, E., 418
Muenchow, S., 540
Muldoon, K. M., 386
Munson, S. M., 47
Murphy, J., 94
Myklebust, H. R., 140, 141
Myles, B. S., 542

Nagel, D., 387
Nania, P. A., 47, 63
Narayan, J. S., 104
Natchez, G., 262
National Advisory Committee on
    Handicapped Children, 67
National Association of the Deaf, 435
National Coalition of Advocates for
    Students, 78, 302, 490
National Commission on Excellence in
    Education, 20
National Council of Teachers of Math-
    ematics, 282
National Council on Disability, 540
National Joint Committee on Learning
    Disabilities, 23, 261, 545
National Society to Prevent Blindness,
    421
NEA survey, 125
Needham, N., 513
Neisworth, J. T., 170, 192, 198, 200,
    201, 206, 211
Nelson, C. M., 175, 335, 336, 338, 339,
    507, 517, 528, 544
Nelson, L. R., 174
Neufeld, J., 336
Nevin, A., 546
Newcomb, M. D., 512, 514, 515, 516
Newcomer, P. L., 363
News beat: Drug abuse, 512

Newsom, C. D., 76
Nietupski, J., 58
Nihira, K., 301
Nirje, B., 10
Nixon, H. L., 419
Nolan, S. M., 282, 354
Norris, W. C., 207
Northcutt, L., 490

Oakland, T., 548
Odle, S. J., 402
Odom, S. L., 160
Oehring, S., 224
Office of Technology Assessment, 220,
    226
Ogden, E. H., 498, 499, 502, 506, 519
O'Leary, S. G., 292
Olsen, L., 500
Olson, J. L., 125
Orlansky, M. D., 15, 18, 70, 71, 76,
    302, 368, 421, 427, 447, 452, 455,
    458, 476
Ortiz, A. A., 475
Orza, M., 541
Osborne, S. S., 542
OSERS, 546
Osguthorpe, R. T., 175
Ostrow, V., 387
Ostrow, W., 387
Outhred, L., 287

Paglieri, R. A., 379
Palfrey, J. S., 541
Pallay, A., 12, 540, 541
Papert, S., 227
Parke, B. N., 449, 455
Parker, J. P., 446
Parson, L. R., 214
Pasanella, A. L., 172, 173, 178, 190,
    427–428, 434
Patrick, J. L., 300
Patros, P. G., 501, 508
Patterson, G. R., 527, 528
Patterson, J. N., 161, 162, 175
Patton, J. R., 166, 196, 198, 211, 299,
    301, 308, 311
Paul, P. V., 281
Payne, J. S., 301
Pearl, R., 68
Pendarvis, E. D., 448, 453, 457, 466

Pepper, F. C., 476, 477, 478
Perreault, H. R., 162
Perske, M., 175
Perske, R., 175
Peters, J. Y., 477, 480
Peterson, R. L., 180, 536
Petreshene, S. S., 202
Peverly, S., 542
Pfeifer, J. K., 507, 508, 509, 511
Pfiffner, L. J., 291
Pflaum, S., 68, 161
Phelps, M. S., 502
Phi Delta Kappa Center on Evaluation, Development, and Research, 107
Phillipo, J., 505
Pirner, C. W., 387
Plaskon, S. P., 376
Platt, J. M., 125, 214
Platt, J. S., 214
Polloway, E. A., 166, 196, 198, 211, 301, 370
Polsgrove, L., 544
Popham, J. P., 519
Postel, C. A., 398
Powers, M. E., 387
Prasad, S., 168
President's Committee on Mental Retardation, 10, 302
Price, M., 499
Prieto, A. G., 472
Prior, M., 379
Prock, G. A., 502
Project seen helping 'disconnected' young, 507
Public Law (P.L.) 101–476, 473
Pugach, M. C., 47, 63
Pullen, P. L., 127, 128
Pumpian, I., 60, 320
Putnam, J. M., 181
Pysh, M., 42

Quality Education Data, Inc., 220
Quay, H. C., 70

Rabe, B., 300
Raison, S. B., 203
Ramig, P. R., 369
Ramsey, E., 527, 528
Randolph, R., 542

Raphael, T. E., 282
Ratleff, J. E., 478, 490
Ray, B. M., 161
Recer, P., 498, 501
Redden, M. R., 536, 538
Rees, T., 436
Reeve, R. E., 261–262, 291, 293
Reeves, C. K., 378, 379
Reeves, M. S., 22, 498, 499, 500, 502
Reis, S. M., 435, 455
Renzulli, J. S., 190, 449, 453
Reschly, D. J., 162, 300
Research and Training Center on Independent Living, 24
Reynolds, C. J., 281
Reynolds, M. C., 5, 23, 82, 111, 386, 388, 389, 394, 420, 428, 432, 436, 456, 457, 458, 543
Reynolds, W. M., 266
Rich, H. L., 103, 541
Richeck, M., 96, 274, 281
Riessman, F., 190
Rieth, R., 94, 101, 104, 121, 196
Rinn, R. C., 178
Rittenmeyer, D. C., 518
Roberts, P. C., 398
Robinson, F. P., 280
Roby, K. M., 263
Rockefeller, N. A., 290
Rodriguez, R. C., 477
Roe, D. L., 40
Roland, P., 182, 183
Rose, L. C., 125, 501, 512
Rosenkoetter, S. E., 104
Rosenshine, B., 87, 94, 100, 101, 103
Rosenthal, H. F., 512
Ross, S. M., 103, 541
Rossett, A., 350
Rubin, R. A., 70, 125
Rucker, C. N., 162
Rude, H. A., 322
Rueda, R., 472
Ruiz, N. T., 488, 489
Russell, B., 501
Russell, S. J., 252
Rutherford, R. B., 528
Ryder, R. J., 278

Saba, F., 244, 284
Sacca, M. K., 175

Sailor, W., 60
Salend, S. J., 174, 541
Salend, S. M., 541
Salpeter, J., 224
Salvia, J., 266, 548
Sander, E. K., 365
Sanford, D., 387
Sanford, J. P., 190, 346
Sansone, J., 541
Sarff, L., 439
Sasso, G., 322
Sattler, J., 454
Saudargas, R. A., 162
Savage, J. G., 162
Sawrey, J. M., 394
Scavarda, M., 518
Schifani, J. W., 402
Schilit, J., 316, 317
Schindler, W. J., 536
Schlicter, C. L., 449
Schlosser, L. Y., 162
Schmidt, P., 477
Schneider, B. H., 541
Schubert, A., 379
Schubert, M., 190, 202
Schulte, A. C., 542
Schultz, J. B., 171
Schulz, J. B., 5, 47, 164, 171, 172, 173
Schumaker, J. B., 160, 165, 168, 178, 282, 354, 545
Schwartz, A. A., 379
Schwartz, S. S., 287
Schwarz, P., 543
Scott, D., 210
Scrogan, L., 220
Scruggs, T. E., 175
Secord, W., 363, 370
Seidel, J. F., 394
Semel, E. M., 363, 370
Semmel, M. I., 23, 351, 545
Senna, J. J., 498, 502, 527
Shames, G. H., 369, 370, 481
Shamoo, T. K., 501, 508
Shea, T. M., 522
Shepard, D. H., 246
Sheras, P. L., 507, 508, 509, 511
Shinn, M. R., 84
Shulman, J., 171
Siegel, L., 287
Siegel, L. J., 468, 502, 527

Subject Index

Environmental adaptations, 46, 190, 192–198
Epilepsy, 384, 386, 390, 391. *See also* Physical and health impairments
Error (work sample) analysis, 114–115, 454
ESL Writer, 487
Etiology, 82
Event recording, 135
Extinction, 129, 130, 348, 349

Facilitated communication, 379
Facilitating learning, 97
Factory, The, 227
Friendship programs, 174–175, 322–324
Full inclusion
  described, 5–6, 10, 320–329, 543–547
Functional practice activities, 315–316
Functional tasks, 96, 311

General education teachers,
  acceptance of special students, 161–162, 180–181
  consultation services from special education, 57–58
  gifted students, 466
  IEP responsibilities, 37–38, 53
  mainstreaming skills, 16, 23–25, 86–87, 107, 180–181, 184–185, 537–538
  management skills, 190
  role in referrals, 37, 40–41, 47–48, 260, 263, 335, 360, 385–386, 417, 448
Generalization, 92, 106, 109, 548
Getting Along with Others: Teaching Social Effectiveness to Children, 178
Gifted and Talented Education Act of 1978. *See Public Law 95-561*
Gifted and talented students
  academic needs, 77
  adaptations for, 456–459, 462, 466–467
  assessment, 453–454
  creativity and problem solving, 458, 459, 462
  described, 8, 76–77, 446–453, 455

educational options, 457–458, 460–461
  social needs, 77
  special services, 454, 456
  underachievement, 462, 466–467
Giftedness, 447
Goals 2000, 22
Goldman-Fristoe Test of Articulation, 363
Goldman-Fristoe-Woodcock Auditory Skills Test Battery, 266
Group contingencies, 153–154, 174

Habilitation, 308
Handicapped students. *See* Special students
Hard-of-hearing, 75, 421. *See also* Hearing impairments
Health impairments. *See* Physical and health impairments
Hearing aids, 249–250, 437–440
Hearing impairments
  academic needs, 74–75
  adaptations for, 427–432, 434, 436–438
  assessment, 422–424
  described, 8, 74–75, 416–417, 420–422, 423
  learning environment, 428
  physical needs, 74–75
  social needs, 74–75
  special services, 425–427
High interest-low vocabulary, 278–280
Homebound and hospital services, 61
Hyperactivity, 292, 335, 348

Identification of special students, 40–43, 46
Illinois Test of Psycholinguistic Abilities, 266
Impulsivity, 292, 335
Inattention, 291–292
Inclusion
  described, 5–6, 10–11, 320–329, 543–547
  preparing for, 163–165
Independent practice, 100
Individualized education program (IEP)
  components of, 51–52

defined, 17, 51–52
  examples of, 18–20, 53–54
  forms, 17–18
  implementation of, 51–52, 55
  responsibilities of the general education teacher, 37–38, 53
Individualized education program (IEP) committee, 30, 32. *See also* Mainstreaming team
Individualized education program (IEP) team, 30, 32, 36. *See also* Mainstreaming team
Individualized family services plan (IFSP), 23, 61
Individualized instruction, 94
Individuals with Disabilities Education Act of 1990. *See Public Law (P.L.) 101-476*
Infant and preschool programs, 61
Informal assessment, 83, 149, 268
Informal reading inventories, 268–269
Information processing, 66
Instruction
  accuracy (increasing), 354–356
  adaptations, 46, 116–120, 271–273
  allocated time, 105
  auto-instructional learning materials, 202, 274, 276
  automaticity, 283
  basic skills, 273–288
  choral responding, 104
  clinical teaching, 84
  compensation, 272
  computer-assisted, 207, 220
  computer-managed, 231
  content area, 288–290
  cooperative learning, 174, 176–177, 253
  differential grading, 318
  direct teaching, 94, 101, 274, 377, 548–549
  engaged time, 102, 105
  error analysis, 114–115, 454
  evaluating materials, 212–213
  functional academics, 311, 314–316
  functional practice activities, 315–316
  functional tasks, 96
  grouping students, 201–202
  guided practice, 117, 119, 274

About the Authors

Dr. Rena B. Lewis earned her Ph.D. at the University of Arizona, with a major in special education and minors in psychology and systems engineering. She currently teaches at San Diego State University in the Departments of Special Education and Educational Technology and serves on the faculty of the Doctoral Program in Education offered jointly by SDSU and Claremont Graduate School.

A prolific author, Dr. Lewis is interested in assessment, bilingual and multicultural education, applications of technology for persons with disabilities, and mainstreaming. In addition to this book, she is the author of *Special Education Technology: Classroom Applications* and co-author with Dr. James A. McLoughlin of *Assessing Special Students* (4th ed.). She was honored with an award by the International Reading Association for her report on research implications for teaching reading to students with learning disabilities.

For several years, Dr. Lewis has coordinated the technology area of San Diego State's program for the preparation of special education teachers. Her current research interests include the use of technology to improve the writing skills of students with learning disabilities, technology-based instructional interventions for students with severe disabilities, and the preparation of teachers to serve students from diverse cultural and linguistic backgrounds. At present, she is the principal investigator in a research project studying the effectiveness of word processing tools in enhancing the writing skills of students with learning disabilities.

Dr. Donald H. Doorlag currently teaches in the Department of Special Education at San Diego State University. He serves as coordinator of a certificate program for teachers working with students with serious emotional disturbances. In addition, he coordinates a credential program that combines training in general and special education so that graduates earn credentials in both areas simultaneously.

After receiving his undergraduate degree in secondary education, Dr. Doorlag worked throughout most of the 1960s as a teacher of students with emotional and behavioral disorders. Following this teaching experience he completed his doctorate at Michigan State University with major concentrations in the areas of emotional disturbance and special education administration and a minor in educational research. He joined the faculty at San Diego State University in 1970 and for a number of years chaired their Department of Special Education. Since coming to San Diego, he has also been very active at the local, regional, and state levels in contributing to the development and improvement of programs related to the training of special education teachers and the delivery of special education services to students with disabilities.

Dr. Doorlag's most recent publications and research interests have focused on the role of the research specialist; learning and behavioral disorders; management of violent individuals; improving spelling and reading instruction for students with learning disabilities; and the recruitment, training, and retention of special education teachers. Currently he is the principal investigator on a major study examining issues related to the attrition and retention of special education teachers in urban settings.